BARRON'S

TOEIC®

Test of English for International Communication

NINTH EDITION

Lin Lougheed, Ed.D.

Teachers College
Columbia University

TOEIC® is a registered trademark of the Educational Testing Service, which neither sponsors nor endorses this product.

ACKNOWLEDGEMENTS

I would like to acknowledge Chris Oliver and his classes at Sophia University Junior College Division, Kanagawa, Japan for their assistance in perfecting the Barron's TOEIC Preparation books.

AUDIO AND AUDIOSCRIPTS

The MP3 files and audioscripts for all listening segments can be found online at
online.barronsbooks.com/

Published by Kaplan, Inc., d/b/a Barron's Educational Series
750 Third Avenue
New York, NY 10017
www.barronseduc.com

ISBN: 978-1-5062-7342-6

10 9 8 7 6 5 4 3 2 1

Kaplan, Inc., d/b/a Barron's Educational Series print books are available at special quantity discounts to use for sales promotions, employee premiums, or educational purposes. For more information or to purchase books, please call the Simon & Schuster special sales department at 866-506-1949.

Contents

TOEIC PRACTICE TESTS

Audio Track List

Overview of the TOEIC

There are two sections on the TOEIC: Listening Comprehension and Reading. Specific information about each section is given in detail in this book. The kinds of questions asked and the strategies you'll need to master in order to perform well are provided in the respective chapters.

TOEIC		
Section 1: Listening Comprehension **Time: Approximately 45 minutes**		
Part	Name	Number of questions
1	Photographs	6
2	Question-Response	25
3	Conversations (13) with and without a visual image	39
4	Talks (10) with and without a visual image	30

TOEIC		
Section 2: Reading **Time: 75 minutes**		
Part	Name	Number of questions
5	Incomplete Sentences	30
6	Text Completion (4)	16
7	Reading Comprehension	
	■ Single passages	29
	■ Multiple passages	25

TO THE TEACHER

Rationale for a TOEIC Preparation Course

Barron's *TOEIC* preparation book may be used as either a self-study course or a class course. In a class situation, this text will provide an excellent structure for helping your students improve their English language skills and prepare for the TOEIC.

Adult learners of English are very goal-oriented. For many adults who are required to take the TOEIC, their goal is a high score. Having a goal that can be easily measured will be very motivating for your students.

Many teachers do not like to "teach to the test." They feel that developing a general knowledge of English will be more useful to the students than reviewing test items. But students want to "study the test." They don't want to spend their time learning something that might not be tested.

Both arguments ignore what actually happens during a TOEIC preparation course. General English is used to discuss how the exam is structured, what strategies should be used, and what skills should be developed. General English is used to explain problems and to expand into other areas. By helping students prepare for an exam, you can't help but improve their general knowledge of English.

A TOEIC preparation course gives the students what they want: a streamlined approach to learning what they need to know for the exam. The course gives the teachers what they want: a scheme to help them improve the English language ability of their students.

Organization of a TOEIC Preparation Course

TIMETABLE

Every test-preparation course faces the same dilemma: how to squeeze a total review of English into a class timetable. Some of you may have an afternoon TOEIC orientation; others may have a one-week intensive class; some may have a ten-week session. However long your class time, one thing is true: no class is ever long enough to cover everything you want to cover.

As a guideline, you might want to follow this plan and expand it as your time allows.

- **First period:** Study Chapter 1, Introduction.
  Have students sign the TOEIC Contract.
- **Next period:** Take a Practice Test.
  Evaluate answers; determine the weak areas of the class.
- **Subsequent periods:** Review Listening Comprehension.
  Take the Mini-Test.
  Review Reading.
  Take the Mini-Test.
  Take additional Practice Tests.
- **Last period:** Take a final Practice Test and note the improvement in scores.

After your students have completed the exercises, the Mini-Tests, or the Practice Tests, they can check the Answer Key for quick access to the correct answer or read the Answer Explanations for reasons why the correct answer is right and the incorrect answers are wrong.

Teaching Listening Comprehension

The more your students hear English, the better their listening comprehension will be. Encourage a lot of discussion about the various strategies mentioned in the Listening Comprehension activities. Have your students work in pairs or small groups to increase the amount of time they will spend listening and speaking.

All tests require the students to choose a correct answer. This means the students must eliminate the incorrect answers. There are common distractors (traps) on an exam that a student can be trained to listen for. And coincidentally, while they are learning to listen for these traps, they are improving their listening comprehension.

The Listening Comprehension activities in this text are a gold mine. You can use them for the stated purpose, which is to help students learn how to analyze photos, answer choices, question types, and language functions. In addition, you can use them for a variety of communicative activities.

PHOTOGRAPH EXERCISES

The photographs can be used to help your students develop their vocabulary. Have them pick a photograph and, in pairs or small groups, name everything they see in the picture.

Then, in the same small groups (or individually) have them use those words in a sentence. They can write a short description of the photograph or, even better, they can write a short narrative. The narratives can be extremely imaginative—the more imaginative the better. Have your students describe what happened before the photograph was taken and what might happen afterward.

Once they have the vocabulary under control, they can make an oral presentation. The other students or groups will then have to retell the narrative. This will help them evaluate their own listening comprehension.

QUESTION-RESPONSE EXERCISES

In this section, there is one short question, followed by an equally short answer. There is sometimes just a statement followed by a short response. Have your students establish a context for the short question or statement. Where are the speakers? Who are they? What are they talking about? What were they doing before? What will they do next? What did they say before? What will they say next?

Have them create a short skit that a pair of students can act out. Then have others in the class try to summarize the dialogue. Again, you are helping them evaluate their own listening comprehension.

CONVERSATIONS EXERCISES

The same technique can work here. Actually, it will be easier, because there is more dialogue for your students to use as a basis. This time have them listen to the skit created by their colleagues and ask "wh" questions. Have them learn to anticipate *who, what, when, where, why,* and *how.*

TALKS EXERCISES

There are a variety of short talks: some are about the weather; others are public service announcements; some are advertisements. Have your students take one of the small talks and rewrite it. If it is a weather announcement, have them take a rainy day and make it sunny; have them change an advertisement for a television into an advertisement for a car.

Then, as with the other activities, have the other students create the "wh" questions. See if they can stump their colleagues. Encourage them to make these talks challenging.

Teaching Reading

Again, the best way for students to improve their reading is to read, read, read. On the TOEIC, even the grammar activities focus on reading. They demand that students understand the whole context of the statement, not just an isolated part. That is why the structure tests are in the Reading section.

As in the Listening Comprehension section, it is as important to know why an answer is wrong as it is to know why an answer is right. Training your students to use the strategies mentioned in these sections will make them more efficient readers.

VOCABULARY EXERCISES

All students want to know as many words as possible. Remind them that it is important to know how to use them. They will learn more by reading and learning words in context than they will from memorizing word lists.

They can and should create their own personal word lists. Every time they encounter an unfamiliar word, they should write it down in a notebook. They should try to use it in a sentence, or even better, in a dialogue. Have your students create their own skits using the words from their own personal word lists.

If your students insist on lists, show them all the charts of words in the various sections of both the Listening and Reading sections. Have them use these words to learn how to use words in context.

GRAMMAR EXERCISES

The grammar reviewed in this text covers those areas that are most likely to be found on the TOEIC and that will be the most challenging. You can help your students focus their attention by having them analyze their mistakes in the Practice Tests.

READING EXERCISES

The strategies emphasized in the Reading review are not only for reading on the TOEIC. They can be, and should be, applied to all reading a student might have to do. Use outside reading materials such as English news magazines and newspapers. Have your students read not only the articles but also the ads, announcements, subscription forms, and tables of contents. In fact, have them scan and read the entire magazine. Everything found in a news magazine, including charts and graphs, is found on the TOEIC.

As your students did in the Listening Comprehension review, have them create "wh" questions for the articles, graphs, tables, and so on that they find. Let them try to stump their colleagues. To make the lesson even more communicative, have them give an oral presentation of what they have read. Let the "wh" questions be oral, too.

> **USE A PRACTICE TEST AS A DIAGNOSTIC**
>
> If your students have several errors on questions testing prepositions, you would suggest they concentrate on the problems dealing with prepositions. Lists in the front of Chapter 2 and Chapter 3 provide an easy way for you to find the specific exercises your students need. (See pages 15 and 105.) By focusing on problem areas, they will be able to study more efficiently and effectively.

Introduction

1

> ### What to Look for in This Chapter
>
> - Questions and Answers Concerning the TOEIC
> - Study Plan for the TOEIC
> - Self-Study Activities
> - On Test Day

QUESTIONS AND ANSWERS CONCERNING THE TOEIC

More than 5 million people take the TOEIC each year, and this number is growing. The TOEIC is administered in Europe, Asia, North America, South America, and Central America. Since the test is relatively new (compared to the TOEFL, which was first given in 1963), many test takers are unfamiliar with the TOEIC. The following are some commonly asked questions about the TOEIC.

TIP

Online Resources You can also learn more at the TOEIC website *www.toeic.com* or at my website *www.lougheed.com.*

What Is the Purpose of the TOEIC?

Since 1979, the TOEIC (the Test of English for International Communication) has been used internationally as a standard assessment of English-language proficiency. The TOEIC has been developed by linguists, language experts, and staff at The Chauncey Group International Ltd. to evaluate the English language skills of nonnative speakers of English in the field of business.

What Skills Are Tested on the TOEIC?

The TOEIC consists of two sections: Listening Comprehension (100 multiple-choice questions) and Reading (100 multiple-choice questions). Audio is used to test Listening Comprehension.

The content of the TOEIC is not specialized; the vocabulary and content are familiar to those individuals who use English in daily activities.

Who Uses the TOEIC?

Government agencies, multinational corporations, and international organizations use the TOEIC to ascertain the English-language capabilities of employees and prospective employees. The scores are used as an independent measure of proficiency and can be helpful in identifying personnel capable of handling language-specific responsibilities, in placing personnel in language-training programs, and in promoting personnel to positions where reliable linguistic standards are met.

Language-training programs use the TOEIC to establish language-training goals and to assess students' progress in overall English ability.

Who Takes the TOEIC?

In addition to the staffs of the companies and organizations previously mentioned, individuals take the TOEIC to document their abilities for personal and professional reasons.

What Is the Format of the TOEIC?

The TOEIC consists of two sections: Listening Comprehension and Reading Comprehension. See the charts on page vi for a description of each section.

There are a total of 200 items; the total time allowed for the test (including administrative tasks) is approximately 2½ hours. The Listening Comprehension section takes 45 minutes; the Reading section takes 75 minutes.

Why Are TOEIC Questions so Tricky?

TOEIC questions are carefully designed to test your knowledge of English. The questions must be difficult in order to discriminate between test takers of varying abilities. That is, the difficult questions separate those who are more proficient in English from those who are less proficient. A test question and the answer options may use one or more of these tricks to test your language competence:

- Use words with similar sounds
- Use homonyms
- Use related words
- Omit a necessary word
- Include unnecessary words
- Alter the correct word order

How Is the TOEIC Score Determined?

Separate scores are given for Listening Comprehension (5 to 495) and Reading (5 to 495). These two sub-scores are added to arrive at the total score. The TOEIC score is represented on a scale of 10 to 990 and is based on the total number of correct answers.

What Do TOEIC Scores Mean?

There is no established minimum passing score; each institution, through experience, sets up its own acceptable score.

How Are TOEIC Scores Obtained?

TOEIC test takers who are sponsored by companies, institutions, or organizations receive their scores from their sponsors. Those examinees who register individually to take the TOEIC receive their scores directly. Scores are valid for two years.

When and Where Can I Take the TOEIC?

The TOEIC is offered worldwide and is generally available upon demand. The dates, times, and locations of the test sites are determined by the local TOEIC representatives. For test fees, test dates, and locations, contact the TOEIC office in your country or contact ETS in the USA. The TOEIC representative offices are listed on the ETS website, *www.ets.org*.

How Can I Prepare for the TOEIC?

If you plan to take the TOEIC, make a concerted effort to use English as much as possible and in many different situations.

The best preparation is using a book/audio combination such as this—a program designed to help you specifically with the TOEIC. Following through with this book will:

- make you aware of certain test-taking skills;
- familiarize you with the format of the test; and
- improve your total score.

Additional suggestions are found in the next section, entitled "Study Plan for the TOEIC."

How Can I Get a Better Score on the TOEIC?

Assuming you have prepared well for the TOEIC, you can maximize your score on test day by following these suggestions:

- Read the directions carefully
- Work quickly
- Do not make notes in the test booklet
- Guess if you're not sure
- Mark only one answer

Additional suggestions are found in the next section, "Study Plan for the TOEIC."

STUDY PLAN FOR THE TOEIC

There is an English expression: "You can lead a horse to water, but you can't make him drink." Similarly, this book can lead you through the TOEIC, but it can't make you think. Learning is a self-motivated activity. Only you can prepare yourself for the TOEIC.

TOEIC Contract

It takes a lot of discipline to learn a foreign language. You need to formalize your commitment by signing a contract with yourself. This contract will obligate you to spend a certain number of hours each week learning English for a certain period of time. You will promise (1) to study Barron's *TOEIC* book and other Barron's TOEIC preparation materials, and (2) to study on your own. Sign the contract below to make your commitment.

- Print your name on line 1.
- Write the time you will spend each week studying English on lines 4–8. Think about how much time you have to study every day and every week and set a realistic schedule.
- Sign your name and date the contract on the last line.
- At the end of each week, add up your hours. Did you meet the requirements of your contract? Did you study both the Barron's *TOEIC* and the self-study activities?

TOEIC STUDY CONTRACT

I, _____, promise to study for the TOEIC. I will begin my study with Barron's *TOEIC*, and I will also study English on my own.

I understand that to improve my English, I need to spend time on English.

I promise to study English _____ hours per week.

I will spend _____ hours per week listening to English.

I will spend _____ hours per week writing English.

I will spend _____ hours per week speaking English.

I will spend _____ hours per week reading English.

This is a contract with myself. I promise to fulfill the terms of this contract.

_____   _____
Signed   Date

Good TOEIC Preparation Tips

1. **STUDY REGULARLY.** Pick the same time of day to practice. If you don't develop a routine, you won't develop good study habits. Tell yourself that you can't watch television at 7:30 because that is your TOEIC time. If you do miss your scheduled time one day, don't worry. Try to make it up later that day, but don't study at a different time every day. You will never get any studying done.

2. **DO A LITTLE AT A TIME.** Tell yourself that you will study for ten minutes on the train every morning or ten minutes just before you go to bed. It is better to learn one thing very well in a short period of time than to spend long periods trying to study everything.

3. **BUDGET YOUR TIME.** The TOEIC is a timed test, so time your study sessions. Give yourself ten minutes to study and then stop. You must use your time effectively. Learn how to take advantage of short periods of time.

4. **WRITE OUT A STUDY SCHEDULE.** If you put something in writing, you are more likely to do it.

5. **KNOW YOUR GOAL.** Why are you taking the TOEIC? If it's to qualify for a better position in your company, picture yourself in that job. What kind of score will you need? Work for that score (or a higher one).

6. **DEVELOP A POSITIVE ATTITUDE.** Before Olympic athletes compete, many shut their eyes and imagine themselves skiing down the mountain, running around the track, or swimming the fastest and passing the finish line first. They imagine themselves performing perfectly, scoring the best, and winning. This is the power of positive thinking. It is not just for athletes. You can use it, too.

   You must have a positive attitude when you take the TOEIC. Every night just before you fall asleep (when the right side of the brain is most receptive) repeat the following sentence ten times. "I understand English very well, and I will score very high on the TOEIC." The subconscious mind is very powerful. If you convince yourself that you can succeed, you are more likely to succeed.

7. **RELAX.** Don't become anxious about the exam. Get a good night's rest the night before the exam. Don't study that night. Relax and have a good time. Your mind will be more receptive if you are calm. Relax before, during, and especially after the exam.

Using Barron's *TOEIC*

1. **BECOME FAMILIAR WITH THE TOEIC QUESTIONS AND DIRECTIONS.** Read the sections on the TOEIC and the introductions to the Listening Comprehension and Reading chapters carefully. They contain information and advice that will help you raise your score.

2. **TAKE A PRACTICE TEST.** Use the Answer Explanations as a guide to help you determine your weaknesses. If you miss more questions about prepositions than about adverbs of frequency, then you should spend your time studying prepositions. Use the skills lists found on pages 15 and 105 to easily find the exercises you need most.

3. **STUDY EFFICIENTLY.** When time is limited, concentrate on what you really need to study. Don't try to do everything if you don't have enough time.

4. **STUDY ALL THE POTENTIAL PROBLEMS.** Know what to look for in the Listening Comprehension and Reading sections. You should learn how to recognize an incorrect answer.

5. **DO THE EXERCISES, REVIEW EXERCISES, AND MINI-TESTS.** All of the exercises are designed like those on the TOEIC. You will develop both your English ability and your test-taking skills by studying these exercises.

6. **REVIEW THE ANSWER EXPLANATIONS.** All of the answers for the review exercises, Mini-Tests, and Practice Tests are explained thoroughly at the end of the chapter in which they appear. Studying these explanations will sharpen your ability to analyze a test question. Knowing why you made an error will help you avoid the error the next time.

   Answer Keys are provided. You can use these keys to quickly find out which questions you did not answer correctly. Then, go to the Answer Explanations to learn where you went wrong. This will help you to focus your studies on the areas in which you need the most practice.

7. **USE OTHER BARRON'S TOEIC PREPARATION MATERIALS.** Improve your TOEIC vocabulary with Barron's *Essential Words for the TOEIC*. Get more test practice with Barron's *TOEIC Practice Exams*. You can order both of these books online at *www.barronseduc.com*.

DO A LITTLE EVERY DAY

It is worth repeating this advice. Following a consistent study routine will help you prepare for the TOEIC. You may not have to study everything in this book. Study the types of questions for which you need additional practice. But do it every day!

SELF-STUDY ACTIVITIES

1. **LISTEN TO AS MUCH ENGLISH AS YOU CAN.** The best way to improve your listening comprehension is by listening. As you listen, ask yourself these questions:

   Who is talking?
   Who are they talking to?
   What are they talking about?
   Where are they talking?
   Why are they talking?

   As you answer these questions, you will improve your ability to understand English through context.

2. **READ AS MUCH ENGLISH AS YOU CAN.** It should be no surprise that the best and easiest way to improve your reading comprehension is by reading. Concentrate on weekly news magazines. Look at the tables of contents, the advertisements, the announcements, and the articles. Read anything in English you can find: classified ads, train schedules, hotel registration forms, etc. Again, always ask yourself questions as you read.

   Use the PSRA reading strategy technique discussed on pages 168–169. It will help you on the TOEIC and every time you read anything—even reading material in your own language!

3. **WRITE AND SPEAK AS MUCH ENGLISH AS YOU CAN.** Every time you listen and ask yourself who, what, when, where, and why, say your answers out loud and then write them down.

4. **KEEP A VOCABULARY NOTEBOOK.** Learning vocabulary in context will help you much more than memorizing long lists of words. Be on the lookout for new vocabulary. Be persistent about it. Get on the Internet and start reading websites. Any English website will be useful, but you can get both reading and listening practice on many of them such as CNN and BBC. Many newspapers, magazines, zines, and blogs are on the Internet. Do a search on an area of interest to you. You may be surprised how many sites are available.

   Here are some ways you can practice your listening, reading, speaking, and writing skills in English. You will find many opportunities to practice English in books and magazines as well as on the Internet. Check the ones you plan to try and add some ideas of your own on the blank lines provided.

Listening

☐ Listen to podcasts on the Internet.

☐ Listen to news websites: CNN, BCC, NBC, ABC, and CBS.

☐ Watch movies and television in English.

☐ Find YouTube videos that interest you.

☐ Find videos and movies that interest you at this website: *http://archive.org/details/movies*.

☐ Listen to CNN and BBC on the radio or on the Internet.

☐ Listen to Pandora or other Internet radio applications.

☐ Listen to music in English.

☐ _____

☐ _____

Speaking

☐ Describe out loud what you see and what you do.

☐ Practice having a conversation with a friend.

☐ Use FaceTime, Zoom, or Skype to talk to English speakers.

☐ _____

☐ _____

Writing

- ☐ Write a daily journal.
- ☐ Write a letter to an English speaker.
- ☐ Make lists of the things that you see every day.
- ☐ Write descriptions of your family and friends.
- ☐ Write e-mails to website contacts.
- ☐ Write a blog.
- ☐ Leave comments on blogs and YouTube.
- ☐ Post messages in a chat room.
- ☐ Use Facebook and Instagram.
- ☐ _____
- ☐ _____

Reading

- ☐ Read newspapers and magazines in English.
- ☐ Read books in English.
- ☐ Read graphic novels in English.
- ☐ Read news and magazine articles online.
- ☐ Do web research on topics that interest you.
- ☐ Follow blogs that interest you.
- ☐ _____
- ☐ _____

Examples of Self-Study Activities

Whether you read an article in a newspaper or on a website, you can use that article in a variety of ways to practice reading, writing, speaking, and listening in English.

- ■ Read about it.
- ■ Paraphrase and write about it.
- ■ Give a talk or presentation about it.
- ■ Record or make a video of your presentation.
- ■ Listen to or watch what you recorded.
- ■ Write down your presentation.
- ■ Correct your mistakes.
- ■ Do it all again.

Here are some specific examples you can do to study on your own.

PLAN A TRIP

Go to *www.fodors.com* or another travel website.

 Choose a city, then choose some sites to visit there (*reading*). Write a report about the city (*writing*). Tell why you want to go there and when you want to go. Tell what sites you plan to visit. Where will you eat? How will you get around?

Now write a letter to someone recommending this place (*writing*). Pretend you have to give a lecture on your planned trip (*speaking*). Make a video of yourself talking about this place, and then watch the video and write down what you said. Correct any mistakes you made and record the presentation again. Then choose another city and do this again.

SHOP FOR AN ELECTRONIC PRODUCT

Go to *www.cnet.com*

 Choose an electronic product and read about it (*reading*). Write a report about the product. Tell why you want to buy the product. Describe its features.

Now write a letter to someone recommending this product (*writing*). Pretend you have to give a talk about this product (*speaking*). Make a video of yourself talking about this product, and then watch the video and write down what you said. Correct any mistakes you made and record the presentation again. Then choose another product and do this again.

DISCUSS A BOOK OR A MOVIE

Go to *www.amazon.com*

 Choose a book, movie, or any product. Read the product's description and reviews (*reading*). Write a report about the product. Tell why you want to buy the product or why it is interesting to you. Describe its features.

Now write a letter to someone recommending this product (*writing*). Pretend you have to give a talk about this product (*speaking*). Make a video of yourself talking about this product, and then watch the video and write down what you said. Correct any mistakes you made and record the presentation again. Then choose another product and do this again.

DISCUSS ANY SUBJECT

Go to *http://simple.wikipedia.org/wiki/Main_Page*

 This website is written in simple English. Pick any subject and read the entry (*reading*).

Write a short essay about the topic (*writing*). Give a presentation on the topic (*speaking*). Record the presentation, and then watch the video and write down what you said. Correct any mistakes you made and record the presentation again. Choose another topic and do this again.

DISCUSS ANY EVENT

Go to *http://news.google.com*

 Google News has a variety of links. Pick one event and read the articles (*reading*).

Write a short essay about the event (*writing*). Give a presentation about the event (*speaking*). Record the presentation, and then watch the video and write down what you said. Correct any mistakes you made and record the presentation again. Then choose another event and do this again.

REPORT THE NEWS

Listen to an English-language news report on the radio or watch a news program on television (*listening*). Take notes as you listen. Write a summary of what you heard (*writing*).

Pretend you are a news reporter. Use the information from your notes to report the news (*speaking*). Record the presentation, and then watch the video and write down what you said. Correct any mistakes you made and record the presentation again. Then listen to another news program and do this again.

EXPRESS AN OPINION

Read a letter to the editor in the newspaper (*reading*). Write a letter in response in which you say whether or not you agree with the opinion expressed in the first letter. Explain why (*writing*).

Pretend you have to give a talk explaining your opinion (*speaking*). Record yourself giving the talk, and then watch the video and write down what you said. Correct any mistakes you made and record the presentation again. Then read another letter to the editor and do this again.

REVIEW A BOOK OR MOVIE

Read a book (*reading*). Think about your opinion of the book. What did you like about it? What didn't you like about it? Who would you recommend it to and why? Pretend you are a book reviewer for a newspaper. Write a review of the book stating your opinion and recommendations (*writing*).

Give an oral presentation about the book. Explain what the book is about and state your opinion (*speaking*). Record yourself giving the presentation, and then watch the video and write down what you said. Correct any mistakes you made and record the presentation again. Then read another book and do this again.

You can do this same activity after watching a movie (*listening*).

SUMMARIZE A TELEVISION SHOW

Watch a television show in English (*listening*). Take notes as you listen. After watching, write a summary of the show (*writing*).

Use your notes to give an oral summary of the show. Explain the characters, setting, and plot (*speaking*). Record yourself speaking, and then watch the video and write down what you said. Correct any mistakes you made and record the presentation again. Then watch another television show and do this again.

LISTEN TO A LECTURE

Listen to an academic or other type of lecture on the Internet. Go to any of the following or similar sites and look for lectures on topics that are of interest to you:

https://academicearth.org/playlists/

http://podcasts.ox.ac.uk

http://freevideolectures.com

www.ted.com/talks

Listen to a lecture and take notes as you listen. Listen again to check and add to your notes (*listening*). Use your notes to write a summary of the lecture (*writing*).

Pretend you have to give a lecture on the same subject. Use your notes to give your lecture (*speaking*). Record yourself as you lecture. Then watch the video and write down what you said. Correct any mistakes you made and record the lecture again. Then listen to another lecture and do this again.

ON TEST DAY

You are well prepared. You studied this book and other Barron's preparation material, and now it is test day. Here are some suggestions that will help you on the day of the test.

1. **BE EARLY.** You should avoid rushing on the test day. Leave yourself plenty of time to get to the testing center.

2. **BE COMFORTABLE.** If you can, choose your own seat; pick one that is away from distractions. You don't want to be near an open door where you can watch people pass outside. On the other hand, you might want to be near a window to get good light. Try, if you can, to sit near the audio player. If you can't hear well, be sure to tell the test administrator.

3. **BRING WHAT YOU NEED.** Your test site may provide pencils with erasers, but to be safe you should bring three or four No. 2 pencils with erasers. You may find a watch useful, too.

4. **LISTEN TO THE DIRECTIONS.** Even though you will know the format after using this book, you should listen to the directions carefully. Listening to the familiar directions will help you relax.

5. **ANSWER ALL QUESTIONS.** Even if you do not know an answer, you should mark your best answer. But try to make it an educated guess. When time is running out, just blacken any letter for the questions you have not answered—even if you didn't have time to read the question. You may be right.

6. **MATCH THE NUMBERS.** Make sure that the number on your answer sheet matches the number in your test book.

7. **MARK ONLY ONE ANSWER PER QUESTION ON THE ANSWER SHEET.** Only one black mark will be counted. If you make a mistake and erase, do it completely. Do not make any other marks on the answer sheet.

8. **LISTEN CAREFULLY.** In Part 2, listen to the entire question and all the answer choices before making a final decision.

9. **FOCUS ATTENTION ON RELEVANT INFORMATION.** In Parts 3 and 4, quickly scan the questions and answer choices, then listen for relevant clues.

10. **ANSWER THE EASY QUESTIONS FIRST.** In the Reading section, you can pace yourself. If you do not immediately know an answer to a question, skip that question and go to one you can answer. At the end of the section, come back and do the more difficult questions. This will give you an opportunity to answer as many questions as you can.

11. **PACE YOURSELF.** The audio player will keep you moving in the Listening Comprehension section. But in the Reading section you will be able to adjust your own pace. You will have less than 45 seconds for each question in the Reading section.

12. **LEAVE TIME AT THE END.** If you can, try to leave a minute at the end to go over your answer sheet and make sure you have filled in every question.

13. **CELEBRATE AFTER THE EXAM.** Go ahead. Have a good time. You deserve it. Congratulations on a job well done.

TOEIC Review

Listening

2

OVERVIEW

There are four parts to the Listening Comprehension section of the TOEIC. You will have approximately 45 minutes to complete this section.

Part 1: Photographs	6 Questions
Part 2: Question-Response	25 Questions
Part 3: Conversations	39 Questions
Part 4: Talks	30 Questions

To prepare for the four parts of the Listening Comprehension section, you must develop certain listening and analytical skills. Most of the skills targeted in this chapter are useful for all parts of the Listening Comprehension section.

SKILLS LIST

Part 1: Photographs
Skill
1. Assumptions
2. People
3. Things
4. Actions
5. General Locations
6. Specific Locations

Part 2: Question-Response
Skill
1. Similar Sounds
2. Related Words
3. Homonyms
4. Same Sound/Same Spelling but Different Meaning
5. Suggestions
6. Offers
7. Requests

Part 3: Conversations
Skill
1. Questions About People
2. Questions About Occupations
3. Questions About Place
4. Questions About Time
5. Questions About Activities
6. Questions About Opinions
7. Graphic
8. Meaning in Context
9. Incomplete Sentences

Part 4: Talks
Skill
1. Questions About Events and Facts
2. Questions About Reasons
3. Questions About Numbers
4. Questions About Main Topics
5. Paraphrases
6. Graphic
7. Implied Meaning
8. Multiple Accents

PART 1: PHOTOGRAPHS

Sample Question

> **Directions:** You will see a photograph. You will hear four statements about the photograph. Choose the statement that most closely matches the photograph, and fill in the corresponding oval on your answer sheet. The statements will not be printed and will be spoken only once.

You will hear: Look at the photo marked number 1 in your test book.

    (A)   They're waiting at the bus stop.   Ⓐ Ⓑ Ⓒ ⬤

    (B)   They're leaving the building.

    (C)   They're selling tickets.

    (D)   They're getting off the bus.

Statement (D), "They're getting off the bus," best describes what you see in the photo. Therefore, you should choose answer (D).

Assumptions

You may have to *make assumptions* when you listen to the TOEIC. These assumptions will be based on what you can infer in the photograph. You will have to determine which of the four statements you hear is true or might be true. One statement (answer choice) will be true or will most likely be true. That choice will be the correct answer.

> **TIP** Listen carefully to the whole sentence and determine which one choice best matches the photo.

PHOTO 1

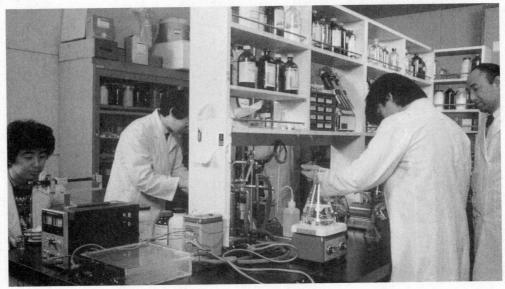

PHOTO 2

➥ Example _____

Look at these statements about Photo 1.

These statements are true.

This is a laboratory.

There are bottles on the shelves.

There is equipment on the counter.

The people are wearing protective clothing.

There are at least four people in the lab.

Wires run from the equipment.

These statements are probably true, but you can't tell for sure.

The people are lab technicians.

They look like technicians, but they could be pharmacists.

The people are students with a teacher.

A teacher may be working with a class, or they may all be employees.

The technicians are doing experiments.

They might be doing experiments, or they might be producing some chemical compound.

PRACTICE

Look at Photo 2 and read the following statements. Mark the statements True (T), Probably True (PT), or False (F).

A. There are five people around the table.
B. It's nighttime.
C. They're business colleagues.
D. They're smiling.
E. There is a bottle on the table.
F. There is water in the bottle.
G. They're drinking coffee.
H. They're eating something.
I. The computer is open.
J. They're reading a report.

EXERCISE

Choose the statement that best describes what you see in the photos on page 18.

Track 2

Photo 1 ⒶⒷⒸⒹ

Photo 2 ⒶⒷⒸⒹ

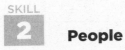

People

You may have to *identify the people* in a photograph. You may identify them by number, gender, location, description, activity, or occupation.

> **TIP** Determine the number, gender, location, description, activity, and occupation of the people as best you can.

PHOTO 3

PHOTO 4

➡ **Example** _____

Look at these statements about Photo 3.

Number:	There are four people in the photo.
Gender:	There are two men and two women in the photo.
Location:	On the left, there are two men.
	On the right, there are two women.
Description:	One of the men is wearing glasses.
	The woman on the right is shorter than the other woman.
Activity:	The group is looking at a map.
	One woman is pointing to the map.
	All four people are leaning on the table.
Occupation:	Their profession is unknown. They are looking at and discussing a map. We can assume they are planners of some sort.

You may not be able to answer all questions. You may not know their occupation, for example. However, the more assumptions you can make, the easier it will be to answer the questions.

PRACTICE

Complete the information about the people in Photo 4.

Number: _____

Gender: _____

Location: _____

Description: _____

Activity: _____

Occupation: _____

EXERCISE

Track 3

Choose the statement that best describes what you see in the photos on page 20.

Photo 3 Ⓐ Ⓑ Ⓒ Ⓓ

Photo 4 Ⓐ Ⓑ Ⓒ Ⓓ

SKILL 3 Things

You may have to *identify things* in a photo. When you look at a photo, try to name everything you see. On the TOEIC, general terms are used. You will not have to know specialized names for objects. For example, in the photo below, you should know the general word "piano." You do not have to know the specific term "grand piano."

> **TIP** Use the context of the photo to help you identify the things.

PHOTO 5

PHOTO 6

➡ **Example** _____

Find the following items in the photo. Keep in mind the context of Photo 5: It is a living room in a private home.

Words to Find

window	window shade	curtain
chair	cushion	carpet
floor	wall	fireplace
mantle	plant	plant
piano	piano bench	vase
candle	piano keys	shelf

PRACTICE

Make a list of the items you see in Photo 6.

_____   _____

_____   _____

_____   _____

_____   _____

_____

Track 4

EXERCISE

Choose the statement that best describes what you see in the photos on page 22.

Photo 5 Ⓐ Ⓑ Ⓒ Ⓓ

Photo 6 Ⓐ Ⓑ Ⓒ Ⓓ

4 Actions

You may have to *identify the actions* in a photo. There may be more than one action happening, even if there is only one person in the photo. If there are several people in the photo, they may all be doing the same thing or they may each be doing something different.

> **TIP** Determine what each person in the photo is doing.

PHOTO 7

PHOTO 8

➥ Example

Identify the following actions in Photo 7:

standing in the trench
standing next to the trench
kneeling in the trench
wearing a hard hat
holding the pipe
looking at the pipe
laying the pipe
leaning against the rocks

PRACTICE

Make a list of the actions you see in Photo 8.

_____   _____

_____   _____

_____   _____

_____   _____

_____

EXERCISE

Choose the statement that best describes what you see in the photos on page 24.

Photo 7   Ⓐ Ⓑ Ⓒ Ⓓ

Photo 8   Ⓐ Ⓑ Ⓒ Ⓓ

5 General Locations

You may have to *identify the general location* of a photograph. When you look at a picture, analyze the clues to determine a location. If you see a car, a mechanic, some tools, and a customer in a photo, you can assume the location is an automobile repair shop. If you see men and women working at desks with computers, you can assume the location is an office. A photo is full of clues to help you identify the general location.

> **TIP** Use the context of the photograph to help you make assumptions about the general location.

PHOTO 9

PHOTO 10

➥ Example _____

The following is a list of context clues in Photo 9. You may hear these words or variations of these words in Part I. Pay attention—the words may differ on the actual test.

Context Clues

Security checkpoint	Security officers
Departure information	Man with mobile phone
Gate sign	Airline names
People with baggage	Names of destinations
Porter with luggage cart	Sign about X-ray
Security personnel	Uniformed personnel

PRACTICE

Determine the general location in Photo 10. List the context clues you used.

Location _____

_____   _____

_____   _____

_____   _____

_____   _____

_____   _____

EXERCISE

Track 6

Choose the statement that best describes what you see in the photos on page 26.

Photo 9   Ⓐ Ⓑ Ⓒ Ⓓ

Photo 10 Ⓐ Ⓑ Ⓒ Ⓓ

6 Specific Locations

You may have to *identify the specific location* of people and things in a photograph. When you look at a photo, analyze the locations of the people and things in relation to each other.

> **TIP** Listen for the correct preposition.

PHOTO 11

PHOTO 12

Prepositions and Phrases of Location

above	beneath	far from	near	over
across	beside	in	next to	to the left of
around	between	in back of	on	to the right of
at	by	in front of	on top of	under
below	close to	inside	outside	underneath

Look at these sentences about specific locations in Photo 11.

The server is <u>next to</u> the table.
There is a bottle <u>in front of</u> the woman.
The forks are <u>on</u> a plate.
There is a plate <u>in</u> the server's hand.
The man is sitting <u>across from</u> a woman.
A woman is sitting <u>next to</u> the man.

PRACTICE

Write sentences about specific locations in Photo 12 using the prepositions and phrases provided.

A. (on) _____

B. (in front of) _____

C. (over) _____

D. (between) _____

E. (to the left of) _____

F. (on top of) _____

EXERCISE

Choose the statement that best describes what you see in the photos on page 28.

Track
7

Photo 11 Ⓐ Ⓑ Ⓒ Ⓓ

Photo 12 Ⓐ Ⓑ Ⓒ Ⓓ

PART 2: QUESTION-RESPONSE

Sample Question

> **Directions:** You will hear a question and three possible responses. Choose the response that most closely answers the question, and fill in the corresponding oval on your answer sheet. The statements will not be printed and will be spoken only once.

You will hear: How can I get to the airport from here?

             (A)   Take a taxi. It's just a short ride.   ● Ⓑ Ⓒ

             (B)   No, I don't.

             (C)   You can get on easily.

The best response to the question "How can I get to the airport from here?" is Choice (A), "Take a taxi. It's just a short ride." Therefore, you should choose answer (A).

Similar Sounds

On the TOEIC, you may have to distinguish between words with *similar sounds*. When you hear the answer choices, pay attention to the meaning. There will be context clues that help you understand the meaning. Do not be confused by words with similar sounds.

> **TIP** Listen carefully to the meaning of the statement or question and determine which answer choice really answers the question.

➡ **Examples** _____

Here are examples of similar sounds:

Different Vowel Sounds			
bass	car	deep	gun
base	core	dip	gone
boots	cart	fall	grass
boats	court	full	grease
bus	drug	fun	letter
boss	drag	phone	later
Different Initial Consonant Sounds			
back	core	race	hair
pack	tore	case	fair
rack	sore	place	tear
Different Final Consonant Sounds			
cab	little	nab	think
cap	litter	nap	thing
Two or More Words That Sound Like One Word			
mark it	sent her	letter	in tents
market	center	let her	intense
Words That Have Sounds That Are Part of a Longer Word			
nation	mind	give	intention
imagination	remind	forgive	unintentional

EXERCISE

Track 8

Choose the best response to each question.

1. Ⓐ Ⓑ Ⓒ

2. Ⓐ Ⓑ Ⓒ

3. Ⓐ Ⓑ Ⓒ

4. Ⓐ Ⓑ Ⓒ

5. Ⓐ Ⓑ Ⓒ

Related Words

On the TOEIC, you may have to determine whether the answer choices contain *related words*. An answer choice that contains a word related to the context of the question is not necessarily the correct answer.

> **TIP** Listen for the choice that completely answers the question.

➡ **Examples** _____

These are some related words:

Airline				
ticket	pilot	reservation	baggage claim	check-in
seat belt	flight attendant	ticket counter	crew	turbulence
Hotel				
room	pool	floor	suite	fitness center
front desk	check in/out	bed	lobby	housekeeping
Restaurant				
table	server	menu	tray	waiter/waitress
dish	napkin	meal	dinner	breakfast
lunch	dessert	tip	plate	bill/check
Bank				
cash	deposit	withdrawal	teller	officer
account	loan	savings	receipt	check
Weather				
sunny	cool	rain	drizzle	wind
cold	sleet	rainstorm	mist	breeze
freezing	warm	hot	cloudy	blizzard
snow	humid	smoggy	thunder	tornado
chilly	humidity	fog	lightning	hurricane

EXERCISE

Choose the best response to each question.

Track
9

1. Ⓐ Ⓑ Ⓒ

2. Ⓐ Ⓑ Ⓒ

3. Ⓐ Ⓑ Ⓒ

4. Ⓐ Ⓑ Ⓒ

5. Ⓐ Ⓑ Ⓒ

Homonyms

On the TOEIC, you may have to determine whether the answer choices contain a word that is a *homonym*. Homonyms are words that are pronounced the same, but have different meanings and different spellings.

> **TIP** Listen for the meaning of the word in the context of the sentence.

➥ **Examples** _____

Homonyms

allowed	feet	male	right	tale
aloud	feat	mail	rite	tail
bear	find	meat	write	threw
bare	fined	meet	sail	through
blew	flew	mind	sale	too
blue	flu	mined	seen	two
bough	flour	morning	scene	to
bow	flower	mourning	sight	wait
buy	for	one	site	weight
by	four	won	sowing	week
do	loan	pale	sewing	weak
due	lone	pail	steak	
dew	made	plane	stake	
fare	maid	plain	steel	
fair			steal	

Track 10

EXERCISE

Choose the best response to each question.

1. Ⓐ Ⓑ Ⓒ
2. Ⓐ Ⓑ Ⓒ
3. Ⓐ Ⓑ Ⓒ
4. Ⓐ Ⓑ Ⓒ
5. Ⓐ Ⓑ Ⓒ

SKILL 4

Same Sound/Same Spelling but Different Meaning

On the TOEIC, you may have to distinguish between *words that have the same sound and same spelling but have a different meaning.* When you hear the answer choices, pay attention to the meaning. Be careful of words with the same sound and same spelling, but with different meaning.

> **TIP** Listen to the context for the word that answers the question.

➡ **Examples**

Different Meanings for the Same Word

Call:	Animal or bird noise Shout Telephone call		*File:*	Folder Row Tool
Class:	Social position Group of students Level of quality		*Hard:*	Difficult Tough Firm
Court:	Tennis court Court of law Royal court		*Note:*	Musical note Short letter Currency
Date:	Type of fruit Meeting with someone Particular day		*Seat:*	A chair Location of power Membership in a club
Band:	Group of musicians Strip of cloth or other material		*Park:*	Open, grassy area in a city Leave your car in a certain place
Bank:	Financial institution Land along a river		*Right:*	Correct Opposite of *left* Just or fair
Left:	Past tense of *leave* Opposite of *right*			

EXERCISE

Track 11

Choose the best response to each question.

1. Ⓐ Ⓑ Ⓒ
2. Ⓐ Ⓑ Ⓒ
3. Ⓐ Ⓑ Ⓒ
4. Ⓐ Ⓑ Ⓒ
5. Ⓐ Ⓑ Ⓒ

Suggestions

Some of the questions in Part 2 may actually be suggestions. They require a certain type of response.

> **TIP** Listen for words that signal suggestions.

➡ Examples _____

If you hear these question types, listen for answers about suggestions.

Suggestions

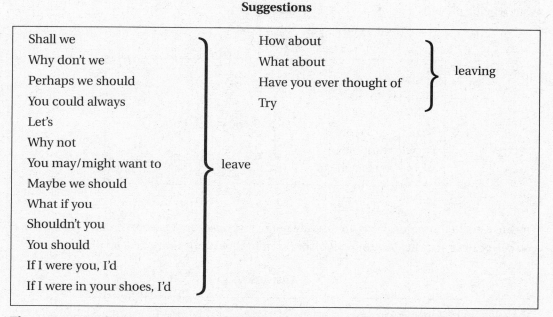

Shall we	How about	
Why don't we	What about	
Perhaps we should	Have you ever thought of	leaving
You could always	Try	
Let's		
Why not		
You may/might want to		
Maybe we should	leave	
What if you		
Shouldn't you		
You should		
If I were you, I'd		
If I were in your shoes, I'd		

The answers to those questions are usually responses to a suggestion. The responses can be positive (*let's go*) or negative (*let's not*). If you see or hear answers like these, look or listen for questions that are suggestions.

Answers

Yes, let's.	What a brilliant idea!
That's a good idea.	No, I haven't yet.
Why not?	OK.
Suits me.	Good idea.

Track 12

EXERCISE

Choose the best response to each question.

1. Ⓐ Ⓑ Ⓒ
2. Ⓐ Ⓑ Ⓒ
3. Ⓐ Ⓑ Ⓒ
4. Ⓐ Ⓑ Ⓒ
5. Ⓐ Ⓑ Ⓒ

SKILL
6   Offers

Some of the questions in Part 2 may actually be offers. Learn to recognize the words, phrases, and suggestions that signal an offer.

> **TIP** Listen for words that signal offers.

➡ **Examples** _____

If you hear these question types, which begin with these common offer markers, listen to see what is being offered.

Offers

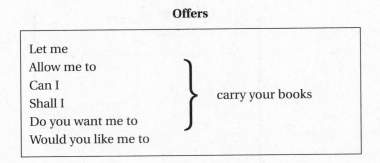

| Let me |
| Allow me to |
| Can I |
| Shall I | } carry your books |
| Do you want me to |
| Would you like me to |

The answers to those questions are usually polite responses that accept or decline an offer. If you see or hear answers like these, look or listen for questions that make an offer.

Answers

Thank you.	You're too kind.
That's very kind of you.	No, thanks. I can manage.
I'd appreciate that.	

Track 13

EXERCISE

Choose the best response to each question.

1. Ⓐ Ⓑ Ⓒ
2. Ⓐ Ⓑ Ⓒ
3. Ⓐ Ⓑ Ⓒ
4. Ⓐ Ⓑ Ⓒ
5. Ⓐ Ⓑ Ⓒ

Requests

A request is a polite way of asking someone to do something. Learn to recognize requests and the information in them.

> **TIP** Listen for words that signal requests.

➥ Examples

If you hear these question types, which begin with these common request markers, listen to see what is being requested.

Requests

Can you	
May I	
Would you	
Could you	speak louder
Do you think you could	
How about	speaking louder
Would you mind	

The answers to those questions are usually polite responses that acknowledge a request. If you see or hear answers like these, look or listen for questions that make a request.

Answers

Of course.	I'm sorry. I can't.
Is this OK?	Regretfully, no.
No problem.	Not at all. I'd be glad to.
Certainly.	I'd be happy to.

EXERCISE

Track 14

Choose the best response to each question.

1. Ⓐ Ⓑ Ⓒ
2. Ⓐ Ⓑ Ⓒ
3. Ⓐ Ⓑ Ⓒ
4. Ⓐ Ⓑ Ⓒ
5. Ⓐ Ⓑ Ⓒ

PART 3: CONVERSATIONS

Sample Questions

> **Directions:** You will hear a short conversation between two or more people. You will see three questions on each conversation and four possible answers. Choose the best answer to each question, and fill in the corresponding oval on your answer sheet. The conversations will not be printed and will be spoken only once.

You will hear:

Man:	We'll need your medical history so take this form and fill it out, please.
Woman:	Will there be a long wait for my appointment?
Man:	No, the doctor is seeing patients on schedule.
Woman:	That's good news. The last time I was here, I waited almost an hour.
Man:	I'd say you won't have to be in the waiting room longer than a few minutes. Certainly not a half an hour. Not even twenty minutes.

Question 1

You will read: Where are the speakers?

(A) At a sidewalk café
(B) In a history class
(C) At an airport check-in counter
(D) In a physician's office

Ⓐ Ⓑ Ⓒ ●

The best response to the question "Where are the speakers?" is Choice (D), "In a physician's office." Therefore, you should choose answer (D).

Question 2

You will read: Who are the speakers?

(A) A doctor and a nurse
(B) A clerk and a shopper
(C) A receptionist and a patient
(D) A pilot and a passenger

Ⓐ Ⓑ ● Ⓓ

The best response to the question "Who are the speakers?" is Choice (C), "A receptionist and a patient." Therefore, you should choose answer (C).

Question 3

You will read: How long will the woman have to wait?

        (A) A little bit

        (B) Twenty minutes

        (C) Thirty minutes

        (D) Over an hour

● Ⓑ Ⓒ Ⓓ

The best response to the question "How long will the woman have to wait?" is Choice (A), "A little bit." Therefore, you should choose answer (A).

1 Questions About People

On the TOEIC, questions about people are common. They ask you to identify the speaker or the performer of an action. Questions about people usually begin with *who*, although some *what* questions may also be about people.

> **TIP** When you see a *who* question, listen for information about people.

➡ Examples

If you see these question types, listen for answers about people.

Questions

> Who are the speakers?
> Who is the man?
> Who will make the photocopies?
> Who delivered the package?
> Who has the tickets?
> Who is the party for?
> Whose office will they use?
> Who are the speakers looking for?

Answers

Proper names	*Identification by activity or role*	*Identification by group*	*Identification by relationship*
Mr. Tanza	A tourist	Business people	His boss
Mrs. Green	A passenger	Family members	Her son
Ms. Hu	A driver	College students	Their teacher
Dr. Shapiro	A jogger		My colleague
			The woman's friend

EXERCISE

Choose the best answer to the question.

1. Who are the speakers?

   (A) Lifeguards at the beach   Ⓐ Ⓑ Ⓒ Ⓓ
   (B) Painters
   (C) Salespeople selling coats
   (D) Bartenders

2. Who will prepare the wall?

   (A) The man   Ⓐ Ⓑ Ⓒ Ⓓ
   (B) The woman
   (C) The boss
   (D) The helper

3. Who owns the house?

   (A) The man's father   Ⓐ Ⓑ Ⓒ Ⓓ
   (B) The man's mother
   (C) The man's brother
   (D) The man's friend

4. Who is the man?

   (A) A waiter   Ⓐ Ⓑ Ⓒ Ⓓ
   (B) A caterer
   (C) A pastry chef
   (D) A restaurant customer

5. Who are the women giving the dinner for?

   (A) Their boss   Ⓐ Ⓑ Ⓒ Ⓓ
   (B) Their friend
   (C) Their client
   (D) Their business partner

6. Who will pay the bill?

   (A) Mary   Ⓐ Ⓑ Ⓒ Ⓓ
   (B) Mary's assistant
   (C) The accountant
   (D) Everyone in the office

SKILL 2 — Questions About Occupations

Questions about a person's occupation are commonly asked on the TOEIC. You should first look at the answer choices to see what four occupations are given. Then you should try to think of words related to those occupations. These words will be clues.

It is important to listen for occupational clues in the conversations and short talks. If a person is an auto mechanic, you might hear references to engines, cars, oil, brakes, gas stations, and so on. If you hear those words, it is likely that the correct answer is *auto mechanic.*

> **TIP** Look for types of occupations in the answer choices BEFORE you hear the audio. Make assumptions about those occupations and listen for the clues.

➡ Examples

If you see these question types, listen for answers about someone's occupation.

Questions

What kind of job does the man have?
What is Mr. Smith's present position?
What type of work does the woman do?
How does this man earn a living?
What is the man's job?
What kind of job is available?
What is the woman's occupation?
Who can benefit from seeing this memo?
What is the man's profession?
Who was interviewed?
What does this woman do?
Who would most likely use the conference hall?

Answers

She's the director.	A dentist
He's a lawyer.	A travel agent
They're accountants.	A hotel clerk
The office manager	A pilot
The personnel director	A flight attendant
The receptionist	A waiter/waitress/server
A computer programmer	A chef

EXERCISE

Choose the best answer to the question.

1. What is the woman's occupation?

   (A) Running coach
   (B) Baseball player
   (C) Telephone operator
   (D) Telephone installer

   Ⓐ Ⓑ Ⓒ Ⓓ

2. What is the man's job?

   (A) Employment counselor
   (B) Tech support specialist
   (C) Website designer
   (D) Accountant

   Ⓐ Ⓑ Ⓒ Ⓓ

3. Who is responsible for answering the phone?

   (A) The man only
   (B) The receptionist
   (C) Everyone at the company
   (D) The customer service specialist

   Ⓐ Ⓑ Ⓒ Ⓓ

4. Who is the man?

   (A) A travel agent
   (B) A tourist
   (C) A tour guide
   (D) A museum director

   Ⓐ Ⓑ Ⓒ Ⓓ

5. What is the woman's job?

   (A) Bus driver
   (B) Taxi driver
   (C) Waiter
   (D) Chef

   Ⓐ Ⓑ Ⓒ Ⓓ

6. Who will call the restaurant?

   (A) The man
   (B) The woman
   (C) The hotel manager
   (D) The front desk clerk

   Ⓐ Ⓑ Ⓒ Ⓓ

Questions About Place

Most questions about place begin with *where*. These questions are generally answered by locations preceded by *in, on,* or *at*.

> **TIP** When you see a *where* question, listen for information about place.

➡ **Examples** _____

If you see these question types, listen for answers about places.

Questions

Where did the conversation probably take place?	Where has the man/woman been?
Where did the conversation likely occur?	Where does the man/woman want to go?
	Where did the man/woman come from?
Where is the man?	
Where is the woman?	Where are they going?
Where is the speaker?	
	Where did the man think the woman was?
Where are the man and woman?	
Where are the speakers?	Where should he call?
Where is the package?	Where did he put his coat?

Answers

Without prepositions	*With prepositions*	
The train station	In the closet	By the door
The store	Under the desk	In the dining room
The office	At the office	At home
The house	Next to the bank	On the bus
	At the train station	At the dentist's
	At the beach	To the airport
	To the store	

EXERCISE

Track 17

Choose the best answer to the question.

1. Where does this conversation take place?

   (A) In a private home
   (B) On a delivery truck
   (C) In a business office
   (D) At a shipping company

   Ⓐ Ⓑ Ⓒ Ⓓ

2. Where will the woman put the package?

   (A) On Jim's keyboard
   (B) On the filing cabinet
   (C) On Jim's desk
   (D) On a table

   Ⓐ Ⓑ Ⓒ Ⓓ

3. Where is Jim now?

   (A) At a conference
   (B) In his office
   (C) On a flight
   (D) On vacation

   Ⓐ Ⓑ Ⓒ Ⓓ

4. Where are the speakers?

   (A) In a taxi
   (B) On a plane
   (C) In a school
   (D) In a private home

   Ⓐ Ⓑ Ⓒ Ⓓ

5. Where is the woman's coat?

   (A) On a chair
   (B) On the floor
   (C) In the lobby
   (D) In the closet

   Ⓐ Ⓑ Ⓒ Ⓓ

6. Where is the woman going?

   (A) To her accountant's office
   (B) To the train station
   (C) To her apartment
   (D) To the bank

   Ⓐ Ⓑ Ⓒ Ⓓ

Questions About Time

Most questions about time begin with the words *when, how long* or *how often*. These questions are generally answered by time words or phrases. *When* questions are answered with a specific point in time, *how long* questions are answered with a length of time, and *how often* questions are answered with a frequency expression.

> **TIP** Look for clues on time in the answer choices BEFORE you hear the audio. Listen carefully for those clues in the audio.

➥ Examples

If you see these question types, listen for answers about time. Note the questions begin with *when* and *how*.

Questions

Questions with **When**	Questions with **How Long**	Questions with **How Often**
When did the conversation take place?	How long will they be in Tokyo?	How often do buses leave?
When is the man's birthday?	How long did the meeting last?	How often are the employees paid?
When is the woman's vacation date?	How long will it take to arrive?	How often is there a conference?
When is the restaurant open?	How long do you spend on the reports?	How often is the magazine published?
When was the meeting?		
When will the increase go into effect?		
When did he join the firm?		

Answers

Points in time	*Lengths of time*	*Frequency*
11:00 A.M.	45 minutes	Every hour
Noon	An hour	Every day
Midnight	Two days	Every other day
At 6:00	A week	Every two weeks
Before 5:30	About a month	Once a month
In the morning	Less than a year	Twice a year
Tomorrow		Three times a week
In the summer		
Next year		
In April		
On January 3rd		

EXERCISE

Choose the best answer to the question.

1. How much longer will the man stay?

(A) 10 minutes
(B) 15 minutes
(C) 30 minutes
(D) 60 minutes

Ⓐ Ⓑ Ⓒ Ⓓ

2. When is the man's appointment?

(A) At 9:00
(B) Tomorrow
(C) In a few minutes
(D) In half an hour

Ⓐ Ⓑ Ⓒ Ⓓ

3. How long will it take the man to get home?

(A) 20 minutes
(B) 25 minutes
(C) 40 minutes
(D) 45 minutes

Ⓐ Ⓑ Ⓒ Ⓓ

4. How often is there a staff meeting?

(A) Every morning
(B) Once a week
(C) Once a month
(D) Twice a month

Ⓐ Ⓑ Ⓒ Ⓓ

5. When will the meeting start?

(A) At 1:00
(B) At 3:00
(C) Before lunch
(D) In a couple of hours

Ⓐ Ⓑ Ⓒ Ⓓ

6. How long will the meeting last?

(A) One hour
(B) Two hours
(C) Three hours
(D) Four hours

Ⓐ Ⓑ Ⓒ Ⓓ

5 Questions About Activities

Most questions about activities begin with *what*. Some questions can begin with *how*. These questions are generally answered by short phrases or complete sentences. You should first look at the answer choices to see what four activities are given. Then you should try to think of words related to those activities. These words will be activity clues.

It is important to listen for activity clues. For example, the activity playing golf might have words such as *golf club*, *bag*, *course*, *fairway*, *hole*, and *green* in the audio.

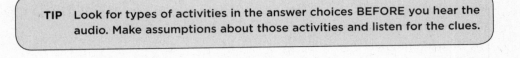

> **TIP** Look for types of activities in the answer choices BEFORE you hear the audio. Make assumptions about those activities and listen for the clues.

➡ Examples

If you see these question types, listen for answers about an activity. Note the questions begin with *what* and *how*.

Questions

Questions with to Do	*Questions about an event or occurrence*
What will the man do?	What happened?
What did the woman do?	What occurred?
What has the customer decided to do?	What took place?
What are they planning to do?	What happened to the woman?
What does the woman have to do?	What will happen next?
What is the man going to do?	
What is Mrs. Park supposed to do?	*Questions with How*
What are they doing?	How can the package be sent?
	How will the room be changed?

Answers

They are having dinner.	Mail a package
They will go to the store.	Wait on the corner
	Take a Spanish course
Seeing a movie	Attend a lecture
Playing golf	Take a day off
Planning a workshop	Leave soon
Making photocopies	Move some furniture

EXERCISE

Choose the best answer to the question.

1. What are they doing?

   (A) Taking a walk
   (B) Taking a nap
   (C) Buying a map
   (D) Driving a car

   Ⓐ Ⓑ Ⓒ Ⓓ

2. What did they do earlier?

   (A) Rested
   (B) Played in the snow
   (C) Had dinner
   (D) Rented a movie

   Ⓐ Ⓑ Ⓒ Ⓓ

3. What will they do next?

   (A) Read
   (B) Go to bed
   (C) See a play
   (D) Go to the movies

   Ⓐ Ⓑ Ⓒ Ⓓ

4. What is the man trying to do?

   (A) Staple copies
   (B) Fix the machine
   (C) Make extra copies
   (D) Make the copies look darker

   Ⓐ Ⓑ Ⓒ Ⓓ

5. What does the woman suggest doing?

   (A) Add toner
   (B) Try again later
   (C) Call a repair person
   (D) Report the problem

   Ⓐ Ⓑ Ⓒ Ⓓ

6. What will the man do next?

   (A) Ask the office manager to do the job
   (B) Use another machine
   (C) Do the job tomorrow
   (D) Buy a new machine

   Ⓐ Ⓑ Ⓒ Ⓓ

SKILL
6   Questions About Opinions

Most questions about opinions begin with the word *what*. They are generally answered with short sentences expressing an opinion about something.

> **TIP** Look for clues on opinions in the answers BEFORE you hear the audio. Listen carefully for those clues.

➡ Examples _____

If you see these question types, listen for answers about an opinion.

Questions

What questions
What did the man think about the play?
What did the speaker think about the talk?
What did the woman say about the presentation?
What was the matter with the conference?
What did the man like about the meal?
What is the woman's opinion of the movie?

Answers

It's boring.
He's highly qualified.
The room is too dark.
It was too expensive.
She was very helpful.
It wasn't long enough.

EXERCISE

Choose the best answer to the question.

1. What did they like about the speaker?

   (A) His short presentation
   (B) His humor
   (C) His clothes
   (D) His folks

   Ⓐ Ⓑ Ⓒ Ⓓ

2. What is the man's opinion of the hotel?

   (A) The décor is nice.
   (B) The food is great.
   (C) The seats are too hard.
   (D) The room is too big.

   Ⓐ Ⓑ Ⓒ Ⓓ

3. What does the woman think of the hotel?

   (A) It's very expensive.
   (B) It's cheaper than she expected.
   (C) The tables are nice.
   (D) It's uncomfortable.

   Ⓐ Ⓑ Ⓒ Ⓓ

4. What does the man say about the meeting?

   (A) It was boring.
   (B) It was too long.
   (C) It was informative.
   (D) It was disorganized.

   Ⓐ Ⓑ Ⓒ Ⓓ

5. What is the women's opinion of the new director?

   (A) He is not qualified for the job.
   (B) He is always busy.
   (C) He is talkative.
   (D) He is shy.

   Ⓐ Ⓑ Ⓒ Ⓓ

6. What does the man think of the cafeteria?

   (A) It has better food.
   (B) It is inexpensive.
   (C) It is too crowded.
   (D) It is quiet.

   Ⓐ Ⓑ Ⓒ Ⓓ

SKILL 7 Graphic

Some of the conversations in Part 3 may include a graphic. The graphic could be a chart, a graph, an agenda, a timetable, or something similar. The speakers could verify the information in the graphic or they could contradict the information.

> **TIP** Scan the questions quickly and look for key words in the visual. Listen for the key words in the conversation.

➡ **Examples** _____

Questions about graphics always begin with the sentence *Look at the graphic,* followed by a *wh-* question.

> Look at the graphic. Who works on Tuesday?
> Look at the graphic. When will the visitor arrive?
> Look at the graphic. Where will they sit?

You cannot answer the question only by looking at the graphic. You need to listen to the conversation for clues that will help you know what information to select from the graphic in order to answer the question.

EXERCISE

Track 21

Listen to the conversation, then choose the best answer to the question.

1. Look at the graphic. When will Sue work at the reception desk?   Ⓐ Ⓑ Ⓒ Ⓓ

   (A) Monday
   (B) Tuesday
   (C) Wednesday
   (D) Thursday

Reception Desk Schedule

Monday	Sue
Tuesday	Sam
Wednesday	Bill
Thursday	Jim
Friday	open

2. Look at the graphic. Which printer will the woman buy?

    (A) Model XX

    (B) Model XZ

    (C) Model Y

    (D) Model WY

Ⓐ Ⓑ Ⓒ Ⓓ

Printer Model	Price
Model XX	$115
Model XZ	$155
Model Y	$175
Model WY	$225

3. Look at the graphic. When was Mr. Kim hired?

    (A) February

    (B) March

    (C) April

    (D) May

Ⓐ Ⓑ Ⓒ Ⓓ

Sales

4. Look at the graphic. What topic will be discussed first at the meeting?

    (A) Budget Report

    (B) Sales Update

    (C) New Ad Campaign

    (D) Hiring Update

Ⓐ Ⓑ Ⓒ Ⓓ

Staff Meeting
January 12 2:00 P.M.

Budget Report .... Robert Franks
Sales Update .... Maya Lopez
New Ad Campaign ..... Sue Lin
Hiring Update .... Ben Ingram

5. Look at the graphic. Where will they meet for lunch?

(A) Location A
(B) Location B
(C) Location C
(D) Location D

(A) (B) (C) (D)

Downtown Shopping Mall

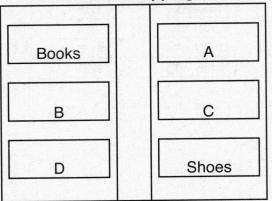

8 Meaning in Context

You will be asked questions about the meaning of a word or phrase used in the conversation. You will have to understand the meaning of the word or phrase in the context of the conversation.

> **TIP** Use the context to help determine the meaning.

➡ **Examples** _____

Meaning-in-context questions contain a word or phrase from the conversation.

> What does the man mean when he says, "I got it"?
> Why does the woman say, "Could you"?

Words and phrases can be used in different ways. When you see a meaning-in-context question, listen for the quoted words in the conversation. Understand how they are used by the speakers.

EXERCISE

Track 22

Listen to the conversation, then choose the best answer to the question.

1. What does the woman mean when she says, "I wouldn't do it like that"?

   (A) The woman thinks the man is working inefficiently. Ⓐ Ⓑ
   (B) The woman thinks the man is working too hard.

2. What does the man mean when he says, "Things have picked up"?

   (A) He got a promotion. Ⓐ Ⓑ
   (B) He is feeling optimistic.

3. What does the man mean when he says, "that color"?

   (A) He likes the color of the carpet. Ⓐ Ⓑ
   (B) He does not like the color of the carpet.

4. What does the woman mean when she says, "I thought that meeting would never end"?

   (A) The meeting was boring. Ⓐ Ⓑ
   (B) The meeting was canceled.

5. What does the woman mean when she says, "I'm on top of it"?

   (A) The woman is aware of the work schedule. Ⓐ Ⓑ
   (B) The woman is confident she can finish the work on time.

9 Incomplete Sentences

In normal conversation, much is understood through context. Speakers do not always use complete sentences.

> **TIP** Use the context to understand the meaning of short, fragmented answers.

➡ Examples

Are you coming to the meeting?
Maybe later.

Maybe later in this case means *Maybe I will come to the meeting later.* The idea *I will come to the meeting* is implied by the context.

I'm going out for lunch. Wanna come?
Sorry. Gotta work.

Wanna come means *Do you want to come*? The *Do* is omitted and *want to come* is shortened in speech only (never in writing) to *Wanna*. Similarly, *Gotta work* means *I have got to work*. The subject *I* and the modal *have to* is shortened in speech only (never in writing) to *Gotta*.

EXERCISE

Choose the correct meaning for the underlined fragments.

1. Woman: So, the meeting day has been changed to Friday?
   Man: <u>Right.</u>

   (A) It's on the right.   Ⓐ Ⓑ
   (B) You are correct.

2. Man: Let's take a break now and finish this later.
   Woman: <u>Fine with me.</u>

   (A) I agree with your plan.   Ⓐ Ⓑ
   (B) That's a bad idea.

3. Woman: Please make ten copies of this report, leave one on my desk, and send the rest to Mr. Sato.
   Man: <u>Got it.</u>

   (A) I have Mr. Sato's address.   Ⓐ Ⓑ
   (B) I understand everything you want me to do.

4. Man: We're having lunch at Café de Oro. Will you join us?
   Woman: <u>Wish I could.</u>

   (A)   I would like to join you, but I can't.   Ⓐ Ⓑ
   (B)   I have always wanted to eat at that café.

5. Woman: Ms. Chang is in a meeting and can't see you now.
   Man: <u>Too bad.</u>

   (A)   The meeting is a bad idea.   Ⓐ Ⓑ
   (B)   I'm sorry she can't see me.

PART 4: TALKS

Sample Questions

> **Directions:** You will hear a short talk given by a single speaker. You will see three questions on each talk, each with four possible answers. Choose the best answer to each question, and fill in the corresponding oval on your answer sheet. The talks will not be printed and will be spoken only once.

You will hear: In five minutes, for one hour only, women's coats and hats go on sale in our fifth-floor Better Fashions department. All merchandise is reduced by twenty-five to forty percent. Not all styles in all sizes, but an outstanding selection nonetheless. You should hurry to the fifth floor now. Last week, we sold out completely in a matter of minutes. We don't want any of you to be disappointed.

Question 1

You will read: When does the sale begin?

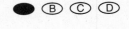

    (A) In five minutes
    (B) In one hour
    (C) At 2:45
    (D) Tomorrow

The best response to the question "When does the sale begin?" is Choice (A), "In five minutes." Therefore, you should choose answer (A).

Question 2

You will read: What is going on sale?

    (A) Men's coats
    (B) Women's hats
    (C) Cosmetics
    (D) Old merchandise

The best response to the question "What is going on sale?" is Choice (B), "Women's hats." Therefore, you should choose answer (B).

Question 3

You will read: How long will the sale last?

(A) Five minutes   Ⓐ Ⓑ ● Ⓓ
(B) Fifteen minutes
(C) Sixty minutes
(D) One week

The best response to the question "How long will the sale last?" is Choice (C), "Sixty minutes." Therefore, you should choose answer (C).

Questions About Events and Facts

Most questions about events and facts begin with *what*. These questions are generally answered by phrases or complete sentences. The strategy for these questions is similar to the strategies for the previous questions. Read the answer choices, make some assumptions about the events listed, and listen for the relevant clues.

> **TIP** Look for clues on events or facts in the answer choices BEFORE you hear the audio. Listen carefully for those clues in the audio.

➡ Examples

If you see these question types, listen for answers about an event or fact. Note that the questions begin with *what*.

Questions

What is the talk mainly about?
What event will take place?
What will happen next week?
What are the tickets for?
What will the speaker do after the meeting?
What will happen after the program?

Answers

A parade
A job fair
A concert
The annual banquet
The budget
Plans for next year

She will sign books.
He will answer questions.
There will be a festival.
Furniture will go on sale.

EXERCISE

Choose the best answer to the question.

1. What event will take place this weekend?

    (A) A book fair
    (B) A conference
    (C) A national celebration
    (D) An international dance

    (A) (B) (C) (D)

2. What will happen on Saturday evening?

    (A) A parade
    (B) A food sale
    (C) A concert
    (D) A circus performance

    (A) (B) (C) (D)

3. What will the mayor do on Sunday?

    (A) Sell tickets
    (B) Address the crowds
    (C) Play basketball
    (D) Buy some baskets

    (A) (B) (C) (D)

4. What event is the speaker celebrating?

    (A) A birthday
    (B) A graduation
    (C) A retirement
    (D) A job promotion

    (A) (B) (C) (D)

5. What will guests do at the celebration?

    (A) Dance
    (B) Play games
    (C) Enjoy a meal
    (D) Receive awards

    (A) (B) (C) (D)

6. What will the speaker do on Sunday?

    (A) Take a walk
    (B) Play tennis
    (C) Get up late
    (D) Go to work

    (A) (B) (C) (D)

Questions About Reasons

Most questions about reasons begin with *why*. Sometimes the question can begin with *what*. These questions are generally answered by complete sentences, but sometimes by short phrases. Use the same strategies that you have been using for the other question types.

> **TIP** Look for clues on reasons in the answer choices BEFORE you hear the audio. Listen carefully for those clues.

➡ Examples

If you see these question types, listen for answers about a reason. Note that most of the questions begin with *why*.

Questions

Why will the bus be late?
Why has the schedule been changed?
Why does the speaker want to have a meeting?
Why does the speaker need to change the appointment?
Why is there a sale this week?
Why did the speaker make the call?
What was the cause of the delay?

Answers

The weather is bad.
The director is away.
Traffic is heavy.
She wants to discuss the project.
He has to go out of town.
The store is closing.
To ask for help

EXERCISE

Choose the best answer to the question.

1. Why is there a delay?

    (A) Workers are staging a work action.   Ⓐ Ⓑ Ⓒ Ⓓ
    (B) The weather is bad.
    (C) There are flight control problems.
    (D) Passengers are boarding slowly.

2. Why should passengers get something to eat now?

    (A) The restaurants will close at midnight.   Ⓐ Ⓑ Ⓒ Ⓓ
    (B) The restaurants won't be open tomorrow.
    (C) There will be no food served on the flight.
    (D) There are some restaurants close to the gate.

3. Why should passengers pay attention to the
    announcements?

    (A) To find out which gate their flight will leave from   Ⓐ Ⓑ Ⓒ Ⓓ
    (B) To hear which restaurants are open
    (C) To keep from getting bored
    (D) To know when it is time to board the flight

4. Why does Mr. Brown have an appointment with Mr. Wilson?

    (A) To interview him for a newspaper article   Ⓐ Ⓑ Ⓒ Ⓓ
    (B) To go look at an apartment for rent
    (C) To review some documents
    (D) To sign some papers

5. Why does Mr. Brown have to cancel the appointment?

    (A) He has to buy a new suit.   Ⓐ Ⓑ Ⓒ Ⓓ
    (B) He has an unexpected meeting.
    (C) He has to go to the hospital emergency room.
    (D) He has not had enough time to prepare for the appointment.

6. Why doesn't Mr. Brown want the listener to call his office
    number today?

    (A) He is not at the office today.   Ⓐ Ⓑ Ⓒ Ⓓ
    (B) His office phone is out of order.
    (C) He is too busy to answer the phone.
    (D) Mr. Wilson only has his cell phone number.

Questions About Numbers

Questions about numbers may begin with *how many, how much, how long, what time,* or *when.* You will have to distinguish between numbers that sound similar to each other. You will also have to distinguish between numbers and other words that sound similar or the same.

> **TIP** Listen carefully for numbers and distinguish them from words that sound similar.

➡ **Examples** _____

Similar-Sounding Numbers

7 and 11
13 and 30
14 and 40
15 and 50
15 and 16
16 and 60
17 and 70
18 and 80
19 and 90
50 and 60

Words That Sound Similar to Numbers

2—to, too
2 days—today, Tuesday
3—free
4—for, forget
6—picks, sick
8—ate, wait
9—fine, time
10—then, when
20—plenty

Useful Phrases

over 20 = more than 20
under 20 = fewer than 20
at least 20 = 20 or more
up to 20 = no more than 20

EXERCISE

Track 25

Choose the best answer to the question.

1. When is the workshop?

    (A) Today   Ⓐ Ⓑ Ⓒ Ⓓ
    (B) In two days
    (C) On Tuesday
    (D) Wednesday

2. How many people will attend the workshop?

    (A) 13   Ⓐ Ⓑ Ⓒ Ⓓ
    (B) Almost 30
    (C) Exactly 30
    (D) More than 30

3. How long does the speaker want to meet with John?

    (A) 15 minutes   Ⓐ Ⓑ Ⓒ Ⓓ
    (B) 50 minutes
    (C) 30 minutes
    (D) 2 hours

4. What time is the program scheduled to start?

    (A) 2:00   Ⓐ Ⓑ Ⓒ Ⓓ
    (B) 7:00
    (C) 9:00
    (D) 10:00

5. How many people will give presentations?

    (A) 5   Ⓐ Ⓑ Ⓒ Ⓓ
    (B) 11
    (C) 13
    (D) 30

6. How much does admission to the program cost?

    (A) $0   Ⓐ Ⓑ Ⓒ Ⓓ
    (B) $3
    (C) $4
    (D) $20

SKILL 4 Questions About Main Topics

Answers to questions are often found among details, but sometimes they are about larger ideas. Questions about the main topic require you to understand the general purpose of the talk.

> **TIP** Look for ideas that indicate the general purpose.

➡ Examples

If you see these question types, listen for answers about the main topic. When you see these types of questions, you should look in the answer choices for the overall subject of what you heard. The question might ask about the identity of the speaker, the context of the talk, the purpose of the talk, or the audience.

Questions

What is this talk about?
Who is this information for?
Who would be interested in this announcement?
What is the purpose of this message?
Where would you hear this talk?

Answers

General categories	Specific examples
A role, job title, or group	A client A ticket clerk The woman's colleagues Airline passengers
A kind of place or a situation	In an office At a convention During a banquet At an airport
Any subject	The new machinery Politics Environmental responsibility An advertising campaign
A purpose	To change an appointment To advertise a business To introduce a speaker To change an order

EXERCISE

Choose the best answer to the question.

1. What changes are taking place in the company?

   (A) The Board of Directors resigned.   Ⓐ Ⓑ Ⓒ Ⓓ
   (B) The Managing Director was fired.
   (C) The workers went on strike.
   (D) All letters will be sent by computer.

2. Who is the speaker addressing?

   (A) Some clients   Ⓐ Ⓑ Ⓒ Ⓓ
   (B) His coworkers
   (C) A server
   (D) The director

3. What does the speaker plan to do soon?

   (A) Become a clothes salesman   Ⓐ Ⓑ Ⓒ Ⓓ
   (B) Start a business
   (C) Go to college
   (D) Work as a restaurant manager

4. Where would you hear this announcement?

   (A) In a store   Ⓐ Ⓑ Ⓒ Ⓓ
   (B) In a hotel
   (C) In a restaurant
   (D) In a train station

5. What is the announcement about?

   (A) A sale   Ⓐ Ⓑ Ⓒ Ⓓ
   (B) How to pay
   (C) Job openings
   (D) Closing time

6. Who is the announcement for?

   (A) All staff   Ⓐ Ⓑ Ⓒ Ⓓ
   (B) Customers
   (C) The manager
   (D) Security guards

5 Paraphrases

The answer to a question is often a paraphrase of what you hear in the talk. A paraphrase is a restatement of information using different words.

> **TIP** Pay attention to synonyms and similar phrases that restate the meaning of a statement.

➥ Examples

Answer choices are often paraphrases of statements in the talk. Look at these examples:

Statement:	Temperatures will be high today.
Paraphrase:	It will be a warm day.
Statement:	Please remain seated.
Paraphrase:	Please stay in your seats.
Statement:	Mr. Johnson has written several books.
Paraphrase:	Mr. Johnson is an author.
Statement:	Houses in this neighborhood don't cost a great deal.
Paraphrase:	It isn't expensive to live in this area.

EXERCISE

Choose the best answer to the question.

1. What is the purpose of the form?

   (A) To make a complaint
   (B) To borrow money
   (C) To apply for a job
   (D) To get a license

   Ⓐ Ⓑ Ⓒ Ⓓ

2. How should the form be submitted?

   (A) By regular mail
   (B) By e-mail
   (C) In person
   (D) Through a website

   Ⓐ Ⓑ Ⓒ Ⓓ

3. When will the listener be contacted?

   (A) In two days
   (B) In four days
   (C) In ten days
   (D) In fourteen days

   Ⓐ Ⓑ Ⓒ Ⓓ

4. Why did the speaker make the call?

   (A) To arrange for a delivery
   (B) To advertise products
   (C) To thank the listener
   (D) To order a table

   Ⓐ Ⓑ Ⓒ Ⓓ

5. What does the speaker say about the listener's address?

   (A) It is near his office.
   (B) It is difficult to find.
   (C) It is listed in his records.
   (D) It has changed recently.

   Ⓐ Ⓑ Ⓒ Ⓓ

6. What does the speaker ask the listener to do?

   (A) Rent a truck
   (B) Call before Friday
   (C) Go to the warehouse
   (D) Provide a phone number

   Ⓐ Ⓑ Ⓒ Ⓓ

SKILL
6

Graphic

Some of the conversations in Part 4 may include a graphic. The graphic could be a chart, an agenda, a timetable, or something similar. The speaker could verify the information in the graphic or the speaker could contradict the information.

> **TIP** Scan the questions quickly and look for key words in the visual. Listen for the key words from the questions.

➥ Examples _____

As in Part 3, questions about graphics in Part 4 always begin with the sentence *Look at the graphic*, followed by a *wh-* question.

> Look at the graphic. Who will speak first?
> Look at the graphic. What will they discuss first?
> Look at the graphic. What time will the bus leave?

You cannot answer the question only by looking at the graphic. You need to listen to the talk for clues that will help you know what information to select from the graphic in order to answer the question.

Track
28

EXERCISE

Listen to the talk, then choose the best answer to the question.

1. Look at the graphic. Which train will Pamela take?

    (A) 30
    (B) 31
    (C) 32
    (D) 33

    (A) (B) (C) (D)

Timetable

Train No.	Lv. Ardale	Arr. Springfield
30	5:00 A.M.	7:17
31	6:45	9:02
32	8:45	11:02
33	10:30	12:47

2. Look at the graphic. Which part of the budget does the speaker want to reduce first?

    (A) Advertising   Ⓐ Ⓑ Ⓒ Ⓓ

    (B) Salaries

    (C) Overhead

    (D) Materials

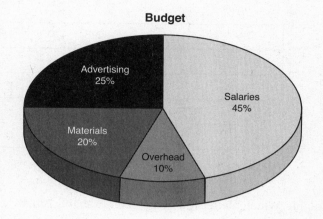

Budget

3. Look at the graphic. Where will the group have lunch?

    (A) Pine Grove   Ⓐ Ⓑ Ⓒ Ⓓ

    (B) Butterfly Garden

    (C) Rose Garden

    (D) Nature Center

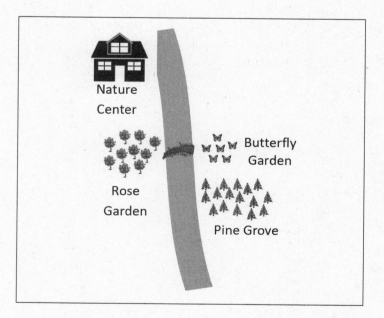

4. Look at the graphic. Which region will the speaker discuss?

(A) Northwest
(B) Southwest
(C) Northeast
(D) Southeast

Ⓐ Ⓑ Ⓒ Ⓓ

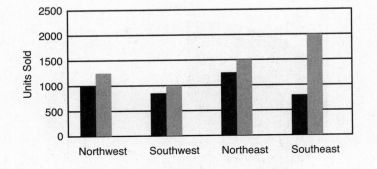

5. Look at the graphic. Which platter will the speaker probably order?

(A) Small
(B) Medium
(C) Large
(D) Extra Large

Ⓐ Ⓑ Ⓒ Ⓓ

Kim's Catering		
Cold Cuts Platter		
Small	....	serves 15
Medium	....	serves 25
Large	....	serves 50
Extra Large	....	serves 75

Implied Meaning

The speaker may not express an idea directly. The speaker may imply something without saying it directly.

> They were a bit disappointed by the turnout.
>
> > implies
>
> They expected more people to be there.

> **TIP** The meaning comes from the context of the talk.

EXERCISE

Track 29

Listen to each talk and answer the question.

1. What does the speaker say about his appointment?

   (A) He has rescheduled this appointment several times already.
   (B) This is the first time he has rescheduled the appointment.

   (A) (B)

2. What does the speaker say about the weather?

   (A) She wishes it were warmer.
   (B) She thinks it is very nice.

   (A) (B)

3. What does the speaker say about the ticket machine?

   (A) It accepts both cash and credit cards.
   (B) The machine accepts credit cards only.

   (A) (B)

4. What does the speaker say about the celebration?

   (A) The event is more crowded than it was last year.
   (B) The stadium isn't big enough to hold the crowds.

   (A) (B)

5. What does the speaker say about the tickets?

   (A) They are discounted for members.
   (B) They are available to members only.

   (A) (B)

Multiple Accents

In the international business world, there are many varieties of English spoken. On the TOEIC, the speakers could have American, British, Australian, South African, Canadian, or Indian accents. You will not have to identify the accent, but you should be able to understand the meaning of what is being said regardless of the speaker's accent.

> **TIP** Use the Internet to listen to news broadcasts from cities in the U.S., the U.K., Australia, Canada, New Zealand, and India. Listen to the same news from different sources.

Track
30

EXERCISE

Listen to these short talks, then write what you hear.

1. _____

_____

2. _____

_____

3. _____

_____

4. _____

_____

5. _____

_____

SUMMARY OF TIPS

Part 1: Photographs

- Listen for the meaning of the whole sentence to determine which choice best matches the photo.
- When you look at the photo, analyze the people. Determine their number, gender, location, occupation, and actions.
- Use the context of the photo to identify objects and location.

Part 2: Question-Response

- Listen for the meaning of the question/statement and answer choices. Do not be confused by words with similar sounds, related words, and homonyms.
- Listen for suggestions, offers, and requests.

Part 3: Conversations and Part 4: Talks

- Learn to recognize different types of questions and what they ask about – people, occupations, place, time, etc.
- Understand the meaning of words and phrases in the context of the conversation or talk.
- Look for paraphrases of words in the conversation or talk.
- Listen for implied meaning.
- In questions with a graphic, scan the graphic, then listen for information in the talk that confirms or contradicts the information in the graphic.
- Practice listening to different accents.

Many thanks to my readers, especially Jean-Pierre Saint-Aimé, who have provided valuable tips on test-taking strategies.

ANSWER SHEET
Listening Comprehension
Mini-Test

Part 1: Photographs

1. Ⓐ Ⓑ Ⓒ Ⓓ 2. Ⓐ Ⓑ Ⓒ Ⓓ 3. Ⓐ Ⓑ Ⓒ Ⓓ 4. Ⓐ Ⓑ Ⓒ Ⓓ

Part 2: Question-Response

5. Ⓐ Ⓑ Ⓒ 8. Ⓐ Ⓑ Ⓒ 11. Ⓐ Ⓑ Ⓒ 14. Ⓐ Ⓑ Ⓒ
6. Ⓐ Ⓑ Ⓒ 9. Ⓐ Ⓑ Ⓒ 12. Ⓐ Ⓑ Ⓒ 15. Ⓐ Ⓑ Ⓒ
7. Ⓐ Ⓑ Ⓒ 10. Ⓐ Ⓑ Ⓒ 13. Ⓐ Ⓑ Ⓒ 16. Ⓐ Ⓑ Ⓒ

Part 3: Conversations

17. Ⓐ Ⓑ Ⓒ Ⓓ 22. Ⓐ Ⓑ Ⓒ Ⓓ 27. Ⓐ Ⓑ Ⓒ Ⓓ 32. Ⓐ Ⓑ Ⓒ Ⓓ
18. Ⓐ Ⓑ Ⓒ Ⓓ 23. Ⓐ Ⓑ Ⓒ Ⓓ 28. Ⓐ Ⓑ Ⓒ Ⓓ 33. Ⓐ Ⓑ Ⓒ Ⓓ
19. Ⓐ Ⓑ Ⓒ Ⓓ 24. Ⓐ Ⓑ Ⓒ Ⓓ 29. Ⓐ Ⓑ Ⓒ Ⓓ 34. Ⓐ Ⓑ Ⓒ Ⓓ
20. Ⓐ Ⓑ Ⓒ Ⓓ 25. Ⓐ Ⓑ Ⓒ Ⓓ 30. Ⓐ Ⓑ Ⓒ Ⓓ
21. Ⓐ Ⓑ Ⓒ Ⓓ 26. Ⓐ Ⓑ Ⓒ Ⓓ 31. Ⓐ Ⓑ Ⓒ Ⓓ

Part 4: Talks

35. Ⓐ Ⓑ Ⓒ Ⓓ 39. Ⓐ Ⓑ Ⓒ Ⓓ 43. Ⓐ Ⓑ Ⓒ Ⓓ 47. Ⓐ Ⓑ Ⓒ Ⓓ
36. Ⓐ Ⓑ Ⓒ Ⓓ 40. Ⓐ Ⓑ Ⓒ Ⓓ 44. Ⓐ Ⓑ Ⓒ Ⓓ 48. Ⓐ Ⓑ Ⓒ Ⓓ
37. Ⓐ Ⓑ Ⓒ Ⓓ 41. Ⓐ Ⓑ Ⓒ Ⓓ 45. Ⓐ Ⓑ Ⓒ Ⓓ 49. Ⓐ Ⓑ Ⓒ Ⓓ
38. Ⓐ Ⓑ Ⓒ Ⓓ 42. Ⓐ Ⓑ Ⓒ Ⓓ 46. Ⓐ Ⓑ Ⓒ Ⓓ

MINI-TEST FOR LISTENING COMPREHENSION

Part 1: Photographs

Track 31

Directions: You will see a photograph. You will hear four statements about the photograph. Choose the statement that most closely matches the photograph, and fill in the corresponding oval on your answer sheet.

1.

2.

3.

4.

Part 2: Question-Response

Directions: You will hear a question and three possible responses. Choose the response that most closely answers the question, and fill in the corresponding oval on your answer sheet.

5. Mark your answer on your answer sheet.

6. Mark your answer on your answer sheet.

7. Mark your answer on your answer sheet.

8. Mark your answer on your answer sheet.

9. Mark your answer on your answer sheet.

10. Mark your answer on your answer sheet.

11. Mark your answer on your answer sheet.

12. Mark your answer on your answer sheet.

13. Mark your answer on your answer sheet.

14. Mark your answer on your answer sheet.

15. Mark your answer on your answer sheet.

16. Mark your answer on your answer sheet.

Part 3: Conversations

Directions: You will hear a conversation between two or more people. You will see three questions on each conversation and four possible answers. Choose the best answer to each question, and fill in the corresponding oval on your answer sheet.

17. What did the woman have at the café?

   (A) Soup and a sandwich
   (B) Soup and a salad
   (C) A sandwich only
   (D) A salad only

18. What did the man imply about the café?

   (A) The food is better than the décor.
   (B) The walls are in need of repair.
   (C) Its menu isn't interesting.
   (D) It's too far from the office.

19. What will the speakers do tomorrow?

   (A) Work on a project together
   (B) Look for a new place to eat
   (C) Paint the walls
   (D) Return to the café

20. What does the man suggest the woman do?

   (A) Spend her vacation at home
   (B) Ask for more time off
   (C) Start packing soon
   (D) Go to Paris

21. How long is the woman's vacation?

   (A) One week
   (B) Two weeks
   (C) Three weeks
   (D) Four weeks

22. What will the woman do this afternoon?

   (A) Read a book
   (B) Go shopping
   (C) Walk her dog
   (D) Make trip reservations

23. What does the woman want to have printed?

   (A) Menus
   (B) Checks
   (C) Order forms
   (D) Advertisements

24. What does the man agree to do?

   (A) Print 24 copies
   (B) Forget the rush charge
   (C) Have the order ready tomorrow
   (D) Print on one side of the page only

25. What does the man want the woman to do?

   (A) Pick up the order at night
   (B) Pay ahead of time
   (C) Check the order
   (D) Use a credit card

26. What do the speakers imply about the new director?

    (A) They admire the director's professional background.

    (B) She is looking for some important documents.

    (C) She is interested in hiring a new director.

    (D) She needs help writing her own résumé.

27. When did the new director begin working at this company?

    (A) Today

    (B) Two days ago

    (C) A week ago

    (D) Last Tuesday

28. What does the woman suggest?

    (A) Going to a staff meeting

    (B) Attending a social event

    (C) Getting something to eat

    (D) Calling the director at noon

Main Street Paints
Interior Paint Price list

Size	Coverage
1-liter can	.... up to 6 sq. meters
2-liter can	.... up to 12 sq. meters
5-liter can	.... up to 30 sq. meters
25-liter bucket	.... up to 150 sq. meters

29. What are they going to paint?

    (A) The closet

    (B) The office

    (C) The hallway

    (D) The stairwell

30. What color paint will they buy?

    (A) Yellow

    (B) Green

    (C) White

    (D) Blue

31. Look at the graphic. Which size paint will they probably buy?

    (A) 1-liter can

    (B) 2-liter can

    (C) 5-liter can

    (D) 25-liter bucket

Springer's Office Store
Store-wide sale

Discounts offered on most items throughout the store!

10% off paper and pens
15% off electronics
20% off office furniture
25% off coffeemakers

This week only!

32. Look at the graphic. How much of a discount will the man get?

    (A) 10%

    (B) 15%

    (C) 20%

    (D) 25%

33. What does the woman offer to do?

    (A) Open the box

    (B) Explain the instructions

    (C) Show the man where to park

    (D) Take the purchase to the cash register

34. How will the man transport his purchase to his office?

    (A) He will ask a colleague to get it.

    (B) He will carry it with him now.

    (C) He will pick it up tomorrow.

    (D) He will have it delivered.

Part 4: Talks

Directions: You will hear a talk given by a single speaker. You will see three questions on each talk, each with four possible answers. Choose the best answer to each question, and fill in the corresponding oval on your answer sheet.

Floor Plan

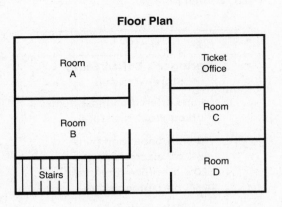

35. Where would you hear this talk?

   (A) Shopping mall
   (B) Sports event
   (C) Museum
   (D) Theater

36. What are the listeners asked to do?

   (A) Buy a ticket
   (B) Watch a play
   (C) Choose a gift
   (D) Move their seats

37. Look at the graphic. Where is the gift shop?

   (A) Room A
   (B) Room B
   (C) Room C
   (D) Room D

38. Why did the speaker make the call?

   (A) To make an appointment
   (B) To solicit a new client
   (C) To ask for directions
   (D) To get information

39. What does the speaker mean when he says, "It would work better for me if you came after hours"?

   (A) He prefers the cleaners to come when the office is closed.
   (B) He thinks the work will take several hours to complete.
   (C) He's at the office just a few hours a day.
   (D) He does a better job later in the day.

40. What does the speaker want the listener to do?

   (A) Come to his office next week
   (B) Wait for another call from him
   (C) Meet him downtown
   (D) Return his call soon

41. What kind of subscription is being offered?

   (A) Movie tickets
   (B) Magazine
   (C) Cable TV
   (D) Video streaming

42. How long does a free subscription last?

(A) Two days
(B) Three days
(C) One month
(D) One year

43. How much does a one-year subscription cost?

(A) $50
(B) $99
(C) $150
(D) $100

---

44. What will happen tomorrow?

(A) Software will be installed.
(B) A new carpet will be laid.
(C) Furniture will be delivered.
(D) The hallway will be painted.

45. What does the speaker mean when he says, "They should be out of here by noon"?

(A) Staff should stay out of the office all morning.
(B) The workers will finish before 12:00.
(C) Employees can take the afternoon off.
(D) Office supplies are running low.

46. What are listeners asked to do?

(A) Arrange the new furniture
(B) Work in the front office
(C) Use the back entrance
(D) Arrive early

| **Hildamire Hotel** |
| Directory |
| **Ground floor** |
| Lobby, Restaurant, Pool |
| **First floor** |
| Conference and Banquet Rooms |
| **Third floor** |
| Administrative Offices |
| **Fourth–Tenth floors** |
| Guest Rooms |

47. What event is the listener planning?

(A) A wedding
(B) A conference
(C) A training seminar
(D) An awards banquet

48. About how many people will attend the event?

(A) 100
(B) 125
(C) 200
(D) 225

49. Look at the graphic. Where is Ms. Jones's office located?

(A) Ground floor
(B) First floor
(C) Second floor
(D) Third floor

ANSWER KEY FOR LISTENING COMPREHENSION SKILLS

Answer Explanations can be found beginning on page 89.

Part 1: Photographs

SKILL 1 ASSUMPTIONS

Practice

A. T	D. T	G. F	J. PT
B. F	E. T	H. F	
C. PT	F. PT	I. T	

Exercise

Photo 1: **B**   Photo 2: **C**

SKILL 2 PEOPLE

Practice

Number: There are two people in the photo.
Gender: There is one man and one woman.
Location: The man is on the right, the woman is on the left.
Description: They are elderly. They have short hair. The man has a mustache.
Activity: They are looking at a computer. The man is pointing at the computer screen. They are sitting on a bench. They have suitcases.
Occupation: They may be retired. They look like tourists.

Exercise

Photo 3: **A**   Photo 4: **B**

SKILL 3 THINGS

Practice

table, chairs, glasses, plates, napkins, forks, vase, flower

Exercise

Photo 5: **A**   Photo 6: **C**

SKILL 4 ACTIONS

Practice

(possible answers)
shopping, holding the fruit, picking up the fruit, looking at the fruit, pushing the cart, choosing fruit, standing in the aisle

Exercise

Photo 7: **D**   Photo 8: **D**

SKILL 5 GENERAL LOCATIONS

Practice

Location: park. Context clues: benches, grass, trees, bushes, walking path, fence, lamppost

Exercise

Photo 9: **B**   Photo 10: **D**

SKILL 6 SPECIFIC LOCATIONS

Practice

(possible answers)
The pen is on the notebook.
The notebook is in front of the computer.
The lamp is over the table.
The computer is between the two speakers.
The books are to the left of the speakers.
The plant is on top of the bookshelf.

Exercise

Photo 11: **A**   Photo 12: **C**

Part 2: Question-Response

Skill 1 Similar Sounds	1. **A**	2. **C**	3. **A**	4. **B**	5. **B**
Skill 2 Related Words	1. **A**	2. **B**	3. **C**	4. **C**	5. **A**
Skill 3 Homonyms	1. **A**	2. **B**	3. **A**	4. **A**	5. **A**
Skill 4 Same Sound/Same Spelling but Different Meaning	1. **B**	2. **C**	3. **B**	4. **C**	5. **B**
Skill 5 Suggestions	1. **C**	2. **A**	3. **C**	4. **B**	5. **A**
Skill 6 Offers	1. **C**	2. **A**	3. **B**	4. **A**	5. **B**
Skill 7 Requests	1. **A**	2. **B**	3. **C**	4. **B**	5. **C**

Part 3: Conversations

Skill 1 Questions About People	1. **B**	2. **B**	3. **A**	4. **B**	5. **A**	6. **B**
Skill 2 Questions About Occupations	1. **D**	2. **D**	3. **C**	4. **C**	5. **A**	6. **D**
Skill 3 Questions About Place	1. **C**	2. **A**	3. **D**	4. **C**	5. **D**	6. **B**
Skill 4 Questions About Time	1. **C**	2. **B**	3. **D**	4. **C**	5. **A**	6. **B**
Skill 5 Questions About Activities	1. **D**	2. **C**	3. **D**	4. **A**	5. **D**	6. **B**
Skill 6 Questions About Opinions	1. **B**	2. **B**	3. **A**	4. **C**	5. **D**	6. **C**
Skill 7 Graphic	1. **D**	2. **A**	3. **B**	4. **B**	5. **A**	

| Skill 8 Meaning in Context | 1. **A** | 2. **B** | 3. **B** | 4. **A** | 5. **B** | |
| Skill 9 Incomplete Sentences | 1. **B** | 2. **A** | 3. **B** | 4. **A** | 5. **B** | |

Part 4: Talks

Skill 1 Questions About Events and Facts	1. **C**	2. **C**	3. **C**	4. **B**	5. **C**	6. **B**
Skill 2 Questions About Reasons	1. **A**	2. **A**	3. **D**	4. **C**	5. **B**	6. **A**
Skill 3 Questions About Numbers	1. **B**	2. **D**	3. **A**	4. **B**	5. **A**	6. **A**
Skill 4 Questions About Main Topics	1. **B**	2. **B**	3. **B**	4. **A**	5. **D**	6. **B**
Skill 5 Paraphrases	1. **B**	2. **A**	3. **D**	4. **A**	5. **C**	6. **B**
Skill 6 Graphic	1. **C**	2. **B**	3. **C**	4. **D**	5. **A**	
Skill 7 Implied Meaning	1. **A**	2. **B**	3. **B**	4. **A**	5. **B**	

Skill 8 Multiple Accents

1. Good evening and welcome to tonight's presentation. We are very excited to have with us tonight a world-famous journalist. I am sure you will enjoy his talk very much.

2. Here is the weather outlook for the weekend. We will have cloudy skies all day Saturday. Expect rain to begin late Saturday evening and continue through Sunday morning. The rain will clear up on Sunday afternoon.

3. Thank you for calling the Acme Company. We value your call. To check your order status, press one. For shipping information, press two. To speak with a customer service representative, press three. To repeat this menu, press four.

4. Attention shoppers. We will be closing the store in ten minutes. Please take your purchases to the checkout area at this time. If you are purchasing ten items or fewer, you may use the express checkout lane

5. The tour will begin in just a few minutes. Please line up by the main entrance. If you don't have a ticket, you can purchase one in the gift shop.

ANSWER EXPLANATIONS FOR LISTENING COMPREHENSION SKILLS

Part 1: Photographs

SKILL 1 ASSUMPTIONS

Photo 1

(B) In Choice (B) you can assume from the context that the people in white laboratory coats are technicians and that they could be doing experiments. Choice (A) is incorrect because the photo shows several people who could be pharmacists but none who could be customers. Choice (C) is incorrect because there are no laboratory animals pictured. Choice (D) is incorrect because the shelves contain bottles, jars, and supplies.

Photo 2

(C) The people are wearing business clothes and appear to be discussing some documents, so you can assume that they are business people having a meeting. Choice (A) correctly mentions the bottle, but no one is washing it. Choice (B) correctly mentions the computer, but the people are not in a store so no one is buying anything. Choice (D) is related to the fact that they are sitting around a table, but there is no food present, instead, there are things you might see at a business meeting—documents and a computer.

SKILL 2 PEOPLE

Photo 3

(A) Choice (A) correctly identifies the number and activity of the people. Choice (B) is incorrect because the men are in short sleeves. Choice (C) is incorrect because one woman is not as tall as the men. Choice (D) is incorrect because one of the women is pointing to the map.

Photo 4

(B) Choice (B) correctly identifies the people and their activity. Choice (A) is incorrect because it incorrectly identifies the man and woman's activity as looking for a bench rather than sitting on one.

Choice (C) incorrectly describes the woman's hair. Choice (D) correctly identifies the suitcases, but no one is carrying them.

SKILL 3 THINGS

Photo 5

(A) Choice (A) correctly identifies the candles and their location—on the mantle. Choice (B) correctly identifies the piano, but there is no man in the photo. Choice (C) correctly identifies the chairs, but there are no people sitting on them. Choice (D) correctly identifies the cushions but not their location.

Photo 6

(C) Choice (C) correctly identifies the vase and its location. Choice (A) correctly identifies the flower, but not its location—it is in the vase, not in a garden. Choice (B) incorrectly identifies the location of the forks—they are on the napkins, not the plates. Choice (D) correctly identifies the table, but there is no food on it.

SKILL 4 ACTIONS

Photo 7

(D) Choice (D) correctly describes what the people (workers) are doing (laying pipeline). Choice (A) is incorrect because the men are *laying pipe*, not *smoking pipes*. Choice (B) identifies an incorrect action. Choice (C) identifies a *previous* action.

Photo 8

(D) Choice (D) correctly describes what the woman is doing. Choice (A) correctly identifies the fruit, but no one is washing it. Choice (B) is incorrect because the woman is pushing a cart, not looking for one. Choice (C) correctly identifies the oranges and the boxes, but no one is packing them.

SKILL 5 GENERAL LOCATIONS

Photo 9

(B) Choice (B) assumes that the people are passengers and are passing through a security checkpoint. Choice (A) incorrectly identifies the scene as a store. Choice (C) incorrectly identifies the scene as a bank. Choice (D) takes place on the plane, not at airport security.

Photo 10

(D) Choice (D) correctly identifies the location as a park and correctly describes the benches. Choice (A) makes an incorrect assumption about the location—there are benches at a bus stop, but everything else in the photo suggests that it is a park. Choice (B) confuses the meaning of the word *park*. Choice (C) correctly identifies the lamppost but not its location—there is no bank in the photo.

SKILL 6 SPECIFIC LOCATIONS

Photo 11

(A) Choice (A) correctly identifies the glasses and their specific location. Choice (B) correctly identifies the activity of the people but not their location—there is no window in the picture. Choice (D) correctly identifies the activity of the server but not her location—she is not near the man. Choice (C) correctly identifies the napkins but not their location—they are on a plate or under the forks.

Photo 12

(C) Choice (C) correctly identifies the location of the small clock. Choice (A) is incorrect because the plant is on top of the bookshelf, not on the desk. Choice (B) is incorrect because the pen is on the notebook, not in the cup. Choice (D) is incorrect because the speakers are next to, or on either side of, the computer, not behind it.

Part 2: Question-Response

SKILL 1 SIMILAR SOUNDS

1. **(A)** Choice (A) answers the *yes–no* question with *Yes*. Choice (B) has related words *delivery/truck* and similar-sounding words *letter/ladder, delivered/delivery*. Choice (C) has similar-sounding words *today/Tuesday, Was the/was he*. Listen for the whole meaning; note the grammar clue such as a *yes–no* question that begins with the auxiliary *was*.

2. **(C)** Choice (C) answers the *Where* question with a place: *on the next block*. Choice (A) has similar-sounding words *office/softest*. Choice (B) has similar-sounding words *fined/find*.

3. **(A)** The tag question *isn't she* asks for agreement. The question states that Mary Ann is *a nice person*, and the answer agrees by restating the idea as *she gets along well*, which has the same meaning. Choice (B) has similar-sounding words *nice/rice*. Choice (C) has similar-sounding words *person/purse*.

4. **(B)** *I sent a check* is a logical response to the question about paying a bill. Choice (A) confuses similar-sounding words *pay* and *play*. Choice (C) confuses similar-sounding words *bill* and *will*.

5. **(B)** This is a polite response to the polite request. Choice (A) confuses similar-sounding words *for me* and *form*. Choice (C) confuses similar-sounding words *report* and *sports*.

SKILL 2 RELATED WORDS

1. **(A)** Listen for the whole meaning; note the grammar clue: *How long* and the verb *married* suggest a length of time. Choice (A) gives the appropriate answer (ten years) to *how long*. Choice (B) has the related words *long/five feet*, but the question refers to time, not distance. Choice (C) has the related words *married/bride*.

2. **(B)** The question *When* is about time. Choice (B) answers with a time: *ten tomorrow morning*. Choice (A) relates the words *flight/ticket*. Choice (C) relates the words *flight/reservation*.

3. **(C)** The question *Where* is about a place. Choice (C) answers the question about a place to eat dinner with *restaurant*. Choice (A) relates the words *dinner/menu* and also repeats the word *like*. Choice (B) relates the words *dinner/meal*.

4. **(C)** This is a logical answer to the *What time* question. Choices (A) and (B) relate the word *bus* with *driver* and *ticket*.

5. **(A)** *It's mine* is a logical response to the *Whose* question. Choices (B) and (C) relate the word *office* with *desk* and *work*.

SKILL 3 HOMONYMS

1. **(A)** The tag question *doesn't he* requires a *yes–no* answer. Choice (A) answers the question and tells when he will leave. Choice (B) has the homonyms *week/weak*. Choice (C) has the homonyms *leaves* (v) / *leaves* (n).

2. **(B)** The question asks about a color of paint. Choice (B) responds with a comment about color. Choice (A) has the homonyms *blue/blew*. Choice (C) has the homonyms *wait (waiting room)/weight*.

3. **(A)** The embedded question *Who* asks about a person. Choice (A) responds with the name of a person, *Mr. Cho*. Choice (B) has the homonyms *won/one*. Choice (C) has the homonyms *do/due*.

4. **(A)** *Only one* answers the *How many* question. Choice (B) confuses the homonyms *buy* and *bye*. Choice (C) confuses the homonyms *buy* and *by*.

5. **(A)** This answers the question about a preference for a meeting time. Choices (B) and (C) confuse the homonyms *week* and *weak*.

SKILL 4 SAME SOUND/SAME SPELLING BUT DIFFERENT MEANING

1. **(B)** The phrase in (B) *Not for me* is a *no* answer to the *yes–no* question. It means, *No, the bed is not too hard for me*. A hard bed is a *firm* bed. Choice (A) incorrectly interprets *hard* to mean *difficult*. In Choice (C) *bed* means *a place for flowers*.

2. **(C)** Choice (C) is a logical response to a complaint about lack of light in the room. Choice (A) incorrectly interprets *light* in this context to mean *not heavy*. Choice (B) incorrectly interprets *room* in this context to mean *space*.

3. **(B)** In Choice (B), *I'll phone you* is a logical response to a request for a call. Choice (A) incorrectly interprets *right* in this context to mean *correct*. Choice (C) incorrectly interprets *right* in this context to mean *opposite of left*.

4. **(C)** *Six o'clock* answers the indirect *When* question, which uses *back* to mean *return*. Choice (A) uses *back* to mean *rear*. Choice (B) uses *back* to mean a part of the body.

5. **(B)** This is a logical response to the statement about running out of paper, that is, coming to the end of the supply of paper. Choices (A) and (C) use the word *run* to mean *operate*.

SKILL 5 SUGGESTIONS

1. **(C)** Choice (C) answers the *yes–no* suggestion with *Yes* and suggests a time to leave. Choice (A) has similar-sounding words and related word phrases *leave more time/left my watch*. Choice (B) confuses similar-sounding words *more/anymore*.

2. **(A)** Choice (A) answers the suggestion *Why don't we?* with *OK*, which is an agreement with the suggestion. Choice (B) confuses similar-sounding words *meet/meat*. Choice (C) repeats the word *three*.

3. **(C)** Choice (C) answers the suggestion *Let's* with *Good idea* and a rephrase of the suggestion. Choice (A) repeats the word *over*. Choice (B) confuses similar-sounding words *decision/precision*.

4. **(B)** *That's a good idea* is a logical response to the suggestion to use the conference room for a meeting. Choice (A) confuses the homonyms *meet* and *meat*. Choice (C) confuses similar-sounding words *meeting* and *reading*.

5. **(A)** *Yes, let's* is a logical response to the suggestion to take a break. Choice (B) uses the word *work* with a different meaning. Choice (C) uses the word *break* with a different meaning.

SKILL 6 OFFERS

1. **(C)** The other choices do not respond to the offer to accompany them out for coffee. Choice (A) uses words associated with *coffee* like *milk* and *sugar*. Choice (B) uses the location for having coffee, *a café*.

2. **(A)** Choice (A) is an appropriate way to respond to an offer. Choice (B) confuses similar-sounding words *arrives/drives*. Choice (C) confuses related words *visitors/visited*.

3. **(B)** Choice (B) thanks the speaker for the offered help and then says what help is needed. Choice (A) confuses similar-sounding words *ready/read*. Choice (C) confuses the meaning of the word *meeting*.

4. **(A)** This is a polite response to the polite offer. Choices (B) and (C) repeat the word *wait*.

5. **(B)** This is a polite response to the polite offer. Choice (A) uses related words *package* and *mail*. Choice (C) confuses similar-sounding words *package* and *packed*.

SKILL 7 REQUESTS

1. **(A)** The other choices do not respond to the request. Choice (B) has related words *window/door*. Choice (C) has related words *window/curtains*.

2. **(B)** Choice (B) is an appropriate way to respond to a request. Choice (A) confuses similar-sounding words *package/packed it*. Choice (C) uses related words *lunch/cafeteria*.

3. **(C)** Choice (C) is an appropriate response to a request. Choice (A) confuses similar-sounding words *collect/recollect*. Choice (B) repeats the word *town*.

4. **(B)** This is a polite response to the polite request to lock the door. Choice (A) relates the words *lock* and *key*. Choice (C) confuses similar-sounding words *door* and *floor*.

5. **(C)** This is a polite response to the polite request for more coffee. Choice (A) confuses similar-sounding words *coffee* and *coughing*. Choice (C) relates the words *coffee* and *cream and sugar.*

Part 3: Conversations

SKILL 1 QUESTIONS ABOUT PEOPLE

1. **(B)** Listen for the context clues such as *sand, wall, first coat of paint,* and *mix the color.* Choice (A) suggests a related word for life-guard: *sand* at the beach as opposed to the verb to *sand* a wall. Choice (C) has a word with the same sound but a different meaning: *coat of paint* (layer) and *coat* (clothing). Choice (D)

has a related expression *to mix paints* (painters) and *to mix drinks* (bartenders).

2. **(B)** The man tells the woman to *sand* the wall. Choice (A) is incorrect because the man tells the woman to do the job. Choice (C) has similar-sounding words *boss* and *gloss*. Choice (D) confuses *helper* with *I'll help you.*

3. **(A)** The speakers talk about the kind of paint the father prefers and the woman says she hopes he will like his house when it's painted, so the house belongs to the father. Choices (B) and (C) confuse *mother* and *brother* with the similar-sounding word *other*. Choice (D) has similar-sounding words *friend* and *end*.

4. **(B)** The women are hiring the man to make a buffet dinner and cake for a retirement party, so the man is a caterer. Choices (A), (C), and (D) are other food-related occupations.

5. **(A)** One of the women says, *It's our boss's retirement party.* Choices (B) and (C) are plausible but not mentioned. Choice (D) is confused with the man's mention of his partner, who decorates cakes.

6. **(B)** Mary says, *Just send the bill to my assistant.* Choice (A) repeats the name *Mary*. Choice (C) relates *accountant* to *account*. Choice (D) is not mentioned.

SKILL 2 QUESTIONS ABOUT OCCUPATIONS

1. **(D)** Look for the context clues such as *put one in each room, wires along the baseboard,* and *phone*. Choice (A) confuses the meanings of *run wires/running* as in jogging. Choice (B) has similar-sounding words *baseboard/baseball*. Choice (C) has related words *phone/telephone operator*.

2. **(D)** The woman says when commenting about the man's business, *Lots of people need accounting services,* so we know that the man is running an accounting business. Choice (A), *employment*, is related to *employee*. Choice (B) repeats the word *support*. Choice (C) repeats the word *website*.

3. **(C)** The man says, *We're all responsible for answering the phone here.* Choice (A) is incorrect because *everyone* is responsible. Choice

(B) is not mentioned. Choice (D) repeats the phrase *customer service*.

4. **(C)** The man is discussing the tour he will guide this morning showing people a historic district and a museum. Choices (A) and (B) are related to the topic but are not the correct answer. Choice (D) repeats the word *museum*.

5. **(A)** The man mentions a *bus*, and the woman mentions several times that she will *drive* the group, so she is a bus driver. Choice (B) is incorrect because the speakers are talking about a bus, not a taxi. Choices (C) and (D) are associated with the mention of a restaurant.

6. **(D)** The man says, *I've asked the front desk clerk here at the hotel to call the restaurant*. Choices (A) and (B) are incorrect because the man has asked someone else to do this. Choice (C) repeats the words *hotel* and *manager*.

SKILL 3 QUESTIONS ABOUT PLACE

1. **(C)** The speakers talk about putting the package in a *conference room*, in an *office*, and on a *desk*, so they are most likely in a business office. Choice (A) is not mentioned. Choices (B) and (D) associate *delivery* and *shipping* with *package*.

2. **(A)** This is where the man suggests putting the package and the woman agrees. Choice (B) associates *filing cabinet* with the *file folders* that are on the desk. Choice (C) is where the woman does not want to put the package. Choice (D) is where the package is now.

3. **(D)** The man says, *He's returning from vacation tomorrow night*. Choice (A) is confused with the mention of the *conference room*. Choice (B) repeats the word *office*. Choice (C) confuses similar-sounding words *flight* and *night*.

4. **(C)** The woman mentions the *teacher's break room*, and the man mentions his *classroom*, so they are in a school. Choice (A) repeats the word *taxi*, which the speakers will use to get to their next destinations. Choice (B) confuses similar-sounding words *plane* and *train*. Choice (D) is a place where one might also find a *hall* and a *closet*.

5. **(D)** The man says about the coat, *I hung it in the closet*. Choice (A) is where the woman left the coat. Choice (B) is what the man wanted to avoid. Choice (C) is where the woman thought the man had put the coat.

6. **(B)** The woman says, *I've got to get to the station to catch a five o'clock train*. Choice (A) is where the man is going. Choice (C) confuses similar-sounding words *apartment* and *appointment*. Choice (D) associates *bank* with *accountant*.

SKILL 4 QUESTIONS ABOUT TIME

1. **(C)** A half-hour is equal to 30 minutes. You may sometimes have to change hours to minutes: for example, one and a half hours is 90 minutes. Choice (A) indicates when the man had planned to leave. Choice (B) is not mentioned. Choice (D) indicates how long the woman asked him to stay.

2. **(B)** The man says, *I have an early appointment tomorrow*. Choice (A) confuses similar-sounding words *nine* and *time*. Choice (C) is not mentioned. Choice (D) is when the man will leave.

3. **(D)** The woman says that the man can get to his house in 45 minutes. Choices (A) and (B) have similar-sounding words *twenty* and *plenty*. Choice (C) sounds similar to the correct answer.

4. **(C)** The woman mentions *the monthly staff meeting*. Choice (A) repeats the word *morning*. Choice (B) repeats the word *week*. Choice (D) repeats the word *month*.

5. **(A)** One of the men asks what time the meeting will start and the woman answers *one*. Choice (B) confuses similar-sounding words *three* and *free*. Choice (C) is when one of the men hopes the meeting will end. Choice (D) repeats *couple of hours*—the length of the meeting.

6. **(B)** The woman says, *It should only last a couple of hours*. Choice (A) is confused with the start time of the meeting. Choice (C) confuses similar-sounding words *three* and *free*. Choice (D) confuses similar-sounding words *before* and *four*.

SKILL 5 QUESTIONS ABOUT ACTIVITIES

1. **(D)** Look for the context clues *turn left, one-way street*, and *map*. Choice (A) is contradicted by *one-way street*. Choice (B) has similar-sounding words *map/nap*. Choice (C) is contradicted by *should have bought a map*.

2. **(C)** The man mentions a restaurant, the woman mentions *dinner*. Choice (A) has similar-sounding words *rested/restaurant*. Choice (B) has similar-sounding words *snow/show*. Choice (D) has similar-sounding words *rent/spent* and repeats the word *movie*.

3. **(D)** They are looking for a movie theater. Choice (A) has similar-sounding words *read/need*. Choice (B) has similar-sounding words *bed/ahead*. Choice (C) associates *play* with *theater*.

4. **(A)** The man is having difficulty getting the machine to work and says, *But the machine is supposed to staple, too. But, look, the copies are all coming out without staples.* Choice (B) would be logical since the machine doesn't work, but it isn't mentioned. Choice (C) repeats the word *copies*. Choice (D) is what the woman thinks the man wants to do.

5. **(D)** The woman says, *You should probably report it to the office manager.* Choice (A) is what the man has already done. Choice (B) repeats the word *later*. Choice (C) is what was done last week.

6. **(B)** The man mentions that there is another machine and says, *I'll just go use that one.* Choice (A) repeats the phrase *office manager*. Choice (C) repeats the word *tomorrow*. Choice (D) is plausible but not mentioned.

SKILL 6 QUESTIONS ABOUT OPINIONS

1. **(B)** The context clues all refer to humor: *funny, laughed, jokes.* Be careful: *I never laughed so hard* means *I laughed harder than ever before.* Choice (A) has the related words *speaker/presentation.* Choice (C) is not mentioned. Choice (D) confuses similar-sounding words *jokes/folks.*

2. **(B)** The man says that the food is great. Choice (A) is the woman's opinion. Choice (C) has similar-sounding words, *seats/eat,* and confuses the meaning of *hard.* Choice (D) is incorrect because it is the portions of food that are big, not the room.

3. **(A)** The woman says, *. . . it's a bit on the expensive side.* Choice (B) is confused with *I'd expected it to be cheaper.* Choice (C) has similar-sounding words *tables/uncomfortable,* and *nice/price.* Choice (D) is how the woman feels about the price, not the hotel.

4. **(C)** The man says, *. . . we got a lot of information in a short time.* Choice (A) is plausible but not mentioned. Choices (B) and (D) are the opposite of what the speakers say.

5. **(D)** The women say, *He's a bit timid, hard to talk to,* and *He is the quiet type.* Choices (A) and (C) are the opposite of what they say. Choice (B) is plausible but not mentioned.

6. **(C)** The man says about the cafeteria, *It's always full of people at lunch time.* Choices (A), (B), and (D) are what one of the women says about the café across the street.

SKILL 7 GRAPHIC

1. **(D)** According to the conversation, Sue will work on Jim's scheduled day, which is Thursday. Choice (A) is the day Sue was originally scheduled to work at the reception desk, but Jim is covering for her on that day. Choices (B) and (C) are days other people will work.

2. **(A)** The man says not to spend more than $150, and Choice (A) is the only model that costs less than that amount. Choices (B), (C), and (D) all cost more than the man authorized the woman to spend.

3. **(B)** The man says, *The month after we hired him, sales were up for the first time all year.* The graph shows that April was the first month sales were up, and the month before that is March. Choices (A), (C), and (D) don't agree with the man's statement.

4. **(B)** The woman asks the man to change the agenda by moving Robert's presentation to last place and starting the meeting with Maya's presentation, and Maya will talk about the sales update. Choice (A) was originally the first item on the agenda. Choices (C) and

(D) are agenda items that will follow the sales update.

5. **(A)** The man says that the café is across from the bookstore. Choices (B), (C), and (D) don't fit this description.

SKILL 8 MEANING IN CONTEXT

1. **(A)** The woman is criticizing the man's work method because she thinks it will take him a long time to finish, that is, he is inefficient.

2. **(B)** The man says, . . . *things are starting to pick up*, meaning *things are getting better*, and he also has a job interview scheduled, so he must be feeling optimistic.

3. **(B)** When the man questions who chose the carpet and then says, *I mean, that color!*, he implies that he doesn't like the color. When the woman says that it's not a color that *would be at the top of my list*, she means it wouldn't be one of her first choices, in fact, it probably wouldn't be on her list of choices at all because she doesn't like it.

4. **(A)** The woman's statement means that the meeting felt long because it was so boring, and the man's statement means that he almost fell asleep from boredom.

5. **(B)** To be on top of something means to have it under control; the woman means that she can finish the work within the amount of time that she has.

SKILL 9 INCOMPLETE SENTENCES

1. **(B)** *Right*, in this case, means *correct*. The man is confirming that the woman correctly understands what he said.

2. **(A)** The response is short for *It's fine with me*, with *fine* used here to mean *good*.

3. **(B)** *Get*, in this case, means *understand*. The man is confirming to the woman that he understands and has made note of her requests.

4. **(A)** *Wish I could* is short for *I wish I could join you*.

5. **(B)** *Too bad* is short for *That's too bad*, a common expression of regret. The man regrets that Ms. Chang is too busy to see him.

Part 4: Talks

SKILL 1 QUESTIONS ABOUT EVENTS AND FACTS

1. **(C)** The speaker says, . . . *our annual celebration of National Day is this weekend.* Choice (A) confuses the meaning of the word *book* (in *book your tickets*) and repeats the word *fair* (*food fair*). Choice (B) is confused with the mention of the conference center. Choice (D) repeats the word *international* (*international cuisine*) and confuses similar-sounding words *chance/dance*.

2. **(C)** The speaker mentions a concert at City Conference Center on Saturday evening. Choice (A) is incorrect because the parade is on Friday. Choices (B) and (D) are incorrect because both those events take place during the day on Saturday.

3. **(C)** The mayor will participate in the basketball tournament on Sunday. Choice (A) repeats the word *tickets*. Choice (B) repeats the word *crowds*. Choice (D) confuses *basketball* with *baskets*.

4. **(B)** The speaker says that she is going to *celebrate my nephew's graduation from high school*. Choices (A) and (C) are other events that people commonly celebrate but are not mentioned. Choice (D) repeats the word *job*.

5. **(C)** The speaker mentions *dinner*. Choice (A) is plausible but not mentioned. Choice (B) repeats the word *play*. Choice (D) repeats the word *awards*.

6. **(B)** The speaker says, *I'll be at the club Sunday morning playing tennis*. Choice (A) confuses similar-sounding words *walk* and *talk*. Choice (C) repeats the word *late*. Choice (D) associates *work* with *job*.

SKILL 2 QUESTIONS ABOUT REASONS

1. **(A)** A work slowdown is a work action. A slowdown is like a strike except workers show up, but do not work at their normal speed. They work more slowly. Choices (B), (C), and (D) do not give the reason *why*.

2. **(A)** The announcer suggests that people should eat now because the restaurants will

close at midnight. Choice (B) is confused with . . . *won't reopen until tomorrow*. Choice (C) repeats the word *flight*, but no mention is made of whether or not there will be food on the flight. Choice (D) confuses *close (near)* with *close (opposite of open)*.

3. **(D)** The announcer suggests listening to the announcements to hear when flights are ready for boarding. Choice (A) repeats the word *gate*. Choice (B) repeats the word *restaurants*. Choice (C) has similar-sounding words *bored/board*.

4. **(C)** Mr. Brown says that he has an appointment with Mr. Wilson *to go over some papers*. Choice (A) confuses *newspaper* with the similar-sounding word *papers*. Choice (B) confuses similar-sounding words *apartment* and *appointment*. Choice (D) repeats the word *papers*.

5. **(B)** Mr. Brown says, *I have an emergency meeting*. Choice (A) repeats the word *suit* with a different meaning. Choice (C) repeats the word *emergency*. Choice (D) relates *prepare* with *preparation*.

6. **(A)** Mr. Brown says, *Don't call me at the office today as I won't be there*. Choices (B) and (C) are plausible but not mentioned. Choice (D) repeats the phrase *cell phone*.

SKILL 3 QUESTIONS ABOUT NUMBERS

1. **(B)** The speaker says, *We only have two days left* to plan the workshop. Choices (A) and (C) sound similar to the correct answer. Choice (D) confuses similar-sounding words *Wednesday* and *when's*.

2. **(D)** The speaker says, . . . *there will be over 30 participants*. Choice (A) sounds similar to the correct answer. Choices (B) and (C) confuse the meaning of *over*.

3. **(A)** The speaker suggests getting together with John, then says, *It'll only take 15 minutes*. Choice (B) sounds similar to the correct answer. Choice (C) is confused with the number of workshop participants. Choice (D) confuses similar-sounding words *two* and *to*.

4. **(B)** The speaker says, . . . *the program is scheduled to go from seven o'clock until nine-thirty*. Choice (A) confuses similar-sounding words *few* and *two*. Choice (C) sounds similar to *9:30*. Choice (D) confuses similar-sounding words *ten* and *then*.

5. **(A)** The speaker says, . . . *we will have a presentation from each of our five speakers*. Choice (B) confuses similar-sounding words *seven* and *eleven*. Choice (C) confuses similar-sounding words *thirty* and *thirteen*. Choice (D) repeats *thirty*.

6. **(A)** The speaker says, . . . *all our programs are free of charge. . . .* Choice (B) confuses similar-sounding words *three* and *free*. Choice (C) confuses similar-sounding words *door* and *four*. Choice (D) confuses similar-sounding words *plenty* and *twenty*.

SKILL 4 QUESTIONS ABOUT MAIN TOPICS

1. **(B)** The phrases *asked me to submit my letter of resignation* and *told me to leave by the close of business today* both indicate that the Managing Director was *fired*. Choice (A) repeats the words *Board of Directors* and *resignation*. Choice (C) is not mentioned. Choice (D) repeats the word *letter*.

2. **(B)** The speaker says, *I will no longer work as your managing director*, so he is speaking to his staff. Choice (A) has related words *clients/business*. Choice (C) confuses the meaning of *serve*. Choice (D) is the speaker's position.

3. **(B)** The speaker says that he hopes to open up a consulting business. Choice (A) has the homonyms *clothes/close*. Choice (C) has similar-sounding words *college/colleague*. Choice (D) has similar-sounding words *restaurant/rest* and related words *manager/managing*.

4. **(A)** The speaker mentions *purchases* and *manager's specials throughout the store*. Choice (B) associates *hotel* with *checkout*. Choice (C) is not mentioned. Choice (D) associates *train* with *express*.

5. **(D)** The speaker says near the beginning of the announcement, *We will be closing in 15 minutes*, and then explains that customers must hurry to make their purchases. Choices (A) and (B) are mentioned but are not the

main topic of the announcement. Choice (C) is not mentioned.

6. **(B)** The announcement is telling customers to make their purchases because the store will be closing soon. Choices (A) and (D) are not mentioned. Choice (C) repeats the word *manager*.

SKILL 5 PARAPHRASES

1. **(B)** The talk says the form is to track your loan application. Choices (A), (C), and (D) are not mentioned.

2. **(A)** The speaker says, . . . *please submit it through the postal service*. Choice (B) is incorrect because the speaker says, *We do not accept e-mailed applications*. Choices (C) and (D) are plausible but not mentioned.

3. **(D)** The speaker says that the listener will be contacted within *two weeks*, which is the same as fourteen days. Choice (A) repeats the word *two*. Choice (B) is the number of copies that will be made. Choice (C) has similar-sounding words *ten/then*.

4. **(A)** The speaker says that a table ordered by the listener is in the warehouse, and that a truck can *drop off* (that is, deliver) *the table at your office*. Choice (B) is plausible but not mentioned. Choice (C) is what the speaker does at the end of the message but is not the purpose of the call. Choice (D) is what the listener has done.

5. **(C)** The speaker says, *We have your address on file*, that is, on record. Choice (A) repeats the word *office*. Choices (B) and (D) are plausible but not mentioned.

6. **(B)** The speaker says, *contact me by phone before Friday*. Choice (A) repeats the word *truck*. Choice (C) repeats the word *warehouse*. Choice (D) repeats the word *phone*.

SKILL 6 GRAPHIC

1. **(C)** The speaker says that her train *gets into Springfield Station at just after 11:00*, which matches the 11:02 scheduled arrival time of train no. 32. Choices (A), (B), and (D) refer to trains that arrive at other times.

2. **(B)** The speaker says, . . . *the most logical place to start cutting is in the category where the largest percentage of our budget has been spent*, that is, *salaries*, which take up 45% of the budget. Choice (A), (C), and (D) are parts of the budget that don't fit this description.

3. **(C)** The tour starts in the Pine Grove, on the right-hand side of the river. The speaker says they will stop for lunch after crossing the foot-bridge, which puts them in the Rose Garden. Choices (A), (B), and (D) are other places on the map.

4. **(D)** The speaker says there was *a significant increase in sales in one part of the country*, and the graph shows the Southeast as the only region with a significant increase in sales. Choices (A), (B), and (C) are other regions shown on the graph that only had small increases in sales.

5. **(A)** The speaker expects *no more than 15* people, and the small platter serves that number. Choices (B), (C), and (D) are sizes that serve larger numbers of people.

SKILL 7 IMPLIED MEANING

1. **(A)** The speaker says that he is rescheduling the appointment *yet again*, which implies that he has done this more than once before.

2. **(B)** The speaker says, *Could we ask for a better day? I don't think so!* meaning that the weather on this day is very good.

3. **(B)** The speaker suggests that those who are paying cash should go to the ticket office, implying that the machine cannot accept cash.

4. **(A)** The speaker says, *It looks like we're going to have a huge turnout, certainly much more than we had a year ago*. A huge turnout means a big crowd.

5. **(B)** The man says that people should show their membership cards to the ticket seller and goes on to say that *tickets cannot be sold to non-cardholders*, that is, people who aren't members.

SKILL 8 MULTIPLE ACCENTS

1. Good evening and welcome to tonight's presentation. We are very excited to have with us tonight a world-famous journalist. I am sure you will enjoy his talk very much.

2. Here is the weather outlook for the weekend. We will have cloudy skies all day Saturday. Expect rain to begin late Saturday evening and continue through Sunday morning. The rain will clear up on Sunday afternoon.

3. Thank you for calling the Acme Company. We value your call. To check your order status, press one. For shipping information, press two. To speak with a customer service representative, press three. To repeat this menu, press four.

4. Attention shoppers. We will be closing the store in ten minutes. Please take your purchases to the checkout area at this time. If you are purchasing ten items or fewer, you may use the express checkout lane.

5. The tour will begin in just a few minutes. Please line up by the main entrance. If you don't have a ticket, you can purchase one in the gift shop.

ANSWER KEY
Listening Comprehension Mini-Test

Answer Explanations can be found beginning on page 100.

Part 1: Photographs

1. **B**   2. **C**   3. **A**   4. **D**

Part 2: Question-Response

5. **B**   8. **C**   11. **A**   14. **C**
6. **A**   9. **B**   12. **C**   15. **B**
7. **A**   10. **B**   13. **A**   16. **A**

Part 3: Conversations

17. **C**   22. **B**   27. **C**   32. **C**
18. **A**   23. **A**   28. **B**   33. **D**
19. **D**   24. **C**   29. **B**   34. **B**
20. **A**   25. **D**   30. **D**
21. **B**   26. **A**   31. **C**

Part 4: Talks

35. **C**   39. **A**   43. **C**   47. **C**
36. **A**   40. **B**   44. **B**   48. **B**
37. **C**   41. **D**   45. **B**   49. **A**
38. **D**   42. **C**   46. **C**

ANSWER EXPLANATIONS FOR MINI-TEST FOR LISTENING COMPREHENSION

Part 1: Photographs

1. **(B)** A pharmacist is wearing a white coat and holding a pill bottle and speaking with a customer. Choice (A) is incorrect because the man is wearing his coat, not hanging it up. Choice (C) correctly mentions the bottle, but the man is not opening it, and he doesn't look like a cook. Choice (D) confuses similar-sounding words *pharmacist* and *farmer*.

2. **(C)** This choice correctly describes the location of the book. Choice (A) correctly identifies the eggs, but not their location. Choice (B) correctly identifies the pencil, but not its location. Choice (D) correctly identifies the flowers, but not their location.

3. **(A)** A man is trimming bushes in a garden. Choice (B) correctly identifies the man's action (cutting = trimming), but he is not cutting hair. Choice (C) associates *mowing* and *cutting*. Choice (D) associates *flowers* and *garden*.

4. **(D)** A woman is looking at a phone that she holds in her hand. Choice (A) correctly identifies her action, but she is reading the phone screen, not a book. Choice (B) correctly identifies her glasses, but she is not putting them on. Choice (C) correctly identifies the computer in her lap, but she is not buying it.

Part 2: Question-Response

5. **(B)** *Two days* answers the *How long* question. Choice (A) would answer *How did you like . . . ?* Choice (C) would answer a *How long* question about distance.

6. **(A)** This is a polite response to the request for help. Choice (B) would answer a *yes–no* question. Choice (C) repeats the word *desk*.

7. **(A)** This is an appropriate response to the question about possession. Choice (B) associates *package* and *mail*. Choice (C) repeats the word *door*.

8. **(C)** *25 employees* answers the *How many* question. Choice (A) repeats the words *work here*. Choice (B) confuses same-sounding words *here* and *hear*.

9. **(B)** *Ten o'clock* answers the *What time* question. Choice (A) would answer a *Where* question. Choice (C) repeats the word *close*.

10. **(B)** This is an appropriate response to a request for an appointment. Choice (A) confuses similar-sounding words *appointment* and *apartment*. Choice (C) confuses the meaning of the word *like* in this context.

11. **(A)** *At his office* answers the *Where* question. Choice (B) would answer a *When* question. Choice (C) repeats the word *meet*.

12. **(C)** This is an appropriate response to the comment about the darkness of the room. Choice (A) confuses similar-sounding words *dark* and *park*. Choice (B) repeats the word *dark*.

13. **(A)** *Two boxes* answers the *How much* question. Choice (B) repeats the word *paper*. Choice (C) confuses the homonyms *buy* and *by*.

14. **(C)** This answers the *When* question. Choice (A) would answer a *How many* question. Choice (B) would answer a *Who* question.

15. **(B)** This is a logical response to a question about a preference. Choice (A) would answer a *Where* question. Choice (C) confuses similar-sounding words *later* and *waiter*.

16. **(A)** This answers the *yes–no* question. Choice (B) confuses similar-sounding words *meeting* and *reading*. Choice (C) repeats the word *yesterday*.

Part 3: Conversations

17. **(C)** The woman says that she had the sandwich of the day. Choice (A) is incorrect because the woman implies that she didn't have soup when she says, *I'd like to try the soup next time.* Choice (B) is what the man had. Choice (D) repeats the word *salad*.

18. **(A)** The man implies that he doesn't like the color of the walls when he says, *After I*

got past those wild colors they've painted on the walls, I actually enjoyed my lunch, and *But those walls!* But he did say that the soup was great and the salad fresh, and he further implies that he likes the food when he says, *at least they've got the food part right*. Choice (B) repeats the word *walls*, but no repairs are mentioned. Choice (C) is incorrect because the man praises the food. Choice (D) is incorrect because the café is *down the street*, that is, nearby.

19. **(D)** The man asks the woman if she would like to try the place (that is, the café) again, and she replies saying, *tomorrow works for me*, meaning that she is available tomorrow. Choice (A) confuses the meaning of the word *work* in this context. Choice (B) repeats the word *place*. Choice (C) refers to the man's dislike of the colors of the walls, but painting them is not mentioned.

20. **(A)** After the woman explains everything she needs to do to get ready for her trip, the man says, *You might be better off staying home*. Choice (B) repeats the phrase *time off*. Choice (C) is plausible but not mentioned. Choice (D) is what the woman plans to do.

21. **(B)** The woman mentions *my two weeks in Paris*. Choice (A) is the amount of time before her vacation begins. Choice (C) confuses similar-sounding words *three* and *free*. Choice (D) confuses same-sounding words *four* and *for*.

22. **(B)** The woman says, *I think I'll take the afternoon off and buy some things for my trip*. Choice (A) confuses the meaning of the word *book*—the woman says she has *booked a trip to Paris*. Choice (C) is confused with the woman's mention that she has to find someone to care for her dog. Choice (D) has already been done.

23. **(A)** The woman says, *This is the new menu for my restaurant*. Choice (B) repeats the word *check*, which is the way the woman wants to pay. Choice (C) repeats the word *order*. Choice (D) is plausible but not mentioned.

24. **(C)** The woman asks if the order can be ready *by tomorrow morning*, and the man replies, *Sure thing*, meaning *yes*. Choice (A) repeats the number *24* (24-hour rush fee). Choice (B) mentions the rush fee, but the man implies it will be charged. Choice (D) is incorrect because the woman asks for two-sided printing and the man does not disagree.

25. **(D)** The woman offers to write a check, and the man says, *we prefer credit cards*. Choice (A) repeats the verb *pick up*. Choice (B) is what the woman wants to do. Choice (C) confuses the meaning of the word *check* and repeats the word *order*.

26. **(A)** The woman continues by saying, *It's very impressive*, and the men agree, adding information about the director's impressive background. Choices (B), (C), and (D) do not fit the context.

27. **(C)** The first man says, *Today makes a week since he started here*. Choice (A) repeats the word *today*. Choices (B) and (D) sound similar to *today*.

28. **(B)** The woman mentions a social hour, and then says, *We should all go*. Choice (A) relates *meet* and *meeting*. Choice (C) confuses similar-sounding words *meet* and *eat*. Choice (D) confuses similar-sounding words *afternoon* and *noon*.

29. **(B)** The woman mentions *this office*. Choice (A) is where they keep the paint left over from painting the hallway. Choice (C) is something they have already painted. Choice (D) is plausible but not mentioned.

30. **(D)** The woman suggests blue and the man says, *Sure. Get it*. Choice (A) is the man's suggestion. Choice (B) confuses similar-sounding words *seem* and *green*. Choice (C) confuses similar-sounding words *bright* and *white*.

31. **(C)** The man says, *We need to cover about 20 or 25 square meters*, and this size will cover that much plus a little more. Choices (A) and (B) don't have enough paint. Choice (D) has too much paint.

32. **(C)** The man is buying a computer table, which is furniture, so he will get the 20% discount. Choices (A), (B), and (D) are discounts on items he is not buying.

33. **(D)** The woman says, *I'll take it up front for you so you can pay.* Choice (A) repeats the word *box*, but she doesn't offer to open it. Choice (B) repeats the word *instructions*; the woman says they are easy to follow, but she doesn't offer to explain them. Choice (C) associates *car*, mentioned by the man, with *park*.

34. **(B)** The man says, *I'll just take it back to the office in my car.* Choices (A) and (C) are plausible but not mentioned. Choice (D) is what the woman suggests.

Part 4: Talks

35. **(C)** *Gallery, painting, prints,* and *sculpture* all indicate that the location is an art museum. Choice (A) is related to the mention of shopping at the gift shop. Choices (B) and (D) are related to the mention of *tickets*.

36. **(A)** The speaker says, *If you haven't purchased a tour ticket yet, please do so now.* Choice (B) is confused with the similar-sounding word *display*. Choice (C) repeats the word *gift*. Choice (D) repeats the word *move*.

37. **(C)** Near the beginning of the talk, the speaker indicates that the group is standing by the ticket counter, and near the end she says that they will finish the tour *right next door to where we are now, at the gift shop.* Location C is the only choice that is next to the ticket counter. Choices (A), (B), and (D) are locations that don't fit the description.

38. **(D)** The caller wants to have his office cleaned and asks about prices and schedules. Choices (A), (B), and (C) are all plausible, but they are not the correct reason.

39. **(A)** The phrase, *It would work better for me,* is used to express a preference, and *after hours* refers to the time when a business is closed. Choices (B), (C), and (D) use words

from the phrase, but they are not the correct meaning and do not fit the context.

40. **(B)** The speaker says, *I'll give you a ring when I get back early next week,* meaning he will call again when he returns from his trip. Choice (A) repeats the phrase *next week*. Choice (C) confuses *out of town* with *downtown*. Choice (D) is related to the topic of phone calls, but it is not the correct answer.

41. **(D)** The talk is an advertisement for Movie Time video streaming service. Choice (A) is associated with the mention of movies. Choice (B) is not mentioned but is something one might subscribe to. Choice (D) is associated with the mention of TV shows.

42. **(C)** The speaker says, *The first month is free.* Choice (A) is confused with the similar-sounding word *today*. Choice (B) confuses similar-sounding words *free/three*. Choice (D) is confused with the mention of a yearly subscription, but that is not free.

43. **(C)** The speaker says, *Subscriptions start at $150 annually.* Choices (A) and (D) sound similar to the correct answer. Choice (B) sounds similar to the word *sign*.

44. **(B)** The speaker says, *A team will be in tomorrow morning to install the carpet in the hallway and front office.* Choice (A) repeats the word *install*. Choice (C) happened last week. Choice (D) repeats the word *hallway*.

45. **(B)** The speaker is referring to the workers who will be laying the carpet. The expression *should be out of here* means that they will probably have left. Choices (A), (C), and (D) do not fit the context or the meaning of the expression.

46. **(C)** The speaker says that the workers *request that you enter the building through the rear doorway.* Choice (A) repeats the phrase *new furniture.* Choice (B) repeats the phrase *front office.* Choice (D) is what the workers will do.

47. **(C)** The speaker says, *You asked about renting a space for a training seminar.* Choice (A) is plausible but not mentioned. Choice (B) repeats the word *conference* from the phrase

conference room, and Choice (D) repeats the word *banquet* from the phrase *banquet room*; these are rooms mentioned by the speaker as places where the event could be held.

48. **(B)** The speaker mentions a room that *has seating for 125 people, which is just the number you are expecting.* Choices (A) and (D) sound similar to the correct answer. Choice (C) is the number of people another room can hold.

49. **(A)** The speaker says, *You'll find my office just behind the front desk in the lobby,* and the directory shows that the lobby is on the ground floor. Choices (B), (C), and (D) are floors where other facilities are located.

Reading

3

OVERVIEW

There are three parts to the Reading Comprehension section of the TOEIC. You will have approximately 75 minutes to complete this section.

Part 5:	Incomplete Sentences	30 Questions
Part 6:	Text Completion	16 Questions
Part 7:	Reading Comprehension	
	■ Single passages	29 Questions
	■ Multiple passages	25 Questions

To prepare for the Reading Comprehension section, you must develop vocabulary, grammar, and reading comprehension skills. The grammar and vocabulary skills targeted in this chapter for Part 5 are also useful in Part 6, and vice versa.

SKILLS LIST

Part 5: Incomplete Sentences
Skill
1. Word Families
2. Similar Meanings
3. Similar Forms
4. Subject-Verb Agreement with Prepositional Phrases
5. Singular and Plural Subjects
6. Verb Tenses
7. Prepositions
8. Prepositions with Verbs and Adjectives
9. Coordinating Conjunctions
10. Parallel Structure
11. Subordinating Conjunctions
12. Future Time Clauses

Part 6: Text Completion
Skill
1. Adverbs of Frequency
2. Gerunds and Infinitives After Main Verbs
3. Gerunds and Infinitives After Prepositions and Adjectives
4. Causative Verbs
5. Real Conditionals
6. Unreal Conditionals
7. Comparisons
8. Pronouns
9. Subject Relative Pronouns
10. Object Relative Pronouns
11. Passive Voice
12. Word Meaning
13. Sentence Choice

Part 7: Reading Comprehension
Skill
1. Advertisements
2. Forms
3. Letters
4. Memos
5. Tables and Charts
6. Graphs
7. Announcements
8. Notices
9. Articles
10. Schedules
11. E-mails
12. Webpages
13. Text Messages and Online Chats

PART 5: INCOMPLETE SENTENCES

Sample Question

> **Directions:** You will see a sentence with a missing word. Four possible answers follow the sentence. Choose the best answer to the question, and fill in the corresponding oval on your answer sheet.

You will read:

They have decided _____ business class.

(A) fly
(B) to fly
(C) flying
(D) flew

The best way to complete the sentence "They have decided _____ business class" is Choice (B), "to fly." Therefore you should choose answer (B).

Word Families

Word families are created by adding endings to a word. These endings will change the word into a noun, verb, adjective, or adverb.

Common Word Endings

noun	verb	adjective	adverb
-ance	-en	-able	-ly
-ancy	-ify	-ible	-ward
-ence	-ize	-al	-wise
-ation		-ful	
-ian		-ish	
-ism		-ive	
-ist		-ous	
-ment			
-ness			
-ship			
-or			
-er			

Common Word Families

| noun | | verb | adjective | adverb |
thing	person	verb	adjective	adverb
application	applicant	apply	applicable	
competition	competitor	compete	competitive	competitively
criticism	critic	criticize	critical	critically
decision		decide	decisive	decisively
economy	economist	economize	economical	economically
finale	finalist	finalize	final	finally
interpretation	interpreter	interpret	interpretive	
maintenance	maintainer	maintain	maintainable	
management	manager	manage	managerial	
mechanism	mechanic	mechanize	mechanical	mechanically
nation	nationalist	nationalize	national	nationally
negotiation	negotiator	negotiate	negotiable	
politics	politician	politicize	political	politically
production	producer	produce	productive	productively
prosperity		prosper	prosperous	prosperously
repetition	repeater	repeat	repetitious	repetitively
simplification		simplify	simple	simply
theory	theoretician	theorize	theoretical	theoretically

➥ Examples

She is a *careful* manager.
She read the report *carefully*.

Careful is an adjective. In the example above it describes the word *manager*. It tells us *what kind* of manager she is.

Carefully is an adverb. In the example above it modifies the verb *read*. It tells us *how* she read the report.

Mr. Kim *applied* for a job at our company.
His *application* contains a lot of information about his background.

Applied is a past tense verb. In the example above, it tells us what Mr. Kim did. *Application* is a noun. In the example above it is the subject of the sentence.

EXERCISE

Choose the one word or phrase that best completes the sentence.

1. The director of purchasing can _____ the best price.

   (A) negotiable   Ⓐ Ⓑ Ⓒ Ⓓ
   (B) negotiate
   (C) negotiator
   (D) negotiation

2. The first day that we advertised the job on our website, there were over 700 _____ for the position.

   (A) applies   Ⓐ Ⓑ Ⓒ Ⓓ
   (B) applicants
   (C) appliances
   (D) applications

3. The ability to act _____ in moments of crisis is the mark of a strong leader.

   (A) decide   Ⓐ Ⓑ Ⓒ Ⓓ
   (B) decision
   (C) decisive
   (D) decisively

4. The two sample colors are so similar that it is difficult
to _____ between them.

(A) differ

(B) difference

(C) different

(D) differentiate

Ⓐ Ⓑ Ⓒ Ⓓ

5. Of all the designers in this department, Ms. Smith is
considered to be the most _____.

(A) compete

(B) competent

(C) competence

(D) competently

Ⓐ Ⓑ Ⓒ Ⓓ

2 Similar Meanings

Some words have similar meanings but cannot be used interchangeably. The meanings or usage may not be exactly the same, or the grammar may be different.

Words with Similar Meanings

affect	effect	affection	effective
borrow	lend	loan	lease
develop	expand	elaborate	enhance
money	cash	currency	coin
obtain	earn	win	achieve
raise	rise	elevate	ascend
say	tell	speak	talk
travel	commute	go	journey
bill	pay	fee	cost
down	decrease	under	descent
like	similar	same	alike
soon	recent	newly	lately

> **TIP** First try to understand the meaning of the sentence. Then determine the correct word in meaning, usage, and spelling for that sentence.

➥ Examples

Sarah *commutes* to her job in the city from the suburbs.
Sarah will *travel* to Tahiti on her vacation.

Commute and *travel* have similar meanings, however, *commute* has a very specific use. It means *travel to and from work every day*. *Travel* has a more general meaning.

I had to *borrow* some money in order to pay for my new car.
John *lent* me the money, and I will pay him back soon.

Borrow means to receive something as a loan. Something that is borrowed has to be returned or repaid to the owner. *Lend* means to let someone use something you own.

They will *raise* the building in order to dig a basement underneath it.
Prices have continued to *rise* throughout the first half of the year.

Raise means to lift or to increase something. It is a transitive verb—a verb with an object. In the example above, the object is *the building*. *Rise* means to go up or to increase. The meaning is very similar to the meaning of *raise*, but *rise* is an intransitive verb—a verb that cannot take an object.

EXERCISE

Choose the one word or phrase that best completes the sentence.

1. New employees _____ only a small salary during the first six months.

   (A) win   Ⓐ Ⓑ Ⓒ Ⓓ
   (B) gain
   (C) reach
   (D) earn

2. Miranda has many more responsibilities at the office now because of her _____ promotion.

   (A) recent   Ⓐ Ⓑ Ⓒ Ⓓ
   (B) lately
   (C) soon
   (D) newly

3. Our costs have gone down this month, but we need to _____ them even more next month.

   (A) fall   Ⓐ Ⓑ Ⓒ Ⓓ
   (B) descent
   (C) decrease
   (D) under

4. A friend _____ me his car while mine was being repaired.

   (A) borrowed   Ⓐ Ⓑ Ⓒ Ⓓ
   (B) leased
   (C) owed
   (D) lent

5. More and more companies are interested in investing in this region as the value of the national _____ is increasing.

   (A) money   Ⓐ Ⓑ Ⓒ Ⓓ
   (B) currency
   (C) coin
   (D) cash

3 Similar Forms

Some words look similar but have different meanings. They may have the same prefix, suffix, or root, or they may simply have similar spelling but are completely unrelated.

Words with Similar Forms

reduce	produce	deduce	induce
except	expect	accept	accent
omit	emit	admit	permit
preference	inference	reference	conference
contact	contract	compact	comport
disk	desk	dusk	discus
particle	participant	participle	partition

> **TIP** First try to understand the meaning of the sentence. Then choose the word that has the correct meaning for that sentence.

➡ **Examples** _____

Don't *omit* any information from the form.
We *permit* our employees to work from home occasionally.

Omit and *permit* both contain the root word *mit*. However, they each have different meanings. *Omit* means to forget or leave out. *Permit* means to allow.

Please put the package on *my desk*.
They walked home *at dusk*.

Desk and *dusk* have almost the same spelling, but they are unrelated words with completely different meanings. *Desk* is a type of office furniture. *Dusk* is the time of evening right before it becomes completely dark.

EXERCISE

Choose the one word or phrase that best completes the sentence.

1. I'll need some time to read over the _____ before I sign it.

   (A) contact   Ⓐ Ⓑ Ⓒ Ⓓ
   (B) contract
   (C) comport
   (D) compact

2. The room is large, but we can use _____ to divide it into smaller work areas.

   (A) partitions   Ⓐ Ⓑ Ⓒ Ⓓ
   (B) participants
   (C) particles
   (D) participles

3. Because of low profits this quarter, we will have to _____ the size of our staff.

   (A) produce   Ⓐ Ⓑ Ⓒ Ⓓ
   (B) induce
   (C) deduce
   (D) reduce

4. The deadline for job applications is March 1, and we will not _____ any resumes that are submitted after that date.

   (A) except   Ⓐ Ⓑ Ⓒ Ⓓ
   (B) expect
   (C) accept
   (D) accent

5. Some people do better when working alone, while others have a _____ for working as part of a team.

   (A) preference   Ⓐ Ⓑ Ⓒ Ⓓ
   (B) inference
   (C) reference
   (D) conference

Subject-Verb Agreement with Prepositional Phrases

The subject and verb of a sentence must agree. They must match in person (*I, we, he, they,* etc.) and in number (singular or plural). A prepositional phrase may come between the subject and verb of a sentence, and the phrase may contain a noun that is different in person or number from the subject. This does not change the need for subject-verb agreement.

> **TIP** Distinguish the subject from other nouns in the sentence.

➡ Examples

The order for office supplies was on my desk.

In the example above, the subject, *order,* is singular. It agrees with the verb, *was.* The subject and verb are separated by a prepositional phrase. The plural noun *supplies* is not the subject of the sentence; it is part of the prepositional phrase *for office supplies.*

The workers in this factory receive many benefits.

In the example above, the subject, *workers,* is plural. It agrees with the verb, *receive.* The subject and verb are separated by a prepositional phrase. The singular noun *factory* is not the subject of the sentence; it is part of the prepositional phrase *in this factory.*

This group of business leaders meets with the mayor every month.

In the example above, the subject, *group,* is singular. It agrees with the verb, *meets.* The subject and verb are separated by a prepositional phrase. The plural noun *leaders* is not the subject of the sentence; it is part of the prepositional phrase *of business leaders.*

EXERCISE

Choose the one word or phrase that best completes the sentence.

1. The officers of the company _____ today at 1:00.

    (A) is meeting   Ⓐ Ⓑ Ⓒ Ⓓ
    (B) meets
    (C) has met
    (D) are meeting

2. The owner of these buildings _____ his tenants a very reasonable rent.

    (A) charges   Ⓐ Ⓑ Ⓒ Ⓓ
    (B) charge
    (C) are charging
    (D) have charged

3. The supplies in that closet _____ there for any staff member to use.

    (A) is   Ⓐ Ⓑ Ⓒ Ⓓ
    (B) has
    (C) are
    (D) was

4. The documents in this folder _____ to be signed by both parties and returned to the attorney right away.

    (A) need   Ⓐ Ⓑ Ⓒ Ⓓ
    (B) needs
    (C) needy
    (D) is needed

5. The carpets in this office _____ before we signed the lease last year.

    (A) replace   Ⓐ Ⓑ Ⓒ Ⓓ
    (B) were replaced
    (C) has been replaced
    (D) was being replaced

SKILL 5   Singular and Plural Subjects

Some nouns appear plural but are actually singular. Other nouns have irregular plurals that look singular. Be careful because the verb must agree with the subject.

> **TIP** Know whether the subject is considered singular or plural.

➡ Examples _____

Thirty dollars **is** a low price for a nice shirt like that.
Five cents **is** added to the price for sales tax.

A sum of money is treated as a singular noun. Even though it may contain a plural noun such as *dollars* or *cents*, it is considered as one sum.

National Autos owns this factory.
United Computers employs most of the workers in this town.

A company name may contain a plural noun but it is the name of one company so it is considered singular.

Everyone wants to have lunch now.
Nobody is ready for the meeting.

Words that begin with *every* or *no,* such as *everybody, everything, nobody,* and *nothing* are singular and take singular verbs even though they refer to a group of people or things.

Few *people understand* these laws.
Children are not allowed in the office without adult supervision.

Irregular plural words may look singular because they don't end with *-s,* but they are plural and take plural verbs.

EXERCISE

Choose the one word or phrase that best completes the sentence.

1. The manager from headquarters _____ this office at least twice a year.

    (A) visiting
    (B) to visit
    (C) visits
    (D) visit

    Ⓐ Ⓑ Ⓒ Ⓓ

2. Most people _____ that Acme, Inc. can be relied on to consistently provide high-quality products.

    (A) agree
    (B) agrees
    (C) has agreed
    (D) is agreeing

    Ⓐ Ⓑ Ⓒ Ⓓ

3. My assistant has assured me that everything _____ in order for the staff meeting.

    (A) have been
    (B) were
    (C) are
    (D) is

    Ⓐ Ⓑ Ⓒ Ⓓ

4. Although relatively young, Rheingold Consultants _____ fast becoming one of the most successful companies in the industry.

    (A) were
    (B) have
    (C) is
    (D) are

    Ⓐ Ⓑ Ⓒ Ⓓ

5. In the past, one thousand dollars _____ considered to be a high rent to pay for an apartment in this part of the city.

    (A) is
    (B) was
    (C) were
    (D) have been

    Ⓐ Ⓑ Ⓒ Ⓓ

SKILL

6   **Verb Tenses**

The main verb of a sentence must be in the correct tense. Often, a time word or time expression indicates the verb tense.

Time Words and Expressions

Simple Present	*Present Continuous*	*Simple Past*
every day	now	an hour ago
every week	at this moment	a month ago
every year	currently	yesterday
always		last week
often		last year
sometimes		
Present Perfect	*Future*	
since last year	tomorrow	
since Tuesday	next month	
for two weeks	next Friday	
for a long time	later this week	
already		
yet		

> **TIP** Look for a time word or expression in the sentence to help you determine the correct tense.

➡ Examples _____

We *hire* an accountant to audit our books at the end of *every year*.
(simple present)

We cannot hold the meeting at our office as we *are currently redecorating*.
(present continuous)

Mr. Brown *traveled* to Japan *last month* in order to visit our branch office there.
(simple past)

Ms. Henderson *has been* a client of ours *for the last fifteen years*.
(present perfect)

The conference room *will be* ready for use *later this afternoon*.
(future)

EXERCISE

Choose the one word or phrase that best completes the sentence.

1. Mr. Cho _____ the new budget at the staff meeting next Friday.

   (A) present   Ⓐ Ⓑ Ⓒ Ⓓ
   (B) will present
   (C) is presenting
   (D) has presented

2. We are planning to repaint the office, but we _____ on a color yet.

   (A) didn't decide   Ⓐ Ⓑ Ⓒ Ⓓ
   (B) don't decide
   (C) haven't decided
   (D) isn't deciding

3. The company _____ a picnic for all staff members at the beginning of every summer.

   (A) host   Ⓐ Ⓑ Ⓒ Ⓓ
   (B) hosts
   (C) is hosting
   (D) to host

4. Even though they _____ on that report since last week, it still isn't finished.

   (A) have been working   Ⓐ Ⓑ Ⓒ Ⓓ
   (B) will be working
   (C) will work
   (D) are working

5. After signing the contract with the new client yesterday, we all _____ to a restaurant to celebrate.

   (A) go   Ⓐ Ⓑ Ⓒ Ⓓ
   (B) will go
   (C) have gone
   (D) went

SKILL

7 **Prepositions**

Prepositions show the relationships between nouns or pronouns and other words. They can indicate time, place, movement, and so on.

> **TIP** Learn the most common uses of prepositions.

Time

Preposition	Use	Example
at	exact time	They arrived *at* 10:30.
on	day or date	They arrived *on* Monday.
in	month or year	We began work *in* April.
from . . . to, from . . . until	beginning and end times	I lived there *from* June *to* December.
by	no later than	Please finish this report *by* noon.

Place

Preposition	Use	Example
at	exact address	He lives *at* 1267 Main Street.
on	street	He lives *on* Main Street.
in	city, country	She worked *in* London.
on	on top of	The phone is *on* my desk.
in	inside of	The pencil is *in* the drawer.
next to, beside, by	to the side of	My desk is *next to* the window.
across . . . from	on the opposite side	His house is *across* the street *from* the bank.

Movement

Preposition	Use	Example
to, toward	in the direction of	She went *to* the bank.
into	to the inside of	They walked *into* the building.
through	from one end to the other	Let's drive *through* the park.
across	from one side to the other	She walked *across* the room.

EXERCISE

Choose the one word or phrase that best completes the sentence.

1. Just put the packages _____ the table and I'll open
   them for you.

   (A) on   Ⓐ Ⓑ Ⓒ Ⓓ
   (B) in
   (C) to
   (D) at

2. They realized the meeting was already in progress the minute
   they walked _____ the room.

   (A) on   Ⓐ Ⓑ Ⓒ Ⓓ
   (B) among
   (C) until
   (D) into

3. The company cafeteria is open for lunch every day from
   11:00 _____ 1:00.

   (A) at   Ⓐ Ⓑ Ⓒ Ⓓ
   (B) for
   (C) until
   (D) by

4. Since the meeting is scheduled to begin _____ noon,
   we will provide sandwiches and snacks for attendees.

   (A) on   Ⓐ Ⓑ Ⓒ Ⓓ
   (B) to
   (C) in
   (D) at

5. Their office is located on the next block, _____ the
   post office and the bank.

   (A) among   Ⓐ Ⓑ Ⓒ Ⓓ
   (B) outside
   (C) between
   (D) through

Prepositions with Verbs and Adjectives

Many verbs and adjectives are commonly paired with certain prepositions.

Verb + Preposition

apologize for	insist on
agree to (something)	object to
agree with (someone)	participate in
ask for (something)	pay for
ask to (do something)	prepare for
believe in	prevent from
blame for	prohibit from
complain about	replace with
decide on	result in
depend on	think about

Adjective + Preposition

afraid of	famous for
angry about (something)	good at
angry at/with (someone)	happy about
aware of	interested in
bored with	late for
busy with	pleased with
curious about	responsible for
different from	serious about
excited about	suitable for
familiar with	tired of

TIP Learn common *verb + preposition* and *adjective + preposition* combinations.

➡ Examples _____

She is *thinking about* applying for a position with another company.

Everyone in the office was able to *participate in* the training session.

I'll be *busy with* some clients for the rest of the afternoon.

This city is *famous for* its wide avenues and pretty parks.

EXERCISE

Choose the one word or phrase that best completes the sentence.

1. Everyone in the office was complaining _____ the noise from the construction site across the street.

   (A) over

   (B) about

   (C) from

   (D) with

   Ⓐ Ⓑ Ⓒ Ⓓ

2. We replaced our old copy machine _____ a newer, more efficient model.

   (A) of

   (B) to

   (C) with

   (D) for

   Ⓐ Ⓑ Ⓒ Ⓓ

3. Ms. Chang is responsible _____ making sure new staff members understand their duties.

   (A) for

   (B) of

   (C) in

   (D) at

   Ⓐ Ⓑ Ⓒ Ⓓ

4. Many local residents objected _____ the developer's plans for building a shopping mall in their neighborhood.

   (A) about

   (B) for

   (C) on

   (D) to

   Ⓐ Ⓑ Ⓒ Ⓓ

5. We have rearranged the office so that we have a comfortable area that is suitable _____ meeting with clients.

   (A) on

   (B) for

   (C) from

   (D) with

   Ⓐ Ⓑ Ⓒ Ⓓ

Coordinating Conjunctions

Coordinating conjunctions are used to join words, phrases, and clauses of equal importance and whose functions are grammatically similar. For example, a coordinating conjunction may join two adjectives, two prepositional phrases, or two independent clauses.

> **TIP** Pay attention to the meaning of the coordinating conjunction.

➡ Examples

Conjunction   and
Use   joins similar ideas

I need some paper *and* a pencil.
He can both dance *and* sing.

Conjunction   but, yet
Use   joins opposite ideas

He eats a lot *but* he never gets fat.
She speaks French fluently, *yet* I never hear her use it.

Conjunction   or, either . . . or, neither . . . nor
Use   joins choices

Would you like coffee *or* tea?
I can give you *either* coffee *or* tea.
I'm sorry but I drink *neither* coffee *nor* tea.

EXERCISE

Choose the one word or phrase that best completes the sentence.

1. Ms. Sam's work is both creative _____ accurate.

    (A) but
    (B) or
    (C) and
    (D) nor

    Ⓐ Ⓑ Ⓒ Ⓓ

2. George worked all night, _____ he wasn't able to finish the report on time.

    (A) yet
    (B) and
    (C) either
    (D) neither

    Ⓐ Ⓑ Ⓒ Ⓓ

3. We can either meet this afternoon _____ wait until later in the week if you prefer.

    (A) but
    (B) or
    (C) nor
    (D) neither

    Ⓐ Ⓑ Ⓒ Ⓓ

4. Neither the bus _____ the subway will get you to the airport on time.

    (A) or
    (B) and
    (C) but
    (D) nor

    Ⓐ Ⓑ Ⓒ Ⓓ

5. We were really interested in seeing the recent play at the National Theater, _____ the tickets sold out too quickly.

    (A) and
    (B) or
    (C) but
    (D) either

    Ⓐ Ⓑ Ⓒ Ⓓ

Parallel Structure

The two words, phrases, or clauses joined by a coordinating conjunction must be alike: two noun forms, two verb forms, two gerunds, and so on.

> **TIP** Learn to recognize the correct grammatical form. Learn to distinguish gerunds from infinitives, nouns from verbs, adjectives from adverbs, and so on.

➥ Examples

Mr. Lee types _quickly_ and _accurately_.
            adverb   adverb

I enjoy both _swimming_ and _sailing_.
         gerund   gerund

You can either _send_ an e-mail or _write_ a letter.
        base form   base form

Neither _the bus_ nor _the subway_ will take you anywhere near his office.
      noun   noun

The manager is _kind_ but _strict_.
       adjective   adjective

EXERCISE

Choose the one word or phrase that best completes the sentence.

1. Prompt and _____ customer service is a priority at
   our business.

   (A) friend   Ⓐ Ⓑ Ⓒ Ⓓ
   (B) friendly
   (C) friendship
   (D) friendliness

2. Sharon is really good at making clients feel comfortable and
   _____ them interested in using our services.

   (A) get   Ⓐ Ⓑ Ⓒ Ⓓ
   (B) got
   (C) gotten
   (D) getting

3. Focus on efficiency and _____ and you will get the job
   done right.

   (A) accurate   Ⓐ Ⓑ Ⓒ Ⓓ
   (B) accurately
   (C) accuracy
   (D) accruing

4. Until the contract is signed, we can neither _____ the
   budget nor begin the research.

   (A) finalize   Ⓐ Ⓑ Ⓒ Ⓓ
   (B) finality
   (C) finalized
   (D) final

5. In order to finish the work on time, we can stay at the office
   _____ today or come in to the office earlier tomorrow.

   (A) lately   Ⓐ Ⓑ Ⓒ Ⓓ
   (B) lateness
   (C) later
   (D) latest

SKILL

11 Subordinating Conjunctions

Subordinating conjunctions are used to join clauses (not words or phrases) that have grammatically different functions. A subordinating conjunction together with its following clause acts like part of the main clause. The subordinate clause may come before or after the main clause.

> **TIP** Pay attention to the meaning of the subordinating conjunction.

➡ Examples

Common Subordinating Conjunctions

Introduce a Reason

because   as   since

I was late to the meeting *because* traffic was heavy.
Since Mr. Kim is out of the office today, I will be taking all his calls.

Introduce a Contradiction

though   although   even though

We decided to hold the conference at this hotel *even though* the rates are higher.
Although Ms. Clark is new at the company, she already knows a lot about our work.

Introduce a Time Clause

before   after   as soon as
when   while   until

I met Mr. Cho *while* I was working in New York.
As soon as the plane landed, all the passengers stood up.

EXERCISE

Choose the one word or phrase that best completes the sentence.

1. The usher allowed Ms. Sello into the concert hall _____ she was late.

   (A) because   Ⓐ Ⓑ Ⓒ Ⓓ
   (B) yet
   (C) even though
   (D) before

2. _____ so few people showed up, we finally decided to cancel the meeting.

   (A) Since   Ⓐ Ⓑ Ⓒ Ⓓ
   (B) Although
   (C) If
   (D) Until

3. Miranda will send a copy of the report to your office _____ it is ready.

   (A) but   Ⓐ Ⓑ Ⓒ Ⓓ
   (B) so
   (C) as soon as
   (D) before

4. Everyone had to use the stairs _____ the elevators were out of order.

   (A) however   Ⓐ Ⓑ Ⓒ Ⓓ
   (B) although
   (C) because
   (D) so

5. I did not get a place in the class _____ I sent my registration form in early.

   (A) as   Ⓐ Ⓑ Ⓒ Ⓓ
   (B) as soon as
   (C) so
   (D) even though

Future Time Clauses

A time clause is a clause that tells when the action in the main clause occurs. A time clause begins with a subordinating conjunction about time, such as *when, while, before, after,* or *until.* In a sentence about the future, the main clause uses a future verb (with *will* or *going to*), but the time clause uses a present tense verb even though it is about the future.

> **TIP** Use a present tense verb in a future time clause.

➡ **Examples** _____

I *will show* you the report as soon as I *finish* writing it.
   main clause   time clause

When the rain *stops*, we *are going to take* a walk in the park.
   time clause   main clause

He is *going to give* everyone copies of his schedule before he *leaves* on his trip.
     main clause   time clause

After they *get* to the hotel, they'*ll call* us.
   time clause   main clause

EXERCISE

Choose the one word or phrase that best completes the sentence.

1. I'll let you know when the train _____.

   (A) arrive   Ⓐ Ⓑ Ⓒ Ⓓ
   (B) arrives
   (C) will arrive
   (D) arriving

2. We'll talk things over with our lawyer before we _____
   the contract.

   (A) sign   Ⓐ Ⓑ Ⓒ Ⓓ
   (B) to sign
   (C) will sign
   (D) signature

3. By the time the meeting _____ over, you'll know everything
   about our marketing plan.

   (A) will be   Ⓐ Ⓑ Ⓒ Ⓓ
   (B) was
   (C) is
   (D) be

4. We will find out the decision on salary increases after the directors
   _____ tomorrow.

   (A) will meet   Ⓐ Ⓑ Ⓒ Ⓓ
   (B) to meet
   (C) met
   (D) meet

5. They _____ ready paint the hallways next week after they
   finish work in the front room.

   (A) are   Ⓐ Ⓑ Ⓒ Ⓓ
   (B) be
   (C) going to
   (D) will be

PART 6: TEXT COMPLETION

Sample Questions

> **Directions:** You will see short passages, each with four blanks. Each blank has four answer options. Choose the word, phrase, or sentence that best completes the passage.

In Part 6, you will answer questions that require you to understand grammar, vocabulary, and the context of the passage. Sometimes you will have to read just the sentence with the blank to answer the question. More often, you will have to look at the surrounding sentences or paragraphs to be able to choose the correct answer.

The skills in this chapter will help you prepare to answer the questions in Part 6. The skills in the chapter for Part 5 will also help you answer grammar and vocabulary questions in Part 6.

Dear Mr. Sanders,

I enjoyed _____ you at the conference last week. I am enclosing the brochures
　　　　　　1

that you requested. I hope _____ are useful to you. If I can be of further assistance,
　　　　　　　　　　　　2

please let me _____.
　　　　　　　3

_____.
4

Sincerely,
Bertha Smith

---

1. (A) met
   (B) meet
   (C) to meet
   (D) meeting

2. (A) it
   (B) they
   (C) we
   (D) its

3. (A) know
   (B) understand
   (C) realize
   (D) learn

4. (A) My assistant is, unfortunately, out of the office this week
   (B) The brochures are a good source for the information you seek
   (C) You can reach me at my office any day between 9:00 A.M. and 5:00 P.M.
   (D) The conference was interesting, and I hope to attend again next year

Question 1

    (A) met
    (B) meet
    (C) to meet
    (D) meeting

The best way to complete the sentence "I enjoyed _____ you at the conference last week" is Choice (D) "meeting." The participle *meeting* follows the verb *enjoyed*. Therefore, you should choose answer (D).

Question 2

    (A) it
    (B) they
    (C) we
    (D) its

The best way to complete the sentence "I hope _____ are useful to you" is Choice (B) "they." You must read beyond this sentence to answer the question. Sometimes you have to look back; sometimes forward. In this case, you look back. The pronoun *they* refers back to the plural noun *brochures*. Therefore, you should choose answer (B).

Question 3

    (A) know
    (B) understand
    (C) realize
    (D) learn

The best way to complete the sentence "If I can be of further assistance, please let me _____ " is Choice (A) "know." All of the words have a similar meaning, but only *know* fits the context. Therefore, you should choose answer (A).

Question 4

    (A) My assistant is, unfortunately, out of the office this week.
    (B) The brochures are a good source for the information you seek.
    (C) You can reach me at my office any day between 9:00 A.M. and 5:00 P.M.
    (D) The conference was interesting, and I hope to attend again next year.

The best sentence to complete the passage is Choice (C), "You can reach me at my office any day between 9:00 A.M. and 5:00 P.M." The previous sentence offers further assistance, and this sentence explains how to get that assistance. Therefore, you should choose answer (C).

1 Adverbs of Frequency

Adverbs of frequency tell *when* or *how often* something happens.

> **TIP** Pay attention to the context in order to choose the correct adverb.

➡ Examples _____

Common Adverbs of Frequency

100% of the time	always
	usually
	frequently
	often
	sometimes
	occasionally
	seldom
	rarely
0% of the time	never

We *always* eat lunch at this café because it is so close to the office.

I *usually* play golf on weekends, but last Saturday I played tennis instead.

The weather is *usually* dry in the summer, but *sometimes* it rains.

Sam *rarely* works late, although last night he stayed at the office until 8:00.

I *never* drink coffee at night, because it keeps me awake.

EXERCISE

Choose the one word or phrase that best completes each sentence.

1. We _____ hold staff meetings on weekends. In fact, I believe this is the first time we've done this, but something very important has come up.

    (A) rarely

    (B) frequently

    (C) often

    (D) sometimes

    Ⓐ Ⓑ Ⓒ Ⓓ

2. Please note that punctuality is very important in this company. We _____ begin our staff meetings on time and don't wait for late arrivals.

    (A) never

    (B) seldom

    (C) occasionally

    (D) always

    Ⓐ Ⓑ Ⓒ Ⓓ

3. Our meetings _____ last about an hour, and I expect this one will, too.

    (A) usually

    (B) sometimes

    (C) rarely

    (D) never

    Ⓐ Ⓑ Ⓒ Ⓓ

4. Mr. Kim will not be present at the meeting. This is unexpected, as he _____ misses meetings.

    (A) generally

    (B) seldom

    (C) frequently

    (D) occasionally

    Ⓐ Ⓑ Ⓒ Ⓓ

5. We _____ serve snacks when the meeting is over. However, we won't have time for that at this meeting.

    (A) rarely

    (B) never

    (C) often

    (D) seldom

    Ⓐ Ⓑ Ⓒ Ⓓ

Gerunds and Infinitives After Main Verbs

The main verb in a sentence can be followed immediately by a second verb. This verb can be a gerund (-*ing* form) or an infinitive (*to* + verb). The main verb determines which form is used.

> **TIP** Pay attention to the main verb to determine whether to use a gerund or an infinitive.

➡ **Examples** _____

Common Verbs Followed by a Gerund

appreciate	I *appreciate* having the opportunity to speak.
avoid	They *avoided* looking us in the eye.
consider	We *considered* staying longer.
delay	We *delayed* writing you until we had more information.
discuss	Have you *discussed* working together on this project?
enjoy	We *enjoyed* having you for dinner.
finish	They will *finish* correcting the report soon.
mind	She didn't *mind* staying late for the meeting.
miss	We *miss* going to the movies with you.
postpone	Could we *postpone* leaving?
quit	He wants to *quit* smoking.
risk	They *risked* losing everything.
suggest	We *suggest* leaving on time.

Common Verbs Followed by an Infinitive

agree	He *agreed* to complete the project.
attempt	They *attempted* to climb Mt. Fuji.
claim	She *claims* to be an expert.
decide	We *decided* to hire her anyway.
demand	He *demanded* to know what we were doing.
fail	We *failed* to give a satisfactory answer.
hesitate	I *hesitated* to tell the truth.
hope	We *hope* to leave before dawn.
intend	She *intends* to start her own club.
learn	They will *learn* to swim at camp.
need	She *needs* to stop smoking.
offer	They *offered* to take us home.
plan	We *plan* to accept their offer.
prepare	She *prepared* to leave.
refuse	He *refused* to come with us.
seem	She *seemed* to be annoyed.
want	He didn't *want* to leave.

EXERCISE

Choose the one word or phrase that best completes each sentence.

1. I talked with our client, Mr. Wilson, over the phone. He has agreed _____ with us in order to discuss the contract.

   (A) met   Ⓐ Ⓑ Ⓒ Ⓓ
   (B) has met
   (C) to meet
   (D) meeting

2. Our schedule is full this week, but Mr. Wilson doesn't mind _____ until next week for an appointment.

   (A) waits   Ⓐ Ⓑ Ⓒ Ⓓ
   (B) waiting
   (C) is waiting
   (D) will wait

3. I've offered _____ a draft of the contract to Mr. Wilson's office. This will give him a chance to review it before our meeting.

   (A) sending   Ⓐ Ⓑ Ⓒ Ⓓ
   (B) to send
   (C) can send
   (D) have sent

4. The contract is not complete yet. However, I should be able to finish _____ it before the end of the day.

   (A) writing   Ⓐ Ⓑ Ⓒ Ⓓ
   (B) written
   (C) to write
   (D) write

5. I hope you will review the contract for me before I forward it to Mr. Wilson. I plan _____ it on your desk tomorrow morning.

   (A) putting   Ⓐ Ⓑ Ⓒ Ⓓ
   (B) will put
   (C) put
   (D) to put

3 Gerunds and Infinitives After Prepositions and Adjectives

In addition to following the main verb of a sentence or clause, gerunds and infinitives can follow other types of words, as well.

> **TIP** Know the kinds of words that gerunds and infinitives can follow.

➡ Examples _____

Harry is interested *in applying* for a position with an international company.
Sara apologized *for arriving* at the meeting late.

A gerund can follow a preposition. See Skill 8 on page 122 for lists of common verb + preposition and adjective + preposition pairs.

They will be *happy to help* you.
He was *eager to start* working on the project.

An infinitive can follow an adjective.

He was *hungry enough to eat* three servings of rice.
They walked *too slowly to get* there in time.

An infinitive can follow phrases with the pattern adjective/adverb + *enough* or adjective/adverb + *too*.

EXERCISE

Choose the one word or phrase that best completes each sentence.

1. Do your employees complain about _____ frequent headaches or constant eye pain? The fault may lie with your lighting system.

   (A) have
   (B) having
   (C) to have
   (D) had

   Ⓐ Ⓑ Ⓒ Ⓓ

2. The bright glare of some kinds of lights is stressful on the eyes. You need a lighting system that creates soft diffused light that is easy on the eyes but still bright enough _____ by.

   (A) read
   (B) reads
   (C) to read
   (D) reading

   Ⓐ Ⓑ Ⓒ Ⓓ

3. With the proper lighting system in place, your employees will sit down at their desks ready _____ in ease and comfort.

   (A) to work
   (B) working
   (C) are working
   (D) have worked

   Ⓐ Ⓑ Ⓒ Ⓓ

4. If you are tired of _____ complaints about the lights in your workplace, it's time to make a change.

   (A) heard
   (B) to hear
   (C) should hear
   (D) hearing

   Ⓐ Ⓑ Ⓒ Ⓓ

5. You could start by changing the lights in just a few places. Or, you could decide on _____ a completely new lighting system in your entire office.

   (A) install
   (B) will install
   (C) installing
   (D) to install

   Ⓐ Ⓑ Ⓒ Ⓓ

4 Causative Verbs

Causative verbs show that one person makes another person do something. A causative is followed by another verb in either the base form or the infinitive.

> **TIP** Learn which causative verbs are followed by the base form and which are followed by the infinitive.

➡ **Examples** _____

Causative Verbs Followed by the Base Form

have	let	make

The manager <u>had</u> Mr. Smith <u>demonstrate</u> the product.
    causative   base form

Our boss <u>lets</u> us <u>leave</u> early on Friday afternoons.
   causative base
        form

The driver <u>will make</u> you <u>get</u> off the bus if you don't have the exact fare.
     causative   base
          form

Causative Verbs Followed by the Infinitive Form

allow	get	require
cause	order	
force	permit	

I'll <u>get</u> my assistant <u>to copy</u> those documents.
 causative   infinitive form

The company never <u>permits</u> employees <u>to make</u> public statements.
       causative   infinitive form

The human resources office <u>requires</u> all job applicants <u>to provide</u> three references.
        causative   infinitive form

EXERCISE

Choose the one word or phrase that best completes each sentence.

1. Our newest staff member, John Greene, appears to have some confusion about ordering supplies. Please make him _____ that he must have authorization before submitting an order.

   (A) understand   Ⓐ Ⓑ Ⓒ Ⓓ
   (B) understands
   (C) to understand
   (D) can understand

2. We cannot permit staff _____ anything at any time they want. That would create havoc with our budget.

   (A) order   Ⓐ Ⓑ Ⓒ Ⓓ
   (B) to order
   (C) ordering
   (D) will order

3. It's time to start planning our annual holiday luncheon. Please have John Greene _____ the caterers before the end of the week.

   (A) call   Ⓐ Ⓑ Ⓒ Ⓓ
   (B) calls
   (C) called
   (D) will call

4. He should get the caterers _____ several menu options. Then together we can decide which one we prefer.

   (A) provide   Ⓐ Ⓑ Ⓒ Ⓓ
   (B) providing
   (C) to provide
   (D) should provide

5. Mr. Greene is a new staff member and is not familiar with the customs of this office. Therefore, I don't think we should let him _____ the menu himself.

   (A) choosing   Ⓐ Ⓑ Ⓒ Ⓓ
   (B) chose
   (C) to choose
   (D) choose

Real Conditionals

Conditional sentences can express two kinds of conditions: real and unreal. Conditional sentences describe a condition and a result and are made up of two clauses: an *if* clause, or condition, and a main clause, or result. Real conditionals express what is true or really possible. The *if* clause in a real conditional is always in the present tense. The main clause may be in the present or future tense or may be a command.

> **TIP** Use present tense in the *if* cause of a real conditional.

➡ Examples

Habit	*If* it rains, *if* clause (real condition)	I drive to work. main clause
Future	*If* it rains, *if* clause (real condition)	I will drive to work. main clause
Command	*If* it rains, *if* clause (real condition)	drive to work. main clause

EXERCISE

Choose the one word or phrase that best completes each sentence.

1. Class registration begins August 21 and classes begin August 29.
   If you _____ for a class after August 28, you will have to pay
   a late fee.

   (A) register
   (B) to register
   (C) will register
   (D) is going to register

   Ⓐ Ⓑ Ⓒ Ⓓ

2. Some classes may not have enough students. If we _____
   a class due to low enrollment, we will contact you.

   (A) to cancel
   (B) cancel
   (C) canceling
   (D) will cancel

   Ⓐ Ⓑ Ⓒ Ⓓ

3. Please remember to provide your phone number and e-mail address on
   your registration form. We _____ able to contact you if we don't
   have this information.

   (A) not be
   (B) aren't
   (C) won't be
   (D) weren't

   Ⓐ Ⓑ Ⓒ Ⓓ

4. We offer classes for working people. If you _____ time to study
   during the day, please check our evening class schedule.

   (A) not have
   (B) didn't have
   (C) won't have
   (D) don't have

   Ⓐ Ⓑ Ⓒ Ⓓ

5. If you bring your registration form to the school bookstore, you
   _____ a discount on the textbooks required for your class.

   (A) receive
   (B) to receive
   (C) will receive
   (D) have received

   Ⓐ Ⓑ Ⓒ Ⓓ

6 Unreal Conditionals

Unreal conditions express something that is not true or is not possible. If the sentence is about a present situation, the verb in the *if* clause borrows the form of the past, but remember that it represents the present. If the situation is about the past, the verb in the *if* clause borrows the form of the past perfect. The main clause uses the auxiliary *would* + verb for a present situation and *would have* + verb for a past situation.

> **TIP** Remember that a past tense verb in the *if* clause indicates a *present* unreal conditional.

➡ Examples

Present

> If George *owned* the company, he *would* accept the project.

This sentence tells us that George doesn't really own the company so he won't really accept the project.

> Sarah *would get* to work on time if she *left* her house earlier every morning.

This sentence tells us that Sarah doesn't really leave her house earlier so she doesn't really get to work on time.

> I *would eat* lunch with you if I *didn't have* so much work to do.

This sentence tells us that I really have a lot of work to do so I won't eat lunch with you.

Past

> If I *had received* the promotion, I *would have bought* a new car.

This sentence tells us that I didn't really receive the promotion so I didn't buy a new car.

> We *would have gone* skiing on our vacation if it *had snowed* in the mountains.

This sentence tells us that it didn't really snow in the mountains so we didn't go skiing.

> If he *hadn't been* so busy, he *would have called* you.

This sentence tells us that he really was busy so he didn't call you.

EXERCISE

Choose the one word or phrase that best completes each sentence.

1. Dear Mr. Klugman, I am terribly sorry about our misunderstanding
   yesterday. If I _____ that space #7 was your assigned parking
   space, I would never have parked there.

   (A) knew   Ⓐ Ⓑ Ⓒ Ⓓ
   (B) had known
   (C) have known
   (D) could know

2. If you _____ for parking elsewhere, I would have reimbursed you.
   Luckily you found another free spot on the staff parking lot.

   (A) have paid   Ⓐ Ⓑ Ⓒ Ⓓ
   (B) had paid
   (C) pay
   (D) will pay

3. I looked for you in the office today but found out that you are away for
   the day. If you _____ here today, I would apologize in person.

   (A) are   Ⓐ Ⓑ Ⓒ Ⓓ
   (B) will be
   (C) were
   (D) had been

4. Parking is a big problem in this part of town. If I didn't live so far
   from the office, I _____ the parking problem by walking to
   work every day.

   (A) avoided   Ⓐ Ⓑ Ⓒ Ⓓ
   (B) had avoided
   (C) would have avoided
   (D) would avoid

5. If I had walked to work yesterday, I _____ in your parking space.

   (A) wouldn't have parked   Ⓐ Ⓑ Ⓒ Ⓓ
   (B) wouldn't park
   (C) didn't park
   (D) hadn't parked

7 Comparisons

Adjectives and adverbs can be used to show the similarities and differences among people, places, things, and actions. There are three degrees of comparison: (1) positive; (2) comparative (-er and more forms); and (3) superlative (-est and most forms).

One-syllable adjectives and two-syllable adjectives that end in -y have the -er and -est forms. Certain other two-syllable adjectives also have these forms. All three-syllable adjectives use more and most. Adverbs follow a similar pattern.

> **TIP** Remember that superlative adjectives and adverbs are preceded by *the*.

➥ Examples

Adjectives and adverbs that have the *-er/-est* forms:

Adjectives and Adverbs

Positive	Comparative	Superlative
pretty	prettier	the prettiest
narrow	narrower	the narrowest
far	farther	the farthest
soon	sooner	the soonest

I think fall is a *prettier* season *than* spring.
No one drives down that street because it is *the narrowest* in the neighborhood.
They arrived *sooner than* we expected.
That hotel is the *farthest* from the convention center

Adjectives and adverbs that have the *more/most* forms:

Adjectives and Adverbs

Positive	Comparative	Superlative
popular	more popular	the most popular
competent	more competent	the most competent
efficiently	more efficiently	the most efficiently
quickly	more quickly	the most quickly

That restaurant is *the most popular* one in town.
Shirley is a *more competent* accountant *than* her colleagues.
She works *more efficiently than* other accountants I know.
Roger finished his presentation *the most quickly*.

Irregular adjectives:

Adjectives

Positive	Comparative	Superlative
good	better	the best
bad	worse	the worst

Adverbs

Positive	Comparative	Superlative
well	better	the best
little	less	the least

This is *the worst* weather we've had all year.

The new copier works *better than* the old one.

EXERCISE

Choose the one word or phrase that best completes each sentence.

1. Techno Business Academy offers intensive, short-term skills training courses for office workers. We guarantee to train you _____ any other business school at a price you can afford.

    (A) faster than   Ⓐ Ⓑ Ⓒ Ⓓ
    (B) nicer than
    (C) longer than
    (D) more costly than

2. Some schools charge hundreds of dollars per course. But at Techno Business Academy, we guarantee _____ prices in town.

    (A) low   Ⓐ Ⓑ Ⓒ Ⓓ
    (B) lowest
    (C) lower than
    (D) the lowest

3. Our recent graduates earn _____ salaries than other office professionals with years of experience.

    (A) high   Ⓐ Ⓑ Ⓒ Ⓓ
    (B) higher
    (C) highest
    (D) the highest

4. If you are looking for a _____ job than the one you have now, Techno Business Academy can help you.

    (A) the best   Ⓐ Ⓑ Ⓒ Ⓓ
    (B) best
    (C) better
    (D) good

5. A certificate from Techno Business Academy will open doors for you. Employers know that _____ workers around are graduates of our program.

    (A) the highest   Ⓐ Ⓑ Ⓒ Ⓓ
    (B) the most skilled
    (C) the least competent
    (D) the least expensive

Pronouns

Pronouns take the place of nouns. A pronoun must agree with its antecedent (the noun it replaces) in person and number. There are several different types of pronouns with different grammatical functions.

> **TIP** Identify the antecedent and make sure the pronoun agrees with it in person and number.

Subject Pronouns		Object Pronouns		Reflexive Pronouns	
I	we	me	us	myself	ourselves
you	you	you	you	yourself	yourselves
he/she/it	they	him/her/it	them	himself/herself/itself	themselves

Possessive Adjectives		Possessive Pronouns			
my	our	mine	ours		
our	your	yours	yours		
his/her/its	their	his/hers/its	theirs		

➡ Examples

Mrs. Kim was at the office yesterday, but I didn't see *her*.

The clients will be here all day tomorrow, and *they* hope to meet with the director.

You should call a repair person instead of trying to fix the machine *yourself*.

I don't think this coat is *mine*.

Bob will present *his* plan at the next staff meeting.

EXERCISE

Choose the one word or phrase that best completes each sentence.

1. Dear Ms. Coleman, I would like thank you for the kind hospitality
   I received during my visit to the branch office last week. Please tell
   _____ staff that I very much appreciated the welcome they
   gave me.

   (A) yourself   Ⓐ Ⓑ Ⓒ Ⓓ
   (B) yours
   (C) you
   (D) your

2. I was impressed by the friendliness and helpfulness of all the employees
   in the office. _____ made my work go smoothly even though I was
   working in an unfamiliar setting.

   (A) I   Ⓐ Ⓑ Ⓒ Ⓓ
   (B) He
   (C) You
   (D) They

3. I would particularly like to mention John Malstrom, who made
   special efforts to make sure I had everything I needed. Please thank
   _____ for me.

   (A) me   Ⓐ Ⓑ Ⓒ Ⓓ
   (B) him
   (C) her
   (D) them

4. Unfortunately, I left behind a folder of important documents during my
   visit. I think I left _____ on the table in the conference room.

   (A) it   Ⓐ Ⓑ Ⓒ Ⓓ
   (B) him
   (C) them
   (D) me

5. Could you please send the forgotten item to my office? I won't have time
   to pick up the folder _____.

   (A) itself   Ⓐ Ⓑ Ⓒ Ⓓ
   (B) yourself
   (C) myself
   (D) themselves

9   Subject Relative Pronouns

A relative pronoun introduces an adjective clause. An adjective clause has the same purpose as an adjective—it modifies a noun in the main clause. The relative pronoun may be the subject or the object of the clause. The correct relative pronoun to use depends on the noun it modifies (the antecedent), on whether it is the subject or the object of the clause, and on whether the clause is restrictive or nonrestrictive.

> **TIP** Remember that the adjective clause immediately follows the noun it modifies. This will help you identify the antecedent.

➡ Examples

A restrictive clause is one that is necessary to identify the noun it modifies. Without the restrictive clause, the identity of the noun is unclear.

Subject Relative Pronouns—Restrictive Clauses

People	*who*
	that
Things	*which*
	that
Possession	*whose*

<u>The woman</u>   <u>who</u>   shares this office is very good with computers.
antecedent   relative
             pronoun

The sentence above is made up of a main clause: *The woman is very good with computers*, and an adjective clause: *who shares this office*.

<u>The packages</u>   <u>that</u>   arrived this morning are on your desk.
antecedent   relative
             pronoun

The sentence above is made up of a main clause: *The packages are on your desk*, and an adjective clause: *that arrived this morning*.

<u>The man</u>   <u>whose</u>   office is next door wants to meet you.
antecedent   relative
             pronoun

The sentence above is made up of a main clause: *The man wants to meet you*, and an adjective clause: *whose office is next door*.

A nonrestrictive clause is one that is not necessary to identify the noun. It just gives some extra information. If we removed the nonrestrictive clause from the sentence, the identity of the noun would remain clear. A nonrestrictive clause is always set off from the rest of the sentence with commas.

Subject Relative Pronouns—Nonrestrictive Clauses

People	*who*
Things	*which*
Possession	*whose*

<u>Mr. Maurice</u>, <u>who</u> has worked here for a long time, will retire soon.
antecedent relative
            pronoun

The sentence above is made up of a main clause: *Mr. Maurice will retire soon,* and an adjective clause: *who has worked here for a long time.*

<u>My car,</u> <u>which</u> is constantly breaking down, is at the mechanic's again today.
antecedent relative
            pronoun

The sentence above is made up of a main clause: *My car is at the mechanic's again today,* and an adjective clause: *which is constantly breaking down.*

<u>My assistant,</u> <u>whose</u> French is excellent, will help with the clients from France.
antecedent relative
            pronoun

The sentence above is made up of a main clause: *My assistant will help with the clients from France,* and an adjective clause: *whose French is excellent.*

EXERCISE

Choose the one word or phrase that best completes each sentence.

1. Ms. McIntyre will be visiting us next week from the London offices. Staff members _____ wish to make an appointment to meet with her may contact the Human Resources office.

   (A) who
   (B) whom
   (C) whose
   (D) which

   (A) (B) (C) (D)

2. A luncheon for Ms. McIntyre will be held on Wednesday at the Flowers Restaurant. Everyone _____ schedule allows is welcome to attend this event.

   (A) who
   (B) their
   (C) whose
   (D) his

   (A) (B) (C) (D)

3. We are all looking forward to Ms. McIntyre's visit, _____ will last ten days.

   (A) who
   (B) that
   (C) whose
   (D) which

   (A) (B) (C) (D)

4. Ms. McIntyre will spend time in each department. If you want to know when she will be in your department, please check the schedule _____ is available on the company website.

   (A) it
   (B) that
   (C) who
   (D) whose

   (A) (B) (C) (D)

5. Ms. McIntyre, _____ does not often get a chance to visit overseas offices, is looking forward to the visit.

   (A) that
   (B) who
   (C) which
   (D) she

   (A) (B) (C) (D)

Object Relative Pronouns

An object relative pronoun is the object of the verb or a preposition in the relative clause. An object relative pronoun, except for *whose*, can be omitted from restrictive clauses.

> **TIP** Identify the subject of the adjective clause. If the relative pronoun is the subject, use a subject relative pronoun. Otherwise, use an object relative pronoun.

➡ **Examples**

Object Relative Pronouns—Restrictive Clauses

People	*whom, who, that,* nothing
Things	*which, that,* nothing
Possession	*whose*

<u>The accountant</u>   <u>whom</u>   we hired last month used to work for Ibex International.
antecedent   relative
                  pronoun

The sentence above is made up of a main clause: *The accountant used to work for Ibex International,* and an adjective clause: *whom we hired last month.*

<u>The office</u>   <u>that</u>   we rented is very close to the subway station.
antecedent   relative
              pronoun

The sentence above is made up of a main clause: *The office is very close to the subway station,* and an adjective clause: *that we rented.*

<u>The person</u>   <u>whose</u>   phone number you requested no longer works here.
antecedent   relative
              pronoun

The sentence above is made up of a main clause: *The person no longer works here,* and an adjective clause: *whose phone number you requested.*

Object Relative Pronouns—Nonrestrictive Clauses

People	*whom, who*
Things	*which*
Possession	*whose*

<u>My neighbor,</u>   <u>who</u>   I have known for many years, is moving away next month.
antecedent   relative
           pronoun

The sentence above is made up of a main clause: *My neighbor is moving away next month,* and an adjective clause: *who I have known for many years.*

<u>The City Museum,</u>   <u>which</u>   I visit almost every day, has many interesting exhibits.
antecedent   relative
                pronoun

The sentence above is made up of a main clause: *The City Museum has many interesting exhibits,* and an adjective clause: *which I visit almost every day.*

<u>Shirley,</u>   <u>whose</u>   office you were using last week, is back at work today.
antecedent   relative
           pronoun

The sentence above is made up of a main clause: *Shirley is back at work today,* and an adjective clause: *whose office you were using last week.*

EXERCISE

Choose the one word or phrase that best completes each sentence.

1. Do you want to know more about global warming and how you can help prevent it? Dr. Herman Friedman, _____ many consider the foremost authority on the subject, will speak at Grayson Hall next Tuesday.

    (A) whose
    (B) which
    (C) who
    (D) him

    Ⓐ Ⓑ Ⓒ Ⓓ

2. Dr. Freidman has written many articles and books on the subject of global warming. The gradual bleaching of the Great Barrier Reef, _____ he has been researching for several years, is the subject of his latest book.

    (A) that
    (B) which
    (C) whom
    (D) it

    Ⓐ Ⓑ Ⓒ Ⓓ

3. Signed copies of his book will be for sale after his talk, along with other books _____ he has written about global warming.

    (A) whose
    (B) that
    (C) them
    (D) who

    Ⓐ Ⓑ Ⓒ Ⓓ

4. Dr. Friedman will be accompanied by a colleague. Dr. Smythe, _____ writings on global warming are also widely known, will present slides of his research visits to coral reefs.

    (A) who
    (B) whom
    (C) that
    (D) whose

    Ⓐ Ⓑ Ⓒ Ⓓ

5. Those interested in understanding more about global warming will not want to miss this event. Drs. Friedman and Smythe, to _____ we owe so much of our knowledge of this subject, are both interesting and informed speakers.

    (A) whom
    (B) whose
    (C) them
    (D) which

    Ⓐ Ⓑ Ⓒ Ⓓ

Passive Voice

Most sentences are in active voice—the subject performs the action. Some sentences are in passive voice—the subject receives the action. We use passive voice when the agent (the one who performs the action) is unknown or unimportant. The passive voice is formed with the verb *be* + the past participle form of the verb.

> **TIP** To identify a passive voice sentence, determine whether the subject performs or receives the action.

➡ Examples

In the passive voice, the verb *be* carries the tense and the negative. The main verb is always in the past participle form.

Simple Present

> Employees <u>are</u> <u>paid</u> every Friday.
>   be   past
>   participle

The subject of the sentence above is *employees* and the action is *pay*. The employees don't perform the action. Somebody else, probably the boss or the company, pays the employees.

> Children <u>aren't</u> <u>allowed</u> in this office without adult supervision.
>   be   past
>   participle

The subject of the sentence above is *children* and the action is *allow*. The children don't perform the action; they aren't the ones who don't allow themselves.

Simple Past

> The mail <u>was</u> <u>delivered</u> at 10:00 this morning.
>   be   past
>   participle

The subject of the sentence above is *mail* and the action is *delivered*. The mail didn't perform the action. It didn't deliver itself. The letter carrier, not mentioned in the sentence, did.

Present Perfect

> The annual conference <u>has been</u> <u>held</u> in this city every year since 2005.
>   be   past
>   participle

The subject of the sentence above is *conference* and the action is *held*. The conference doesn't perform the action; it doesn't hold itself. Some organization or group of people holds the conference.

Future

Copies of the report <u>will be</u> <u>distributed</u> at tomorrow's meeting.
               be   past
                         participle

The subject of the sentence above is *copies of the report* and the action is *distributed*. The copies of the report will not perform the action; they will not distribute themselves.

Sometimes the agent, the one that performs the action, is mentioned in the sentence. In that case, we use the preposition *by*.

The letter was signed *by* everyone in the office.

All receipts are inspected *by* the accountant.

EXERCISE

Choose the one word or phrase that best completes each sentence.

1. We have just put a good deal of effort, not to mention money, into to renovating the conference room. In addition to new tables and chairs, the walls _____ painted last month.

   (A) was   Ⓐ Ⓑ Ⓒ Ⓓ
   (B) are
   (C) were
   (D) have been

2. We had a problem with the carpet company, but we have worked that out, and they have promised us that the new carpet will be _____ before the end of this week.

   (A) installs   Ⓐ Ⓑ Ⓒ Ⓓ
   (B) installed
   (C) installing
   (D) installation

3. The only thing in the room that isn't new is the curtains. We determined that they just needed a thorough cleaning. We sent them out to a professional cleaning facility where the stains _____, and now they are as good as new.

   (A) remove   Ⓐ Ⓑ Ⓒ Ⓓ
   (B) removed
   (C) have removed
   (D) were removed

4. Now that the conference room _____, we hope everyone will find it to be a pleasant place to work.

   (A) has been renovated Ⓐ Ⓑ Ⓒ Ⓓ
   (B) has renovated
   (C) is renovating
   (D) renovated

5. We thank you for your patience during the renovation process. In order to celebrate the new conference room, a party _____ next month.

   (A) will give Ⓐ Ⓑ Ⓒ Ⓓ
   (B) is giving
   (C) to be given
   (D) will be given

SKILL 12 Word Meaning

In order to choose the correct vocabulary word to complete a sentence, you will have to understand the context. You will have to look at the surrounding sentences to understand the context and know which word best fits the passage.

> **TIP** Understand the context to choose the correct answer.

➥ Examples

1. The workshop begins at 9:00 A.M. sharp. Therefore, we ask _____ to arrive early so that we can begin on time.

   (A) consultants
   (B) participants
   (C) customers
   (D) reviewers

This information is directed at people who will attend a workshop, asking them to arrive ahead of time. People who attend a workshop may be referred to as *participants*, so Choice (B) is the correct answer. The other choices do not fit the context.

2. The doctor is very busy and it is difficult to get a chance to see him. I was _____ to be given an appointment for two months from now.

   (A) wise
   (B) necessary
   (C) persistent
   (D) fortunate

The information states that it is difficult to get an appointment with the doctor. Therefore, the person who was given an appointment feels lucky, or *fortunate*. Choice (D) is the correct answer. The other choices do not fit the context.

EXERCISE

Choose the one word or phrase that best completes each sentence.

1. This is a very well-maintained building. The _____ keeps all public areas clean and recently had the hallways re-carpeted.

   (A) landlord   Ⓐ Ⓑ Ⓒ Ⓓ
   (B) tenant
   (C) resident
   (D) architect

2. We had our apartment painted last year. The rooms are dark, so we _____ a light color to brighten things up.

   (A) acknowledged   Ⓐ Ⓑ Ⓒ Ⓓ
   (B) possessed
   (C) selected
   (D) enjoyed

3. The building is in a great location. The subway station is just a block away, and there are many nice shops and restaurants in the neighborhood. The good location is one reason why the rent is so _____.

   (A) reasonable   Ⓐ Ⓑ Ⓒ Ⓓ
   (B) unusual
   (C) fair
   (D) high

4. Many people come to this part of the city for the _____ activities. In addition to the museums and theaters, there are concerts in the park every summer.

   (A) athletic   Ⓐ Ⓑ Ⓒ Ⓓ
   (B) cultural
   (C) dramatic
   (D) performance

5. Many of the events are free for city residents. You will not be _____ an entrance fee if you can prove that you live in the city.

(A) allowed
(B) charged
(C) purchased
(D) demanded

Ⓐ Ⓑ Ⓒ Ⓓ

Sentence Choice

Some questions ask you to choose the sentence that best fits the context. The context includes both the topic and the purpose of the passage. The topic of a memo may be a staff meeting, for example, while the purpose might be to inform staff that the meeting will be held, explain the content of the meeting, or ask for evaluations of a meeting already held.

> **TIP** Identify both the topic and the purpose of the passage.

➡ Examples

1. There will be a meeting about our new health insurance policy next Wednesday afternoon. Attendance is not mandatory, but it is recommended. If you have any questions about this new policy, this is your opportunity to get them answered. _____.

   (A) If you need a few days off work for health reasons, please inform your supervisor
   (B) We hope that the new policy will save everyone some money and will be easier to understand

The paragraph announces a meeting to explain the new health insurance policy. Choice (A) mentions health, but it is not related to health insurance or the meeting, so it does not fit the context. Choice (B) fits the context because it explains the reason for a new policy, so Choice (B) is the best choice to complete the blank.

2. I am sending you a draft of the new contract with the XZ Company. _____. Please review it and send me your comments as soon as possible. Your help with this matter is greatly appreciated.

   (A) The XZ Company has been our client for several years now
   (B) I would like your feedback before I meet with the client on Thursday

The writer of this note is sending a draft of a contract and would like someone to review it, or give feedback, so Choice (B) fits the context. Choice (A) mentions information about the client that is not relevant to the request for a contract review.

EXERCISE

Choose the sentence that best completes each paragraph.

1. The elevators in this building will undergo routine maintenance during the week of September 15. _____. When this occurs, please use another elevator or the stairs. We apologize for any inconvenience this may cause.

   (A) There are three elevators in this building, each with a capacity of 15 passengers
   (B) During this week, there may be one or two elevators out of service from time to time
   (C) Some people prefer to use the stairs because they enjoy the exercise
   (D) Each elevator is equipped with a red emergency phone

   (A) (B) (C) (D)

2. Thank you for agreeing to meet with me next week. _____. I look forward to the opportunity to discuss my company and the services we can offer you. We have served many satisfied clients like yourself in the past, and I feel confident we can provide you with satisfactory services, as well.

   (A) I enjoy social get-togethers from time to time
   (B) I have a full schedule of meetings and little time for anything else
   (C) I will look for you at the Golden Café at 10:00
   (D) I have been unable to reach you by either phone or e-mail

   (A) (B) (C) (D)

3. Thank you for sending your resume to us. You have exactly the kind of education and experience we are looking for. I would like you to come in for an interview soon. _____.

   (A) Please call my office to set up a time for an appointment
   (B) There are several places in the city where you can get the training you need
   (C) We generally go through an employment agency when we need to hire new staff
   (D) Many young people are looking for a position in this field

   (A) (B) (C) (D)

4. Thank you for your interest in using the services of Spick and Span Office Cleaners. We have set up an appointment for you for next Monday morning. _____. As we discussed over the phone, we expect the job will take 3–4 hours. We will vacuum and dust all rooms. Payment is due at the time of services.

   (A) We have been cleaning offices in this city for over five years
   (B) Monday is generally our busiest day of the week
   (C) Most clients hire us on a weekly basis
   (D) We will arrive at 8:00 A.M. ready to clean

   (A) (B) (C) (D)

PART 6: SKILLS PRACTICE

Read each passage and choose the best word, phrase, or sentence to complete each blank.

Questions 1–4 refer to the following letter.

Dear Client,

We _____ invite you to attend our 3rd annual open house party on the
                1
afternoon of December 2. This is our way of showing our appreciation

to our clients, as well as an opportunity for you to get to know us _____
                                                                        2
better. Please come to our offices any time between 3:00 and 7:00 P.M. to

enjoy refreshments, _____ entertainment, and good company. _____.
                        3   4

---

1. (A) cordial
   (B) cordially
   (C) cordiality
   (D) cordialness

2. (A) any
   (B) some
   (C) a few
   (D) a little

3. (A) live
   (B) alive
   (C) liven
   (D) living

4. (A) Please call for an appointment
   (B) It will be charged to your account
   (C) We look forward to seeing you
   (D) Tickets are available at the front desk

Questions 5–8 refer to the following e-mail.

To: Richard Simms (rsimms@acmeinc.com)
From: Ethel Burt (eburt@acmeinc.com)

Richard,
I have received _____ request for time off during the last week of May to attend a training seminar. I applaud
                5
your initiative in taking advantage of this professional development opportunity. Unfortunately, the timing is a
problem as your absence would occur right at the beginning of our busy _____ , when I really need to have
                                                                         6
you in the office every day. Perhaps you could take a look at the seminar schedule and find an appropriate one
that _____ at some time later in the year. _____. Let me know if I can be of any further help.
     7   8

5. (A) you
    (B) your
    (C) yours
    (D) you'll

6. (A) venue
    (B) location
    (C) season
    (D) calendar

7. (A) give
    (B) gives
    (C) will give
    (D) will be given

8. (A) Last month's seminar was very successful
    (B) We are already making plans for the end of May
    (C) Please submit requests for time off to your supervisor
    (D) I am sorry to have to turn down your request at this time

Questions 9–12 refer to the following notice.

NOTICE

_____ in this lot is for employees of the Zip Zap Company only. Cars not bearing a
 9
Zip Zap parking sticker on the lower passenger side windshield will be _____ at the
                                                                        10
owner's expense. The Zip Zap Company will not be held responsible for any _____ that
                                                                          11
may occur. If you are a Zip Zap employee, you can apply for a parking sticker at the Zip Zap

Human Resources Office. _____.
                         12

---

9. (A) Park
    (B) To park
    (C) Parking
    (D) Car park

10. (A) towed
    (B) relocated
    (C) maintained
    (D) detailed

11. (A) happenings
    (B) damages
    (C) delays
    (D) hindrances

12. (A) Cleaning the lot is the responsibility of the building manager
    (B) The parking lot is open to the public 24 hours a day
    (C) The front row is reserved for compact cars only
    (D) Parking stickers are free and valid for one year

Questions 13–16 refer to the following announcement.

See page 200 for the Answer Key and page 208 for the Answer Explanations for TOEIC practice Part 6.

The Farnsworth Group announces the opening of the new Farnsworth Towers Office Center in the downtown business district. ____.
13
We offer a prime location in the ____ of the business district, close to public
14
transportation. Building amenities include a parking garage, 24-hour security, a fitness center, and more. Office sizes ____ from 200 sq. feet to over 2000 sq.
15
feet. Design your office layout to suit your needs! Call now for an appointment to view ____ model offices and discuss your rental options.
16

13. (A) Rental space is now available for offices of all sizes
    (B) The hallways and lobby have already been painted
    (C) There are several other large office buildings in the area
    (D) Investors in the project include some well-known business leaders

14. (A) edge
    (B) heart
    (C) structure
    (D) completion

15. (A) multiply
    (B) enlarge
    (C) create
    (D) range

16. (A) your
    (B) their
    (C) our
    (D) his

PART 7: READING COMPREHENSION

In Part 7: Reading Comprehension of the TOEIC, you will answer a total of 54 reading comprehension questions—29 based on single passages and 25 based on multiple-passage sets. The questions will be about the main idea, details, vocabulary, sentence insertion, and meaning in context.

Sample Questions

PASSAGE

> If you are planning a visit to Wilmington, consider staying at the Bougainvillea Inn. –[1]– This charming hotel is located in the Park View neighborhood, one of the loveliest areas of the city. –[2]– The lobby features a mural by a local artist, and each guest room is decorated with a floral theme. The staff is friendly and helpful and have many good suggestions for sights to see and places to eat. –[3]– The prices are a little higher than similar hotels in the area, but the excellent service makes it well worth the cost. –[4]–

Main Idea

Who is this article for?

(A) Travel agents
(B) Hotel staff
(C) Neighbors
(D) Tourists

The purpose of this article is to recommend a hotel to people planning to visit a particular city, that is, *tourists*. Therefore, the best response is Choice (D).

Detail

What is indicated about the hotel?

(A) It is more expensive than other hotels.
(B) It is located close to downtown.
(C) It has many guest rooms.
(D) It has a large lobby.

The article says "The prices are a little higher than similar hotels . . ." Therefore, the best response is Choice (A).

Vocabulary

The word "loveliest" in line 3 is closest in meaning to

(A) most popular
(B) most historic
(C) prettiest
(D) quietest

Loveliest means *prettiest*. Therefore, the best response is Choice (C).

Sentence Insertion

In which of the following positions marked [1], [2], [3], and [4] does the following sentence best belong?

"The artistically designed interior is a delight to the eye."

(A) [1]
(B) [2]
(C) [3]
(D) [4]

The sentence to be inserted introduces the idea that the inside of the hotel is artistic and pretty. The sentence following position [2] gives examples of the artistic features inside the hotel. Therefore, the best response is Choice (B).

Certain types of passages—text messages and online chats—will always include one question about meaning in context. You will need to determine the meaning of a phrase or word as it is used in the passage.

PASSAGE

SAM SMITH	10:10
Are you at the store now?	
MARY CLARK	10:12
Yes. Why?	
SAM SMITH	10:13
Would you pick up a box of envelopes for me?	
MARY CLARK	10:15
What size did you want?	
SAM SMITH	10:16
The large ones. Business size.	
MARY CLARK	10:18
Got it.	
SAM SMITH	10:20
Thanks. Just leave them on my desk when you get back.	

Meaning in Context

At 10:18, what does Ms. Clark mean when she writes, "Got it"?

(A) She understands what kind of envelopes Mr. Smith wants.
(B) She already has envelopes in her office.
(C) She is almost ready to leave the store.
(D) She knows where Mr. Smith's desk is.

Got it can be used to mean *I understand*, and this is Ms. Clark's reply to Mr. Smith explaining what size envelope he wants. Therefore, the best response is Choice (A).

THE PSRA STRATEGY

An important strategy for reading comprehension is learning to approach a passage in an organized way. First make a *Prediction* about the passage; then *Scan* it; next *Read* it; and finally *Answer* the questions. We can abbreviate this strategy as **PSRA**.

Prediction

Learning how to make predictions about what you are going to read BEFORE you read will help you establish a context for understanding the passage. This will improve your reading score.

Before you begin to read one of the reading passages, you should first look at the question introduction line. This line looks like this:

Questions 161–163 refer to the following office memo.

In the question introduction line, you will learn how many questions there are and what kind of reading passage it is (in this case an office memo). The look of the reading passage will also give you a clue: a fax will look like a fax, a phone message like a phone message, and a graph like a graph. This will help you PREDICT what the passage is about.

There are generally two or three questions for every reading passage, although there may be up to five. Look at the questions and the four answer options. This will give you a clue what to look for. These clues will help you PREDICT what the passage is about.

According to the memo, which equipment has multiple uses?

(A)   Desktop computers
(B)   Fax machines
(C)   Answering machines
(D)   Tablet computers

Scan

We can predict that the memo has something to do with electronics. When we *Scan* the passage, we look for the Key Words. You may not find the exact words, but you might find words with similar meanings. Try to think of words that have meanings similar to the Key Words in the question and answer options. The Key Words for this question are:

Questions		Answer Options
Key words	*Similar meanings*	Desktop computers
equipment	electronic tools; hardware	Fax machines
multiple uses	useful in a variety of settings	Answering machines
		Tablet computers

Look first for the Key Words from the question; then look around the Question Key Words for the Key Words from the answer options. When you find the Answer Option Key Words, see if the words answer the question. Try to answer the question (in your head, NOT on the answer sheet). Here's a sample:

MEMORANDUM

To: Lafite, Pierre
        Purchasing Department

From: Clement, Marie France
        Personnel

We need **desktop computers** for use in the office, **answering machines** for our consultants, **fax machines** for the shipping department, and **tablet computers** for everyone. This **last piece of hardware** can be used in a variety of ways.

According to the memo, which equipment has multiple uses?

(A)   Desktop computers
(B)   Fax machines
(C)   Answering machines
(D)   Tablet computers

The correct answer is (D). Tablet computers are the **last** piece of hardware mentioned. *This last piece of hardware can be used in a variety of ways.*

Note how much different the answer would be if the last sentence were:

This **first piece of hardware** can be **used in a variety** of ways.

The word "first" changes the answer completely from (D) Tablet computers to (A) Desktop computers. This is why you must NOT rely on Prediction and Scanning alone.

Read

You must READ the passage as well. But when you read, read quickly. Read to confirm your predictions.

You should not make any mark on your answer sheet until you have made a PREDICTION based on all of the questions, SCANNED the passage looking for key words, answered the questions in your head, and READ the passage to confirm your answer choices. The answer to the first question is found in the first part of the reading passage. The answer to the second question is found in the next part and so on. The questions follow the sequence of the passage.

Answer

Now you are ready to mark your answer sheet. ANSWER the easy questions first. If you don't know an answer, scan the passage again, look for the key words, read parts of the passage. If you still don't know, GUESS. Do NOT leave any answer blank.

1 Advertisements

Advertisements on the TOEIC are similar to those found in magazines or newspapers. You can find other examples in English-language newspapers and magazines and ask yourself questions about the products being advertised.

EXERCISE

Questions 1–2 refer to the following advertisement. Choose the one best answer to each question.

ATTENTION MANUFACTURERS!

We introduce and distribute your products
to 125,000 distributors in 155 countries, FREE!

For a FREE information kit call:

Tel: (310) 553-4434 Ext. 105 • Fax (310) 553-5555
GRAND TECHNOLOGIES LIMITED

---

1. Who is the advertisement written for?

    (A) Distributors   Ⓐ Ⓑ Ⓒ Ⓓ
    (B) Sales representatives
    (C) Manufacturers
    (D) Information specialists

2. How many countries are mentioned?

    (A) 125   Ⓐ Ⓑ Ⓒ Ⓓ
    (B) 155
    (C) 310
    (D) 501

Forms

A form is a template: a standard form that an individual adds information to. These could include magazine subscription forms, purchase orders, immigration forms, hotel check-in forms, telephone message blanks, and so on.

EXERCISE

Questions 1–4 refer to the following form. Choose the one best answer to each question.

Special Subscription Offer

Subscribe to the journal that recently received the Editorial Excellence Award from the Society of Industrial Designers

☑ **YES!** send me INTERNATIONAL INDUSTRY for 1 year (12 issues) at just $48, a savings of 20% off the full cover price of $5.00.

☐ Payment enclosed   ☑ Bill me.

Name: _Anne Kwok_
Title: _Design Specialist_
Company: _Pharmaceutical Supply Co._
Address: _Tong Chong Street_
Quarry Bay Hong Kong

Please allow four weeks for first issue.

---

1. Why did Anne Kwok complete this form?

   (A) To win an award
   (B) To apply for a design job
   (C) To enroll in design school
   (D) To receive a journal

2. How much is the full cover price per issue?

   (A) $4
   (B) $5
   (C) $12
   (D) $48

3. How long will it take for the first issue to arrive?

   (A) One week
   (B) One month
   (C) One year
   (D) Unknown

4. The magazine comes

   (A) daily
   (B) weekly
   (C) monthly
   (D) once a year

Letters

In a letter, the important information is generally contained in the body of the letter—the part between the greeting (*Dear . . .*) and the closing (*Sincerely yours*).

EXERCISE

Questions 1–3 refer to the following letter. Choose the one best answer to each question.

```
                    EUTECH, s.r.o.
              Zborovská  23,150 00 Praha 5
                    Czech Republic
            Tel: (02) 513.2343 Fax: (02) 513.2334

December 3, 20—

Post Comptoir
43 Griffith Road
Dinsdale, Hamilton
North Island, New Zealand

Dear Sir or Madam:

We are interested in becoming distributors for your
software products in the Czech Republic. Would you
please send us your latest catalogs, descriptive
brochures, and terms?

We are a hardware company that would like to add
software to our sales offerings. Our annual report
is enclosed.

We look forward to hearing from you soon.

Sincerely yours,

Peter Zavel
Peter Zavel
Chairman
```

1. Which items were NOT requested?

    (A) Catalogs   Ⓐ Ⓑ Ⓒ Ⓓ
    (B) Brochures
    (C) Samples
    (D) Pricing information

2. What does EUTECH sell now?

    (A) Software   Ⓐ Ⓑ Ⓒ Ⓓ
    (B) Computers
    (C) Financial reports
    (D) Printing services

3. EUTECH wants to

    (A) distribute software   Ⓐ Ⓑ Ⓒ Ⓓ
    (B) manufacture computers
    (C) purchase hardware
    (D) receive an annual report

Memos

A memorandum (memo) is an internal form of communication that is sent from one member of a company to a member of the same company. Today these memos (memoranda) are often sent by computer as e-mail. To learn more about computer-generated language, see Skills 11 and 12 on pages 180–181.

EXERCISE

Questions 1–4 refer to the following memorandum. Choose the one best answer to each question.

MEMORANDUM

To: All Employees

From: Simon Gonzales
        Personnel Officer

Date: May 15, 20—

Sub: Company Travel

Effective June 1 all personnel traveling on company business must use the most economical means possible. No flights under five hours can be booked in Business Class. No flights regardless of duration can be booked in First Class.

---

1. If a flight is over five hours, what class can be booked?

    (A) Economy
    (B) Economy Plus
    (C) Business
    (D) First

    Ⓐ Ⓑ Ⓒ Ⓓ

2. When will this rule go into effect?

    (A) In about two weeks
    (B) At the end of the summer
    (C) At the first of the year
    (D) In five months

    Ⓐ Ⓑ Ⓒ Ⓓ

3. Why was this memo written?

    (A) To save time
    (B) To save money
    (C) To reward the employees
    (D) To increase company travel

    Ⓐ Ⓑ Ⓒ Ⓓ

4. Who is affected by this memo?

    (A) Only the Board of Directors
    (B) Only frequent travelers
    (C) Only the personnel department
    (D) All personnel

    Ⓐ Ⓑ Ⓒ Ⓓ

Tables and Charts

Tables and charts show a compilation of data that are useful for quick comparison. They can be about almost any subject. You can find examples in English-language newspapers and magazines.

EXERCISE

Questions 1–4 refer to the following table. Choose the one best answer to each question.

WORLD TEMPERATURES
January 5

	Hi (C/F)	Lo (C/F)	Weather
Amsterdam	6/41	3/37	c
Athens	13/55	8/46	sh
Bangkok	32/90	27/80	sh
Beijing	12/53	1/34	pc
Brussels	4/39	1/34	sh
Budapest	3/37	0/32	r
Frankfurt	3/37	1/34	r
Jakarta	29/84	24/75	sh
Kuala Lampur	31/88	24/75	t
Madrid	9/48	1/34	sh
Manila	33/91	21/70	pc
Seoul	9/48	−2/29	s
Taipei	21/70	14/57	c
Tokyo	9/48	−2/29	pc

Weather: s-sunny; pc-partly cloudy; c-cloudy; sh-showers; t-thunderstorms; r-rain

1. Which two cities were cloudy on January 5?

   (A) Amsterdam and Taipei
   (B) Beijing and Manila
   (C) Athens and Tokyo
   (D) Bangkok and Seoul

   Ⓐ Ⓑ Ⓒ Ⓓ

2. Which city had the highest temperature?

   (A) Athens
   (B) Bangkok
   (C) Jakarta
   (D) Manila

   Ⓐ Ⓑ Ⓒ Ⓓ

3. Which city had the closest spread between high and low temperature?

   (A) Brussels
   (B) Frankfurt
   (C) Seoul
   (D) Tokyo

   Ⓐ Ⓑ Ⓒ Ⓓ

4. Kuala Lampur had

   (A) sun
   (B) thunderstorms
   (C) rain
   (D) showers

   Ⓐ Ⓑ Ⓒ Ⓓ

SKILL 6 — Graphs

A graph is a drawing that shows the relationship between variables. On the TOEIC there can be line graphs, bar graphs, or pie graphs.

EXERCISE

Questions 1–2 refer to the following graph. Choose the one best answer to each question.

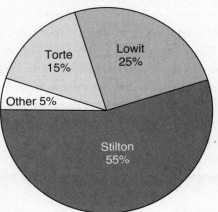

Hotel Chain Market Share

1. Who would be most interested in reading this graph?

   (A) Tourists
   (B) Competing hotels
   (C) Landscape architects
   (D) Job hunters

   Ⓐ Ⓑ Ⓒ Ⓓ

2. According to this graph, Lowit

   (A) is the top-ranking hotel chain
   (B) is only in Latin America
   (C) has less of a share than Torte
   (D) has one-quarter of the market

   Ⓐ Ⓑ Ⓒ Ⓓ

Announcements

An announcement is a formal statement made to the public about a specific piece of news. It might be about such things as people accepting or resigning from high positions, the opening of a new building, the launch of a new product, or a special event.

EXERCISE

Questions 1–4 refer to the following announcement. Choose the one best answer to each questions.

The City Chamber of Commerce announces this year's City Job Fair, to be held on March 11 at the City Convention Center –[1]–. This is a unique opportunity to find out where the jobs are and to meet people who are hiring now. There will also be workshops on résumé writing, interview skills, resources for job hunters, and more. –[2]– There is no charge for the workshops, but pre-registration is required. –[3]– Visit the Chamber of Commerce website for more information on workshops. This event is open to the public, so come on down and get the information you need for a successful job search. –[4]–

---

1. How often is this event held?

   (A) One time only   Ⓐ Ⓑ Ⓒ Ⓓ
   (B) Once a month
   (C) Twice a year
   (D) Once a year

2. What is indicated about the workshops?

   (A) They will be given online.   Ⓐ Ⓑ Ⓒ Ⓓ
   (B) A small fee will be charged.
   (C) Participants must sign up ahead of time.
   (D) All the spaces have already been filled.

3. The word "unique" in line 2 of the passage is closest in meaning to

   (A) interesting   Ⓐ Ⓑ Ⓒ Ⓓ
   (B) important
   (C) limited
   (D) rare

4. In which of the following positions marked [1], [2], [3], and [4] does the following sentence best belong?

"Employers from all over the region and representing a variety of industries will be present."

(A) [1]
(B) [2]
(C) [3]
(D) [4]

Ⓐ Ⓑ Ⓒ Ⓓ

8 Notices

A notice is information that the writer feels the general public or specific product users must be made aware of. There are often notices attached to walls and public buildings or enclosed with product literature.

EXERCISE

Questions 1–2 refer to the following notice. Choose the one best answer to each question.

Corporate Policy Change

Moving Expenses. You can be reimbursed for your expenses of moving to a new home only if your new home is at least 50 miles away from your former home. In addition, expenses are limited to the costs of moving your household goods and personal effects from your former home to your new home. Meals, pre-move house-hunting expenses, and temporary-quarters expenses are no longer reimbursable.

---

1. Who would be most affected by this notice?

(A) Hotel chains
(B) Furniture rental companies
(C) Real estate agents
(D) New employees moving from another city

Ⓐ Ⓑ Ⓒ Ⓓ

2. Which of the following will be reimbursed?

(A) Lunch for the movers
(B) Shipping household goods
(C) Gas used looking for a house
(D) Hotel expenses

Ⓐ Ⓑ Ⓒ Ⓓ

Articles

An article is a passage written for a newspaper, magazine, or newsletter. It may be about a current news item or about a topic of general or specific interest, depending on the publication where it appears.

EXERCISE

Questions 1–4 refer to the following article.

> Restaurateurs, like other business owners, are constantly seeking ways to expand their clientele and keep their restaurants filled. –[1]– Various types of advertising, networking, and discounts and special offers are all tried-and-true ways of attracting more business. Recently, many restaurant owners have had great success with offering cooking classes.
>
> Customers are willing to pay to eat food prepared in your restaurant. They are also willing, it turns out, to pay to learn to prepare the meal themselves. –[2]– Cooking classes are most successful when they offer the opportunity to learn something unusual. Classes might focus on demonstrating a specialized cooking technique or showing ways to use seasonal ingredients. –[3]– Classes that explain how to prepare some unusual regional dish are the ones that tend to fill up most quickly.
>
> Cooking classes can be seen as a sideline, but they are also an effective means of advertising your business. –[4]– Organizing cooking classes takes a little extra effort, but the costs are low and the return can be quite high.

1. What is this passage mainly about?

   (A) How to organize a cooking class   Ⓐ Ⓑ Ⓒ Ⓓ
   (B) The costs of running a restaurant
   (C) A way for restaurants to increase business
   (D) Different methods of attracting customers

2. Which cooking classes are most popular?

   (A) The ones that cost the least   Ⓐ Ⓑ Ⓒ Ⓓ
   (B) The ones about regional cooking
   (C) The ones that use seasonal ingredients
   (D) The ones that explain special techniques

3. The word "sideline" in paragraph 3, line 1 of the passage is closest in meaning to

   (A) extra activity   Ⓐ Ⓑ Ⓒ Ⓓ
   (B) small task
   (C) expense
   (D) distraction

4. In which of the following positions marked [1], [2], [3], and [4] does the following sentence best belong?

   "Cooking class participants usually become loyal customers who recommend your restaurant to others."

   (A) [1]   Ⓐ Ⓑ Ⓒ Ⓓ
   (B) [2]
   (C) [3]
   (D) [4]

Schedules

A schedule is a list of times or dates when events will take place or tasks will be carried out, such as train and bus schedules, payment schedules, class schedules, project schedules, and so on.

EXERCISE

Questions 1–4 refer to the following schedule. Choose the one best answer to each question.

7th & Market	East Rise P&R	Tunnel	122nd East & 16th
7:11 W	**7:21**	**7:36 T**	**8:01**
7:22 W	**7:32**	**7:47 T**	**8:12**
7:30 W	**7:41**	**7:59 T**	**8:21**
7:40	**7:51**	**8:06**	**8:32**
8:02 W	**8:13**	**8:25**	**8:53**
8:25	8:35	8:49	9:14
8:51 W	9:01	9:15	9:40
9:21	9:32	9:48	10:11
9:51 W	10:10	10:24	10:40

Key:

T = Tunnel opens at 8:00 A.M. Buses prior to this time stop on 12th and Meridian.

W = Bus departs at this time. It arrives about 5 minutes earlier.

Boldface indicates peak fare.

1. What time do off-peak fares probably start?

    (A) Before 7 A.M.   Ⓐ Ⓑ Ⓒ Ⓓ
    (B) 8:25 A.M.
    (C) 8:30 A.M.
    (D) 8:51 A.M.

2. What time does the 7:30 bus arrive at 7th & Market?

    (A) 7:00   Ⓐ Ⓑ Ⓒ Ⓓ
    (B) 7:22
    (C) 7:25
    (D) 7:30

3. Why doesn't the 7:30 use the tunnel?

    (A) Because it's rush hour   Ⓐ Ⓑ Ⓒ Ⓓ
    (B) Bus heights exceed limits for the tunnel.
    (C) The tunnel is closed at that time.
    (D) Early buses are rarely full enough to use the tunnel.

4. How long is the trip from 7th & Market to 122nd & 16th?

    (A) A quarter hour   Ⓐ Ⓑ Ⓒ Ⓓ
    (B) A half hour
    (C) Almost an hour
    (D) An hour

E-mails

E-mail means *electronic mail* and refers to computer mail. E-mail can be used to send any type of correspondence, form, or questionnaire, so an e-mail reading item may include any type of content. One distinctive feature of e-mail is its heading, which includes information about the sender, the receiver, and the transmission. A second feature of e-mail is that its language is usually more casual than that of formal paper correspondence.

EXERCISE

Questions 1–2 refer to the following e-mail. Choose the one best answer to each question.

From: Melinda Ligos
To: Misha Polentesky
Subject: Meeting in Orlando

Misha,

The meeting went better than expected. The client loved our proposal and didn't ask for any changes. They will get the necessary paperwork to us by the end of the week.

By the way, thanks for suggesting Sparazza's. I had dinner there Thursday after leaving the client's office. Loved it, and so close to my hotel.

I'll be back at the home office tomorrow. See you then.

Melinda

---

1. What is the purpose of the email?

   (A) To report on the results of a meeting   Ⓐ Ⓑ Ⓒ Ⓓ
   (B) To ask for a signature on paperwork
   (C) To explain the contents of a proposal
   (D) To set up a new meeting with Ms. Polentesky

2. Where did the writer of the email go after the client meeting?

   (A) To another meeting   Ⓐ Ⓑ Ⓒ Ⓓ
   (B) To her home office
   (C) To a restaurant
   (D) To her hotel

Webpages

You may see webpages in Part 7 of the TOEIC. You can find an unlimited number of webpages on the Internet to familiarize yourself with their layout and terminology.

EXERCISE

Questions 1–2 refer to the following webpage. Choose the one best answer to each question.

DOMESTIC DESIGNS

| HOME | ABOUT | FAQ | PRICING | REVIEWS |

You want your home or office to reflect who you are. At Domestic Designs, our designers are concerned with creating the look you want. That is why we work closely with you every step of the way, from choosing a color scheme to finding the right paint, carpets, furniture, and accessories that will create the atmosphere you want.

Why should you choose Domestic Designs for your redecorating needs? Our 20 years of experience in the business and hundreds of satisfied customers are the reason! The first consultation is free. Call our office at 800-123-4567 to make your appointment today.

<u>Click here</u> to see our portfolio of past projects.

1. What kind of business is Domestic Designs?

   (A) Architects   Ⓐ Ⓑ Ⓒ Ⓓ
   (B) Furniture designer
   (C) Custom-made paints
   (D) Interior decorations

2. How can a customer see examples of the company's work?

   (A) Click on the link at the bottom of the page   Ⓐ Ⓑ Ⓒ Ⓓ
   (B) Make an appointment with a consultant
   (C) Call past customers
   (D) Call the office

Text Messages and Online Chats

Text messages and online chats are common forms of communication. You will see examples of these in Part 7 of the TOEIC. These types of passage always include a meaning in context question, asking you to determine the meaning of a word or phrase in the context of the passage.

PRACTICE

Directions: Read each passage and answer the questions.

Questions 1–2 refer to the following text message chain.

Lin Lee Where are you?	1:29
Jim Hart Traffic is heavy. The bus can hardly move. I'll be there in 10–15.	1:30
Lin Lee The client's just arriving.	1:32
Lin Lee We'll have to start without you.	1:33
Jim Hart No problem. I'll be there shortly.	1:35
Lin Lee You have the papers, right?	1:37
Jim Hart I'm sorry?	1:38
Lin Lee The work agreement for the client to sign.	1:40
Jim Hart Right, yes.	1:41

1. Why is Jim Hart late?

   (A) He missed the bus.

   (B) His bus is slow.

   (C) His client canceled.

   (D) He forgot about the meeting.

   Ⓐ Ⓑ Ⓒ Ⓓ

2. What does Jim Hart mean when he writes, "I'm sorry"?

   (A) He lost the papers.

   (B) He wants to apologize to the client.

   (C) He doesn't understand Lin Lee's text message.

   (D) He wishes he could get there more quickly.

   Ⓐ Ⓑ Ⓒ Ⓓ

SUMMARY OF TIPS

Part 5: Incomplete Sentences and Part 6: Text Completion

- Distinguish between words that have similar but different meanings or forms.
- Determine the correct word, phrase, or sentence for the context.
- Recognize different verb forms.
- Recognize different adjective and adverb forms.
- Recognize singular and plural nouns.
- Recognize different kinds of clauses.
- Understand the different uses of prepositions.

Part 7: Reading Comprehension

- Know how to read the different types of reading passages found on the TOEIC.
- Know the different types of reading comprehension questions found on the TOEIC.
- Know how to use the PSRA strategy: Predict, Scan, Read, Answer.

ANSWER SHEET
Reading Mini-Test

Part 5: Incomplete Sentences

1. Ⓐ Ⓑ Ⓒ Ⓓ   5. Ⓐ Ⓑ Ⓒ Ⓓ   9. Ⓐ Ⓑ Ⓒ Ⓓ   13. Ⓐ Ⓑ Ⓒ Ⓓ
2. Ⓐ Ⓑ Ⓒ Ⓓ   6. Ⓐ Ⓑ Ⓒ Ⓓ   10. Ⓐ Ⓑ Ⓒ Ⓓ   14. Ⓐ Ⓑ Ⓒ Ⓓ
3. Ⓐ Ⓑ Ⓒ Ⓓ   7. Ⓐ Ⓑ Ⓒ Ⓓ   11. Ⓐ Ⓑ Ⓒ Ⓓ   15. Ⓐ Ⓑ Ⓒ Ⓓ
4. Ⓐ Ⓑ Ⓒ Ⓓ   8. Ⓐ Ⓑ Ⓒ Ⓓ   12. Ⓐ Ⓑ Ⓒ Ⓓ

Part 6: Text Completion

16. Ⓐ Ⓑ Ⓒ Ⓓ   18. Ⓐ Ⓑ Ⓒ Ⓓ   20. Ⓐ Ⓑ Ⓒ Ⓓ   22. Ⓐ Ⓑ Ⓒ Ⓓ
17. Ⓐ Ⓑ Ⓒ Ⓓ   19. Ⓐ Ⓑ Ⓒ Ⓓ   21. Ⓐ Ⓑ Ⓒ Ⓓ   23. Ⓐ Ⓑ Ⓒ Ⓓ

Part 7: Reading Comprehension

24. Ⓐ Ⓑ Ⓒ Ⓓ   30. Ⓐ Ⓑ Ⓒ Ⓓ   36. Ⓐ Ⓑ Ⓒ Ⓓ   42. Ⓐ Ⓑ Ⓒ Ⓓ
25. Ⓐ Ⓑ Ⓒ Ⓓ   31. Ⓐ Ⓑ Ⓒ Ⓓ   37. Ⓐ Ⓑ Ⓒ Ⓓ   43. Ⓐ Ⓑ Ⓒ Ⓓ
26. Ⓐ Ⓑ Ⓒ Ⓓ   32. Ⓐ Ⓑ Ⓒ Ⓓ   38. Ⓐ Ⓑ Ⓒ Ⓓ   44. Ⓐ Ⓑ Ⓒ Ⓓ
27. Ⓐ Ⓑ Ⓒ Ⓓ   33. Ⓐ Ⓑ Ⓒ Ⓓ   39. Ⓐ Ⓑ Ⓒ Ⓓ   45. Ⓐ Ⓑ Ⓒ Ⓓ
28. Ⓐ Ⓑ Ⓒ Ⓓ   34. Ⓐ Ⓑ Ⓒ Ⓓ   40. Ⓐ Ⓑ Ⓒ Ⓓ   46. Ⓐ Ⓑ Ⓒ Ⓓ
29. Ⓐ Ⓑ Ⓒ Ⓓ   35. Ⓐ Ⓑ Ⓒ Ⓓ   41. Ⓐ Ⓑ Ⓒ Ⓓ   47. Ⓐ Ⓑ Ⓒ Ⓓ

MINI-TEST FOR READING

Part 5: Incomplete Sentences

> **Directions:** You will see a sentence with a missing word. Four possible answers follow the sentence. Choose the best answer to the question, and fill in the corresponding oval on your answer sheet.

1. Rice Enterprises _____ some of the most talented design specialists in the field.

   (A) employ
   (B) employs
   (C) employees
   (D) have employed

2. The directors are happy to report that the advertising campaign has been _____ successful.

   (A) huge
   (B) huger
   (C) hugely
   (D) hugeness

3. Procom Industries has announced plans to _____ production by opening up a new manufacturing plant.

   (A) increase
   (B) enlarge
   (C) curtail
   (D) diminish

4. _____ the new restaurant has recently received a lot of attention from the press, business continues to be slow.

   (A) Because
   (B) Therefore
   (C) Although
   (D) Nevertheless

5. All information provided by clients will be kept entirely _____ and will never be shared with anyone outside the office.

   (A) professional
   (B) confidential
   (C) essential
   (D) intact

6. You may use the health club _____ you are employed by this company, but membership eligibility ends if you leave your position.

   (A) in the meantime
   (B) according to
   (C) in order to
   (D) as long as

7. Ms. Yamamoto is in charge of organizing the office party, so please let _____ know if you have any suggestions.

   (A) her
   (B) hers
   (C) she
   (D) herself

8. The sign posted just outside the front door _____ the history and architectural significance of the building.

   (A) recounts
   (B) explains
   (C) instructs
   (D) advises

9. The director had not expected to hear so much _____ to the proposed policy changes.

(A) opposition
(B) opponents
(C) opposing
(D) opposed

10. The manager asked everyone in the office _____ in the time sheets by noon on Friday.

(A) turn
(B) turns
(C) turning
(D) to turn

11. He received a job offer from this company, but we don't know _____ he will accept it or turn it down

(A) either
(B) neither
(C) whether
(D) however

12. The client is considering the offer and will give us a _____ answer by the end of the week.

(A) define
(B) definite
(C) definitely
(D) definition

13. You'll notice that the new accounting system is different _____ the old one in several ways.

(A) to
(B) for
(C) than
(D) from

14. Each table must be _____ cleaned before seating the next group of diners.

(A) thoroughly
(B) permanently
(C) directly
(D) finally

15. If the client isn't completely satisfied with the terms of the contract, some _____ can be made.

(A) introductions
(B) developments
(C) modifications
(D) permissions

Part 6: Text Completion

> **Directions:** You will see four passages, each with three sets of blanks. Under each blank are four options. Choose the word or phrase that best completes the statement.

Questions 16–19 refer to the following flyer.

Stellar Professional Training

The following seminar _____ in your area on April 10: **Webpage Design**. At this
16

all-day seminar for business professionals, interns, and current business

students, find out how you can create a webpage that presents your business

in the most attractive way. The price _____ lunch and materials as well as
17

instruction. Visit us at *www.stellar.com/seminars* to sign up. _____ ends March 31.
18

While you are there, take a look at what else we have to offer. _____.
19

We look forward to seeing you at Stellar!

---

16. (A) offers
    (B) will offer
    (C) will be offered
    (D) will be offering

17. (A) participates
    (B) covers
    (C) accounts
    (D) charges

18. (A) Register
    (B) Registrar
    (C) Registered
    (D) Registration

19. (A) Stellar provides staff training, custom web-
        page design, and more
    (B) You can contact us any time, day or night
    (C) The seminar lasts about seven hours
    (D) Our clients have given our seminars top
        ratings

Questions 20–23 refer to the following flyer.

The Springdale Community Center offers services for all members of the Springdale community. _____ include recreational activities for children, teens, and adults, parenting
                    20
workshops, arts and crafts classes, a teen drop-in center, and a daycare center. We
are _____ looking for volunteers to help out with any of the above-mentioned programs.
       21
Interested people should contact our volunteer _____, Mabel Rivera (mrivera@commcenter.
                                                22
org), for further information. _____.
                               23

20. (A) These
    (B) There
    (C) Them
    (D) That

21. (A) lately
    (B) probably
    (C) currently
    (D) eventually

22. (A) coordinate
    (B) coordinator
    (C) coordinating
    (D) coordination

23. (A) Please indicate which program you would like
        to work in
    (B) All our programs are free for Springdale
        residents
    (C) The next workshop session begins in one week
    (D) Ms. Rivera is a long-time employee of the
        community center

Part 7: Reading Comprehension

Directions: You will see single and multiple reading passages followed by several questions. Each question has four answer choices. Choose the best answer to the question, and fill in the corresponding oval on your answer sheet.

Questions 24–25 refer to the following e-mail.

To: frank.knockaert@crestco.com
From: grombach@hamburgpaper.com
Subj: re: recent order

Dear Mr. Knockaert,

I sincerely regret the inconvenience caused to you by the error we made in the shipment of your recent order. The additional 1000 cases of all-purpose paper that we neglected to include in the shipment will be sent to you immediately. We will not charge you for that part of your order.

We value our relationship with your company and are very sorry for any difficulties our error may have caused you. You can be assured that this will not happen in the future.

Sincerely,
Gertrude Rombach
Customer Service Specialist
Hamburg Paper Company

24. What is the purpose of the e-mail?

(A) To place a new order
(B) To give an apology
(C) To make a complaint
(D) To introduce new services

25. What was the problem with the shipment?

(A) It arrived late.
(B) It was damaged.
(C) It was not complete.
(D) It was sent to the wrong address.

Questions 26–27 refer to the following article.

September 1, Zurich: RADD, A.G., the Swiss chemical company purchased the European polypropylene business of Royal Chemical Industries, P.L.C., of Britain. No price was disclosed, but RCI said the deal represented 1 to 2 percent of its net assets and would be paid in cash. Based on net assets, the price would be between $100 million and $160 million. The acquisition includes RCI production plants in England, Denmark, Norway, and Poland. The plants alone are valued at $60 million to $80 million. Polypropylene, a tough, flexible plastic, has uses that range from rope fibers to bottles.

26. What is this article mostly about?

(A) International trade agreements
(B) The business climate in Europe
(C) The value of a particular company
(D) The acquisition of one company by another

27. What does the Royal Chemical Industries company manufacture?

(A) Different kinds of rope
(B) Glass beverage bottles
(C) A type of plastic
(D) Cotton fabric

Questions 28–30 refer to the following webpage.

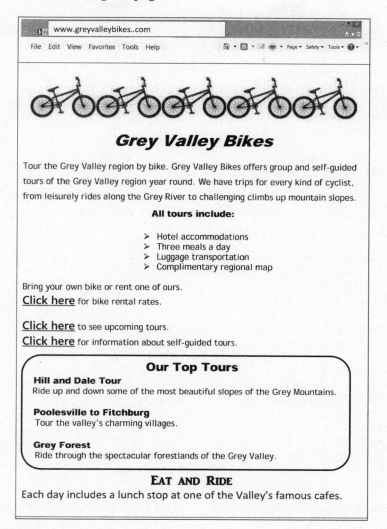

Grey Valley Bikes

Tour the Grey Valley region by bike. Grey Valley Bikes offers group and self-guided tours of the Grey Valley region year round. We have trips for every kind of cyclist, from leisurely rides along the Grey River to challenging climbs up mountain slopes.

All tours include:

➢ Hotel accommodations
➢ Three meals a day
➢ Luggage transportation
➢ Complimentary regional map

Bring your own bike or rent one of ours.
Click here for bike rental rates.

Click here to see upcoming tours.
Click here for information about self-guided tours.

Our Top Tours

Hill and Dale Tour
Ride up and down some of the most beautiful slopes of the Grey Mountains.

Poolesville to Fitchburg
Tour the valley's charming villages.

Grey Forest
Ride through the spectacular forestlands of the Grey Valley.

EAT AND RIDE
Each day includes a lunch stop at one of the Valley's famous cafes.

28. What is NOT included in the cost of a tour?

(A) Hotel
(B) Food
(C) Map
(D) Bicycle

29. What is indicated about Grey Valley Bikes tours?

(A) They last a week or more.
(B) They are only for experienced cyclists.
(C) They are for both individuals and groups.
(D) They take place in spring and summer only.

30. Which tours are listed on this webpage?

(A) The most popular
(B) The most difficult
(C) The most lengthy
(D) The most expensive

Questions 31–33 refer to the following online chat discussion.

Yoko Ota You've ordered the fabric for the shirts, right?	9:15
Anders Larsen Yes. 4 bolts of printed cotton.	9:15
Milla Colby 4 bolts? Didn't we say 6?	9:16
Anders Larsen We always order 4 bolts.	9:17
Yoko Ota We got an extra order for shirts this time. We need 6 bolts. When did you make the order?	9:18
Anders Larsen Yesterday afternoon. But I'm sure they haven't processed it yet. I can call them back.	9:20
Yoko Ota Please call them back right away. We can't wait on those extra two bolts.	9:21
Milla Colby I've got people lined up to start working on those shirts the minute we get the fabric. We really have to get going on this order.	9:21
Yoko Ota Yes. Those shirts have to be on their way by the end of the month.	9:23

31. What kind of business are they involved in?

    (A) Clothing manufacturer
    (B) Fabric wholesaler
    (C) Shipping service
    (D) Shirt retailer

32. What does Anders have to do now?

    (A) Ship the order
    (B) Cancel the order
    (C) Add to the order
    (D) Process the order

33. What does Yoko mean when she writes at 9:23, "Those shirts have to be on their way"?

    (A) The fabric for making shirts has to be available.
    (B) The shirts have to be shipped to the customer.
    (C) The workers have to start making the shirts.
    (D) The designs for the shirts have to be ready.

Questions 34–37 refer to the following article.

Amy Ann's Kitchen opened its doors just three months ago, but the owner is already talking about expanding. The reason? Business is booming. –[1]– Customers line up daily to buy freshly made bread, cakes, cookies and other tasty delights at Amy Ann's. –[2]– Owner Amy Ann Anderson is pleased but surprised at the high sales volume. –[3]– In fact, she has brought in close to half that amount in the first quarter alone. –[4]– To keep up with the demand, Anderson says she will need to add at least two ovens and take on extra staff. "I am not sure I can fit all that into my current space," she says. She is looking around the neighborhood for a larger space.

34. What kind of business is Amy Ann's Kitchen?

   (A) Bakery
   (B) Restaurant
   (C) Grocery store
   (D) Kitchen supplies

35. What is indicated about the business?

   (A) It has been around for a long time.
   (B) It is very popular.
   (C) It has high prices.
   (D) Its staff is large.

36. The word "volume" in line 4 of the passage is closest in meaning to

   (A) amount
   (B) loudness
   (C) products
   (D) price

37. In which of the following positions marked [1], [2], [3], and [4] does the following sentence best belong?

   "She says that she originally hoped to make about $40,000 a year in profits."

   (A) [1]
   (B) [2]
   (C) [3]
   (D) [4]

Questions 38–42 refer to the following notice and memo.

Notice to tenants of South Ridge Office Complex   August 25, 20—

Reconstruction of the parking garage will begin at the end of next month and is scheduled to last three months. During this time there will be no parking for anyone in the building garage. The city has temporarily designated the parking spaces on the streets surrounding our building as all-day parking spaces for our use. A special pass is required to use these spaces. Since the number of parking spaces is limited, we will distribute four passes to each office in this building. Building tenants are asked to encourage their employees to use public transportation until the garage reconstruction is completed. There are also two public parking garages within five blocks of here where parking spaces can be rented on a daily, weekly, or monthly basis. Thank you for your cooperation.

South Ridge Office Complex Building Management Team

Memo
Parrot Communications, Inc.

To: All Office Personnel
From: Dena Degenaro
             Office Manager
Date: August 28, 20—
Re: Parking

I am sure you have all seen the recent notice about the parking garage reconstruction by now. Since we have five times as many employees as allotted parking passes, we will reserve the parking passes for clients and ask our employees to make alternative plans. For your convenience, we have obtained subway passes that are valid for the entire amount of time that the garage reconstruction will last. They are available at a 25% discount to all Parrot Communications employees. Please see me before the end of this week if you are interested in getting one. Thank you.

38. When will the parking garage reconstruction begin?

    (A) This week
    (B) Next month
    (C) In three months
    (D) In August

39. How many employees work for Parrot Communications, Inc.?

    (A) Four
    (B) Five
    (C) Twenty
    (D) Twenty-five

40. Who can park next to the building during the garage reconstruction?

    (A) Parrot Communications clients
    (B) Parrot Communications employees
    (C) All South Ridge tenants
    (D) Dena Degenaro

41. Who should Parrot Communications employees contact to get a subway pass?

    (A) The city manager
    (B) Their office manager
    (C) The building manager
    (D) The subway station manager

42. How long are the subway passes valid?

    (A) One week
    (B) Three weeks
    (C) One month
    (D) Three months

Questions 43–47 refer to the following webpage, e-mail, and article.

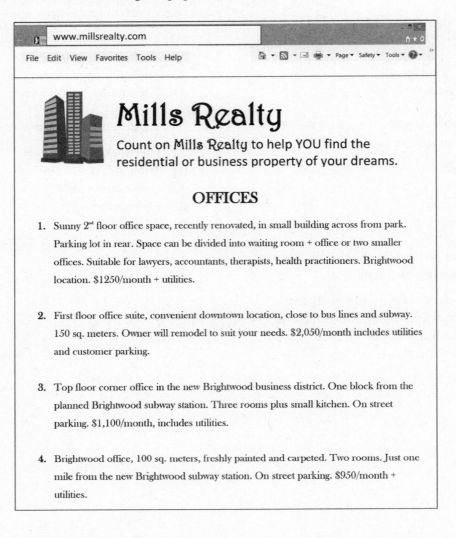

Mills Realty

Count on Mills Realty to help YOU find the residential or business property of your dreams.

OFFICES

1. Sunny 2nd floor office space, recently renovated, in small building across from park. Parking lot in rear. Space can be divided into waiting room + office or two smaller offices. Suitable for lawyers, accountants, therapists, health practitioners. Brightwood location. $1250/month + utilities.

2. First floor office suite, convenient downtown location, close to bus lines and subway. 150 sq. meters. Owner will remodel to suit your needs. $2,050/month includes utilities and customer parking.

3. Top floor corner office in the new Brightwood business district. One block from the planned Brightwood subway station. Three rooms plus small kitchen. On street parking. $1,100/month, includes utilities.

4. Brightwood office, 100 sq. meters, freshly painted and carpeted. Two rooms. Just one mile from the new Brightwood subway station. On street parking. $950/month + utilities.

To: Steve Mills
From: Elsa Roper
Date: July 25
Subject: Seeking office space

Mr. Mills,

I am interested in seeing some offices advertised on your website. I run a small accounting firm and am looking for a space of about 100–125 square meters. Unfortunately, downtown is a bit out of reach for me, but I think the Brightwood neighborhood would be very suitable. Ideally, I'd like a place with its own parking lot, but if it's close enough to the new subway station, that might not be an issue. I'd like to go no higher than $1,000/month on the rent, expecting to pay utilities on top of that. I'd like to see several of your listings this week, if possible. I am busy most mornings, but I am available any day after 1:00 PM. Please let me know when you can show me these properties.

Elsa Roper, CPA

Brightwood: Up and Coming

The new Brightwood business district is fast becoming the city's hottest new neighborhood. As rapidly rising rents are driving business owners out of the popular downtown area, many are turning to much more affordable Brightwood. This neighborhood has become even more appealing since the city announced plans to extend the subway line to its center. The new Brightwood Avenue subway station is scheduled to open early next year. Already, several offices have opened their doors along Brightwood Avenue and two new restaurants catering specifically to office workers have appeared recently, as well. The beautiful Lilac Park area of the neighborhood, with its wide streets and gardens, is also a draw. Look for a new café and several boutiques to be opening there soon.

43. What is NOT true about the advertised downtown office?

(A) The rent covers electricity and heat.
(B) It has recently been remodeled.
(C) It is near public transportation.
(D) The building has a parking lot.

44. Which advertised office will Ms. Roper probably prefer?

(A) #1
(B) #2
(C) #3
(D) #4

45. When does Ms. Roper want to look at offices?

(A) Any afternoon
(B) Any morning
(C) Next week
(D) Today

46. In the article, the word *driving* in line 2, is closest in meaning to

(A) operating
(B) traveling
(C) leading
(D) forcing

47. What is suggested about the Brightwood neighborhood?

(A) It is less expensive than downtown.
(B) The streets are not attractive.
(C) It has a bad reputation.
(D) The rents are going up.

ANSWER KEY FOR READING SKILLS

Answer Explanations can be found beginning on page 202.

Part 5: Incomplete Sentences

Skill 1 Word Families	1. **B**	2. **B**	3. **D**	4. **D**	5. **B**
Skill 2 Similar Meanings	1. **D**	2. **A**	3. **C**	4. **D**	5. **B**
Skill 3 Similar Forms	1. **B**	2. **A**	3. **D**	4. **C**	5. **A**
Skill 4 Subject-Verb Agreement with Prepositional Phrases	1. **D**	2. **A**	3. **C**	4. **A**	5. **B**
Skill 5 Singular and Plural Subjects	1. **C**	2. **A**	3. **D**	4. **C**	5. **B**
Skill 6 Verb Tenses	1. **B**	2. **C**	3. **B**	4. **A**	5. **D**
Skill 7 Prepositions	1. **A**	2. **D**	3. **C**	4. **D**	5. **C**
Skill 8 Prepositions with Verbs and Adjectives	1. **B**	2. **C**	3. **A**	4. **D**	5. **B**
Skill 9 Coordinating Conjunctions	1. **C**	2. **A**	3. **B**	4. **D**	5. **C**
Skill 10 Parallel Structure	1. **B**	2. **D**	3. **C**	4. **A**	5. **C**
Skill 11 Subordinating Conjunctions	1. **C**	2. **A**	3. **C**	4. **C**	5. **D**
Skill 12 Future Time Clauses	1. **B**	2. **A**	3. **C**	4. **D**	5. **D**

Part 6: Text Completion

Skill 1 Adverbs of Frequency	1. **A**	2. **D**	3. **A**	4. **B**	5. **C**
Skill 2 Gerunds and Infinitives After Main Verbs	1. **C**	2. **B**	3. **B**	4. **A**	5. **D**
Skill 3 Gerunds and Infinitives After Prepositions and Adjectives	1. **B**	2. **C**	3. **A**	4. **D**	5. **C**
Skill 4 Causative Verbs	1. **A**	2. **B**	3. **A**	4. **C**	5. **D**
Skill 5 Real Conditionals	1. **A**	2. **B**	3. **C**	4. **D**	5. **C**
Skill 6 Unreal Conditionals	1. **B**	2. **B**	3. **C**	4. **D**	5. **A**
Skill 7 Comparisons	1. **A**	2. **D**	3. **B**	4. **C**	5. **B**
Skill 8 Pronouns	1. **D**	2. **D**	3. **B**	4. **A**	5. **C**
Skill 9 Subject Relative Pronouns	1. **A**	2. **C**	3. **D**	4. **B**	5. **B**
Skill 10 Object Relative Pronouns	1. **C**	2. **B**	3. **B**	4. **D**	5. **A**
Skill 11 Passive Voice	1. **C**	2. **B**	3. **D**	4. **A**	5. **D**
Skill 12 Word Meaning	1. **A**	2. **C**	3. **D**	4. **B**	5. **B**
Skill 13 Sentence Choice	1. **B**	2. **C**	3. **A**	4. **D**	

Part 6: Skills Practice

1. **B**	5. **B**	9. **C**	13. **A**
2. **D**	6. **C**	10. **A**	14. **B**
3. **A**	7. **D**	11. **B**	15. **D**
4. **C**	8. **D**	12. **D**	16. **C**

Part 7: Reading Comprehension

Skill 1 Advertisements	1. **C**	2. **B**					
Skill 2 Forms	1. **D**	2. **B**	3. **B**	4. **C**			
Skill 3 Letters	1. **C**	2. **B**	3. **A**				
Skill 4 Memos	1. **C**	2. **A**	3. **B**	4. **D**			
Skill 5 Tables and Charts	1. **A**	2. **D**	3. **B**	4. **B**			
Skill 6 Graphs	1. **B**	2. **D**					
Skill 7 Announcements	1. **D**	2. **C**	3. **D**	4. **A**			
Skill 8 Notices	1. **D**	2. **B**					
Skill 9 Articles	1. **C**	2. **B**	3. **A**	4. **D**			
Skill 10 Schedules	1. **C**	2. **C**	3. **C**	4. **C**			
Skill 11 E-mails	1. **A**	2. **C**					
Skill 12 Webpages	1. **D**	2. **A**					
Skill 13 Text Messages and Online Chats	1. **B**	2. **C**					

ANSWER EXPLANATIONS FOR READING SKILLS

Part 5: Incomplete Sentences

SKILL 1 WORD FAMILIES

1. **(B)** *Negotiate* is a verb. Choice (A) is an adjective. Choices (C) and (D) are nouns.

2. **(B)** *Applicants* is a noun referring to people. Choice (A) is a verb. Choice (C) is a noun that looks like it belongs to this word family, but it has a completely different meaning. Choice (D) is a noun, but it doesn't refer to people.

3. **(D)** *Decisively* is an adverb of manner modifying the verb act. Choice (A) is a verb. Choice (B) is a noun. Choice (C) is an adjective.

4. **(D)** This is a verb meaning *distinguish*. Choice (A) is a verb meaning *be different*. Choice (B) is a noun. Choice (C) is an adjective.

5. **(B)** This is an adjective referring to the noun *designer*. Choice (A) is a verb and has a completely different meaning. Choice (C) is a noun. Choice (D) is an adverb.

SKILL 2 SIMILAR MEANINGS

1. **(D)** *Earn* is often used to mean *gain money by working*. Choice (A), *win*, means *be first in a competition*. Choice (B), *achieve*, means *accomplish something*. Choice (C), *obtain*, means *acquire something*.

2. **(A)** *Recent* is an adjective referring to something that happened a very short while ago. In this sentence, it modifies the noun *promotion*. Choices (B) and (D) are adverbs, so they cannot be used in this way. Choice (C) refers to something that will happen in the future.

3. **(C)** *Decrease* means to make smaller or less. The sentence means *We will make our costs smaller*. Choices (A) and (B) mean *go down*. They don't fit the sentence because they are intransitive verbs. Choice (D) is a preposition, but a transitive verb is needed in this sentence.

4. **(D)** *Lend* means to let someone use something that belongs to you. Choice (A), *borrow*, means to use something that belongs to someone else. Choice (B), *lease*, refers to a business transaction that involves signing a contract and paying to use something that doesn't belong to you. Choice (C), *owe*, means to be obligated to pay back money or a favor that someone has done for you.

5. **(B)** *Currency* means the system of money used in a country. Choice (A) is a more general term and is not generally used to refer to the currency of any particular country. Choice (C) refers to the round pieces of metal used to represent currency. Choice (D) refers to coins and bills (paper money).

SKILL 3 SIMILAR FORMS

1. **(B)** A *contract* is a legal document. Choice (A) means *communicate with*. Choice (C) means *behave*. Choice (D) means *small* or *tightly packed*.

2. **(A)** *Partitions* are walls used to divide a room into separate areas. Choice (B) refers to people who *participate* in something. Choice (C) means *very small pieces*. Choice (D) refers to a type of verb form.

3. **(D)** *Reduce* means *make smaller or less*. Choice (A) means *make or create something*. Choice (B) means *persuade*. Choice (C) means *make a logical conclusion*.

4. **(C)** *Accept* means *receive*. Choice (A) means *not include*. Choice (B) means to believe that something will happen. Choice (D) refers to a style of pronunciation.

5. **(A)** To have a *preference* means to like one particular thing more than other choices. Choice (B) refers to a conclusion or implication. Choice (C) means *mention*. Choice (D) is a type of meeting.

SKILL 4 SUBJECT-VERB AGREEMENT WITH PREPOSITIONAL PHRASES

1. **(D)** This plural verb agrees with the plural subject of the sentence, *officers*. Choices (A), (B), and (C) are singular verbs.

2. **(A)** The singular verb *charges* agrees with the singular subject *owner*. Choices (B), (C), and (D) are plural verb forms.

3. **(C)** The plural verb *are* agrees with the plural subject *supplies*. Choices (A), (B), and (D) are singular verb forms.

4. **(A)** This plural verb agrees with the plural subject *documents*. Choices (B) and (D) don't agree with the subject. Choice (C) is an adjective.

5. **(B)** This plural verb agrees with the plural subject *carpets*. Choices (A), (C), and (D) don't agree with the subject.

SKILL 5 SINGULAR AND PLURAL SUBJECTS

1. **(C)** The verb *visits* agrees with the singular subject *manager*. Choice (A) is a gerund. Choice (B) is an infinitive verb. Choice (D) needs a plural subject.

2. **(A)** The plural verb *agree* agrees with the plural subject *people*. Choices (B), (C), and (D) are singular verb forms.

3. **(D)** The singular verb *is* agrees with the singular subject *everything*. Choices (A), (B), and (C) are plural verb forms.

4. **(C)** *Rheingold Consultants* is the name of a company; therefore, it is considered singular and takes a singular verb. Choices (A), (B), and (D) are all plural verbs.

5. **(B)** One thousand dollars is a quantity of money and, therefore, treated as a singular noun. Choice (A) is singular but present tense, and this sentence requires a past tense verb. Choices (C) and (D) are plural verbs.

SKILL 6 VERB TENSES

1. **(B)** The time expression *next Friday* indicates that a future tense verb is needed. Choice (A) is simple present. Choice (C) is present continuous. Choice (D) is simple present.

2. **(C)** The time word *yet* indicates that a present perfect verb is needed. Choice (A) is simple past. Choice (B) is simple present. Choice (D) is present continuous and doesn't agree with the plural subject.

3. **(B)** The time expression *every summer* indicates that a simple present verb is needed. Choice (A) is simple present, but it doesn't agree with the singular subject. Choice (C) is

present continuous. Choice (D) is an infinitive verb, a form that can't be used as a main verb.

4. **(A)** The present perfect continuous tense is used to refer to an action that started in the past and is still in progress. Choices (B) and (C) are future forms. Choice (D) is present continuous.

5. **(D)** The action took place *yesterday*, so simple past tense is required. Choice (A) is simple present. Choice (B) is future. Choice (C) is present perfect.

SKILL 7 PREPOSITIONS

1. **(A)** *On* is a preposition of place that means *on top of*. Choices (B), (C), and (D) are prepositions that do not make sense in this context.

2. **(D)** *Into* indicates movement to the inside of something. Choices (A), (B), and (C) are prepositions that don't make sense in this context.

3. **(C)** In this sentence, *until* is paired with *from* to indicate beginning and end times of an action. Choices (A), (B), and (D) are prepositions that don't make sense in this context.

4. **(D)** *At* is used for a specific point in time, such as *noon*. Choices (A), (B), and (C) are not used for a specific point in time.

5. **(C)** *Between* indicates a position with one thing (*post office*) on one side and another thing (*bank*) on the other. Choice (A) is used when there are more than two reference points. Choice (B) is incorrect because an office would not normally be outside. Choice (D) indicates movement, not location.

SKILL 8 PREPOSITIONS WITH VERBS AND ADJECTIVES

1. **(B)** The preposition *about* correctly follows the verb *complain*. Choices (A), (C), and (D) are prepositions that are not generally used with *complain*.

2. **(C)** The preposition *with* correctly follows the verb *replace*, even when there is an object (*our old copy machine*) between. Choices (A), (B), and (D) are prepositions that are not generally used with *replace*.

3. **(A)** The preposition *for* correctly follows the adjective *responsible*. Choices (B), (C), and (D) are prepositions that are not generally used with *responsible*.

4. **(D)** The verb *object* is followed by the preposition *to*. Choices (A), (B), and (C) are prepositions that don't normally follow this verb.

5. **(B)** The adjective *suitable* is followed by the preposition *for*. Choices (A), (C) and (D) are prepositions that don't normally follow this adjective.

SKILL 9 COORDINATING CONJUNCTIONS

1. **(C)** *And* joins two similar ideas—*creative* and *accurate*—which are both positive descriptions of Ms. Sam's work. Choice (A), *but*, joins two opposite ideas. Choice (B), *or*, joins two choices. Choice (D), *nor*, must be used together with *neither*.

2. **(A)** *Yet* joins two opposite ideas—you would expect that George would finish the report after working all night, but he didn't. Choice (B) joins two similar ideas. Choice (C) indicates a choice and must be used with *or*. Choice (D) indicates a lack of choice and must be used with *nor*.

3. **(B)** Together with *either, or* indicates a choice, in this case between two meeting times. Choice (A) joins two opposite ideas. Choice (C) must be used with *neither* to indicate a lack of choice. Choice (D) must be used with *nor*.

4. **(D)** *Nor* is the conjunction paired with *neither*. Choices (A), (B), and (C) are not used with *neither*.

5. **(C)** *But* joins two opposite ideas: (1) we wanted to see the play, and (2) we couldn't get tickets (therefore, we did not see the play). Choice (A) joins two similar ideas. Choice (B) joins two choices. Choice (D) is also used to join choices and must be paired with *or*.

SKILL 10 PARALLEL STRUCTURE

1. **(B)** *Friendly* is an adjective and is parallel with the adjective *prompt*. Choices (A), (C), and (D) are nouns.

2. **(D)** The gerund *getting* is parallel with the gerund *making*. The sentence tells us that Sharon is good at two things—(1) *making clients feel comfortable* and (2) *getting them interested in our services*. Choice (A) is base form. Choice (B) is past tense. Choice (C) is a past participle.

3. **(C)** The noun *accuracy* is parallel with the noun *efficiency*. Choice (A) is an adjective. Choice (B) is an adverb. Choice (D) is a gerund and, although it looks similar, is not related in meaning to the other choices or the correct answer.

4. **(A)** The present tense verb *finalize* is parallel with the present tense verb *begin*. Choice (B) is a noun. Choice (C) is a past tense verb. Choice (D) is an adjective

5. **(C)** The comparative adjective *later* is parallel with the comparative adjective *earlier*. Choice (A) is an adverb. Choice (B) is a noun. Choice (D) is a superlative adjective.

SKILL 11 SUBORDINATING CONJUNCTIONS

1. **(C)** Usually people cannot enter a concert hall after the concert has started, so this clause describes a situation that contradicts expectations. Choice (A) introduces a reason. Choice (B) is a coordinating conjunction. Choice (D) introduces a time clause.

2. **(A)** *Since* introduces a reason, and this clause describes the reason for canceling the meeting. Choice (B) introduces a contradiction. Choice (C) introduces a condition. Choice (D) introduces a time clause.

3. **(C)** *As soon as* introduces a time clause and means *immediately after*. This clause tells when Miranda will send the report. Choice (A) is a coordinating conjunction that joins opposite ideas. Choice (B) introduces a result. Choice (D) introduces a time clause, but the meaning does not make sense in this context—you cannot send a report before it is ready.

4. **(C)** *Because* introduces a cause or reason. Choices (A) and (B) introduce a contradiction. Choice (D) introduces a result.

5. **(D)** *Even though* introduces a contradiction—the expected result of registering early is to get a place in the class, so not getting a place is a contradiction. Choice (A) introduces a reason. Choice (B) introduces a time clause. Choice (C) introduces a result.

SKILL 12 FUTURE TIME CLAUSES

1. **(B)** This is a present tense verb in a future time clause, and it agrees with the subject of the clause, *train*. Choice (A) is present tense but doesn't agree with the subject. Choice (C) is future tense. Choice (D) is a gerund.

2. **(A)** The main clause has a future verb, so a present tense verb is needed in the time clause. Choice (B) is an infinitive verb, a form that cannot be used as the main verb of a clause. Choice (C) is a future verb. Choice (D) is a noun.

3. **(C)** The main clause has a future verb, so a present tense verb is needed in the time clause. Choice (A) is future. Choice (B) is past. Choice (D) is base form.

4. **(D)** A present tense verb is required in a future time clause. Choice (A) is a future verb. Choice (B) is an infinitive. Choice (C) is past tense.

5. **(D)** This is the main clause of a future sentence (the action will take place *next week*), so a future verb is required. Choice (A) is present tense. Choice (B) is base form. Choice (C) is an incomplete future form—it should be *are going to be*.

Part 6: Text Completion

SKILL 1 ADVERBS OF FREQUENCY

1. **(A)** *Rarely* means *almost never*. The information states that this is the first time a meeting has been held on the weekend. Choices (B), (C), and (D) indicate greater frequency.

2. **(D)** *Always* means *all the time*. The context makes it clear that meetings begin on time all the time. Choices (A), (B), and (C) indicate lesser frequency.

3. **(A)** *Usually* means *most of the time*. Choices (B), (C), and (D) indicate lesser frequency.

4. **(B)** *Seldom* means *almost never*. The information that Mr. Kim's absence is *unexpected* implies that he almost never misses a meeting. Choices (A), (C), and (D) indicate greater frequency.

5. **(C)** The word *however* introducing the information that snacks will not be served implies that snacks are *often*, that is, frequently, served at meetings. Choices (A), (B), and (D) indicate lesser frequency.

SKILL 2 GERUNDS AND INFINITIVES AFTER MAIN VERBS

1. **(C)** *Agree* is followed by an infinitive. Choices (A), (B), and (D) are not in the infinitive form.

2. **(B)** *Mind* is followed by a gerund. Choices (A), (C), and (D) are not gerunds.

3. **(B)** *Offer* is followed by an infinitive. Choices (A), (C), and (D) are not infinitives.

4. **(A)** *Finish* is followed by a gerund. Choices (B), (C), and (D) are not gerunds.

5. **(D)** *Plan* is followed by an infinitive. Choices (A), (B), and (C) are not infinitives.

SKILL 3 GERUNDS AND INFINITIVES AFTER PREPOSITIONS AND ADJECTIVES

1. **(B)** *About* is a preposition, so it is followed by a gerund. Choices (A), (C), and (D) are not gerunds.

2. **(C)** *Bright enough* follows the adjective + *enough* pattern, which is followed by an infinitive verb. Choices (A), (B), and (D) are not infinitives.

3. **(A)** *Ready* is an adjective, so it is followed by an infinitive. Choices (B), (C), and (D) are not infinitives.

4. **(D)** *Of* is a preposition, so it is followed by a gerund. Choices (A), (B), and (C) are not gerunds.

5. **(C)** *On* is a preposition, so it is followed by a gerund. Choices (A), (B), and (D) are not gerunds.

SKILL 4 CAUSATIVE VERBS

1. **(A)** The causative verb *make* is followed by the base form. Choices (B), (C), and (D) are not in the base form.
2. **(B)** The causative verb *permit* is followed by the infinitive form. Choices (A), (C), and (D) are not infinitives.
3. **(A)** The causative verb *have* is followed by the base form. Choices (B), (C), and (D) are not in the base form.
4. **(C)** The causative verb *get* is followed by the infinitive form. Choices (A), (B), and (D) are not infinitives.
5. **(D)** The causative verb *let* is followed by the base form. Choices (A), (B), and (C) are not base form.

SKILL 5 REAL CONDITIONALS

1. **(A)** The verb in the *if* clause in a real conditional sentence must be in the present tense. Choice (B) is an infinitive verb. Choices (C) and (D) are future verbs.
2. **(B)** The verb in the *if* clause in a real conditional sentence must be in the present tense. Choice (A) is an infinitive verb. Choice (C) is a gerund. Choice (D) is future tense.
3. **(C)** The verb in the main clause in a real conditional sentence must be in the future tense. Choice (A) is the base form. Choice (B) is present tense. Choice (D) is past tense.
4. **(D)** The verb in the *if* clause in a real conditional sentence must be in the present tense. Choice (A) is the base form. Choice (B) is past tense. Choice (C) is future tense.
5. **(C)** The verb in the main clause in a real conditional sentence must be in the future tense. Choice (A) is present tense or base form. Choice (B) is an infinitive. Choice (D) is future perfect.

SKILL 6 UNREAL CONDITIONALS

1. **(B)** In an unreal conditional about the past, the *if* clause uses a past perfect verb. Choice (A) is simple past. Choice (C) is present perfect. Choice (D) would be correct in an unreal conditional about the present.
2. **(B)** In an unreal conditional about the past, the *if* clause uses a past perfect verb. Choice (A) is present perfect tense. Choice (C) is present tense. Choice (D) is future tense.
3. **(C)** In an unreal conditional about the present, the *if* clause uses a past tense verb. Choice (A) is present tense. Choice (B) is future tense. Choice (D) is past perfect.
4. **(D)** In an unreal conditional about the present, the main clause uses *would* + base form verb. Choice (A) is past tense. Choice (B) is past perfect. Choice (C) is the form for an unreal conditional about the past.
5. **(A)** In an unreal conditional about the past, the main clause uses *would have* + past participle verb. Choice (B) the form for an unreal conditional about the present. Choice (C) is past tense. Choice (D) is past perfect.

SKILL 7 COMPARISONS

1. **(A)** *Faster than* is a correct comparative form using the -*er* ending and *than*, and it makes sense in the context. Choice (B) does not fit the context of business training. Choice (C) is incorrect because the courses are *short-term*, not long. Choice (D) is incorrect because the courses are offered *at a price you can afford*, that is, they are not *costly*.
2. **(D)** This is a correct superlative form using *the* and the -*est* ending. Choice (A) is an adjective but it is not superlative. Choice (B) is a superlative form but is missing *the*. Choice (C) is a comparative, not superlative, form.
3. **(B)** *Higher* is a correct comparative form used in a sentence that already contains *than*. Choices (A), (C), and (D) cannot be used with *than*.
4. **(C)** *Better* pairs with *than* to form a comparative. Choices (A) and (B) are superlative forms. Choice (D) is a positive adjective.
5. **(B)** Employers would most likely be looking for *the most skilled* workers. Choice (A) is not used to describe workers. Choices (C) and (D) are not qualities that an employer would look for.

SKILL 8 PRONOUNS

1. **(D)** *Your* is a possessive pronoun describing the adjective *staff*, with the antecedent *you*. Choice (A) is a reflexive pronoun. Choice (B) is a possessive pronoun. Choice (C) is a subject or object pronoun.

2. **(D)** The antecedent is *employees*, a third person plural noun, so the correct pronoun is the third person plural *they*. Choice (A) is first person singular. Choice (B) is third person singular. Choice (C) is second person singular or plural.

3. **(B)** The antecedent is *John Malstrom*, a third person singular noun, so the correct pronoun is the third person singular *him*. Choice (A) is first person singular. Choice (C) is third person singular, but it refers to a woman, not a man, and *John* is a man's name. Choice (D) is third person plural.

4. **(A)** The antecedent is *folder*, a third person singular noun referring to a thing. Choice (B) is also third person singular but refers to a person. Choice (C) is third person plural. Choice (D) is first person singular.

5. **(C)** *Myself* is a first person reflexive pronoun with the antecedent *I*. Choices (A), (B), and (D) are not first person.

SKILL 9 SUBJECT RELATIVE PRONOUNS

1. **(A)** The antecedent, *staff members*, is a group of people so *who* is the correct pronoun. Choice (B) is an object relative pronoun but a subject relative pronoun is required here. Choice (C) refers to a possessive. Choice (D) refers to a thing.

2. **(C)** *Whose* is a possessive relative pronoun, referring to *everyone's schedule*. Choice (A) refers to a person, not to a possessive. Choices (B) and (D) are not relative pronouns.

3. **(D)** The antecedent, *visit*, is a thing. Choice (A) refers to a person. Choice (B) refers to a thing but cannot be used in a nonrestrictive clause. Choice (C) refers to a possessive.

4. **(B)** *That* introduces the restrictive clause and has the antecedent *schedule*, a thing. Choice (A) is not a relative pronoun. Choices (C) and

(D) refer to people, not things.

5. **(B)** Relative pronoun *who* refers to a person, in this case, *Ms. McIntyre*. Choice (A) can only be used in a restrictive clause but this is a non-restrictive clause. Choice (C) refers to a thing. Choice (D) is not a relative pronoun.

SKILL 10 OBJECT RELATIVE PRONOUNS

1. **(C)** The antecedent is a person, *Dr. Herman Friedman*. Choice (A) refers to a possessive. Choice (B) refers to a thing. Choice (D) is not a relative pronoun.

2. **(B)** The antecedent is a thing, *the gradual bleaching of the Great Barrier Reef*. Choice (A) refers to a thing but can only be used in restrictive clauses and this is a nonrestrictive clause. Choice (C) refers to a person. Choice (D) is not a relative pronoun.

3. **(B)** The antecedent is a thing, *books*, and this is a restrictive clause. Choice (A) refers to a possessive. Choice (C) is not a relative pronoun. Choice (D) refers to a person.

4. **(D)** *Whose* is a possessive relative pronoun referring to *Dr. Smythe's writings*. Choices (A), (B), and (C) are not possessives.

5. **(A)** The antecedent is two people, *Drs. Friedman and Smythe*. Choice (B) refers to a possessive. Choice (C) is not a relative pronoun. Choice (D) refers to a thing.

SKILL 11 PASSIVE VOICE

1. **(C)** This is a passive verb in the past, *last month*, with a plural subject, *walls*. Choice (A) is singular. Choice (B) is present tense. Choice (D) is present perfect.

2. **(B)** This is passive voice. The subject, *carpet*, does not install itself. A past participle is required after the verb *be*. Choice (A) is an active form. Choice (C) is a gerund. Choice (D) is a noun.

3. **(D)** This is passive voice. The subject, *stains*, do not remove themselves. Choices (A), (B), and (C) are all active forms.

4. **(A)** This is passive voice. The subject, *conference room*, has not renovated itself. Choices (B), (C), and (D) are active forms.

5. **(D)** This is passive voice. The subject, *party*, will not give itself. The action takes place in the future, *next month*. Choices (A) and (B) are active forms. Choice (C) is an infinitive, not future.

SKILL 12 WORD MEANING

1. **(A)** *Landlord* means the building's owner, the logical person to keep the building clean and re-carpet the hallways. Choices (B), (C), and (D) are people who would not be responsible for these things.
2. **(C)** *Selected* means *chose*. Choices (A), (B), and (D) have meanings that do not fit the context.
3. **(D)** People generally have to pay a *high* rent to live in a desirable location. Choices (A), (B), and (C) have meanings that do not fit the context.
4. **(B)** *Cultural* activities are activities that involve such things as art, music, and theater. Choices (A), (C), and (D) have meanings that do not fit the context.
5. **(B)** *Charged* means *asked to pay*. Choices (A), (C), and (D) have meanings that do not fit the context.

SKILL 13 SENTENCE CHOICE

1. **(B)** This sentence logically fits in a paragraph notifying people of scheduled elevator maintenance and the disruption it might cause to elevator use. Choices (A), (C), and (D) do not fit the context.
2. **(C)** This sentence describing the details of the meeting place and time logically follows the sentence mentioning that a meeting will take place. Choices (A), (B), and (D) do not fit the context.
3. **(A)** This sentence explaining how to make an appointment logically follows the sentence asking a job seeker to come in for an interview. Choices (B), (C), and (D) do not fit the context.
4. **(D)** This sentence telling the time of the appointment logically follows the sentence telling the day of the appointment. Choices (A), (B), and (C) do not fit the context.

Part 6: Skills Practice

1. **(B)** This is an adverb modifying the verb *invite*. Choice (A) is an adjective. Choices (C) and (D) are nouns.
2. **(D)** This is an adverb modifying the adjective *better*. Choices (A) and (B) have meanings that don't fit the context. Choice (C) is not an adverb.
3. **(A)** *Live* is an adjective referring to something that is done in front of the audience rather than recorded in a studio. Choices (B) and (D) are adjectives that mean the *opposite of dead*. Choice (C) is a verb meaning *make more interesting or exciting*.
4. **(C)** The purpose of the letter is to extend an invitation to a social event, and Choice (C) is an appropriate way to conclude an invitation. Choice (A) is incorrect because appointments are not normally made for social events. Choices (B) and (D) are incorrect because guests are not normally asked to pay or get tickets for social events.
5. **(B)** This is a possessive adjective modifying the noun *request*. Choice (A) is a subject pronoun. Choice (C) is a possessive pronoun. Choice (D) is a contraction of *you will*.
6. **(C)** The request for time off is being turned down because it is at the wrong time of year; *season* means *time of year*. Choices (A) and (B) refer to a place. Choice (D) is something that shows specific dates.
7. **(D)** The implied subject of the verb is *seminar*, and a seminar does not give itself but is given by someone, so a passive voice verb is needed here. Choices (A), (B), and (C) are all active verb forms,
8. **(D)** The purpose of the e-mail is to explain the reason for turning down a request, so apologizing is appropriate near the end of the message. Choice (A) is not logical as it is a about a past seminar and the message is about future seminars. Choice (B) is out of place; it could possibly fit in with the mention of the May busy season. Choice (C) does not make sense as clearly the recipient of the message knows this as he has already done it.

9. **(C)** This is a gerund used as the subject of the sentence. Choice (A) is the base form or present tense. Choice (B) is an infinitive. Choice (D) is a noun that means the same as *parking lot* and doesn't make sense in the sentence.

10. **(A)** *Tow* describes a way of removing a car and taking it to another place. Choice (B) describes what will happen, but it is not usually used in the context of moving illegally parked cars. Choices (C) and (D) don't fit the context.

11. **(B)** *Damages*, or harm, may happen to a car when it is towed. Choices (A), (C), and (D) don't fit the context.

12. **(D)** The purpose of the notice is to explain that only cars with a sticker can park in the lot, so this sentence explaining how to get a sticker fits the purpose and context. Choices (A), (B), and (C) are about the parking lot, but they are not about parking stickers.

13. **(A)** The notice is directed toward people who might be interested in renting office space in a particular building, so this sentence fits the context. Choices (B), (C), and (D) are also about the building, but they are not specifically related to renting space there.

14. **(B)** *Heart* in this sentence means *center*. Choice (A) is not likely to be described as a *prime location*. Choices (C) and (D) don't make sense.

15. **(D)** *Range* refers to a series of numbers, in this case, from the smallest to the largest office sizes. Choices (A), (B), and (C) don't fit the context.

16. **(C)** *Our* refers to the owners of the building, previously referred to in the announcement as *we*. The owners are the ones who have model offices. Choice (A) would refer to the reader of the announcement. Choices (B) and (D) refer to other people.

Part 7: Reading Comprehension

SKILL 1 ADVERTISEMENTS

1. **(C)** *Attention Manufacturers* indicates that the writers want manufacturers to read the ad. Choice (A) confuses the writers of the ad with the readers. Choices (B) and (D) are not mentioned.

2. **(B)** It indicates they can distribute in 155 countries. Choice (A) is less than the number mentioned. Choices (C) and (D) are more than the number mentioned.

SKILL 2 FORMS

1. **(D)** To *subscribe* means that you will start to receive a periodical. Choices (A), (B), and (C) are contradicted by the heading *Special Subscription Offer*.

2. **(B)** The full cover price is $5 an issue ($60 divided by 12 months). Choice (A) is less than the price. Choices (C) and (D) are more than the price.

3. **(B)** *Allow four weeks for first issue* means about *one month*. Choice (A) is shorter than a month. Choices (C) and (D) are not logical.

4. **(C)** If there are 12 issues in one year, the magazine comes *monthly*. Choices (A) and (B) are more often. Choice (D) is less often.

SKILL 3 LETTERS

1. **(C)** *Samples* are not requested. Choices (A), (B), and (D) are explicitly requested. (*Terms* means *pricing information*.)

2. **(B)** *Hardware* includes computers. Choice (A) is contradicted by the fact that they are *adding software to their sales offerings*. Choices (C) and (D) are not mentioned.

3. **(A)** *Add software to our sales offerings* means *distribute software*. Choice (B) is not mentioned. Choice (C) confuses *selling hardware* with *purchasing hardware*. Choice (D) confuses *sending* an annual report with *receiving* an annual report.

SKILL 4 MEMOS

1. **(C)** *No flights under five hours can be booked in Business Class*, but flights over five hours can be. Choices (A) *Economy* and (B) *Economy Plus* can probably be booked. Choice (D) is contradicted by *No flights . . . can be booked in First Class.*

2. **(A)** If it is written *May 15* and goes into effect *June 1*, it goes into effect in *two weeks*. Choices (B) and (C) are contradicted by *June 1*. Choice (D) confuses *five hours* with *five months.*

3. **(B)** The memo is about using *economical means*, or *saving money*. Choices (A), (C), and (D) are not mentioned.

4. **(D)** The memo affects *all employees*, or *all personnel*. Choices (A), (B), and (C) are contradicted by *all personnel.*

SKILL 5 TABLES AND CHARTS

1. **(A)** Amsterdam and Taipei are both coded *C* for cloudy. Choice (B) cities were partly cloudy. Choices (C) and (D) had different weather but were not cloudy.

2. **(D)** Manila had a high of *33/91*. Choices (A), (B), and (C) had lower temperatures.

3. **(B)** Frankfurt had a spread from *3/37* to *1/34*. Choices (A), (C), and (D) had wider spreads.

4. **(B)** Kuala Lampur is coded *t* for thunderstorms. Choices (A), (C), and (D) are not mentioned for this city.

SKILL 6 GRAPHS

1. **(B)** Competing hotels would be most interested in market share information. Choices (A), (C), and (D) are unlikely to be interested.

2. **(D)** Lowit has 25%, or one-quarter, of the market. Choice (A) is incorrect because Stilton is the top-ranking chain. Choice (B) is incorrect because location information is not given in the graph. Choice (C) is incorrect because Torte has only 15% of the market.

SKILL 7 ANNOUNCEMENTS

1. **(D)** The event is described as *this year's City Job Fair*, the phrase *this year's* implying that the event takes place every year. Choices (A), (B), and (C) do not match the meaning of this phrase.

2. **(C)** The passage states, *pre-registration is required*. Choice (A) is confused with the suggestion to visit the website for more information. Choice (B) is incorrect because the passage states, *There is no charge for the workshops*. Choice (D) is plausible but not mentioned.

3. **(D)** *Unique* means *rare*. Choices (A), (B), and (C) are not the correct meaning for this word.

4. **(A)** The first sentence states that there will be a job fair, then this sentence follows giving a general idea of what the fair is about. The rest of the paragraph describes details of the fair. Choices (B), (C), and (D) are not a good context for this sentence.

SKILL 8 NOTICES

1. **(D)** Employees moving from other cities are most affected. Choices (A), (B), and (C) are not affected by these changes.

2. **(B)** *Moving household items* is reimbursed. Choices (A), (C), and (D) are *no longer reimbursable.*

SKILL 9 ARTICLES

1. **(C)** The article talks about giving cooking classes as a way for restaurants to attract customers. Choices (A) and (B) are related to the topic but are not discussed. Choice (D) is mentioned but is not the main idea.

2. **(B)** Paragraph 2 explains that this type of cooking class usually *fills up most quickly*, that is, many people want to take it. Choice (A) is not mentioned. Choices (C) and (D) are mentioned but not as the most popular.

3. **(A)** A *side line* is an activity or job done in addition to one's main job. Choices (B), (C), and (D) are not the correct meaning for this phrase.

4. **(D)** The sentence that precedes this explains that cooking classes are *an effective means of advertising your business*, and this sentence goes on to explain that idea in further detail.

Choices (A), (B), and (C) are not logical locations for this sentence.

SKILL 10 SCHEDULES

1. **(C)** Off-peak fares start somewhere between 8:25 and 8:32; 8:30 is a reasonable guess. Choice (A) is not mentioned. Choices (B) and (D) are times in the schedule, but neither is the start of off-peak fares.

2. **(C)** Buses marked with a *W* arrive at this stop five minutes earlier than others, so the 7:30 arrives at 7:25. Choices (A) and (B) are not mentioned. Choice (D) is the bus's departure time.

3. **(C)** The tunnel isn't open until 8:00. Choice (A) is probably true, but it isn't mentioned in the schedule. Choices (B) and (D) are not mentioned.

4. **(C)** Each trip is 50 minutes, or *almost an hour*. This question requires some quick math computation. Choice (A) means 15 minutes. Choice (B) means 30 minutes. Choice (D) is incorrect.

SKILL 11 E-MAILS

1. **(A)** The subject line says *Orlando meeting* and the first paragraph of the email explains the results of a meeting with a client. Choice (B) repeats the word *paperwork*. Choice (C) repeats the word *proposal*. Choice (D) refers to the recipient of the email but no meeting with her is mentioned.

2. **(C)** The writer mentions a place where she had dinner after leaving the meeting with the client. Choice (A) is plausible but not mentioned. Choice (B) is where she will go tomorrow. Choice (D) is mentioned but not as the place she went to following the meeting.

SKILL 12 WEBPAGES

1. **(D)** The company chooses colors, carpet, and furniture for homes and offices and says that it helps clients with *redecorating*, all things that interior decorators do. Choice (A) is related but refers to the exterior, not the interior, design of a building. Choice (B) repeat the word *furniture*. Choice (C) repeats the word paint.

2. **(A)** Customers are asked to click on a link to see a portfolio, that is, a set of examples, of the company's work. Choice (B) is something that customers are asked to do but presumably to discuss their decorating needs. Choices (C) and (D) are confused with the suggestion to call the office, but the call would be for the purpose of consulting on decorating needs.

SKILL 13 TEXT MESSAGES AND ONLINE CHATS

1. **(B)** Jim Hart says *the bus can hardly move* due to heavy traffic. Choices (A), (B), and (C) are logical, but incorrect.

2. **(C)** *I'm sorry?*, said or written as a question, is short for *I'm sorry, but I don't understand*. Lin Lee's response, explaining which papers she is referring to, makes it clear that Jim Hart was asking for an explanation. Choice (A) is related to the mention of papers. Choice (B) is another meaning of the phrase *I'm sorry*. Choice (D) is another way of apologizing.

ANSWER KEY
Reading Mini-Test

Answer Explanations can be found beginning on page 213.

Part 5: Incomplete Sentences

1. **B**	5. **B**	9. **A**	13. **D**
2. **C**	6. **D**	10. **D**	14. **A**
3. **A**	7. **A**	11. **C**	15. **C**
4. **C**	8. **B**	12. **B**	

Part 6: Text Completion

16. **C**	18. **D**	20. **A**	22. **B**
17. **B**	19. **A**	21. **C**	23. **A**

Part 7: Reading Comprehension

24. **B**	30. **A**	36. **A**	42. **D**
25. **C**	31. **A**	37. **C**	43. **B**
26. **D**	32. **C**	38. **B**	44. **C**
27. **C**	33. **B**	39. **C**	45. **A**
28. **D**	34. **A**	40. **A**	46. **D**
29. **C**	35. **B**	41. **B**	47. **A**

ANSWER EXPLANATIONS FOR MINI-TEST FOR READING

Part 5: Incomplete Sentences

1. **(B)** This third person singular verb agrees with the singular subject, *Rice Enterprises*, which is the name of a company. Choices (A) and (D) are verbs that don't agree with the subject. Choice (C) is a noun.

2. **(C)** This is an adverb modifying the adjective *successful*. Choices (A) and (B) are adjectives. Choice (D) is a noun.

3. **(A)** *Increase* means *make bigger*, and we know from the context—opening up a new manufacturing plant—that that is what the plans are about. Choice (B) also means *make bigger*, but only refers to size, not to amount or quantity. Choices (C) and (D) mean *make smaller*.

4. **(C)** *Although* introduces a contradictory cause—one would expect that press attention would cause more business, but that isn't what happened. Choice (A) introduces a cause or reason. Choice (B) introduces a result. Choice (D) introduces a contradictory result—it could be used with the second clause of this sentence.

5. **(B)** *Confidential* means *private* or *secret*. Choices (A), (C), and (D) have meanings that don't fit the context.

6. **(D)** *As long as* means *during the time*. Choices (A), (B), and (C) have meanings that don't fit the context.

7. **(A)** This is an object pronoun (follows the verb) referring to a woman, *Ms. Yamamoto*. Choice (B) is a possessive pronoun. Choice (C) is a subject pronoun. Choice (D) is a reflexive pronoun.

8. **(B)** In this context, *explain* means *give information about*. Choices (A), (C), and (D) have meanings that don't fit the context.

9. **(A)** A noun is needed as an object of the verb *hear* and following the adjective *much*. Choice (B) is a noun but refers to people, not a situation, and as a plural noun cannot follow *much*. Choice (C) is a gerund or present participle. Choice (D) is past tense or past participle.

10. **(D)** The main verb *ask* is followed by an infinitive. Choice (A) is the base form or present tense. Choice (B) is present tense. Choice (C) is a gerund or present participle.

11. **(C)** *Whether* introduces possible alternatives. Choice (A) is also used with alternatives, but it comes after the subject of the clause. Choice (B) gives a negative meaning to the sentence. Choice (D) introduces a contradiction.

12. **(B)** *Definite* is an adjective defining the noun *answer*. Choice (A) is a verb. Choice (C) is an adverb. Choice (D) is a noun.

13. **(D)** *Different* is followed by the preposition *from*. Choices (A), (B), and (C) are prepositions that don't normally follow *different*.

14. **(A)** *Thoroughly* means *completely*. Choices (B), (C), and (D) have meanings that don't fit the context.

15. **(C)** *Modifications* means *changes*. Choices (A), (B), and (D) have meanings that don't fit the context.

Part 6: Text Completion

16. **(C)** The passive form is required here because the subject, *seminar*, is not active—the seminar doesn't offer itself, it is offered by Stellar. Choices (A), (B), and (D) are all active verbs.

17. **(B)** *Covers* in this context means *includes*. In this case, the things that the price pays for are lunch and materials, as well as the seminar itself. Choices (A), (C), and (D) have meanings that don't fit the context.

18. **(D)** A noun is needed here to act as the subject of the sentence. Choices (A) and (C) are verbs. Choice (B) is a noun, but it refers to a person, not a process, which is the meaning here.

19. **(A)** The preceding sentence says, *take a look at what else we have to offer*, and Choice (A) gives examples of services that are offered. Choices (B), (C), and (D) don't fit the context.

20. **(A)** *These* is a pronoun for the plural noun *services* and is the subject of the sentence. Choice (B) is not a pronoun. Choice (C) is an object pronoun. Choice (D) is singular.

21. **(C)** *Currently* means *now*. Choice (A) means *recently*, so it refers to a past time. Choice (B) means *maybe*. Choice (D) means *at some time in the future*.

22. **(B)** *Coordinator* is a noun referring to a person. Choice (A) is a verb. Choice (C) is a gerund or present participle. Choice (D) is a noun, but it doesn't refer to a person.

23. **(A)** The previous sentence suggests contacting someone about volunteering, and this sentence mentions specific information to include related to volunteering. Choices (B), (C), and (D) are about the community center, but they are not about becoming a volunteer there.

Part 7: Reading Comprehension

24. **(B)** The company made an error with a shipment, and the writer of the e-mail *regrets the inconvenience it caused* and is *very sorry for any difficulties our error may have caused*. Choices (A) and (C) are what the recipient of the e-mail has already done. Choice (D) is not mentioned.

25. **(C)** The shipment was missing 1,000 cases of all-purpose paper. Choices (A), (B), and (D) are other problems shipments can have but are not mentioned.

26. **(D)** The article explains that a Swiss company has purchased the Royal Chemical Industries company. Choice (A) refers to the many countries mentioned but no trade agreements are mentioned. Choice (B) refers to the mention of the names of several European countries. Choice (C) is confused with the discussion of the purchase price and the value of the plants, but these are not the main topic of the article.

27. **(C)** The company manufactures polypropylene, which is described as a type of *tough, flexible plastic*. Choices (A) and (B) are confused with the mention of the products that can be made with this plastic. Choice (D) is not mentioned.

28. **(D)** The information states, *Bring your own bike or rent one of ours*, and then a link to rental rates is provided. Choices (A), (B), and (C) are all listed as part of a tour.

29. **(C)** Both group and self-guided (that is, an individual could take the tour without a guide) are offered. Choice (A) is incorrect because the length of the tours is not mentioned. Choice (B) is incorrect because tours are offered *for every kind of cyclist*. Choice (D) is incorrect because tours are offered *year round*.

30. **(A)** The page ends with a list of *top tours*, that is, the most popular tours. Choices (B), (C), and (D) do not have the same meaning as *top*.

31. **(A)** They are discussing ordering fabric to make shirts, so they work for a clothing manufacturer. Choice (B) is where they are buying the fabric. Choice (C) is related to the discussion of making an order. Choice (D) repeats the word *shirt*.

32. **(C)** Anders ordered 4 bolts of fabric, but they need 6, so he offers to *call them back*, in order to, we can assume, order 2 more bolts of fabric. Choices (A), (B), and (D) are related to the situation of making orders, but they are not the correct answer.

33. **(B)** Milla mentions the need to work quickly to fulfill the order, so Yoko mentions the next step—shipping it. The expression *on their way* means *traveling toward a specific place*. Choices (A), (C), and (D) don't fit the context.

34. **(A)** Customers go to Amy Ann's to buy *freshly made bread, cakes, and cookies*, so it is a bakery. Choices (B), (C), and (D) are other food-related businesses but are not the correct answer.

35. **(B)** The article states, *Customers line up daily*, meaning that there are so many customers, they have to wait on line to be served, so the business is popular. Choice (A) is incorrect because the business opened just three months ago. Choice (C) is not mentioned. Choice (D) is not likely since the owner mentions the need to hire more staff to keep up with the demand for the products.

36. **(A)** In this context, *volume* refers to the amount of sales, which is much larger than the owner expected. Choice (B) is another meaning of the word but does not fit the context.

Choices (C) and (D) are not the correct meaning of the word.

37. **(C)** The sentence following this position mentions *close to half that amount*, which refers to the $40,000 mentioned in the inserted sentence. Choices (A), (B), and (D) are not an appropriate context for this sentence.

38. **(B)** The notice says that the work will begin *at the end of next month.* Choice (A) is confused with when employees should ask for a subway pass. Choice (C) is confused with the amount of time the work will last. Choice (D) is this month.

39. **(C)** Each office in the building will get four parking passes, and Parrot Communications has five times as many employees as that. Choice (A) is confused with the number of parking passes. Choice (B) is confused with *five times as many employees.* Choice (D) is confused with the size of the discount on the subway passes.

40. **(A)** The parking passes allow parking on the streets around the building, and Parrot Communications will reserve its parking passes for its clients. Choice (B) is incorrect because Parrot Communications employees will not be given passes. Choice (C) is incorrect because there are only four passes allowed per office. Choice (D) is incorrect because Dena Degenaro is a Parrot Communications employee, and as such will not get a parking pass.

41. **(B)** The memo was sent by the office manager and asks employees to *see me* to ask for a subway pass. Choice (A) is confused with the city's allotting certain parking spaces for building tenants. Choice (C) is confused with the people who posted the notice. Choice (D) is a logical place to get a subway pass, but it is not mentioned.

42. **(D)** The subway passes will be valid for the entire length of the garage reconstruction, which is three months. Choices (A), (B), and (C) are not mentioned.

43. **(B)** The ad states, *Owner will remodel to suit your needs*, so we can assume that remodeling has not been done recently. Choice (A) is true because the rent includes utilities. Choice (C) is true because the office is near bus and subway lines. Choice (D) is true because the rent includes parking.

44. **(C)** Ms. Roper wants to pay $1,000 a month rent plus utilities. She also prefers a place with parking, but she could do without this if it is near the subway. Office #3 costs $1,100 with utilities and is one block from the subway, so it fits her criteria. Choices (A) and (B) are too expensive. Choice (D) doesn't have parking and isn't close to the subway.

45. **(A)** Ms. Roper is available *any day after 1:00 P.M.*, that is, any afternoon. Choice (B) is incorrect because she is busy in the mornings. Choice (C) is incorrect because she wants to look this week. Choice (D) is not mentioned.

46. **(D)** Businesses are being forced out of downtown because the rents are becoming too high. Choices (A), (B), and (C) are other uses of the word *driving*, but they are not the correct answer.

47. **(A)** The article explains that businesses are leaving downtown because of high rents and then describes Brightwood as *affordable*, that is, not too expensive. Also, in the e-mail, Ms. Roper describes downtown as *a bit out of reach*, that is, more expensive than she can pay for, and goes on to say that Brightwood is suitable for her. Choice (B) is incorrect, as the article mentions wide streets, gardens, and a park as attractions. Choice (C) is incorrect because the article shows the neighborhood as a place that is enjoying increasing popularity. Choice (D) is true of downtown, not Brightwood.

TOEIC
Practice Tests

SUMMARY OF TIPS

Part 1: Photographs

- Listen for the meaning of the whole sentence to determine which choice best matches the photo.
- When you look at the photo, analyze the people. Determine their number, gender, location, occupation, and actions.
- Use the context of the photo to identify objects and location.

Part 2: Question-Response

- Listen for the meaning of the question/statement and answer choices. Do not be confused by words with similar sounds, related words, and homonyms.
- Listen for suggestions, offers, and requests.

Part 3: Conversations and Part 4:Talks

- Learn to recognize different types of questions and what they ask about – people, occupations, place, time, etc.
- Understand the meaning of words and phrases in the context of the conversation or talk.
- Look for paraphrases of words in the conversation or talk.
- Listen for implied meaning.
- In questions with a graphic, scan the graphic, then listen for information in the talk that confirms or contradicts the information in the graphic.
- Practice listening to different accents.

Part 5: Incomplete Sentences and Part 6: Text Completion

- Distinguish between words that have similar but different meanings or forms.
- Determine the correct word, phrase, or sentence for the context.
- Recognize different verb forms.
- Recognize different adjective and adverb forms.
- Recognize singular and plural nouns.
- Recognize different kinds of clauses.
- Understand the different uses of prepositions.

Part 7: Reading Comprehension

- Know how to read the different types of reading passages found on the TOEIC.
- Know the different types of reading comprehension questions found on the TOEIC.
- Know how to use the PSRA strategy: Predict, Scan, Read, Answer.

*Many thanks to my readers, especially Jean-Pierre Saint-Aimé, who have provided valuable tips on test-taking strategies.

ANSWER SHEET
Practice Test 1

LISTENING COMPREHENSION

Part 1: Photographs

1. Ⓐ Ⓑ Ⓒ Ⓓ   3. Ⓐ Ⓑ Ⓒ Ⓓ   5. Ⓐ Ⓑ Ⓒ Ⓓ
2. Ⓐ Ⓑ Ⓒ Ⓓ   4. Ⓐ Ⓑ Ⓒ Ⓓ   6. Ⓐ Ⓑ Ⓒ Ⓓ

Part 2: Question-Response

7. Ⓐ Ⓑ Ⓒ   14. Ⓐ Ⓑ Ⓒ   21. Ⓐ Ⓑ Ⓒ   28. Ⓐ Ⓑ Ⓒ
8. Ⓐ Ⓑ Ⓒ   15. Ⓐ Ⓑ Ⓒ   22. Ⓐ Ⓑ Ⓒ   29. Ⓐ Ⓑ Ⓒ
9. Ⓐ Ⓑ Ⓒ   16. Ⓐ Ⓑ Ⓒ   23. Ⓐ Ⓑ Ⓒ   30. Ⓐ Ⓑ Ⓒ
10. Ⓐ Ⓑ Ⓒ   17. Ⓐ Ⓑ Ⓒ   24. Ⓐ Ⓑ Ⓒ   31. Ⓐ Ⓑ Ⓒ
11. Ⓐ Ⓑ Ⓒ   18. Ⓐ Ⓑ Ⓒ   25. Ⓐ Ⓑ Ⓒ
12. Ⓐ Ⓑ Ⓒ   19. Ⓐ Ⓑ Ⓒ   26. Ⓐ Ⓑ Ⓒ
13. Ⓐ Ⓑ Ⓒ   20. Ⓐ Ⓑ Ⓒ   27. Ⓐ Ⓑ Ⓒ

Part 3: Conversations

32. Ⓐ Ⓑ Ⓒ Ⓓ   42. Ⓐ Ⓑ Ⓒ Ⓓ   52. Ⓐ Ⓑ Ⓒ Ⓓ   62. Ⓐ Ⓑ Ⓒ Ⓓ
33. Ⓐ Ⓑ Ⓒ Ⓓ   43. Ⓐ Ⓑ Ⓒ Ⓓ   53. Ⓐ Ⓑ Ⓒ Ⓓ   63. Ⓐ Ⓑ Ⓒ Ⓓ
34. Ⓐ Ⓑ Ⓒ Ⓓ   44. Ⓐ Ⓑ Ⓒ Ⓓ   54. Ⓐ Ⓑ Ⓒ Ⓓ   64. Ⓐ Ⓑ Ⓒ Ⓓ
35. Ⓐ Ⓑ Ⓒ Ⓓ   45. Ⓐ Ⓑ Ⓒ Ⓓ   55. Ⓐ Ⓑ Ⓒ Ⓓ   65. Ⓐ Ⓑ Ⓒ Ⓓ
36. Ⓐ Ⓑ Ⓒ Ⓓ   46. Ⓐ Ⓑ Ⓒ Ⓓ   56. Ⓐ Ⓑ Ⓒ Ⓓ   66. Ⓐ Ⓑ Ⓒ Ⓓ
37. Ⓐ Ⓑ Ⓒ Ⓓ   47. Ⓐ Ⓑ Ⓒ Ⓓ   57. Ⓐ Ⓑ Ⓒ Ⓓ   67. Ⓐ Ⓑ Ⓒ Ⓓ
38. Ⓐ Ⓑ Ⓒ Ⓓ   48. Ⓐ Ⓑ Ⓒ Ⓓ   58. Ⓐ Ⓑ Ⓒ Ⓓ   68. Ⓐ Ⓑ Ⓒ Ⓓ
39. Ⓐ Ⓑ Ⓒ Ⓓ   49. Ⓐ Ⓑ Ⓒ Ⓓ   59. Ⓐ Ⓑ Ⓒ Ⓓ   69. Ⓐ Ⓑ Ⓒ Ⓓ
40. Ⓐ Ⓑ Ⓒ Ⓓ   50. Ⓐ Ⓑ Ⓒ Ⓓ   60. Ⓐ Ⓑ Ⓒ Ⓓ   70. Ⓐ Ⓑ Ⓒ Ⓓ
41. Ⓐ Ⓑ Ⓒ Ⓓ   51. Ⓐ Ⓑ Ⓒ Ⓓ   61. Ⓐ Ⓑ Ⓒ Ⓓ

Part 4: Talks

71. Ⓐ Ⓑ Ⓒ Ⓓ   79. Ⓐ Ⓑ Ⓒ Ⓓ   87. Ⓐ Ⓑ Ⓒ Ⓓ   95. Ⓐ Ⓑ Ⓒ Ⓓ
72. Ⓐ Ⓑ Ⓒ Ⓓ   80. Ⓐ Ⓑ Ⓒ Ⓓ   88. Ⓐ Ⓑ Ⓒ Ⓓ   96. Ⓐ Ⓑ Ⓒ Ⓓ
73. Ⓐ Ⓑ Ⓒ Ⓓ   81. Ⓐ Ⓑ Ⓒ Ⓓ   89. Ⓐ Ⓑ Ⓒ Ⓓ   97. Ⓐ Ⓑ Ⓒ Ⓓ
74. Ⓐ Ⓑ Ⓒ Ⓓ   82. Ⓐ Ⓑ Ⓒ Ⓓ   90. Ⓐ Ⓑ Ⓒ Ⓓ   98. Ⓐ Ⓑ Ⓒ Ⓓ
75. Ⓐ Ⓑ Ⓒ Ⓓ   83. Ⓐ Ⓑ Ⓒ Ⓓ   91. Ⓐ Ⓑ Ⓒ Ⓓ   99. Ⓐ Ⓑ Ⓒ Ⓓ
76. Ⓐ Ⓑ Ⓒ Ⓓ   84. Ⓐ Ⓑ Ⓒ Ⓓ   92. Ⓐ Ⓑ Ⓒ Ⓓ   100. Ⓐ Ⓑ Ⓒ Ⓓ
77. Ⓐ Ⓑ Ⓒ Ⓓ   85. Ⓐ Ⓑ Ⓒ Ⓓ   93. Ⓐ Ⓑ Ⓒ Ⓓ
78. Ⓐ Ⓑ Ⓒ Ⓓ   86. Ⓐ Ⓑ Ⓒ Ⓓ   94. Ⓐ Ⓑ Ⓒ Ⓓ

ANSWER SHEET
Practice Test 1

READING

Part 5: Incomplete Sentences

101. Ⓐ Ⓑ Ⓒ Ⓓ	109. Ⓐ Ⓑ Ⓒ Ⓓ	117. Ⓐ Ⓑ Ⓒ Ⓓ	125. Ⓐ Ⓑ Ⓒ Ⓓ
102. Ⓐ Ⓑ Ⓒ Ⓓ	110. Ⓐ Ⓑ Ⓒ Ⓓ	118. Ⓐ Ⓑ Ⓒ Ⓓ	126. Ⓐ Ⓑ Ⓒ Ⓓ
103. Ⓐ Ⓑ Ⓒ Ⓓ	111. Ⓐ Ⓑ Ⓒ Ⓓ	119. Ⓐ Ⓑ Ⓒ Ⓓ	127. Ⓐ Ⓑ Ⓒ Ⓓ
104. Ⓐ Ⓑ Ⓒ Ⓓ	112. Ⓐ Ⓑ Ⓒ Ⓓ	120. Ⓐ Ⓑ Ⓒ Ⓓ	128. Ⓐ Ⓑ Ⓒ Ⓓ
105. Ⓐ Ⓑ Ⓒ Ⓓ	113. Ⓐ Ⓑ Ⓒ Ⓓ	121. Ⓐ Ⓑ Ⓒ Ⓓ	129. Ⓐ Ⓑ Ⓒ Ⓓ
106. Ⓐ Ⓑ Ⓒ Ⓓ	114. Ⓐ Ⓑ Ⓒ Ⓓ	122. Ⓐ Ⓑ Ⓒ Ⓓ	130. Ⓐ Ⓑ Ⓒ Ⓓ
107. Ⓐ Ⓑ Ⓒ Ⓓ	115. Ⓐ Ⓑ Ⓒ Ⓓ	123. Ⓐ Ⓑ Ⓒ Ⓓ	
108. Ⓐ Ⓑ Ⓒ Ⓓ	116. Ⓐ Ⓑ Ⓒ Ⓓ	124. Ⓐ Ⓑ Ⓒ Ⓓ	

Part 6: Text Completion

131. Ⓐ Ⓑ Ⓒ Ⓓ	135. Ⓐ Ⓑ Ⓒ Ⓓ	139. Ⓐ Ⓑ Ⓒ Ⓓ	143. Ⓐ Ⓑ Ⓒ Ⓓ
132. Ⓐ Ⓑ Ⓒ Ⓓ	136. Ⓐ Ⓑ Ⓒ Ⓓ	140. Ⓐ Ⓑ Ⓒ Ⓓ	144. Ⓐ Ⓑ Ⓒ Ⓓ
133. Ⓐ Ⓑ Ⓒ Ⓓ	137. Ⓐ Ⓑ Ⓒ Ⓓ	141. Ⓐ Ⓑ Ⓒ Ⓓ	145. Ⓐ Ⓑ Ⓒ Ⓓ
134. Ⓐ Ⓑ Ⓒ Ⓓ	138. Ⓐ Ⓑ Ⓒ Ⓓ	142. Ⓐ Ⓑ Ⓒ Ⓓ	146. Ⓐ Ⓑ Ⓒ Ⓓ

Part 7: Reading Comprehension

147. Ⓐ Ⓑ Ⓒ Ⓓ	161. Ⓐ Ⓑ Ⓒ Ⓓ	175. Ⓐ Ⓑ Ⓒ Ⓓ	189. Ⓐ Ⓑ Ⓒ Ⓓ
148. Ⓐ Ⓑ Ⓒ Ⓓ	162. Ⓐ Ⓑ Ⓒ Ⓓ	176. Ⓐ Ⓑ Ⓒ Ⓓ	190. Ⓐ Ⓑ Ⓒ Ⓓ
149. Ⓐ Ⓑ Ⓒ Ⓓ	163. Ⓐ Ⓑ Ⓒ Ⓓ	177. Ⓐ Ⓑ Ⓒ Ⓓ	191. Ⓐ Ⓑ Ⓒ Ⓓ
150. Ⓐ Ⓑ Ⓒ Ⓓ	164. Ⓐ Ⓑ Ⓒ Ⓓ	178. Ⓐ Ⓑ Ⓒ Ⓓ	192. Ⓐ Ⓑ Ⓒ Ⓓ
151. Ⓐ Ⓑ Ⓒ Ⓓ	165. Ⓐ Ⓑ Ⓒ Ⓓ	179. Ⓐ Ⓑ Ⓒ Ⓓ	193. Ⓐ Ⓑ Ⓒ Ⓓ
152. Ⓐ Ⓑ Ⓒ Ⓓ	166. Ⓐ Ⓑ Ⓒ Ⓓ	180. Ⓐ Ⓑ Ⓒ Ⓓ	194. Ⓐ Ⓑ Ⓒ Ⓓ
153. Ⓐ Ⓑ Ⓒ Ⓓ	167. Ⓐ Ⓑ Ⓒ Ⓓ	181. Ⓐ Ⓑ Ⓒ Ⓓ	195. Ⓐ Ⓑ Ⓒ Ⓓ
154. Ⓐ Ⓑ Ⓒ Ⓓ	168. Ⓐ Ⓑ Ⓒ Ⓓ	182. Ⓐ Ⓑ Ⓒ Ⓓ	196. Ⓐ Ⓑ Ⓒ Ⓓ
155. Ⓐ Ⓑ Ⓒ Ⓓ	169. Ⓐ Ⓑ Ⓒ Ⓓ	183. Ⓐ Ⓑ Ⓒ Ⓓ	197. Ⓐ Ⓑ Ⓒ Ⓓ
156. Ⓐ Ⓑ Ⓒ Ⓓ	170. Ⓐ Ⓑ Ⓒ Ⓓ	184. Ⓐ Ⓑ Ⓒ Ⓓ	198. Ⓐ Ⓑ Ⓒ Ⓓ
157. Ⓐ Ⓑ Ⓒ Ⓓ	171. Ⓐ Ⓑ Ⓒ Ⓓ	185. Ⓐ Ⓑ Ⓒ Ⓓ	199. Ⓐ Ⓑ Ⓒ Ⓓ
158. Ⓐ Ⓑ Ⓒ Ⓓ	172. Ⓐ Ⓑ Ⓒ Ⓓ	186. Ⓐ Ⓑ Ⓒ Ⓓ	200. Ⓐ Ⓑ Ⓒ Ⓓ
159. Ⓐ Ⓑ Ⓒ Ⓓ	173. Ⓐ Ⓑ Ⓒ Ⓓ	187. Ⓐ Ⓑ Ⓒ Ⓓ	
160. Ⓐ Ⓑ Ⓒ Ⓓ	174. Ⓐ Ⓑ Ⓒ Ⓓ	188. Ⓐ Ⓑ Ⓒ Ⓓ	

Practice Test 1

LISTENING COMPREHENSION

In this section of the test, you will have the chance to show how well you understand spoken English. There are four parts to this section, with special directions for each part. You will have approximately 45 minutes to complete the Listening Comprehension sections.

Part 1: Photographs

Track 35

Directions: You will see a photograph. You will hear four statements about the photograph. Choose the statement that most closely matches the photograph, and fill in the corresponding oval on your answer sheet.

1.

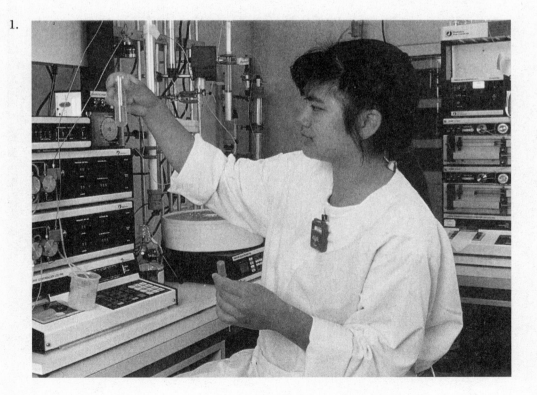

2.

3.

4.

5.

6.

Part 2: Question-Response

Track 36

Directions: You will hear a question and three possible responses. Choose the response that most closely answers the question, and fill in the corresponding oval on your answer sheet.

7. Mark your answer on your answer sheet.

8. Mark your answer on your answer sheet.

9. Mark your answer on your answer sheet.

10. Mark your answer on your answer sheet.

11. Mark your answer on your answer sheet.

12. Mark your answer on your answer sheet.

13. Mark your answer on your answer sheet.

14. Mark your answer on your answer sheet.

15. Mark your answer on your answer sheet.

16. Mark your answer on your answer sheet.

17. Mark your answer on your answer sheet.

18. Mark your answer on your answer sheet.

19. Mark your answer on your answer sheet.

20. Mark your answer on your answer sheet.

21. Mark your answer on your answer sheet.

22. Mark your answer on your answer sheet.

23. Mark your answer on your answer sheet.

24. Mark your answer on your answer sheet.

25. Mark your answer on your answer sheet.

26. Mark your answer on your answer sheet.

27. Mark your answer on your answer sheet.

28. Mark your answer on your answer sheet.

29. Mark your answer on your answer sheet.

30. Mark your answer on your answer sheet.

31. Mark your answer on your answer sheet.

Part 3: Conversations

Directions: You will hear a conversation between two or more people. You will see three questions on each conversation and four possible answers. Choose the best answer to each question, and fill in the corresponding oval on your answer sheet.

32. When will the speakers meet?

   (A) Before lunch
   (B) At 2:00
   (C) After the conference
   (D) Tomorrow

33. Where will they meet?

   (A) At the bus stop
   (B) Downstairs
   (C) In the man's office
   (D) In the waiting room

34. What will the woman bring to the meeting?

   (A) Coffee
   (B) A letter
   (C) Photographs
   (D) Copies of a report

35. What does the man want to do?

   (A) Sell his apartment
   (B) Rent an apartment
   (C) Clean his apartment
   (D) Remodel his apartment

36. What does the woman imply about downtown apartments?

   (A) They cost more than other apartments.
   (B) There aren't many available right now.
   (C) Few people want to rent them.
   (D) They are not very large.

37. What does the woman suggest the man do?

   (A) Meet her at the library
   (B) Call back later
   (C) Look online
   (D) Visit her office

38. Where does this conversation take place?

   (A) At a store
   (B) At a hotel
   (C) At a restaurant
   (D) At the man's house

39. What does the man ask for?

   (A) Keys
   (B) More soup
   (C) A better room
   (D) Towels and soap

40. What does the woman mean when she says, "Not a bit"?

   (A) She does not mind helping the man.
   (B) She does not like her job.
   (C) She does not have what the man asked for.
   (D) She does not have time to help the man right now.

41. When did the brochures arrive?

   (A) Yesterday afternoon
   (B) Last night
   (C) This morning
   (D) This afternoon

42. What will Mary do now?

   (A) Prepare the address labels
   (B) Work on a presentation
   (C) Read the brochures
   (D) Call the printer

43. What does Jim offer to do?

   (A) Take the brochures to the post office
   (B) Drive Mary to her home
   (C) Look up some addresses
   (D) Phone customers

44. What kind of job is the man probably applying for?

(A) Waiter
(B) Chef
(C) Newspaper editor
(D) Advertising executive

45. What does the woman ask the man about?

(A) His work experience
(B) His education
(C) His food preferences
(D) His salary requirements

46. What does the man want to know?

(A) The exact job title
(B) The start date of the job
(C) The woman's address
(D) The name of the woman's company

47. Why can't the man play golf tomorrow?

(A) His wife is sick.
(B) It's going to rain.
(C) He has to take a test.
(D) He's feeling tired.

48. What does the man mean when he says, "What a bore"?

(A) He does not like making phone calls.
(B) He is looking for some entertainment.
(C) He is sorry that he has to cancel the golf game.
(D) He thinks golf is not an interesting game.

49. What will he do tomorrow?

(A) Talk on the phone
(B) Go to the movies
(C) Move some furniture
(D) Stay home

50. Where does the woman want to go?

(A) To a fast food restaurant
(B) To a parking lot
(C) To a bank
(D) To a park

51. Where is this place located?

(A) On a corner
(B) Behind a parking lot
(C) Next door to a library
(D) Across the street from a store

52. What does the man say about this place?

(A) The woman will not be able to park there.
(B) Most people are not familiar with it.
(C) It is not very far away.
(D) It may be difficult to find.

53. What does Jane imply about Sam?

(A) He does not like to wait.
(B) He is not a good driver.
(C) He is a hard worker.
(D) He is usually late.

54. How did Sam get to work this morning?

(A) By bus
(B) On foot
(C) In a carpool
(D) By subway

55. What will Sam do next time?

(A) Stay home
(B) Drive his car
(C) Leave earlier
(D) Take the train

56. What is probably the purpose of the woman's trip?

(A) To visit family
(B) To take a class
(C) To interview for a job
(D) To meet with business colleagues

57. What does the man say about the trip?

(A) It is expensive.
(B) It is too long.
(C) It will be fun.
(D) It will be uncomfortable.

58. How will the woman pay for the trip?

(A) Cash
(B) Check
(C) Credit card
(D) Money order

59. Where is Joe?

(A) Away on a business trip
(B) In the break room
(C) In his office
(D) At the airport

60. What does the woman want Joe to do?

(A) Write a check
(B) Look at a report
(C) Meet her for lunch
(D) Make photocopies

61. When will Joe return?

(A) Later this afternoon
(B) Tomorrow
(C) At 10:00
(D) By 12:00

62. Why doesn't the woman want to eat at the cafeteria?

(A) She does not like the food.
(B) She does not have time.
(C) It is too expensive.
(D) It is too far away.

63. What does the woman ask the man to do for her?

(A) Bring her a sandwich
(B) Mail a package
(C) Pick up her mail
(D) Go to the mall

64. What will the man do after lunch?

(A) Take a walk
(B) Meet with a client
(C) Go to his apartment
(D) Go to a doctor appointment

65. What does the woman plan to do tomorrow morning?

(A) Go shopping
(B) Look for work
(C) Plan a vacation
(D) Attend a workshop

66. Who is George, most likely?

(A) A travel agent
(B) A workshop presenter
(C) The woman's assistant
(D) The woman's husband

67. Look at the graphic. What time will the woman take the train?

(A) 10:20
(B) 11:20
(C) 11:55
(D) 1:55

Trains to Brookfield

Lv.	Arr.
10:20	12:40
11:20	1:40
11:55	2:15
1:55	4:15

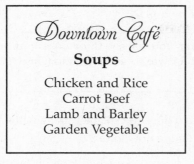

Downtown Café

Soups

Chicken and Rice
Carrot Beef
Lamb and Barley
Garden Vegetable

68. What does the man say about the café?

(A) It is new.
(B) It is small.
(C) It is popular.
(D) It is well known.

69. Look at the graphic. Which soup will the woman order?

(A) Chicken and Rice
(B) Carrot Beef
(C) Lamb and Barley
(D) Garden Vegetable

70. Where does the man want to eat his lunch?

(A) Inside the café
(B) On the patio
(C) At his office
(D) At the park

Part 4: Talks

Directions: You will hear a talk given by a single speaker. You will see three questions on each talk, each with four possible answers. Choose the best answer to each question, and fill in the corresponding oval on your answer sheet.

71. Where is this train located?

    (A) In an airport
    (B) In a city
    (C) Along the coast
    (D) At an amusement park

72. Where should passengers stand when in a train car?

    (A) By the doors
    (B) By the windows
    (C) In the center
    (D) At either end

73. When can passengers get off the train?

    (A) When they see an exit sign
    (B) Before the bell rings
    (C) After the bell rings
    (D) After the colored light goes on

---

74. When on Sundays is the museum open?

    (A) In the morning
    (B) In the afternoon
    (C) In the evening
    (D) All day

75. What is the lecture series probably about?

    (A) Sculpture
    (B) Museum administration
    (C) Local history
    (D) How to photograph art

76. Who doesn't have to pay to enter the museum?

    (A) Members
    (B) Adults over 65
    (C) Children under twelve
    (D) Children under five

77. What does the speaker mean when he says, "You are not alone"?

    (A) Some people work better by themselves.
    (B) Most people need help to solve problems.
    (C) Lonely people often have trouble with organization.
    (D) Many people have difficulty organizing their day.

78. What is the first step in getting organized?

    (A) Set a timeline
    (B) Get clutter out of your life
    (C) Buy a calendar
    (D) Make a list of things to be done

79. What is the last task of the day?

    (A) Review the list
    (B) Finish uncompleted tasks
    (C) Write a new list
    (D) Throw the list away

---

80. What is being advertised?

    (A) A new learning system
    (B) A job for professional teachers
    (C) An opportunity to help children
    (D) A special training program

81. What are listeners asked to do?

    (A) Fill out an application
    (B) Visit an office
    (C) Contact a school
    (D) Complete their schoolwork

82. What must people have to participate?

   (A) A college degree
   (B) Special training
   (C) Age of at least 18
   (D) Experience with children

83. What does the speaker imply when she says, ". . . it's about time"?

   (A) The weather report will be longer than usual.
   (B) The weather depends on the time of day.
   (C) The weather has been bad for a while.
   (D) The weather is nicer at this time of year.

84. What does the speaker suggest?

   (A) Stay inside
   (B) Go outdoors
   (C) Take sunglasses
   (D) Wear a sweater

85. What will the weather be like tomorrow?

   (A) Cloudy
   (B) Foggy
   (C) Rainy
   (D) Sunny

86. Why did the speaker make the call?

   (A) To inquire about ski lessons
   (B) To make a hotel reservation
   (C) To reserve a pair of rental skis
   (D) To find out the snow conditions

87. How does the speaker plan to get to the hotel?

   (A) By bus
   (B) By car
   (C) By train
   (D) By plane

88. What does the speaker imply about the hotel?

   (A) He often recommends it to his friends.
   (B) It is more expensive than other hotels.
   (C) He has never been there before.
   (D) It is in a popular area.

89. What are Greenville residents complaining about?

   (A) A new mall
   (B) The cost of living
   (C) Traffic regulations
   (D) A construction delay

90. Where are they making their complaint?

   (A) On neighborhood streets
   (B) In the newspaper
   (C) On TV
   (D) At City Hall

91. What will the mayor do later this week?

   (A) Visit the construction site
   (B) Meet with protesters
   (C) Announce new plans
   (D) Go shopping

92. When is this talk happening?

   (A) At the end of class
   (B) In the middle of class
   (C) At the beginning of class
   (D) Before class starts

93. What should students do before the next class?

   (A) Take a test
   (B) Read a chapter
   (C) Talk to Dr. Lyons
   (D) Answer a question

94. What kind of class is this, most likely?

   (A) Photography
   (B) Museum studies
   (C) Mathematics
   (D) Drawing

The Coleman Company

Prices

1 room	$50
2–3 rooms	$75
4 rooms	$100
5+ rooms	$125

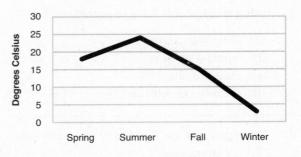

95. What kind of business is the Coleman Company, most likely?

(A) House painters
(B) Carpet installers
(C) Furniture sales
(D) House cleaners

96. Look at the graphic. How much will the speaker pay for Coleman's services?

(A) $50
(B) $75
(C) $100
(D) $125

97. What does the speaker plan to do with her apartment?

(A) Sell it
(B) Live in it
(C) Rent it out
(D) Redecorate it

98. What kind of business is being discussed?

(A) Hotel
(B) Travel agency
(C) Advertising agency
(D) Swimming equipment

99. Look at the graphic. At what time of year is the company busiest?

(A) Spring
(B) Summer
(C) Winter
(D) Fall

100. What are listeners asked to do next?

(A) Create a slide
(B) Ask questions
(C) Write something
(D) Talk with a partner

This is the end of the Listening Comprehension portion of the test. Turn to Part 5 in your test book.

READING

In this section of the test, you will have the chance to show how well you understand written English. There are three parts to this section, with special directions for each part.

**YOU WILL HAVE ONE HOUR AND FIFTEEN MINUTES
TO COMPLETE PARTS 5, 6, AND 7 OF THE TEST.**

Part 5: Incomplete Sentences

> **Directions:** You will see a sentence with a missing word. Four possible answers follow the sentence. Choose the best answer to the question, and fill in the corresponding oval on your answer sheet.

101. If the customer _____ not satisfied, please have him call the manager.

    (A) am
    (B) is
    (C) are
    (D) be

102. We _____ him to think things over carefully before agreeing to accept the new position.

    (A) recommended
    (B) suggested
    (C) proposed
    (D) advised

103. Our boss plans to _____ a party in her home for several staff members who will retire this year.

    (A) entertain
    (B) invite
    (C) host
    (D) guest

104. The seminar was canceled because the invitations were not _____ in time.

    (A) printer
    (B) printed
    (C) printing
    (D) print

105. If the waiter cannot handle your request, the captain _____ assist you.

    (A) will
    (B) has
    (C) did
    (D) is

106. Mr. Wong has been recognized by the local business community for his knowledge and _____.

    (A) leading
    (B) lead
    (C) leadership
    (D) leader

107. According to the most recent figures, our costs are expected to _____ by about five percent this year.

    (A) ascend
    (B) increase
    (C) escalate
    (D) raise

108. Any good business manager will tell you that _____ is the key to efficiency.

    (A) organized
    (B) organize
    (C) organizer
    (D) organization

109. They had to postpone the meeting with the client _____ Mr. Tan's plane was late.

    (A) although
    (B) while
    (C) because
    (D) with

110. Any information that a client provides us with will be kept completely _____ and not shared with anyone outside the office.

    (A) considerable
    (B) confidential
    (C) constructed
    (D) conferred

111. By the time Mr. Sato _____ in San Diego, the convention will have already begun.

    (A) arrives
    (B) arrived
    (C) has arrived
    (D) will arrive

112. Because Ms. Kimura has a long _____, she will always leave work at 5:30.

    (A) commute
    (B) commune
    (C) community
    (D) compost

113. You'll find the restaurant on the next block, _____ the bank and the bookstore.

    (A) among
    (B) outside
    (C) between
    (D) through

114. We hope to begin interviewing _____ applicants by the end of next week.

    (A) job
    (B) occupation
    (C) chore
    (D) positioning

115. When you need supplies, _____ a request with the office manager.

    (A) filling
    (B) fell
    (C) fallen
    (D) file

116. All cabin attendants must lock the cabin door _____ leaving the room.

    (A) afterwards
    (B) after
    (C) later than
    (D) late

117. _____ it was Mr. Guiton's birthday, his staff took him to lunch.

    (A) Although
    (B) During
    (C) Because
    (D) That

118. In order to respect our guests' privacy, employees at the Palms Hotel are _____ to knock before entering rooms for any reason.

    (A) requited
    (B) required
    (C) requisite
    (D) repulsed

119. The billing clerk was not able to find the invoice _____ the order.

    (A) or
    (B) and
    (C) but
    (D) though

120. Before he wrote the check, Jim visited his bank's website to find out his account _____.

    (A) size
    (B) money
    (C) supply
    (D) balance

121. Please forward a copy of the report to Mr. Maxwell as soon as it becomes _____.

    (A) avail
    (B) available
    (C) availability
    (D) availing

122. The bell captain suggested that more porters _____ hired.

    (A) are
    (B) have
    (C) be
    (D) do

123. The _____ parking spaces for company employees are located on the first level of the parking garage.

    (A) signed
    (B) assignment
    (C) assigned
    (D) significant

124. You'll find all the association members listed in the directory in _____ order.

    (A) alphabet
    (B) alphabetize
    (C) alphabetically
    (D) alphabetical

125. Raymond has been working on that account for just a few days, but he is _____ completely familiar with the client's background.

    (A) yet
    (B) since
    (C) already
    (D) soon

126. Everyone seeking entry to the premises must _____ an identification card to the security guard.

    (A) showed
    (B) showing
    (C) shows
    (D) show

127. According to several studies, _____ tasks often lead to muscular fatigue and injury.

    (A) repeat
    (B) repetitive
    (C) repetition
    (D) repetitively

128. Visitors are reminded _____ name tags at all times.

    (A) to wear
    (B) wear
    (C) be worn
    (D) is wearing

129. The position in the publicity department requires knowledge of foreign languages and _____ experience with international clients.

    (A) exciting
    (B) expectant
    (C) exquisite
    (D) extensive

130. The factory's policy is that visitors are _____ allowed to enter the manufacturing area without hard hats, for safety reasons.

    (A) rare
    (B) ever
    (C) never
    (D) no time

Part 6: Text Completion

> **Directions:** You will see four passages, each with four blanks. Each blank has four answer choices. For each blank, choose the word, phrase, or sentence that best completes the passage.

Questions 131–134 refer to the following notice.

International Airport Policy Regarding Security and Baggage

In accordance with international security regulations, passengers are not _____ to take the following items onto a plane, either in carry-on
131
bags or in checked luggage: weapons of any kind, dynamite, or fireworks.

The following items may be placed in checked luggage but not in carry-on bags: Tools, including hammers, screwdrivers, and wrenches; sports equipment _____ golf clubs, baseball bats, and skis and ski poles.
132
When you pass through the _____ line, all bags will go through our X-ray
133
machines. _____.
134
Thank you for your cooperation. Have a safe and pleasant flight.

---

131. (A) permitted
     (B) permitting
     (C) permits
     (D) permission

132. (A) so
     (B) such as
     (C) example
     (D) instance

133. (A) ticket
     (B) arrival
     (C) security
     (D) reservations

134. (A) These machines are delicate and very costly
     (B) Check with your airline about size limits for bags
     (C) Most airlines allow just one carry-on bag per person
     (D) Some bags will be manually checked by personnel, as well

This holiday season, computer retailers hope to increase sales of tablet computers. A heavy advertising campaign began this week, with several computer _____ placing ads on TV, radio, newspapers, and the Internet. The advertising campaign will continue through the holiday season.
135

Tablet computers are gaining popularity because of their _____. Because they are lighter and smaller than laptops, they are much easier to carry around and are filling a growing need for mobility. _____.
136
137

The trend toward giving electronic items as holiday gifts is also growing. The old-fashioned approach to holiday celebrations is giving way to the _____ for new technology.
138

135. (A) manufacturers
(B) purchasers
(C) consumers
(D) trainers

136. (A) fame
(B) quantity
(C) appearance
(D) convenience

137. (A) Some people find them difficult to use because of the small screens
(B) An additional benefit is that they cost less than most laptops
(C) Laptops continue to be popular, however, in many areas
(D) They can be connected to keyboards and printers

138. (A) enthusiast
(B) enthusiasm
(C) enthusiastic
(D) enthusiastically

To: Marguerite Michelson
From: Ambar Patel
Date: September 22, 20—
Subject: Money due

I am writing in regard to _____ payment. We sent an invoice in July but
           139
still have not received a check. _____. If we don't hear from you soon
                                140
regarding this payment, we _____ to take action. Please contact me
                           141
by phone before the end of the week, so we can discuss how best to
resolve this matter. The details of your _____, including items and prices,
                                         142
are attached.

139. (A) a remitted
     (B) an overdue
     (C) a transferrable
     (D) an enclosed

140. (A) Payment by credit card is also
         acceptable
     (B) We hope you were satisfied with
         our services
     (C) Please be sure to make the check
         out in the correct amount
     (D) Our phone messages inquiring
         about the reason for the delay
         have not been answered

141. (A) will have
     (B) have had
     (C) would have
     (D) going to have

142. (A) form
     (B) credit
     (C) order
     (D) rebate

Questions 143–146 refer to the following e-mail.

From: Andrew Devon
Subject: Office Manager Position
Date: April 1
To: Richard Byron

Dear Mr. Byron,

I am contacting you in ____ to the job posted on your company's website
                        143

for an office manager. ____. I feel that I thoroughly understand the opera-
                       144

tions of an office, and that my years of experience ____ me to work as
                                                    145

an office manager. I have good organizational and people skills, and I am

familiar with most current office technology. I am also a responsible and

reliable worker. I am enclosing my resume and two letters of reference.

I look forward ____ hearing from you.
               146

Sincerely,

Andrew Devon

143. (A) response
     (B) repose
     (C) resort
     (D) respite

144. (A) Office managers are essential to the smooth
         running of an office
     (B) As part of my job search, I look at job listings
         on the Internet almost daily
     (C) I would be interested in knowing more
         about the duties of an office manager at your
         company
     (D) I have worked as an administrative assistant at
         a local company for the past ten years

145. (A) qualify
     (B) qualifies
     (C) is qualifying
     (D) has qualified

146. (A) at
     (B) of
     (C) to
     (D) on

Part 7: Reading Comprehension

> **Directions:** You will see single and multiple reading passages followed by several questions. Each question has four answer choices. Choose the best answer to the question, and fill in the corresponding oval on your answer sheet.

Questions 147–148 refer to the following invoice.

Cooper & Allen, Architects
149 Bridge Street, Suite 107
Harrisville, Colorado 76521

April 5, 20__
INVOICE NUMBER _3892_
PROJECT NAME _ Headquarters—Final Design_
PROJECT NUMBER _925639_

The Williams Corporation
5110 Falls Avenue
Thomaston, Colorado 76520

The following amounts for the period ending March 30 are due the end of this month.

Current period fees___$8,200.00_
Unpaid prior balance___$362.00_
Total due at this time_$8,562.00_

We value the opportunity to service you. Your prompt payment is greatly appreciated.

147. When is the payment due?

(A) March 1
(B) March 30
(C) April 5
(D) April 30

148. What is owed in addition to current fees?

(A) Prepayment on the next project
(B) Taxes on the current fees
(C) Service charges on current fees
(D) Money not paid on a previous invoice

Questions 149–150 refer to the following notice.

The company provides a pension plan covering all employees with a minimum of five years of service at the company. Payments are based on years of service and the highest salary level reached. Both the company and the employee make contributions to the plan monthly, the amount determined by government regulations. Pension payments are made bimonthly.

149. What is the notice about?

(A) A job promotion plan
(B) A retirement benefit
(C) A loan program
(D) A salary scale

150. Who is eligible to participate?

(A) Employees with at least five years at the company
(B) Employees earning a certain salary level
(C) Government employees only
(D) Any company employee

Questions 151–152 refer to the following text message chain.

SAM CHAN	9:10
Where are you? We're about to go into the meeting.	
PAT LOPEZ	9:11
Sorry. I'm stuck on the train.	
SAM CHAN	9:13
Where?	
PAT LOPEZ	9:14
We just left Middlebury. Apparently there was an accident near the bridge. All the trains are running late.	
PAT LOPEZ	1:16
I made sure to leave home early, but that didn't help.	
SAM CHAN	1:17
The client is already here.	
PAT LOPEZ	1:18
Go ahead and start without me. I should be there in 30 minutes.	
SAM CHAN	1:20
I'd rather not present the proposal alone.	
PAT LOPEZ	1:21
You'll do fine. Just start with the slide show.	
SAM CHAN	1:22
OK. But hurry. We really want to please this client. It's one of our biggest accounts.	
PAT LOPEZ	1:23
You're telling me! I'll be there soon.	

151. Why is Ms. Lopez late for the meeting?

(A) Sam didn't remind her about the meeting.
(B) She didn't leave home on time.
(C) The train has been delayed.
(D) She took the wrong train.

152. At 1:23, what does Ms. Lopez mean when she writes, "You're telling me!"?

(A) She understands how important the client is.
(B) She doesn't know what to say to the client.
(C) She doesn't like Sam to give her orders.
(D) She wants Sam to tell her what to do.

We're changing our name! We are excited to announce that effective December 5, 20--, our official name will be:

GREEN MILES WEST

The substitution of "West" in our name—replacing "California"—is the result of an agreement we reached with the California Gardening Association, following a protest over the original use of "California" in our name.

We hope this does not create any confusion among our loyal consumers. While this represents a change from our initial name introduction, it does not change the quality of products we offer our customers.

153. What was the original name of the company?

(A) Miles West
(B) Green Miles California
(C) Green Miles West
(D) Green California

154. According to the announcement, why was the name changed?

(A) The corporate offices were relocated.
(B) There was a conflict with another organization.
(C) They did not like the initial choice.
(D) Loyal consumers were confused.

Questions 155–157 refer to the following webpage.

www.palmfrondsresort.com

File Edit View Favorites Tools Help   Page ▾ Safety ▾ Tools ▾

| HOME | ABOUT | ROOMS | ACTIVITIES | FAQ |

Palm Fronds Resort

The Palm Fronds Resort is pleased to welcome you and your entire family to a relaxing, fun-filled vacation with us. We offer spacious, comfortable rooms, fine dining, and a private beach. You can enjoy a range of beach and water sports, or just relax and enjoy the peace and quiet away from the hustle and bustle of the city.

Our all-inclusive vacation package for groups of up to four people includes

❖ An elegant two-room suite that sleeps four comfortably
❖ Breakfast and dinner daily
❖ Beach access
❖ Pool access

We offer on-site equipment rental for snorkeling, scuba diving, surfing, and tennis. **Click here** for prices.

Our world-class instructors are available for private and group lessons. **Click here** for fee schedule.

How to get here

The nearest airport is located on the mainland in Palm City. From there, you can take a shuttle or taxi to the ferry dock. **Click here** for ferry schedules.

155. Where is the Palm Fronds Resort probably located?

(A) In a city
(B) On an island
(C) Next to an airport
(D) On a mountain

156. What is included in the vacation package?

(A) Transportation from the airport
(B) Swimming lessons
(C) Two meals a day
(D) Sports equipment

157. Which one of the following activities can guests do at the resort?

(A) Go fishing
(B) Rent a bicycle
(C) Go swimming
(D) Take cooking lessons

Questions 158–160 refer to the following e-mail.

From: Alan Scheider
To: All Staff
Subj: Answering your questions
Date: September 2

Everyday my inbox is full of messages concerning the transfer to the Paris office. Rather than responding to each of you individually, I am explaining the process here. Please follow the directions below and do not omit anything. And please refrain from asking me more questions. Everything you need to know is explained below.

- Pack all items in and on your desk in boxes.
- Label all boxes clearly with your name and department.
- Notify maintenance to clean your desk so it will be ready for the next occupant.
- Change the outgoing message in your voicemail to notify clients of your transfer.
- Provide the network manager with your old password and computer ID number.
- Notify clients by e-mail of your new location and contact information.

Packing supplies are available for your use. Please ask Ms. Quimby for any supplies you need.

Thank you for your cooperation.
Alan

158.   What is the purpose of the e-mail?

(A)   To propose procedures for layoffs
(B)   To announce the opening of a Paris office
(C)   To give instructions for preparing to move
(D)   To suggest ways to improve workspace organization

159.   What are the e-mail recipients asked to do?

(A)   Buy their own packing supplies
(B)   Complete every one of the steps
(C)   E-mail their questions to Mr. Scheider
(D)   Help colleagues pack up their workspaces

160.   What should each employee do for the person who will use his desk next?

(A)   Move boxes to the edge of the room
(B)   Notify clients of the new occupant
(C)   Get a computer password
(D)   Have the desk cleaned

MEETINGS

People often feel that staff meetings are a waste of time. However, by keeping the following points in mind, you can make sure your meetings run smoothly and use time well. Every meeting should have an agenda. –[1]– This seems obvious, and yet it is a detail so often overlooked. Think about what items need to be covered and how much time should be allocated to each. Make sure everyone has a copy, so they know what to expect. –[2]– As each item is discussed, keep the conversation moving. Thank each speaker for her ideas, then move on to the next speaker. –[3]– This encourages people to keep their remarks brief. When the time allocated for a specific item has passed, move the discussion on to the next item. –[4]– Your staff will feel that their time has been used well. They will return to work with fresh ideas and energy.

---

161. What is this article mostly about?

(A) How to run a meeting efficiently
(B) Different formats for staff meetings
(C) Reasons for having regular staff meetings
(D) Ways to make a meeting more interesting

162. What is said about speaking in a meeting?

(A) People should be allowed to comment as often as they like.
(B) Everyone should be encouraged to make comments.
(C) Comments should be about agenda items only.
(D) People should keep their comments short.

163. In which of the following positions marked [1], [2], [3], and [4] does the following sentence best belong?

"By keeping on schedule, you can ensure that the meeting will end on time."

(A) [1]
(B) [2]
(C) [3]
(D) [4]

Silvia Prieto [1:15]
I just had a phone call from the caterers. Since we want lunch to start at 12:00, they want to start setting up at 11:00.

George Croft [1:16]
That shouldn't be a problem. They can set up in the large conference room. The trainers said the other conference room would work for them.

Marcella Lu [1:17]
Has anyone reserved the conference rooms yet?

George Croft [1:18]
Yes. I did that yesterday. It's all set.

Marcella Lu [1:19]
And the tables and chairs? The projector?

George Croft [1:21]
I've taken care of everything.

Silvia Prieto [1:22]
I also received an e-mail from the trainers this morning with some documents attached. They want each participant to have copies for the morning session.

Marcella Lu [1:23]
I can take care of that. Do we know yet how many of the staff have signed up?

George Croft [1:25]
I have the sign up sheet. Twenty. It's full.

Marcella Lu [1:26]
Fantastic. I'll take care of those copies now. You arranged for enough chairs, right? George?

George Croft [1:27]
Relax. I have it all under control.

164. What kind of event are the chatters organizing, most likely?

(A) An awards banquet
(B) A weekly staff meeting
(C) An association conference
(D) A professional development workshop

165. What did Ms. Prieto do a few minutes ago?

(A) She spoke with the caterers.
(B) She sent an e-mail to the trainers.
(C) She reserved the conference rooms.
(D) She created some documents.

166. What will Ms. Lu probably do next?

(A) Count the participants
(B) Go to George's office
(C) Make photocopies
(D) Arrange the chairs

167. At 1:27, what does Mr. Croft mean when he writes, "Relax"?

(A) Ms. Lu should take a break.
(B) Ms. Lu can sit in the chairs.
(C) Ms. Lu has no need to worry.
(D) Ms. Lu's job is not very hard.

–[1]– ABC Foods Corporation has reported that it is planning to raise prices by an average of 3 percent on 19 different brands of fruit cakes, pies, and other fruit-based sweets. –[2]– The company claims that this is the result of higher fruit prices resulting from the combination of a late freeze and a long drought last spring.

ABC Foods Corporation products with the higher prices will hit the supermarket shelves early next month. Other companies are expected to follow suit and raise prices on their canned fruit and vegetable products by the end of the year. –[3]– Consumers can expect to feel the effects in their pocketbooks throughout the winter.

–[4]– "We can only hope that the weather will improve in the next growing season," said Louella Pearson, president of Consumers United. "If not, and if prices continue to rise, some families will really suffer," she added.

PRACTICE TEST 1

168. On which ABC food products will prices rise?

(A) Canned vegetables
(B) All brands of food
(C) Jams and jellies
(D) Fruit desserts

169. What is the cause of the rise in price of fruit?

(A) Poor growing conditions
(B) Increased consumer spending
(C) Competition from other companies
(D) Demand for more money by farmers

170. What will probably happen before next year?

(A) The weather will improve.
(B) There will be more price increases.
(C) Consumers will demand more fruit.
(D) More varieties of canned products will be available.

171. In which of the following positions marked [1], [2], [3], and [4] does the following sentence best belong?

"This is the second increase by ABC Foods this year."

(A) [1]
(B) [2]
(C) [3]
(D) [4]

Many hotels these days are changing their wasteful habits. For example, it is not unusual for hotel guests to find shampoo in glass dispensers instead of plastic bottles, or for hotels to encourage guests to use towels and sheets more than once before they are washed.

And it is not just the hotels. It is often the tourists themselves who seek out a "greener" way to vacation. The business of eco-tours—guided vacations with an environmental focus—is growing exponentially. Expeditions to the Amazon rainforest and similar places where participants learn about environmental issues are growing in popularity. Such trips may include lectures on the area's natural wonders, an opportunity to help scientists in the field, or a project to clean up a natural area.

Participants on these trips already have a high level of environmental awareness. A study of litter in Antarctica found that the entire collection of litter left by visitors over a two-year period could fit into one small plastic sandwich bag. Compare that amount of litter with what is usually found on the streets around most hotels.

Hotel owners and managers would be wise to pay attention to this trend. The green movement is growing everywhere. Something as simple as placing bottle recycling bins in rooms can be enough to attract the interest of environmentally conscious guests, and you'll be helping to save the planet at the same time. It's a win-win.

172. What is this article mainly about?

   (A) Ways to reduce waste
   (B) A popular type of tour
   (C) A trend in the travel industry
   (D) How to advertise a travel business

173. According to the article, what is something travelers might do on an eco-tour?

   (A) Teach a class
   (B) Build something
   (C) Assist researchers
   (D) Camp in a natural setting

174. What is indicated about travelers to Antarctica?

   (A) They enjoy collecting things.
   (B) They rarely leave behind trash.
   (C) They prefer not to use plastic bags.
   (D) They complain about the mess in their hotels.

175. What is suggested that hotel owners do?

   (A) Provide a way for guests to recycle bottles
   (B) Use glass shampoo dispensers
   (C) Paint their guest rooms green
   (D) Relocate to the rainforest

Questions 176–180 refer to the following e-mail and graph.

To: v.goldsmith@placeco.com
From: gpmills@temppower.com
Subject: Your Career
Att: Temp Power Employment Graph

Dear Vanessa,

Thank you for attending this past week's complimentary workshop, Secretary 101 Skills, where you learned important career skills. If you're looking for a job, we want to help you. Temp Power prides itself on staffing our city's offices with top-notch administrative professionals, and we line our team up with high paying jobs and offer affordable health insurance! Many of our team go on to be hired permanently and then move up the job ladder.

Are you interested in starting your interview process? The next step is to come into our office for skills tests. You'll want to take these tests soon, while the skills you learned in our workshop tutorials are still fresh in your head.

Please click below to select a time to come to our office.

Click here to go to our Registration Page.

Please see the attached graph. We know it will convince you that you will find success as part of the Temp Power team.

Thank you,

George Mills

for Temp Power

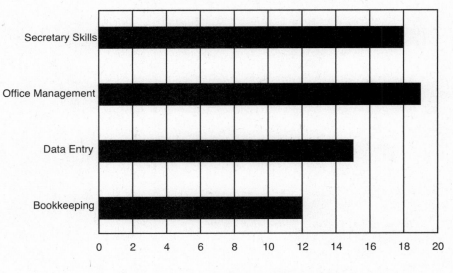

Temp Power Workshop Participants Employment

Average days per month

176. What was the ultimate purpose of the workshop?

(A) To recruit workers
(B) To find new clients
(C) To introduce a college
(D) To gather data for a graph

177. What does the message ask Vanessa to do next?

(A) Call the company
(B) Take a tutorial
(C) Send test results
(D) Sign up for a test

178. How much did Vanessa pay for the workshop?

(A) The workshop was free.
(B) It cost $20.
(C) It cost $50.
(D) The cost is unknown.

179. Which workshop led to the highest average amount of employment?

(A) Bookkeeping
(B) Data Entry
(C) Office Management
(D) Secretary Skills

180. If Vanessa signs up as a Temp Power employee, how much can she expect to work, on average?

(A) 15 days a month
(B) 18 days a month
(C) 18 days a year
(D) 12 months a year

Contract #991YL
Hospitality Consultants Inc.

Hospitality Consultants Inc. (hereafter referred to as Contractor) agrees to perform the following duties as outlined by Cracker Barrel Winery (hereafter called the Client):

A. Statistics Analysis
1) Review the Client's wine sales over the past five years, using monthly inventory charts.
2) Review the Client's food and gift sales over the past five years.
3) Record a summary and chart for proposed sales this year, based on a five-year review.

B. Staff Review
1) Interview one staff member from each department, including the vineyards and cellar.
2) Record duties and responsibilities for each job position.
3) Suggest ways for the Client to cut staffing costs.

C. Decor
1) Meet with board members to discuss year-end renovations.
2) Research materials and costs for all indoor renovations.
3) Provide an estimate for indoor renovations by October 1st.

Any changes to this contract must be agreed upon by both parties in writing.

Contractor: _Hanson Carter_

Client: _Julia Morris_

Date: August 7th, 20—

181. What type of service does this Contractor agree to provide?

(A) Labor assistance in the vineyards
(B) Consulting related to the winery's operations
(C) Inventory on glassware and dishes
(D) Taste tests of competitors' wines

182. Which is NOT an example of a person the Contractor may need to speak with to fulfill his duties?

(A) A medical professional
(B) A wine seller
(C) A board member
(D) A part-time grape picker

183. What is the reason for the addendum to the contract?

(A) The Client is not satisfied with the Contractor's work.
(B) The Contractor can't complete the job because of illness.
(C) The Client wants to add to the Contractor's duties.
(D) The Contractor was able to complete the job ahead of schedule.

Addendum to Contract #991YL dated August 7, 20—
between the following parties:

Contractor: **Hospitality Consultants Inc.**

Client: **Cracker Barrel Winery**

The Contractor initiates the following addendum:

1) Due to unforeseen circumstances the Contractor will be unable to provide services to Cracker Barrel Winery after October 9th, 20—. The Contractor does not expect any payment for any project work that is left incomplete as of today.

2) Before December 1st, 20— the Contractor will provide the Client with the names of three alternate consulting firms capable of completing the work set out in Contract #991YL.

3) The Contractor will submit a report of all work that has been completed, including any important data collected since August 7th 20—.

4) The Client agrees to write a reference for the Contractor, stating that Contract #991YL was broken due to illness in the family, and has no reflection on the Contractor's ability to do his job.

Date: October 9th, 20—

(Contractor) Signature: _____

(Client) Signature: _____

184. If the Contractor honored the contract up until now, what has definitely been completed?

(A) A sales chart based on a five-year review
(B) A count of all wine bottles in the cellar
(C) A calculation of proposed renovation costs
(D) An interview with at least one staff member

185. What is the Client obliged to do in the future if he signs the addendum to the contract?

(A) Rehire the Contractor when his health returns
(B) Provide a letter that states the reasons this contract was broken
(C) Write a positive reference letter about the Contractor's personality
(D) Suggest alternative companies that may hire the Contractor in the future

PRACTICE TEST 1

Parking Violation Notice
Springfield City Police Department

Violation:	Exceeding time limit in a 20-minute parking zone
Location:	500 block of North Main Street
Vehicle type:	Minivan
License Plate No.:	MG097
Registered owner:	Tanaka Kazuya
Date:	April 1, 20—
Amount:	$75

Pay within 30 days. See reverse for payment instructions.

Reminder Notice
Springfield City Police Department

Date: <u>April 21</u>

You have not yet paid a parking ticket issued on <u>April 1</u>. Payment is due by May 1. Unpaid fines are subject to a penalty equivalent to the amount of the original ticket. You have the right to appeal. Appeals must be received by the Parking Division within 30 days of issuance of the ticket. Please use Form 25 available from the Parking Division office or online at *springfieldpkingdiv.org*

Form 25
Notice of Appeal

STEP 1
Reason for Appeal
Please check the legal grounds that apply. Please check ONE option only.

___ This parking violation did not occur.
___ The parking meter was out of order.
___ I am not the owner of this vehicle.
✔ My vehicle was stolen on the day of the violation.

STEP 2
Complete the personal information form on page two with your name and address and contact information and mail it together with this page and a photocopy of your ticket. You will hear back from the Parking Division within 20 business days. If your appeal is granted, you may have to appear in court. If your appeal is denied, you will have fifteen days from the date of denial to pay the original fine.

186. Why did Mr. Kazuya receive this ticket?

 (A) His car was parked in a spot for too long.
 (B) His car was parked in a no-parking zone
 (C) He did not have a parking pass.
 (D) He paid for only 20 minutes.

187. Where will Mr. Kazuya find directions for paying the fine?

 (A) On the other side of the ticket
 (B) On the Parking Division website
 (C) At the police department
 (D) On Form 25

188. What happens if Mr. Kazuya fails to pay the fine or submit an appeal by May 1?

 (A) He must fill out a special form.
 (B) He must pay an additional $75.
 (C) He will lose his driver's license.
 (D) He will lose his parking privileges.

189. Why was Mr. Kazuya probably unaware of the original ticket?

 (A) The police officer forgot to leave it on his car.
 (B) The ticket was stolen from his parked car.
 (C) He thought he had parked legally.
 (D) Someone else was driving his car on April 1.

190. What does Mr. Kazuya have to include with his notice of appeal?

 (A) A check for $75
 (B) A photo of his car
 (C) A copy of his ticket
 (D) His license number

Questions 191–195 refer to the following travel itinerary, e-mail, and shuttle schedule.

Itinerary for: Rosalind Wilson

Monday, June 1
Skyhigh Air flight 234
- Depart New York 8:20 A.M.
- Arrive Winchester 3:40 P.M.
Transportation by company car to Sunrise Hotel, Winchester

Tuesday, June 2 – Friday, June 5
At the Spring Wells, Inc. Headquarters

Saturday, June 6
Express Railways train #45
- Depart Winchester 9:00 A.M.
- Arrive Pottsburgh 1:00 P.M.
Afternoon tour of Spring Wells factory

Sunday, June 7
Skyhigh Air flight 987
- Depart Pottsburgh 7:45 A.M.
- Arrive New York 1:30 P.M.

To: Rosalind Wilson
From: Tom Lee
Subject: Your visit

Hi Rosalind,
I received your itinerary from your office. Everything looks good. The only problem is that no one from our office will be available to meet you at the airport on Monday, as we will all be in a meeting that, unfortunately, cannot be rescheduled. You have several options for getting to your hotel. The airport shuttle is very convenient and will take you to the train station, which is just half a block from your hotel. I am attaching a schedule for you. Another option would be to take a taxi, although that could cost $45 or $50, and since the shuttle is so easy, in my opinion it is not worth the cost. There are also city buses, but they are complicated if you are not familiar with them.

We look forward to seeing you next week. Have a safe flight, and call me as soon as you are settled in your room.

Tom

AIRPORT SHUTTLE SCHEDULE
To Winchester Railway Station

The Airport Shuttle is a free transportation service provided by the Winchester Transportation Authority (WTA). No tickets are required. Seating is on a first come, first served basis.

	1A	2A	3A	4A
Departs airport	11:20 A.M.	1:30 P.M.	4:10 P.M.	6:45 P.M.
Arrives Winchester Station	12:05 P.M.	2:15 P.M.	4:55 P.M.	7:30 P.M.

---

191. What will Ms. Wilson be doing on June 4?

(A) Visiting the Spring Wells headquarters
(B) Touring the Spring Wells factory
(C) Returning home
(D) Riding a train

192. Why won't Mr. Lee meet her at the airport?

(A) He doesn't know how to get there.
(B) He has another commitment.
(C) He can't pay the bus fare.
(D) He won't be working that day.

193. The word "settled" in paragraph 2, line 2 of the e-mail is closest in meaning to

(A) agreed
(B) finished
(C) decisive
(D) comfortable

194. If Ms. Wilson takes the shuttle to her hotel, which one will she probably take?

(A) 1A
(B) 2A
(C) 3A
(D) 4A

195. How much will Ms. Wilson pay for the shuttle?

(A) Nothing
(B) At least $45
(C) Between $45 and $50
(D) $50 exactly

Questions 196–200 refer to the following notice, price list, and e-mail.

The Hanover Business Association (HBA)

presents a lecture by

Stephanie du Bois, MBA

Ms. du Bois will discuss tips and strategies for
investors in the current business climate.
Ms. du Bois received her MBA from
Pickerel University. She is the author of
Successful Investing and other popular titles.

August 18, 3:00 P.M.
Refreshments will be served

RSVP
This event is open to the public. Admission is free,
but space is limited. Please let us know if you plan to
attend by calling our office at 604-0939.

**Hanover Bakery
Cookie Trays**

# of guests	price
up to 10	$10
up to 25	$20
up to 50	$38
up to 75	$55

Coffee and tea are also available.
Please call us to discuss options.

To: Carlos Vasquez
From: Serena Stanley
Subject: Refreshments for lecture

Carlos,

I'm still working on the arrangements for the lecture next week. Would you please call the bakery and order the cookies? We had only about 20 people show up at our last lecture, but Ms. du Bois is so popular, I think we can expect a much larger crowd this time. I'm still getting RSVPs, and I think we should be prepared for 40 or 50 guests. We'll make the coffee and tea here, so no need to order that. I think that's all you need to do. I've checked the room we'll be using, and everything is fine there. I think we'll have plenty of space, even for a large crowd, and there are more than enough chairs. I even tried out the sound system, and it seems to be in working order. I think that's it for now. Thanks.

Serena

196. What should people do if they want to attend the lecture?

   (A) Buy a ticket
   (B) Call the HBA office
   (C) Arrive 30 minutes early
   (D) Become a member of the HBA

197. What is indicated about Ms. du Bois?

   (A) She has written several books.
   (B) She is a university professor.
   (C) She is a member of the HBA.
   (D) She is not well known.

198. How much will Mr. Vasquez pay for the cookies?

   (A) $20
   (B) $20, plus the cost of coffee and tea
   (C) $38
   (D) $38, plus the cost of coffee and tea

199. The phrase "show up" in line 2 of the e-mail is closest in meaning to

   (A) arrive
   (B) display
   (C) look at
   (D) guide

200. What does Ms. Stanley say about the room where the lecture will be held?

   (A) It is too small.
   (B) It is disorganized.
   (C) The chairs are very comfortable.
   (D) The sound system is in good condition.

This is the end of the test. If you finish before time is called, you may go back to Parts 5, 6, and 7 and check your work.

ANSWER KEY
Practice Test 1

LISTENING COMPREHENSION

Part 1: Photographs

1. **B**	3. **B**	5. **D**
2. **B**	4. **A**	6. **A**

Part 2: Question-Response

7. **A**	14. **C**	21. **C**	28. **C**
8. **A**	15. **B**	22. **B**	29. **B**
9. **C**	16. **C**	23. **A**	30. **C**
10. **B**	17. **A**	24. **B**	31. **A**
11. **C**	18. **A**	25. **B**	
12. **B**	19. **B**	26. **A**	
13. **A**	20. **C**	27. **C**	

Part 3: Conversations

32. **C**	42. **A**	52. **C**	62. **A**
33. **C**	43. **A**	53. **D**	63. **C**
34. **D**	44. **B**	54. **A**	64. **B**
35. **B**	45. **A**	55. **B**	65. **D**
36. **A**	46. **C**	56. **A**	66. **C**
37. **D**	47. **B**	57. **A**	67. **B**
38. **B**	48. **C**	58. **C**	68. **B**
39. **D**	49. **D**	59. **D**	69. **D**
40. **A**	50. **C**	60. **B**	70. **C**
41. **C**	51. **A**	61. **D**	

Part 4: Talks

71. **A**	79. **A**	87. **D**	95. **D**
72. **C**	80. **C**	88. **C**	96. **B**
73. **C**	81. **A**	89. **A**	97. **C**
74. **B**	82. **C**	90. **D**	98. **A**
75. **C**	83. **C**	91. **B**	99. **B**
76. **D**	84. **B**	92. **A**	100. **C**
77. **D**	85. **D**	93. **B**	
78. **D**	86. **A**	94. **B**	

ANSWER KEY
Practice Test 1

READING

Part 5: Incomplete Sentences

101. **B**	109. **C**	117. **C**	125. **C**
102. **D**	110. **B**	118. **B**	126. **D**
103. **C**	111. **A**	119. **A**	127. **B**
104. **B**	112. **A**	120. **D**	128. **A**
105. **A**	113. **C**	121. **B**	129. **D**
106. **C**	114. **A**	122. **C**	130. **C**
107. **B**	115. **D**	123. **C**	
108. **D**	116. **B**	124. **D**	

Part 6: Text Completion

131. **A**	135. **A**	139. **B**	143. **A**
132. **B**	136. **D**	140. **D**	144. **D**
133. **C**	137. **B**	141. **A**	145. **A**
134. **D**	138. **B**	142. **C**	146. **C**

Part 7: Reading Comprehension

147. **D**	161. **A**	175. **A**	189. **D**
148. **D**	162. **D**	176. **A**	190. **C**
149. **B**	163. **D**	177. **D**	191. **A**
150. **A**	164. **D**	178. **A**	192. **B**
151. **C**	165. **A**	179. **C**	193. **D**
152. **A**	166. **C**	180. **B**	194. **C**
153. **B**	167. **C**	181. **B**	195. **A**
154. **B**	168. **D**	182. **A**	196. **B**
155. **B**	169. **A**	183. **B**	197. **A**
156. **C**	170. **B**	184. **C**	198. **C**
157. **C**	171. **B**	185. **B**	199. **A**
158. **C**	172. **C**	186. **A**	200. **D**
159. **B**	173. **C**	187. **A**	
160. **D**	174. **B**	188. **B**	

TEST SCORE CONVERSION TABLE

Count your correct responses. Match the number of correct responses with the corresponding score from the Test Score Conversion Table (below). Add the two scores together. This is your Total Estimated Test Score. As you practice taking the TOEIC practice tests, your scores should improve. Keep track of your Total Estimated Test Scores.

# Correct	Listening Score	Reading Score	# Correct	Listening Score	Reading Score	# Correct	Listening Score	Reading Score	# Correct	Listening Score	Reading Score
0	5	5	26	110	65	51	255	220	76	410	370
1	5	5	27	115	70	52	260	225	77	420	380
2	5	5	28	120	80	53	270	230	78	425	385
3	5	5	29	125	85	54	275	235	79	430	390
4	5	5	30	130	90	55	280	240	80	440	395
5	5	5	31	135	95	56	290	250	81	445	400
6	5	5	32	140	100	57	295	255	82	450	405
7	10	5	33	145	110	58	300	260	83	460	410
8	15	5	34	150	115	59	310	265	84	465	415
9	20	5	35	160	120	60	315	270	85	470	420
10	25	5	36	165	125	61	320	280	86	475	425
11	30	5	37	170	130	62	325	285	87	480	430
12	35	5	38	175	140	63	330	290	88	485	435
13	40	5	39	180	145	64	340	300	89	490	445
14	45	5	40	185	150	65	345	305	90	495	450
15	50	5	41	190	160	66	350	310	91	495	455
16	55	10	42	195	165	67	360	320	92	495	465
17	60	15	43	200	170	68	365	325	93	495	470
18	65	20	44	210	175	69	370	330	94	495	480
19	70	25	45	215	180	70	380	335	95	495	485
20	75	30	46	220	190	71	385	340	96	495	490
21	80	35	47	230	195	72	390	350	97	495	495
22	85	40	48	240	200	73	395	355	98	495	495
23	90	45	49	245	210	74	400	360	99	495	495
24	95	50	50	250	215	75	405	365	100	495	495
25	100	60									

Number of Correct Listening Responses _____ = Listening Score _____

Number of Correct Reading Responses _____ = Reading Score _____

Total Estimated Test Score _____

ANSWER EXPLANATIONS

Listening Comprehension

PART 1: PHOTOGRAPHS

1. **(B)** The scientist is holding a test tube in her hand. Choice (A) uses the associated word *examining* for *looking* but there is no *patient* in the picture. Choice (C) uses the associated word *preparing* as in *preparing an experiment*. Choice (D) uses the associated word *watching* as in *looking at the test tube*.

2. **(B)** Choice (B) identifies the action *speaker explaining a chart*. Choice (A) confuses the man's outstretched hand with handshaking. Choice (C) confuses the coffee cups on the table with a meal. Choice (D) confuses the whiteboard with a TV.

3. **(B)** The field workers are loading produce onto a truck. Choice (A) correctly identifies the fruit in the photo but not the action of the men. Choice (C) confuses similar-sounding words *box* and *socks*. Choice (D) is incorrect because the workers are standing in the sunshine, not the rain.

4. **(A)** The photo shows a set of stairs leading up to the flagpole in the foreground. Choice (B) correctly identifies the roofs, but there is no soldier in the photo. Choice (C) correctly identifies the courtyard, but there are no tourists in the photo. Choice (D) is incorrect because there is no ten-story building in the photo.

5. **(D)** The woman in the photo is pushing a cart with some boxes on it. Choice (A) correctly identifies the gates in the picture, but no one is opening them. Choice (B) confuses similar-sounding words *cart* and *car*. Choice (C) incorrectly describes the location of the boxes.

6. **(A)** This correctly describes the man's action. Choice (B) correctly identifies the plant, but no one is trimming it. Choice (C) confuses the pot that the plant is in with a cooking pot. Choice (D) associates *plant* with *gardener*.

PART 2: QUESTION-RESPONSE

7. **(A)** Choice (A) is a logical response to a question about *food*. Choice (B) answers *Who's coming to dinner?* Choice (C) answers *When is dinner?*

8. **(A)** Choice (A) is a logical response to a question about *location*. Choice (B) confuses time: *this weekend* (present-future) and *last week* (past). Choice (C) confuses duration of time *will last a week* with past time *last week*.

9. **(C)** Choice (C) is a logical response to a question about *frequency*. Choice (A) confuses words with same sound and different meaning: *play* (verb) with *play* (performance). Choice (B) confuses similar-sounding words *and often* and *get off*.

10. **(B)** The second speaker thanks the first speaker for the generous offer to pay for dinner. Choice (A) confuses *thinner* with the similar-sounding word *dinner*. Choice (C) repeats the word *pay*.

11. **(C)** Choice (C) is a logical response to a question about *messages*. Choice (A) confuses massage (rubbing muscles) with message. Choice (B) confuses similar-sounding words *messages* with *any of us*.

12. **(B)** Choice (B) answers the question *What*. Choice (A) answers a *Where* question. Choice (C) confuses similar-sounding words *buy/good-bye*.

13. **(A)** *Ten* answers the question *How many*. Choice (B) repeats the idea of *hand out*. Choice (C) confuses the question about quantity (*how many*) with a question about price (*how much*).

14. **(C)** Choice (C) is a logical response to a question about *time*. Choice (A) identifies place (*airport*) but not time. Choice (B) has the related phrase *take off* but does not answer *when*.

15. **(B)** Choice (B) is a logical response to a question about *taking a break*. Choice (A) confuses *coffee break* with *broken (coffee) cup*. Choice (C) confuses *break* with *brakes* on a car and with *won't work* (broken).

16. **(C)** Choice (C) is a logical response to the question asking whether there is anything

more that needs to be done. Choice (A) would be a logical response to an offer of cake. Choice (B) answers the question *What kind.*

17. **(A)** Choice (A) is a logical response to a question about *location.* Choice (B) gives the price of the rooms, not the location of the hotel. Choice (C) confuses similar-sounding words *el(evator)* with *(ho)tel.*

18. **(A)** The first speaker says there was a call, so the second speaker wants to know if the caller left a message. Choice (B) confuses *cold* with the similar-sounding word *called* and repeats the word *out.* Choice (C) confuses *file* with the similar-sounding word *while.*

19. **(B)** Choice (B) is a logical response to a question about *which.* Choice (A) confuses similar-sounding words *hours* with *ours.* Choice (C) has the related word *seat* but does not answer *which.*

20. **(C)** The first speaker feels cold so the second speaker offers to close the window. Choice (A) associates *winter* with *cold.* Choice (B) confuses *sold* with the similar-sounding word *cold* and *year* with the similar-sounding word *here.*

21. **(C)** Choice (C) is a logical response to a question about *location.* Choice (A) confuses similar-sounding words *ear* with *here.* Choice (B) confuses *closed* with *near* (*close*).

22. **(B)** Choice (B) is a logical response to a question about a meeting starting time. Choice (A) associates *meeting* and *agenda,* but it doesn't answer the question. Choice (C) confuses similar-sounding words *meeting* and *reading.*

23. **(A)** Choice (A) is a logical response to the request of a favor. Choice (B) confuses the use of the word *favor.* Choice (C) repeats the word *music.*

24. **(B)** Choice (B) is a logical response to the question about a place to hang a coat. Choice (A) confuses similar-sounding words *leave/live.* Choice (C) repeats the word *leave.*

25. **(B)** Choice (B) is a logical response to the question about the type of people at the conference. Choice (A) would answer a question about the dates of the conference. Choice (C) relates the words *conference/workshop.*

26. **(A)** Choice (A) is a logical response to a question about *asking your father.* Choice (B) confuses similar-sounding words *far* with *father.* Choice (C) confuses similar-sounding words *ask* with *task.*

27. **(C)** Choice (C) is a logical response to the question about work preferences—*by myself* means the same as *alone.* Choice (A) confuses similar-sounding words *team/seem.* Choice (B) would answer a simple *yes–no* question, but this *or* question asks for a choice to be made.

28. **(C)** The second speaker agrees to eat at the restaurant that the first speaker suggests. Choice (A) confuses *rest* with the similar-sounding word *restaurant.* Choice (B) confuses *ice* with the similar-sounding word *nice.*

29. **(B)** Choice (B) is a logical response to the question about the contents of the chart. Choice (A) confuses similar-sounding words *chart/part.* Choice (C) repeats the words *page 8.*

30. **(C)** *Research and Development* answers the question about Fred's department. Choice (A) confuses similar-sounding words *department/apartment.* Choice (B) answers the question *Where.*

31. **(A)** Choice (A) answers the question *How much.* Choices (B) and (C) relate the word *account* with *money* and *check.*

PART 3: CONVERSATIONS

32. **(C)** The woman says, *I'll be in a conference until five,* and the man suggests they meet *then,* that is, at 5:00. Choice (A) repeats the word *lunch,* which is what the man will be doing earlier. Choice (B) is when the man will be free. Choice (D) is when the man doesn't want to meet.

33. **(C)** The man says, *I'll wait for you in my office.* Choice (A) confuses *bus stop* with the similar-sounding word *budget.* Choice (B) is confused with where the man will be earlier. Choice (D) confuses *waiting room* with *I'll wait for you . . . .*

34. **(D)** The woman says that she'll bring photocopies of the budget report. Choice (A) confuses *coffee* with the similar-sounding word *copy*. Choice (B) confuses *letter* with the similar-sounding word *better*. Choice (C) confuses *photographs* with *photocopies*.

35. **(B)** The man says that he is looking for an apartment and wants to sign a lease. Choices (A), (C), and (D) all repeat the word *apartment* but are not what the man wants to do.

36. **(A)** The man says he wants an apartment downtown, and the woman says, *you know that neighborhood isn't the cheapest*. Choice (B) is incorrect because the woman says that there are several vacancies. Choice (C) repeats the word *few*—the man wants to see a few apartments. Choice (D) repeats the word *large*—the man wants a one-bedroom or larger apartment.

37. **(D)** The woman says, *Why don't you stop by my office later today*. Choice (A) repeats the word *library*, which is near the woman's office. Choice (B) repeats the word *later*. Choice (C) repeats the word *online*, which the man mentions.

38. **(B)** The man asks for towels and soap to be brought to his room. Choices (A) and (C) are places where a person might ask for something, but they are not the correct answer. Choice (D) is incorrect because rooms in houses don't normally have numbers.

39. **(D)** The man asks for towels and soap. Choice (A) confuses *keys* with the similar-sounding word *please*. Choice (B) confuses *soup* with the similar-sounding word *soap*. Choice (C) repeats the word *room*.

40. **(A)** *Not a bit* is in response to the man's hope that his request is not too much trouble and means *It is not a bit of trouble*. Choice (B) repeats the word *job*. Choices (C) and (D) confuse the meaning of the expression.

41. **(C)** The woman says that the brochures arrived this morning. Choices (A) and (D) confuse *afternoon* with the similar-sounding word *soon*. Choice (B) is not mentioned.

42. **(A)** Mary mentions the address labels and then says, *I'll go print those out right now.*

Choice (B) is what one of the men will do. Choice (C) repeats the word *brochures*, but no mention is made of reading them. Choice (D) relates the words *print* and *printers*.

43. **(A)** Jim says, *I could drive them down to the post office for you*. Choice (B) repeats the word *drive*. Choice (C) repeats the word *addresses*. Choice (D) repeats the word *customers*.

44. **(B)** The man is applying for a job at a catering company, and he has worked as an assistant cook, so he is probably applying for a position as a chef. Choice (A) confuses related words *wait* and *waiter*. Choice (C) repeats *newspaper*, which is where the man saw the job ad. Choice (D) confuses related words *ad* and *advertising*.

45. **(A)** The woman asks, *Have you ever had a job in the food industry before?* Choice (B) is mentioned by the man, but the woman doesn't ask about it. Choice (C) repeats the word *food*. Choice (D) is related to the topic of a job search but is not mentioned.

46. **(C)** The man says, *Can you tell me exactly where you're located?* Choices (A), (B), and (D) are all related to the topic but are not mentioned.

47. **(B)** He can't play golf because rain is predicted. Choice (A) confuses *sick* with the similar-sounding word *predict*. Choice (C) confuses *test* with the similar-sounding word *rest*. Choice (D) uses the word *tired* out of context.

48. **(C)** *What a bore* can be used to refer to something that someone does not want to do, in this case, the man does not want to cancel the golf game, but he has to. Choice (A) is how the man will cancel the golf game. Choices (B) and (D) confuse the expression, *What a bore*, with the literal meaning of *bore*: something that is not interesting or entertaining.

49. **(D)** Since the man can't play golf tomorrow, he says he wants to stay home and rest. Choice (A) confuses *phone* with the similar-sounding word *home*. Choice (B) is what the woman wants him to do. Choice (C) confuses *move* with the similar-sounding word *movies*.

50. **(C)** The man is giving the woman directions to a bank. Choice (A) associates *fast food restaurant* with *drive-in window*. Choice (B) is what is next to the bank. Choice (D) is what the woman will pass on her way to the bank.

51. **(A)** The man says that the bank is on a corner. Choice (B) is confused with *a parking lot next door*. Choices (C) and (D) are confused with *across the street from the library*.

52. **(C)** The man says, *It's just five minutes from here.* Choice (A) is incorrect because the man mentions a nearby parking lot. Choice (B) is not mentioned. Choice (D) is the opposite of what the man says.

53. **(D)** Jane complains about Sam's late arrival and says, *Why can't you ever arrive on time?* Choice (A) confuses similar-sounding words *late* and *wait*. Choice (B) confuses similar-sounding words *arrive* and *drive*. Choice (C) repeats the word *hard*.

54. **(A)** Sam says he is late because his bus was delayed. Choices (B) and (D) are plausible but not mentioned. Choice (C) repeats the word *car*.

55. **(B)** The man says he will drive his car because it's faster. Choice (A) repeats the word *home*. Choice (C) is what the woman suggests. Choice (D) confuses *train* with the similar-sounding word *rain*.

56. **(A)** The man asks, *Will your cousins meet you at the airport?* Choice (B) confuses the meaning of the word *class*. Choice (C) is plausible but not mentioned. Choice (D) repeats the word *business*.

57. **(A)** The woman says she is flying first class and the man says, *That's a bit pricy, isn't it?* Choice (B) repeats the word *long*. Choice (C) is plausible but not mentioned. Choice (D) is confused with the related word *comfortable*, which is how the woman describes first class.

58. **(C)** The woman says that she is going to put it on her credit card. Choice (A) is not mentioned. Choice (B) confuses the meaning of the word *check*. Choice (D) confuses the meaning of the word *order*.

59. **(D)** The man says that Joe has *gone to pick up Evelyn at the airport*. Choice (A) associates *business trip* with *airport* and *flight*. Choices (B) and (C) are where the woman has looked for Joe.

60. **(B)** The woman says, *I need him to check my figures on the monthly report.* Choice (A) confuses the meaning of the word *check*. Choice (C) is confused with the man's lunch date with Joe. Choice (D) is what the woman will do after Joe looks at the report.

61. **(D)** The man says about Joe, *He'll be back before noon.* Choice (A) confuses similar-sounding words *noon* and *afternoon*. Choice (B) is when the woman needs photocopies of the report. Choice (C) is when Evelyn's flight arrives.

62. **(A)** The woman says, *I don't really care for the food there.* Choices (B) and (C) are plausible but not mentioned. Choice (D) is confused with the man saying he has to go all the way downtown.

63. **(C)** The woman says, *. . . could you get my mail from the mail room?* Choice (A) is what the woman brought from home. Choice (B) repeats the words *package* and *mail*. Choice (D) confuses similar-sounding words *mail* and *mall*.

64. **(B)** The man says, *I've got an appointment with a client at two.* Choice (A) repeats the word *take*. Choice (C) confuses similar-sounding words *appointment* and *apartment*. Choice (D) repeats the word *appointment*.

65. **(D)** The woman says she wants to go to Brookfield *as soon as tomorrow morning's workshop is over.* Choices (A) and (B) confuse *workshop* with *shopping* and *work*. Choice (C) is incorrect because the woman's trip is for business not for a vacation.

66. **(C)** George is planning the woman's business travel, so he is probably her assistant. Choice (A) is not correct because in addition to making travel arrangements, George will notify the office staff, not something a travel agent would likely do. Choice (B) repeats the word *workshop*. Choice (D) is incorrect because George is making arrangements for the woman's work life, not her personal life.

67. **(B)** The woman cannot leave until after 11:00 and wants to arrive before 2:00, and this is the only train that fits that schedule. Choices (A), (C), and (D) do not fit the woman's schedule.

68. **(B)** The man says, . . . *it isn't large.* Choice (A) is incorrect because the man says, *It's been here for quite a while.* Choice (C) is plausible but not mentioned. Choice (D) repeats the word *know.*

69. **(D)** The man mentions that the woman is a vegetarian, and this is the only soup that doesn't have meat. Choices (A), (B), and (C) all have some kind of meat.

70. **(C)** The man says, *I think we'd better just take our food back to work and eat at our desks.* Choice (A) is logical but not mentioned. Choice (B) is what the woman suggests. Choice (D) repeats the word *park.*

PART 4: TALKS

71. **(A)** *Arrival and departure gates, baggage claims,* and *ticketing areas* all suggest an airport. Choices (B) and (C) are not specific enough. Choice (D) is incorrect because an amusement park train would not lead to *baggage claims.*

72. **(C)** The instructions say you should be in the *center of the car.* Choice (A) is contradicted by *away from the doors.* Choice (B) is incorrect because *windows* are not mentioned. Choice (D) is contradicted by *in the center.*

73. **(C)** Passengers are asked to wait until they hear a bell ring before they exit the train. Choice (A) repeats the word *sign.* Choice (B) is contradicted by the correct answer. Choice (D) repeats the word *color.*

74. **(B)** The museum is open from *one until five on Sundays;* this is afternoon. Choices (A) and (C) are not mentioned. Choice (D) contradicts the fact that the museum is open from *one until five on Sundays.*

75. **(C)** The lecture series is *in conjunction with* the special exhibit, which consists of paintings showing *the early history of our city.* Choices (A) and (D) are confused with the subjects of classes taught at the museum.

Choice (B) repeats the word *museum.*

76. **(D)** According to the message, *children under five are not charged admission.* Choice (A) are the people who get a 25% discount. Choice (B) are the people who pay $15. Choice (C) are the people who pay $10.

77. **(D)** The speaker mentions the problem of organizing the work day and then says, *You are not alone,* meaning, *You are not the only person with this problem.* Choice (A) repeats the word *work.* Choice (B) repeats the word *problems.* Choice (C) uses the related word *lonely.*

78. **(D)** The passage says to *start the morning by making a list.* Choices (A), (B), and (C) are not mentioned.

79. **(A)** According to the talk, you should review your list at the end of the day. Choice (B) is incorrect because listeners are told to leave uncompleted tasks for the next day. Choice (C) repeats the word *list,* but nothing is mentioned about writing a new one. Choice (D) confuses *away* with the similar-sounding word *day.*

80. **(C)** The advertisement is asking for volunteers to help school children. Choice (A) repeats the word *learning.* Choice (B) is incorrect because the ad asks for *volunteers.* Choice (D) repeats the phrase *special training.*

81. **(A)** Listeners are asked to complete an application on a website. Choice (B) repeats the words *visit* and *website.* Choice (C) repeats the word *school.* Choice (D) repeats the words *complete* and *schoolwork.*

82. **(C)** The announcement says that participants must be at least eighteen. Choices (A) and (B) are mentioned as not necessary. Choice (D) repeats the word *children,* but experience with children is not mentioned.

83. **(C)** The speaker says, *we've finally got some nice weather coming in today,* and then says, *it's about time,* implying that people have been waiting a while for the weather to become nice. Choices (A), (B), and (D) don't fit the context.

84. **(B)** The meteorologist says to *spend some time outdoors.* Choice (A) is contradicted by

spend some time outdoors. Choices (C) and (D) are possible, but they are not mentioned.

85. **(D)** The weather tomorrow will be like the weather today, which is sunny. Choices (A), (B), and (C) describe the weather later in the week.

86. **(A)** The speaker says, *I wanted to know about ski lessons,* and goes on to talk about when he wants classes and what his level is. Choice (B) is incorrect because he says he already has reservations. Choice (C) is what he says he doesn't need. Choice (D) is incorrect because he already knows the snow conditions.

87. **(D)** The speaker says, *I'll be flying in.* Choices (A), (B), and (C) are not mentioned.

88. **(C)** The speaker says, *I'm looking forward to seeing the hotel. All my friends recommend it,* which implies he has not seen it before. Choice (A) is incorrect because it is the friends who recommend it, not the other way around. Choice (B) is not mentioned. Choice (D) repeats the word *area.*

89. **(A)** Residents of the Greenville district filed a complaint protesting the construction of a shopping mall. Choice (B) repeats the word *cost,* as in *the cost of the project.* Choice (C) repeats the word *traffic,* which is what residents are afraid will be increased by the mall. Choice (D) is what the Greenville residents caused by their complaint.

90. **(D)** Greenville residents filed their complaint at City Hall. Choice (A) refers to the complaint that the mall will bring noise to neighborhood streets. Choices (B) and (C) are not mentioned.

91. **(B)** The speaker says, *The mayor has agreed to meet with protestors to discuss their concerns later on this week.* Choice (A) repeats the word *construction.* Choice (C) repeats the word *plans.* Choice (D) repeats the word *shopping.*

92. **(A)** The speaker says, *Before you go,* meaning that the students are getting ready to leave but the speaker wants to tell them something first. Choices (B), (C), and (D) are contradicted by the correct answer.

93. **(B)** The speaker says to read Chapter 10 in the textbook *ahead of time.* Choice (A) is not

mentioned. Choice (C) is what will happen during the class trip. Choice (D) is confused with the request to, *Come up with a few questions to ask him.*

94. **(B)** The trip is to a museum to speak with a museum manager, and the required reading is about museum management. Choice (A) is confused with the mention that photography is not allowed in the museum. Choice (C) is not mentioned. Choice (D) is confused with the suggestion to bring a sketchpad.

95. **(D)** The speaker says if, . . . *you could come clean* . . . , and also mentions vacuuming the floors, so it is probably a housecleaning company. Choices (A) and (B) are mentioned but are not the services the speaker is asking for in the message. Choice (C) repeats the word *furniture.*

96. **(B)** The speaker says her apartment has three rooms, and $75 is the price shown for 2–3 rooms. Choices (A), (C), and (D) are prices for other sizes of apartments.

97. **(C)** The speaker says about her apartment, *I hope to have it ready to show to prospective tenants.* Choices (A), (B), and (D) are all plausible but not mentioned.

98. **(A)** The speaker mentions *empty rooms* and the need to *attract more guests,* so it is a hotel. Choice (B) relates *travel* with *beach vacation.* Choice (C) repeats the word *advertising.* Choice (D) repeats the word *swimming.*

99. **(B)** The speaker says the company's busy season is *when temperatures are highest.* Choices (A), (C), and (D) don't fit this description.

100. **(C)** The speaker says, *I'd like you now to pick up a pen and jot down a few ideas.* Choice (A) repeats the word *slide.* Choice (B) is incorrect because they are asked to answer, not ask, a question. Choice (D) is not mentioned.

Reading

PART 5: INCOMPLETE SENTENCES

101. **(B)** *Customer* is singular, so it takes a singular verb; it is also third person, so it takes the third person form of *is.* Choice (A) is singular

but first person. Choice (C) is plural. Choice (D) is the simple form of the verb.

102. **(D)** Although all the choices have similar meanings, Choice (D), *advised*, is the only one that fits the grammatical structure of the sentence. Choices (A), (B), and (C) require a different grammatical pattern: *We _____ that he think things over* . . . .

103. **(C)** *Host* means to organize a social event. Choices (A) and (B) is what is done to the guests—you *invite* guests or *entertain* guests. Choice (D) refers to a person who is invited to a party and does not fit the sentence because it is a noun, and a verb is needed here.

104. **(B)** *Were not* requires a past participle to complete the verb. Choice (A) is a noun. Choice (C) is in the progressive form. Choice (D) is the simple form.

105. **(A)** The present tense in the *if* clause can be matched with future tense in the second clause; *will* can also be used with *assist* to make a complete verb. Choices (B) and (C) are past tense. Choice (D) is present tense, and must be used with either the *past participle* or the *progressive form*.

106. **(C)** The noun *knowledge* followed by *and* should be joined to another noun. Choices (A) and (B) are verbs. Choice (D) is a noun, but it refers to a person rather than a thing.

107. **(B)** *Increase* is the most common verb meaning *go up* used with *costs*. Choices (A), (C), and (D) mean *go up*, but they are not used for nouns related to percentages.

108. **(D)** The subject position requires a noun. Choices (A) and (B) are verbs. Choice (C) refers to a person or thing and doesn't make sense here.

109. **(C)** *Because* establishes a logical cause and effect relationship between the two events. Choice (A) indicates contrast; it is not logical unless the plane *was on time*. Choice (B) suggests a simultaneous relationship, not possible because of present tense *is* and past tense *was*. Choice (D) is a preposition and cannot be used to join clauses.

110. **(B)** *Confidential* means *private*. Choices (A), (C), and (D) have meanings that do not fit the context.

111. **(A)** This is a future time clause, so a present tense verb is required. Choice (B) is past tense. Choice (C) is present perfect tense. Choice (D) is future tense.

112. **(A)** *Commute* means to travel from home to work. Choices (B), (C), and (D) do not fit the context of the sentence.

113. **(C)** *Between* indicates that one object has another object on each side. Choice (A) is most often used when one hard-to-count group is indicated (*among the paper clips, among the office equipment*). Choices (B) and (D) are not logical.

114. **(A)** *Job* is used here to refer to an individual position. Choice (B) implies professional standing greater than individual jobs. (*In his career (occupation) as an insurance investigator, he held jobs with several companies.*) Choice (C) implies unpleasant work smaller than an individual job. (*I like my job as a secretary, but it's a chore to sort the boss's mail.*) Choice (D) uses a related word, *position*, but in an inappropriate form.

115. **(D)** *File* has the same meaning here as *submit*. Choice (A) is a form of the verb *fill*. Choices (B) and (C) are forms of the verb *fall*.

116. **(B)** *After* establishes a logical time relationship between the two events. Choice (A) is an adverb, indicating a period of time after a specific event. Choice (C) indicates a comparison. (*His fax arrived later than mine.*) Choice (D) is an adjective and cannot be used to join clauses.

117. **(C)** *Because* indicates a cause and effect relationship between the two events. Choice (A) implies contrast. Choice (B) *during* cannot be followed by a sentence. Choice (D) doesn't make sense.

118. **(B)** *Required* means to be obliged. Choices (A), (C), and (D) do not fit the context of the sentence.

119. **(A)** *Or* is logical and can join two nouns. Choice (B) is not usually used in a negative

relationship. Choices (C) and (D) are not logical.

120. **(D)** *Balance* refers to the amount of money left in a bank account. Choices (A), (B), and (C) are words not normally used in this context.

121. **(B)** The blank requires an adjective; *available* is the only one given. Choices (A) and (D) are verbs. Choice (C) is a noun.

122. **(C)** The causative *suggest* is followed by the simple form of the verb. Choice (A) is the plural form. Choices (B) and (D) are simple forms, but are not logical.

123. **(C)** *Spaces* must be modified by an adjective. Choices (A) and (D) are adjectives, but they are not logical. Choice (B) is a noun.

124. **(D)** *Order* must be modified by an adjective. Choice (A) is a noun. Choice (B) is a verb. Choice (C) is an adverb.

125. **(C)** *Already* can refer to something that has happened earlier than expected. In this case, Raymond learned about the clients in a very short time. Choices (A), (B), and (D) have no meaning in this context.

126. **(D)** *Must* requires the simple form of the verb. Choice (A) is the past tense. Choice (B) is the progressive form. Choice (C) is the third-person singular form.

127. **(B)** *Tasks* must be modified by an adjective. Choice (A) is a verb. Choice (C) is a noun. Choice (D) is an adverb.

128. **(A)** *Reminded* requires the infinitive form. Choice (B) is the simple form. Choice (C) is the past participle. Choice (D) is the progressive form.

129. **(D)** *Extensive* means *broad* or *a lot of.* Choices (A), (B), and (C) have meanings that do not fit the context.

130. **(C)** *Never* can come between the auxiliary and the verb. Choice (A) is an adjective and does not fit here. Choice (B) does not make sense. Choice (D) would fit if it were *at no time.*

PART 6: TEXT COMPLETION

131. **(A)** The subject, *passengers*, does not perform the action. The past participle form of the verb is needed to complete the passive

verb. Choice (B) is a present participle or a gerund. Choice (C) is an active verb. Choice (D) is a noun.

132. **(B)** *Such as* can begin a list of examples. Choice (A) cannot be used in this context. Choices (C) and (D) would have to be preceded by the word *for* in order to be used in this sentence.

133. **(C)** Passengers go through a security line to have their bags checked for unallowed items. Choices (A), (B), and (D) are lines that passengers may have to pass through, but they don't fit the context.

134. **(D)** This sentence continues the explanation in the previous sentence about what happens when bags go through security. Choices (A), (B), and (C) don't fit the context.

135. **(A)** Computer manufacturers are companies that make and sell computers. Choices (B) and (C) mean *buyers.* Choice (D) refers to a type of person who might use computers but probably wouldn't sell them.

136. **(D)** Tablet computers are easy to carry around, and this makes them convenient. Choices (A), (B), and (C) don't fit the context.

137. **(B)** The paragraph discusses a benefit of tablet computers—convenience—and this sentence mentions an additional benefit. Choices (A), (C), and (D) don't fit the context.

138. **(B)** Following the article *the* a noun is required. Choice (A) is a noun, but it refers to a person, not a situation. Choice (C) is an adjective. Choice (D) is an adverb.

139. **(B)** The invoice was sent in July, it is now September, and the message is asking about a delay, so the payment is *overdue*, or *late.* Choices (A), (C), and (D) don't fit the context.

140. **(D)** The e-mail is about an unpaid invoice. This sentence describes attempts at communication with the person who owes the money, and the following sentence indicates that the writer has not received any communication from that person. Choices (A), (B), and (C) don't fit the context.

141. **(A)** This is the main clause of a future real conditional, requiring a future verb form. Choice (B) is present perfect tense. Choice

(C) is an unreal conditional. Choice (D) is an incomplete future form, missing the word *are*.

142. **(C)** An order contains items and prices, as the e-mail mentions. The other choices are related to making orders but are not the correct answer.

143. **(A)** *Response* means answer; the letter answers an ad. Choices (B), (C), and (D) look similar to the correct answer but have very different meanings.

144. **(D)** This choice describes the writer's work experience, which he refers back to in the following sentence. The other choices don't fit this context.

145. **(A)** The present tense verb *qualify* agrees with the plural subject *years*. Choices (B), (C), and (D) agree with singular, not plural, subjects.

146. **(C)** The expression *look forward to* means *anticipate* or *hope for*. Choices (A), (B) and (D) cannot be correctly used with this expression.

PART 7: READING COMPREHENSION

147. **(D)** *At the end of this month* means April 30. Choice (A) is not mentioned. Choice (B) is the last day of the period covered by the invoice. Choice (C) is the date of the invoice.

148. **(D)** *Unpaid prior balance* means they owe money on the last invoice. Choice (A) is not mentioned. Choices (B) and (C) are incorrect because charges are not broken down into taxes and other charges.

149. **(B)** The notice is about a *pension plan*, that is, money paid to retirees. Choice (A) relates *job* and *employees*. Choice (C) relates *loan* and *payments*. Choice (D) repeats the word *salary*.

150. **(A)** The plan covers *employees with a minimum of five years of service*. Choice (B) repeats the word *salary*. Choice (C) repeats the word *government*. Choice (D) is incorrect because employees with less than five years service are not eligible.

151. **(C)** Pat explains that all trains are late because there was an accident. Choice (A) is not mentioned. Choice (B) is incorrect because she says she left home early. Choice (D) is not mentioned.

152. **(A)** "You're telling me" is an expression that means "You don't have to tell me because I already know." This is Pat's response to Sam's writing that he wants to please the client because it is a big account. Choices (B), (C), and (D) are incorrect interpretations of the meaning of the expression.

153. **(B)** The original name of the company was Green Miles California and the announcement explains that "California" was replaced with "West." Choices (A) and (B) combine different words from the company name. Choice (C) is the new name.

154. **(B)** The California Gardening Association did not like the similarity of the corporations' names. Choice (A) confuses *offices* with *brands*. Choice (C) repeats the word *initial*. Choice (D) confuses the hope that they not be confused with the actual reason the names were changed.

155. **(B)** It is by a beach, the nearest airport is described as being on the mainland, and visitors must take a ferry to get there, so *island* is the logical conclusion. Choices (A) and (C) are mentioned as being on the mainland. Choice (D) is not mentioned.

156. **(C)** Things that are included in the vacation package are listed in the middle of the page and include breakfast and dinner daily. Choice (A) is mentioned but not as part of the vacation. Choice (B) refers to the mention of beach access, pool access, and private and group lessons, but the lessons mentioned cost a fee. Choice (D) is available for rental, so costs extra.

157. **(C)** The webpage mentions beach and pool access, so it is logical to conclude that guests can go swimming. Choices (A), (B), and (D) are plausible but not mentioned.

158. **(C)** The e-mail is about the *transfer*, or move, to the Paris office. Choices (A) and (D) describe other situations in which employees might pack up their desks. Choice (B) repeats the word *Paris*.

159. **(B)** The e-mail says, *Please follow the directions below and do not omit anything.* Choice (C) is incorrect because the e-mail states, *please refrain from asking me more questions.* Choice (A) is incorrect because the e-mail states, *Packing supplies are available for your use.* Choice (D) is not mentioned.

160. **(D)** The e-mail states, *Notify maintenance to clean your desk, so it will be ready for the next occupant.* Choices (A) and (C) use words from the passage but don't correctly interpret the information. Choice (B) is mentioned but not as something to do for the next person to use the desk.

161. **(A)** The second sentence says, . . . *you can make sure your meetings run smoothly and use time well.* The article is about how to use meeting time well and not waste it, that is, efficiently. Choices (B), (C), and (D) are related to the topic of staff meetings but are not specifically what the article is about.

162. **(D)** The article says that speakers should be encouraged to keep their *remarks*, that is, comments, *brief*, or short. Choices (A), (B), and (C) are not mentioned.

163. **(D)** This is a detail that supports the preceding sentence. The preceding sentence states that it is important to keep to the schedule and the inserted sentence explains a reason why. Choices (A), (B), and (C) are not a logical context for this sentence.

164. **(D)** The event will be run by trainers and it is for staff, so it is likely a professional development workshop. Choice (A) associates *banquet* with the lunch that is mentioned. Choice (B) is incorrect because it is not likely that a weekly staff meeting would involve such complicated arrangements or a catered lunch. Choice (C) is not likely as the event is just for staff.

165. **(A)** Ms. Prieto writes, *I just had a phone call from the caterers.* Choice (B) is confused with the e-mail she received. Choice (C) is what George has done. Choice (D) is incorrect because documents were sent to her, not created by her.

166. **(C)** Ms. Lu writes, *I'll take care of those copies now*, referring to the requested copies of the documents. Choice (A) refers to her question about the number of participants, but George has already counted them. Choice (B) is not mentioned. Choice (D) is what George will do.

167. **(C)** *Relax* is often used to mean *don't worry.* Choices (A), (B), and (D) confuse the meaning of *relax* in this context.

168. **(D)** ABC Foods will raise prices on *fruit cakes, pies, and other fruit-based sweets.* Choice (A) is mentioned as something on which other companies will soon raise prices. Choice (B) repeats the word *brands.* Choice (C) are fruit-based foods but are not mentioned specifically.

169. **(A)** The article states that the higher prices are due to *a late freeze and a long drought.* Choices (B), (C), and (D) are plausible but not mentioned.

170. **(B)** The article states, *Other companies are expected to . . . raise prices on their canned fruit and vegetable products by the end of the year.* Choices (A), (C), and (D) are plausible but not mentioned.

171. **(B)** This is a detail adding information to the previous statement that prices will rise. Choices (A), (C), and (D) do not provide a proper context for this sentence.

172. **(C)** The article describes a growing interest among hotels and travelers in environmentally friendly practices. Choices (A) and (B) describe details of the article, not the main idea. Choice (D) is related to the topic but is not mentioned.

173. **(C)** One tour activity is described as *an opportunity to help scientists in the field.* Choices (A), (B), and (D) are all plausible but not mentioned.

174. **(B)** The article mentions a study that found that litter left behind by travelers to Antarctica *could fit into one small plastic sandwich bag.* Choice (A) relates *collecting* and *collected.* Choice (C) repeats the words *plastic bag.* Choice (D) is confused with the mention of litter often found near hotels.

175. **(A)** The article suggests *placing bottle recycling bins in rooms*. Choice (B) is confused with the mention of glass dispensers commonly used in hotels these days. Choice (C) confuses the use of the word *green*. Choice (D) repeats the word rainforest, mentioned as a popular tourist destination.

176. **(A)** The e-mail encourages Vanessa, as a workshop participant, to start the process toward becoming an employee. Choices (B) and (C) are not mentioned. Choice (D), a graph, is mentioned, but it is included to encourage Vanessa to become an employee.

177. **(D)** The e-mail says, *The next step is to come into our office for skills tests*. Choice (A) is incorrect because Vanessa is asked to contact the company through the website, not by phone. Choice (B) is what Vanessa has already done. Choice (C) repeats the word *test*.

178. **(A)** The e-mail mentions the *complimentary*, or *free*, workshop. Choices (B), (C), and (D) are contradicted by the correct answer.

179. **(C)** Participants in the Office Management workshop worked an average of 19 days a month. Choices (A), (B), and (D) all worked less than 19 days a month on average.

180. **(B)** Vanessa took the Secretary Skills workshop, which, according to the graph, led to an average of 18 hours a week employment. Choice (A) refers to the Data Entry workshop. Choices (C) and (D) are incorrect because the graph is about a month, not days or months a year.

181. **(B)** The Contractor will provide consulting services for different aspects of the winery's operations. Choices (A), (C), and (D) mention things that are related to a winery's business but that are not mentioned in the texts.

182. **(A)** The contract was not fulfilled because of a medical emergency, but the duties outlined in the contract have no relationship to anything medical. Choices (B) and (D) are examples of winery staff members, and the contract specifies speaking with staff members. Choice (C) is an example of someone the Contractor will speak with, mentioned in Clause C of the contract.

183. **(B)** Clause 1 states that the Contractor is unable to provide services after a certain date, and Clause 4 states the reason as being illness. Choices (A), (C), and (D) are plausible reasons, but they are not the correct answer.

184. **(C)** The contract states that an estimate of renovation costs must be completed by October 1. Choices (A), (B), and (D) are tasks that have no specific deadline assigned.

185. **(B)** This is what Clause 4 of the addendum to the contract states. Choice (A) is not mentioned. Choice (C) looks similar to the correct answer, but there is no mention made of the Contractor's personality. Choice (D) is what the Contractor must do.

186. **(A)** The ticket notes that the violation was *Exceeding time limit in a 20-minute parking zone*. Choices (B), (C), and (D) are plausible reasons for getting a parking ticket but are not the correct answer.

187. **(A)** The ticket states, *See reverse for payment instructions*. Choices (B), (C), and (D) repeat words and phrases from the passages but are not the correct answer.

188. **(B)** The Reminder Notice states, *Unpaid fines are subject to a penalty equivalent to the amount of the original ticket*, and the amount of the original ticket is $75. Choice (A) is what is required to make an appeal. Choices (C) and (D) are plausible but not mentioned.

189. **(D)** On the form, the reason for the appeal that is checked is *My vehicle was stolen on the day of the violation*. Choices (A), (B), and (C) use words from the passages but are not the correct answer.

190. **(C)** Step 2 of the form includes the information that a photocopy of the ticket must be mailed in with the form. Choices (A), (B), and (D) use words from the passages but are not the correct answer.

191. **(A)** According to the itinerary, Ms. Wilson will be at the company headquarters from June 2–June 7, so that is where she will be on June 4. Choices (B) and (D) are what she will be doing on June 6. Choice (C) is what she will be doing on June 7.

192. **(B)** Mr. Lee explains in his e-mail, . . . *no one from our office will be available to meet you at the airport on Monday, as we will all be in a meeting* . . . . Choices (A) and (C) are not mentioned. Choice (D) is incorrect because he writes that he will be in a meeting, that is, working.

193. **(D)** To be *settled* into a hotel room means to have arranged things so that you are comfortable. Choices (A), (B), and (C) don't fit the meaning of the word in this context.

194. **(C)** Ms. Wilson's flight arrives at 3:40, and shuttle 3A is the soonest to leave after her arrival. Choices (A) and (B) leave too early and choice (D) leaves too late.

195. **(A)** The information on the shuttle schedule explains that it is a free service. Choices (B), (C), and (D) are confused with the discussion of taxi fare in the e-mail.

196. **(B)** The notice says, *Please let us know if you plan to attend by calling our office* . . . . Choice (A) is incorrect because the notice states, *Admission is free.* Choices (C) and (D) are not mentioned.

197. **(A)** The notice states that Ms. du Bois *is the author of* <u>Successful Investing</u> *and other popular titles.* Choice (B) is confused with the mention that Ms. du Bois has a university degree. Choice (C) is not mentioned. Choice (D) is incorrect because in the e-mail, Ms. Stanley mentions that Ms. du Bois is very popular.

198. **(C)** In the e-mail, Ms. Stanley writes that she is expecting 40–50 guests, and the cookie tray that costs $38 serves up to 50 people. Choices (A) and (B) mention the price for a tray that serves up to 20 people only. Choice (D) is incorrect because Ms. Stanley tells Mr. Vasquez not to order coffee and tea.

199. **(A)** *Show up* in this context means *arrive.* Ms. Stanley mentions the number of people who arrived for the last lecture. Choices (B), (C), and (D) don't fit the context.

200. **(D)** Ms. Stanley writes that the sound system is *in working order.* Choice (A) is incorrect because Ms. Stanley says there will be *plenty of space.* Choice (B) is incorrect because Ms. Stanley says about the room, *everything is fine.* Choice (C) is incorrect because the only thing Ms. Stanley mentions about the chairs is that *there are more than enough.*

ANSWER SHEET
Practice Test 2

LISTENING COMPREHENSION

Part 1: Photographs

1. (A) (B) (C) (D)　　3. (A) (B) (C) (D)　　5. (A) (B) (C) (D)
2. (A) (B) (C) (D)　　4. (A) (B) (C) (D)　　6. (A) (B) (C) (D)

Part 2: Question-Response

7. (A) (B) (C)　　14. (A) (B) (C)　　21. (A) (B) (C)　　28. (A) (B) (C)
8. (A) (B) (C)　　15. (A) (B) (C)　　22. (A) (B) (C)　　29. (A) (B) (C)
9. (A) (B) (C)　　16. (A) (B) (C)　　23. (A) (B) (C)　　30. (A) (B) (C)
10. (A) (B) (C)　　17. (A) (B) (C)　　24. (A) (B) (C)　　31. (A) (B) (C)
11. (A) (B) (C)　　18. (A) (B) (C)　　25. (A) (B) (C)
12. (A) (B) (C)　　19. (A) (B) (C)　　26. (A) (B) (C)
13. (A) (B) (C)　　20. (A) (B) (C)　　27. (A) (B) (C)

Part 3: Conversations

32. (A) (B) (C) (D)　　42. (A) (B) (C) (D)　　52. (A) (B) (C) (D)　　62. (A) (B) (C) (D)
33. (A) (B) (C) (D)　　43. (A) (B) (C) (D)　　53. (A) (B) (C) (D)　　63. (A) (B) (C) (D)
34. (A) (B) (C) (D)　　44. (A) (B) (C) (D)　　54. (A) (B) (C) (D)　　64. (A) (B) (C) (D)
35. (A) (B) (C) (D)　　45. (A) (B) (C) (D)　　55. (A) (B) (C) (D)　　65. (A) (B) (C) (D)
36. (A) (B) (C) (D)　　46. (A) (B) (C) (D)　　56. (A) (B) (C) (D)　　66. (A) (B) (C) (D)
37. (A) (B) (C) (D)　　47. (A) (B) (C) (D)　　57. (A) (B) (C) (D)　　67. (A) (B) (C) (D)
38. (A) (B) (C) (D)　　48. (A) (B) (C) (D)　　58. (A) (B) (C) (D)　　68. (A) (B) (C) (D)
39. (A) (B) (C) (D)　　49. (A) (B) (C) (D)　　59. (A) (B) (C) (D)　　69. (A) (B) (C) (D)
40. (A) (B) (C) (D)　　50. (A) (B) (C) (D)　　60. (A) (B) (C) (D)　　70. (A) (B) (C) (D)
41. (A) (B) (C) (D)　　51. (A) (B) (C) (D)　　61. (A) (B) (C) (D)

Part 4: Talks

71. (A) (B) (C) (D)　　79. (A) (B) (C) (D)　　87. (A) (B) (C) (D)　　95. (A) (B) (C) (D)
72. (A) (B) (C) (D)　　80. (A) (B) (C) (D)　　88. (A) (B) (C) (D)　　96. (A) (B) (C) (D)
73. (A) (B) (C) (D)　　81. (A) (B) (C) (D)　　89. (A) (B) (C) (D)　　97. (A) (B) (C) (D)
74. (A) (B) (C) (D)　　82. (A) (B) (C) (D)　　90. (A) (B) (C) (D)　　98. (A) (B) (C) (D)
75. (A) (B) (C) (D)　　83. (A) (B) (C) (D)　　91. (A) (B) (C) (D)　　99. (A) (B) (C) (D)
76. (A) (B) (C) (D)　　84. (A) (B) (C) (D)　　92. (A) (B) (C) (D)　　100. (A) (B) (C) (D)
77. (A) (B) (C) (D)　　85. (A) (B) (C) (D)　　93. (A) (B) (C) (D)
78. (A) (B) (C) (D)　　86. (A) (B) (C) (D)　　94. (A) (B) (C) (D)

ANSWER SHEET
Practice Test 2

READING

Part 5: Incomplete Sentences

101. Ⓐ Ⓑ Ⓒ Ⓓ
102. Ⓐ Ⓑ Ⓒ Ⓓ
103. Ⓐ Ⓑ Ⓒ Ⓓ
104. Ⓐ Ⓑ Ⓒ Ⓓ
105. Ⓐ Ⓑ Ⓒ Ⓓ
106. Ⓐ Ⓑ Ⓒ Ⓓ
107. Ⓐ Ⓑ Ⓒ Ⓓ
108. Ⓐ Ⓑ Ⓒ Ⓓ

109. Ⓐ Ⓑ Ⓒ Ⓓ
110. Ⓐ Ⓑ Ⓒ Ⓓ
111. Ⓐ Ⓑ Ⓒ Ⓓ
112. Ⓐ Ⓑ Ⓒ Ⓓ
113. Ⓐ Ⓑ Ⓒ Ⓓ
114. Ⓐ Ⓑ Ⓒ Ⓓ
115. Ⓐ Ⓑ Ⓒ Ⓓ
116. Ⓐ Ⓑ Ⓒ Ⓓ

117. Ⓐ Ⓑ Ⓒ Ⓓ
118. Ⓐ Ⓑ Ⓒ Ⓓ
119. Ⓐ Ⓑ Ⓒ Ⓓ
120. Ⓐ Ⓑ Ⓒ Ⓓ
121. Ⓐ Ⓑ Ⓒ Ⓓ
122. Ⓐ Ⓑ Ⓒ Ⓓ
123. Ⓐ Ⓑ Ⓒ Ⓓ
124. Ⓐ Ⓑ Ⓒ Ⓓ

125. Ⓐ Ⓑ Ⓒ Ⓓ
126. Ⓐ Ⓑ Ⓒ Ⓓ
127. Ⓐ Ⓑ Ⓒ Ⓓ
128. Ⓐ Ⓑ Ⓒ Ⓓ
129. Ⓐ Ⓑ Ⓒ Ⓓ
130. Ⓐ Ⓑ Ⓒ Ⓓ

Part 6: Text Completion

131. Ⓐ Ⓑ Ⓒ Ⓓ
132. Ⓐ Ⓑ Ⓒ Ⓓ
133. Ⓐ Ⓑ Ⓒ Ⓓ
134. Ⓐ Ⓑ Ⓒ Ⓓ

135. Ⓐ Ⓑ Ⓒ Ⓓ
136. Ⓐ Ⓑ Ⓒ Ⓓ
137. Ⓐ Ⓑ Ⓒ Ⓓ
138. Ⓐ Ⓑ Ⓒ Ⓓ

139. Ⓐ Ⓑ Ⓒ Ⓓ
140. Ⓐ Ⓑ Ⓒ Ⓓ
141. Ⓐ Ⓑ Ⓒ Ⓓ
142. Ⓐ Ⓑ Ⓒ Ⓓ

143. Ⓐ Ⓑ Ⓒ Ⓓ
144. Ⓐ Ⓑ Ⓒ Ⓓ
145. Ⓐ Ⓑ Ⓒ Ⓓ
146. Ⓐ Ⓑ Ⓒ Ⓓ

Part 7: Reading Comprehension

147. Ⓐ Ⓑ Ⓒ Ⓓ
148. Ⓐ Ⓑ Ⓒ Ⓓ
149. Ⓐ Ⓑ Ⓒ Ⓓ
150. Ⓐ Ⓑ Ⓒ Ⓓ
151. Ⓐ Ⓑ Ⓒ Ⓓ
152. Ⓐ Ⓑ Ⓒ Ⓓ
153. Ⓐ Ⓑ Ⓒ Ⓓ
154. Ⓐ Ⓑ Ⓒ Ⓓ
155. Ⓐ Ⓑ Ⓒ Ⓓ
156. Ⓐ Ⓑ Ⓒ Ⓓ
157. Ⓐ Ⓑ Ⓒ Ⓓ
158. Ⓐ Ⓑ Ⓒ Ⓓ
159. Ⓐ Ⓑ Ⓒ Ⓓ
160. Ⓐ Ⓑ Ⓒ Ⓓ

161. Ⓐ Ⓑ Ⓒ Ⓓ
162. Ⓐ Ⓑ Ⓒ Ⓓ
163. Ⓐ Ⓑ Ⓒ Ⓓ
164. Ⓐ Ⓑ Ⓒ Ⓓ
165. Ⓐ Ⓑ Ⓒ Ⓓ
166. Ⓐ Ⓑ Ⓒ Ⓓ
167. Ⓐ Ⓑ Ⓒ Ⓓ
168. Ⓐ Ⓑ Ⓒ Ⓓ
169. Ⓐ Ⓑ Ⓒ Ⓓ
170. Ⓐ Ⓑ Ⓒ Ⓓ
171. Ⓐ Ⓑ Ⓒ Ⓓ
172. Ⓐ Ⓑ Ⓒ Ⓓ
173. Ⓐ Ⓑ Ⓒ Ⓓ
174. Ⓐ Ⓑ Ⓒ Ⓓ

175. Ⓐ Ⓑ Ⓒ Ⓓ
176. Ⓐ Ⓑ Ⓒ Ⓓ
177. Ⓐ Ⓑ Ⓒ Ⓓ
178. Ⓐ Ⓑ Ⓒ Ⓓ
179. Ⓐ Ⓑ Ⓒ Ⓓ
180. Ⓐ Ⓑ Ⓒ Ⓓ
181. Ⓐ Ⓑ Ⓒ Ⓓ
182. Ⓐ Ⓑ Ⓒ Ⓓ
183. Ⓐ Ⓑ Ⓒ Ⓓ
184. Ⓐ Ⓑ Ⓒ Ⓓ
185. Ⓐ Ⓑ Ⓒ Ⓓ
186. Ⓐ Ⓑ Ⓒ Ⓓ
187. Ⓐ Ⓑ Ⓒ Ⓓ
188. Ⓐ Ⓑ Ⓒ Ⓓ

189. Ⓐ Ⓑ Ⓒ Ⓓ
190. Ⓐ Ⓑ Ⓒ Ⓓ
191. Ⓐ Ⓑ Ⓒ Ⓓ
192. Ⓐ Ⓑ Ⓒ Ⓓ
193. Ⓐ Ⓑ Ⓒ Ⓓ
194. Ⓐ Ⓑ Ⓒ Ⓓ
195. Ⓐ Ⓑ Ⓒ Ⓓ
196. Ⓐ Ⓑ Ⓒ Ⓓ
197. Ⓐ Ⓑ Ⓒ Ⓓ
198. Ⓐ Ⓑ Ⓒ Ⓓ
199. Ⓐ Ⓑ Ⓒ Ⓓ
200. Ⓐ Ⓑ Ⓒ Ⓓ

Practice Test 2

LISTENING COMPREHENSION

In this section of the test, you will have the chance to show how well you understand spoken English. There are four parts to this section, with special directions for each part. You will have approximately 45 minutes to complete the Listening Comprehension sections.

Part 1: Photographs

Track 39

> **Directions:** You will see a photograph. You will hear four statements about the photograph. Choose the statement that most closely matches the photograph, and fill in the corresponding oval on your answer sheet.

1.

2.

3.

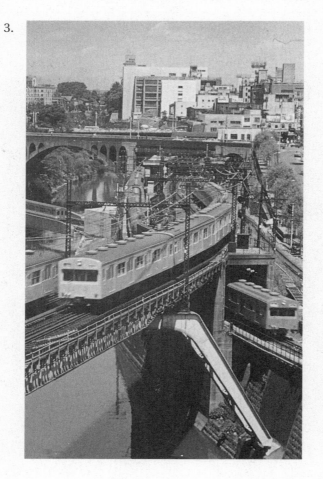

4.

5.

6.

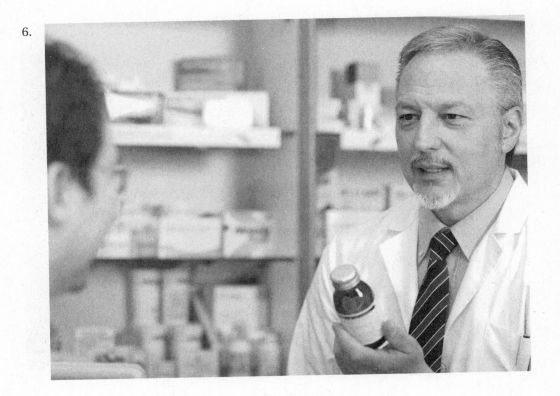

Part 2: Question-Response

Directions: You will hear a question and three possible responses. Choose the response that most closely answers the question, and fill in the corresponding oval on your answer sheet.

7.   Mark your answer on your answer sheet.

8.   Mark your answer on your answer sheet.

9.   Mark your answer on your answer sheet.

10.   Mark your answer on your answer sheet.

11.   Mark your answer on your answer sheet.

12.   Mark your answer on your answer sheet.

13.   Mark your answer on your answer sheet.

14.   Mark your answer on your answer sheet.

15.   Mark your answer on your answer sheet.

16.   Mark your answer on your answer sheet.

17.   Mark your answer on your answer sheet.

18.   Mark your answer on your answer sheet.

19.   Mark your answer on your answer sheet.

20.   Mark your answer on your answer sheet.

21.   Mark your answer on your answer sheet.

22.   Mark your answer on your answer sheet.

23.   Mark your answer on your answer sheet.

24.   Mark your answer on your answer sheet.

25.   Mark your answer on your answer sheet.

26.   Mark your answer on your answer sheet.

27.   Mark your answer on your answer sheet.

28.   Mark your answer on your answer sheet.

29.   Mark your answer on your answer sheet.

30.   Mark your answer on your answer sheet.

31.   Mark your answer on your answer sheet.

Part 3: Conversations

Track 41

Directions: You will hear a conversation between two or more people. You will see three questions on each conversation and four possible answers. Choose the best answer to each question, and fill in the corresponding oval on your answer sheet.

32. What does the woman want to do?

    (A) Clean the coffeepot
    (B) Sit down
    (C) Wash her hands
    (D) Sweep the floor

33. Where are the speakers?

    (A) On the sixth floor
    (B) Above the sixth floor
    (C) Below the sixth floor
    (D) On the ground floor

34. What does the man want to drink?

    (A) Milk
    (B) Coffee
    (C) Cocoa
    (D) Tea

35. What does the man suggest about the shirts?

    (A) They are a popular item.
    (B) They only come in two colors.
    (C) The are good for warm weather.
    (D) They will be discounted next week.

36. How much does the woman have to pay?

    (A) $42.05
    (B) $45
    (C) $60
    (D) $245

37. How will the woman pay?

    (A) Check
    (B) Cash
    (C) Credit card
    (D) Gift certificate

38. What is the woman photocopying?

    (A) A menu
    (B) An agenda
    (C) An invitation
    (D) An address list

39. Why does the woman say, "Would you?"

    (A) To make a request
    (B) To ask for information
    (C) To make a suggestion
    (D) To accept an offer

40. What will the woman do when the copies are made?

    (A) Mail them
    (B) Read them
    (C) Show them to her boss
    (D) Take them to a meeting

41. Where does this conversation take place?

    (A) In a hotel
    (B) In a fish store
    (C) In a restaurant
    (D) In someone's house

42. What is the problem with the fish?

    (A) It is not fresh.
    (B) It is not available this evening.
    (C) It takes a long time to prepare.
    (D) It costs more than other dishes.

43. What will the man do while he waits?

    (A) Have a drink
    (B) Sit and think
    (C) Go fishing
    (D) Wash the dishes

44. Where does the woman most likely work?

(A) In a dentist's office
(B) In a surgeon's office
(C) At a real estate agency
(D) At a rug cleaning service

45. Where is Mr. Wu now?

(A) In his office
(B) Out of town
(C) At a meeting
(D) On a flight

46. What does the woman want Mr. Wu to do?

(A) Make a new appointment
(B) Visit an apartment
(C) Check her schedule
(D) Meet her downtown

47. Where did the woman leave her briefcase?

(A) At a meeting
(B) In her office
(C) On her desk
(D) In a cab

48. What does Jim offer to do?

(A) Take some papers to the bank
(B) Lend the woman his briefcase
(C) Let the woman use his desk
(D) Call the cab company

49. What is in the briefcase?

(A) A cell phone
(B) A passport
(C) A report
(D) A sign

50. Why does the man want to wake up early?

(A) He has to catch an early train.
(B) He wants to make a phone call.
(C) He's going to take a morning plane.
(D) He wants to hear the weather report.

51. How will the weather be tomorrow?

(A) Snowy
(B) Rainy
(C) Cold
(D) Hot

52. What does the man mean when he says, "I don't think I'll bother"?

(A) He doesn't mind traveling on an early flight.
(B) He is not disturbed by the other hotel guests.
(C) He hopes he isn't causing an inconvenience.
(D) He won't have breakfast at the hotel.

53. What does the man say about the plane trip?

(A) It was uncomfortable.
(B) It was expensive.
(C) It was overnight.
(D) It was long.

54. Why is the man annoyed?

(A) They have to go to baggage claim.
(B) He doesn't have enough money.
(C) The woman's bag is heavy.
(D) They are stuck in traffic.

55. What will the man do next?

(A) Look for a taxi
(B) Wait for the woman
(C) Pick up the woman's bag
(D) Check the subway schedule

56. What did the man send the woman?

(A) A program schedule
(B) A personnel file
(C) A finance report
(D) A rent check

57. What does the woman ask the man to do?

(A) Look in a folder
(B) Use a different address
(C) Explain something to her
(D) Get some documents ready

58. What does the woman say about the man?

(A) He is reliable.
(B) He is often late.
(C) He is a bit strange.
(D) He is good with numbers.

59. What sport does the man enjoy?

(A) Golf
(B) Tennis
(C) Biking
(D) Swimming

60. Where does he practice it?

(A) At the hotel
(B) At the park
(C) At the exercise club
(D) At the community center

61. What do the women invite the man to do?

(A) Have lunch
(B) Walk in the park
(C) Play a game of pool
(D) Join the country club

62. What most likely is the man's job?

(A) Artist
(B) Landscaper
(C) Tour guide
(D) Photographer

63. What will the speakers do tomorrow?

(A) Bike through a valley
(B) Meet in an alley
(C) Fish in a river
(D) Ride on a bus

64. What should people bring?

(A) A dress
(B) Cold drinks
(C) Some books
(D) Warm clothes

Mall

Bookstore	Store A
Store B	Store C
Store D	Cafe

65. What does the man need to buy?

(A) Another kind of paper
(B) Notebooks and easels
(C) Green markers
(D) Books

66. Look at the graphic. Which is the supply store?

(A) Store A
(B) Store B
(C) Store C
(D) Store D

67. What will the woman do next?

(A) Go to the mall
(B) Speak with Joe
(C) Give the man instructions
(D) Arrange the conference room

Parking Prices	
up to 1 hour	$5
up to 2 hours	$8
up to 3 hours	$12
over 3 hours	$15

68. What is the man worried about?

(A) Finding a parking space
(B) Getting to the movie late
(C) Waiting on line for tickets
(D) Paying too much for parking

69. Look at the graphic. How much will the speakers probably pay for parking?

(A) $5
(B) $8
(C) $12
(D) $15

70. What does the man want to do?

(A) Leave the theater early
(B) Sit in the front row
(C) Buy tickets online
(D) Eat snacks later

Part 4: Talks

Directions: You will hear a talk given by a single speaker. You will see three questions on each talk, each with four possible answers. Choose the best answer to each question, and fill in the corresponding oval on your answer sheet.

71. Who is the audience for this advertisement?

    (A) Families
    (B) Businesspeople
    (C) Tourists
    (D) Students

72. What is the advertisement for?

    (A) Suitcases
    (B) Computers
    (C) Clothes
    (D) Travel agency

73. How can a customer get a discount?

    (A) By ordering online
    (B) By shopping at a retail store
    (C) By completing an application
    (D) By ordering next month

74. What best describes the weather conditions the area is facing?

    (A) Cold
    (B) Fog
    (C) Snow and ice
    (D) Wind and rain

75. What problems will this weather cause tomorrow?

    (A) People will have trouble getting to work.
    (B) People won't have enough heat.
    (C) Flights will be canceled.
    (D) People should buy plenty of food.

76. What does the speaker mean when he says, "It's not all bad news"?

    (A) The weather will improve soon.
    (B) People will enjoy a day off from work.
    (C) The news report will follow the weather report.
    (D) City officials will work to clear the roads quickly.

77. What is the first thing a receptionist should do for a visitor?

    (A) Greet her
    (B) Have her sign in
    (C) Ask for an ID card
    (D) Let her take a seat

78. Where should the visitor wait?

    (A) By the receptionist's desk
    (B) Outside the office
    (C) Next to the door
    (D) In the lobby

79. What should visitors never do?

    (A) Go upstairs
    (B) Carry books
    (C) Wait too long
    (D) Walk around alone

80. Who is Lynn?

    (A) A historian
    (B) A tour guide
    (C) A guidebook writer
    (D) A property owner

81. Where does the tour take place?

    (A) A village
    (B) A school
    (C) A city
    (D) A farm

82. What are listeners asked to do?

    (A) Carry their own suitcases
    (B) Avoid touching the displays
    (C) Purchase items in a store
    (D) Play some games

83. What is the purpose of this talk?

   (A) To describe library services
   (B) To introduce a tour of the library
   (C) To compare the new and old libraries
   (D) To explain how to reach each floor of the library

84. What is on the second floor?

   (A) Magazines and periodicals
   (B) Young adult books
   (C) Activity rooms
   (D) Offices

85. What does the speaker mean when he says, "It's not to be missed"?

   (A) There is nothing interesting on the sixth floor.
   (B) Everyone should visit the sixth floor.
   (C) No one is allowed on the sixth floor.
   (D) He has never visited the sixth floor.

86. What is the destination for this flight?

   (A) Dallas
   (B) Houston
   (C) Madison
   (D) Wilmington

87. What does the captain say about the flight?

   (A) It will be late.
   (B) There will be turbulence.
   (C) It will be smooth.
   (D) The flying altitude will be low.

88. What does the captain say about the final destination?

   (A) It is a popular place to visit.
   (B) The people there are friendly.
   (C) It is a good place for clothes shopping.
   (D) The weather there will be pleasant.

89. Who will give the keynote address?

   (A) The association president
   (B) A university professor
   (C) A financial expert
   (D) A journalist

90. What will take place in the Garden Room?

   (A) A wedding
   (B) A workshop
   (C) A lunch
   (D) A market

91. What is the audience asked to do?

   (A) Speak with George Williams
   (B) Leave boxes by the door
   (C) Pay for lunch
   (D) Complete a form

92. What will take place in seven days?

   (A) The voicemail system will change.
   (B) This customer will get a new telephone.
   (C) This customer will get a new telephone number.
   (D) The telephone company's web address will change.

93. How can a customer save a message?

   (A) Press two
   (B) Press four
   (C) Press seven
   (D) Press nine

94. How can a customer learn about all of the new codes?

   (A) Press ten
   (B) Press the star key
   (C) Visit the company's website
   (D) Listen to the entire message

<table>
<tr><td colspan="2">

City Caterers
Lunch Prices

15 guests $150
20 guests. $200
25 guests $250
50 guests. $450

</td></tr>
</table>

Building Directory

Ground Floor ...... Lobby
First Floor............ City Bank
Second Floor .... Silverton Company
Third Floor .... City Sports Equipment, Inc.

95. What event is the speaker arranging?

(A) A staff party
(B) A training session
(C) A client luncheon
(D) An awards banquet

96. What does the speaker ask Evelyn to do?

(A) Order the lunch
(B) Count the guests
(C) Pick up the lunch
(D) Arrange the dining room

97. Look at the graphic. How much will the speaker pay for lunch?

(A) $150
(B) $200
(C) $250
(D) $450

98. Who is this talk for?

(A) All building tenants
(B) Department heads
(C) New employees
(D) Job applicants

99. Look at the graphic. Where is the fitness room located?

(A) Ground Floor
(B) First Floor
(C) Second Floor
(D) Third Floor

100. What will the listeners do next?

(A) Tour the building
(B) Break for lunch
(C) Ask questions
(D) View a slide

This is the end of the Listening Comprehension portion of the test. Turn to Part 5 in your test book.

READING

In this section of the test, you will have the chance to show how well you understand written English. There are three parts to this section, with special directions for each part.

**YOU WILL HAVE ONE HOUR AND FIFTEEN MINUTES
TO COMPLETE PARTS 5, 6, AND 7 OF THE TEST.**

Part 5: Incomplete Sentences

> **Directions:** You will see a sentence with a missing word. Four possible answers follow the sentence. Choose the best answer to the question, and fill in the corresponding oval on your answer sheet.

101. By Friday, twenty-five applications had been submitted _____ the position of desk clerk.

    (A) at
    (B) on
    (C) for
    (D) by

102. The deeply discounted prices offered on that line of products is sure to _____ many new customers.

    (A) offer
    (B) attract
    (C) enjoy
    (D) expect

103. Mr. Cruz needs someone to _____ him with the conference display.

    (A) assume
    (B) assign
    (C) assent
    (D) assist

104. The workshop will be repeated next week for everyone who was not able to be _____ yesterday.

    (A) resent
    (B) present
    (C) content
    (D) intent

105. One downside of living in the countryside is the long _____ to get to work.

    (A) travel
    (B) relay
    (C) commute
    (D) extension

106. The final purchase price was higher than the investors _____.

    (A) had expected
    (B) expect
    (C) are expecting
    (D) will expect

107. The new waitress made hardly any mistakes on her first day, so I imagine _____ will be hired full time.

    (A) she
    (B) him
    (C) her
    (D) they

108. The new insurance plan is especially _____ with employees who have families.

    (A) popularized
    (B) popular
    (C) populated
    (D) popularity

109. The provisions officer buys supplies in _____ quantities because the fishing boat is at sea for weeks at a time.

(A) largely
(B) largest
(C) larger
(D) large

110. The airline will refund your money as _____ as your travel agent cancels your reservation.

(A) well
(B) far
(C) soon
(D) little

111. Did Mr. Fisk _____ the reference guide from the company library?

(A) loan
(B) borrow
(C) lend
(D) sent

112. _____ they were ordered, the brochures and business cards were never printed.

(A) Although
(B) Even
(C) However
(D) Despite

113. The operator does not remember receiving a fax from the Madrid office _____ from the Paris office.

(A) or
(B) and
(C) either
(D) but

114. Most of our staff have not used this type of copy machine _____.

(A) before
(B) prior
(C) advance
(D) previous

115. The housekeepers will need to be paid overtime for their work over the holidays, _____?

(A) won't they
(B) will she
(C) aren't they
(D) they will

116. The printer in Mr. Daaka's office uses a special _____ cartridge that comes in four different colors.

(A) dye
(B) ink
(C) paper
(D) tray

117. The receptionist receives packages and _____ them until the proper department is notified.

(A) is holding
(B) held
(C) hold
(D) holds

118. The purpose of our conference is to help employees _____ our policies.

(A) understood
(B) understanding
(C) understand
(D) are understanding

119. _____ none of us were familiar with the city, Mr. Gutman drove us to the meeting.

(A) Although
(B) Because
(C) Therefore
(D) However

120. The gas station attendant suggests _____ a boat from a local to save money.

(A) rent
(B) rents
(C) rented
(D) renting

121. If this report is sent by overnight delivery, it _____ Milan by noon tomorrow.

(A) reaches
(B) will reach
(C) is reaching
(D) has reached

122. Yamamoto Sushi is across town and _____ near our hotel, so we should take a taxi.

(A) nowhere
(B) anywhere
(C) somewhere
(D) everywhere

123. Employees who _____ attending the conference can get a discount on travel arrangements.

(A) have going
(B) are going to
(C) will
(D) will be

124. Mr. Vasco has developed his _____ in electronics over many years of experience and hard work.

(A) technician
(B) professional
(C) expertise
(D) authorization

125. The city is asking for funding _____ five parks and three recreational centers.

(A) on renovating
(B) for renovation
(C) by renovating
(D) to renovate

126. The head housekeeper is going to ask Ms. Chang how much time she _____ available.

(A) will have had
(B) is having
(C) have
(D) has

127. The hotel marketing director is quite _____ about advertising in Europe.

(A) knowing
(B) knowledge
(C) knowledgeable
(D) knows

128. We _____ to know the size of the banner before we can start designing it.

(A) must
(B) need
(C) could
(D) should

129. The operator _____ Mr. Smith if she knew where to reach him.

(A) will call
(B) had called
(C) called
(D) would call

130. The trainers for the seminar had the crew _____ their equipment to the conference center.

(A) move
(B) moving
(C) mover
(D) moved

Part 6: Text Completion

Directions: You will see four passages, each with four blanks. Each blank has four answer choices. For each blank, choose the word, phrase, or sentence that best completes the passage.

Questions 131–134 refer to the following letter.

Creek and Chung, Accountants
1040 Stone Way
Seattle, Washington 93108-2662

July 12, 20—

Mr. Hugh Ferrer
Unity Health Care
400 East Pine Street
Seattle, Washington 93129-2665

Dear Mr. Ferrer:

We are a mid-sized accounting firm. Our staff members have expressed dissatisfaction with our current insurance plan, so we are looking into other _____. The insurance
                                                            131
company we use now has recently raised its rates, while at the same time the quality of service has gotten worse. Naturally, we are not happy about paying more and more money for poor service. _____, we are interested in learning more about Unity
                                       132
Health Care (UHC). Could you please mail a packet of information to me? _____.
                                                                         133
First, our employees want to choose their own doctors. Does your program allow this?
Second, do your doctors have weekend and evening hours? Our employees have busy work schedules, and it is not always _____ for them to go to appointments during regular
                                        134
business hours.

Thank you for your help.
Sincerely,

Felicia Braddish
Human Resources Manager

---

131. (A) employees
     (B) positions
     (C) activities
     (D) options

132. (A) Therefore
     (B) However
     (C) Moreover
     (D) Nevertheless

133. (A) Most insurance plans offer a variety of options to their clients
     (B) I would also appreciate it if you could answer the following questions
     (C) We have several reasons for changing our insurance
     (D) I have outlined the most important points here

134. (A) enjoyable
     (B) difficult
     (C) convenient
     (D) interesting

Questions 135–138 refer to the following e-mail.

From: Simon Yan
To: Mingmei Lee
Subject: Monday Meeting

Dear Mingmei,

I have to leave town for a business trip _____ there is an emergency in our
                                        135
Singapore office. I am sorry that I will have to miss our Monday morning meeting,

especially because I am eager to see your progress on my company's new financial

center. This is an important project for National Bank.

My coworker, Hugh Harrison, will _____ me. Hugh plans to look for you
                                 136
at the construction site at 9:00 A.M. _____. Please talk with Hugh about this. While
                                      137
we don't want to spend a lot of extra money on this building, it is going to be our

company's headquarters and needs to look good. You have an excellent reputation

as a Construction Project Manager, so I'm _____ that you can manage the budget
                                          138
and build a fantastic center for us at the same time.

I will return one week from today. You can e-mail me until I return. Thank you.

135. (A) so
     (B) if
     (C) as
     (D) by

136. (A) escort
     (B) replace
     (C) assist
     (D) accompany

137. (A) Please be sure to arrive on time
     (B) This is a convenient time and place for both of us
     (C) Construction has been going on for quite a while now
     (D) You told me that you have some concerns about the project's budget

138. (A) doubtful
     (B) positive
     (C) wondering
     (D) concerned

Questions 139–142 refer to the following memorandum.

Memorandum

From: Belinda Beilby, Company President
To: Company Vice-Presidents
Re: Reducing electricity expenses

The electric company is ____ its rates by 25% next month, so we need to look at
     139
ways to reduce our electricity usage. Below is a list of recommendations. Please
distribute this list to the departments in your area.

Ways to Reduce Electricity Expenses

1. Lights: Turn off the lights in meeting rooms when your meeting ends. Turn off
   the lights in the offices before you leave for the day.

2. Computers: At the day's end, turn off your computer.

3. Photocopying: Don't photocopy and fax documents. Most documents can
   ____ electronically.
   140

4. Fans/Heaters: Using fans or heaters in the office should not be necessary.
   ____. If you feel that your office is too cool or too warm, please contact the
   141
   maintenance staff.

5. Home Office Option: ____ employees to work at home one or more
        142
   days a week saves money in many ways, including on electricity. Employees who
   are interested in this option should speak to their supervisors.

139. (A) cutting
(B) increasing
(C) dividing
(D) improving

140. (A) send
(B) sent
(C) to send
(D) be sent

141. (A) The building temperature is set at a level that most people find
comfortable
(B) However, you may bring a small space heater or fan from home if you
wish
(C) Temperatures in this region vary, depending on the time of year
(D) Fans and heaters do not adequately control room temperature

142. (A) Allow
(B) Allowing
(C) To allow
(D) Will allow

Questions 143–146 refer to the following announcement.

_____. The company announced last Friday that its president, Shirley Ocampo,
143
will succeed Louis Freeland as chief executive officer starting in September.

Ms. Ocampo will be the first female chief executive in the company's history.

Sunrise Manufacturers is _____ manufacturer of farming equipment in the country.
144
This is a sector that has been traditionally dominated by men, making Ms. Ocampo's

appointment particularly _____. Mr. Freeland, who will retire from Sunrise
145
when Ms. Ocampo takes over his position next month, _____ at the company
146
for 25 years.

143. (A) Employees at Sunrise Manufacturers, Inc. will be getting a new boss soon
     (B) Customers of Sunrise Manufacturing, Inc. give the products high ratings
     (C) Sunrise Manufacturers, Inc. has branches in several parts of the country
     (D) Sunrise Manufacturer's, Inc. has several new positions open

144. (A) large
     (B) larger
     (C) the larger
     (D) the largest

145. (A) recent
     (B) common
     (C) significant
     (D) profitable

146. (A) works
     (B) worked
     (C) had worked
     (D) has been working

Part 7: Reading Comprehension

Directions: You will see single and multiple reading passages followed by several questions. Each question has four answer choices. Choose the best answer to the question, and fill in the corresponding oval on your answer sheet.

Questions 147–148 refer to the following advertisement.

Data Entry/Clerk

Insurance firm seeks reliable, detail-oriented person for operations division. Responsibilities include data entry, filing, and word processing. Good salary and benefits. Pleasant atmosphere. Room to advance.

---

147. What is one responsibility of this job?

   (A) Answering the phone
   (B) Data entry
   (C) Selling insurance
   (D) Operating a division

148. What is one benefit of the position?

   (A) They'll give you your own office later.
   (B) You can work toward promotions.
   (C) Benefits apply to dependents.
   (D) You can earn commissions.

Questions 149–150 refer to the following memo.

MEMORANDUM

To: All Employees
From: Donetta Muscillo
       Safety Coordinator
Date: June 5, 20—

Sub: Fire doors

Employees are reminded that doors designated as fire doors must stay closed at all times. The purpose of fire doors is to help direct smoke away from areas where people are working in case of a fire in the building. Even though the weather is hot and the repairs to the company's air conditioner are not complete, keeping the fire doors open is strictly prohibited.

149. What is the purpose of the memo?

(A) To explain the function of the fire doors
(B) To explain how to keep the fire doors closed
(C) To explain that the fire doors should stay closed
(D) To explain why the building is warmer than usual

150. Why were employees probably keeping the fire doors open?

(A) To get to a higher floor
(B) To look at the view
(C) To go from office to office
(D) To let in cool air

Questions 151–152 refer to the following text message chain.

MYRA LEE Just letting you know I'll be a bit late.	4:10
HIRO MATSUO Was your flight delayed?	4:11
MYRA LEE No. It was early, in fact. And I got a cab right away, but I left my suitcase behind at the baggage claim.	4:13
HIRO MATSUO What? Where?	4:14
MYRA LEE At the airport. We were halfway to the office when I realized it. I had to make the cab driver turn around.	4:16
HIRO MATSUO Wow. You must be tired.	4:17
MYRA LEE It's been a long week. I hope they don't delay the staff meeting for me. Would you mind letting the boss know I'll be late? You don't have to tell him why.	4:18
HIRO MATSUO Sure thing. See you soon.	4:20
MYRA LEE Thanks. Expect me in 30 minutes or so.	4:21

151. What problem does Ms. Lee have?

(A) She lost her suitcase.
(B) She missed her flight.
(C) She couldn't find a taxi.
(D) She forgot to pick up her bag.

152. At 4:20, what does Mr. Matsuo mean when he writes, "Sure thing"?

(A) He will talk to Ms. Lee's boss.
(B) He knows Ms. Lee will arrive soon.
(C) He understands why Ms. Lee is arriving late.
(D) He is certain Ms. Lee's boss won't mind delaying the meeting.

Questions 153–154 refer to the following announcement.

ESTATE AUCTION

An auction for the estate of *Raul Diega*
will be held on

Saturday, October 3, at 11:00 A.M.
(preview starts at 10:00 A.M.)

Location: 5667 North Hedge Lane

Some of the items to be auctioned
* 2004 Mercedes
* China and crystal
* Oriental rugs
* Jewelry
* Stamp collection

Questions? Please call Estate Planners at
778-0099 between noon and 5 P.M.

---

153. Which of the following items will be auctioned?

(A) Chinese antiques
(B) Rare books
(C) Bracelets
(D) Wall-to-wall carpeting

154. When can you start to look at things?

(A) October 3, 11:00 A.M.
(B) By appointment after calling 778-0099
(C) Any day from noon to five
(D) October 3, 10:00 A.M.

Questions 155–157 refer to the following pie chart.

First Impressions Art Gallery

Review of April Finances

Total Expenses: $75,275
Total Income: $228,566

Expenses

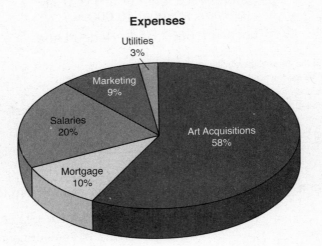

155. When was this graph created?

(A) Before April
(B) After April
(C) In early April
(D) In late April

156. What can be said about the gallery?

(A) It is earning about three times what it is spending.
(B) It is spending more than it is earning.
(C) It is spending the same amount as it is earning.
(D) It is earning half of what it is spending.

157. What is the greatest expense for the gallery?

(A) New inventory
(B) Money paid to employees
(C) Money paid to advertise
(D) Electricity and water costs

Questions 158–160 refer to the following e-mail.

From: Human Resources
To: Transferring Staff
Subj: Information about Transfer
Date: April 10

As you know, you are among the 60 technical and management-level employees who will be making the move to our new manufacturing plant. This is our first overseas plant, and we hope to make the transition as smooth as possible for you and your families. To this end, we are offering a series of seminars designed to help you adjust to life overseas and in a small town. The seminars will address such issues as regional customs, diet, language, and cross-cultural communication. While attendance is not mandatory, it is strongly suggested that you attend as many of these seminars as possible. I have attached a schedule. Please share it with your family members and put them on your calendar. These seminars are suitable for everyone aged 14 and over. Please contact the HR office if you have any questions or concerns.

Amanda Jones
HR officer

158. Where is the new manufacturing plant?

(A) Near the mountains
(B) In another country
(C) In a large city
(D) On the coast

159. What is the purpose of the e-mail?

(A) To give information about a seminar series
(B) To help employees plan their move to the new plant
(C) To announce the opening of a new manufacturing plant
(D) To explain the importance of cross-cultural understanding

160. What is indicated about the seminars?

(A) They are a requirement for new employees.
(B) They are for both employees and their families.
(C) They will take place at the new plant.
(D) They will begin right away.

Questions 161–163 refer to the following announcement.

VAL D'OR CATERING SUPPLY

Val D'Or is pleased to announce its purchase of Gourmet Galore, a company focusing on specialty food products, cookware, and kitchen accessories. –[1]– Plans for Gourmet Galore include the opening of five more stores across Europe. Ten of the original sixteen stores were remodeled last year, and similar plans are in the works for the remaining six. –[2]– Gourmet Galore will also be expanding its reach with a new line of cooking schools. These schools will take advantage of the current interest in health improvement by focusing on gourmet foods that are both delicious and nutritious. –[3]– Regional specialties will also be included, and guest chefs from all over Europe will act as consultants. –[4]–

161. What plans does Val D'Or have for six of the Gourmet Galore stores?

(A) Remodel them
(B) Buy them
(C) Sell them
(D) Relocate them

162. What will be emphasized in the cooking classes?

(A) Recipes from one region
(B) Use of specialty cookware
(C) Food from around the world
(D) Healthful foods

163. In which of the following positions marked [1], [2], [3], and [4] does the following sentence best belong?

"Val D'Or aims to expand the business and offerings of this already popular brand."

(A) [1]
(B) [2]
(C) [3]
(D) [4]

Questions 164–167 refer to the following online chat discussion.

Marco Silva [11:15]
I just got a call from Shipping. They have a return from a client, Sunrise, Inc.

Jane Kim [11:16]
What? Why?

Sabine Kohl [11:17]
I had an e-mail from Sunrise this morning. They said we shipped them the wrong items. It was five bolts of dark blue cotton.

Marco Silva [11:20]
OK. I've checked the files. That's not what they ordered.

Jane Kim [11:22]
That's their usual order.

Marco Silva [11:23]
Right. But they're working on a new line of summer dresses. They wanted lighter colors for that.

Sabine Kohl [11:25]
What should I tell them?

Jane Kim [11:27]
You'll have to apologize, of course. And offer them free shipping on this order and their next order.

Sabine Kohl [11:30]
Someone should contact Shipping and find out what the story is. We can't let this happen again.

Marco Silva [11:31]
I'm on it.

Jane Kim [11:32]
Great. Let us know what you find out.

164. What kind of company do the chatters most likely work for?

(A) Shipping
(B) Clothing retail
(C) Fashion design
(D) Fabric manufacturer

165. What is indicated about the order made by the client?

(A) It was made several weeks ago.
(B) It was larger than the previous order.
(C) It was different from the client's usual order.
(D) It was changed by the client at the last minute.

166. What was the problem with the shipment?

(A) It was shipped too late.
(B) It took too long to arrive.
(C) It was sent to the wrong address.
(D) It did not contain what the client ordered.

167. At 11:31, what does Mr. Silva mean when he writes, "I'm on it"?

(A) He will let the client know what happened.
(B) He will talk with the shipping department.
(C) He is on the shipping department staff.
(D) He is good at solving problems.

BUSINESS ASSOCIATION
FUTURE BUSINESS LEADERS EDUCATION FUND
P.O. BOX 1205, WILLIAMSTOWN

July 8, 20—

Mr. Gregory Harrison
78 North Main Street
Riverdale

Dear Mr. Harrison,

As you know, the Business Association has been supporting aspiring young professionals in our community for over 25 years through our Future Business Leaders Education Fund. In addition to our scholarship program, we offer a variety of workshops to help young business professionals acquire the skills and experience they need to advance along their career paths. Furthermore, through our awards program, we recognize young professionals in the field. This year at our annual banquet on May 1, ten young professionals from our city were the recipients of awards between $500–$2,000 recognizing their career achievements.

As a long-time member of the Business Association, you have been a generous supporter of the Future Business Leaders Education Fund. We ask that you once again make a commitment to support our work by making a cash donation. This year, our goal is to raise $25,000 from among our membership. Your generosity, along with that of your fellow Business Association members, will allow us to continue our important work in training the business leaders of tomorrow.

Please complete the information requested on the enclosed sheet and return it, along with your check, to our office. We hope to receive all donations before the first of next month. Thank you once again for your generous support.

Sincerely,

Elisabeth Larsen

Elisabeth Larsen

168. What is the purpose of this letter?

(A) To describe a scholarship program
(B) To give thanks for a donation
(C) To announce a new program
(D) To ask for money

169. What is indicated about Mr. Harrison?

(A) He has given money to the Education Fund in the past.
(B) He is a new member of the Business Association.
(C) He gives business training workshops.
(D) He is a young business professional.

170. What happened on May 1?

(A) A workshop was given.
(B) There was an awards dinner.
(C) Some scholarships were granted.
(D) The fund received new donations.

171. What is enclosed with the letter?

(A) A program description
(B) A schedule
(C) A form
(D) A check

Questions 172–175 refer to the following article.

If you want to advance in your career, you will have to make some careful decisions, especially regarding job offers. –[1]– It is important to evaluate each offer in terms of the overall value it has for your career. –[2]– For instance, you might have to move to a new region to take a job that you feel is right for you in every other way. You may have to work late hours or even accept a decrease in salary for a job that offers you the experience you need.

–[3]– Agreeing to accept a job that is not within your career path is usually a mistake. Such a decision will not give you the training and experience you want. Moreover, you will feel frustrated because you are not working toward your goals. This will affect your colleagues, who will feel as if you are not acting as part of a team. On the other hand, if you take a position that may not be all you want in terms of salary or location but that moves you closer to your career goals, you will feel satisfied. –[4]– Study after study has shown that job satisfaction, far more than salary or other factors, results in the highest level of performance.

172. What is this advice about?

(A) Choosing a job
(B) Hiring staff
(C) Getting job training
(D) Completing a job application

173. The word "position" in paragraph 2, line 5 is closest in meaning to

(A) opinion
(B) location
(C) level
(D) job

174. According to the article, which workers perform best?

(A) Those who have the right training
(B) Those who work on a team
(C) Those who enjoy their jobs
(D) Those who earn the most

175. In which of the following positions marked [1], [2], [3], and [4] does the following sentence best belong?

"You may have to make some sacrifices at first."

(A) [1]
(B) [2]
(C) [3]
(D) [4]

HORIZON OFFICE PRODUCTS, INC.
COMMITTEE MEETING ON MARKETING
THURSDAY, JUNE 15, 20— 9:30 A.M.–11:30 A.M.
PLACE: ROOM 2

AGENDA

1. REVIEW OF CURRENT STRATEGY   BEN NGUYEN
2. GOALS FOR NEW STRATEGY   BO PARK
3. FOCUS GROUPS   MARTY TAYLOR
4. PROJECTS TO BEGIN   BARBARA SPENCER
5. PLANS FOR THE YEAR   RITA PALMER

To: Max Kohler
From: Bo Park
Subject: Committee Meeting

There were serious problems at today's meeting. We began on time, but Ben wasn't there, so we had to begin with the second agenda item. Then, thirty minutes after we began, Ben finally arrived and gave his presentation. Marty never came at all. I found out later that he's been out sick, but in any case his topic was never discussed. Barbara tried to explain her topic, but it was confusing. She did the best she could, but we really needed to hear from Marty first for her presentation to make sense. We couldn't agree on our next step, so we ended the meeting early, right after Barbara's talk. When will you return from this business trip? I know none of this would have happened if you had been here.

176. What was the topic of the June 15 meeting?

   (A) Marketing
   (B) Business trips
   (C) Work schedules
   (D) Ordering office supplies

177. What topic was discussed first?

   (A) Review of current strategy
   (B) Goals for new strategy
   (C) Focus groups
   (D) Projects to begin

178. What time did Ben start his presentation?

   (A) 9:00
   (B) 9:30
   (C) 10:00
   (D) 11:30

179. Who gave the last presentation?

   (A) Rita Palmer
   (B) Barbara Spencer
   (C) Marty Taylor
   (D) Bo Park

180. Why didn't Max attend the meeting?

   (A) He was out sick.
   (B) He wasn't invited.
   (C) He couldn't arrive on time.
   (D) He was away on a business trip.

Questions 181–185 refer to the following notice and e-mail.

TRANSIT PASS INFORMATION
City of Springfield

Now it is easier and more affordable than ever to use the City of Springfield Pubic Transportation System (CSPTS). Choose the pass that best fits your needs.

C-PASSES
C-passes are good for unlimited rides anytime of day or night, Monday through Friday, except holidays.

SUBWAY C-PASS		BUS C-PASS		SUBWAY/BUS C-PASS	
Two weeks:	$60	Two weeks :	$45	Two weeks :	$75
Six months:	$650	Six months:	$500	Six months:	$850

A-PASSES
A-passes can be used seven days a week, 24 hours a day, any day of the year.

SUBWAY A-PASS		BUS A-PASS		SUBWAY/BUS A-PASS	
Two weeks:	$100	Two weeks :	$75	Two weeks :	$125
Six months:	$950	Six months:	$700	Six months:	$1,050

Passes are available for sale at all CSPTS subway stations, at the CSPTS downtown office, at designated banks throughout the city, and online at *www.cspts.go*.

From: Janet Jones
To: All Staff
Subj: Transit Passes
Date: November 9

In order to do our part to decrease congestion on our local roads, we are now offering all Smith Company staff members CSTPS transit passes at a reduced price. These can be used for bus and/or subway travel on all routes in the CSPTS system. To apply for the pass at the reduced price, obtain a Transit Pass Request Form from my office. After you have completed the form, have it authorized by your department head and return it to me. You can choose between a two-week and a six-month pass. Please keep in mind, however, that a new form will have to be submitted each time you need a new pass. As an added incentive to those of you who currently drive to work, we are raising the cost of parking in the company garage to $15/day starting on the first of next month.

Please let me know if you have any questions.

181. Which transit passes can be used on weekends and holidays?

(A) Any C-pass
(B) Any A-pass
(C) Subway passes only
(D) Subway/Bus passes only

182. The word "good" in line 6 of the notice is closest in meaning to

(A) nice
(B) fresh
(C) valid
(D) correct

183. Who can get a discounted transit pass?

(A) CSPTS staff
(B) Springfield residents
(C) Anyone who wants one
(D) Smith Company employees

184. Where are the discounted transit passes available?

(A) On the Internet
(B) In certain banks
(C) At the CSPTS office
(D) In Ms. Jones's office

185. What is the reason for the increased parking fee in the Smith Company garage?

(A) To encourage the use of public transportation
(B) To cover the rising cost of maintenance
(C) To fund the expansion of the garage
(D) To pay for the discounted passes

Questions 186–190 refer to the following notice and two e-mails.

**Business Journalist's Convention
Accommodations**

In the Convention Center neighborhood:
The Cascade Hotel—105 North Main St. (*www.cascadeho.com*)
The Willowmere Inn—12 Flower Avenue (*www.willowmereinn.com*)
Both of these hotels are within walking distance of the Convention Center.

For a more economical option, try:
Royal Hotel—234 Park Avenue (*www.parkviewho.com*)
Take the Green Line subway to the Park Avenue stop and walk east one block.

All three hotels offer a reduced rate to convention attendees. Reservations must be made before August 15 to receive this benefit.

From: Yvonne Wu
To: Royal Hotel
Subject: Room Reservation
Date: August 1

I will be attending the Business Journalist's Convention next month and would like to reserve a single room at your hotel for that time, September 15–18. I'd prefer a room on an upper floor with a queen-sized bed, if possible. Also, do you have a pool and exercise room? I couldn't find any information about this on your website. Finally, is there a restaurant in or near the hotel?

Thank you for your help.

From: Royal Hotel
To: Yvonne Wu
Subject: re: Room Reservation
Date: August 2

Dear Ms. Wu,

We will be happy to accommodate you during your stay to attend the Business Journalist's Convention. The type of room you requested is available. With your discount, it will cost just $100 a night. However, for the first night of your stay only, we will have to give you a room with a king-sized bed, as there are no queens available that night. It costs an extra $25. I hope this will suit you. To answer your questions, our pool is currently closed for renovations, and we hope to have it reopened by the first of next year. There is a full-service restaurant located in the hotel, and our guests are entitled to a free breakfast there. Lunch and dinner are also served and can be charged to your room for your convenience. If you would like to go ahead with your reservation, please send me your credit card information. Thank you for choosing the Royal Hotel.

Bob Jimenez
Reservations Manager

186. What is indicated about the Royal Hotel?

(A) It is the closest hotel to the convention center.
(B) It costs less than the other hotels mentioned.
(C) It has no rooms available after August 15.
(D) It is popular among business travelers.

187. What kind of room does Ms. Wu request?

(A) A room on the ground floor
(B) A room with two beds
(C) A room for one person
(D) A room near the pool

188. Why will Ms. Wu get a discounted price on her hotel room?

(A) She is attending the convention.
(B) She will stay for several nights.
(C) She is a former employee of the hotel.
(D) She will have to change rooms after the first night.

189. What is the extra $25 charge for?

(A) Transportation to the convention center
(B) A reservation cancellation fee
(C) A room with a larger bed
(D) Use of the hotel pool

190. What is indicated about breakfast?

(A) It is available at the convention center.
(B) It is served all day in the hotel restaurant.
(C) It costs extra to order it through room service.
(D) It is included in the price of the hotel room.

Festival Café Reopens

The Festival Café has recently reopened following renovations that doubled its size. Located in the heart of the downtown commercial district, the cafe is known for its homemade ice cream. Customers have been accustomed to seeing the crowd extend along the entire length of the block on warm days, as people line up to buy this tasty frozen treat. The café is also famous for its homemade baked goods and innovative sandwiches. "Now we can accommodate many more customers at a time," said owner Bertha Maguire. "We'll have outdoor seating in warm weather as well," she added. Ms. Maguire assures loyal customers that all their old favorites are still on the menu. "We look forward to seeing old customers and new in our new space," she said.

The Festival Café

is proud to announce its

GRAND REOPENING

Come celebrate with us.

April 10, 3–8 P.M.

Free ice cream samples!
Live music! Games and prizes!

Bakery and sandwich counters
will be open.

Use the coupon below
to enjoy a free drink on us!

Festival Café	Festival Café
Good for ONE COFFEE Any size Expires April 30	Good for ONE SODA Any size Expires April 30

★★★★★

by Sydney Seldman on April 12
The new Festival Café is better than ever. My family and I attended the grand reopening, and it was so much fun. The kids really loved the games and, of course, the free ice cream. The new space is nice, although, I think the colors are a bit dark. But it is quite comfortable, and there is plenty of seating. The sandwiches are still fantastic, and the cake we tried was delicious and affordable. I was surprised to find that the prices had not been raised. If you are a long-time fan of the Festival, you will enjoy it as much as ever in its new space.

191. What happened at the Festival Café?

   (A) The menu was changed.
   (B) The space was enlarged.
   (C) Old customers were lost.
   (D) A new branch was opened.

192. What is implied about the Festival Café?

   (A) It is very popular.
   (B) It is a new business.
   (C) It sells desserts only.
   (D) It has several locations.

193. How can customers get a free drink?

   (A) Win it as a prize
   (B) Go to the grand reopening
   (C) Pay for an ice cream sample
   (D) Use a coupon before the end of April

194. When did Ms. Seldman go to the Festival Café?

   (A) On April 10
   (B) On April 12
   (C) Last night
   (D) Last week

195. What does Ms. Seldman say about the Festival Café?

   (A) There aren't enough chairs.
   (B) The prices are too high.
   (C) The food is very good.
   (D) The décor has improved.

Wickford Realty Co.
For Sale
Two Retail Spaces

1. Ideal Main Street location in the heart of the downtown shopping district. Large display windows front street. Recently renovated. Near bus and subway lines. 1,500 sq ft.

2. Warren Avenue. Attractive location in the Greenwood School neighborhood. Near bus and subway lines. Customer parking on site.

Contact Wickford Realty for more information.

The Printing Press

Dear Ms. Clark:

I have been a customer at your bank for more than ten years. I am a small business owner and have been renting a space for my operations. My company is now ready to expand, and I am looking into buying a small building.

I am interested in two buildings. The one I prefer is on Main Street. It would require a $200,000 loan, and I'm not sure if I qualify for that large a loan. There is another building that would suit my needs. The size is right although the location is not as good. I would need to borrow only $130,000 to purchase this building.

I have a good credit record and am carrying only two debts at this time—$5,000 on my car loan and $120,000 on my house. I am hoping to get a thirty-year loan at 5% interest.

I would like to meet with you to discuss this as soon as possible. Would Tuesday, April 21 suit you? If not, I am available any other day that week. I look forward to hearing from you.

Sincerely,
Jeremiah Hernandez
Jeremiah Hernandez

FEDERAL BANK

8244 Centergate Street
San Antonio, TX 78217-0099

April 10, 20—

Jeremiah Hernandez
The Printing Press
111 Acorn Parkway
San Antonio, TX 78216-7423

Dear Mr. Hernandez:

Thank you for your interest in getting a loan from Federal Bank. We appreciate your business.

It is possible for us to lend you enough money for the cheaper building. We cannot give you a larger loan because you already have more than $100,000 in debt. We can offer you a loan at the interest rate and for the term you want.

I am happy to meet with you to discuss this. I am not available on the date you mentioned. Can we meet the following day? Please let me know.

Best Wishes,

Anneliese Clark

Anneliese Clark

196. What is indicated about the Warren Street property?

(A) It includes a parking lot.
(B) It is close to downtown.
(C) It is near a bus stop.
(D) It is very small.

197. What kind of business does Mr. Hernandez own, most likely?

(A) A real estate office
(B) A restaurant
(C) A store
(D) A school

198. Why does Mr. Hernandez prefer the Main Street Building?

(A) It is bigger.
(B) It is less expensive.
(C) It is in a better location.
(D) It is in better condition.

199. How much money will the bank lend him?

(A) $100,000
(B) $130,000
(C) $200,000
(D) $330,000

200. When does Ms. Clark want to meet with Mr. Hernandez?

(A) April 10
(B) April 11
(C) April 21
(D) April 22

STOP

This is the end of the test. If you finish before time is called, you may go back to Parts 5, 6, and 7 and check your work.

PRACTICE TEST 2

ANSWER KEY
Practice Test 2

LISTENING COMPREHENSION

Part 1: Photographs

1.	C	3.	B	5.	D
2.	A	4.	C	6.	A

Part 2: Question-Response

7.	A	14.	A	21.	B	28.	C
8.	C	15.	B	22.	A	29.	A
9.	A	16.	A	23.	B	30.	B
10.	A	17.	B	24.	A	31.	A
11.	C	18.	C	25.	A		
12.	A	19.	A	26.	B		
13.	B	20.	C	27.	B		

Part 3: Conversations

32.	A	42.	C	52.	D	62.	C
33.	B	43.	A	53.	D	63.	D
34.	C	44.	A	54.	A	64.	D
35.	A	45.	C	55.	B	65.	C
36.	B	46.	A	56.	C	66.	A
37.	D	47.	D	57.	B	67.	D
38.	C	48.	D	58.	A	68.	B
39.	D	49.	B	59.	B	69.	C
40.	A	50.	C	60.	D	70.	B
41.	C	51.	B	61.	A		

Part 4: Talks

71.	B	79.	D	87.	B	95.	B
72.	A	80.	B	88.	D	96.	A
73.	A	81.	D	89.	C	97.	C
74.	C	82.	B	90.	A	98.	C
75.	A	83.	B	91.	D	99.	B
76.	A	84.	C	92.	A	100.	D
77.	A	85.	B	93.	D		
78.	D	86.	B	94.	B		

READING

Part 5: Incomplete Sentences

101. **C**	109. **D**	117. **D**	125. **D**
102. **B**	110. **C**	118. **C**	126. **D**
103. **D**	111. **B**	119. **B**	127. **C**
104. **B**	112. **A**	120. **D**	128. **B**
105. **C**	113. **A**	121. **B**	129. **D**
106. **A**	114. **A**	122. **A**	130. **A**
107. **A**	115. **A**	123. **D**	
108. **B**	116. **B**	124. **C**	

Part 6: Text Completion

131. **D**	135. **C**	139. **B**	143. **A**
132. **A**	136. **B**	140. **D**	144. **D**
133. **B**	137. **D**	141. **A**	145. **C**
134. **C**	138. **B**	142. **B**	146. **D**

Part 7: Reading Comprehension

147. **B**	161. **A**	175. **B**	189. **C**
148. **B**	162. **D**	176. **A**	190. **D**
149. **C**	163. **A**	177. **B**	191. **B**
150. **D**	164. **D**	178. **C**	192. **A**
151. **D**	165. **C**	179. **B**	193. **D**
152. **A**	166. **D**	180. **D**	194. **A**
153. **C**	167. **B**	181. **B**	195. **C**
154. **D**	168. **D**	182. **C**	196. **A**
155. **B**	169. **A**	183. **D**	197. **C**
156. **A**	170. **B**	184. **D**	198. **C**
157. **A**	171. **C**	185. **A**	199. **B**
158. **B**	172. **A**	186. **B**	200. **D**
159. **A**	173. **D**	187. **C**	
160. **B**	174. **C**	188. **A**	

TEST SCORE CONVERSION TABLE

Count your correct responses. Match the number of correct responses with the corresponding score from the Test Score Conversion Table (below). Add the two scores together. This is your Total Estimated Test Score. As you practice taking the TOEIC practice tests, your scores should improve. Keep track of your Total Estimated Test Scores.

# Correct	Listening Score	Reading Score	# Correct	Listening Score	Reading Score	# Correct	Listening Score	Reading Score	# Correct	Listening Score	Reading Score
0	5	5	26	110	65	51	255	220	76	410	370
1	5	5	27	115	70	52	260	225	77	420	380
2	5	5	28	120	80	53	270	230	78	425	385
3	5	5	29	125	85	54	275	235	79	430	390
4	5	5	30	130	90	55	280	240	80	440	395
5	5	5	31	135	95	56	290	250	81	445	400
6	5	5	32	140	100	57	295	255	82	450	405
7	10	5	33	145	110	58	300	260	83	460	410
8	15	5	34	150	115	59	310	265	84	465	415
9	20	5	35	160	120	60	315	270	85	470	420
10	25	5	36	165	125	61	320	280	86	475	425
11	30	5	37	170	130	62	325	285	87	480	430
12	35	5	38	175	140	63	330	290	88	485	435
13	40	5	39	180	145	64	340	300	89	490	445
14	45	5	40	185	150	65	345	305	90	495	450
15	50	5	41	190	160	66	350	310	91	495	455
16	55	10	42	195	165	67	360	320	92	495	465
17	60	15	43	200	170	68	365	325	93	495	470
18	65	20	44	210	175	69	370	330	94	495	480
19	70	25	45	215	180	70	380	335	95	495	485
20	75	30	46	220	190	71	385	340	96	495	490
21	80	35	47	230	195	72	390	350	97	495	495
22	85	40	48	240	200	73	395	355	98	495	495
23	90	45	49	245	210	74	400	360	99	495	495
24	95	50	50	250	215	75	405	365	100	495	495
25	100	60									

Number of Correct Listening Responses _____ = Listening Score _____

Number of Correct Reading Responses _____ = Reading Score _____

Total Estimated Test Score _____

ANSWER EXPLANATIONS

Listening Comprehension

PART 1: PHOTOGRAPHS

1. **(C)** Choice (C) makes the assumption that the location is an *airport* and that the people waiting are *passengers*. Choice (A) misidentifies the location of the passengers—they are at the airport, not on a plane. Choice (B) is contradicted by *empty*; there are many people on the concourse. Choice (D) does not describe the location of the *bags*, which are on the *floor*, not on a *truck*.

2. **(A)** Choice (A) correctly describes the action, looking at their laptop, and the background shows they are outdoors. Choice (B) confuses the action: There are two people and there is a coffee cup on the table, but they are not making the coffee. Choice (C) is incorrect because you cannot see their hands. Choice (D) is incorrect because they are already seated at a table.

3. **(B)** Choice (B) identifies the specific locations of the *trains*. Choice (A) confuses the sound of *train* with *crane* and uses the related word to *bridge, water*. Choice (C) uses words related to *train (narrow* and *tunnel)*, but it does not describe the picture and confuses the sound of *cart* with *train car*. Choice (D) is incorrect because it is trains, not pedestrians, that are crossing the bridge.

4. **(C)** A man is holding a microphone and talking into it. Choice (A) confuses similar-sounding words *microphone* and *telephone*. Choice (B) confuses similar-sounding words *talking* and *walking* and *microphone* and *telephone*. Choice (D) mentions the man's hand, but he isn't waving it.

5. **(D)** Two men in business suits are wearing nametags. Choice (A) correctly identifies the table, but there is no waiter in the photo. Choice (B) correctly identifies the chairs, but nobody is painting them. Choice (C) correctly identifies the ties the men are wearing, but there is no salesclerk selling anything.

6. **(A)** A pharmacist is holding a bottle of pills, or medicine, and talking with a customer. Choice (B) incorrectly describes the customer's action. He is talking with the pharmacist and possibly looking at the pills, but the pills are still in the bottle and the customer doesn't appear to be counting them. Choice (C) confuses similar-sounding words *pharmacist* and *farmer*. Choice (D) mentions the shelves in the photo, but there is no one stocking them.

PART 2: QUESTION-RESPONSE

7. **(A)** Choice (A) is a logical response to the request for a hotel recommendation. Choice (B) relates *hotel* and *manager*. Choice (C) relates *Los Angeles* and *place*.

8. **(C)** Choice (C) is a logical response to the question about *family origins*. Choice (A) confuses similar-sounding words *family* and *famous*. Choice (B) uses related words *children* and gives an answer to a *Where* question: *at school*.

9. **(A)** Choice (A) is a logical response to the question *How soon*. Choice (B) confuses similar-sounding words *soon* and *son*. Choice (C) confuses similar-sounding words *ready* and *red*.

10. **(A)** The response agrees with the opinion about the restaurant. Choice (B) repeats the word *excellent*. Choice (C) confuses similar-sounding words *excellent* and *spell it*.

11. **(C)** Choice (C) is a logical response to the question about *a train departure*. Choice (A) uses the related word *stop* and the similar-sounding words of *train* and *rain*. Choice (B) repeats the words *train* and *time*.

12. **(A)** The context is a phone call. The caller is asked to *hold*, or wait, and the caller chooses instead to *call back later*. Choice (B) uses the word *hold* in a different way. Choice (C) confuses similar-sounding words *hold/cold*.

13. **(B)** This is a logical response to the *Who* question. Choice (A) confuses similar-sounding words *shift/lift*. Choice (C) confuses similar-sounding words *working/walking* and repeats the word *night*.

14. **(A)** Choice (A) is a logical response to the question about *the date an invoice was sent*. Choice (B) confuses similar-sounding words *invoice* and *voice*. Choice (C) confuses similar-sounding words *sent* and *went*, and has a date (*in March*) but doesn't answer the question about when the *invoice* was sent.

15. **(B)** The first speaker lost a cell phone and the second speaker says that it is on a desk. Choice (A) associates *call* with *phone*. Choice (C) confuses *home* with the similar-sounding word *phone*.

16. **(A)** Choice (A) is a logical response to the *invitation for tonight*. Choice (B) uses similar-sounding words *tonight* and *tight*. Choice (C) also uses similar-sounding words *tonight* and *light*.

17. **(B)** Choice (B) is a logical response to the question of *preference*. Choice (A) confuses *tea* and *team*. Choice (C) confuses (*favo*)*rite* and *right*, and *team* and *seem*.

18. **(C)** The second speaker says that rain is the cause of the heavy traffic mentioned by the first speaker. Choice (A) uses the word *heavy* out of context. Choice (B) repeats the word *traffic*.

19. **(A)** Choice (A) is a logical response to the question about the existence of the fax machine. Choices (B) and (C) confuse *fax* with the similar-sounding words *tax* and *facts*.

20. **(C)** Tuesday answers the question *What day*. Choice (A) confuses similar-sounding words *dentist/dent*. Choice (B) answers the question *Who*.

21. **(B)** Choice (B) is a logical response to the question about the need for a reservation. Choice (A) refers to the number of people the reservation might be for. Choice (C) confuses similar-sounding words *need/read*.

22. **(A)** Choice (A) answers the question *Where*. Choice (B) answers a *How* question. Choice (C) answers a *Why* question.

23. **(B)** The question is about time—a *deadline*, and Choice (B) answers the question with a time—*by Thursday*. Choice (A) answers a *Where* question about a project. Choice (C) confuses similar-sounding words *deadline/ signed*.

24. **(A)** The second speaker thinks the first speaker is a fast reader because of having read a book in three days. Choice (B) confuses the phrase *free days* with the similar-sounding phrase *three days*. Choice (C) confuses *red* with the similar-sounding word *read*.

25. **(A)** *A client* answers the *Who* question. Choice (B) confuses similar-sounding words *standing/sanding*. Choice (C) repeats the word *door*.

26. **(B)** The second speaker thinks that the package contains something he ordered. Choice (A) confuses *packed* with the similar-sounding word *package*. Choice (C) associates *post office* with *package*.

27. **(B)** Choice (B) is a logical response to the question about *laundry service*. Choice (A) confuses similar-sounding words *pressed* and *depressed*. Choice (C) uses related words *pants* and *pair*.

28. **(C)** Choice (C) is a logical response to the question about *time*. Choice (A) uses related words *exercise* and *healthful*. Choice (B) confuses *exercises* (n) with *exercise* (v).

29. **(A)** Choice (A) answers the *yes/no* question. Choice (B) confuses similar-sounding words *reach/beach* and repeats the word *month*. Choice (C) confuses the usage of the word *reach*.

30. **(B)** Choice (B) is a logical response to the question about a journal article. Choice (A) confuses similar-sounding words *seen/green*. Choice (C) repeats the word *journal*.

31. **(A)** Choice (A) is a logical response to the question about *location*. Choice (B) repeats the word *go* and answers the question *When*. Choice (C) confuses *recommend* with *comment* and *go* with *memo*.

PART 3: CONVERSATIONS

32. **(A)** The woman says that the coffeepot is *filthy*, that is, dirty, and that she wants to *wash it out*. Choice (B) repeats the word *down*. Choice (C) is incorrect because it is the

coffeepot, not her hands, that she wants to wash. Choice (D) repeats the word *floor*.

33. **(B)** The man says that there is a kitchen *down on the sixth floor*, implying that the speakers are on some higher floor. Choices (A), (C), and (D) are contradicted by the correct answer.

34. **(C)** The man says, *I think I'd prefer cocoa*. Choice (A) is what will be used to make the cocoa. Choice (B) is what the woman will drink. Choice (D) is plausible but not mentioned.

35. **(A)** The man says, *. . . these shirts are just flying off the shelves*, meaning that they are selling fast, that is, they are popular among customers. Choice (B) is confused with the colors that the woman asks for, but there is nothing to indicate that these are the only colors available. Choice (C) repeats the word *warm*. Choice (D) is confused with the man's mentioning that everything in the store is discounted *this week*.

36. **(B)** The man says she owes forty-five dollars. Choices (A) and (D) sound similar to the correct answer. Choice (C) confuses *sixty* with the similar-sounding word *sixteen*, which is the size of the shirts.

37. **(D)** The woman says she has a gift certificate. Choice (A) uses the word *check* out of context. Choices (B) and (C) are what the man asks.

38. **(C)** The woman says she is making copies related to a banquet, and the man says, *Right. The invitations*. Choice (A) associates *menu* with *banquet*. Choice (B) is what the man is photocopying. Choice (C) is confused with the man's mention of address labels.

39. **(D)** This is in reply to the man's offer to help the woman with the address labels. Choices (A), (B), and (C) don't fit the context.

40. **(A)** The woman says that she has to put the copies in the mail. Choice (B) confuses *read* with the similar-sounding word *ready*. Choice (C) repeats the word *boss*. Choice (D) is what the man will do with his copies.

41. **(C)** The man is ordering food from a waitress, so he is in a restaurant. Choice (A) is not mentioned. Choice (B) repeats the word *fish*.

Choice (D) uses the word *house* out of context.

42. **(C)** The woman tells the man that he will have to wait 20 minutes while the fish is cooked. Choice (A) is incorrect because the woman says that the fish is fresh. Choice (B) is incorrect because the woman suggests the fish as something the man could have. Choice (D) is not mentioned.

43. **(A)** The man says he will have a drink. Choice (B) confuses *think* with the similar-sounding word *drink*. Choice (C) associates *fishing* with *fish*. Choice (D) confuses *dish* with the similar-sounding word *fish*.

44. **(A)** The woman works for Dr. Soto and is calling about Mr. Wu's appointment to have his teeth cleaned, so she must work for a dentist. Choice (A) associates *doctor* and *dentist*. Choice (C) is not mentioned. Choice (D) repeats the word *clean*.

45. **(C)** The man says that Mr. Wu is at a meeting. Choice (A) is confused with *out of the office*. Choice (B) confuses *out of town* with *downtown*. Choice (D) confuses *flight* with the similar-sounding word *right*.

46. **(A)** The woman asks the man to ask Mr. Wu to *please have him call our office to reschedule*. Choice (B) confuses similar-sounding words *appointment* and *apartment*. Choice (C) repeats the word *schedule*. Choice (D) repeats the word *downtown*.

47. **(D)** The woman says that she left her briefcase in a cab. Choices (A), (B), and (C) all repeat words used in other parts of the conversation.

48. **(D)** The man mentions the cab company then says, *I could phone them for you*. Choice (A) is what the woman has already done. Choice (B) repeats the word *briefcase* but is not mentioned. Choice (C) repeats the word *desk* but is not mentioned.

49. **(B)** The woman says that her passport, in addition to some papers, is in her briefcase. Choice (A) repeats the word *phone*. Choice (C) repeats the word *report*, but uses it as a noun instead of as a verb. (The woman will have to *report* the loss of her passport.)

Choice (D) confuses the meaning of the word *sign*. (The woman had the papers signed; she was not carrying a sign.)

50. **(C)** The man says he has to catch an eight-o'clock flight. Choice (A) confuses *train* with the similar-sounding word *rain*. Choice (B) repeats the word *call*. Choice (D) repeats the word *weather*.

51. **(B)** The woman says it will rain. Choice (A) confuses *snow* with the similar-sounding word *know*. Choice (C) confuses *cold* with the similar-sounding word *call*. Choice (D) is not mentioned.

52. **(D)** The woman mentions the early breakfast at the hotel, and the man's reply means that it will be easier for him not to eat there but at the airport instead. Choices (A), (B), and (C) don't fit the context.

53. **(D)** The man says, *I thought that flight would never end.* Choices (A), (B), and (C) are plausible but not mentioned.

54. **(A)** The woman says she has to pick up her bag from baggage claim and the man says, *That means we'll be stuck here forever*, meaning he expects they will have to wait a long time for her bag. Choice (B) repeats the word *money*—he says they could save money by taking a cab but doesn't say whether or not he has enough money. Choice (C) mentions the woman's bag, but no one says whether or not it is heavy. Choice (D) repeats the word *stuck*.

55. **(B)** The woman says to the man, *You stay here while I get the bag*, so we can assume he will wait for her. Choice (A) repeats the word *taxi*, but they haven't decided yet how they will travel. Choice (C) is what the woman will do. Choice (D) repeats the word *subway*, but no mention is made of the schedule.

56. **(C)** The man sent the woman an e-mail with a finance report attached. Choice (A) confuses the usage of the word *program*. Choice (B) confuses similar-sounding words *personal/personnel*. Choice (D) confuses the usage of the word *check* and confuses similar-sounding words *sent/rent*.

57. **(B)** The woman asks the man to resend the document and says, *This time try my personal e-mail address.* Choice (A) is what the man asks the woman to do. Choice (C) is not mentioned. Choice (D) confuses similar-sounding words *already* and *ready*.

58. **(A)** The woman says, *I know I can always count on you.* Choice (B) repeats the word *late*, but it is not used to refer to the man. Choice (C) repeats *a bit strange*, which is what the woman says about the situation of not receiving the document. Choice (D) confuses the meaning of *count* in this context.

59. **(B)** The man says, *Tennis is my sport.* Choice (A) is what the woman asks him about. Choice (C) confuses *biking* with the similar-sounding word *like*. Choice (D) is the woman's sport.

60. **(D)** The man plays tennis with a group at the community center. Choice (A) is where the woman swims. Choice (B) is where the woman used to play tennis. Choice (C) repeats the word *club*.

61. **(A)** The women ask the man to *join* them for a *bite* to eat and then mentions a *great lunch place*. Choice (B) repeats the word *park*, which is where one of the women took tennis lessons. Choice (C) confuses the meaning of the word *pool*—one of the speakers mentions a swimming pool. Choice (D) is incorrect because the women ask the man to join them for lunch, not to join the country club.

62. **(C)** The man is explaining a bus tour and telling people how to prepare for it, so he is a tour guide. Choices (A) and (B) are associated with the mention of the *landscapes* that will be seen on the tour. Choice (D) repeats the word *photographers*—some of the tour members may be amateur photographers.

63. **(D)** The man says everyone should be at the bus by 8:00 A.M., so they will ride on a bus. Choice (A) repeats the word *valley*, but they will see it by bus, not bike. Choice (B) confuses similar-sounding words *valley* and *alley*. Choice (C) repeats the word *river*, but no mention is made of fishing.

64. **(D)** The man says, *Just remember to dress warmly.* Choice (A) misuses the word *dress*. Choice (B) repeats the word *cold*, which is

used to describe the day, not drinks. Choice (C) is not mentioned.

65. **(C)** The man says that he needs to get green markers for the afternoon presentation. Choices (A) and (B) are things that the woman says can be bought at the office supply store. Choice (D) is confused with the mention of the bookstore.

66. **(A)** The woman says that the office supply store is across the corridor from the bookstore. Choices (B), (C), and (D) don't fit this description.

67. **(D)** The woman says, *I'll start getting the conference room set up.* Choice (A) is what the man will do. Choice (B) repeats the name *Joe*, who is mentioned twice but there is no mention of planning to speak with him. Choice (C) repeats the word *instructions*, what the woman says she has gotten from Joe.

68. **(B)** The man says, *I'm afraid we're not going to get to the movie on time.* Choice (A) is incorrect because they have just found a parking space. Choice (C) is incorrect because the woman has already bought the tickets. Choice (D) is incorrect because the only mention of the parking prices is when the woman says that parking won't cost much.

69. **(C)** The woman says, *We'll only be here 3 hours, or maybe a little less,* and the price for parking up to 3 hours is $12. Choices (A), (B), and (D) are prices for parking other amounts of time.

70. **(B)** The man says, *I want to make sure we get front row seats.* Choice (A) is not mentioned. Choice (C) is what the woman has already done. Choice (D) is incorrect because even though the man mentions snacks, he says nothing about when he wants to eat them.

PART 4: TALKS

71. **(B)** The ad is for people concerned about their "professional look." Choices (A), (C), and (D) are other types of people who use luggage but are not identified with the need to look professional.

72. **(A)** The speaker says the ad is for Legerton's luggage, that is, suitcases. Overnight cases, computer carriers, and garment bags—all types of luggage are also mentioned. Choice (B) repeats the word *computers*. Choice (C) is a synonym for *garment*. Choice (D) is associated with the mention of travel.

73. **(A)** Orders made through the website receive the discount. Choice (B) mentions a place where the products can be bought, but the discount is not available there. Choice (C) uses the word *apply* (application) out of context. Choice (D) is confused with *before the end of the month*, when the discount will end.

74. **(C)** The report says, *rain . . . turning to snow . . . will create ice hazards.* Choice (A) is true, but it is not complete. Choice (B) is not mentioned. Choice (D) is incorrect because wind is not mentioned.

75. **(A)** People *go to and from work* during *rush hour.* Choices (B), (C), and (D) are not mentioned.

76. **(A)** *It's not all bad news* is usually used to introduce a piece of good information after presenting some bad or unwelcome information. In this case, the description of icy weather is followed by the description of the warm weather that will come next. Choices (B), (C), and (D) do not fit the meaning of the expression in this context.

77. **(A)** The speaker advises, *As soon as a visitor comes through the door, say "hello."* Choices (B) and (D) are suggested but not as the first thing to do. Choice (C) is not mentioned.

78. **(D)** The speaker says, *Make sure the visitor stays in the lobby.* Choices (A), (B), and (C) use words from the talk but are not mentioned.

79. **(D)** The speaker says, *Remember, visitors should never be allowed to wander around the building unaccompanied.* Choices (A), (B), and (C) use words from the talk but are not mentioned.

80. **(B)** The speaker, Lynn, is guiding a tour of the Janteck Homestead, so she is a tour guide. Choice (A) repeats the word *historian*, which refers to the people who restored the homestead. Choice (C) is related to the context of the talk—a tour. Choice (D) repeats the word *property*.

81. **(D)** The speaker mentions that the Janteck's bought a farm outside of the city, and a homestead is a type of farm. Choice (A) is a place where a tour might go through several buildings, as this tour does. Choice (B) confuses similar-sounding words *rule/school*. Choice (C) repeats the word *city*.

82. **(B)** The speaker says, *keep your hands away from the display cases.* Choice (A) confuses *display cases* with *suitcases*. Choice (C) confuses *restored* with *store*. Choice (D) confuses *display* with *play*.

83. **(B)** The speaker says, *I look forward to showing you around this evening as part of our grand opening,* so he is getting ready to take listeners on a library tour. Choice (A) is not mentioned. Choice (C) is mentioned only as a detail—the speaker compares the sizes of the two libraries, but that is not the purpose of the talk. Choice (D) is confused with the descriptions of what is on each floor of the library.

84. **(C)** The speaker says that children's room and activity rooms are on the second floor. Choices (A), (B), and (D) are things that are mentioned as being on other floors.

85. **(B)** *It's not to be missed* is used to describe something that should be seen or experienced, in the speaker's opinion. Choices (A), (C), and (D) confuse the meaning of the expression in this context.

86. **(B)** The flight is to *Houston*. Choices (A), (C), and (D) are not mentioned.

87. **(B)** Because of the *turbulence*, passengers should remain seated with their seat belts on. We can conclude that the flight will be bumpy. Choices (A), (C), and (D) repeat words from the talk, but none of these is expected by the captain.

88. **(D)** The captain says about Houston, the final destination, *the skies will be clear and the sun bright. In fact you'll have cloudless, sunny skies all week.* Choices (A), (B), and (C) are all plausible but not mentioned.

89. **(C)** The speaker says that the keynote speaker is *George Williams, one of our country's top financial experts.* Choice (A) is the person making the announcement. Choices (B) and (D) are plausible but not mentioned.

90. **(A)** The speaker says that the Garden Room has been reserved for a wedding. Choice (B) is the original plan for the Garden Room. Choice (C) will take place in the Rooftop Restaurant. Choice (D) is confused with the topic of the workshop.

91. **(D)** The speaker asks listeners to fill out the evaluation form that is in their packets. Choice (A) is confused with the fact that George Williams is the *keynote speaker.* Choice (B) is confused with what listeners should do with a completed form—*leave it in the box by the door.* Choice (C) repeats the word *lunch,* but no payment is mentioned in connection with it.

92. **(A)** The message is about changes in the phone company's voicemail system. Choice (B) associates *telephone* with *voicemail.* Choice (C) repeats the phrase *new number.* Choice (D) is associated with *website.*

93. **(D)** A customer can save a message by pressing nine. Choice (A) confuses *two* with the similar-sounding word *new.* Choice (B) confuses *four* with the similar-sounding word *or.* Choice (C) is for deleting a message.

94. **(B)** The message instructs the listener to press the star key in order to hear the new codes. Choice (A) is confused with the number of new codes. Choice (C) repeats the name of the company, but nothing is mentioned about calling it. Choice (D) is confused with *read the entire message* on the website.

95. **(B)** The speaker says that he is making arrangements for *next week's professional development session.* Choices (A), (C), and (D) are all events which could include lunch but are not mentioned.

96. **(A)** The speaker explains which caterers she would like to get lunch from and then asks Evelyn (the listener), *could you call them and arrange it?* Choice (B) is confused with the mention of how many people they should order lunch for. Choice (C) is incorrect because the speaker says that the lunch will be delivered. Choice (D) repeats the

word *dining room* but no mention is made of arranging it.

97. **(C)** The speaker asks for the lunch that serves 25 people. Choices (A), (B), and (D) do not match with what the speaker asked for.

98. **(C)** The speaker is addressing people who have been at the company less than a week, that is, new employees. Choice (A) refers to the people who can use the fitness room. Choice (B) refers to the people who will help new employees with concerns and questions. Choice (D) is plausible but not mentioned.

99. **(B)** The speaker says that the fitness room *is located just below our offices, across the hall from the bank*, which places it on the first floor. Choices (A), (C), and (D) don't fit this description.

100. **(D)** The speaker says, *Now, if you'll just look at this slide* . . . . Choice (A) is confused with the discussion of where the fitness room is located. Choice (B) is confused with the suggestion that employees use the fitness room during their lunch break. Choice (C) is confused with the suggestion to ask questions to the department heads.

Reading

PART 5: INCOMPLETE SENTENCES

101. **(C)** *For* means *with regard to*. Choices (A) and (B) illogically indicate location. Choice (D) means *through the means of*.

102. **(B)** *Attract* means to *pull in* or *get the attention of*. Choices (A), (C), and (D) have meanings that don't fit the context.

103. **(D)** *Assist* means *help*. Choice (A) means *guess*. Choice (B) means to *give a person work or responsibility*. Choice (C) means *agree* or *allow*.

104. **(B)** *Present* means at *a particular place*. Choices (A), (C), and (D) have meanings that don't fit the context.

105. **(C)** *Commute* refers to the regular trip between home and work. Choice (A) is related in meaning, but it is a verb, and a noun is needed here. Choices (B) and (D) have meanings that don't fit the context.

106. **(A)** *Was higher* is already past tense, so to establish an earlier past use the past participle *had expected*. Choice (B) is the simple form. Choice (C) is present progressive tense. Choice (D) is future tense.

107. **(A)** *She* is a singular subject pronoun referring to a woman, in this case, *waitress*. Choice (B) is a masculine object pronoun. Choice (C) is a possessive adjective or object pronoun. Choice (D) is a plural pronoun.

108. **(B)** The adjective *popular* can modify *plan*; the adverb *especially* can modify *popular*. Choices (A) and (C) are verbs. Choice (D) is a noun.

109. **(D)** A simple adjective is required here to modify the noun *quantities*. Choice (A) is an adverb. Choices (B) and (C) are superlative and comparative adjectives, but no comparison is being made here.

110. **(C)** *As soon as* means *immediately after*. Choices (A), (B), and (D) have no meaning in this context.

111. **(B)** *Borrow* means *to take temporarily*. Choice (A) is *what* you take (*the reference guide is a loan*). Choice (C) means *to give temporarily*. Choice (D) means *gone away*.

112. **(A)** *Although* is a subordinate conjunction that indicates that one thing (*business cards not being printed*) happened in spite of another (*ordering the cards*). Choices (B), (C), and (D) do not fit the context of the sentence.

113. **(A)** *Or* allows a choice between the items joined. Choice (B) would mean *both*. Choice (C) should be used with *or*. Choice (D) *but* would imply a contrast (*from the Madrid office but not from the Paris office*).

114. **(A)** *Before* is an adverb and tells when the machine might have been used. Choices (B), (C), and (D) do not fit the context of the sentence.

115. **(A)** The negative tag question *won't they* matches the affirmative future sentence. Choice (B) would match a negative sentence. Choice (C) is not future tense. Choice (D) is not a tag question.

116. **(B)** *Ink* is used in a printer cartridge and comes in colors. Choice (A) comes in colors,

but it is not a word used when referring to printers. Choices (C) and (D) are associated with printers, but they do not fit the meaning of the sentence.

117. **(D)** *Holds* matches *receives* (*receives and holds*). Choice (A) is present progressive tense. Choice (B) is past tense. Choice (C) is present tense, but does not match the subject.

118. **(C)** *Help* is followed by the simple form (or the infinitive) when one thing (*the conference*) helps another (*employees*) do something. Choice (A) is past tense. Choice (B) is a gerund. Choice (D) is present progressive tense.

119. **(B)** *Because* establishes a logical relationship between the two events. Choices (A) and (D) are illogical without a contrast (*Although we knew the city . . . ; We knew the city, however, . . .*). Choice (C) would belong in a result clause (. . . *therefore, Mr. Gutman drove . . .*).

120. **(D)** The verb *suggest* is followed by a gerund. Choice (A) is the base form or present tense. Choice (B) is present tense. Choice (C) is past tense.

121. **(B)** Present tense in a real condition in the *if* clause requires future tense in the other clause. Choice (A) is present tense. Choice (C) is present progressive tense. Choice (D) is present perfect tense.

122. **(A)** *Nowhere* means *in no place*. Choice (B) is used in negative sentences and questions. Choice (C) means *in some place*, however, if the destination were *in some place* near the hotel, a taxi would not be required. Choice (D) means *in all places*.

123. **(D)** *Attending* forms the future progressive with *will be* (*will be attending*). Choices (A), (B), and (C) do not form logical tenses with *attending*.

124. **(C)** *Expertise* is related to the word *expert*, and the sentence means that Mr. Vasco has great abilities in electronics. Choices (A), (B), and (D) do not fit the sentence.

125. **(D)** This is an infinitive of purpose; the sentence explains the purpose of the funding. Choices (A), (B), and (C) don't fit the context.

126. **(D)** Present tense and simple future are possible; only present tense is given. *Ms. Chang* requires third person *has*. Choice (A) is future perfect tense. Choice (B) is present progressive tense. Choice (C) is plural.

127. **(C)** The adjective *knowledgeable* modifies *director*; *quite* modifies *knowledgeable*. Choice (A) is a gerund. Choice (B) is a noun. Choice (D) is a verb.

128. **(B)** *Need* is followed by an infinitive verb. Choices (A), (C), and (D) are modals, which are followed by a base form verb.

129. **(D)** Past tense in the *if* clause of an unreal condition requires *would + simple verb* in the other clause. Choice (A) is future tense. Choice (B) is past perfect tense. Choice (C) is past tense.

130. **(A)** *Have* requires the simple form of the second verb when one or more person(s) (*trainers*) *have* another (*crew*) do something. Choice (B) is a gerund. Choice (C) is a noun. Choice (D) is past tense.

PART 6: TEXT COMPLETION

131. **(D)** The firm doesn't like its current insurance plan, so it wants to make a different choice. Choice (A) is mentioned in the letter, but the company isn't looking for new employees. Choices (B) and (C) could be related to the work of an accounting firm, but they aren't mentioned in the text.

132. **(A)** *Therefore* introduces a result. Wanting to learn more about Unity Health Care is the result of being unhappy with the current insurance plan. Choices (B) and (D) both have a similar meaning to *but*, introducing a contradictory idea. Choice (C) means *additionally*.

133. **(B)** This sentence introduces what comes next, which is some questions the letter writer has for the insurance company. Choices (A), (C), and (D) don't fit the context.

134. **(C)** It is not easy, or *convenient*, for employees to visit the doctor during their working hours. Choices (A) and (D) are not words generally used to describe doctors'

appointments. Choice (B) is the opposite of the correct meaning.

135. **(C)** *As* means *because* and introduces a reason. Choice (A) introduces a result. Choice (B) introduces a condition. Choice (D) is a preposition and cannot introduce a clause.

136. **(B)** Simon Yan cannot go to the meeting, so Hugh Harrison will go in his place. Choices (A) and (D) mean *go with*. Choice (C) means *help*.

137. **(D)** The writer then goes on to say, *Please talk with Hugh about this*, and then mentions issues about money. This sentence is the only one with a subject that would be logical to discuss with Hugh and is the only one that mentions money (budget) concerns. Choices (A), (B), and (C) don't fit the context.

138. **(B)** Positive means *sure* or *certain*. Mr. Yan is certain that Mingmei can do the job because of her good reputation. Choices (A), (C), and (D) all give the sentence the opposite of the correct meaning.

139. **(B)** The company president wants to reduce use of electricity because the cost is *going up*, or *increasing*. Choices (A) and (C) give the sentence the opposite of the correct meaning. Choice (D) doesn't make sense in this sentence.

140. **(D)** The passive voice is necessary here because the subject of the sentence is not the actor. Choices (A), (B), and (C) are all active voice.

141. **(A)** This is a detail that explains the idea presented in the previous sentence—the reason why fans and heaters are not needed. Choices (B), (C), and (D) do not fit the context.

142. **(B)** This is a gerund form used as the subject of the sentence. Choices (A), (C), and (D) are all verb forms that cannot be used in the subject position of the sentence.

143. **(A)** This presents the main idea of the passage, which is about the company's new chief executive officer, or boss. Choices (B), (C), and (D) don't fit the context.

144. **(D)** *The largest* is a superlative adjective, comparing this company to all the other companies in the nation. Choice (A) is an adjective, but it is not a superlative form. Choices (B) and (C) are comparative forms.

145. **(C)** *Significant* means *meaningful* or *important*. The sentence points out the importance of having a female executive in a field where traditionally only men have held such a position. Choices (A), (B), and (D) don't fit the context.

146. **(D)** *Has been working* is a present perfect verb describing an action that began in the past (25 years ago) and continues into the present. Choice (A) is present tense. Choice (B) simple past tense and Choice (C) past perfect tense describe actions that are already completed.

PART 7: READING COMPREHENSION

147. **(B)** *Data entry* is explicitly mentioned as a job responsibility. Choices (A), (C), and (D) are not mentioned.

148. **(B)** *Room to advance* means *opportunity for promotions*. Choices (A), (C), and (D) are all benefits, but not of this job.

149. **(C)** The memo begins and ends with saying that the doors should stay closed and not be kept open. The rest of the memo supports this idea by explaining the reasons for it. Choices (A), (B), and (D) refer to details mentioned in the memo.

150. **(D)** If the weather is hot and the air conditioner is not repaired, employees were probably opening fire doors to let in cool air. Choices (A), (B), and (C) are all purposes of doors, but they do not relate to fire safety.

151. **(D)** Ms. Lee writes, *I left my suitcase behind at the baggage claim*. Choice (A) is incorrect because she knows that her suitcase is at the baggage claim. Choice (B) is incorrect because she was on a flight that arrived on time. Choice (C) is incorrect because she said she got a cab right away.

152. **(A)** *Sure thing* means that Ms. Lee can rely on Mr. Matsuo to do what she asked, which is to tell her boss that she will be late. Choices

(B), (C), and (D) don't fit the meaning of the expression or the context.

153. **(C)** Since *jewelry* is on the list of items to be auctioned, you will probably find *bracelets* for sale. Choice (A) confuses *Chinese antiques* with *china* (dishes). Choice (B) is not mentioned, although you might relate *stamps* and *rare books*. Choice (D) confuses *wall-to-wall carpeting* and *Oriental rugs*.

154. **(D)** The preview starts at *10 A.M. on Saturday, October 3*. Choice (A) is when the auction begins. Choice (B) is not mentioned. Choice (C) is when you can call Estate Planners with questions.

155. **(B)** The graph is a review of money spent in April, so it must have been created after April. Choices (A), (C), and (D) are not possible.

156. **(A)** The gallery had an income of $228,566 and $75,275 in expenses, so it earned more than it spent. Choices (B), (C), and (D) are contradicted by the correct answer.

157. **(A)** In April, 58% of expenses went to *art acquisitions*, which is what the gallery sells, that is, its inventory. Choice (B) refers to *salaries*, which made up 20% of expenses. Choice (C) refers to *marketing*, which made up 9% of expenses. Choice (D) refers to *utilities*, which made up 3% of expenses.

158. **(B)** The new manufacturing plant is overseas, that is, in another country. Choice (A) is not mentioned. Choice (C) is incorrect because the e-mail mentions that the plant is in a small town. Choice (D) confuses *overseas* with *coast*.

159. **(A)** The e-mail explains the reason for and the topics of the seminars. Choice (B) is confused with the purpose of the seminars. Choice (C) is incorrect because we can assume this has already been done. Choice (D) is the content of the seminars.

160. **(B)** The seminars are meant to help both employees and their families adjust to life in their new situation. Choice (A) is incorrect because the e-mail says that the seminars are not mandatory. Choices (C) and (D) are incorrect because neither the location nor the time of the seminars is mentioned.

161. **(A)** The passage states that ten stores were remodeled last year, and there are similar plans for the other six. Choice (B) has already been done. Choices (C) and (D) are not mentioned.

162. **(D)** The passage states that the cooking classes will focus *on foods that are delicious and nutritious at the same time*. Choice (A) is incorrect because chefs from different regions of Europe will participate. Choice (B) is confused with one kind of product sold by the company. Choice (C) is incorrect because only Europe is mentioned.

163. **(A)** This position is followed by details of how the company will expand the brand. Choices (B), (C), and (D) don't fit this context.

164. **(D)** Their company sells bolts of cotton, so it is probably a fabric manufacturer. Choice (A) is not the correct answer because Shipping is a department within the company, not the entire business of the company. Choices (B) and (C) are related to the client's business, which is probably a clothing manufacturer or fashion designer.

165. **(C)** The client usually orders dark blue cotton, but this time asked for lighter colors. Choices (A), (B), and (D) are not mentioned.

166. **(D)** Ms. Kohl writes that the shipment was returned because *we shipped them the wrong items*. Choices (A), (B), and (C) are possible problems with a shipment but are not mentioned.

167. **(B)** Ms. Kohl writes that someone should talk with the people in the shipping department and find out how the problem occurred. When Mr. Silva writes *I'm on it*, he means he is ready to do what Ms. Kohl suggests. Choices (A), (C), and (D) don't fit the meaning of the expression or the context.

168. **(D)** The letter states that the recipient has been a supporter of the fund in the past, asks him to continue being a supporter, and then states a fundraising goal of $25,000, so it is asking for money. Choice (A) is one of the

things the fund is raising money for. Choice (B) is related to the topic of asking for a donation. Choice (C) is incorrect because the programs mentioned in the letter are not new.

169. **(A)** The letter states, *As a long-time member of the Business Association, you have been a generous supporter of the Future Business Leaders Education Fund,* meaning the recipient (Mr. Harrison) has donated money in the past. Choice (B) is incorrect because Mr. Harrison is a long-time member. Choice (C) mentions the workshops, but there is no indication that any have been given by Mr. Harrison. Choice (D) is incorrect because he is being asked to help support young professionals, so it is not likely he is one himself. In addition, he has been a member of the association for a long time, implying that he is probably an older, experienced professional.

170. **(B)** The letter explains that ten young professionals received awards at the annual banquet on May 1. Choices (A), (C), and (D) are other details mentioned in the letter, but they did not happen on May 1.

171. **(C)** The letter says to *complete the information requested on the enclosed sheet.* Complete the information means *fill out the form.* Choices (A) and (B) are related to other details mentioned in the letter. Choice (D) is what should be sent in along with the form.

172. **(A)** The main idea is presented in the first sentence, *. . . you will have to make some careful decisions, especially regarding job offers.* Choices (B), (C), and (D) are topics related to jobs and careers but are not the main topic of this article.

173. **(D)** *Take a position* in this sentence means *accept a job.* Choices (A), (B), and (C) are other meanings of the word *position* but do not fit the context.

174. **(C)** The last sentences states that *job satisfaction, far more than salary or other factors, results in the highest level of performance.* Choices (A), (B), and (D) are other points mentioned in the article but not as things that result in the best job performance.

175. **(B)** This position is followed by a sentence that gives an example of a sacrifice. Choices (A), (C), and (D) are not the right context for the inserted sentence.

176. **(A)** According to the agenda heading, the meeting topic is marketing. Choice (B) is confused with Max's business trip. Choice (C) is confused with the discussion of the meeting schedule. Choice (D) is confused with the name of the company.

177. **(B)** Point 2 was discussed first because the first scheduled speaker didn't arrive on time. Choice (A) is the item that was scheduled to be first. Choices (C) and (D) are later items on the agenda.

178. **(C)** The meeting began at 9:30, and Ben started his presentation thirty minutes after that. Choice (A) is thirty minutes before the meeting began. Choice (B) is when the meeting began. Choice (D) is when the meeting was scheduled to end.

179. **(B)** The meeting ended after Barbara's talk. Choice (A) is the person who was scheduled to give the last presentation. Choices (C) and (D) are people who were scheduled to talk earlier in the meeting.

180. **(D)** Max is away on a business trip. Choice (A) is the reason Marty didn't attend the meeting. Choice (B) is a plausible reason but not mentioned. Choice (C) is true of Ben, not Max.

181. **(B)** The notice states, *A-passes can be used seven days a week, 24 hours a day, any day of the year.* Choice (A) is incorrect because C-passes are only good *Monday through Friday, except holidays.* Choices (C) and (D) are incorrect because all A-passes can be used weekends and holidays.

182. **(C)** The sentence means that the passes are valid, that is, that they can be used as described. Choices (A), (B), and (D) are other meanings of the word *good* but don't fit the context.

183. **(D)** The e-mail explains that Smith Company employees can get passes at a *reduced price.* Choices (A), (B), and (C) are all people who

can get passes but no discount is mentioned for them.

184. **(D)** Ms. Jones, the writer of the e-mail, explains that forms to apply for passes are available from her office and should be returned to her office. Choices (A), (B), and (C) are not mentioned.

185. **(A)** The e-mail explains that discounted passes are being offered in order to encourage people to use public transportation. The cost of garage parking is being raised *As an added incentive*, that is, a further encouragement. Choices (B), (C), and (D) are all plausible but not mentioned.

186. **(B)** The Royal Hotel is listed as *a more economical option*. Choice (A) is incorrect because it is the only hotel not within walking distance of the center. Choice (C) is confused with the latest date to get the discount. Choice (D) is not mentioned.

187. **(C)** Ms. Wu asks for a single room. Choice (A) is incorrect because she asks for a room on an upper floor. Choice (B) is incorrect because she asks for one bed. Choice (D) repeats the word *pool*, but Ms. Wu only asks whether there is one, not to be near one.

188. **(A)** The notice states that there is a *reduced rate* for convention attendees at the hotels. Choices (B) and (C) are plausible reasons but are not mentioned. Choice (D) is something Ms. Wu will do, but no discount is offered for this; in fact, she will have to pay extra.

189. **(C)** The manager writes in the e-mail that he will have to give Ms. Wu a room with a king-sized bed instead of the queen-sized bed she requested for one night, and that this costs $25 more. Choices (A) and (B) are not mentioned. Choice (D) is not possible because the pool is closed.

190. **(D)** The manager mentions the restaurant and then writes, *our guests are entitled to a free breakfast there.* Choices (A), (B), and (C) are all plausible but not mentioned.

191. **(B)** The article says that the café has been renovated and has *doubled its size.* Choice (A) is incorrect because the café owner is quoted as saying that *their old favorites are still on the menu.* Choice (C) repeats the word *customers*, but no indication is given that any have been lost. Choice (D) is not mentioned.

192. **(A)** There are long lines of customers waiting to buy ice cream, and the café is expanded to accommodate more customers, so the implication is that it is a popular place. Choice (B) is incorrect because it has been renovated, not newly built. Choice (C) is incorrect because it sells sandwiches as well as ice cream and baked goods. Choice (D) is not mentioned.

193. **(D)** The ad has coupons for a free coffee and a free soda that are good until April 30. Choice (A) is confused with the mention of prizes at the grand reopening. Choices (B) and (C) are confused with the offer of free ice cream samples at the grand reopening.

194. **(A)** Ms. Seldman writes that she went to the grand reopening, which, according to the ad, was on April 10. Choice (B) is the date Ms. Seldman wrote the review. Choices (C) and (D) are not mentioned.

195. **(C)** Ms. Seldman writes, *The sandwiches are still fantastic, and the cake we tried was delicious.* Choice (A) is incorrect because she writes, *there is plenty of seating.* Choice (B) is incorrect because she writes that the food is *affordable* and *I was surprised to find that the prices had not been raised.* Choice (D) is incorrect because she does not compare the renovated café with the way it looked before.

196. **(A)** The ad says, *Customer parking on site.* Choice (B) is confused with the downtown location of the Main Street property. Choice (C) describes the Main Street property. Choice (D) is incorrect because the size of this property is not mentioned.

197. **(C)** The properties he is interested in are described as *retail spaces.* Choice (A) is confused with the company that placed the ads. Choice (B) is not mentioned. Choice (D) is confused with the name of the neighborhood.

198. **(C)** Mr. Hernandez says that the location of the other building is not as good as that of the Main Street building. Choice (A) is

incorrect because he says the size of the other building is right. Choice (B) is incorrect because the Main Street building is more expensive. Choice (D) is a plausible reason but not mentioned.

199. **(B)** The bank will lend Mr. Hernandez enough money to buy the cheaper building. Choice (A) is confused with *you already have over $100,000 in debt*. Choice (C) is the amount he would need for the Main Street building. Choice (D) is the cost of both buildings together.

200. **(D)** Mr. Hernandez suggests meeting on April 21, and Ms. Clark says she prefers to meet the day after that. Choice (A) is the date of Ms. Clark's letter. Choice (B) is the day following the date of Ms. Clark's letter. Choice (C) is the date Mr. Hernandez suggests meeting.

ANSWER SHEET
Practice Test 3

LISTENING COMPREHENSION

Part 1: Photographs

1. Ⓐ Ⓑ Ⓒ Ⓓ
2. Ⓐ Ⓑ Ⓒ Ⓓ
3. Ⓐ Ⓑ Ⓒ Ⓓ
4. Ⓐ Ⓑ Ⓒ Ⓓ
5. Ⓐ Ⓑ Ⓒ Ⓓ
6. Ⓐ Ⓑ Ⓒ Ⓓ

Part 2: Question-Response

7. Ⓐ Ⓑ Ⓒ
8. Ⓐ Ⓑ Ⓒ
9. Ⓐ Ⓑ Ⓒ
10. Ⓐ Ⓑ Ⓒ
11. Ⓐ Ⓑ Ⓒ
12. Ⓐ Ⓑ Ⓒ
13. Ⓐ Ⓑ Ⓒ
14. Ⓐ Ⓑ Ⓒ
15. Ⓐ Ⓑ Ⓒ
16. Ⓐ Ⓑ Ⓒ
17. Ⓐ Ⓑ Ⓒ
18. Ⓐ Ⓑ Ⓒ
19. Ⓐ Ⓑ Ⓒ
20. Ⓐ Ⓑ Ⓒ
21. Ⓐ Ⓑ Ⓒ
22. Ⓐ Ⓑ Ⓒ
23. Ⓐ Ⓑ Ⓒ
24. Ⓐ Ⓑ Ⓒ
25. Ⓐ Ⓑ Ⓒ
26. Ⓐ Ⓑ Ⓒ
27. Ⓐ Ⓑ Ⓒ
28. Ⓐ Ⓑ Ⓒ
29. Ⓐ Ⓑ Ⓒ
30. Ⓐ Ⓑ Ⓒ
31. Ⓐ Ⓑ Ⓒ

Part 3: Conversations

32. Ⓐ Ⓑ Ⓒ Ⓓ
33. Ⓐ Ⓑ Ⓒ Ⓓ
34. Ⓐ Ⓑ Ⓒ Ⓓ
35. Ⓐ Ⓑ Ⓒ Ⓓ
36. Ⓐ Ⓑ Ⓒ Ⓓ
37. Ⓐ Ⓑ Ⓒ Ⓓ
38. Ⓐ Ⓑ Ⓒ Ⓓ
39. Ⓐ Ⓑ Ⓒ Ⓓ
40. Ⓐ Ⓑ Ⓒ Ⓓ
41. Ⓐ Ⓑ Ⓒ Ⓓ
42. Ⓐ Ⓑ Ⓒ Ⓓ
43. Ⓐ Ⓑ Ⓒ Ⓓ
44. Ⓐ Ⓑ Ⓒ Ⓓ
45. Ⓐ Ⓑ Ⓒ Ⓓ
46. Ⓐ Ⓑ Ⓒ Ⓓ
47. Ⓐ Ⓑ Ⓒ Ⓓ
48. Ⓐ Ⓑ Ⓒ Ⓓ
49. Ⓐ Ⓑ Ⓒ Ⓓ
50. Ⓐ Ⓑ Ⓒ Ⓓ
51. Ⓐ Ⓑ Ⓒ Ⓓ
52. Ⓐ Ⓑ Ⓒ Ⓓ
53. Ⓐ Ⓑ Ⓒ Ⓓ
54. Ⓐ Ⓑ Ⓒ Ⓓ
55. Ⓐ Ⓑ Ⓒ Ⓓ
56. Ⓐ Ⓑ Ⓒ Ⓓ
57. Ⓐ Ⓑ Ⓒ Ⓓ
58. Ⓐ Ⓑ Ⓒ Ⓓ
59. Ⓐ Ⓑ Ⓒ Ⓓ
60. Ⓐ Ⓑ Ⓒ Ⓓ
61. Ⓐ Ⓑ Ⓒ Ⓓ
62. Ⓐ Ⓑ Ⓒ Ⓓ
63. Ⓐ Ⓑ Ⓒ Ⓓ
64. Ⓐ Ⓑ Ⓒ Ⓓ
65. Ⓐ Ⓑ Ⓒ Ⓓ
66. Ⓐ Ⓑ Ⓒ Ⓓ
67. Ⓐ Ⓑ Ⓒ Ⓓ
68. Ⓐ Ⓑ Ⓒ Ⓓ
69. Ⓐ Ⓑ Ⓒ Ⓓ
70. Ⓐ Ⓑ Ⓒ Ⓓ

Part 4: Talks

71. Ⓐ Ⓑ Ⓒ Ⓓ
72. Ⓐ Ⓑ Ⓒ Ⓓ
73. Ⓐ Ⓑ Ⓒ Ⓓ
74. Ⓐ Ⓑ Ⓒ Ⓓ
75. Ⓐ Ⓑ Ⓒ Ⓓ
76. Ⓐ Ⓑ Ⓒ Ⓓ
77. Ⓐ Ⓑ Ⓒ Ⓓ
78. Ⓐ Ⓑ Ⓒ Ⓓ
79. Ⓐ Ⓑ Ⓒ Ⓓ
80. Ⓐ Ⓑ Ⓒ Ⓓ
81. Ⓐ Ⓑ Ⓒ Ⓓ
82. Ⓐ Ⓑ Ⓒ Ⓓ
83. Ⓐ Ⓑ Ⓒ Ⓓ
84. Ⓐ Ⓑ Ⓒ Ⓓ
85. Ⓐ Ⓑ Ⓒ Ⓓ
86. Ⓐ Ⓑ Ⓒ Ⓓ
87. Ⓐ Ⓑ Ⓒ Ⓓ
88. Ⓐ Ⓑ Ⓒ Ⓓ
89. Ⓐ Ⓑ Ⓒ Ⓓ
90. Ⓐ Ⓑ Ⓒ Ⓓ
91. Ⓐ Ⓑ Ⓒ Ⓓ
92. Ⓐ Ⓑ Ⓒ Ⓓ
93. Ⓐ Ⓑ Ⓒ Ⓓ
94. Ⓐ Ⓑ Ⓒ Ⓓ
95. Ⓐ Ⓑ Ⓒ Ⓓ
96. Ⓐ Ⓑ Ⓒ Ⓓ
97. Ⓐ Ⓑ Ⓒ Ⓓ
98. Ⓐ Ⓑ Ⓒ Ⓓ
99. Ⓐ Ⓑ Ⓒ Ⓓ
100. Ⓐ Ⓑ Ⓒ Ⓓ

ANSWER SHEET
Practice Test 3

READING

Part 5: Incomplete Sentences

101. Ⓐ Ⓑ Ⓒ Ⓓ	109. Ⓐ Ⓑ Ⓒ Ⓓ	117. Ⓐ Ⓑ Ⓒ Ⓓ	125. Ⓐ Ⓑ Ⓒ Ⓓ
102. Ⓐ Ⓑ Ⓒ Ⓓ	110. Ⓐ Ⓑ Ⓒ Ⓓ	118. Ⓐ Ⓑ Ⓒ Ⓓ	126. Ⓐ Ⓑ Ⓒ Ⓓ
103. Ⓐ Ⓑ Ⓒ Ⓓ	111. Ⓐ Ⓑ Ⓒ Ⓓ	119. Ⓐ Ⓑ Ⓒ Ⓓ	127. Ⓐ Ⓑ Ⓒ Ⓓ
104. Ⓐ Ⓑ Ⓒ Ⓓ	112. Ⓐ Ⓑ Ⓒ Ⓓ	120. Ⓐ Ⓑ Ⓒ Ⓓ	128. Ⓐ Ⓑ Ⓒ Ⓓ
105. Ⓐ Ⓑ Ⓒ Ⓓ	113. Ⓐ Ⓑ Ⓒ Ⓓ	121. Ⓐ Ⓑ Ⓒ Ⓓ	129. Ⓐ Ⓑ Ⓒ Ⓓ
106. Ⓐ Ⓑ Ⓒ Ⓓ	114. Ⓐ Ⓑ Ⓒ Ⓓ	122. Ⓐ Ⓑ Ⓒ Ⓓ	130. Ⓐ Ⓑ Ⓒ Ⓓ
107. Ⓐ Ⓑ Ⓒ Ⓓ	115. Ⓐ Ⓑ Ⓒ Ⓓ	123. Ⓐ Ⓑ Ⓒ Ⓓ	
108. Ⓐ Ⓑ Ⓒ Ⓓ	116. Ⓐ Ⓑ Ⓒ Ⓓ	124. Ⓐ Ⓑ Ⓒ Ⓓ	

Part 6: Text Completion

131. Ⓐ Ⓑ Ⓒ Ⓓ	135. Ⓐ Ⓑ Ⓒ Ⓓ	139. Ⓐ Ⓑ Ⓒ Ⓓ	143. Ⓐ Ⓑ Ⓒ Ⓓ
132. Ⓐ Ⓑ Ⓒ Ⓓ	136. Ⓐ Ⓑ Ⓒ Ⓓ	140. Ⓐ Ⓑ Ⓒ Ⓓ	144. Ⓐ Ⓑ Ⓒ Ⓓ
133. Ⓐ Ⓑ Ⓒ Ⓓ	137. Ⓐ Ⓑ Ⓒ Ⓓ	141. Ⓐ Ⓑ Ⓒ Ⓓ	145. Ⓐ Ⓑ Ⓒ Ⓓ
134. Ⓐ Ⓑ Ⓒ Ⓓ	138. Ⓐ Ⓑ Ⓒ Ⓓ	142. Ⓐ Ⓑ Ⓒ Ⓓ	146. Ⓐ Ⓑ Ⓒ Ⓓ

Part 7: Reading Comprehension

147. Ⓐ Ⓑ Ⓒ Ⓓ	161. Ⓐ Ⓑ Ⓒ Ⓓ	175. Ⓐ Ⓑ Ⓒ Ⓓ	189. Ⓐ Ⓑ Ⓒ Ⓓ
148. Ⓐ Ⓑ Ⓒ Ⓓ	162. Ⓐ Ⓑ Ⓒ Ⓓ	176. Ⓐ Ⓑ Ⓒ Ⓓ	190. Ⓐ Ⓑ Ⓒ Ⓓ
149. Ⓐ Ⓑ Ⓒ Ⓓ	163. Ⓐ Ⓑ Ⓒ Ⓓ	177. Ⓐ Ⓑ Ⓒ Ⓓ	191. Ⓐ Ⓑ Ⓒ Ⓓ
150. Ⓐ Ⓑ Ⓒ Ⓓ	164. Ⓐ Ⓑ Ⓒ Ⓓ	178. Ⓐ Ⓑ Ⓒ Ⓓ	192. Ⓐ Ⓑ Ⓒ Ⓓ
151. Ⓐ Ⓑ Ⓒ Ⓓ	165. Ⓐ Ⓑ Ⓒ Ⓓ	179. Ⓐ Ⓑ Ⓒ Ⓓ	193. Ⓐ Ⓑ Ⓒ Ⓓ
152. Ⓐ Ⓑ Ⓒ Ⓓ	166. Ⓐ Ⓑ Ⓒ Ⓓ	180. Ⓐ Ⓑ Ⓒ Ⓓ	194. Ⓐ Ⓑ Ⓒ Ⓓ
153. Ⓐ Ⓑ Ⓒ Ⓓ	167. Ⓐ Ⓑ Ⓒ Ⓓ	181. Ⓐ Ⓑ Ⓒ Ⓓ	195. Ⓐ Ⓑ Ⓒ Ⓓ
154. Ⓐ Ⓑ Ⓒ Ⓓ	168. Ⓐ Ⓑ Ⓒ Ⓓ	182. Ⓐ Ⓑ Ⓒ Ⓓ	196. Ⓐ Ⓑ Ⓒ Ⓓ
155. Ⓐ Ⓑ Ⓒ Ⓓ	169. Ⓐ Ⓑ Ⓒ Ⓓ	183. Ⓐ Ⓑ Ⓒ Ⓓ	197. Ⓐ Ⓑ Ⓒ Ⓓ
156. Ⓐ Ⓑ Ⓒ Ⓓ	170. Ⓐ Ⓑ Ⓒ Ⓓ	184. Ⓐ Ⓑ Ⓒ Ⓓ	198. Ⓐ Ⓑ Ⓒ Ⓓ
157. Ⓐ Ⓑ Ⓒ Ⓓ	171. Ⓐ Ⓑ Ⓒ Ⓓ	185. Ⓐ Ⓑ Ⓒ Ⓓ	199. Ⓐ Ⓑ Ⓒ Ⓓ
158. Ⓐ Ⓑ Ⓒ Ⓓ	172. Ⓐ Ⓑ Ⓒ Ⓓ	186. Ⓐ Ⓑ Ⓒ Ⓓ	200. Ⓐ Ⓑ Ⓒ Ⓓ
159. Ⓐ Ⓑ Ⓒ Ⓓ	173. Ⓐ Ⓑ Ⓒ Ⓓ	187. Ⓐ Ⓑ Ⓒ Ⓓ	
160. Ⓐ Ⓑ Ⓒ Ⓓ	174. Ⓐ Ⓑ Ⓒ Ⓓ	188. Ⓐ Ⓑ Ⓒ Ⓓ	

Practice Test 3

LISTENING COMPREHENSION

In this section of the test, you will have the chance to show how well you understand spoken English. There are four parts to this section, with special directions for each part. You will have approximately 45 minutes to complete the Listening Comprehension sections.

Part 1: Photographs

Track 43

Directions: You will see a photograph. You will hear four statements about the photograph. Choose the statement that most closely matches the photograph, and fill in the corresponding oval on your answer sheet.

1.

2.

3.

4.

5.

6.

Part 2: Question-Response

Directions: You will hear a question and three possible responses. Choose the response that most closely answers the question, and fill in the corresponding oval on your answer sheet.

7. Mark your answer on your answer sheet.

8. Mark your answer on your answer sheet.

9. Mark your answer on your answer sheet.

10. Mark your answer on your answer sheet.

11. Mark your answer on your answer sheet.

12. Mark your answer on your answer sheet.

13. Mark your answer on your answer sheet.

14. Mark your answer on your answer sheet.

15. Mark your answer on your answer sheet.

16. Mark your answer on your answer sheet.

17. Mark your answer on your answer sheet.

18. Mark your answer on your answer sheet.

19. Mark your answer on your answer sheet.

20. Mark your answer on your answer sheet.

21. Mark your answer on your answer sheet.

22. Mark your answer on your answer sheet.

23. Mark your answer on your answer sheet.

24. Mark your answer on your answer sheet.

25. Mark your answer on your answer sheet.

26. Mark your answer on your answer sheet.

27. Mark your answer on your answer sheet.

28. Mark your answer on your answer sheet.

29. Mark your answer on your answer sheet.

30. Mark your answer on your answer sheet.

31. Mark your answer on your answer sheet.

Part 3: Conversations

Directions: You will hear a conversation between two or more people. You will see three questions on each conversation and four possible answers. Choose the best answer to each question, and fill in the corresponding oval on your answer sheet.

32. Where did the man learn about the event?

    (A) In a newspaper
    (B) On the Internet
    (C) On the radio
    (D) From a friend

33. Why can't they go on Saturday?

    (A) The man promised to help someone.
    (B) The woman has plans to go to a dance.
    (C) The man has to look for a new apartment.
    (D) The woman has to work that day.

34. What does the woman want to do?

    (A) Not go
    (B) Go on Sunday
    (C) Go to next year's event
    (D) Wait until their friend can go

35. What is the appointment for?

    (A) A medical checkup
    (B) A sales meeting
    (C) A possible presentation
    (D) A job interview

36. When will the appointment take place?

    (A) On Tuesday morning
    (B) At 8:30 in the evening
    (C) Tomorrow at ten
    (D) Today at noon

37. What should the man bring?

    (A) An application
    (B) A finished test
    (C) His résumé
    (D) Nothing

38. Where is the woman?

    (A) At a department store
    (B) At a repair shop
    (C) At a hotel
    (D) At home

39. What will the man do?

    (A) Turn the TV on
    (B) Take the TV away
    (C) Have someone fix the TV
    (D) Show the woman a different TV

40. What does the woman ask the man to do?

    (A) Wait half an hour
    (B) Come back at 10:00
    (C) Send her a package
    (D) Take a picture

41. Why do the speakers need Mr. Chung?

    (A) To deliver some letters
    (B) To speak at a meeting
    (C) To announce the date
    (D) To loan them his car

42. Why is Mr. Chung late?

    (A) He lost the address.
    (B) He's stuck in traffic.
    (C) His car broke down.
    (D) He's making a phone call.

43. What will the man do next?

    (A) Look for Mr. Chung
    (B) Prepare to show a film
    (C) Take Mr. Chung's place
    (D) Start the meeting

44. What was painted?

    (A) The cafeteria
    (B) The office
    (C) The lobby
    (D) The hallways

45. What does the woman say about
    the elevator?

    (A) It is very messy.
    (B) It runs too slowly.
    (C) Its color makes her feel sad.
    (D) It needs a new set of lights.

46. What will the woman do next week?

    (A) Choose paint colors
    (B) Meet a new client
    (C) Eat in the cafeteria
    (D) Go away on a trip

47. What does the woman say about the man?

    (A) He's an excellent golfer.
    (B) He cooks every day.
    (C) He is often bored.
    (D) He's very busy.

48. What does the woman like to do?

    (A) Run
    (B) Eat
    (C) Cook
    (D) Read

49. What does the woman mean when she says,
    "That's no good"?

    (A) She can't meet the man tomorrow.
    (B) She thinks the man doesn't cook well.
    (C) She doesn't enjoy going out in the
        evening.
    (D) She doesn't want to have dinner with
        the man.

50. What is the man's problem?

    (A) He wants something to drink.
    (B) He needs to change the oil.
    (C) He has run out of gas.
    (D) He has a flat tire.

51. Where is the service station?

    (A) On the other side of the road
    (B) Several miles away
    (C) In the next town
    (D) Near a bridge

52. How will the man get to the service station?

    (A) He will walk.
    (B) He will take a bus.
    (C) He will drive his car.
    (D) He will ride with the woman.

53. What does the woman want to do?

    (A) Go on a diet
    (B) Get more exercise
    (C) Get a gym membership
    (D) Find a better place to eat lunch

54. What does the man say about the gym?

    (A) It is crowded.
    (B) It is expensive.
    (C) It is far away.
    (D) It is cold.

55. Where does the man eat his lunch?

    (A) At home
    (B) At his desk
    (C) In the park
    (D) In the cafeteria

56. What does Maria mean when she says, "I know"?

    (A) She is familiar with the offices on the fifth floor.
    (B) She agrees with what the other woman said.
    (C) She understands how to get a good office.
    (D) She has some important information.

57. What describes the man's office?

    (A) It is near a park.
    (B) It is bright and sunny.
    (C) It overlooks a vacant lot.
    (D) It has a view of the parking lot.

58. What is suggested about the man?

    (A) He is unhappy with his job.
    (B) He is worried about his work.
    (C) He has been at his job a short time.
    (D) He often works until late at night.

59. What is the woman doing?

    (A) Ordering a meal
    (B) Planning a menu
    (C) Cooking some food
    (D) Shopping for groceries

60. What time of day is it?

    (A) Morning
    (B) Noon
    (C) Afternoon
    (D) Night

61. What will the man do next?

    (A) Bring ice cream
    (B) Bring a menu
    (C) Serve coffee
    (D) Look for jelly

62. Where does this conversation take place?

    (A) On a cruise ship
    (B) On a tour bus
    (C) On a plane
    (D) On a train

63. What does the woman ask about?

    (A) The length of the trip
    (B) The cost of tickets
    (C) The arrival time
    (D) The weather

64. What does the man recommend?

    (A) Taking a guided tour
    (B) Walking around
    (C) Leaving the city
    (D) Going to a café

Conference Room Schedule

Monday	Tuesday	Wednesday	Thursday
Training Session	Staff Meeting	Job Interviews	Workshop

65. What has to be cleaned?

    (A) The furniture
    (B) The windows
    (C) The walls
    (D) The carpet

66. Look at the graphic. When will the cleaning be done?

    (A) Monday
    (B) Tuesday
    (C) Wednesday
    (D) Thursday

67. What was the problem with the previous cleaners?

    (A) They charged too much.
    (B) They always arrived late.
    (C) They never finished the job.
    (D) They were difficult to schedule.

Clark's Department Store

Don't miss our storewide sale!

School supplies....................10% off
Housewares..........................15% off
Clothing.................................20% off
Books and toys.....................25% off

68. Look at the graphic. How much of a discount will the woman get on her purchase?

(A) 10%
(B) 15%
(C) 20%
(D) 25%

69. What does the woman ask the man for?

(A) Another color
(B) A larger size
(C) Gift wrapping
(D) More discounts

70. What does the man say about the item the woman is purchasing?

(A) It is very popular.
(B) It is of high quality.
(C) It is a new item in the store.
(D) It is available this week only.

Part 4: Talks

Directions: You will hear a talk given by a single speaker. You will see three questions on each talk, each with four possible answers. Choose the best answer to each question, and fill in the corresponding oval on your answer sheet.

71. What kind of event is being announced?

    (A) A garden tour
    (B) A high school graduation
    (C) The opening of a new park
    (D) The inauguration of a new mayor

72. When will the event take place?

    (A) Next Thursday
    (B) Next week
    (C) Next weekend
    (D) Next year

73. How can you get a ticket for the ceremony?

    (A) Line up at the park
    (B) Pay three dollars
    (C) Order it online
    (D) Call City Hall

74. What kind of training does the school provide?

    (A) Computer skills
    (B) Business management
    (C) Personnel training
    (D) Teacher preparation

75. What is indicated about the school?

    (A) It is very popular.
    (B) It has many students.
    (C) It has recently opened.
    (D) It is for working people.

76. What service does the school provide?

    (A) Help finding employment
    (B) Tutoring for individuals
    (C) Free parking on site
    (D) Tuition assistance

77. Why is Mr. Robertson going to Boston?

    (A) To be a radio show guest
    (B) To attend a workshop
    (C) To meet with a client
    (D) To enjoy a vacation

78. How will Mr. Robertson get to Boston?

    (A) By train
    (B) By taxi
    (C) By plane
    (D) By car

79. What is in the e-mail?

    (A) A travel ticket
    (B) A trip schedule
    (C) A hotel reservation
    (D) A question list

80. What kind of business most likely is Whitman's Downtown?

    (A) Delivery service
    (B) Furniture store
    (C) Interior decorator
    (D) Rug cleaning service

81. What does the speaker mean when he says, "that was taken care of"?

    (A) The order has been placed.
    (B) The invoice has been prepared.
    (C) The rug has already been paid for.
    (D) The store will handle the rug carefully.

82. What does the speaker ask the listener to do?

    (A) Call to make an appointment
    (B) Check the delivery schedule
    (C) Visit Whitman's by 5:30
    (D) Review the records

83. What is a requirement for job applicants?

   (A) A professional certificate
   (B) Availability on weekends
   (C) A high school diploma
   (D) Previous experience

84. What is mentioned as a job benefit?

   (A) Possible promotions
   (B) Regular salary raises
   (C) Paid vacation time
   (D) Insurance

85. How should you apply for these jobs?

   (A) Send a résumé
   (B) Go to the hotel
   (C) Write a letter
   (D) Make a phone call

86. Where would you hear this message?

   (A) At a bus station
   (B) At a train station
   (C) At an airport
   (D) At a subway station

87. What should the customer do first?

   (A) Insert a credit card
   (B) Check the ticket price
   (C) Enter the travel schedule
   (D) Select one-way or round trip

88. How can a customer pay cash?

   (A) Show an ID card
   (B) Go to the ticket office
   (C) Insert dollar bills in the slot
   (D) Buy the ticket from the driver

89. What is the purpose of this talk?

   (A) To compare different work methods
   (B) To describe some relaxation techniques
   (C) To explain how to organize work schedules
   (D) To give advice about relaxing during the work day

90. According to the speaker, how can you keep others from disturbing you?

   (A) Work at home
   (B) Close the door
   (C) Take a vacation
   (D) Put up a "Do not disturb" sign

91. What does the speaker mean when he says, "They don't consider that a poor use of time"?

   (A) Efficiency is a common goal.
   (B) Taking naps can be very useful.
   (C) Executives don't often have free time.
   (D) It is important to organize your time well.

92. Who are the awards for?

   (A) Professional musicians
   (B) Orchestra members
   (C) Young musicians
   (D) Music teachers

93. What kind of award is being given?

   (A) Cash
   (B) Trophy
   (C) A trip
   (D) A musical instrument

94. What are listeners asked to do?

   (A) Pay their bills
   (B) Give money
   (C) Teach music
   (D) Practice more

Highbury House

Blue Room	Red Room
Maps	**Documents**
Main Hall	Green Room
Paintings	**History Displays**

Painting Schedule

Monday	Tuesday	Wednesday	Thursday
Reception Area	Staff Break Room	Conference Room	Front Office

95. What was the original use of Highbury House?

(A) Private family home
(B) Office building
(C) Museum
(D) Hotel

96. Look at the graphic. Which exhibit will listeners be unable to see today?

(A) Maps
(B) Paintings
(C) Documents
(D) History displays

97. What does the speaker suggest listeners do?

(A) Check the concert schedule
(B) Visit the flower gardens
(C) Return later in the year
(D) Have lunch soon

98. What event will take place next week?

(A) A luncheon
(B) Inventory
(C) A staff meeting
(D) Conference registration

99. Look at the graphic. Which day will the event take place?

(A) Monday
(B) Tuesday
(C) Wednesday
(D) Thursday

100. What are listeners asked to do next?

(A) Put the tables away
(B) Check the schedule
(C) Return their cups
(D) Have some coffee

This is the end of the Listening Comprehension portion of the test. Turn to Part 5 in your test book.

READING

In this section of the test, you will have the chance to show how well you understand written English. There are three parts to this section, with special directions for each part.

**YOU WILL HAVE ONE HOUR AND FIFTEEN MINUTES
TO COMPLETE PARTS 5, 6, AND 7 OF THE TEST.**

Part 5: Incomplete Sentences

Directions: You will see a sentence with a missing word. Four possible answers follow the sentence. Choose the best answer to the question, and fill in the corresponding oval on your answer sheet.

101. The office would look much better with a new coat of paint _____ a few pictures hanging on the walls.

    (A) but
    (B) and
    (C) as
    (D) though

102. Most people in the department are _____ that staffing cuts will have to be made.

    (A) aware
    (B) await
    (C) awaken
    (D) awe

103. The itinerary _____ the time and location of each meeting Dr. Richards has while he is visiting the department.

    (A) contain
    (B) contains
    (C) containing
    (D) have contained

104. Passengers can check in for the charter flight _____ 8:00 and 12:00 tomorrow.

    (A) between
    (B) with
    (C) through
    (D) from

105. The landscaper made several _____, including the installation of an automatic watering system.

    (A) recommends
    (B) recommended
    (C) recommendations
    (D) recommendable

106. It is _____ to transfer a document by e-mail than by fax.

    (A) fast
    (B) fastest
    (C) the faster
    (D) faster

107. You can pay your bill online, _____ you can send a check by regular mail.

    (A) so
    (B) or
    (C) but
    (D) since

108. All conference speakers need to be notified that their allowed time has been _____ from 30 minutes to 25 minutes.

    (A) heightened
    (B) lengthened
    (C) shortened
    (D) widened

109. I will ask my assistant _____ the necessary forms to you at your office.

    (A) to send
    (B) sending
    (C) will send
    (D) sends

110. Ms. Chang is very frugal and buys most of _____ business suits at large discount stores.

    (A) that
    (B) them
    (C) our
    (D) her

111. With so much light pollution in the city, it's difficult _____ many stars at night.

    (A) see
    (B) sees
    (C) to see
    (D) seeing

112. Once every three months, all stockroom employees are _____ to work overnight to do inventory.

    (A) required
    (B) suggested
    (C) preferred
    (D) appreciated

113. The variety of insurance benefits _____ very broad under this policy.

    (A) are
    (B) is
    (C) being
    (D) be

114. The purpose of the awards banquet is to _____ the many achievements of our talented staff.

    (A) acknowledge
    (B) determine
    (C) entertain
    (D) discern

115. Please leave your luggage _____ the bus for the driver to load.

    (A) among
    (B) between
    (C) from
    (D) beside

116. The hotel offers a discount for guests who stay a _____ of three nights.

    (A) podium
    (B) optimum
    (C) minimum
    (D) premium

117. If we were not certain about the safety of the product, we _____ it.

    (A) had sold
    (B) don't sell
    (C) will sell
    (D) would not sell

118. The company handbook _____ the department's policies on building customer relationships.

    (A) explains
    (B) is explaining
    (C) explain
    (D) explaining

119. Model 34 is on backorder with the _____ and probably won't be here until spring.

    (A) candidate
    (B) transportation
    (C) manufacturer
    (D) customer

120. Mr. Larsen says that he will _____ consider military veterans for the foreman position.

   (A) all
   (B) only
   (C) some
   (D) except

121. _____ we checked the budget twice, the managers found a mistake in our calculations.

   (A) Unless
   (B) However
   (C) Since
   (D) Even though

122. Everyone else left the office early, so Harry had to finish up the report by _____.

   (A) alone
   (B) just
   (C) himself
   (D) single

123. Ethel's economic predictions for the coming year _____ by her colleagues with some skepticism.

   (A) were received
   (B) were receiving
   (C) had received
   (D) received

124. Doctors _____ have recently been licensed use the medical association's website to find jobs.

   (A) what
   (B) who
   (C) whose
   (D) which

125. The only difference _____ the two flights your assistant suggested is the time of departure.

   (A) with
   (B) then
   (C) between
   (D) among

126. _____ careful planning, the caterers did not bring enough linens for the tables.

   (A) During
   (B) Because
   (C) In spite of
   (D) Although

127. The project manager is responsible for _____ every step of the project.

   (A) organization
   (B) organizing
   (C) organized
   (D) organize

128. The head of accounts _____ to sit in on the client meeting tomorrow.

   (A) decisions
   (B) are deciding
   (C) has decided
   (D) decide

129. The promotional message needs to emphasize that our product is better _____ all similar products on the market.

   (A) much
   (B) than
   (C) off
   (D) to

130. Mr. Kim spent most of the week preparing _____ his new idea to the director.

   (A) present
   (B) presented
   (C) presenting
   (D) to present

Part 6: Text Completion

> **Directions:** You will see four passages, each with four blanks. Each blank has four answer choices. For each blank, choose the word, phrase, or sentence that best completes the passage.

Questions 131–134 refer to the following letter.

Green Office Renovators
Da'an District, Taipei City 106-03
TAIWAN

Kao Su Mei, Vice President
377 Chiang An Road
Da'an District, Taipei City 106-03
TAIWAN

Dear Ms. Kao,

Thank you for considering Green Office Renovators for your upcoming office renovation project. I hope you will take the time to read through the enclosed brochure, which explains the materials we use and the measures we take to meet the highest standards for environmental protection. _____ also outlines the services we provide, as well
131
as our pricing system. Please note that Green Office Renovators _____ a minimum
132
deposit before work can begin on any project. The initial costs of installing energy-efficient systems can be high. _____.
133
In addition, statistics show that companies that demonstrate _____ the environment
134
are more popular among customers.

I look forward to discussing the renovation needs of your company.
Sincerely,

Cai Mi
Cai Mi

131. (A) You
(B) He
(C) It
(D) We

132. (A) requires
(B) require
(C) have required
(D) are requiring

133. (A) Fortunately, the installation process is not overly complicated
(B) Our workers are highly trained in all aspects of these systems
(C) Nevertheless, these systems are used in both residences and businesses
(D) However, they save money in the long run

134. (A) concern for
(B) happiness about
(C) placement in
(D) knowledge of

To: clementinebooks@learning.org
From: rep990@gaspower.net
Subject: Equal Payment Billing Plan

Dear Sheldon Murray,

It has come to my attention that your business is still paying its gas bills using our Monthly Plan. During the past year, your _____ bill was for $400 in the
135
month of January. However, your bills were as low as $23 in the summer months.

_____. We believe that you are an excellent candidate for our Equal Billing Plan.
136
Approximately 78% of our customers have switched to this option since it became available three years ago. Though the amount of money you spend in the year will be identical, your higher bills will be _____ throughout the year. This makes it easier to
137
budget your finances.

With the Equal Billing Plan, the amount you pay per month is based on an approximation. To do this we take an average from the bills in your previous year. After six months on the Equal Billing Plan we will adjust this amount depending on whether or not you use more or less gas than we _____. At the end of the year
138
you will receive a debit or credit from us to balance the amount owed with the amount used.

135. (A) high
(B) higher
(C) highest
(D) most high

136. (A) We appreciate that you paid all of your monthly bills on time
(B) The majority of your annual fees occurred in the four coldest months of the year
(C) In fact, your summer bills were among the lowest of all our customers'
(D) You may be aware that we now offer electronic billing for customers in your region

137. (A) marked down
(B) built up
(C) spread out
(D) topped off

138. (A) estimated
(B) permitted
(C) inquired
(D) ordered

Questions 139–142 refer to the following article.

Airport Lounge Removes Free Internet Service
By Kelly Christie

As of this Friday, passengers at Port Elizabeth Airport will no longer _____ free Internet service in the business travelers' lounge. Since
139
January of last year, free Internet access has been available in the airport business lounge to travelers who have purchased a VIP card. VIP card holders enjoy numerous _____ in the business lounge in addition to Inter-
140
net access, including coffee, snacks, newspapers, and the use of printers. _____. Now users of the business lounge will need to purchase Internet
141
access at a cost of $5 per hour, with a two-hour _____.
142

---

139. (A) offer
    (B) offered
    (C) be offered
    (D) be offering

140. (A) utilities
    (B) furniture
    (C) benefits
    (D) functions

141. (A) Business travelers spend hours each month waiting in airports
    (B) The Airport Authority has plans to renovate the lounge next year
    (C) Prices at the airport are notoriously higher than in other parts of the city
    (D) The lounges also provide an escape from crowded waiting rooms

142. (A) minimum
    (B) minimal
    (C) minimize
    (D) minimally

Questions 143–146 refer to the following e-mail.

From: shih-yismith@techworld.com
Subject: Technology conference
Date: October 10
To: yi-fangwu@techworld.com

Are you interested in going to that international technology conference in
Taipei in December? I've never been, but everyone ____ it's the
                                                    143
place to go to learn about the latest technology. I missed going last year
because I just ____ find the time, but I know I can make it work this
              144
year. I really hope you'll be able to join me. ____. If you want to attend the
                                               145
conference, then we should talk to our ____ as soon as possible to make
                                       146
sure we can get permission. Please get back to me soon.

Shih-Yi

143. (A) say
     (B) says
     (C) are saying
     (D) have said

144. (A) can't
     (B) mustn't
     (C) shouldn't
     (D) couldn't

145. (A) I think you would get a lot out of it
     (B) I like keeping up with the new technology
     (C) It takes place in a different country every year
     (D) You have taught me a lot about technology development

146. (A) colleagues
     (B) supervisors
     (C) assistants
     (D) customers

Part 7: Reading Comprehension

> **Directions:** You will see single and multiple reading passages followed by several questions. Each question has four answer choices. Choose the best answer to the question, and fill in the corresponding oval on your answer sheet.

Questions 147–148 refer to the following advertisement.

WHY WAIT FOR A BETTER JOB?

Get a great job now!

National Air

is hiring full-time representatives for
Sales & Reservations. Talk to our employees
and discover why we're the best thing in the air.
Interviews on the spot!
Bring your résumé.

OPEN HOUSE

National Air Headquarters
Southeast Regional Airport
Thursday, June 15 7:30 P.M.

147. What is the purpose of this ad?

   (A) To advertise a job training program
   (B) To sell airline tickets
   (C) To recruit potential employees
   (D) To introduce the new headquarters

148. Where will the event be held?

   (A) At company headquarters
   (B) At a private home
   (C) On an airplane
   (D) At the company's regional office

Questions 149–150 refer to the following notice.

ATTENTION RIDERS

- Pay exact fare when boarding. Drivers cannot make change.
- Upon boarding, move to the rear. Stand in the passenger area. Do not block doors.
- Allow senior citizens and disabled riders to use the priority seating area near the front.
- Earphones must be used when listening to music.
- No food or open beverages. No smoking.

Thank you for riding with us!

149. Where would you see this notice?

   (A) At a train station
   (B) On an airplane
   (C) In a taxi
   (D) On a bus

150. Which of the following is permitted?

   (A) Smoking by the door
   (B) Listening to music
   (C) Having a snack
   (D) Drinking coffee

| LI CHEN | 11:20 |
| They have the paper you wanted. Two packs, right? | |

LINA GIAMETTI 11:21
Right. And the envelopes?

LI CHEN 11:22
They have the size you wanted, but not in red.

LI CHEN 11:24
They can order them for you, but it takes 5–7 days.

LINA GIAMETTI 11:26
That's no good. The mailing has to go out by
Thursday, at the latest.

LI CHEN 11:27
The only color they have in stock in that size is ivory.

LINA GIAMETTI 11:29
That will have to do.

LI CHEN 11:31
OK. Do you still want me to get two boxes?

LINA GIAMETTI 11:32
Yes. And don't forget to put it on the company
credit card.

151. Where is Mr. Chen?

(A) At home
(B) At a store
(C) In his office
(D) In the supply room

152. At 11:29, what does Ms. Giametti mean when she writes, "That will have to do"?

(A) She will use the ivory envelopes.
(B) She doesn't want the envelopes now.
(C) She has to complete the mailing on time.
(D) She wants Mr. Chen to order red envelopes.

Questions 153–154 refer to the following table.

Results of Study on Time Distribution of Tasks for Sales Managers	
Training new personnel	20%
Identifying possible clients	20%
Reviewing sales data	28%
Resolving customer problems	5%
Making sales assignments	15%
Coordinating with technical staff	7%
Administrative duties	5%

153. What do sales managers spend the most time on?

(A) Training staff
(B) Going over sales records
(C) Making sales assignments
(D) Performing administrative duties

154. What can be concluded from this information?

(A) Too much time is spent with technical staff
(B) Finding new customers is a low priority
(C) There are few customer problems
(D) Sales are going down

Summer is a great time to return to school!
If you need better business skills, let us help.

Each summer Claybourne University School of Business Administration offers special courses for experienced managers who want to sharpen their existing business skills or learn new ones. You will study with your peers in a week-long intensive session that simulates the world of international commerce. You will learn new theories and study the way business is conducted around the world. Students in previous sessions have reported that what they learned was immediately applicable to their own work situations.

Only one person from a company is accepted into this special program. All applications require a letter of recommendation from your current supervisor.

For more information, call the

Summer Education Center
School of Business Administration
Claybourne University
903-477-6768 Fax: 903-477-6777

155. Who is this course for?

(A) Professional managers
(B) College professors changing careers
(C) Undergraduate business students
(D) Administrative support staff

156. What is required for admission?

(A) An entrance exam
(B) A business degree
(C) International experience
(D) A reference from your boss

157. How long is the course?

(A) All summer long
(B) One week
(C) Three evenings a month
(D) Two years

Questions 158–160 refer to the following webpage.

| Home | Shop | About Us | My Cart |

Ginger's Botanical Designs

Our Story
For 25 years, Ginger's has been helping to beautify the homes and businesses of Burkettsville. Whatever occasion you are celebrating—from a simple birthday greeting to a lavish wedding—our bouquets, baskets, wreathes, and garlands will transform it into a beautifully memorable experience. –[1]–

Ginger's was founded by Ginger Carpenter in a small store front on Main Street. It quickly became popular and the business thrived. –[2]– It soon grew out of its small downtown space, and Ginger purchased the property on Willow Road. The company's main store and offices are now located there. The Main Street space continues as a branch store. –[3]– Our consultants are waiting to help you choose the right look and designs to celebrate your special occasion.

Ginger's is happy to deliver your order. –[4]– We charge no fee for deliveries in the local area, including most addresses in Burkettsville, Springdale, and Rosslyn. There is a mileage charge for other areas. Orders placed before 11:00 A.M. will be delivered the same day. Orders placed after 11:00 A.M. will be delivered the following day.

Click on your preferred category and start shopping!

| Celebrations | Romance | Roses and Orchids |

158. What kind of business is Ginger's?

(A) Florist
(B) Landscaper
(C) Party planner
(D) Interior designer

159. What is said about deliveries?

(A) Deliveries usually take 24 hours or longer.
(B) Deliveries are only made in the local area.
(C) No deliveries are made after 11:00 A.M.
(D) There is no charge for local deliveries.

160. In which of the following positions marked [1], [2], [3], and [4] does the following sentence best belong?

"We are ready to serve you at either of our two locations."

(A) [1]
(B) [2]
(C) [3]
(D) [4]

Questions 161–163 refer to the following e-mail.

From: Ravi Niazi
To: F. Omoboriowo
Subj: Re: Shipping question

Dear Mr. Omoboriowo,

Thank you for your interest in Dawn Products. I am attaching a table that shows the current prices of our most popular products for your information.

To answer your question, yes, all our products are available at wholesale prices to registered retailers and on orders of $1,000 or more. Shipping times and costs depend on your location, as well as on the size of your order. You may also be interested in knowing that all our products are manufactured here at our company facilities under the supervision of our trained managers. We do not subcontract any of our production.

Please contact me if you would like any further assistance in placing an order.

Sincerely,
Ravi Niazi
Customer Relations Manager
Dawn Products

161. What does the e-mail attachment contain?

(A) A price list
(B) An order form
(C) Shipping information
(D) Staff contact information

162. What does Mr. Niazi say about shipping?

(A) It is always done by air.
(B) It is free on large orders.
(C) It requires insurance.
(D) Its price varies.

163. What kind of business does Mr. Omoboriowo probably work for?

(A) Shipping
(B) Retail
(C) Advertising
(D) Manufacturing

Questions 164–167 refer to the following memo.

MEMO

To: All employees
From: K. Osafo
         Director, Personnel

Date: November 23, 20—
Subject: Charitable Leave

   The corporation is pleased to announce a new policy which will allow employees to take paid time off for unpaid community service. Employees may take up to eight hours of paid leave per month to volunteer for charity organizations. Employees are eligible for this program if they are full-time and have been employed here for at least one year. Charitable leave must be requested in advance; otherwise, employees will not be paid for that time. Charitable leave must also be approved by the employee's supervisor.

164. What does the new policy allow employees to do?

   (A) Take paid leave for professional training
   (B) Have more holidays
   (C) Get paid for volunteer work
   (D) Go home early

165. How much time may an employee take under this program?

   (A) One hour per week
   (B) Three hours per week
   (C) Six hours per month
   (D) Eight hours per month

166. Who can participate in the program?

   (A) Full-time employees
   (B) Part-time employees
   (C) New employees
   (D) All employees

167. What must an employee do to get paid for time off?

   (A) Complete an absence form
   (B) Have a good attendance record
   (C) Be recommended by a supervisor
   (D) Get advance supervisor approval

Ruby Stone [2:10]
Has anyone noticed any problems with the carpet?

Glen Blake [2:12]
Yes. There is a big bump in the middle of my office floor. It looks like they didn't nail it down correctly.

Ruby Stone [2:13]
Right. I have the exact same problem in my office.

Kaylee O'Hara [2:14]
In the conference room, I noticed a big gap between the edge of the carpet and the wall.

Ruby Stone [2:15]
We paid a lot to get this new carpet installed. We are going to have to contact the carpet company and have them come back and do the job right.

Glen Blake [2:16]
Leave that to me. I can get to it this afternoon.

Kaylee O'Hara [2:18]
See if they can come back before the end of the week. We have the representatives from Wilson, Inc. coming for that meeting first thing Monday morning.

Ruby Stone [2:20]
I know. The new clients. We have to have everything in order before then. Why did we use this carpet company, anyway?

Glen Blake [2:23]
Don't you remember? You said it is important to give an opportunity to a business that is just starting out.

Kaylee O'Hara [2:25]
Next time I think we should give the opportunity to the business with the experience to do the job right.

168. What is the problem with the carpet?

(A) It was installed incorrectly.
(B) It is old and worn out.
(C) It is the wrong color.
(D) It needs cleaning.

169. What will happen on Monday?

(A) Office supplies will be ordered.
(B) There will be a staff meeting.
(C) Clients will visit the office.
(D) The office will be cleaned.

170. What is indicated about the carpet company?

    (A) It has relatively high fees.
    (B) It has a good reputation.
    (C) It has many employees.
    (D) It is a new business.

171. At 2:16, what does Mr. Blake mean when he writes, "Leave that to me"?

    (A) He plans to fix the carpet.
    (B) He will call the carpet company.
    (C) He will pay the bill for the carpet.
    (D) He wants to be left alone for the afternoon.

Questions 172–175 refer to the following article.

The New Target for Hackers

    Is your company a sitting duck for hackers? When did you last change your passwords? How strong are your security systems?

    According to the International Network Security Association, there's a new breed of hacker out there. And, there's a new target, too.

    In the past, hackers gained notoriety by breaking into the networks of large companies. The bigger the company, the bigger the success in the eyes of the hackers. –[1]– When hackers broke into Infelmax's notoriously secure system several yeas ago, they made headline news around the world.

    The big "successes" came with a major drawback, however—international teams of investigators and serious criminal charges. Several former hackers are now sitting behind bars or working to pay off hefty fines. –[2]–

    Now hackers have changed their focus. Smaller companies make an attractive target because of their less sophisticated security systems. –[3]– Also, a breached system in a smaller company may attract little attention as investigators pursue bigger problems, making the consequences less problematic for the hackers. –[4]–

---

172. Which is a likely victim for the new breed of hackers?

    (A) Well-known companies
    (B) Small companies
    (C) International companies
    (D) Technology companies

173. According to the article, what was one probable motive for hackers of Infelmax's network?

    (A) Money
    (B) Power
    (C) Fame
    (D) Fun

174. What has happened to some former hackers?

    (A) They have been hired by software companies.
    (B) They have been found innocent of crimes.
    (C) They are working with investigators.
    (D) They are in prison.

175. In which of the following positions marked [1], [2], [3], and [4] does the following sentence best belong?

"They may even be lax about simple security measures, such as changing their passwords frequently."

    (A) [1]
    (B) [2]
    (C) [3]
    (D) [4]

MARKETING REPRESENTATIVE

New Zealand's fastest-growing women's clothing company seeks a marketing representative. Position requires travel approximately one week per month, representing the company at conferences and media events.

Required qualifications
- a degree from a four-year college or university, preferably in marketing.
- at least one year of experience in sales, preferably clothing.
- excellent communication skills, including experience giving presentations.

Send your resume and cover letter to Camilla Crowe: ccrowe@nzworld.com

From: Camilla Crowe
To: Akiko Sasaki
Subject: Your application

Dear Ms. Sasaki:

Thank you for applying for the position of marketing representative. We appreciate your interest in NZ World.

Although your résumé shows that you have good preparation for a career in marketing, unfortunately you don't meet all our required qualifications. You have the degree we are looking for, but not the experience. Your sales experience in an electronics store is a good background, but your time there is just half of what we ask for as a minimum. In addition, you have no experience in clothing sales.

However, your résumé also shows some of your strengths. You have excellent grades and have been active in your campus' marketing club. Therefore, we would like to offer you a position as an intern.

This is a three-month, unpaid internship. Since you just graduated last month, I think this would be a great opportunity for you. It would give you some of the experience you will need to start your career. For example, your internship would give you some practice with public speaking, an important marketing skill that is lacking on your résumé.

Contact me by April 1 if you are interested in accepting this position. I look forward to hearing from you.

Sincerely,

Camilla Crowe

HR Director
NZ World

176. Which of the following is NOT a duty of the advertised job?

(A) Recruiting new staff
(B) Giving presentations
(C) Traveling every month
(D) Attending conferences

177. What field did Akiko get her degree in?

(A) Electronics
(B) Marketing
(C) Communications
(D) Clothing design

178. When did Akiko get her degree?

(A) February
(B) March
(C) April
(D) May

179. What type of work experience does Akiko have?

(A) Clothing sales
(B) Electronics sales
(C) Career counselor
(D) Marketing representative

180. What did Camilla Crowe offer Akiko?

(A) A job
(B) An interview
(C) An internship
(D) A club membership

This year, try something different for your company's annual party. Visit the Front Street Theater.

An afternoon or evening at the Front Street Theater includes a delicious meal prepared by our Paris-trained chef, Jacques, and a show preformed by some of the region's finest actors. A tour of this historic theater is also offered before the meal. Groups of 250 or more can reserve the entire theater for their group. This option is available on Sunday afternoons only. Groups of 300–350 receive a 10% discount. Groups over 350 receive a 15% discount.

Shows are selected based on the time of the year: January–April, tragedy; May–July, drama; August–October, musical; and November–December, comedy.

Reservations are available at the following times:

Monday–Thursday: Dinner and evening show
                        6–10 P.M.

Friday–Saturday   Lunch and afternoon show
                        12–4 P.M.
                        Dinner and evening show
                        6–10 P.M.

Sunday   Only large groups renting the entire theater. Both lunch
                        and dinner schedules are available. It is recommended to
                        make large group reservations one month ahead of time.

Come to the Front Street Theater for food, entertainment, and fun. To make a reservation, e-mail us or call us at 216-707-2268.

To: Front Street Theater, Reservations
From: Constance Hekler, Events Coordinator
Date: October 25, 20—
Subject: Holiday party

I saw your advertisement in this week's *Business Journal*. I am interested in renting your theater for Federal Bank's annual employee party.

We have set the date for our party as Sunday, December 20. Is the theater available then? We prefer the lunch and afternoon show. There will be 325 guests.

Please fax the menu, a description of the shows, and the price list to me. And let me know about the availability of dates in December.

Thank you.

181. What is included in a visit to the theater?

(A) Meeting the chef
(B) Talking with the actors
(C) Touring the theater
(D) Selecting shows

182. When is the theater open to individuals and small groups?

(A) Monday through Thursday only
(B) Friday and Saturday only
(C) Monday through Saturday only
(D) Sunday only

183. What time does Ms. Hekler prefer the Federal Bank party to begin?

(A) 10 A.M.
(B) 12 P.M.
(C) 4 P.M.
(D) 6 P.M.

184. What type of discount will the Federal Bank get for this party?

(A) 0%
(B) 10%
(C) 15%
(D) 20%

185. What type of show will guests at the Federal Bank party see?

(A) Tragedy
(B) Drama
(C) Musical
(D) Comedy

PRACTICE TEST 3

Retiring Soon?

Attend a Retirement Workshop. This workshop will explain available retirement benefits and how to determine which you are eligible for.

Choose the date that is most convenient for you.

- ✓ August 1
- ✓ August 15
- ✓ August 29
- ✓ September 13

All workshops take place from 8:30–10:30 A.M. in Meeting Room F. Registration is not required. Just show up!

From: Marcus Mains
To: Jae Sun Oh
Subj: Retirement questions
Date: July 20

Mr. Oh,

I am thinking about retiring soon and have some questions about my retirement benefits. I saw the notice about retirement workshops, and I tried to attend one, but the room was empty when I showed up. That was this morning at 8:30 in Room F.

My main question is this: I am 63 years old and have been working with this company for 20 years. Since I am not yet 65, will there be a reduction in my benefits if I retire now? Also, I have some questions about taxes after I retire. Who can help me with that?

Thank you.

Marcus Mains

From: Jae Sun Oh
To: Marcus Mains
Subj: re: Retirement questions
Date: July 20

Hello Mr. Mains,

Thank you for your questions. Here is the basic information about retirement benefits:

- You can retire with full benefits if you are age 65 or over and have worked at the company for at least 20 years, or if you have worked at the company for at least 25 years, you can retire no matter what your age.

- If you are age 55–64 and have worked here for at least 20 years but less than 25 years, you can retire but with a reduction in your retirement fund. It will be reduced by 2% for each year of age under 65. For example, if you are 63, it will be reduced by 4%.

I encourage you to attend a workshop. It is led by Augusta James, who does a very good job of presenting all the possible scenarios. As far as tax issues go, I suggest you contact Fred Lee in Accounting. He is a tax specialist and should be able to answer your concerns.

Let me know if you have any more questions.

Jae Sun Oh

Human Resources Office

186. How long does each workshop last?

(A) 1 hour
(B) 2 hours
(C) All morning
(D) All day

187. How many workshops should a potential retiree attend?

(A) 1
(B) 2
(C) 3
(D) 4

188. What mistake did Mr. Mains make about the workshop?

(A) He arrived too late.
(B) He went to the wrong room.
(C) He went on the wrong date.
(D) He forgot to register ahead of time.

189. If Mr. Mains retires now, what will be the reduction in his retirement fund?

(A) 0%
(B) 2%
(C) 4%
(D) 10%

190. What does Mr. Oh suggest that Mr. Mains do about his tax questions?

(A) Hire a tax specialist
(B) Attend a workshop
(C) Send them to Mr. Oh
(D) Call the Accounting Department

Questions 191–195 refer to the following notice, course information, and e-mail.

Professional Development Credits Update

As you know, all ABC, Inc. staff are required to earn 20 hours of professional development credits per year. You can now use coursework at the Central Technical Institute toward your required professional development credit hours. Only courses in the Office Skills category are eligible. Each course is worth 15 hours of credit. You must receive a passing grade to get credit. At the end of the course, please have your records forwarded to the Human Resources Office.

Classes offered at Central Technical Institute
CATEGORY: Office Skills

Accounting
ACTG 101   Financial Accounting, Part One
ACTG 102   Financial Accounting, Part Two*
ACTG 670   Accounting for Small Businesses

Business
BUSI 100   Introduction to Business
BUSI 200   Principles of Business

Computers
COMP 104   Introduction to Microsoft Word
COMP 207   Microsoft Excel: Basics
COMP 300   Computers in the Office**

Marketing
MARK 500   Global Marketing Strategies
MARK 600   Marketing on the Internet

Classes last from January 3 until March 15. Classes at the same level are offered on the same day: 100—Monday, 200—Tuesday, 300 and 400—Wednesday, and 500 and higher—Thursday. All classes are offered from 6:00—8:00 in the evening.
  The fee for each course is $300. To register, go to: *www.cti.org* and click on the "Registration" link.

*Students must take ACTG 101 and earn a grade of 75 or better before taking ACTG 102.
**This course will be offered on Tuesday evenings.

From: Amanda Minh
To: Roberto Guzman
Subj: Professional development credits

Mr. Guzman,

I have received your records from the Central Technical Institute for the Accounting 101 course you took last term. Unfortunately, we cannot count this course toward your professional development credits as your grade was too low. I see that you have signed up for Computer 207 and Business 100 this term. You can use these for professional development credits as long as you get a passing grade. Work hard! I look forward to seeing your course records at the end of this term.

Amanda Minh
HR Assistant

191. How many professional development hours can an ABC, Inc. employee earn for courses at the Central Technical Institute?

(A) No more than 15
(B) No more than 20
(C) 15 per course
(D) 20 per year

192. What time does the Accounting 102 class start?

(A) 6:00 A.M.
(B) 8:00 A.M.
(C) 6:00 P.M.
(D) 8:00 P.M.

193. How much will Roberto pay for each class he takes?

(A) Nothing; his company will pay.
(B) $300
(C) $600
(D) It depends on the level.

194. Why won't Roberto get professional development credits for the accounting course he took last term?

(A) He did not get a passing grade .
(B) It is not in the Office Skills category.
(C) It was not offered at the Central Technical Institute.
(D) He did not have his records forwarded to the HR office.

195. Which days will Roberto be in class this term?

(A) Monday only
(B) Monday and Tuesday
(C) Tuesday and Wednesday
(D) Wednesday only

MITCHELL LANDSCAPERS
DESIGN • PLANT • MAINTAIN
We do it all!

❖ We can turn your residential or business property into a place of beauty and elegance. We will create a landscape design specifically for you and your property. Our expert gardeners will install and maintain your new garden to keep it looking beautiful.

❖ Are you a do-it-yourselfer? We will develop a design and help you pick plants that will give you the look you want, while at the same time being easy for you to care for.

Initial consultation is free!
Call today for an appointment,
or visit us at *www.mitchelllandscapes.com*

From: Scott Holmes
To: Shelley Silva
Subj: Landscaping Broad Street
Date: May 10

Shelley,

Do you know anything about Mitchell Landscapers? I saw their ad the other day and thought they might be able to do something for the front of our new property on Broad Street. It looks sadly neglected. The shrubbery on either side of the door needs to be replaced with some healthier-looking bushes, and it would be nice to have some sort of flowers along the walkway. There is already a nice-looking cherry tree on one side of the walkway, and I would like to add another on the other side. Find out if they could do the work for under $3,000 and have it done before the end of the month. We have that open house for prospective tenants on June1, and I would like to have the place in shape by then.

Let me know what they say.

Scott

MITCHELL LANDSCAPERS
DESIGN • PLANT • MAINTAIN

Project estimate for: Scott Holmes Properties

Location: 156 Broad Street

Summary:
Create design for front of property, remove
shrubs, plant bushes, create flower beds along
walkway, add cherry tree

COST ESTIMATE

Design work		$500
Materials		$1,000
Labor		$650
	Total	**$2,150**

Project date:
Work to begin June 2, to be completed by June 4

---

196. What is indicated about the landscaping business?

(A) It works at both private homes and commercial properties.
(B) It has worked with Mr. Holmes in the past.
(C) It has been in business for many years.
(D) It has several branches.

197. The word "pick" in paragraph 2, line 2 of the advertisement is closest in meaning to

(A) harvest
(B) choose
(C) pull
(D) lift

198. Who is Mr. Holmes?

(A) An interior decorator
(B) A real estate agent
(C) A city planner
(D) A landlord

199. What problem will Mr. Holmes have with the project estimate?

(A) The project cost is too high.
(B) It doesn't include a new tree.
(C) The job will be completed too late.
(D) He doesn't want shrubs to be removed.

200. How much will Mitchell Landscapers pay the workers for the Broad Street project?

(A) $500
(B) $650
(C) $1,000
(D) $2,150

This is the end of the test. If you finish before time is called, you may go back to Parts 5, 6, and 7 and check your work.

ANSWER KEY
Practice Test 3

LISTENING COMPREHENSION

Part 1: Photographs

1. **C**	3. **A**	5. **B**
2. **D**	4. **B**	6. **C**

Part 2: Question-Response

7. **C**	14. **B**	21. **A**	28. **B**
8. **A**	15. **C**	22. **C**	29. **C**
9. **C**	16. **C**	23. **B**	30. **A**
10. **A**	17. **B**	24. **A**	31. **A**
11. **C**	18. **C**	25. **C**	
12. **C**	19. **A**	26. **B**	
13. **B**	20. **A**	27. **A**	

Part 3: Conversations

32. **C**	42. **B**	52. **D**	62. **A**
33. **A**	43. **B**	53. **B**	63. **C**
34. **B**	44. **C**	54. **A**	64. **B**
35. **D**	45. **C**	55. **B**	65. **D**
36. **A**	46. **D**	56. **B**	66. **B**
37. **D**	47. **D**	57. **D**	67. **B**
38. **C**	48. **B**	58. **C**	68. **C**
39. **C**	49. **A**	59. **A**	69. **A**
40. **A**	50. **C**	60. **A**	70. **A**
41. **B**	51. **D**	61. **C**	

Part 4: Talks

71. **C**	79. **B**	87. **C**	95. **A**
72. **C**	80. **B**	88. **B**	96. **D**
73. **D**	81. **C**	89. **D**	97. **B**
74. **A**	82. **C**	90. **B**	98. **A**
75. **D**	83. **B**	91. **B**	99. **D**
76. **A**	84. **A**	92. **C**	100. **C**
77. **B**	85. **B**	93. **A**	
78. **A**	86. **B**	94. **B**	

ANSWER KEY
Practice Test 3

READING

Part 5: Incomplete Sentences

101. **B**	109. **A**	117. **D**	125. **C**
102. **A**	110. **D**	118. **A**	126. **C**
103. **B**	111. **C**	119. **C**	127. **B**
104. **A**	112. **A**	120. **B**	128. **C**
105. **C**	113. **B**	121. **D**	129. **B**
106. **D**	114. **A**	122. **C**	130. **D**
107. **B**	115. **D**	123. **A**	
108. **C**	116. **C**	124. **B**	

Part 6: Text Completion

131. **C**	135. **C**	139. **C**	143. **B**
132. **A**	136. **B**	140. **C**	144. **D**
133. **D**	137. **C**	141. **D**	145. **A**
134. **A**	138. **A**	142. **A**	146. **B**

Part 7: Reading Comprehension

147. **C**	161. **A**	175. **C**	189. **C**
148. **A**	162. **D**	176. **A**	190. **D**
149. **D**	163. **B**	177. **B**	191. **C**
150. **B**	164. **C**	178. **A**	192. **C**
151. **B**	165. **D**	179. **B**	193. **B**
152. **A**	166. **A**	180. **C**	194. **A**
153. **B**	167. **D**	181. **C**	195. **B**
154. **C**	168. **A**	182. **C**	196. **A**
155. **A**	169. **C**	183. **B**	197. **B**
156. **D**	170. **D**	184. **B**	198. **D**
157. **B**	171. **B**	185. **D**	199. **C**
158. **A**	172. **B**	186. **B**	200. **B**
159. **D**	173. **C**	187. **A**	
160. **C**	174. **D**	188. **C**	

TEST SCORE CONVERSION TABLE

Count your correct responses. Match the number of correct responses with the corresponding score from the Test Score Conversion Table (below). Add the two scores together. This is your Total Estimated Test Score. As you practice taking the TOEIC practice tests, your scores should improve. Keep track of your Total Estimated Test Scores.

# Correct	Listening Score	Reading Score	# Correct	Listening Score	Reading Score	# Correct	Listening Score	Reading Score	# Correct	Listening Score	Reading Score
0	5	5	26	110	65	51	255	220	76	410	370
1	5	5	27	115	70	52	260	225	77	420	380
2	5	5	28	120	80	53	270	230	78	425	385
3	5	5	29	125	85	54	275	235	79	430	390
4	5	5	30	130	90	55	280	240	80	440	395
5	5	5	31	135	95	56	290	250	81	445	400
6	5	5	32	140	100	57	295	255	82	450	405
7	10	5	33	145	110	58	300	260	83	460	410
8	15	5	34	150	115	59	310	265	84	465	415
9	20	5	35	160	120	60	315	270	85	470	420
10	25	5	36	165	125	61	320	280	86	475	425
11	30	5	37	170	130	62	325	285	87	480	430
12	35	5	38	175	140	63	330	290	88	485	435
13	40	5	39	180	145	64	340	300	89	490	445
14	45	5	40	185	150	65	345	305	90	495	450
15	50	5	41	190	160	66	350	310	91	495	455
16	55	10	42	195	165	67	360	320	92	495	465
17	60	15	43	200	170	68	365	325	93	495	470
18	65	20	44	210	175	69	370	330	94	495	480
19	70	25	45	215	180	70	380	335	95	495	485
20	75	30	46	220	190	71	385	340	96	495	490
21	80	35	47	230	195	72	390	350	97	495	495
22	85	40	48	240	200	73	395	355	98	495	495
23	90	45	49	245	210	74	400	360	99	495	495
24	95	50	50	250	215	75	405	365	100	495	495
25	100	60									

Number of Correct Listening Responses _____ = Listening Score _____

Number of Correct Reading Responses _____ = Reading Score _____

Total Estimated Test Score _____

ANSWER EXPLANATIONS

Listening Comprehension

PART 1: PHOTOGRAPHS

1. **(C)** This identifies the *customers* in the restaurant and their action: *enjoying their meal*. Choice (A) is incorrect because there is food on the plates. Choice (B) incorrectly identifies the waiter's action—he is serving food. Choice (D) associates *menu* with the restaurant scene, but there is no menu in the photo.

2. **(D)** The scientist is wearing gloves to protect his hands while he works. Choice (A) correctly identifies the test tube, but he is pouring something into it, not washing it. Choice (B) correctly identifies his coat, but he is not taking it off. Choice (C) correctly identifies his action, *pouring*, but he is pouring something into a test tube, not into a glass or cup for drinking.

3. **(A)** The photo shows heavy traffic on a highway. Choice (B) correctly identifies the cars, but not their location. Choice (C) associates *cars* with *parking lot*. Choice (D) correctly identifies the bridge, but it goes across a highway, not a river.

4. **(B)** Choice (B) identifies *the passengers* and the action *ready to board* a train. Choice (A) confuses similar-sounding words *rain* with *train*. Choice (C) confuses similar-sounding words *plane* and *train*. Choice (D) confuses similar-sounding words *grain* and *train*.

5. **(B)** Many trucks are pulled up to the loading docks of a large warehouse. Choice (A) confuses similar-sounding words *duck* and *truck*. Choice (C) uses the associated word *ship* for *shipping*, sending things by truck. Choice (D) uses the word *shoppers*, but there are no shoppers in the photo, nor is an *aisle* visible.

6. **(C)** There are two men at the front of the class by the blackboard. Choices (A), (B), and (D) all use words associated with a school, but the context is not correct: *students, classroom, professor*.

PART 2: QUESTION-RESPONSE

7. **(C)** Choice (C) is a logical response to a question about the *subject*. Choice (A) gives the location of the book, not *its subject*. Choice (B) gives the price.

8. **(A)** The suggestion to go on Monday is a logical response to the remark that City Hall is *closed over the weekend*. Choice (B) relates *countryside* with *city*. Choice (C) implies that the speaker's sister works at City Hall, but it is not a logical response to the remark.

9. **(C)** Choice (C) is a logical response to a question about *which train*. Choice (A) confuses similar-sounding words *train* and *rain*. Choice (B) answers the question, *Which class should I take*.

10. **(A)** Choice (A) answers the question *Why*. Choice (B) confuses the meaning of the word *permit*. Choice (C) confuses similar-sounding words *ready* and *already*.

11. **(C)** Choice (C) is a logical response to a question about *When*. Choice (A) tells *How long*, not *When*. Choice (B) confuses similar-sounding words *is he* and *she* and related words *too long* and *when*.

12. **(C)** Choice (C) is a logical response to a question about *How much*. Choice (A) answers the question *How you paid*. Choice (B) answers the question *How many* (stories the hotel had).

13. **(B)** Since the rent is going up, the second speaker suggests looking for a cheaper place to live. Choice (A) confuses *lent* with the similar-sounding word *rent*. Choice (C) repeats the phrase *going up*.

14. **(B)** The possessive word *Robert's* answers the possessive question *Whose*. Choice (A) relates *handwriting* with *cursive*. Choice (C) relates *handwriting* with *sign*.

15. **(C)** The second speaker will arrive at the meeting in a minute. Choice (A) associates *conference room* with *meeting*. Choice (B) uses the word *meeting* out of context.

16. **(C)** Choice (C) is a logical response to a question about *winning a tennis game*. Choice (A) has related the word *smoke* to another meaning of *match*. Choice (B) confuses *ten* with

tennis. Only Choice (C) concerns the game, *tennis.*

17. **(B)** Choice (B) is a logical response to a question about *purpose of a visit.* Choice (A) uses related words *visitors* and *visit.* Choice (C) confuses *proposal* with *purpose* and *list* with *visit.*

18. **(C)** Choice (C) is a logical response to a question about *seasonal preference.* Choice (A) confuses the related word *seasoning* with *season.* Choice (B) confuses similar-sounding words *refer* and *prefer.*

19. **(A)** The first speaker mentions seeing Jim at a party, so the second speaker asks how Jim is. Choice (B) associates *dancing* with *party.* Choice (C) confuses *part* with the similar-sounding word *party.*

20. **(A)** Choice (A) is a logical response to a question about *when the mail comes.* Choice (B) confuses similar-sounding words *milk* and *mail c(ome).* Choice (C) confuses similar-sounding words *come* and *welcome.*

21. **(A)** Choice (A) is a logical response to a question about *where the bank is.* Choice (B) confuses similar-sounding words *where* and *nowhere.* Choice (C) confuses the homonyms *where* and *wear.*

22. **(C)** Choice (C) is a logical response to a question about *the weather.* Choice (A) may seem close with its verb *is going* and the adverb *today.* Choice (B) confuses similar-sounding words *rain* and *complain.*

23. **(B)** Choice (B) is a logical response to a question about the *amount of a tip.* Choice (A) has related words *tip* (v) and *tip* (n). Choice (C) confuses the words *water* and *waded* with *waiter,* and has an answer to *How many,* not *How much.*

24. **(A)** Choice (A) is a logical response to a question about *who was the designer.* Choice (B) confuses the word *resign* with *design.* Choice (C) confuses the word *house* with *mouse.*

25. **(C)** This is a logical response to the tag question about whether or not Ken eats meat. Choice (A) relates *meat* and *steak.* Choice (B)

confuses similar-sounding words *meat* and *neat.*

26. **(B)** Choice (B) is a logical response to a question about *the fabric a shirt is made of.* Choice (A) changes the preposition from *made of* to *made in.* Choice (C) confuses similar-sounding words *this shirt* and *dessert.*

27. **(A)** This is a logical response to the negative question about the view. Choice (B) confuses similar-sounding words *view* and *too.* Choice (C) confuses similar-sounding words *view* and *knew.*

28. **(B)** Choice (B) is a logical response to a question about *where you study English.* Choice (A) confuses the related word *students* with *study* and *England* with *English.* Choice (C) answers *How long.*

29. **(C)** Choice (C) is a logical response to a question about *which sweater fits better.* Choice (A) confuses the word *sweater* with *sweat pants* and the concept of *fit* with something that is *too large.* Choice (B) confuses the word *sweater* with *weather.*

30. **(A)** Choice (A) is a logical response to a question about *the time.* Choice (B) answers another *do you have* question. Choice (C) answers *what time do you have to leave.*

31. **(A)** Choice (A) is a logical response to a request *to close the window.* Choice (B) confuses the word *close* with *clothes.* Choice (C) has the related word *open.*

PART 3: CONVERSATIONS

32. **(C)** The man says that he heard it on the radio. Choice (A) is not mentioned. Choice (B) sounds similar to *I bet.* Choice (D) sounds similar to *Fred,* the person that the man is going to help.

33. **(A)** The man promised to help Fred move to his new apartment. Choice (B) confuses similar-sounding words *chance* and *dance.* Choice (C) repeats the word *apartment.* Choice (D) is not mentioned.

34. **(B)** The woman says, *Let's go on Sunday.* Choice (A) is plausible, but it is contradicted by the correct answer. Choice (C) repeats

the phrase *next year*. Choice (D) confuses similar-sounding words *Fred* and *friend*.

35. **(D)** *Résumé* and *possible positions* suggest a job interview. Choices (A), (B), and (C) are all scheduled by appointment, but they would not involve a résumé.

36. **(A)** The woman suggests Tuesday at 8:30 A.M., and the man agrees. Choice (B) is incorrect because the woman says A.M., not P.M. Choice (C) confuses similar-sounding words *ten* and *then*. Choice (D) confuses similar-sounding words *noon* and *soon*.

37. **(D)** The man asks if he should bring anything and the woman says no. Choice (A) is related to the word *applicant*, mentioned by the woman. Choice (B) is incorrect because the man will take the test at the time of the interview. Choice (C) is incorrect because the woman says she has already read his résumé.

38. **(C)** The man answers the phone *front desk* and is providing help to a guest in *room 624*, so he is most likely working in a hotel. Choices (A) and (B) are related to the discussion about the problem with the TV. Choice (D) is incorrect because a home doesn't have a front desk or rooms with numbers.

39. **(C)** After the woman describes the problem with the TV, the man says, *I'll send someone up right away*. Choice (A) is incorrect because the woman says she has already tried doing this. Choice (B) is confused with the expression *right away*. Choice (D) is something the man might do if the conversation were in a department store.

40. **(A)** The woman says, *I'll be going out in about half an hour. Could you send someone then?* Choice (B) confuses similar-sounding words *ten* and *then*. Choice (C) is not mentioned. Choice (D) is confused with the woman's description of the problem with the TV, which doesn't have a *picture*.

41. **(B)** The woman says she is looking for Mr. Chung because *He's due to address the meeting this morning*. Choice (A) confuses the meaning of *address*. Choice (C) is not mentioned. Choice (D) is confused with the mention of Mr. Chung's calling from his car.

42. **(B)** Mr. Chung called to explain that he's stuck in traffic. Choice (A) uses the word *address* out of context. Choice (C) associates *car* with *traffic*. Choice (D) is the result of his lateness, not its cause.

43. **(B)** The speakers agree to show a film while waiting for Mr. Chung, and the man says, *I can have it ready to go in ten minutes*. Choice (A) is incorrect because the speakers know where Mr. Chung is. Choice (C) is incorrect because the speakers say they will wait for Mr. Chung, not replace him. Choice (D) is incorrect because the man has to prepare the film before starting the meeting.

44. **(C)** The first speaker says, *I like the way the lobby looks now*, and the second speaker mentions the fact that *they painted it white*. Choice (A) will be painted in the future. Choices (B) and (D) are other places mentioned but not as having been painted.

45. **(C)** The woman says about the elevator, *The color is really depressing*. Choice (A) is confused with the woman's mention of the mess to be caused when the cafeteria is painted. Choice (B) is plausible but not mentioned. Choice (D) is confused with the discussion of how dark the lobby used to look.

46. **(D)** After one of the men mentions that the cafeteria will be painted *next week*, the woman says, *I'll be out of town then*. Choice (A) is related to the discussion of paint colors in the lobby and elevator, but no mention is made of the woman choosing any. Choice (B) repeats the word *client*. Choice (C) repeats the word *cafeteria*.

47. **(D)** The woman says the man's job keeps him *well occupied* and that he probably doesn't have much free time. Choice (A) is related to how the man says he likes to play golf but there is no mention of how well he plays. Choice (B) is incorrect because the man says he likes to cook *when I have the time*, implying that he doesn't always have time. Choice (C) is not likely since the man is busy at work and also has at least two hobbies—golfing and cooking.

48. **(B)** The woman says, *I certainly love eating*. Choices (A) and (D) are not mentioned. Choice (C) is what the man likes to do.

49. **(A)** This is in reply to the man's invitation to cook for her tomorrow and is followed by the women's suggesting an alternative day, so it means that the plan does not fit her schedule. Choices (B), (C), and (D) don't fit the context.

50. **(C)** The man says, *. . . my gas tank is empty*. Choice (A) is not mentioned. Choice (B) repeats the word *change*—the woman offers to help change a flat tire. Choice (D) is what the woman thinks the problem is.

51. **(D)** The woman says that the service station is *just this side of the bridge*. Choice (A) repeats *side* and *road*. Choice (B) is incorrect because the woman says the service station is *about a mile or so from here*. Choice (C) is plausible but not mentioned.

52. **(D)** The woman says, *I'll drive you*. Choice (A) considers going before the woman offers to drive him. Choice (B) is not mentioned. Choice (C) is incorrect because the man's car is out of gas.

53. **(B)** The woman says, *I wish I had more time to exercise*. Choice (A) could be associated with getting more exercise, but it is not mentioned. Choice (C) is associated with the discussion of using the gym, but membership is not mentioned. Choice (D) is associated with the discussion of lunch.

54. **(A)** The man says, *. . . there usually are a lot of people using the gym at lunch time*. Choice (B) is incorrect because the use of the gym is free. Choices (C) and (D) are not mentioned.

55. **(B)** The man says, *I have a quick bite at my desk*. Choice (A) is not mentioned. Choice (C) is where he takes a walk. Choice (D) is where the woman eats lunch.

56. **(B)** The other woman says that Maria was fortunate to get such a nice office, and Maria agrees with her. Choices (A), (C), and (D) don't fit the context.

57. **(D)** The man says, *My office faces the parking lot*. Choices (A) and (B) describe Maria's office. Choice (C) repeats the word *lot*.

58. **(C)** One of the women says, *You've been at the company only a few months*, and the other adds, *. . . you'll probably get a better office after a while*. Both comments indicate that the man has not been at his job for long. Choices (A) and (B) are incorrect because the man says he likes his job. Choice (D) is not mentioned.

59. **(A)** The woman looks at a menu and asks the man to bring her some food, so she is ordering a meal in a restaurant. Choices (B), (C), and (D) are all related to the topic of a meal but are not the correct answer.

60. **(A)** The woman says, *it's still not noon yet*; that is, it is morning. Choices (B), (C), and (D) are times of day that don't fit this description.

61. **(C)** The man says, *Be right back with your beverage*, and the beverage the woman ordered was coffee. Choice (A) is confused with the cream the woman requests for her coffee. Choice (B) is incorrect because the woman has already seen the menu. Choice (D) repeats the word *jelly*, which the woman wants with her toast, but it is not what the man says he will bring right away.

62. **(A)** The man mentions *docking* and *go ashore*, so the speakers are on a ship. Choice (B) is confused with the bus tour of the city that will happen after the passengers go ashore. Choices (C) and (D) are also places where there would be passengers, but they don't fit the context of the conversation.

63. **(C)** The woman asks, *Can you tell me when we're due in Boston?* Choice (A) is associated with the context of travel but is not mentioned. Choice (B) associates *tickets* with ships and tour buses but is not mentioned. Choice (D) is confused with the woman's mention of the good weather.

64. **(B)** The man says, *I think it'd be more fun to just walk around*. Choices (A) and (D) are mentioned by the woman. Choice (C) repeats the word *city* but no one mentions leaving it.

65. **(D)** The man says, *the carpet still needs shampooing*. Choice (A) is not mentioned.

Choices (B) and (C) have already been cleaned.

66. **(B)** The man suggests scheduling the cleaning on the day of the staff meeting, which, according to the graphic, is on Tuesday. Choices (A), (C), and (D) are days when other events will be taking place in the conference room.

67. **(B)** The man says, *They never showed up on time.* Choice (A) is not likely since the woman says about the new cleaners, *It's worth the extra cost*, implying that the old cleaners cost less. Choices (C) and (D) use words from the conversation but are not mentioned.

68. **(C)** The woman is buying shirts, a type of clothing, and the discount on clothing is 20%. Choices (A), (B), and (D) are discounts on other types of items.

69. **(A)** The woman says, *Do you have them in green?* Choice (B) is incorrect because the woman is buying two shirts of the same size. Choice (C) refers to the fact that one of the shirts will be a gift, but the woman does not ask for it to be wrapped. Choice (D) is incorrect because the woman seems happy with the discount offered. In fact, she asks for a second shirt because of it.

70. **(A)** The man says, *These shirts are selling fast. Everyone seems to want one.* Choices (B) and (C) are plausible but not mentioned. Choice (D) is incorrect because it is the discount, not the shirt, that is available this week only.

PART 4: TALKS

71. **(C)** The speaker says, . . . *it's the inauguration of the new City Garden Park*, that is, a celebration of a park opening. Choice (A) repeats the word *garden*. Choice (B) repeats the words *high school*. Choice (D) repeats the words *inauguration* and *mayor*.

72. **(C)** The speaker says, *We'll be celebrating all next weekend* . . . Choice (A) is the last day to get a ticket. Choice (B) sounds similar to the correct answer. Choice (D) repeats the word

year, which refers to the time leading up to the event.

73. **(D)** The speaker says to phone City Hall for tickets. Choice (A) confuses similar-sounding words *fine* and *line* and repeats the word *park*. Choice (B) confuses similar-sounding words *free* and *three*, and it is incorrect because the tickets are free. Choice (C) confuses similar-sounding words *fine* and *online*.

74. **(A)** A *computer school* provides *computer training*. Choice (B) is incorrect; the school trains in *business software*, not *business management*. Choice (C) confuses the ideas of *job placement* and *personnel*. Choice (D) is incorrect; the school *teaches*, but it doesn't *train teachers*.

75. **(D)** The speaker says, *Are you bored with your current job?* and mentions the class schedule designed for *working people like you*. Choice (A) repeats the word *popular* used to describe software. Choices (B) and (C) are plausible but not mentioned.

76. **(A)** The speaker says, *Job placement assistance is available.* Choices (B), (C), and (D) are plausible but not mentioned.

77. **(B)** The speaker says, *I've arranged your travel to Boston for this weekend's workshop.* Choice (A) confuses the meaning of the word *station*—it refers to a *train station*, not a *radio station*. Choices (C) and (D) are reasons people travel but are not mentioned.

78. **(A)** The speaker says, . . . *take Train 3425* . . . . Choice (B) is how the traveler will travel after arriving in Boston. Choice (C) sounds similar to the correct answer. Choice (D) is related to the word *drive* and is how the traveler will get to the train station on the day he returns home.

79. **(B)** The speaker says, *Please check your e-mail for your complete itinerary.* Choice (A) is related to the topic of the message, but no ticket is mentioned. Choice (C) repeats the word *hotel*. Choice (D) repeats the word *question*.

80. **(B)** The speaker, calling from Whitman's Downtown, has sold a rug, a desk, and some chairs to the listener, so the business is most

likely a furniture store. Choice (A) is confused with the mention that the *rug* was delivered last night. Choice (C) associates new furniture with interior decorating. Choice (D) repeats the word *rug*, but it is clear that the rug is being sold, not cleaned.

81. **(C)** The speaker says, *no payment is due on the rug as that was taken care of when you placed the order*; that is, the customer has already paid for the rug. Choice (A) repeats *order* and *placed*. Choice (B) associates *invoice* with *payment*. Choice (D) is plausible but not mentioned.

82. **(C)** The speaker says the customer can come by and pick up the rug, and then says, *Someone will be here all day until five thirty*, implying that the business will close at that time, so the customer should pick up the rug before then. Choice (A) repeats the word *call*. Choice (B) repeats the word *delivery*. Choice (D) repeats the word *records*.

83. **(B)** The speaker says, *You must be over 18 and willing to work weekends*. Choices (A), (C), and (D) are common job requirements but are not mentioned.

84. **(A)** The speaker says that they offer *opportunity for advancement*. Choices (B), (C), and (D) are common job benefits but are not mentioned.

85. **(B)** *Apply in person* means *go to the hotel*. Choice (A) is not required. Choices (C) and (D) are unnecessary if you apply in person.

86. **(B)** The speaker mentions the *City Bus Service*, and later on mentions a *driver*. Choices (A), (C), and (D) are all things for which one might buy tickets, but they are not the correct answer.

87. **(C)** The speaker says, *To begin, enter the date and time of your travel*, that is, the travel schedule. Choices (A), (B), and (D) are later steps in the process.

88. **(B)** The speaker says, *Please approach the ticket office if you wish to pay cash*. Choice (A) is confused with the mention of a credit *card*. Choice (C) is not correct because the speaker says *the machine does not accept cash*. Choice

(D) is not correct because the speaker says *drivers cannot issue tickets*.

89. **(D)** The talk explains the importance of taking regular breaks and gives advice on how to do this. Choices (A), (B), and (C) are not the purpose of the talk.

90. **(B)** The speaker recommends *closing your door*. Choice (A) is related to the topic, but it is not mentioned. Choice (C) is confused with *take a break*, but it is a one-hour break that is recommended, not a vacation. Choice (D) is plausible but not mentioned.

91. **(B)** This phrase refers to the suggestion to take naps, and means that this activity is actually a good way to use time. Choices (A), (C), and (D) don't fit the context or the meaning of the phrase.

92. **(C)** The speaker says, *honoring teenage musicians* and *honor our fine young musicians*. Choices (A), (B), and (D) are other types of people involved in music careers but are not the correct answer.

93. **(A)** The speaker says, *The money we award today* and *Each honoree will receive five thousand dollars*. Choices (B), (C), and (D) are other types of awards but are not mentioned.

94. **(B)** Listeners are asked to make donations so that awards can continue to be given in the future. Choices (A), (C), and (D) are confused with the various things winners might do with their money.

95. **(A)** The speaker says that the building *was first constructed as a residence for the Highbury family*. Choices (B), (C), and (D) are mentioned as later uses of the building.

96. **(D)** The speaker says, *the Green Room is closed today*, and the graphic shows that the exhibit in this room is *history displays*. Choices (A), (B), and (C) are exhibits in the other rooms, which the speaker says are all open today.

97. **(B)** The speaker says, *After the tour, you may want to look at the gardens on your own*. Choice (A) is confused with the mention of the concert scheduled for today. Choice (C) repeats the word *year*. Choice (D) is confused

with *lunchtime*, the time the concert will be held.

98. **(A)** The speaker says, *you are invited to a special staff luncheon next week.* Choices (B), (C), and (D) repeat words from the talk but are not the correct answer.

99. **(D)** The speaker explains that the luncheon will take place in the conference room the day after it is painted. The conference room will be painted on Wednesday, so the luncheon will take place on Thursday. Choices (A), (B), and (C) don't fit this explanation.

100. **(C)** The speaker asks listeners to *put your coffee cups back on the snack table before you leave.* Choices (A), (B), and (D) repeat words from the talk but are not the correct answer.

Reading

PART 5: INCOMPLETE SENTENCES

101. **(B)** *Paint* and *pictures* are equal items joined with *and.* Choices (A), (C), and (D) join clauses, not nouns.

102. **(A)** *Aware* is the only adjective among the options. Choices (B), (C), and (D) do not fit the context of the sentence.

103. **(B)** The verb agrees with the singular third person subject *itinerary.* Choices (A) and (D) are not singular forms. Choice (C) is a gerund, so it cannot be used as a main verb.

104. **(A)** *Between* expresses beginning and ending points. Choice (B) indicates *in the company of or by means of.* Choice (C) indicates movement across something. Choice (D) indicates source.

105. **(C)** *Recommendations* is a noun, and in this sentence it acts as the object of the verb *made.* Choices (A) and (B) are verbs. Choice (D) is an adjective.

106. **(D)** The comparative form is *faster.* Choice (A) is an adjective. Choice (B) is the superlative. Choice (C) has an unnecessary article, *the.*

107. **(B)** *Or* refers to a choice between two things, in this case, two ways of paying a bill. Choice (A) introduces a result. Choice (C) introduces

a contradiction. Choice (D) can introduce either a reason or a time expression.

108. **(C)** The time for the speakers has been *made shorter,* or *shortened.* Choice (A) means *make higher.* Choice (B) means *make longer.* Choice (D) means *make wider.*

109. **(A)** The causative *ask* requires a following infinitive. Choice (B) is the gerund. Choice (C) is future tense. Choice (D) is present tense.

110. **(D)** The third person singular feminine possessive adjective *her* agrees with the antecedent *Ms. Chang,* and modifies the noun *business suits.* Choices (A) and (B) are not possessive adjectives. Choice (C) doesn't agree with the antecedent.

111. **(C)** The adjective *difficult* is followed by an infinitive verb. Choices (A) and (B) are present tense verbs. Choice (D) is a gerund.

112. **(A)** This is a passive causative construction. Choices (B), (C), and (D) cannot be used as causative verbs.

113. **(B)** The subject *variety* requires a singular verb. Choice (A) is plural. Choice (C) is a gerund. Choice (D) is the simple form.

114. **(A)** *Acknowledge* means *recognize.* Choices (B), (C), and (D) have meanings that don't fit the context.

115. **(D)** *Beside* means *next to.* Choices (A) and (B) need more than one bus as a reference point. Choice (C) means *direction away;* it is not logical.

116. **(C)** *A minimum of* means *at least.* Choices (A), (B), and (D) have meanings that don't fit the context.

117. **(D)** An unreal condition requires *would* in the clause without *if.* Choice (A) is the wrong tense. Choices (B) and (C) do not use *would.*

118. **(A)** Habitual action uses present tense; *handbook* requires third person singular forms. Choice (B) is the present progressive tense. Choice (C) is the simple form. Choice (D) is a gerund.

119. **(C)** The sentence means that the manufacturer, or maker, of the product (model 34) will fulfill the order in the spring. Choices (A), (B),

and (D) are not entities from which you could order a product.

120. **(B)** *Only* is an adverb modifying the verb *consider*—Mr. Larsen will consider veterans and nobody else. Choices (A), (C), and (D) cannot be used in this position in a sentence.

121. **(D)** *Even though* establishes a logical link between clauses. Choices (A), (B), and (C) are not logical.

122. **(C)** *By himself* means *alone* or *without help*. Choices (A), (B), and (D) cannot be used following *by*.

123. **(A)** The subject of the sentence, *predictions*, does not perform the action, so a passive verb is needed. Choices (B), (C), and (D) are all active verbs.

124. **(B)** In this sentence, *who* is a subject relative pronoun with *doctors* as the antecedent. Choice (A) cannot be used as a relative pronoun. Choice (C) is possessive. Choice (D) is used as a pronoun for things, not people.

125. **(C)** Use *between* with two items. Choice (A) means *together*. Choice (B) indicates time. Choice (D) is used with three or more items.

126. **(C)** *In spite of* means *despite*. It is a prepositional phrase, so it must be followed by a noun or a gerund. Choice (A) doesn't make sense in this context. Choices (B) and (D) must introduce a clause.

127. **(B)** *Organizing* is a gerund, the object of the preposition *for*. Choice (A) is a noun. Choices (C) and (D) are verbs.

128. **(C)** This third person singular verb agrees with the subject *head of accounts*. Choice (A) is a noun, not a verb. Choices (B) and (D) are plural verbs, so they don't agree with the subject.

129. **(B)** *Than* completes the comparative adjective *better*. Choice (A) could precede the adjective, but it cannot follow it. Choices (C) and (D) are not used to form comparisons.

130. **(D)** *Prepare* as a main verb is followed by an infinitive. Choice (A) is base form or present tense. Choice (B) is past tense. Choice (C) is a gerund.

PART 6: TEXT COMPLETION

131. **(C)** The pronoun *it* agrees with the verb *outlines* and has the antecedent *brochure*. Choices (A) and (D) don't agree with the verb. Choice (B) refers to a person.

132. **(A)** The verb *requires* agrees with the singular subject, *Green Office Renovators*, the name of a single company. Choices (B), (C), and (D) don't agree with the subject.

133. **(D)** The previous sentence mentions high costs, and this sentence explains why the costs are not as high as they may seem. Choices (A), (B), and (C) don't fit the context.

134. **(A)** To *demonstrate concern* for something means to *care* about it. Choices (B), (C), and (D) have meanings that do not fit the context.

135. **(C)** This is the correct superlative form for a one-syllable adjective. Choice (A) is not a superlative adjective. Choice (B) is the comparative form. Choice (D) is an incorrect form for a one-syllable adjective.

136. **(B)** This sentence sums up the main point of the paragraph—that the customer's bills are much larger during one particular part of the year. Choices (A), (C), and (D) don't fit the context.

137. **(C)** *Spread out* can mean divided up; the customer will not pay the highest bills at one time of the year, but instead divide the bills into smaller pieces and pay them throughout the year. Choice (A) means *reduced in price*. Choice (B) means *increased*. Choice (D) means *added to*.

138. **(A)** The company *estimates*, or *guesses*, how much gas the customer will use in a year based on use in past years. Choice (B) means *allowed*. Choice (C) means *asked about*. Choice (D) means *asked for*.

139. **(C)** A passive voice form is needed because the subject, *passengers*, is not active. It is the airport that offers the Internet service. Choices (A), (B), and (D) are all active voice forms.

140. **(C)** VIP card holders receive *benefits*, that is, special *advantages* or *favors* because they have purchased the card. Choices (A), (B), and (D) don't fit the context.

141. **(D)** The previous sentence lists some of the benefits of using the lounge, and this sentence describes an additional one. Choices (A), (B), and (C) don't fit the context.

142. **(A)** A noun is needed here. Choice (B) is an adjective. Choice (C) is a verb. Choice (D) is an adverb.

143. **(B)** *Everyone* takes the singular verb, *says*. Choices (A), (C), and (D) are plural verbs.

144. **(D)** *Couldn't* in this sentence means *wasn't able to*. Choices (A), (B), and (C) do not have meanings that fit the context.

145. **(A)** This follows the previous sentence, explaining why the writer thinks his friend should go to the conference. Choices (B), (C), and (D) don't fit the context.

146. **(B)** Supervisors are people who can give permission to go to a conference. Choices (A), (C), and (D) don't fit the context.

PART 7: READING COMPREHENSION

147. **(C)** The ad says, *get a great job now*, mentions that the company *is hiring*, and says, *bring your résumé*. Choice (A) is related to the topic but is not the correct answer. Choice (B) is related to the location of the company headquarters (the airport). Choice (D) repeats the word *headquarters*.

148. **(A)** National Headquarters is mentioned with the *time* and *date*, so it must be the place. Choice (B) is not mentioned. Choice (C) is not a logical location for an open house. Choice (D) is incorrect; the airport is regional, not the office.

149. **(D)** You would see this notice in a place where passengers can stand and where there is a driver; bus is the only choice that fits these criteria. Choices (A), (B), and (C) are all places where you might see passengers but do not match the criteria.

150. **(B)** Music is permitted with earphones. Choice (A) is incorrect because the notice says, *No smoking*. Choices (C) and (D) are incorrect because the notice says, *No food or open beverages*.

151. **(B)** Mr. Chen has the option of ordering envelopes and will use a credit card, so he is at a store. Choices (A), (C), and (D) are all places where one might look for paper and envelopes, but they don't fit this description.

152. **(A)** This means that Ms. Giametti will use the ivory envelopes because her preferred color is not available. Choices (B), (C), and (D) don't fit the meaning of the expression or the context.

153. **(B)** *Reviewing sales data* takes up 28% of time, the most of any task listed. Choices (A), (C), and (D) all take up less time.

154. **(C)** *Resolving customer problems* takes up very little time—just 5%. Choice (A) only takes up 7% of time, so it is not a likely conclusion that too much time is spent on this. Choice (B) takes up 20% of time, not a low number compared with the time spent on other tasks, so it does not seem to be a low priority. Choice (D) is incorrect because the table has no information on sales at all.

155. **(A)** The ad states, *You will study with your peers*. *Peers* are defined here as *other experienced managers*. Choices (B), (C), and (D) are not mentioned.

156. **(D)** The ad states, *All applications require a letter of recommendation from your current supervisor*. Choices (A), (B), and (C) are not mentioned.

157. **(B)** The course is a *week-long* intensive one. The other periods of time are not mentioned.

158. **(A)** Ginger's sells bouquets, baskets, wreathes, and garlands, which are different types of flower arrangements. Choice (B) is associated with flowers, but it is a service and does not focus on selling individual items. Choice (C) is associated with the mention of celebrating special occasions. Choice (D) is confused with the mention of designs, but it is floral designs that is referred to.

159. **(D)** The information states, *There is no fee for deliveries in the local area*. Choice (A) is incorrect because orders placed in the morning are delivered the same day. Choice (B) is incorrect because other areas are mentioned.

Choice (C) is confused with the deadline for same-day deliveries.

160. **(C)** This follows the information in the two previous sentences, which describe the two locations of the business. Choices (A), (B), and (D) do not provide the proper context for this detail.

161. **(A)** Mr. Niazi writes, *I am attaching a table that shows the current prices* . . . . Choices (B) and (C) are related to other things mentioned in the e-mail. Choice (D) is not mentioned.

162. **(D)** Mr. Niazi writes, *Shipping times and costs depend on your location as well as on the size of your order.* Choices (A), (B), and (C) are plausible but not mentioned.

163. **(B)** The company he has written to sells products to retailers. Choices (A) and (D) are related to other topics mentioned in the e-mail. Choice (C) is not mentioned.

164. **(C)** It *allows employees to take paid time off for volunteer activities.* Choices (A), (B), and (D) concern other types of *time off.*

165. **(D)** They may take *up to eight hours of paid leave per month.* Choices (A) and (C) are all less than the allowed time. Choice (B) is more than the allowed time.

166. **(A)** The memo says that to be eligible, employees must be full time and employed at the company for at least one year. Choices (B), (C), and (D) are contradicted by the correct answer.

167. **(D)** Volunteer leave must be *requested in advance* and *approved by the supervisor.* Choices (A), (B), and (C) are not mentioned as requirements.

168. **(A)** The carpet has bumps and a gap, and Ms. Stone writes, *We paid a lot to get this new carpet installed*, and then writes that the company should come back and redo the job. Choices (B), (C) and (D) are all problems a carpet might have but are not mentioned.

169. **(C)** Ms. O'Hara mentions visitors on Monday morning, and Ms. Stone refers to them as *the new clients.* Choices (A), (B) and (D) use words from the passage but are not the correct answer.

170. **(D)** Mr. Blake refers to the business as *just starting out*, that is, that it is new, and Ms. O'Hara implies that it does not have experience. Choices (A), (B), and (C) are plausible but not mentioned.

171. **(B)** Ms. Stone writes that someone will have to contact the carpet company, and Mr. Blake replies, *Leave that to me*, meaning that he will take responsibility for that task. Choices (A), (C) and (D) don't fit the context.

172. **(B)** The article discusses how hackers used to target large companies but have now turned their attention to smaller companies. Choices (A), (C), and (D) are plausible but not the correct answer.

173. **(C)** *Notoriety* means *fame.* Choices (A), (B), and (D) are likely reasons for a hacker to do his work, but none is mentioned in the article.

174. **(D)** Sitting behind bars means in prison. Choice (A) is associated with the topic of *security systems.* Choice (B) is associated with the mention of *criminal charges.* Choice (C) repeats the word *investigators.*

175. **(C)** This is a detail adding information to the previous statement that smaller companies have less sophisticated security systems. Choices (A), (B), and (D) do not provide a proper context for this sentence.

176. **(A)** This is confused with Camilla Crowe's title of *Recruiting Coordinator*, but is not mentioned as part of the advertised job. Choices (B), (C), and (D) are all mentioned in the ad as duties of the job.

177. **(B)** Camilla Crow says that Akiko has the degree they are looking for, which, according to the ad, is a degree in marketing. Choice (A) is confused with the store where Akiko worked. Choice (C) is confused with the communications skills asked for in the ad. Choice (D) is confused with the conferences mentioned in the ad as a job duty.

178. **(A)** Camilla Crowe mentions that Akiko graduated last month; since the letter has a March date, last month was February. Choice (B) is the month the letter was written. Choice (C) is confused with the date by which Akiko

must contact Camilla about the internship. Choice (D) is not mentioned.

179. **(B)** The letter mentions Akiko's *sales experience in an electronics store*. Choice (A) is the type of experience the company is looking for. Choice (C) is not mentioned. Choice (D) is the job Akiko applied for.

180. **(C)** Camilla offered Akiko a three-month unpaid internship. Choice (A) is what Akiko applied for, but Camilla says she is not experienced enough. Choice (B) is associated with a job application, but it is not mentioned. Choice (D) is confused with the Marketing Club.

181. **(C)** The ad says that a tour of the theater is included. Choice (A) is confused with the mention of the French chef. Choice (B) is confused with the mention of the region's finest actors. Choice (D) is done by the theater, not the guests.

182. **(C)** Sundays are for large groups only, so it follows that all the other days are for individuals and small groups. Choice (A) are the days when only evening shows are available. Choice (B) are the days that both afternoon and evening shows are available. Choice (D) is the day reserved for large groups.

183. **(B)** In her e-mail, Ms. Hekler says she prefers the lunch and afternoon show, which runs from 12–4 P.M. Choice (A) is not mentioned. Choice (C) is the time the event will end. Choice (D) is the time the evening events begin.

184. **(B)** The group from the Federal Bank is 325 people, so they will get the 10% discount. Choice (A) applies to groups smaller than 300. Choice (C) applies to groups larger than 350. Choice (D) is confused with the date of the party.

185. **(D)** The Federal Bank party is in December, so they will see a comedy. Choice (A) is the type of show available January–April. Choice (B) is the type of show available May–July. Choice (C) is the type of show available August–October.

186. **(B)** The workshops are scheduled from 8:30 to 10:30. Choices (A), (C) and (D) are not mentioned.

187. **(A)** The notice says, *Choose the date that is most convenient for you*, which implies that it is the same workshop repeated each time. Choices (B) and (C) are not mentioned. Choice (D) is confused with the number of times the workshop is given.

188. **(C)** In his e-mail, Mr. Mains says he tried to attend a workshop *this morning*, which would be July 20, the date of his e-mail. The first workshop is given on August 1. Choices (A) and (B) are incorrect because the time and place he mentions match the information on the notice. Choice (D) is incorrect because the notice states that registration is not required.

189. **(C)** Mr. Mains states that he is 63, and Mr. Oh writes, *if you are 63, it* (meaning the retirement fund) *will be reduced by 4%*. Choice (B) is the amount it is reduced for each year of age under 65. Choices (A) and (D) are not mentioned.

190. **(D)** Mr. Oh writes, *As far as tax issues go, I suggest you contact Fred Lee in Accounting*. Choice (A) repeats the words *tax specialist*, which describes Fred Lee. Choice (B) is suggested but not for answering tax questions. Choice (C) is not mentioned.

191. **(C)** The notice states, *Each course is worth 15 hours of credit*. Choices (A) and (B) are incorrect because there is no limit put on the number of credits earned. Choice (D) is confused with the required number of credits per year.

192. **(C)** The course information states that all classes take place from 6:00–8:00 in the evening. Choices (A) and (B) are incorrect because the classes are in the evening not the morning. Choice (D) is the time the classes end.

193. **(B)** The course information says that the fee is $300 per course. Choices (A) and (D) are not mentioned. Choice (D) is what Roberto will pay for his two courses together.

194. **(A)** The notice states, *You must receive a passing grade to get credit,* and in the e-mail, Ms. Minh writes, *we cannot count this course toward your professional development credits as your grade was too low.* Choices (B), (C), and (D) all state incorrect information.

195. **(B)** According to the e-mail, Roberto will take a 100 level and a 200 level course, and according to the course information, these courses are given on Monday and Tuesday. Choices (A), (C), and (D) don't match this description.

196. **(A)** The ad mentions *residential* (private home) and *business* (commercial) property. Choice (B) is incorrect because Mr. Holmes' question in his e-mail, *Do you know anything about Mitchell Landscapers?,* implies that he is not familiar with the business. Choices (C) and (D) are not mentioned.

197. **(B)** The ad explains that the business will help customers choose appropriate plants.

Choices (A), (C), and (D) are other meanings for *pick* but don't fit the context.

198. **(D)** Mr. Holmes owns property on Broad Street and is planning an open house for prospective tenants, so he is a landlord. Choice (A) is associated with the mention of *design*. Choice (B) is associated with the mention of *property*. Choice (C) is not mentioned.

199. **(C)** In his e-mail, Mr. Holmes says he wants the job done by June 1, and the project estimate shows the dates of the job to be June 2–4. Choice (A) is incorrect because Mr. Holmes is willing to spend $3,000, and the job will cost less than that. Choice (B) is incorrect because the estimate mentions a new tree. Choice (D) is incorrect because Mr. Holmes writes that he wants the shrubbery replaced.

200. **(B)** This is the cost for labor listed on the project estimate. Choice (A) is the cost of the design work. Choice (C) is the cost of materials. Choice (D) is the total cost of the project.

ANSWER SHEET
Practice Test 4

LISTENING COMPREHENSION

Part 1: Photographs

1. Ⓐ Ⓑ Ⓒ Ⓓ
2. Ⓐ Ⓑ Ⓒ Ⓓ
3. Ⓐ Ⓑ Ⓒ Ⓓ
4. Ⓐ Ⓑ Ⓒ Ⓓ
5. Ⓐ Ⓑ Ⓒ Ⓓ
6. Ⓐ Ⓑ Ⓒ Ⓓ

Part 2: Question-Response

7. Ⓐ Ⓑ Ⓒ
8. Ⓐ Ⓑ Ⓒ
9. Ⓐ Ⓑ Ⓒ
10. Ⓐ Ⓑ Ⓒ
11. Ⓐ Ⓑ Ⓒ
12. Ⓐ Ⓑ Ⓒ
13. Ⓐ Ⓑ Ⓒ
14. Ⓐ Ⓑ Ⓒ
15. Ⓐ Ⓑ Ⓒ
16. Ⓐ Ⓑ Ⓒ
17. Ⓐ Ⓑ Ⓒ
18. Ⓐ Ⓑ Ⓒ
19. Ⓐ Ⓑ Ⓒ
20. Ⓐ Ⓑ Ⓒ
21. Ⓐ Ⓑ Ⓒ
22. Ⓐ Ⓑ Ⓒ
23. Ⓐ Ⓑ Ⓒ
24. Ⓐ Ⓑ Ⓒ
25. Ⓐ Ⓑ Ⓒ
26. Ⓐ Ⓑ Ⓒ
27. Ⓐ Ⓑ Ⓒ
28. Ⓐ Ⓑ Ⓒ
29. Ⓐ Ⓑ Ⓒ
30. Ⓐ Ⓑ Ⓒ
31. Ⓐ Ⓑ Ⓒ

Part 3: Conversations

32. Ⓐ Ⓑ Ⓒ Ⓓ
33. Ⓐ Ⓑ Ⓒ Ⓓ
34. Ⓐ Ⓑ Ⓒ Ⓓ
35. Ⓐ Ⓑ Ⓒ Ⓓ
36. Ⓐ Ⓑ Ⓒ Ⓓ
37. Ⓐ Ⓑ Ⓒ Ⓓ
38. Ⓐ Ⓑ Ⓒ Ⓓ
39. Ⓐ Ⓑ Ⓒ Ⓓ
40. Ⓐ Ⓑ Ⓒ Ⓓ
41. Ⓐ Ⓑ Ⓒ Ⓓ
42. Ⓐ Ⓑ Ⓒ Ⓓ
43. Ⓐ Ⓑ Ⓒ Ⓓ
44. Ⓐ Ⓑ Ⓒ Ⓓ
45. Ⓐ Ⓑ Ⓒ Ⓓ
46. Ⓐ Ⓑ Ⓒ Ⓓ
47. Ⓐ Ⓑ Ⓒ Ⓓ
48. Ⓐ Ⓑ Ⓒ Ⓓ
49. Ⓐ Ⓑ Ⓒ Ⓓ
50. Ⓐ Ⓑ Ⓒ Ⓓ
51. Ⓐ Ⓑ Ⓒ Ⓓ
52. Ⓐ Ⓑ Ⓒ Ⓓ
53. Ⓐ Ⓑ Ⓒ Ⓓ
54. Ⓐ Ⓑ Ⓒ Ⓓ
55. Ⓐ Ⓑ Ⓒ Ⓓ
56. Ⓐ Ⓑ Ⓒ Ⓓ
57. Ⓐ Ⓑ Ⓒ Ⓓ
58. Ⓐ Ⓑ Ⓒ Ⓓ
59. Ⓐ Ⓑ Ⓒ Ⓓ
60. Ⓐ Ⓑ Ⓒ Ⓓ
61. Ⓐ Ⓑ Ⓒ Ⓓ
62. Ⓐ Ⓑ Ⓒ Ⓓ
63. Ⓐ Ⓑ Ⓒ Ⓓ
64. Ⓐ Ⓑ Ⓒ Ⓓ
65. Ⓐ Ⓑ Ⓒ Ⓓ
66. Ⓐ Ⓑ Ⓒ Ⓓ
67. Ⓐ Ⓑ Ⓒ Ⓓ
68. Ⓐ Ⓑ Ⓒ Ⓓ
69. Ⓐ Ⓑ Ⓒ Ⓓ
70. Ⓐ Ⓑ Ⓒ Ⓓ

Part 4: Talks

71. Ⓐ Ⓑ Ⓒ Ⓓ
72. Ⓐ Ⓑ Ⓒ Ⓓ
73. Ⓐ Ⓑ Ⓒ Ⓓ
74. Ⓐ Ⓑ Ⓒ Ⓓ
75. Ⓐ Ⓑ Ⓒ Ⓓ
76. Ⓐ Ⓑ Ⓒ Ⓓ
77. Ⓐ Ⓑ Ⓒ Ⓓ
78. Ⓐ Ⓑ Ⓒ Ⓓ
79. Ⓐ Ⓑ Ⓒ Ⓓ
80. Ⓐ Ⓑ Ⓒ Ⓓ
81. Ⓐ Ⓑ Ⓒ Ⓓ
82. Ⓐ Ⓑ Ⓒ Ⓓ
83. Ⓐ Ⓑ Ⓒ Ⓓ
84. Ⓐ Ⓑ Ⓒ Ⓓ
85. Ⓐ Ⓑ Ⓒ Ⓓ
86. Ⓐ Ⓑ Ⓒ Ⓓ
87. Ⓐ Ⓑ Ⓒ Ⓓ
88. Ⓐ Ⓑ Ⓒ Ⓓ
89. Ⓐ Ⓑ Ⓒ Ⓓ
90. Ⓐ Ⓑ Ⓒ Ⓓ
91. Ⓐ Ⓑ Ⓒ Ⓓ
92. Ⓐ Ⓑ Ⓒ Ⓓ
93. Ⓐ Ⓑ Ⓒ Ⓓ
94. Ⓐ Ⓑ Ⓒ Ⓓ
95. Ⓐ Ⓑ Ⓒ Ⓓ
96. Ⓐ Ⓑ Ⓒ Ⓓ
97. Ⓐ Ⓑ Ⓒ Ⓓ
98. Ⓐ Ⓑ Ⓒ Ⓓ
99. Ⓐ Ⓑ Ⓒ Ⓓ
100. Ⓐ Ⓑ Ⓒ Ⓓ

READING

Part 5: Incomplete Sentences

101. Ⓐ Ⓑ Ⓒ Ⓓ
102. Ⓐ Ⓑ Ⓒ Ⓓ
103. Ⓐ Ⓑ Ⓒ Ⓓ
104. Ⓐ Ⓑ Ⓒ Ⓓ
105. Ⓐ Ⓑ Ⓒ Ⓓ
106. Ⓐ Ⓑ Ⓒ Ⓓ
107. Ⓐ Ⓑ Ⓒ Ⓓ
108. Ⓐ Ⓑ Ⓒ Ⓓ

109. Ⓐ Ⓑ Ⓒ Ⓓ
110. Ⓐ Ⓑ Ⓒ Ⓓ
111. Ⓐ Ⓑ Ⓒ Ⓓ
112. Ⓐ Ⓑ Ⓒ Ⓓ
113. Ⓐ Ⓑ Ⓒ Ⓓ
114. Ⓐ Ⓑ Ⓒ Ⓓ
115. Ⓐ Ⓑ Ⓒ Ⓓ
116. Ⓐ Ⓑ Ⓒ Ⓓ

117. Ⓐ Ⓑ Ⓒ Ⓓ
118. Ⓐ Ⓑ Ⓒ Ⓓ
119. Ⓐ Ⓑ Ⓒ Ⓓ
120. Ⓐ Ⓑ Ⓒ Ⓓ
121. Ⓐ Ⓑ Ⓒ Ⓓ
122. Ⓐ Ⓑ Ⓒ Ⓓ
123. Ⓐ Ⓑ Ⓒ Ⓓ
124. Ⓐ Ⓑ Ⓒ Ⓓ

125. Ⓐ Ⓑ Ⓒ Ⓓ
126. Ⓐ Ⓑ Ⓒ Ⓓ
127. Ⓐ Ⓑ Ⓒ Ⓓ
128. Ⓐ Ⓑ Ⓒ Ⓓ
129. Ⓐ Ⓑ Ⓒ Ⓓ
130. Ⓐ Ⓑ Ⓒ Ⓓ

Part 6: Text Completion

131. Ⓐ Ⓑ Ⓒ Ⓓ
132. Ⓐ Ⓑ Ⓒ Ⓓ
133. Ⓐ Ⓑ Ⓒ Ⓓ
134. Ⓐ Ⓑ Ⓒ Ⓓ

135. Ⓐ Ⓑ Ⓒ Ⓓ
136. Ⓐ Ⓑ Ⓒ Ⓓ
137. Ⓐ Ⓑ Ⓒ Ⓓ
138. Ⓐ Ⓑ Ⓒ Ⓓ

139. Ⓐ Ⓑ Ⓒ Ⓓ
140. Ⓐ Ⓑ Ⓒ Ⓓ
141. Ⓐ Ⓑ Ⓒ Ⓓ
142. Ⓐ Ⓑ Ⓒ Ⓓ

143. Ⓐ Ⓑ Ⓒ Ⓓ
144. Ⓐ Ⓑ Ⓒ Ⓓ
145. Ⓐ Ⓑ Ⓒ Ⓓ
146. Ⓐ Ⓑ Ⓒ Ⓓ

Part 7: Reading Comprehension

147. Ⓐ Ⓑ Ⓒ Ⓓ
148. Ⓐ Ⓑ Ⓒ Ⓓ
149. Ⓐ Ⓑ Ⓒ Ⓓ
150. Ⓐ Ⓑ Ⓒ Ⓓ
151. Ⓐ Ⓑ Ⓒ Ⓓ
152. Ⓐ Ⓑ Ⓒ Ⓓ
153. Ⓐ Ⓑ Ⓒ Ⓓ
154. Ⓐ Ⓑ Ⓒ Ⓓ
155. Ⓐ Ⓑ Ⓒ Ⓓ
156. Ⓐ Ⓑ Ⓒ Ⓓ
157. Ⓐ Ⓑ Ⓒ Ⓓ
158. Ⓐ Ⓑ Ⓒ Ⓓ
159. Ⓐ Ⓑ Ⓒ Ⓓ
160. Ⓐ Ⓑ Ⓒ Ⓓ

161. Ⓐ Ⓑ Ⓒ Ⓓ
162. Ⓐ Ⓑ Ⓒ Ⓓ
163. Ⓐ Ⓑ Ⓒ Ⓓ
164. Ⓐ Ⓑ Ⓒ Ⓓ
165. Ⓐ Ⓑ Ⓒ Ⓓ
166. Ⓐ Ⓑ Ⓒ Ⓓ
167. Ⓐ Ⓑ Ⓒ Ⓓ
168. Ⓐ Ⓑ Ⓒ Ⓓ
169. Ⓐ Ⓑ Ⓒ Ⓓ
170. Ⓐ Ⓑ Ⓒ Ⓓ
171. Ⓐ Ⓑ Ⓒ Ⓓ
172. Ⓐ Ⓑ Ⓒ Ⓓ
173. Ⓐ Ⓑ Ⓒ Ⓓ
174. Ⓐ Ⓑ Ⓒ Ⓓ

175. Ⓐ Ⓑ Ⓒ Ⓓ
176. Ⓐ Ⓑ Ⓒ Ⓓ
177. Ⓐ Ⓑ Ⓒ Ⓓ
178. Ⓐ Ⓑ Ⓒ Ⓓ
179. Ⓐ Ⓑ Ⓒ Ⓓ
180. Ⓐ Ⓑ Ⓒ Ⓓ
181. Ⓐ Ⓑ Ⓒ Ⓓ
182. Ⓐ Ⓑ Ⓒ Ⓓ
183. Ⓐ Ⓑ Ⓒ Ⓓ
184. Ⓐ Ⓑ Ⓒ Ⓓ
185. Ⓐ Ⓑ Ⓒ Ⓓ
186. Ⓐ Ⓑ Ⓒ Ⓓ
187. Ⓐ Ⓑ Ⓒ Ⓓ
188. Ⓐ Ⓑ Ⓒ Ⓓ

189. Ⓐ Ⓑ Ⓒ Ⓓ
190. Ⓐ Ⓑ Ⓒ Ⓓ
191. Ⓐ Ⓑ Ⓒ Ⓓ
192. Ⓐ Ⓑ Ⓒ Ⓓ
193. Ⓐ Ⓑ Ⓒ Ⓓ
194. Ⓐ Ⓑ Ⓒ Ⓓ
195. Ⓐ Ⓑ Ⓒ Ⓓ
196. Ⓐ Ⓑ Ⓒ Ⓓ
197. Ⓐ Ⓑ Ⓒ Ⓓ
198. Ⓐ Ⓑ Ⓒ Ⓓ
199. Ⓐ Ⓑ Ⓒ Ⓓ
200. Ⓐ Ⓑ Ⓒ Ⓓ

Practice Test 4

LISTENING COMPREHENSION

In this section of the test, you will have the chance to show how well you understand spoken English. There are four parts to this section, with special directions for each part. You will have approximately 45 minutes to complete the Listening Comprehension sections.

Part 1: Photographs

Directions: You will see a photograph. You will hear four statements about the photograph. Choose the statement that most closely matches the photograph, and fill in the corresponding oval on your answer sheet.

1.

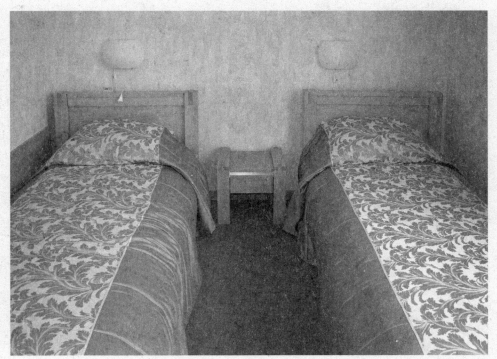

2.

3.

4.

5.

6.

Part 2: Question-Response

Track 48

Directions: You will hear a question and three possible responses. Choose the response that most closely answers the question, and fill in the corresponding oval on your answer sheet.

7.   Mark your answer on your answer sheet.

8.   Mark your answer on your answer sheet.

9.   Mark your answer on your answer sheet.

10. Mark your answer on your answer sheet.

11. Mark your answer on your answer sheet.

12. Mark your answer on your answer sheet.

13. Mark your answer on your answer sheet.

14. Mark your answer on your answer sheet.

15. Mark your answer on your answer sheet.

16. Mark your answer on your answer sheet.

17. Mark your answer on your answer sheet.

18. Mark your answer on your answer sheet.

19. Mark your answer on your answer sheet.

20. Mark your answer on your answer sheet.

21. Mark your answer on your answer sheet.

22. Mark your answer on your answer sheet.

23. Mark your answer on your answer sheet.

24. Mark your answer on your answer sheet.

25. Mark your answer on your answer sheet.

26. Mark your answer on your answer sheet.

27. Mark your answer on your answer sheet.

28. Mark your answer on your answer sheet.

29. Mark your answer on your answer sheet.

30. Mark your answer on your answer sheet.

31. Mark your answer on your answer sheet.

Part 3: Conversations

Directions: You will hear a conversation between two or more people. You will see three questions on each conversation and four possible answers. Choose the best answer to each question, and fill in the corresponding oval on your answer sheet.

32. What time did the man call the woman?

    (A) 2:00
    (B) 7:00
    (C) 8:00
    (D) 10:00

33. Why didn't the woman hear the phone?

    (A) She was out.
    (B) She was singing.
    (C) She was sleeping.
    (D) She was watching TV.

34. Why did the man call the woman?

    (A) To ask her to go to a party
    (B) To ask her to see a movie
    (C) To ask her to go on a walk
    (D) To ask her to help him with work

35. What does the woman say about Room 365?

    (A) It is large.
    (B) It has two beds.
    (C) It is not available.
    (D) It has a good view.

36. What kind of room does the man ask for?

    (A) A room by the pool
    (B) A room that is quieter
    (C) A room near the garden
    (D) A room with a king-sized bed

37. What will the man do now?

    (A) Put on his sweater
    (B) Swim in the pool
    (C) Have dinner
    (D) Take a rest

38. What is the problem?

    (A) A door is locked.
    (B) A car was stolen.
    (C) An alarm went off.
    (D) A man is lost.

39. Who is Jerry?

    (A) An ambulance driver
    (B) A firefighter
    (C) A thief
    (D) A coworker

40. What will the man do?

    (A) Check the time
    (B) Fix his phone
    (C) Call Jerry
    (D) Take a break

41. What is the man's complaint?

    (A) The tour was too fast.
    (B) They didn't see any paintings.
    (C) His back hurt.
    (D) He didn't like the paintings.

42. What does the woman suggest to the man?

    (A) Take another tour
    (B) Hurry up
    (C) Return to the museum alone
    (D) Get a painting of his own

43. What does the man say about the museum?

    (A) The tour guides are knowledgeable.
    (B) The admission price is high.
    (C) There are too many rooms.
    (D) The paintings are unusual.

44. Why does the man take the train?

(A) Driving is too expensive.
(B) He sometimes needs his car.
(C) The train is faster than driving.
(D) He doesn't like to park in the city.

45. Where does Isabel keep her car all day?

(A) At the park
(B) In a garage
(C) On the street
(D) At the train station

46. What does the man think of Isabel's parking place?

(A) The cost is too high.
(B) It is always crowded.
(C) The spaces are too small.
(D) It is conveniently located.

47. Why is the man disappointed?

(A) The post office is closed.
(B) The post office isn't close.
(C) The post office is hard to find.
(D) The post office is underground.

48. How does the woman recommend getting to the post office?

(A) By car
(B) By bus
(C) By foot
(D) By taxi

49. What does the man mean when he says, "That's not so bad"?

(A) He prefers walking.
(B) He does not get lost easily.
(C) The post office is not too far away.
(D) The woman's directions are easy to follow.

50. Who is the woman talking to?

(A) Her manager
(B) Her assistant
(C) A travel agent
(D) A new employee

51. How often do employees at this company get paid?

(A) Once a week
(B) Twice a week
(C) Once a month
(D) Twice a month

52. What is the man excited about?

(A) The number of insurance benefits
(B) The length of the vacation
(C) The size of his pay check
(D) The type of job duties

53. Where are the speakers going?

(A) Home
(B) To the store
(C) To the airport
(D) To the train station

54. What time does the man want to leave?

(A) At noon
(B) At 2:00
(C) At 3:00
(D) At 10:00

55. Why does he want to leave at this time?

(A) He likes to arrive early.
(B) He doesn't like to hurry.
(C) He's afraid traffic will be bad.
(D) He wants to try a new way of getting there.

56. Where does this conversation take place?

    (A) Library
    (B) Bookstore
    (C) Airplane
    (D) Dentist's office

57. What does the woman want?

    (A) A video
    (B) A book
    (C) A magazine
    (D) A newspaper

58. What does the woman say she will do?

    (A) Return at 9:00
    (B) Wait for the man
    (C) Give the man 25 cents
    (D) Avoid paying a fine

59. What does the woman want to do?

    (A) Have lunch outside
    (B) Drink some coffee
    (C) Make a sandwich
    (D) Go home

60. Where are the speakers going to meet?

    (A) At a café
    (B) In the park
    (C) At the office
    (D) On the sidewalk

61. Why does the man say, "If it's not a problem"?

    (A) To make a suggestion
    (B) To explain a reason
    (C) To accept an offer
    (D) To make a request

62. How many nights did the woman stay at the hotel?

    (A) One
    (B) Two
    (C) Three
    (D) Four

63. What was the problem with her bill?

    (A) The woman misplaced the bill.
    (B) The man added the bill wrong.
    (C) The man gave her the wrong bill.
    (D) The woman read the bill incorrectly.

64. What does the woman want to do?

    (A) Cash a check
    (B) Go to the bank
    (C) Pay her bill by check
    (D) Leave her business card

www.sportstown.com

Sports Town

Discount Coupon

Take 25% off of any purchase of $150 or more

Coupon good for online or in-store purchases.

Coupon expires June 30.
Type in code: A106

65. What does the woman want to buy?

    (A) Skis
    (B) Shoes
    (C) Boots
    (D) Books

66. Look at the graphic. Why did the woman have a problem with the coupon?

    (A) It has expired.
    (B) She used the wrong code.
    (C) She didn't spend enough money.
    (D) It is not valid for online purchases.

67. What does the man offer to do?

(A) Give the woman a full refund
(B) Take 20% off the shipping fee
(C) Give a discount on the current order
(D) Send a coupon for a discount on a future order

Small Office Tables

One drawer	$75
Two drawers	$100
Three drawers	$115
Four drawers	$125

68. Which room do the speakers want to buy chairs for?

(A) Conference room
(B) Break room
(C) Front office
(D) Cafeteria

69. What do the speakers say about shipping?

(A) The delivery is slow.
(B) The fee is very high.
(C) Next day delivery costs extra.
(D) The shipping company is unreliable.

70. Look at the graphic. Which table will the speakers probably order?

(A) One drawer
(B) Two drawers
(C) Three drawers
(D) Four drawers

Part 4: Talks

Directions: You will hear a talk given by a single speaker. You will see three questions on each talk, each with four possible answers. Choose the best answer to each question, and fill in the corresponding oval on your answer sheet.

71. Who can get on the plane during priority boarding?

    (A) People with connecting flights
    (B) Large groups
    (C) Elderly people
    (D) Airline personnel

72. What should be given to the gate agent?

    (A) A ticket
    (B) Extra luggage
    (C) A boarding pass
    (D) Requests for assistance

73. What are other passengers asked to do?

    (A) Stand near the door
    (B) Assist the flight attendants
    (C) Make their phone calls now
    (D) Listen for their row number

74. What kind of books does this store carry?

    (A) Novels
    (B) Children's books
    (C) Professional books
    (D) Textbooks

75. If the store doesn't have the book in stock, what will it do?

    (A) Refer you to another store
    (B) Look it up in the master list
    (C) Give you a different book at a discount
    (D) Order it

76. What else does this store sell?

    (A) Newspapers
    (B) Carry-alls
    (C) Journals
    (D) CDs

77. What does the speaker mean when he says, "I've got some good news for you"?

    (A) The news report is next.
    (B) He is about to report good weather.
    (C) He has already read the newspaper.
    (D) He has been given a job promotion.

78. When will the weather change?

    (A) Today
    (B) Tonight
    (C) Tomorrow morning
    (D) Tomorrow afternoon

79. What will the weather be like on Monday?

    (A) Sunny
    (B) Cloudy
    (C) Windy
    (D) Rainy

80. Where is this train going?

    (A) Into the city
    (B) To the hospital
    (C) To the business district
    (D) To the shopping mall

81. Which subway line goes to the airport?

    (A) The gray line
    (B) The green line
    (C) The red line
    (D) The blue line

82. How often do airport trains leave?

    (A) Every two minutes
    (B) Every five minutes
    (C) Every fifteen minutes
    (D) Every sixteen minutes

83. Why are these closings taking place?

    (A) It's Sunday.
    (B) There is no transportation.
    (C) It's a federal holiday.
    (D) The weather is bad.

84. What service is the transportation system eliminating for the day?

    (A) Rush hour service
    (B) Weekend service
    (C) Service into the city
    (D) Service to recreation areas

85. Where is parking free today?

    (A) In public garages
    (B) In private garages
    (C) On downtown streets
    (D) At the bus stations

86. Who participated in this survey?

    (A) Hotel owners
    (B) Secretaries
    (C) Housekeepers
    (D) Business travelers

87. Where would travelers prefer to have hotels located?

    (A) In the business district
    (B) Close to parks and museums
    (C) Near shopping and entertainment
    (D) Beside the airport

88. What additional service should the hotels provide at night?

    (A) Access to exercise and recreation rooms
    (B) Movies in the rooms
    (C) Light snacks in the lobby
    (D) Transportation services

89. Where does this talk take place?

    (A) In an auditorium
    (B) In a museum
    (C) At a café
    (D) On a bus

90. What will listeners do after lunch?

    (A) Drive through the historic district
    (B) Visit the botanical gardens
    (C) Tour some buildings
    (D) Return to the hotel

91. What does the speaker mean when she says, "Please don't worry"?

    (A) She enjoys her job.
    (B) She knows her way around the city.
    (C) She is prepared to answer questions.
    (D) She doesn't expect any problems will occur.

92. What is the first step in packing?

    (A) Get your suitcase
    (B) Wash your clothes
    (C) Choose your outfits
    (D) Check your medicine

93. What should go into the suitcase first?

    (A) Underwear
    (B) Heavy items
    (C) Smaller items
    (D) Jeans and slacks

94. What should you use to help airport security?

    (A) Travel guides
    (B) Light items
    (C) Plastic bags
    (D) Slip-on shoes

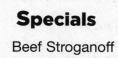

Kayla Sanchez
Sound Engineer

kayla@kaylas.com   456-7890

Specials

Beef Stroganoff
★ Pasta Primavera
Roast Lamb
★ Eggplant Stew

95. What does the speaker say about the ink color?

(A) It is too dark.
(B) She likes it a lot.
(C) It looks too heavy.
(D) She would prefer black.

96. Look at the graphic. Which information does the speaker want moved?

(A) The logo
(B) Her name
(C) Her job title
(D) The e-mail address

97. What does the speaker ask the listener to do?

(A) Send her the bill
(B) Deliver the cards
(C) Cancel the order
(D) Return the call

98. Who is the speaker talking to?

(A) Restaurant customers
(B) Restaurant servers
(C) Food wholesalers
(D) Cooking students

99. Look at the graphic. What does the speaker say about the eggplant stew?

(A) It is a popular dish.
(B) It is a new dish.
(C) It is a vegetarian dish.
(D) It is the least expensive dish.

100. What does the speaker imply about Saturday night?

(A) The prices are always higher.
(B) Most restaurants close late.
(C) There are more specials.
(D) It is a very busy night.

This is the end of the Listening Comprehension portion of the test. Turn to Part 5 in your test book.

READING

In this section of the test, you will have the chance to show how well you understand written English. There are three parts to this section, with special directions for each part.

YOU WILL HAVE ONE HOUR AND FIFTEEN MINUTES TO COMPLETE PARTS 5, 6, AND 7 OF THE TEST.

Part 5: Incomplete Sentences

> **Directions:** You will see a sentence with a missing word. Four possible answers follow the sentence. Choose the best answer to the question, and fill in the corresponding oval on your answer sheet.

101. If the weather is any worse tomorrow, we _____ the client lunch.

    (A) canceled
    (B) will cancel
    (C) have canceled
    (D) are canceling

102. We cannot process the order _____ we get a copy of the purchase order.

    (A) because
    (B) that
    (C) until
    (D) when

103. Although he met many new people at the party, William was able to _____ all their names.

    (A) recall
    (B) remind
    (C) review
    (D) remark

104. After completing the questionnaire, use the _____ envelope to return it to our office.

    (A) is enclosed
    (B) enclose
    (C) enclosing
    (D) enclosed

105. When buying a home, a licensed realtor is your best source for _____.

    (A) guide
    (B) consultant
    (C) advice
    (D) lawyer

106. Check the delivery service's website to _____ out when the package will be delivered.

    (A) bring
    (B) find
    (C) get
    (D) point

107. Because of the drop in oil prices, the cost of our raw materials is expected to _____.

    (A) increase
    (B) decrease
    (C) escalate
    (D) even out

108. Using a checklist is an _____ way to make plans.

    (A) effective
    (B) effect
    (C) effectiveness
    (D) effectively

109. Lunch has been ordered, _____ the delivery person has not arrived yet.

   (A) or
   (B) since
   (C) because
   (D) but

110. It is almost impossible to schedule an appointment with Ms. Grimm at this time of year because she is busy _____ the annual report.

   (A) in
   (B) for
   (C) with
   (D) from

111. The head of operations _____ to the convention and will be away from the factory all week long.

   (A) going
   (B) are going
   (C) go
   (D) is going

112. Customers can speak with a sales _____ by calling our 1-800 number.

   (A) representation
   (B) representative
   (C) represented
   (D) represents

113. Guests can find a telephone directory and a binder with information about local attractions _____ their rooms.

   (A) around
   (B) below
   (C) in
   (D) on

114. _____ smoking nor flash photography is allowed inside the museum.

   (A) Either
   (B) Neither
   (C) But
   (D) Or

115. As part of her annual evaluation, the supervisor had Ms. Balla _____ down her job responsibilities.

   (A) to write
   (B) wrote
   (C) written
   (D) write

116. State law _____ that residents change the address on their driver's license within 30 days of moving.

   (A) submits
   (B) ignores
   (C) mandates
   (D) requests

117. Glenda _____ to arrive at work late, but she makes up the time by staying late or working over the weekend.

   (A) tends
   (B) is scheduled
   (C) is supposed
   (D) attempts

118. We hope that the new marketing _____ for the county's recycling program will encourage residents to participate.

   (A) competence
   (B) candidate
   (C) collusion
   (D) campaign

119. Mr. and Mrs. Xiao decided to stay at the hotel that _____ travel agent suggested.

    (A) their
    (B) they
    (C) them
    (D) they're

120. The YRTL-32 is our most reliable model, mostly because it is hardly every brought in for _____.

    (A) despair
    (B) compares
    (C) impairs
    (D) repairs

121. The _____ to get into the building is 4-5-2-6.

    (A) reason
    (B) method
    (C) code
    (D) dial

122. Mr. Phelps suggested _____ a committee to research which kind of trucks we should add to our fleet.

    (A) formed
    (B) forming
    (C) form
    (D) to form

123. Human resources asks employees _____ one months' notice when leaving their job.

    (A) to give
    (B) will give
    (C) giving
    (D) gave

124. This list of contributors is more _____ the one on the computer server.

    (A) current
    (B) currently
    (C) current than
    (D) current as

125. Stuart isn't able to use his corporate credit card _____ it was stolen along with his wallet while he was in London.

    (A) until
    (B) because
    (C) although
    (D) once

126. The ship's captain requests that all passengers _____ emergency procedures.

    (A) reviewing
    (B) reviews
    (C) review
    (D) to review

127. The person _____ lost a briefcase may claim it in the lobby.

    (A) whose
    (B) which
    (C) whom
    (D) who

128. This memo about the new schedule is _____ the one you prepared yesterday.

    (A) as confusing
    (B) confusing as
    (C) as confusing as
    (D) as confused as

129. Ms. Friel _____ about her promotion before it was announced.

    (A) knew
    (B) known
    (C) is knowing
    (D) has known

130. Please _____ me at any time if you have any questions at all about the software.

    (A) are calling
    (B) call
    (C) calls
    (D) will call

Part 6: Text Completion

> **Directions:** You will see four passages, each with four blanks. Each blank has four answer choices. For each blank, choose the word, phrase, or sentence that best completes the passage.

Questions 131–134 refer to the following letter.

Modern Tech Inc.
St. No 2, Sector H 1/6, Hunter Complex
Islamabad, Pakistan

April 13th, 20—

Vaqas Mahmood
21, Sharah-e-Iran, Clifton
Karachi, Pakistan

Dear Mr. Mahmood,

Thank you for purchasing the XY40 USB digital speakers. _____.
                                                          131

Unfortunately, we will not be able to honor it because the rebate offer had already

_____ when you mailed it. Rebates must be mailed within three days of purchase.
132

However, you sent yours in almost two weeks after your purchase was made. Please

understand that we value your business, and in place of the rebate, we would like

_____ you a book of coupons that can be used toward other Modern Tech, Inc.
133

products. You will find great _____ on many of our products, including our new speaker
                              134

phone with improved sound quality.

Thank you for choosing Modern Tech, Inc. for all your technology needs.

Sincerely,

Tarik Khan

Tarik Khan
President

---

131. (A) Some items may be returned for a
        complete refund
     (B) Many companies offer rebates on
        certain products
     (C) All our products are guaranteed
        for one full year
     (D) We received your mail-in rebate
        card this week

132. (A) launched
     (B) initiated
     (C) expired
     (D) transferred

133. (A) to offer
     (B) offering
     (C) offered
     (D) will offer

134. (A) explanations
     (B) discounts
     (C) packages
     (D) instructions

To: benlivingston@accountantsgroup.ca
Copy: Kyle; Cheryl; Leslie
From: ryanedison@accountantsgroup.ca
Subject: Golf Tournament

Hi Everyone,

I'm starting the planning for the _____ company golf tournament in May. I know
135
it's more than two months away, but I wanted to get going early this year. I'd
like to get everyone's input, so I am drawing up a list of points to discuss. I
will hand it _____ at our next staff meeting so we can go over it together. Last
136
year's tournament was a great success. We _____ over $7,000 for charity.
137
This year we are aiming for $10,000. _____.
138

Thanks,
Ryan

135. (A) daily
     (B) weekly
     (C) monthly
     (D) annual

136. (A) in
     (B) out
     (C) over
     (D) down

137. (A) spent
     (B) saved
     (C) raised
     (D) invested

138. (A) With your support, we can do it
     (B) I expect everyone to attend the staff meeting
     (C) Many other companies hold similar charity
         events
     (D) The golf tournament has always proved to
         be a popular event

Questions 139–142 refer to the following article.

Indoor Air Pollution

New studies on air quality inside office buildings show that the indoor air quality is ____ to human health than the polluted air outside. According to the Committee on the Environment, the air quality in approximately 30% of buildings ____ unsafe.

139

140

The most common reason for Sick Building Syndrome, a medical condition that has been blamed on poor indoor air quality, is the ____ opening of businesses. When a building opens too early, paint fumes and cleaning products don't have enough time to disperse. ____.

141

142

---

139. (A) hazardous
     (B) more hazardous
     (C) most hazardous
     (D) the most hazardous

140. (A) is
     (B) are
     (C) seem
     (D) are becoming

141. (A) premeditated
     (B) premature
     (C) premium
     (D) prevented

142. (A) As a general rule, carpets should be installed after painting is finished
     (B) It is possible these days to purchase less toxic cleaning products
     (C) This is especially a problem if the space is not well ventilated
     (D) Air quality can be controlled with a good air exchange system

Questions 143–146 refer to the following e-mail.

To: Bill O'Hara
From: Edie Saunders
Subject: Workshop

Bill,

I am trying to finalize plans for next Friday's workshop. Please let me _____ how
                                                                        143
many people you expect to attend so that I can know how much food to order. Also, how

long do you expect the workshop to last? In addition to lunch, should I order afternoon coffee

and snacks _____? _____. I also need to know expected numbers so I can decide which
            144   145
conference room to reserve. Conference Room 2 is _____ than Conference Room 1, but it might
                                                  146
not be big enough.

Please get back to me as soon as possible because I need to take care of this soon.

Thanks.

Edie

143. (A) know
     (B) knows
     (C) to know
     (D) knowing

144. (A) moreover
     (B) instead
     (C) furthermore
     (D) as well

145. (A) I am also wondering if I should set up more than one table in the room
     (B) I have already ordered the pens, notepads, and other supplies you requested
     (C) I find that afternoon is not the best time for a workshop as people are often
         tired then
     (D) If a workshop goes all day, people usually expect some sort of midafternoon
         refreshment

146. (A) pleasant
     (B) pleasanter
     (C) pleasantly
     (D) pleasantest

Part 7: Reading Comprehension

> **Directions:** You will see single and multiple reading passages followed by several questions. Each question has four answer choices. Choose the best answer to the question, and fill in the corresponding oval on your answer sheet.

Questions 147–148 refer to the following form.

The Griffith Hotel
Reservation Form

Name:	Charles Winston
Room type:	queen
Length of stay:	3 nights
Dates:	September 10–12
Cost:	$100/night
Total charges:	$300

A deposit equivalent to the cost of one night's stay is required to hold the reservation and must be paid within 14 days of the reservation date. The remainder is due at check-in. Cancellation must be made within 7 days of check-in date in order for the deposit to be refunded.

---

147. How much must Mr. Winston pay two weeks before his arrival at the hotel?

(A) $0
(B) $100
(C) $200
(D) $300

148. What happens if Mr. Winston cancels his reservation on September 9?

(A) He will lose his deposit.
(B) He will receive a partial refund.
(C) He will receive a credit to be used for a future hotel stay.
(D) He will have to pay the entire cost of the three-night stay.

Questions 149–150 refer to the following announcement.

> Trust Line cordially invites you to attend a morning seminar to learn how you can predict the trends that will assist your clients with the success of their investments.
>
> To reserve a seat, fill out the attached card and mail it with your registration fee.
>
> Don't miss this chance to learn about the resources that drive successful fiduciary service management firms.
>
> For further information, please call 676-9980.

149. Who would be likely to attend the seminar?

(A) A private investor
(B) A manager in a not-for-profit organization
(C) A stockbroker
(D) A newspaper publisher

150. What will be discussed at the seminar?

(A) Building client relationships
(B) Fiduciary service management firms
(C) How to foresee good investments
(D) How to get new clients

Questions 151–152 refer to the following schedule.

BUS FARES

		Peak	Off Peak
Effective March 1, 20___	Any one zone	1.00	.75
Peak hours,	Between zones 1 and 2	1.35	1.00
Weekdays 5:30–9:30 A.M.	zones 1 and 3	1.70	1.35
and 3:00–7:00 P.M.	zones 2 and 3	1.35	1.00

151. When do these bus fares take effect?

(A) Immediately
(B) On March 1
(C) On February 28
(D) Next week

152. What is indicated about peak hours?

(A) They are the same on weekends as on weekdays.
(B) They are effective only in certain zones.
(C) They will no longer exist after March 1.
(D) They occur twice a day.

SAMANTHA ARNAULT Are you going to the dinner tonight?	1:30
BARRY GELLER I wish I could. I have to finish this report, so I'll be working late.	1:32
SAMANTHA ARNAULT Too bad. We'll miss you. I was hoping we could drive together because my car is in the shop.	1:34
BARRY GELLER Sorry. Wish I could.	1:37
SAMANTHA ARNAULT Do you know if Liz is going? Maybe I could ride with her.	1:40
BARRY GELLER I'll check. Hold on.	1:42
BARRY GELLER She says she'll pick you up at 6:30.	1:46
SAMANTHA ARNAULT Perfect. Thanks.	1:48

153. Why did Ms. Arnault contact Mr. Geller?

(A) To ask him for a ride
(B) To give him an invitation
(C) To check the time of the dinner
(D) To remind him about the dinner

154. At 1:42, what does Mr. Geller mean when he writes, "Hold on"?

(A) He thinks that riding with Liz is a bad idea.
(B) He thinks Ms. Arnault should not go to the dinner.
(C) He might change his mind about going to the dinner.
(D) He is going to find the answer to Ms. Arnault's question.

Questions 155–157 refer to the following advertisement.

Leading TV-Advertising
company with broadcast interests worldwide seeks a Specialist in Audience Research. The Specialist will design studies to determine consumer preferences and write reports for use within the company. Candidates must have a college degree with courses in research. Must also have experience in advertising. Outstanding oral, written, and computer skills are necessary. Downtown location. Excellent benefits.

155. What does this job involve?

(A) Making TV commercials
(B) Discovering what consumers like
(C) Advertising products
(D) Testing products

156. Who will use the reports the Specialist writes?

(A) The consumer
(B) The television station
(C) The manufacturers
(D) The TV-advertising company

157. What qualifications should the candidate have?

(A) Education in research and experience in advertising
(B) Experience in television audiences
(C) Ability in accounting
(D) A degree in broadcasting

Questions 158–160 refer to the following fax.

Starling Brothers Investment Firm
145 East 45th Street
New York NY 10019

```
To:    All airline investors          BY FAX
Fm:    Alfonso O'Reilly               Pages: 1 of 1
       Broker
```

Stock Alert   Stock Alert   Stock Alert   Stock Alert

—[1]— Southern Regional Airlines earned $9.8 million in the
fourth quarter, compared with a loss of $584.1 million in
the previous year. —[2]— The profit was due to reduced costs
and an increase in profitable routes. If the present
management does not change, we assume the cost-reduction
measures and their choice of routes will continue to have a
positive effect on earnings. It seems likely they will
continue to eliminate the less traveled routes across the
Atlantic. —[3]— Thus, they should be able to focus more on
the short-haul routes, where the airline has built a strong
base and where most of its revenue is generated. —[4]— If
there is any change in the forecast, we will advise you.

---

158. Why are airline profits up?

(A) New marketing strategies
(B) Lower cost and better routes
(C) Greater ticket sales
(D) Changes in the competition

159. Which routes have been most profitable for the airline?

(A) Cross-Atlantic routes
(B) International routes
(C) Shorter routes
(D) Freight routes

160. In which of the following positions marked [1], [2], [3], and [4] does the following sentence best belong?

"We suggest holding on to stock in this airline at this time."

(A) [1]
(B) [2]
(C) [3]
(D) [4]

Questions 161–163 refer to the following memo.

From: Mazola Sawarani
Sent: Thursday, June 03, 20— 9:30 A.M.

To: All Employees

Sub: Vacation

Supervisors must approve any and all
vacation periods longer than one week.
Approval is not automatic. If (1) your
absence would create a heavy workload
for your team, or cause your team to
miss deadlines; (2) you fail to give
at least one week's advance notice;
(3) there are problems with your job
performance; or (4) you have had other
frequent absences, your request could
be denied. In that case, please
contact the Personnel Review Board.

161. What is said about vacations?

(A) Only one-week vacations are
allowed.
(B) Vacations may be taken just once
a year.
(C) Approval is required for vacations over
one week.
(D) There are no paid vacations for
temporary employees.

162. Why might a supervisor deny a vacation
request?

(A) The employee is a team leader.
(B) The employee often misses work.
(C) The employee is not a hard worker.
(D) The employee has been recently hired.

163. What can an employee do if a vacation
request has been denied?

(A) Discuss the matter with the Personnel
Review Board
(B) Request a transfer to another
department
(C) Resubmit the request after one week
(D) Report the supervisor to the labor union

Questions 164–167 refer to the following webpage.

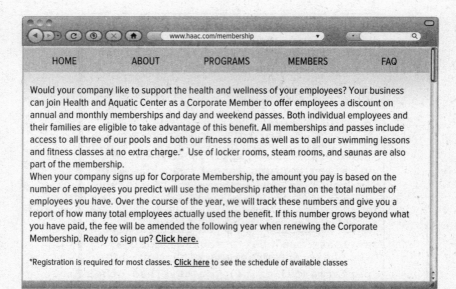

HOME   ABOUT   PROGRAMS   MEMBERS   FAQ

Would your company like to support the health and wellness of your employees? Your business can join Health and Aquatic Center as a Corporate Member to offer employees a discount on annual and monthly memberships and day and weekend passes. Both individual employees and their families are eligible to take advantage of this benefit. All memberships and passes include access to all three of our pools and both our fitness rooms as well as to all our swimming lessons and fitness classes at no extra charge.* Use of locker rooms, steam rooms, and saunas are also part of the membership.

When your company signs up for Corporate Membership, the amount you pay is based on the number of employees you predict will use the membership rather than on the total number of employees you have. Over the course of the year, we will track these numbers and give you a report of how many total employees actually used the benefit. If this number grows beyond what you have paid, the fee will be amended the following year when renewing the Corporate Membership. Ready to sign up? Click here.

*Registration is required for most classes. Click here to see the schedule of available classes

164. What is the purpose of this information?

(A) To advertise the services of a health club
(B) To tell how to sign up for health club membership
(C) To describe a health and wellness program for corporate staff
(D) To explain how businesses can get membership discounts for employees

165. What is said about the facilities at the center?

(A) They include swimming pools and fitness rooms.
(B) Saunas and steam rooms were recently added.
(C) There is a separate pool for small children.
(D) There is an outdoor pool.

166. What is said about the fitness classes?

(A) They are for adults only.
(B) Weekend classes cost extra.
(C) They are a benefit of membership
(D) The class schedule frequently changes.

167. Why would the cost of a Corporate Membership increase?

(A) If the number of employees using this benefit changes.
(B) If employees' families use the membership.
(C) If the company renews its membership late.
(D) If the company increases its staff size.

Questions 168–171 refer to the following announcement.

NewTech Equipment Company has announced that it expects to cut 4,000 jobs at its branch in Brazil within the next six months. –[1]– NewTech has been struggling to make a profit after two years of losses worldwide.

The reduction in its labor force comes as a surprise to business analysts, who had been impressed with the performance of the company in recent months. –[2]– Although its revenues have not matched those of its first two years in business, they had been increasing steadily since June.

New competition was blamed for the loss of revenue, but sources close to the company put the blame on the lack of direction from the chairman of the company, Pierre Reinartz. Mr. Reinartz has been with the company for only three years, but he will probably resign soon. –[3]–

It is expected that Elizabeth Strube, a current company VP, will succeed him. –[4]– Ms. Strube was responsible for opening the international offices, which have been more profitable than those in Brazil. NewTech employs about 25,000 people in Brazil, another 20,000 in Asia, and 10,000 in Europe. The international office will not be affected by the staff reductions.

168. What has been happening since June?

(A) The number of employee layoffs has been rising.
(B) The customer base has been growing.
(C) Earnings have been going up.
(D) Losses have been getting worse.

169. What is the current NewTech chairman likely to do?

(A) Sell the company
(B) Quit his job
(C) Increase profits
(D) Open new offices

170. What describes the international branches of NewTech?

(A) They earn more money than the Brazilian office.
(B) They are less cost-effective.
(C) They are older than the Brazilian branch.
(D) They will be closed within six months.

171. In which of the following positions marked [1], [2], [3], and [4] does the following sentence best belong?

"This is part of a strategy to reorganize the money-losing business."

(A) [1]
(B) [2]
(C) [3]
(D) [4]

KAIA JONES	9:15
I need some help figuring out an order.	
ANN ADAMS	9:16
Sure. What's up?	
KAIA JONES	9:19
It's for the Bigelow wedding next month. They wanted chocolate-dipped strawberries, but I am not sure about our usual source for the berries. Didn't we decide to not use them anymore?	
ANN ADAMS	9:24
You mean Berry Vale Farm? Do not order from them. Last time half the berries they sent were rotten. We couldn't use them.	
ANN ADAMS	9:27
Chocolate-dipped strawberries are our specialty. We need the best berries. And we need a new source because the Smith's also want the strawberries for their party next month.	
KAIA JONES	9:29
Right. Do you think I should try Hammond Orchards?	
ANN ADAMS	9:32
Why don't you contact them and find out their prices. In the meantime, I'll ask around and see if anyone else has had experience with them.	
ANN ADAMS	9:35
How about the menu for the Wilson graduation party this weekend?	
KAIA JONES	9:38
I've ordered the meat and the vegetables, and we've already started on the cake.	
ANN ADAMS	9:41
Good. That's all set. So, let me know what you learn from Hammond Farm.	
KAIA JONES	9:45
I'll get back to you this afternoon as soon as I've talked to them.	
ANN ADAMS	9:47
Fine.	

172. What kind of business do Ms. Jones and Ms. Adams probably work for?

(A) A farm
(B) A cooking school
(C) A food wholesaler
(D) A catering company

173. What was the problem with the last order from the strawberry supplier?

(A) It cost too much.
(B) It arrived too late.
(C) The fruit was poor quality.
(D) There was too much fruit.

174. At 9:41, what does Ms. Adams mean when she writes, "That's all set"?

(A) The date for the party has been decided.
(B) Everything is organized for the party.
(C) The client has agreed to the menu.
(D) The client has signed the contract.

175. What will Ms. Jones do this afternoon?

(A) Find out the price of strawberries
(B) Visit Hammond Farm
(C) Finish making the cake
(D) Call the client

FAX

To: Management
From: Unhappy customer
Date: Friday, February 4th

To Whom It May Concern:

I'm sending this complaint by fax because I haven't been able to reach anyone at your company by telephone. I am extremely disappointed with the service that Concord's call center provides. I called yesterday at 10: 30 A.M. for help with my new dishwasher. I was immediately put on hold. I listened to some annoying music for 35 minutes before I finally hung up and called again. The same person, he said his name was Kazuki, told me that he was with another caller and that my call was important to him. If my call was important, someone would have been available to help me.

     The worst part is, my call really was important. I had a major flood yesterday after I turned my new dishwasher on, and I couldn't figure out how to get the water to stop running. There is a lot of damage to my kitchen floor. I would appreciate a personal phone call explaining why nobody was available to answer my call. I will not be purchasing from your store in the future.

Suzuki Kana

NOTICE

Date: February 7, 20—
For: Call center employees
Re: Weekly meetings

As of March 1, call center employees will no longer be required to attend weekly Concord staff meetings. The minutes from each meeting will be posted in the staff room for all employees to view after the Thursday morning meetings.

There are two reasons for this change:

1) Our current arrangement of using one employee to cover all ten phones during the meeting hour is not working. We have had numerous complaints from customers saying that they wait up to half an hour to have a call answered on Thursday mornings.

2) We are losing up to $300 in sales every Thursday morning because we don't have all the phones working. Call center representatives generate extra sales while handling help line calls. You are also losing money, because commission is lost when you have to take time out for meetings.

If you have any questions regarding these changes, please contact Itou Saki at manager3@concord.org.

176. Which of the following is NOT true about the caller?

 (A) She recently purchased an appliance from Concord.
 (B) She was calling for advice about how to clean up a flood.
 (C) She was upset with the length of time she waited on the phone.
 (D) She disliked the music that played while she was on hold.

177. Why are call center employees no longer required to attend weekly staff meetings?

 (A) The content of the meetings is not relevant to them.
 (B) They need to be available to answer the help line.
 (C) They complained about the frequency of staff meetings.
 (D) They are worried about the loss of sales commissions during meeting time.

178. How many people were working the phones when Suzuki called this company?

 (A) None
 (B) One
 (C) Nine
 (D) Ten

179. How will call center employees learn about what happened at the weekly meetings?

 (A) A memo will be delivered two days later.
 (B) There will be one call center representative taking notes.
 (C) A summary will be available in the staff room.
 (D) Itou Saki will send out an e-mail with the details.

180. How did management handle this complaint?

 (A) By putting the customer on hold
 (B) By phoning the call center employees
 (C) By changing the company procedures
 (D) By sending a notice to the customer

To: Operator 7, Operator 9, Operator 11
Sender: Park Gi
Subject: Recorded names and titles

I have recently discovered that a number of you have reprogrammed your telephones and changed the information on your voice mail. You have replaced the generic title, *systems operator*, with your own name, or worse for at least one of you, a nickname. Not only is this unprofessional, it is against the rules set out in your manual. The original recordings were set up with generic names and titles for a good reason. Your supervisor may ask you to change stations or departments at any time in order for you to learn a new position at the office. New interns will take your desk and the duties that go along with it.

 Please refer to page 14 of your manual, which starts, "As temporary employees, you do not have the right to reprogram the telephone on your desk or the settings on your computer."

Thank you,
Park Gi

To: parkgi@financialguide.net
From: student7@financialguide.net
Subject: Answering machines

Dear Mr. Park,

 I want to apologize for reprogramming the voice mail for desk 12. After being referred to as Operator 7 several times by repeat customers, I decided to change the recorded name to my own. I don't believe the message I recorded was unprofessional in any way. I simply gave my full name and my title, *student intern*.

 I changed the recording because I got a message from a customer who said, "It would be nice to know your name. It feels impersonal to say thank you to a number."

 Would you like me to change the message back to a generic one, or do you plan to do this yourself? I know how to do it, but I don't want to break the rule again.

 Finally, I didn't realize that we would be moving to other stations, but I look forward to trying new positions. I am enjoying my internship so far.

All the best,
Chong Dae

181. Who was the first e-mail written to?

    (A) All temporary employees

    (B) Three student trainers

    (C) Selected student interns

    (D) All systems operators

182. How does Park Gi suggest interns find out the rules about voice mail?

    (A) By reading their manuals

    (B) By asking their supervisors

    (C) By e-mailing Park Gi

    (D) By talking with other temporary employees

183. What did Chong Dae record on her voice mail?

    (A) Her nickname

    (B) Her telephone number

    (C) Her name and job title

    (D) Her desk number

184. What excuse does Chong use to defend her actions?

    (A) Her own name is easy to pronounce.

    (B) She thought she would be offered full-time work.

    (C) A customer commented on her telephone's voice mail message.

    (D) She didn't read the training package manual.

185. What does Park forget to mention in his e-mail?

    (A) Where the rule for interns was written

    (B) If interns should change the voice mail message back

    (C) Whether or not interns are temporary employees

    (D) Why the policy was made in the first place

www.busybusinessworkers.com

It's time to take a break, relax, and enjoy some time away from the office. This month we're offering three holiday packages especially for busy business workers like you. May is the best month for travel. While students are busy with their exams, you can enjoy beaches and resorts in peace. Book a vacation this month and receive 25% off the regular price. Packages do not include tax. Cancellation insurance is recommended.

Click on any packages for full details. Prices are per person.
Package A: twelve nights. five-star hotel in Portugal. includes all meals. $1,650
Package B: five nights. Caribbean Cruise. $1,400
Package C: Angelino's Spa and Golf Getaway. from $600.
Package D: Sorry. No longer available.

Don't wait until the end of the year. Take a break now. You deserve it.

To: manager@marketpro.com
From: francogerard@marketpro.com
Subj: vacation

Hi Alain,

I recently saw an ad for a travel company that is offering some great deals on vacations, and I'd really like to take advantage of the opportunity. My wife and I have been wishing for some time to travel to the islands, and now we have a chance to do it comfortably and affordably. These trips appear to be quite popular, and early May is the soonest we can get reservations. I know that it is a busy time of year here at Market Pro; however, I only plan to be away for a week, and I am sure Stephen can cover my duties quite competently during that time. It's been some time since I last took a vacation, and I hope you will be able to approve this request. Please let me know soon, so we can finalize our reservations.

Thank you.
Franco

Reservation Form

Name: Franco Gerard

Address: 123 Main Street, Springfield

Phone: 456-1234

E-mail: francogerard@marketpro.com

Vacation: Package B

No. of travelers: 2

Dates of trip: May 3–May 10

Payment method:

☒ ☐ ☐ ☐ ☐ ☐ check (mail to address below)

☐ credit card no. _____

---

186. Who is the audience for the advertisement?

(A) Golfers
(B) Families
(C) Students
(D) Office workers

187. How can a customer get a discount on a vacation?

(A) Make a reservation this month
(B) Pay before the end of the year
(C) Reserve a trip for two people
(D) Travel in May

188. What is indicated about Package C?

(A) It includes golf lessons.
(B) It does not include meals.
(C) It could cost more than $600.
(D) It is not available at this time.

189. Why did Mr. Gerard write the e-mail?

(A) To ask who can cover his duties during vacation
(B) To tell Alain about the vacation deals
(C) To ask for vacation recommendations
(D) To request time off from work for vacation

190. Which vacation will Mr. Gerard take?

(A) Caribbean Cruise
(B) Trip to Portugal
(C) Spa and Golf Getaway
(D) Stay in a five-star hotel

Questions 191–195 refer to the following notice, ticket, and e-mail.

The North Star Center for the Performing Arts

presents its new season

October 5–30:   The City Ballet performs Swan Lake
November 7–21:   Romeo and Juliet, a play by Wm. Shakespeare
December 2–18:   The City Orchestra performs weekly concerts
January 4–30:   Carmen, an opera by Georges Bizet

All tickets must be bought in advance at *www.nscpa.org*. Tickets are available for individual performances, or you can subscribe to the entire season.

Ticket prices (individual performances)

Weekdays:
- Matinee: $40
- Evening: $55

Weekends:
- Matinee: $50
- Evening: $65

Print At Home Ticket

Instructions
You must print this ticket and bring it to the event.

January 4, 7:30 P.M.
North Star Center for the Performing Arts

DESCRIPTION	PRICE
Row F, seat 10	$65
Row F, seat 12	$65

All sales are final. Ticket is nonrefundable. In the event that there is a cancellation by the theater, a refund for this ticket may be issued.

To: Peter Richards
From: Amanda Osann
Subj: Tickets

Hi Pete,

Thank you so much for getting the tickets for next week. I'm really looking forward to seeing the performance. You mentioned getting dinner before the show. Unfortunately, I don't think I will be able to leave the office in time for that. We are all working late these days to get the year-end report finished. But a light supper after the show would be fun, if you're up for that. I'll have my car with me, so I can swing by your office and pick you up at around 7:00. Let me know if that works for you.

Amanda

191. How much does it cost to see a performance on a Thursday afternoon?

(A) $40
(B) $55
(C) $50
(D) $65

192. What is indicated about tickets for performances at the North Star Center?

(A) They are available online only.
(B) They can be picked up at the box office.
(C) They are discounted for senior citizens.
(D) They are no longer available for certain performances.

193. When can a customer get a refund on a ticket?

(A) If the refund is requested before the day of the performance
(B) If the ticket was not bought at a discount price
(C) If the performance is canceled
(D) Refunds are never given.

194. What kind of performance will Mr. Richards and Ms. Osann see?

(A) Ballet
(B) Play
(C) Concert
(D) Opera

195. What does Ms. Osann offer to do?

(A) Print the tickets
(B) Pay for supper after the show
(C) Help Mr. Richards write a report
(D) Give Mr. Richards a ride to the theater

Questions 196–200 refer to the following real estate listings and two e-mails.

To: melissa.davenport@myjob.com
From: sydneya@someplace.com
Subj: re: apartments

Hi Sydney,

I have great news. I recently accepted a position with the Sylvan Company, which means I will be moving to Winchester very soon. It will be so great to be in the same city as you. Anyhow, I was wondering if you could give me some suggestions about where to look for an apartment for my family. We'd like to live somewhere safe and quiet. We'd also like to be near a good school for our two children. We would need at least two bedrooms, although three would be better. Since we're planning to bring our car, we won't need to be near public transportation. That will give us more choices in terms of location, but we would prefer garage parking. Let me know if you have any ideas, and if you could recommend a real estate agent, that would be great.

Thanks, and I look forward to seeing you soon!

Melissa

HASKELL REALTY COMPANY
Winchester Apartments

Listing A
Bright and sunny one-bedroom near Riverside Park. Small building, tenant parking lot in rear. Near schools, transportation. $1,000/month

Listing B
Charming two-bedroom apartment near university. Party room and fitness room in building. Garage parking. Near schools, stores. $1,800/month

Listing C
Spacious and affordable three-bedroom apartment on the Greenville Subway line. Street parking. Near schools, stores. $2,000/month

Listing D
Newly-renovated two-bedroom apartment close to downtown. On bus and subway lines. Near shopping, parks, museums. $1,500.

```
To:      melissa.davenport@myjob.com
From:    bob@haskellrealty.com
Subj:    re: apartments

Dear Ms. Davenport,

Thank you for your e-mail. I would be very happy to show you apartments for
rent here in Winchester. We have several listings that I think would interest you.
You mentioned that you will be in town next week and that your afternoons will
be free. Why don't we meet on Wednesday afternoon. If you will let me know the
address where you will be staying, I will pick you up at 1:30, and we can go look
at apartments from there. I look forward to meeting you.

Bob Haskell
```

196. Why is Ms. Davenport moving?

(A) She got a new job.
(B) She needs a bigger apartment.
(C) She wants to be closer to her family.
(D) She does not like her current neighborhood.

197. What is indicated about apartment Listing D?

(A) It is close to schools.
(B) It has a fitness room.
(C) It has the lowest rent.
(D) It is near public transportation.

198. Which apartment will Ms. Davenport most likely prefer?

(A) Listing A
(B) Listing B
(C) Listing C
(D) Listing D

199. Why did Mr. Haskell write the e-mail?

(A) To find out when Ms. Davenport is free
(B) To recommend places to live
(C) To make an appointment
(D) To advertise his business

200. What does Mr. Haskell ask Ms. Davenport to do?

(A) Meet him at his office
(B) Give him her address
(C) Pick him up in her car
(D) Choose some apartments to see

STOP

*This is the end of the test. If you finish before time is called,
you may go back to Parts 5, 6, and 7 and check your work.*

ANSWER KEY
Practice Test 4

LISTENING COMPREHENSION

Part 1: Photographs

1. **C**	3. **C**	5. **C**
2. **A**	4. **D**	6. **C**

Part 2: Question-Response

7. **B**	14. **A**	21. **A**	28. **B**
8. **A**	15. **B**	22. **C**	29. **A**
9. **C**	16. **A**	23. **B**	30. **A**
10. **C**	17. **C**	24. **A**	31. **C**
11. **A**	18. **A**	25. **B**	
12. **B**	19. **C**	26. **A**	
13. **B**	20. **A**	27. **C**	

Part 3: Conversations

32. **B**	42. **C**	52. **B**	62. **A**
33. **D**	43. **B**	53. **C**	63. **C**
34. **A**	44. **D**	54. **C**	64. **C**
35. **A**	45. **B**	55. **C**	65. **C**
36. **B**	46. **A**	56. **A**	66. **A**
37. **D**	47. **B**	57. **B**	67. **D**
38. **C**	48. **B**	58. **D**	68. **A**
39. **D**	49. **C**	59. **A**	69. **B**
40. **C**	50. **D**	60. **B**	70. **A**
41. **A**	51. **D**	61. **C**	

Part 4: Talks

71. **C**	79. **A**	87. **C**	95. **B**
72. **B**	80. **D**	88. **A**	96. **C**
73. **D**	81. **A**	89. **D**	97. **A**
74. **C**	82. **C**	90. **B**	98. **B**
75. **D**	83. **C**	91. **C**	99. **C**
76. **C**	84. **A**	92. **C**	100. **D**
77. **B**	85. **C**	93. **B**	
78. **D**	86. **D**	94. **C**	

ANSWER KEY
Practice Test 4

READING

Part 5: Incomplete Sentences

101. **B**	109. **D**	117. **A**	125. **B**
102. **C**	110. **C**	118. **D**	126. **C**
103. **A**	111. **D**	119. **A**	127. **D**
104. **D**	112. **B**	120. **D**	128. **C**
105. **C**	113. **C**	121. **C**	129. **A**
106. **B**	114. **B**	122. **B**	130. **B**
107. **B**	115. **D**	123. **A**	
108. **A**	116. **C**	124. **C**	

Part 6: Text Completion

131. **D**	135. **D**	139. **B**	143. **A**
132. **C**	136. **B**	140. **A**	144. **D**
133. **A**	137. **C**	141. **B**	145. **D**
134. **B**	138. **A**	142. **C**	146. **B**

Part 7: Reading Comprehension

147. **B**	161. **C**	175. **A**	189. **D**
148. **A**	162. **B**	176. **B**	190. **A**
149. **C**	163. **A**	177. **B**	191. **A**
150. **C**	164. **D**	178. **B**	192. **A**
151. **B**	165. **A**	179. **C**	193. **C**
152. **D**	166. **C**	180. **C**	194. **D**
153. **A**	167. **A**	181. **C**	195. **D**
154. **D**	168. **C**	182. **A**	196. **A**
155. **B**	169. **B**	183. **C**	197. **D**
156. **D**	170. **A**	184. **C**	198. **B**
157. **A**	171. **A**	185. **B**	199. **C**
158. **B**	172. **D**	186. **D**	200. **B**
159. **C**	173. **C**	187. **A**	
160. **D**	174. **B**	188. **C**	

TEST SCORE CONVERSION TABLE

Count your correct responses. Match the number of correct responses with the corresponding score from the Test Score Conversion Table (below). Add the two scores together. This is your Total Estimated Test Score. As you practice taking the TOEIC practice tests, your scores should improve. Keep track of your Total Estimated Test Scores.

# Correct	Listening Score	Reading Score	# Correct	Listening Score	Reading Score	# Correct	Listening Score	Reading Score	# Correct	Listening Score	Reading Score
0	5	5	26	110	65	51	255	220	76	410	370
1	5	5	27	115	70	52	260	225	77	420	380
2	5	5	28	120	80	53	270	230	78	425	385
3	5	5	29	125	85	54	275	235	79	430	390
4	5	5	30	130	90	55	280	240	80	440	395
5	5	5	31	135	95	56	290	250	81	445	400
6	5	5	32	140	100	57	295	255	82	450	405
7	10	5	33	145	110	58	300	260	83	460	410
8	15	5	34	150	115	59	310	265	84	465	415
9	20	5	35	160	120	60	315	270	85	470	420
10	25	5	36	165	125	61	320	280	86	475	425
11	30	5	37	170	130	62	325	285	87	480	430
12	35	5	38	175	140	63	330	290	88	485	435
13	40	5	39	180	145	64	340	300	89	490	445
14	45	5	40	185	150	65	345	305	90	495	450
15	50	5	41	190	160	66	350	310	91	495	455
16	55	10	42	195	165	67	360	320	92	495	465
17	60	15	43	200	170	68	365	325	93	495	470
18	65	20	44	210	175	69	370	330	94	495	480
19	70	25	45	215	180	70	380	335	95	495	485
20	75	30	46	220	190	71	385	340	96	495	490
21	80	35	47	230	195	72	390	350	97	495	495
22	85	40	48	240	200	73	395	355	98	495	495
23	90	45	49	245	210	74	400	360	99	495	495
24	95	50	50	250	215	75	405	365	100	495	495
25	100	60									

Number of Correct Listening Responses _____ = Listening Score _____

Number of Correct Reading Responses _____ = Reading Score _____

Total Estimated Test Score _____

PRACTICE TEST 4

ANSWER EXPLANATIONS

Listening Comprehension

PART 1: PHOTOGRAPHS

1. **(C)** Choice (C) correctly identifies the location of the table. Choice (A) is incorrect because the lamps are on the wall, not on the table. Choice (B) is incorrect because there is no picture on the wall in the photo. Choice (D) is incorrect because both pillows are on, not next to, the beds.

2. **(A)** Choice (A) makes assumptions: *it looks like a restaurant*, so *the customers must be holding a menu* and *ordering food*. Choice (B) confuses *reading a menu* and *learning to read*. Choice (C) is incorrect because the waiter has already approached the customer. Choice (D) is incorrect because the guest is ordering, not waiting to order.

3. **(C)** Choice (C) identifies the correct action: A woman is putting a suitcase into the trunk of the car. Choice (A) correctly identifies the luggage but not the woman's location. Choices (B) and (D) correctly identify the bag/baggage, but not the woman's action.

4. **(D)** Choice (D) correctly identifies the condition of the gate—all the doors are shut. Choice (A) correctly identifies the gate, but there is no car in the photo. Choice (B) correctly identifies the lamps, but not their location. Choice (C) relates *gate* with *lock*, but there is no man in the photo.

5. **(C)** The delivery person is knocking on a door in order to deliver a package. Choice (A) correctly identifies the boxes, but the man is not opening them. Choice (B) correctly identifies the glass in the doors, but the man is not washing it. Choice (D) correctly identifies the man's action, but not the object he is delivering—he is delivering boxes or packages, not his hat.

6. **(C)** Choice (C) identifies the action *unloading cargo*. Choices (A) and (B) misidentify the cargo (*shopping bags, pillows*). Choice (D) does not match the photo.

PART 2: QUESTION-RESPONSE

7. **(B)** Choice (B) is a logical response to the question about packing for a camping trip. Choice (A) relates *camping trip* with *light a fire*. Choice (C) relates *camping trip* with *backpack*.

8. **(A)** Choice (A) is a logical response to a question about *weather*. Choice (B) contains the same verb *was* and might be related to *weather* (bad weather causes some people to wear hats), but it does not describe the weather. Choice (B) also confuses similar-sounding words *weather* and *wearing*. Choice (C) confuses similar-sounding words *weather* and *wet*.

9. **(C)** Choice (C) is a logical response to a question about *coffee*. Choice (A) confuses similar-sounding words *coffee* and *cough*. Choice (B) confuses similar-sounding words *coffee* and *fee*.

10. **(C)** Choice (C) is a logical response to the *yes-no* question about paying a bill—*I took care of it* means *I paid it*. Choice (A), *I opened it*, refers to something you might do with a bill that comes in the mail. Choice (B) confuses similar-sounding words *paid* and *pain*.

11. **(A)** Since the first speaker doesn't want cake, the second speaker offers fruit in its place. Choice (B) associates *baking* with cake. Choice (C) confuses the phrase *buy it* with the similar-sounding word *diet*.

12. **(B)** Choice (B) is a logical response to a question about *time*. Choice (A) confuses related words *time* and *watch*. Choice (C) confuses related words *morning* and *get up*.

13. **(B)** Choice (B) is a logical response to a question about *duration of time*. Choice (A) confuses similar-sounding words *ride* and *bride* and related words *long* with *tall*. Choice (C) describes *how long the train is* (ten cars), not *how long the ride is* (two hours).

14. **(A)** Choice (A) is a logical response to a question about *occupation*. Choice (B) confuses similar-sounding words *occupation* and *attention*. Choice (C) confuses similar-sounding words *occupied* with *occupation*.

15. **(B)** Choice (B) is a logical response to a question about *coming*. Choice (A) confuses *not coming* with *are coming* or *not* (coming) and does not match the subject (*you–he*). Choice (C) confuses *didn't come* with *are coming* or *not* (coming) and does not match subject (*you–they*) or tense.

16. **(A)** Choice (A) is a logical response to a question about *seat location*. Choice (B) confuses similar-sounding words *sitting* and *city*. Choice (C) confuses similar-sounding words *sitting* and *sitter*.

17. **(C)** The first speaker wants to take a walk, so the second speaker suggests going to the park. Choice (A) confuses *work* with the similar-sounding word *walk*. Choice (B) confuses *talk* with the similar-sounding word *walk*.

18. **(A)** Choice (A) is a logical response to the question about a relative. Choice (B) confuses similar-sounding words *brother* and *bother*. Choice (D) confuses similar-sounding words *busy* and *isn't he*.

19. **(C)** Choice (C) is a logical response to the negative question about the length of the meeting. Choice (A) confuses similar-sounding words *meeting* and *seating*. Choice (B) confuses the meaning of the word *rather*.

20. **(A)** The second speaker suggests leaving at 6:00 in order to get to the airport on time. Choice (B) associates *plane tickets* with *airport*. Choice (C) confuses *court* with the similar-sounding word *airport*.

21. **(A)** Choice (A) is a logical response to a question about *what color*. Choice (B) confuses similar-sounding words *hall* and *tall*. Choice (C) confuses related words *paint* and *painting* and similar-sounding words *wall* with *hall*.

22. **(C)** Choice (C) is a logical response to a question about *Which*. Choice (A) confuses similar-sounding words *my gray* and *migraine*. Choice (B) confuses similar-sounding words *tie* and *tried* and *suit* and *do it*.

23. **(B)** Choice (B) is a logical response to the *How* question. Choice (A) repeats the word *visitor*. Choice (C) would be an answer to a *yes–no* question.

24. **(A)** Choice (A) is a logical response to a question about *When*. Choice (B) is incorrect; *finished* (past tense) does not match the tense of the question—*will be finished* (future). Choice (C) is incorrect; *thought* (past tense) does not match the tense of the question—*think* (present tense).

25. **(B)** Choice (B) is a logical response to a question about *not coming with us*. Choice (A) has the related word *go*, but it does not answer *Why*. Choice (C) is incorrect; *didn't come* (past tense) does not match *aren't coming* (present tense) and does not answer *Why*.

26. **(A)** Choice (A) answers the tag question about possession of a key. Choice (B) confuses the meaning of the word *key*. Choice (C) would be a response to a remark about not having a key.

27. **(C)** Choice (C) is a logical response to a tag question about *what page*. Choice (A) answers *when*, not *what page*. Choice (B) confuses *on* with *under* and does not answer *what page*.

28. **(B)** Choice (B) is a logical response to a question about *Where*. Choice (A) confuses similar-sounding words *wait* and *weigh*. Choice (C) is incorrect; *waited* (past tense) does not match *should wait* (present-future) and answers *How long* (an hour) but not *Where*.

29. **(A)** Choice (A) answers the *How long* question. Choice (B) confuses similar-sounding words *cord* and *card*. Choice (C) would answer a *When* question.

30. **(A)** Choice (A) is a logical response to a question about *sending a memo*. Choice (B) confuses sending with *shipping department* (any department can send and receive memos). Choice (C) confuses related words *departments* with *department store*.

31. **(C)** The second speaker offers to give the first speaker money for the bus. Choice (A) confuses *rush* with the similar-sounding word *bus*. Choice (B) uses the word *change* out of context.

PART 3: CONVERSATIONS

32. **(B)** The man says that he called at 7:00. Choice (A) is the time that the man got home. Choice (C) confuses *eight* with the similar-sounding word *great*. Choice (D) is the time that the woman went to bed.

33. **(D)** The woman says she didn't hear the phone because she had the TV on. Choice (A) is the man's guess. Choice (B) confuses *singing* with the similar-sounding word *ringing*. Choice (C) is what the woman did later on.

34. **(A)** The man says that he wanted to invite the woman to a party. Choice (B) is what the woman was watching on TV. Choice (C) confuses *walk* with the similar-sounding word *work*. Choice (D) repeats the word *work*.

35. **(A)** The woman says that the room is *quite spacious*. Choice (B) is incorrect because she only mentions one bed in that room. Choice (C) is confused with *available*, which she says about room 217. Choice (D) is what she says about room 217.

36. **(B)** The man is concerned about crowds at the pool and says, *Could you give me something less noisy?* Choice (A) is what he does not want. Choices (C) and (D) describe the rooms suggested by the woman.

37. **(D)** The man says he wants to get some rest. Choice (A) confuses the word *sweater* with the similar-sounding word *better*. Choice (B) repeats the word *pool*. Choice (C) is what he will do later.

38. **(C)** The man says he needs someone to turn off the alarm on the emergency exit door. Choice (A) is incorrect because the door was opened. Choice (B) is related to *alarm*. Choice (D) is confused with the fact that they are looking for Jerry, but he isn't lost.

39. **(D)** The speakers are responsible for getting the alarm turned off, and Jerry will help them, so they must all work together. Choices (A) and (B) are related to *accident* and *emergency*. Choice (C) could be a reason for an alarm going off, but it is not the cause here.

40. **(C)** The man says he will try to contact Jerry on his cell phone. Choice (A) repeats the word *time*. Choice (B) repeats the word *phone*. Choice (D) is what Jerry is doing now.

41. **(A)** The man complains that the tour guide was in a hurry. Choice (B) confuses *any* with the similar-sounding word *many*. Choice (C) uses the word *back* out of context. Choice (D) repeats the word *paintings*.

42. **(C)** The woman suggests that the man go back on his own. Choice (A) repeats the word *tour*. Choice (B) repeats the word *hurry*. Choice (D) uses the word *own* out of context.

43. **(B)** The man says, *it costs so much to get in*. Choices (A) and (D) repeat words from the conversation. Choice (C) is not mentioned.

44. **(D)** The man says that he doesn't like to park in the city. Choice (A) is associated with the fact that the woman pays a lot for parking, but the man doesn't give it as a reason. Choice (B) is the reason the woman drives. Choice (C) repeats the word *train*.

45. **(B)** The woman parks in the garage downstairs. Choice (A) uses the word *park* out of context. Choice (C) is the man's guess. Choice (D) repeats the word *train*.

46. **(A)** The man says, *Who can afford that?*, meaning he thinks it is too expensive for most people. Choices (B), (C), and (D) are plausible but not mentioned.

47. **(B)** The man was looking for a post office close enough to walk to. Choice (A) confuses *closed* with the similar-sounding word *close*. Choice (C) is incorrect because the woman says, *You can't miss it*. Choice (D) confuses *underground* with the similar-sounding word *around*.

48. **(B)** The woman tells the man to take the bus. Choice (A) confuses *car* with the similar-sounding word *far*. Choice (C) is how the man wanted to go. Choice (D) is not mentioned.

49. **(C)** This is the man's response to the woman's saying that to get to the post office takes *just a five-minute bus ride*. He means it seems like a short and easy trip. Choices (A), (B), and (D) don't fit the context.

50. **(D)** The woman is explaining company benefits to a new employee. Choice (A) repeats the word *manager*. Choice (B) repeats the

word *assistant.* Choice (C) associates *travel agent* with *vacation.*

51. **(D)** Employees get paid *every two weeks,* which amounts to twice a month. Choice (A) repeats the word *once.* Choice (B) confuses *twice a week* with *every two weeks.* Choice (C) is what the man says he doesn't prefer.

52. **(B)** When the woman explains that the man will get three weeks paid vacation, he responds, *Three weeks? Fantastic.* Choice (A) is mentioned by the woman, but the man makes no response to this information. Choice (C) is incorrect because the only thing mentioned about paychecks is how often they are issued. Choice (D) is not mentioned.

53. **(C)** The man says they will leave for the airport. Choice (A) is where they will leave from. Choice (B) confuses *store* with the similar-sounding word *more.* Choice (D) confuses *train* with the similar-sounding word *rain.*

54. **(C)** The man says he wants to leave at 3:00. Choice (A) confuses *noon* with the similar-sounding word *soon.* Choice (B) confuses *two* with the similar-sounding word *too.* Choice (D) confuses *ten* with the similar-sounding word *then.*

55. **(C)** The man mentions the *heavy traffic.* Choice (A) repeats the word *early.* Choice (B) confuses *hurry* with the similar-sounding word *worry.* Choice (D) uses the word *way* out of context.

56. **(A)** The speakers are discussing borrowing books and videos and reading magazines and newspapers and there is a fine for things that are overdue, so it is a library. Choice (B) is incorrect because you buy, not borrow, books at a bookstore. Choices (C) and (D) are other places where you might read magazines and newspapers.

57. **(B)** The woman says she will take a novel, which is a type of book. Choices (A), (C), and (D) are other types of reading material mentioned in the conversation.

58. **(D)** After the man mentions the fine for overdue materials, the woman says, *I'll be sure to return it on time,* and if she does this, she won't owe a fine. Choice (A) confuses similar-sounding words *nine* and *fine.* Choice (B) is not mentioned. Choice (C) is the amount of the fine that the woman wants to avoid paying.

59. **(A)** The woman suggests lunch at a sidewalk café and then says, *We could sit outside* . . . . Choice (B) associates *coffee* and *café.* Choice (C) refers to what the man brought for lunch. Choice (D) repeats the word *home.*

60. **(B)** The man says he is planning to have lunch in the park, and the woman agrees to meet him there. Choice (A) is what the woman originally suggested. Choice (C) is where they will return after lunch. Choice (D) is confused with the description of the café.

61. **(C)** This is the man's response to the woman's offer—*Should I bring you a cookie, too?* Choices (A), (B), and (D) don't fit the context.

62. **(A)** The woman says, *I was charged for three nights, but I stayed only one.* Choices (B) and (D) are not mentioned. Choice (C) is the number of nights she was charged for.

63. **(C)** The man says, *I gave you another guest's bill by mistake.* Choices (A) and (D) are not mentioned. Choice (B) is what the man originally guesses might be the problem.

64. **(C)** The woman asks, *Will you take a personal check?* Choice (A) is confused with the mention of *check* and *cash.* Choice (B) repeats the word *bank.* Choice (D) confuses *business card* with *credit card.*

65. **(C)** The woman says she was trying to order *ski boots.* Choices (A) and (D) sound similar to the correct answer. Choice (B) is not mentioned.

66. **(A)** The coupon expires June 30 and the man says, *Today's July 3rd.* Choice (B) is incorrect because the code that the woman gives the man is the same as the code on the coupon. Choice (C) is incorrect because the charge for the order is $175, and the coupon is good, for purchases over $150. Choice (D) is incorrect because the coupon states it is good for online purchases.

67. **(D)** The man says, *I'll e-mail you a coupon for 20 percent off your next order.* Choice (A) is incorrect because no refund is mentioned.

Choice (B) is incorrect because shipping fees are not mentioned. Choice (C) is what the woman thought she would get.

68. **(A)** The man says the chairs are for the conference room. Choices (B) and (D) are not mentioned. Choice (C) is where they will put the table.

69. **(B)** The woman says, *look how much they charge for shipping*, and the man says, *It is more than most companies charge*. Choice (A) is incorrect because they say there is next day delivery. Choice (C) is incorrect because no extra fee is mentioned for the next day delivery. Choice (D) is not mentioned.

70. **(A)** The woman says not to spend more than $75, and this is the only table that fits that description. Choices (B), (C), and (D) all cost too much.

PART 4: TALKS

71. **(C)** *Senior citizens* means *elderly people*. Choices (A), (B), and (D) are not mentioned.

72. **(B)** The speaker reminds passengers that only one carry-on bag per passenger is allowed and then says, *Please give any extra bags to the gate agent before boarding the plane*. Choices (A) and (C) are plausible but not mentioned. Choice (D) is what should be asked of the flight attendants.

73. **(D)** The other passengers are asked to stay away from the door until they hear their row numbers called. Choice (A) is the opposite of the correct answer. Choice (B) is confused with *request assistance from a flight attendant*. Choice (C) uses the word *call* out of context.

74. **(C)** This ad is for *professional* books. Choices (A) and (B) would not be sold at such a store. Choice (D) is incorrect; textbooks are for students who are not yet professionals.

75. **(D)** They will *order it*. Choice (A) is unnecessary if they can order it. Choice (B) would not help in getting the book. Choice (C) is not logical.

76. **(C)** The store sells scientific and technical journals. Choice (A) confuses *newspapers* with

the similar-sounding word *newest*. Choice (B) confuses *carry-alls* with *carry all*. Choice (D) is not mentioned.

77. **(B)** The speaker is a weather reporter and follows this sentence with a report of good weather: *The fantastic weather we've been enjoying all week will continue for a while longer*. Choices (A), (C), and (D) don't fit the context.

78. **(D)** The speaker reports warm and sunny weather for today, then says, *Tomorrow morning will be the same, but by early afternoon we'll have cloudy skies and scattered rain showers*. Choice (A) repeats the word *today*. Choice (B) confuses similar-sounding words *tonight* and *overnight*. Choice (C) is when the weather will be the same.

79. **(A)** The speaker says that on Monday *the skies should be clear and sunny once more*. Choices (B) and (D) are how the weather will be from tomorrow afternoon until Monday. Choice (C) is not mentioned.

80. **(D)** The subway is *to the shopping mall and suburbs*. Choices (A) and (C) are contradicted by *to the northern suburbs*. Choice (B) is not mentioned.

81. **(A)** The announcement says to catch *the gray line to the airport*. Choice (B) is the current line. Choices (C) and (D) are not mentioned.

82. **(C)** The announcer says that airport trains leave every fifteen minutes. Choices (A) and (B) are confused with *2:05*, the time that the next train is due. Choice (D) sounds similar to the correct answer.

83. **(C)** *Things will close* because of *the federal holiday*. Choice (A) is incorrectly suggested by *weekend schedule*. Choice (B) is contradicted by *public transportation will operate*. Choice (D) is not mentioned.

84. **(A)** The announcement says there will be *no additional buses or trains for rush hour service*. Choice (B) is confused with *operate on a weekend schedule*. Choices (C) and (D) are unlikely if transportation follows weekend service.

85. **(C)** The announcer says that parking is free downtown. Choice (A) is incorrect because public garages are closed today. Choice (B) is incorrect because some of them will be charging weekend rates. Choice (D) is associated with *buses*.

86. **(D)** This was a *survey of business travelers*. Choices (A), (B), and (C) do not travel much on business.

87. **(C)** Hotels should be located close to *shopping and entertainment facilities*. Choice (A) is where they don't want hotels located. Choices (B) and (D) are not mentioned.

88. **(A)** *To provide access* means that *facilities should be open*. Choice (B) is not mentioned. Choice (C) confuses *light snacks* and serving *lighter meals*. Choice (D) is not mentioned.

89. **(D)** The speaker is a tour guide speaking to a group of tourists; she mentions that listeners have found their seats and says that the tour will get started as *soon as our driver is ready*, so they are on a bus. Choice (A) is associated with *seats*. Choices (B) and (C) are where they will go later.

90. **(B)** The speaker explains where they will eat lunch, then says, *then we'll head over to the botanical gardens*. Choice (A) is what they will do earlier. Choice (C) repeats the word *buildings*. Choice (D) is plausible but not mentioned.

91. **(C)** Before saying this phrase, the speaker mentions that listeners may want to find out more about something. Then she says, *I'm happy to explain anything you want to know*, meaning that she will gladly answer questions. Choices (A), (B), and (D) do not fit the context.

92. **(C)** The speaker says, *Select your clothes*. Choice (A) repeats the word *suitcase*. Choice (B) repeats the word *clothes*. Choice (D) repeats the word *medicine*.

93. **(B)** The speaker suggests packing heavier items first. Choices (A), (C), and (D) are other things mentioned by the speaker.

94. **(C)** The speaker suggests that clear plastic bags let security officers see what's inside them. Choices (A) and (B) are other things

mentioned by the speaker. Choice (D), shoes, are mentioned, but slip-on shoes are not.

95. **(B)** The speaker says about the ink, *The dark blue looks great*, that is, she likes it. Choice (A) repeats the word *dark*. Choice (C) is what she says about the black ink and is why she prefers the blue. Choice (D) is the ink color that she does not prefer.

96. **(C)** The speaker says, *I think it would look better if you dragged the words that are under my name just a bit lower*. The words under her name are *sound engineer*, a job title. Choices (A), (B), and (D) are other kinds of information on the card, but the speaker does not ask for them to be moved.

97. **(A)** The speakers says, *send the invoice to my e-mail address*. Choices (B), (C), and (D) are plausible but not mentioned.

98. **(B)** The speaker is a restaurant manager or chef explaining the evening's specials to the servers. Choices (A), (C), and (D) are related to the topic of restaurant meals but not mentioned.

99. **(C)** The speaker says that some of the menu items are starred, and that *Those are the vegetarian dishes*, and eggplant stew is one of the starred items. Choices (A), (B) and (D) are plausible things to say about a menu item but not mentioned.

100. **(D)** The speaker says, *it's Saturday, and that means we can expect the biggest crowd of the week*. Choices (A), (B), and (C) are plausible but not mentioned.

Reading

PART 5: INCOMPLETE SENTENCES

101. **(B)** The present tense in the *if* clause of a real condition can use future tense in the other clause. Choice (A) is past tense. Choice (C) is past perfect tense. Choice (D) is present progressive tense.

102. **(C)** *Until* joins the clauses; it is logical. Choices (A) and (D) are not logical. Choice (B) is used in relative clauses or in time clauses.

103. **(A)** *Recall* means *remember*. Choices (B), (C), and (D) have meanings that don't fit the context.

104. **(D)** Someone else *enclosed* the envelope; use the past participle. Choice (A) has an unnecessary *is*. Choice (B) is the simple form of the verb. Choice (C) is the present participle.

105. **(C)** *Advice* is something a realtor (a professional who helps people buy and sell houses) can provide. Choices (A), (B), and (D) all refer to a person, not something a realtor can provide.

106. **(B)** The phrasal verb *find out* means *learn* or *discover*. Choices (A), (C), and (D) can also be used with *out*, but they have meanings that don't fit the context.

107. **(B)** *Decrease* means *go down*. It is logical to expect that when oil prices drop, or go down, the overall cost of raw materials will also go down. Choices (A) and (C) both mean *go up* or *get bigger*. Choice (D) means *flatten* or *become balanced*.

108. **(A)** The adjective *effective* modifies *way*. Choices (B) and (C) are nouns. Choice (D) is an adverb.

109. **(D)** Join contrasting clauses with *but*. Choices (A), (B), and (C) are not logical.

110. **(C)** The adjective *busy* is generally used with the preposition *with*. Choices (A), (B), and (D) are prepositions, but they are not generally used with *busy*.

111. **(D)** *Head of operations* requires a singular verb. Choice (A) is a gerund. Choice (B) is plural. Choice (C) is the simple form.

112. **(B)** *Representative* is a noun referring to a person. Choice (A) is a noun, but it does not refer to a person. Choices (C) and (D) are verbs.

113. **(C)** *In* means *inside*. Choices (A), (B), and (D) do not fit the context.

114. **(B)** *Neither* pairs with *nor* to refer to a negative choice. Choices (A), (C), and (D) cannot be used with *nor*.

115. **(D)** The causative *had* is followed by the simple form. Choice (A) is an infinitive. Choice (B) is past tense. Choice (C) is the past participle.

116. **(C)** *Mandates* means *demands* and is often used when talking about a law. Choices (A), (B), and (D) have meanings that don't fit the context.

117. **(A)** *Tends* means *has the habit of*. Choices (B), (C), and (D) have meanings that don't fit the context.

118. **(D)** A marketing *campaign* is a planned course of action designed to sell a product. Choices (A), (B), and (C) have meanings that don't fit the context.

119. **(A)** *Their* is a possessive adjective with the antecedent *Mr. and Mrs. Xiao*. Choice (B) is a subject pronoun. Choice (C) is an object pronoun. Choice (D) is a contraction with a subject pronoun.

120. **(D)** *Repairs* is the only noun among the options. Choices (A), (B), and (C) do not fit the context of the sentence.

121. **(C)** In this sentence, a *code* is a set of numbers used to unlock a door. Choices (A), (B), and (D) do not fit the context.

122. **(B)** The causative *suggest* is followed by a gerund. Choice (A) is past tense. Choice (C) is present tense. Choice (D) is an infinitive.

123. **(A)** The main verb *ask* is followed by an infinitive. Choice (B) is future tense. Choice (C) is a gerund. Choice (D) is past tense.

124. **(C)** The comparative *more* is followed by an adjective and *than*. Choice (A) omits *than*. Choice (B) is an adverb. Choice (D) is an incomplete *as-as* comparison.

125. **(B)** *Because* establishes a cause-and-effect relationship. Choices (A), (C), and (D) are not logical.

126. **(C)** The causative *request* is followed by the simple form of the verb. Choice (A) is a gerund. Choice (B) is present tense. Choice (D) is an infinitive.

127. **(D)** *Who* refers to the subject *person*. Choice (A) is possessive. Choice (B) refers to things. Choice (C) is objective.

128. **(C)** Equal comparisons use *as* + adjective + *as*; *the memo* is causing people to become confused, so the adjective must be the present participle. Choice (A) omits the second *as*. Choice (B) omits the first *as*. Choice (D) uses the past participle.

129. **(A)** Since *know* happened before *was*, it must also be past tense. Choice (B) is the past participle. Choice (C) is present progressive tense. Choice (D) is past perfect tense.

130. **(B)** Commands are in the simple form of the verb. Choice (A) is present progressive tense. Choice (C) is present tense. Choice (D) is the future tense.

PART 6: TEXT COMPLETION

131. **(D)** The letter is about a rebate on a product. This sentence logically precedes the sentence explaining that the company cannot honor *it* (meaning the rebate card) because it was mailed in too late. Choices (A), (B), and (C) do not fit the context.

132. **(C)** The date for using the rebate card had passed; this is the meaning of *expired*. Choices (A), (B), and (D) don't fit the context.

133. **(A)** *Would like* is followed by an infinitive verb. Choice (B) is a gerund. Choice (C) is simple past tense. Choice (D) is a future form.

134. **(B)** The company is sending the customer a page of coupons; coupons are a form of *discount*. Choices (A), (C), and (D) are words that are related to *products*, but they don't have the correct meaning.

135. **(D)** This is probably a yearly, or *annual*, tournament. Since the tournament is two months away, Choices (A), (B), and (C) are not likely.

136. **(B)** *Hand out* means to *distribute* or *give away*. Choice (A) creates a word that means *submit*. Choice (C) creates a word that means *give up possession*. Choice (D) creates a word that means *give away something no longer useful*.

137. **(C)** During the tournament, the company *raised*, or *collected money that it needed* to give to charity. Choices (A), (B), and (D) are all words that are related to money, but they don't fit the context.

138. **(A)** This sentence is a logical conclusion to an e-mail asking for staff help to plan an event to raise money for charity and logically follows the sentence setting a goal. Choices (B), (C), and (D) do not fit the context.

139. **(B)** This is a comparison using the word *than*, so an adjective with *more* is needed. Choice (A) is an adjective, but it is not a comparative form. Choices (C) and (D) are superlative adjectives, which are not used with *than*.

140. **(A)** The verb must agree with the singular subject *air quality*. Choices (B), (C), and (D) are verbs that agree with a plural subject.

141. **(B)** Premature means *too early*. Choices (A), (C), and (D) look similar to the correct answer but have very different meanings.

142. **(C)** The preceding sentence mentions the problem of poor air quality created by new paint and cleaning products, and this sentence adds further information to that, mentioning the need for good ventilation to disperse the fumes. Choices (A), (B), and (D) do not fit the context.

143. **(A)** The verb *let* is followed by the base form of a verb. Choice (B) is simple present tense. Choice (C) is an infinitive. Choice (D) is a gerund.

144. **(D)** *As well* means also. Choices (A) and (C) are used to introduce additional information to a paragraph. Choice (B) means *in place of*.

145. **(D)** In the preceding sentence, the writer asks whether snacks should be ordered, and this sentence explains the reason for that suggestion. Choices (A), (B), and (C) do not fit the context.

146. **(B)** The sentence compares Conference Room 2 to Conference Room 1, so a comparative adjective is used. Choice (A) is a simple adjective. Choice (C) is an adverb. Choice (D) is a superlative form.

PART 7: READING COMPREHENSION

147. **(B)** The information states, *A deposit equivalent to the cost of one night's stay is required to hold the reservation and must be paid within 14 days*, and the cost of one night's stay is $100. Choice (A) is incorrect because a deposit is required. Choice (C) is not mentioned. Choice (D) is the cost of a three-night's stay.

148. **(A)** The information states, *Cancellation must be made within 7 days of check-in date in order for the deposit to be refunded*, but September 9 is only one day before the check-in date. Choices (B), (C), and (D) are plausible but not mentioned.

149. **(C)** A stockbroker is likely to attend to learn how he/she can better assist clients. Choice (A) is contradicted by *clients*. Choice (B) confuses *manager* and *management firm*. Choice (D) is not likely.

150. **(C)** The seminar will help you learn about how you can predict trends for successful investments. Choices (A) and (B) are mentioned, but they are not what will be discussed. Choice (D) repeats the word *clients*.

151. **(B)** The schedule says *effective March 1*. Choices (A), (C), and (D) are not mentioned.

152. **(D)** Peak hours are listed as occurring on weekdays 5:30–9:30 A.M. and 3:00–7:00 P.M., that is, twice a day. Choice (A) is incorrect because only weekdays are mentioned, so we can assume there are no peak hours on weekends. Choice (B) repeats the word *zone*. Choice (C) repeats *March 1*.

153. **(A)** Ms. Arnault needs a ride to the dinner because her car is in the shop, and when Mr. Geller can't help her, she decides to ride with Liz. Choices (B), (C), and (D) are related to the topic of going to a dinner but are not mentioned.

154. **(D)** *Hold on* can mean *wait*, and Mr. Geller is asking Ms. Arnault to wait while he talks with Liz to find out the answer to Ms. Arnault's question, *Do you know if Liz is going?* Choices (A), (B), and (C) do not fit the meaning of the phrase or the context.

155. **(B)** *Consumer preferences* means *what consumers like*. Choices (A) and (C) are likely uses for this information, but they are not the duties of the Specialist. Choice (D) is incorrect; product testing is a way to discover consumer preferences, but it is not explicitly mentioned.

156. **(D)** The Specialist will write reports *for use within the company*. Choice (A) is incorrect; the reports will be *about* the consumer. Choices (B) and (C) are contradicted by *within the company*.

157. **(A)** The qualifications are *a college degree in research and experience in advertising*. Choice (B) is not logical. Choice (C) is not mentioned. Choice (D) is related, but not necessary.

158. **(B)** *Reduced costs* and *lowered costs* have the same meaning; they also had a higher number of *profitable routes*. Choices (A), (C), and (D) are not mentioned.

159. **(C)** The fax describes the improved routes as *short-haul markets where it [the airline] has built its strong base*. This means that the company already has many customers on its shorter routes. Choice (A) is the routes the company is cutting out. Choices (B) and (D) are not mentioned.

160. **(D)** This sentence advising to keep this stock is a logical conclusion to the fax describing the forecast for this stock. Choices (A), (B), and (C) are not a logical context for this sentence.

161. **(C)** The passage states, *Supervisors must approve any and all vacations longer than one week*. Choice (A) is incorrect because longer vacations are allowed, with approval. Choices (B) and (D) are plausible but not mentioned.

162. **(B)** The passage gives one reason for denial as *you have had other frequent absences*. Choice (A) repeats the word *team*. Choice (C) confuses *hard worker* with *heavy workload*. Choice (D) is plausible but not mentioned.

163. **(A)** The passage states that if a vacation request has been denied, *please contact the Personnel Review Board*. Choices (B), (C), and (D) are plausible but not mentioned.

164. **(D)** This information explains how a company an offer *employees a discount on annual and monthly memberships and day and weekend passes* by becoming a Corporate Member. Choice (A) is incorrect because this is not an advertisement. Choice (B) is too general – the information is about a specific type of membership. Choice (C) is incorrect because the information is about membership rather than the specifics of a health and wellness program.

165. **(A)** The membership description mentions *all three of our pools and both our fitness rooms.* Choice (B) refers to the mention of the steam rooms and saunas but no mention is made of when they were added. Choices (C) and (D) are both incorrect because no specifics are given about the location or uses of the pools.

166. **(C)** The membership description mentions *swimming lessons and fitness classes at no extra charge.* Choices (A) and (B) are not mentioned. Choice (D) refers to the class schedule but not mention is made of whether or how often it changes.

167. **(A)** The information explains that the cost of Corporate Membership is based on the number of employees that use it and that *if this number grows beyond what you have paid, the fee will be amended the following year.* Choice (B) is incorrect because the membership is for both individuals and families. Choice (C) is not mentioned. Choice (D) is confused with the mention of the increase of staff that use the benefit. This does not refer to the size of the entire staff. Only to those who use the membership.

168. **(C)** The passage states, *Although its revenues have not matched those of its first two years in business, they had been increasing steadily since June. Revenues* means *earnings*, so earnings have been increasing, or going up, since June. Choices (A), (B), and (D) are related to the topic of the article but are not mentioned.

169. **(B)** The article states that Mr. Reinartz, the chairman, *will probably resign soon.* Choice (A) is not likely as the article mentions job cuts and the probability of a new chairman. Choice (C) is exactly what the chairman has been unable to do. Choice (D) is confused with the international offices that were opened by the current vice president.

170. **(A)** Ms. Strube has made the international branches more profitable. Choices (B), (C), and (D) are not mentioned in the passage.

171. **(A)** In this sentence, *this* refers to the cutting of 4,000 jobs mentioned in the previous sentence. Cutting jobs is part of an attempt to fix this business that has been losing money. Choices (B), (C), and (D) are not a logical context for this sentence.

172. **(D)** Ms. Jones and Ms. Adams are talking about preparing food for a wedding and some parties, so they are probably caterers. Choice (A) is confused with the suppliers they use. Choices (B) and (C) are other types of food-related businesses.

173. **(C)** Ms. Adams writes, *Last time half the berries they sent were rotten.* Choices (A), (B), and (D) are plausible but not mentioned.

174. **(B)** *All set* can mean ready, and this is Ms. Adams' response to Ms. Jones' writing that she has ordered the food for the Wilson party. Choices (A), (C), and (D) do not fit the meaning of the phrase or the context.

175. **(A)** Ms. Adams asks Ms. Jones to contact the farm and ask about the price of strawberries and later when again discussing Hammond farm, Ms. Jones writes, *I'll get back to you this afternoon as soon as I've talked to them.* Choice (B) is incorrect because she only mentions contacting the farm, not visiting it. Choice (C) refers to the cake for the Wilson party, but no mention is made of when it will be finished. Choice (D) is not mentioned.

176. **(B)** The caller wanted advice for turning off the water to stop the flood, not for cleaning up. Choice (A) is true because a problem with a new dishwasher was the reason for the call. Choices (C) and (D) are both things the caller mentioned as upsetting her.

177. **(B)** The meeting policy was changed because of problems with handling the help line calls. Choice (A) is not true; the minutes of each meeting will be posted, probably because all employees will want to be able to see them. Choice (C) is also not true. Customers have complained about having to wait to get help but there is no mention of staff members complaining. Choice (D) is mentioned in the memo as a disadvantage of attending meetings, but this comes from management, not from the employees themselves and is mentioned as a side effect, not as the main reason.

178. **(B)** She called on a Thursday morning, which, according to the notice is when staff meetings are held and therefore only one person is available to work the phones. Choice (A) is not true because somebody answered the phone even though they immediately put the caller on hold. Choice (C) is the number of unattended phones. Choice (D) is the number of phones normally in operation.

179. **(C)** The meeting minutes will be posted in the staff room. Choices (A), (B) and (D) are not mentioned.

180. **(C)** The company handled the problem by releasing call center employees from the weekly meetings so that there would be enough people to answer the phones. Choice (A) was a complaint made in the customer's fax. Choice (B) uses words from the texts but is not mentioned. Choice (D) confuses a notice for the customer with the notice for call center employees.

181. **(C)** The operators are all student interns. Choice (A) is incorrect because the e-mail is addressed to three people only. Choice (B) is incorrect because the operators are interns, or trainees, not trainers. Choice (D) is incorrect because the e-mail is addressed to three operators only.

182. **(A)** Park Gi refers the interns to a page in their manuals that states the rules. Choices (B), (C), and (D) are all people mentioned in the texts, but Park Gi does not refer the interns to them.

183. **(C)** Chong Dae says that she changed the message to include her own name and her job title. Choice (A) is what another intern put in her voice mail message. Choice (B) is not mentioned. Choice (D) is mentioned but she did not include this information in her voice mail message.

184. **(C)** Chong Dae changed the recording after a customer said that calling a person by a number instead of a name was impersonal. Choices (A), (B), and (D) are related to the topic, but they are not mentioned.

185. **(B)** Chong Dae says she hasn't changed the recording back to the original one because she wasn't sure if this was allowed. Choice (A) is mentioned; the rule is in the manual. Choice (C) is implied by the wording of the rule in the manual. Choice (D) is explained very clearly—the interns may be asked to move to a new department at any time, leaving their phone and voice mail to be used by another person.

186. **(D)** The ad mentions time away from the office and *busy business workers like you*. Choice (A) is confused with the golf vacation, but it is not the only kind of vacation listed. Choice (B) is not mentioned. Choice (C) repeats the word *students*.

187. **(A)** The ad states, *Book a vacation this month and receive 25% off the regular price*. Choice (B) repeats the phrase *the end of the year*. Choice (C) is plausible but not mentioned. Choice (D) is the recommended time to travel but is not associated with the discount.

188. **(C)** The information states, *from $600*, meaning the price starts at $600 and goes up from there, presumably depending on which features the customer chooses. Choice (A) repeats the word *golf*, but no lessons are mentioned, so we don't know whether or not they are included. Choice (B) is incorrect because meals are not mentioned, so we don't know whether or not they are included. Choice (D) describes vacation Package D.

189. **(D)** Mr. Gerard explains why he wants to take a vacation in May and writes, *I hope you will be able to approve this request*. Choice (A) is incorrect because Mr. Gerard writes that he already knows who can do this. Choice (B) mentions the vacation deals, but they are not the purpose of the e-mail. Choice (C) is confused with Mr. Gerard's describing the vacation he wants to take.

190. **(A)** The form indicates that Mr. Gerard wants to take Package B, which is, according to the ad, the Caribbean Cruise. Choices (B), (C), and (D) refer to other vacations mentioned in the ad.

191. **(A)** According to the notice, a ticket for a weekday matinee (that is, afternoon

performance) costs $40. Choices (B), (C), and (D) are prices of other kinds of tickets.

192. **(A)** The notice says, *All tickets must be bought in advance at www.nscpa.org,* that is, online. Choice (B) is incorrect because all tickets must be bought through a website. Choices (C) and (D) are plausible but not mentioned.

193. **(C)** The information on the ticket states, *In the event that there is a cancellation by the theater, a refund for this ticket may be issued.* Choices (A) and (B) are plausible but not mentioned. Choice (D) is incorrect because even though the ticket states that it is nonrefundable, this is followed by the mention that there may be refunds if an event is canceled.

194. **(D)** The date on the ticket is January 4, and, according to the notice, an opera will be performed on that date. Choices (A), (B), and (C) are performances that will take place on other dates.

195. **(D)** Ms. Osann writes, *I'll have my car with me, so I can swing by your office and pick you up.* Choice (A) is related to the discussion of the tickets but is not mentioned. Choice (B) repeats the word *supper,* but Ms. Osann does not offer to pay for it. Choice (C) is confused with the report that Ms. Osann is working on for her job.

196. **(A)** Ms. Davenport writes, *I recently accepted a position with the Sylvan Company, which means I will be moving to Winchester.* Choices

(B) and (D) are plausible but not mentioned. Choice (C) repeats the word *family.*

197. **(D)** The listing says, *On bus and subway lines.* Choices (A) and (B) are mentioned in other listings. Choice (C) is incorrect because Listing A has the lowest rent.

198. **(B)** Ms. Davenport's e-mail indicates that she wants a two- or three-bedroom apartment with garage parking that is near schools, and this is the only listing that meets all those criteria. Choices (A), (C), and (D) meet some but not all of these criteria.

199. **(C)** Mr. Haskell is responding to Ms. Davenport's request that he show her some apartments, and he suggests a time for that. Choice (A) is incorrect because the e-mail indicates that he already knows this information. Choice (B) is not mentioned and is presumably what he will do when they meet. Choice (D) is incorrect because he is writing to someone who already knows about his business.

200. **(B)** Mr. Haskell writes, *If you will let me know the address where you will be staying . . . .* Choice (A) is incorrect because he offers to meet her at the place where she is staying. Choice (C) is incorrect because it is Mr. Haskell who will pick up Ms. Davenport. Choice (D) is not mentioned and is presumably what Mr. Haskell will do.

ANSWER SHEET
Practice Test 5

LISTENING COMPREHENSION

Part 1: Photographs

1. Ⓐ Ⓑ Ⓒ Ⓓ
2. Ⓐ Ⓑ Ⓒ Ⓓ
3. Ⓐ Ⓑ Ⓒ Ⓓ
4. Ⓐ Ⓑ Ⓒ Ⓓ
5. Ⓐ Ⓑ Ⓒ Ⓓ
6. Ⓐ Ⓑ Ⓒ Ⓓ

Part 2: Question-Response

7. Ⓐ Ⓑ Ⓒ
8. Ⓐ Ⓑ Ⓒ
9. Ⓐ Ⓑ Ⓒ
10. Ⓐ Ⓑ Ⓒ
11. Ⓐ Ⓑ Ⓒ
12. Ⓐ Ⓑ Ⓒ
13. Ⓐ Ⓑ Ⓒ
14. Ⓐ Ⓑ Ⓒ
15. Ⓐ Ⓑ Ⓒ
16. Ⓐ Ⓑ Ⓒ
17. Ⓐ Ⓑ Ⓒ
18. Ⓐ Ⓑ Ⓒ
19. Ⓐ Ⓑ Ⓒ
20. Ⓐ Ⓑ Ⓒ
21. Ⓐ Ⓑ Ⓒ
22. Ⓐ Ⓑ Ⓒ
23. Ⓐ Ⓑ Ⓒ
24. Ⓐ Ⓑ Ⓒ
25. Ⓐ Ⓑ Ⓒ
26. Ⓐ Ⓑ Ⓒ
27. Ⓐ Ⓑ Ⓒ
28. Ⓐ Ⓑ Ⓒ
29. Ⓐ Ⓑ Ⓒ
30. Ⓐ Ⓑ Ⓒ
31. Ⓐ Ⓑ Ⓒ

Part 3: Conversations

32. Ⓐ Ⓑ Ⓒ Ⓓ
33. Ⓐ Ⓑ Ⓒ Ⓓ
34. Ⓐ Ⓑ Ⓒ Ⓓ
35. Ⓐ Ⓑ Ⓒ Ⓓ
36. Ⓐ Ⓑ Ⓒ Ⓓ
37. Ⓐ Ⓑ Ⓒ Ⓓ
38. Ⓐ Ⓑ Ⓒ Ⓓ
39. Ⓐ Ⓑ Ⓒ Ⓓ
40. Ⓐ Ⓑ Ⓒ Ⓓ
41. Ⓐ Ⓑ Ⓒ Ⓓ
42. Ⓐ Ⓑ Ⓒ Ⓓ
43. Ⓐ Ⓑ Ⓒ Ⓓ
44. Ⓐ Ⓑ Ⓒ Ⓓ
45. Ⓐ Ⓑ Ⓒ Ⓓ
46. Ⓐ Ⓑ Ⓒ Ⓓ
47. Ⓐ Ⓑ Ⓒ Ⓓ
48. Ⓐ Ⓑ Ⓒ Ⓓ
49. Ⓐ Ⓑ Ⓒ Ⓓ
50. Ⓐ Ⓑ Ⓒ Ⓓ
51. Ⓐ Ⓑ Ⓒ Ⓓ
52. Ⓐ Ⓑ Ⓒ Ⓓ
53. Ⓐ Ⓑ Ⓒ Ⓓ
54. Ⓐ Ⓑ Ⓒ Ⓓ
55. Ⓐ Ⓑ Ⓒ Ⓓ
56. Ⓐ Ⓑ Ⓒ Ⓓ
57. Ⓐ Ⓑ Ⓒ Ⓓ
58. Ⓐ Ⓑ Ⓒ Ⓓ
59. Ⓐ Ⓑ Ⓒ Ⓓ
60. Ⓐ Ⓑ Ⓒ Ⓓ
61. Ⓐ Ⓑ Ⓒ Ⓓ
62. Ⓐ Ⓑ Ⓒ Ⓓ
63. Ⓐ Ⓑ Ⓒ Ⓓ
64. Ⓐ Ⓑ Ⓒ Ⓓ
65. Ⓐ Ⓑ Ⓒ Ⓓ
66. Ⓐ Ⓑ Ⓒ Ⓓ
67. Ⓐ Ⓑ Ⓒ Ⓓ
68. Ⓐ Ⓑ Ⓒ Ⓓ
69. Ⓐ Ⓑ Ⓒ Ⓓ
70. Ⓐ Ⓑ Ⓒ Ⓓ

Part 4: Talks

71. Ⓐ Ⓑ Ⓒ Ⓓ
72. Ⓐ Ⓑ Ⓒ Ⓓ
73. Ⓐ Ⓑ Ⓒ Ⓓ
74. Ⓐ Ⓑ Ⓒ Ⓓ
75. Ⓐ Ⓑ Ⓒ Ⓓ
76. Ⓐ Ⓑ Ⓒ Ⓓ
77. Ⓐ Ⓑ Ⓒ Ⓓ
78. Ⓐ Ⓑ Ⓒ Ⓓ
79. Ⓐ Ⓑ Ⓒ Ⓓ
80. Ⓐ Ⓑ Ⓒ Ⓓ
81. Ⓐ Ⓑ Ⓒ Ⓓ
82. Ⓐ Ⓑ Ⓒ Ⓓ
83. Ⓐ Ⓑ Ⓒ Ⓓ
84. Ⓐ Ⓑ Ⓒ Ⓓ
85. Ⓐ Ⓑ Ⓒ Ⓓ
86. Ⓐ Ⓑ Ⓒ Ⓓ
87. Ⓐ Ⓑ Ⓒ Ⓓ
88. Ⓐ Ⓑ Ⓒ Ⓓ
89. Ⓐ Ⓑ Ⓒ Ⓓ
90. Ⓐ Ⓑ Ⓒ Ⓓ
91. Ⓐ Ⓑ Ⓒ Ⓓ
92. Ⓐ Ⓑ Ⓒ Ⓓ
93. Ⓐ Ⓑ Ⓒ Ⓓ
94. Ⓐ Ⓑ Ⓒ Ⓓ
95. Ⓐ Ⓑ Ⓒ Ⓓ
96. Ⓐ Ⓑ Ⓒ Ⓓ
97. Ⓐ Ⓑ Ⓒ Ⓓ
98. Ⓐ Ⓑ Ⓒ Ⓓ
99. Ⓐ Ⓑ Ⓒ Ⓓ
100. Ⓐ Ⓑ Ⓒ Ⓓ

ANSWER SHEET
Practice Test 5

READING

Part 5: Incomplete Sentences

101. Ⓐ Ⓑ Ⓒ Ⓓ
102. Ⓐ Ⓑ Ⓒ Ⓓ
103. Ⓐ Ⓑ Ⓒ Ⓓ
104. Ⓐ Ⓑ Ⓒ Ⓓ
105. Ⓐ Ⓑ Ⓒ Ⓓ
106. Ⓐ Ⓑ Ⓒ Ⓓ
107. Ⓐ Ⓑ Ⓒ Ⓓ
108. Ⓐ Ⓑ Ⓒ Ⓓ

109. Ⓐ Ⓑ Ⓒ Ⓓ
110. Ⓐ Ⓑ Ⓒ Ⓓ
111. Ⓐ Ⓑ Ⓒ Ⓓ
112. Ⓐ Ⓑ Ⓒ Ⓓ
113. Ⓐ Ⓑ Ⓒ Ⓓ
114. Ⓐ Ⓑ Ⓒ Ⓓ
115. Ⓐ Ⓑ Ⓒ Ⓓ
116. Ⓐ Ⓑ Ⓒ Ⓓ

117. Ⓐ Ⓑ Ⓒ Ⓓ
118. Ⓐ Ⓑ Ⓒ Ⓓ
119. Ⓐ Ⓑ Ⓒ Ⓓ
120. Ⓐ Ⓑ Ⓒ Ⓓ
121. Ⓐ Ⓑ Ⓒ Ⓓ
122. Ⓐ Ⓑ Ⓒ Ⓓ
123. Ⓐ Ⓑ Ⓒ Ⓓ
124. Ⓐ Ⓑ Ⓒ Ⓓ

125. Ⓐ Ⓑ Ⓒ Ⓓ
126. Ⓐ Ⓑ Ⓒ Ⓓ
127. Ⓐ Ⓑ Ⓒ Ⓓ
128. Ⓐ Ⓑ Ⓒ Ⓓ
129. Ⓐ Ⓑ Ⓒ Ⓓ
130. Ⓐ Ⓑ Ⓒ Ⓓ

Part 6: Text Completion

131. Ⓐ Ⓑ Ⓒ Ⓓ
132. Ⓐ Ⓑ Ⓒ Ⓓ
133. Ⓐ Ⓑ Ⓒ Ⓓ
134. Ⓐ Ⓑ Ⓒ Ⓓ

135. Ⓐ Ⓑ Ⓒ Ⓓ
136. Ⓐ Ⓑ Ⓒ Ⓓ
137. Ⓐ Ⓑ Ⓒ Ⓓ
138. Ⓐ Ⓑ Ⓒ Ⓓ

139. Ⓐ Ⓑ Ⓒ Ⓓ
140. Ⓐ Ⓑ Ⓒ Ⓓ
141. Ⓐ Ⓑ Ⓒ Ⓓ
142. Ⓐ Ⓑ Ⓒ Ⓓ

143. Ⓐ Ⓑ Ⓒ Ⓓ
144. Ⓐ Ⓑ Ⓒ Ⓓ
145. Ⓐ Ⓑ Ⓒ Ⓓ
146. Ⓐ Ⓑ Ⓒ Ⓓ

Part 7: Reading Comprehension

147. Ⓐ Ⓑ Ⓒ Ⓓ
148. Ⓐ Ⓑ Ⓒ Ⓓ
149. Ⓐ Ⓑ Ⓒ Ⓓ
150. Ⓐ Ⓑ Ⓒ Ⓓ
151. Ⓐ Ⓑ Ⓒ Ⓓ
152. Ⓐ Ⓑ Ⓒ Ⓓ
153. Ⓐ Ⓑ Ⓒ Ⓓ
154. Ⓐ Ⓑ Ⓒ Ⓓ
155. Ⓐ Ⓑ Ⓒ Ⓓ
156. Ⓐ Ⓑ Ⓒ Ⓓ
157. Ⓐ Ⓑ Ⓒ Ⓓ
158. Ⓐ Ⓑ Ⓒ Ⓓ
159. Ⓐ Ⓑ Ⓒ Ⓓ
160. Ⓐ Ⓑ Ⓒ Ⓓ

161. Ⓐ Ⓑ Ⓒ Ⓓ
162. Ⓐ Ⓑ Ⓒ Ⓓ
163. Ⓐ Ⓑ Ⓒ Ⓓ
164. Ⓐ Ⓑ Ⓒ Ⓓ
165. Ⓐ Ⓑ Ⓒ Ⓓ
166. Ⓐ Ⓑ Ⓒ Ⓓ
167. Ⓐ Ⓑ Ⓒ Ⓓ
168. Ⓐ Ⓑ Ⓒ Ⓓ
169. Ⓐ Ⓑ Ⓒ Ⓓ
170. Ⓐ Ⓑ Ⓒ Ⓓ
171. Ⓐ Ⓑ Ⓒ Ⓓ
172. Ⓐ Ⓑ Ⓒ Ⓓ
173. Ⓐ Ⓑ Ⓒ Ⓓ
174. Ⓐ Ⓑ Ⓒ Ⓓ

175. Ⓐ Ⓑ Ⓒ Ⓓ
176. Ⓐ Ⓑ Ⓒ Ⓓ
177. Ⓐ Ⓑ Ⓒ Ⓓ
178. Ⓐ Ⓑ Ⓒ Ⓓ
179. Ⓐ Ⓑ Ⓒ Ⓓ
180. Ⓐ Ⓑ Ⓒ Ⓓ
181. Ⓐ Ⓑ Ⓒ Ⓓ
182. Ⓐ Ⓑ Ⓒ Ⓓ
183. Ⓐ Ⓑ Ⓒ Ⓓ
184. Ⓐ Ⓑ Ⓒ Ⓓ
185. Ⓐ Ⓑ Ⓒ Ⓓ
186. Ⓐ Ⓑ Ⓒ Ⓓ
187. Ⓐ Ⓑ Ⓒ Ⓓ
188. Ⓐ Ⓑ Ⓒ Ⓓ

189. Ⓐ Ⓑ Ⓒ Ⓓ
190. Ⓐ Ⓑ Ⓒ Ⓓ
191. Ⓐ Ⓑ Ⓒ Ⓓ
192. Ⓐ Ⓑ Ⓒ Ⓓ
193. Ⓐ Ⓑ Ⓒ Ⓓ
194. Ⓐ Ⓑ Ⓒ Ⓓ
195. Ⓐ Ⓑ Ⓒ Ⓓ
196. Ⓐ Ⓑ Ⓒ Ⓓ
197. Ⓐ Ⓑ Ⓒ Ⓓ
198. Ⓐ Ⓑ Ⓒ Ⓓ
199. Ⓐ Ⓑ Ⓒ Ⓓ
200. Ⓐ Ⓑ Ⓒ Ⓓ

Practice Test 5

LISTENING COMPREHENSION

In this section of the test, you will have the chance to show how well you understand spoken English. There are four parts to this section, with special directions for each part. You will have approximately 45 minutes to complete the Listening Comprehension sections.

Part 1: Photographs

Track 51

> **Directions:** You will see a photograph. You will hear four statements about the photograph. Choose the statement that most closely matches the photograph, and fill in the corresponding oval on your answer sheet.

1.

2.

3.

4.

5.

6.

Part 2: Question-Response

Track
52

Directions: You will hear a question and three possible responses. Choose the response that most closely answers the question, and fill in the corresponding oval on your answer sheet.

7. Mark your answer on your answer sheet.

8. Mark your answer on your answer sheet.

9. Mark your answer on your answer sheet.

10. Mark your answer on your answer sheet.

11. Mark your answer on your answer sheet.

12. Mark your answer on your answer sheet.

13. Mark your answer on your answer sheet.

14. Mark your answer on your answer sheet.

15. Mark your answer on your answer sheet.

16. Mark your answer on your answer sheet.

17. Mark your answer on your answer sheet.

18. Mark your answer on your answer sheet.

19. Mark your answer on your answer sheet.

20. Mark your answer on your answer sheet.

21. Mark your answer on your answer sheet.

22. Mark your answer on your answer sheet.

23. Mark your answer on your answer sheet.

24. Mark your answer on your answer sheet.

25. Mark your answer on your answer sheet.

26. Mark your answer on your answer sheet.

27. Mark your answer on your answer sheet.

28. Mark your answer on your answer sheet.

29. Mark your answer on your answer sheet.

30. Mark your answer on your answer sheet.

31. Mark your answer on your answer sheet.

Part 3: Conversations

Directions: You will hear a conversation between two or more people. You will see three questions on each conversation and four possible answers. Choose the best answer to each question, and fill in the corresponding oval on your answer sheet.

32. Why did the man call Mr. Wilson's office?

    (A) To make an appointment
    (B) To cancel an appointment
    (C) To ask for directions
    (D) To speak with Mr. Wilson

33. What does the woman mean when she says, "Nothing easier"?

    (A) The office isn't close to the subway station.
    (B) The streets are pleasant to walk along.
    (C) The directions are difficult to explain.
    (D) The office isn't hard to find.

34. Where is Mr. Wilson's office?

    (A) On Main Street
    (B) On Green Street
    (C) On the corner
    (D) Next to the subway station

35. What is the conversation mainly about?

    (A) An apartment
    (B) A plane ticket
    (C) A hotel room
    (D) An office

36. What is the man's problem about?

    (A) The view
    (B) The price
    (C) The size
    (D) The location

37. What does the woman suggest that the man do?

    (A) Call back later
    (B) Choose another date
    (C) Make a payment now
    (D) Look elsewhere

38. What is the purpose of the man's trip?

    (A) To take a vacation
    (B) To attend a meeting
    (C) To go to a job interview
    (D) To see a sports event

39. How is he traveling?

    (A) By plane
    (B) By train
    (C) By car
    (D) By bus

40. What does the woman imply about the man's method of travel?

    (A) It's uncomfortable.
    (B) It's expensive.
    (C) It's boring.
    (D) It's slow.

41. Where is the man going tonight?

    (A) To a dinner
    (B) To a party
    (C) To a meeting
    (D) To the office

42. Why doesn't the woman like the suit?

    (A) It isn't clean.
    (B) It is too dark.
    (C) It doesn't fit.
    (D) It has a rip in it.

43. What will the man do next?

    (A) Send the suit to the cleaner's
    (B) Ask for another opinion
    (C) Change into a new suit
    (D) Put on another tie

44. What does the woman invite the man to do?

   (A) Take a walk
   (B) Go to a play
   (C) Play golf
   (D) Have lunch

45. When does she want to do it?

   (A) Sunday
   (B) Monday
   (C) Tuesday
   (D) Saturday

46. What will the woman do tonight?

   (A) Change the meeting time
   (B) Visit her friends
   (C) Go to bed early
   (D) Call the club

Evening Bus Schedule

Lv. Winwood Street	Arr. Berksville
7:10	8:00
7:40	8:30
8:10	9:00
8:40	9:30

47. What does the man ask the woman to help with?

   (A) Finding a bus schedule
   (B) Making photocopies
   (C) Finishing a report
   (D) Reviewing a record

48. What problem does the man mention?

   (A) The photocopier needs replacement.
   (B) The office has too few employees.
   (C) The woman usually arrives late.
   (D) The bus station is too far away.

49. Look at the graphic. What time will the woman get on the bus?

   (A) 8:10
   (B) 8:30
   (C) 8:40
   (D) 9:30

50. What are the speakers discussing?

   (A) A place to meet
   (B) A time to meet
   (C) A client appointment
   (D) The weekly schedule

51. What does the woman mean when she says, "That's no good"?

   (A) She can't meet at that time.
   (B) The presentation has problems.
   (C) She doesn't like her office.
   (D) The work is too difficult.

52. What do the men imply about the presentation?

   (A) It will be well received by the client.
   (B) It will take a long time to prepare.
   (C) It is going very well so far.
   (D) It has to be finished soon.

53. What does the woman want to do?

   (A) Buy a new car
   (B) Mail a package
   (C) Order business cards
   (D) Make an appointment

54. What does the man recommend?

(A) Increasing the order
(B) Using only one color
(C) Returning on Tuesday
(D) Consulting an expert

55. What does the woman ask the man to do?

(A) Look up an address
(B) Pick up something
(C) Make a delivery
(D) Call her up

56. Who is the woman?

(A) A bank officer
(B) A real estate agent
(C) A financial advisor
(D) A business owner

57. What does the man want to do?

(A) Buy a house
(B) Borrow money
(C) Start a business
(D) Get a credit card

58. What is the man's complaint?

(A) The forms are too long.
(B) The situation is too risky.
(C) He needs more information.
(D) His accountant is not available.

59. What is the new parking policy?

(A) Employees can't park in the garage.
(B) Employees are charged a fee to park.
(C) Employees must park in assigned spaces.
(D) Employees aren't allowed to park in the lot.

60. Why do the women like the policy?

(A) Public transportation is quicker.
(B) The parking lot is too crowded.
(C) Traffic is a problem in the city.
(D) They don't like driving.

61. What does the man mean when he says, "This idea isn't going to go over"?

(A) The parking policy won't be popular.
(B) The parking policy won't get city approval.
(C) The parking policy won't be in effect very long.
(D) The parking policy won't be adopted by other companies.

Conference Room

Table A Table B

Table C Table D

62. What is the conversation mainly about?

(A) A luncheon
(B) A trip to Tokyo
(C) A conference
(D) A staff meeting

63. When will Ms. Yamamoto arrive?

(A) At noon
(B) At 4:00
(C) Next week
(D) In a month

64. Look at the graphic. Where will Ms. Yamamoto sit?

(A) Table A
(B) Table B
(C) Table C
(D) Table D

_____

65. What is the woman hiring the man to do?

(A) Rearrange furniture
(B) Clean the office
(C) Paint the walls
(D) Lay a carpet

66. When will the job be done?

(A) This afternoon
(B) Tomorrow
(C) Thursday
(D) Tuesday

67. What will the woman do now?

(A) Check her calendar
(B) Finish her work
(C) Greet a client
(D) Pay the man

68. What is the man looking for?

(A) A new job
(B) A place to live
(C) A business suit
(D) An office to rent

69. What do the speakers imply about the café?

(A) It's too noisy for conversation.
(B) The prices are very high.
(C) The food tastes bad.
(D) It's too far away.

70. What does the man suggest?

(A) Taking a walk
(B) Going to his house
(C) Meeting at his office
(D) Chatting on the phone

Part 4: Talks

Directions: You will hear a talk given by a single speaker. You will see three questions on each talk, each with four possible answers. Choose the best answer to each question, and fill in the corresponding oval on your answer sheet.

71. What will the guest speak about?

    (A) Mountain climbing
    (B) Novel writing
    (C) Photography
    (D) Sales

72. How long will the program last?

    (A) 15 minutes
    (B) 50 minutes
    (C) One hour
    (D) One and a half hours

73. What will happen after the program?

    (A) The speaker will read from her book.
    (B) There will be a photography exhibit.
    (C) Refreshments will be served.
    (D) Signs will be removed.

74. What was the cause of the delay?

    (A) An accident
    (B) Equipment repair
    (C) Crowds on the train
    (D) Construction in the station

75. What are passengers asked to do now?

    (A) Sit in the boarding area
    (B) Travel with a group
    (C) Buy their tickets
    (D) Line up at the gate

76. Where should passengers put large suitcases?

    (A) At the luggage counter
    (B) At the gate
    (C) In the boarding area
    (D) Under their seats

77. What is the purpose of this talk?

    (A) To explain registration procedures
    (B) To announce schedule changes
    (C) To describe a workshop
    (D) To announce lunch

78. What should people interested in the Best Hiring Practices workshop do?

    (A) Wait in the Terrace Room
    (B) Check the schedule
    (C) Register now
    (D) Go to Room C

79. What does the speaker mean when she says, "I wouldn't miss that event"?

    (A) She plans to be there.
    (B) She wants to go but can't.
    (C) She recommends attending.
    (D) She expects it to be crowded.

80. Where would you hear this talk?

    (A) On a tour bus
    (B) At a theater
    (C) At a museum
    (D) In a private home

81. What is everyone asked to do now?

    (A) Save questions for later
    (B) Pay for their tickets
    (C) Stop talking
    (D) Sit down

82. What will happen at noon?

    (A) A talk will be heard.
    (B) Lunch will be served.
    (C) A tour will be given.
    (D) The schedule will be reviewed.

83. What is being advertised?

(A) A school
(B) Bank loans
(C) An employment agency
(D) Financial planning services

84. Who would be interested in this announcement?

(A) Small business owners
(B) Bank employees
(C) Business assistants
(D) Police officers

85. How can someone get more information?

(A) Make a phone call
(B) Visit the office
(C) Take a workshop
(D) Read a brochure

Awards Banquet
March 17 – Winchester Hotel

Social hour	6:30–7:30
Dinner	7:30–8:30
Awards Ceremony	8:30–9:30
Music and Dancing	9:30–11:30

86. What is the purpose of this talk?

(A) To organize an event
(B) To choose a location
(C) To get ideas for an event
(D) To decide who will get awards

87. Look at the graphic. When will the speaker arrive at the banquet?

(A) 6:30
(B) 7:30
(C) 8:30
(D) 9:30

88. What will happen next?

(A) The speaker will call the hotel.
(B) The guests will receive invitations.
(C) People will volunteer for different jobs.
(D) Someone will check the sound system.

89. What does the speaker mean when he says, "Things are finally looking up"?

(A) His predictions are based on research.
(B) Temperatures were higher yesterday.
(C) The condition of the sky is changing.
(D) The bad weather is now improving.

90. What will the weather be like today?

(A) It will be rainy.
(B) It will cool down.
(C) It will get warmer.
(D) It will get cloudier.

91. What does the speaker suggest listeners do on Saturday?

(A) Carry an umbrella in case of rain
(B) Dress for cold temperatures
(C) Go out to enjoy the weather
(D) Notice the spring flowers

92. Who is Joe Roberts?

(A) A banker
(B) A doctor
(C) An assistant
(D) An accountant

93. What is the purpose of the message?

(A) To ask for information
(B) To explain a procedure
(C) To make an appointment
(D) To change an appointment

94. What does the speaker want the listener to do?

   (A) Return the call
   (B) Explain some concerns
   (C) Provide an office address
   (D) Submit a financial statement

Montrose Station Map

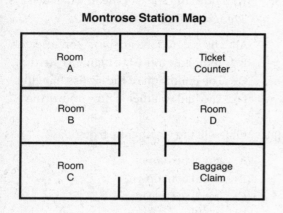

95. What has been found?

   (A) A large package
   (B) A piece of clothing
   (C) A train ticket
   (D) A blue bag

96. Where was it found?

   (A) On the track
   (B) By a door
   (C) In a waiting room
   (D) Outside the station

97. Look at the graphic. Where is the station manager's office?

   (A) A
   (B) B
   (C) C
   (D) D

98. Where would you hear this announcement?

   (A) At a farm
   (B) At a bank
   (C) At a clothing store
   (D) At a grocery store

99. How long will the special offer last?

   (A) One day
   (B) Two days
   (C) All week
   (D) Until Tuesday

100. What does the speaker suggest shoppers do?

   (A) Write a check
   (B) Return next week
   (C) Count their change
   (D) Go to the checkout counter

This is the end of the Listening Comprehension portion of the test. Turn to Part 5 in your test book.

READING COMPREHENSION

In this section of the test, you will have the chance to show how well you understand written English. There are three parts to this section, with special directions for each part.

**YOU WILL HAVE ONE HOUR AND FIFTEEN MINUTES
TO COMPLETE PARTS 5, 6, AND 7 OF THE TEST.**

Part 5: Incomplete Sentences

> **Directions:** You will see a sentence with a missing word. Four possible answers follow the sentence. Choose the best answer to the question, and fill in the corresponding oval on your answer sheet.

101. Registration for the computer training workshops _____ the first week of April.

   (A) begin
   (B) begins
   (C) beginning
   (D) have begun

102. ColPro, Inc. announced yesterday that Priscilla Perkins has _____ from her position as Chief Financial Officer after fifteen years with the company.

   (A) contracted
   (B) resigned
   (C) dismissed
   (D) retreated

103. It is your responsibility to let your supervisor know _____ you will be unable to attend next week's staff meeting.

   (A) if
   (B) so
   (C) then
   (D) but

104. I don't plan to _____ my contract with the company next year unless they are willing to discuss a raise.

   (A) subscribe
   (B) affirm
   (C) renew
   (D) employ

105. The agreement must _____ by both parties before work on the project can proceed.

   (A) sign
   (B) signed
   (C) to sign
   (D) be signed

106. The office manager has decided to buy a new printer for the marketing department and _____ for the front office.

   (A) either
   (B) any
   (C) another
   (D) this

107. _____ of the increasing rents in this neighborhood, Apex Market is considering relocating to another part of the city.

   (A) Because
   (B) Instead
   (C) Despite
   (D) Due

108. Staff members plan to _____ in the lobby at 5:00 for a small party in honor of Martha's retirement.

   (A) join
   (B) gather
   (C) attend
   (D) combine

109. You should always _____ your work carefully before turning it in to your supervisor.

    (A) review
    (B) reviewing
    (C) to review
    (D) reviewed

110. The directors are expecting to hear an answer _____ the client before the end of the week.

    (A) of
    (B) to
    (C) from
    (D) over

111. A sound _____ in improving manufacturing facilities now will result in increased profits over the next few years.

    (A) invest
    (B) investor
    (C) investiture
    (D) investment

112. Rising fuel costs have _____ many companies to seek alternative sources of energy for their facilities.

    (A) desired
    (B) expected
    (C) motivated
    (D) generated

113. An ad posted on the company's website resulted _____ hundreds of applicants for the vacant position.

    (A) on
    (B) in
    (C) of
    (D) about

114. The low attendance at the business conference last month was _____ due to the bad weather conditions affecting that part of the country.

    (A) largely
    (B) almost
    (C) because
    (D) usually

115. According to economic forecasters, a significant increase in transportation costs is _____ to occur in the next quarter.

    (A) like
    (B) likely
    (C) likeable
    (D) dislike

116. You should take the time to talk the matter over with your colleagues before _____ a final decision.

    (A) make
    (B) made
    (C) making
    (D) had made

117. This is a part-time position, but it requires _____ during evening hours as well as on occasional weekends.

    (A) avail
    (B) availing
    (C) available
    (D) availability

118. There is a _____ chance that the company will increase salaries this year, but it is not probable.

    (A) slight
    (B) normal
    (C) good
    (D) huge

119. _____ we have hired several new workers at the factory, we are still not able to meet our weekly quotas.

   (A) Since
   (B) Following
   (C) Although
   (D) Therefore

120. The board meeting had to be canceled at the last minute because so few people _____ for it.

   (A) turned in
   (B) showed up
   (C) stood by
   (D) took over

121. We will need to _____ in several areas if we want to stay within the budget.

   (A) economy
   (B) economize
   (C) economist
   (D) economics

122. We have been assured that the person _____ is giving the workshop is an expert in international finance.

   (A) who
   (B) whom
   (C) whose
   (D) which

123. If you accept a job offer from another company, please _____ the personnel director as soon as possible.

   (A) signify
   (B) testify
   (C) notify
   (D) dignify

124. Everybody _____ to find out whether an agreement about the new contract has been reached.

   (A) have waited
   (B) are waiting
   (C) is waiting
   (D) wait

125. You don't have to accept an initial salary offer because it is almost always _____.

   (A) negotiate
   (B) negotiation
   (C) negotiator
   (D) negotiable

126. I would have signed up for that workshop if I _____ it on the schedule.

   (A) saw
   (B) had seen
   (C) would see
   (D) would have seen

127. Everyone in the department _____ Mr. Hammersmith was present at last night's awards banquet.

   (A) expect
   (B) accept
   (C) except
   (D) accent

128. We chose this photocopier because it is a good deal _____ the one it is replacing.

   (A) fast
   (B) faster
   (C) the fastest
   (D) faster than

129. Ms. Soto would like you to call _____ back before 5:00 this afternoon.

   (A) her
   (B) she
   (C) hers
   (D) herself

130. We asked the designer to come up with several options so that we could _____ the best one.

   (A) select
   (B) selective
   (C) selectively
   (D) selection

Part 6: Text Completion

> **Directions:** You will see four passages, each with four blanks. Each blank has four answer choices. For each blank, choose the word, phrase, or sentence that best completes the passage.

Questions 131–134 refer to the following e-mail.

To: "Stevens, Dan"
From: "Markston, Phil"
Date: June 12
Subject: Changes to Registration Form

We have a problem with our e-mail mailing list. The problem isn't with the list _____,
131

but with how people can sign up. Our sign up form is buried so far down on our website

that it is impossible to find. We need _____ it easier for people to subscribe.
132

_____. While we are making this change, I want to edit the form slightly. There are five
133

questions on the form, and each must be answered to submit the form. I think these should

be optional—only _____ name and e-mail address fields should be required to subscribe.
134

Let's talk about this tomorrow. Come to my office when you have a moment.

Phil

131. (A) its
     (B) it's
     (C) itself
     (D) its self

132. (A) make
     (B) to make
     (C) making
     (D) will make

133. (A) One option might be to move the registration form to the home page
     (B) Most people don't mind taking a few minutes to complete the form
     (C) The number of subscribers is growing faster than we expected
     (D) Our newsletter is enjoying widespread popularity

134. (A) a
     (B) an
     (C) the
     (D) this

Questions 135–138 refer to the following notice.

NOTICE TO MOVERS

While picking up and lifting furniture from a client's home to the moving van is often ____ quickest option, I am asking that movers also consider pushing
135

furniture when possible. ____. Please use hand carts to move stacks of boxes
136

and furniture with a ____ base. Alternatively, a piece of cardboard can be placed
137

under heavy furniture so that you can more easily slide it along the floor. ____
138

option you choose, remember not to track dirt into a client's home and not to

damage the client's valuables.

---

135. (A) their
     (B) her
     (C) his
     (D) our

136. (A) Speed and efficiency are the
         company's top priorities
     (B) This will reduce your risk of
         injury and save you energy
     (C) The ability to lift heavy items is a
         requirement of this job
     (D) We are fully insured for any
         damage done to a client's property

137. (A) solid
     (B) solidly
     (C) solidify
     (D) solidity

138. (A) However
     (B) Whenever
     (C) Whichever
     (D) Whomever

Dear Ms. Thompson,

We have received your job _____ and resume. Thank you for your
                          139
interest in working with us here at the Amet Corporation. Unfortunately,

we do not currently have any _____ positions for which you would
                             140
be qualified. _____ , we will keep your information on file and will
              141
contact you when a suitable position becomes available.

_____. In the meantime, if you have any questions, please contact
142
Ms. Garcia, our Human Resources Manager.

Again, thank you for your interest.

Sincerely,
Michel Boudreau

---

139. (A) request
     (B) solicitation
     (C) application
     (D) petition

140. (A) vacate
     (B) vacant
     (C) vacancy
     (D) vacated

141. (A) However
     (B) While
     (C) As long as
     (D) Even though

142. (A) Please call my assistant this week to make an appointment
     (B) We are looking for someone with your exact training and background
     (C) Job application forms are available on the careers page of our website
     (D) If you have not heard from us in six months, you may resubmit your
         résumé

Questions 143–146 refer to the following e-mail.

From: Vanessa Holden
To: All department staff
Subject: Away next week
cc: Kyle Rogers

I will be out of the office for all of next week, attending a conference in Rome. During my _____, my assistant, Kyle Rogers, will be handling
143
all my correspondence. He will also be available _____ with any
144
issues that may arise while I am away. I understand that some of you wish to meet with me to discuss your annual evaluation. I will be happy to do this when I _____ from the conference. _____.
145   146

Vanessa Holden

143. (A) tenure
     (B) absence
     (C) pursuit
     (D) engagement

144. (A) will help
     (B) can help
     (C) to help
     (D) help

145. (A) go over
     (B) get back
     (C) come up
     (D) turn in

146. (A) The evaluations will be ready for your review next week
     (B) I plan to do some sightseeing after the conference is over
     (C) There will be many worthwhile workshops at the conference
     (D) I will be available for appointments the week after I return

Part 7: Reading Comprehension

> **Directions:** You will see single and multiple reading passages followed by several questions. Each question has four answer choices. Choose the best answer to the question, and fill in the corresponding oval on your answer sheet.

Questions 147–148 refer to the following advertisement.

ATTENTION JOB SEEKERS

Businesses throughout the region are hiring computer programmers every day.

You could be one of them.

Start a new career as a computer programmer by enrolling in the Computer School at City College.

Complete the program in as little as two years.

Day, evening, and weekend classes are available.

Why wait?

Call now to find out how you can become a computer programmer.

- Open to all high school graduates.
- No previous experience necessary!

---

147. What is being advertised?

    (A) A job opening
    (B) A training course
    (C) An employment agency
    (D) A computer programming business

148. What is a requirement?

    (A) A college degree
    (B) Computer training
    (C) Previous experience
    (D) A high school diploma

Questions 149–150 refer to the following text message chain.

Pam Spurr	10:45
I am really enjoying this conference. The exhibits are fantastic.	
Kai Noda	10:46
How was your meeting with Bruce?	
Pam Spurr	10:46
Great. We had coffee in the café and talked quite a while.	
Pam Spurr	10:47
I'm still here, drinking my second cup. Are you still in the Finance Workshop?	
Kai Noda	10:48
It's product promotion. It just finished.	
Pam Spurr	10:50
Where are you going next?	
Kai Noda	10:50
Sales Seminar. Should I take notes for you?	
Pam Spurr	10:52
Don't bother. Just save me a seat.	
Kai Noda	10:55
Will do.	

149. Where is Ms. Spurr now?

   (A) In a meeting
   (B) In the café
   (C) In a workshop
   (D) In the exhibit hall

150. At 10:52, what does Ms. Spurr mean when she writes, "Just save me a seat"?

   (A) She is on her way to a meeting.
   (B) She will wait for her friend in the café.
   (C) She is going back to the exhibit hall.
   (D) She will attend the Sales Seminar.

Save $15

On your next purchase of $100 or more on select
Pennwell office products. Offer includes shipping at
no charge for purchases of ink, toner, and paper.

Coupon code: POS97865
Expires April 30

Make your selection at *www.pennwelloffice.com*
or call 800-123-4567 to place your order today.

Pennwell is *the* leading supplier of printers and copiers,
office furniture, and other essential office supplies.

151. What is the coupon good for?

(A) Any Pennwell product
(B) Office furniture only
(C) A purchase of at least $100
(D) Printers and copiers only

152. What do you have to do to get the discount?

(A) Purchase your products by April 30
(B) Purchase your products on online
(C) Purchase your products by phone
(D) Purchase at least $15 worth of products

Questions 153–154 refer to the following invoice.

Invoice

SMITHFIELD KITCHEN SUPPLIES
Supplying restaurants and offices for over 50 years!

Order # 40291   Date: April 10

Your customer service representative: Pamela Jones
Thank you for your order. Please keep this invoice for your records.

Ship to: **Bill to:**
Mark Gillman   The Hubert Restaurant Group
Park House Restaurant   Attn: Rita Spofford
85 South Street   74 Belt Avenue
Greensboro, NH   Hudson, MA

Product	Quantity	Price/ea.	Total
Kringle Deluxe coffeemaker	1	$250	$250
Kringle bread machine	1	$425	$425
Extended warranties	0		$0
		Shipping	$35
		Expedited shipping surcharge	$20
		Sales tax	$30
		Total due	$760

Payment due upon receipt of order.

153. Who will pay the invoice?

(A) Mark Gillman
(B) Pamela Jones
(C) Park House Restaurant
(D) The Hubert Restaurant Group

154. What is the $20 charge for?

(A) Holiday and weekend delivery
(B) Sending the order quickly
(C) Shipping heavy items
(D) Special packaging

PRACTICE TEST 5

Dorchester Towers
Tenant Application

Name   Howard Danes

Address   113 Fordham Road

            Winesburg, OH

Apartment type

____ studio   _X_ one-bedroom   ____ two-bedroom   ____ three-bedroom

Number of occupants   2

Desired move-in date   November 15

Application fee	$100
First month's rent*	$800
Security deposit	$600
Total due on signing of lease	$1500

All apartments will be cleaned, repainted, and re-carpeted prior to move in. Return of security deposit upon termination of the lease is contingent upon an apartment inspection. Questions and repair requests should be directed by phone or e-mail to the building manager:

Michael Lee

548-9982

michaell@redbird.com

*Rent does not include parking. A limited number of parking spaces are available in the garage for a fee. Please contact the manager for further information.

---

155. What is this purpose of this form?

(A) To ask for repairs
(B) To make a payment
(C) To request an apartment
(D) To give notification of lease termination

156. What is the monthly rent for a one-bedroom apartment?

(A) $100
(B) $600
(C) $800
(D) $1500

157. What is included with all apartments?

(A) A parking space
(B) A repair
(C) A phone
(D) A new carpet

Questions 158–160 refer to the following webpage.

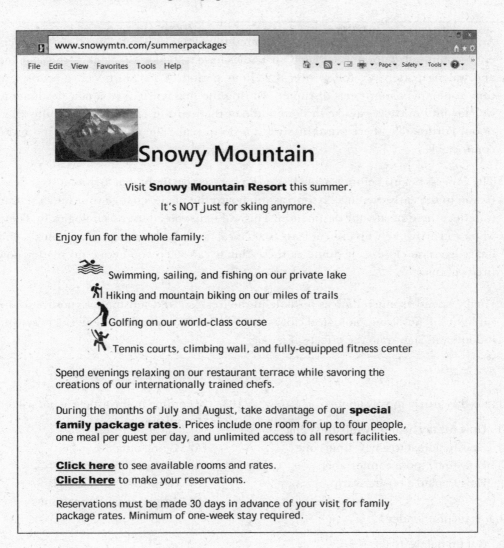

www.snowymtn.com/summerpackages

File   Edit   View   Favorites   Tools   Help

Snowy Mountain

Visit **Snowy Mountain Resort** this summer.

It's NOT just for skiing anymore.

Enjoy fun for the whole family:

Swimming, sailing, and fishing on our private lake

Hiking and mountain biking on our miles of trails

Golfing on our world-class course

Tennis courts, climbing wall, and fully-equipped fitness center

Spend evenings relaxing on our restaurant terrace while savoring the creations of our internationally trained chefs.

During the months of July and August, take advantage of our **special family package rates**. Prices include one room for up to four people, one meal per guest per day, and unlimited access to all resort facilities.

Click here to see available rooms and rates.
Click here to make your reservations.

Reservations must be made 30 days in advance of your visit for family package rates. Minimum of one-week stay required.

158. What is suggested about Snowy Mountain Resort?

(A) It is known as a ski resort.
(B) It is only open in the summer.
(C) It has luxurious accommodations.
(D) It is less expensive than other resorts.

159. Which of the following is NOT mentioned as a resort activity?

(A) Dining
(B) Cycling
(C) Water sports
(D) Horseback riding

160. When must reservations be made to get the special rate?

(A) A week ahead of time
(B) A month ahead of time
(C) In July or August
(D) Any time

Questions 161–163 refer to the following article.

Any business person who has traveled around the globe has experienced the phenomenon commonly known as jet lag. Our bodies have a "biological clock"—the sleeping and waking pattern we follow over a 24-hour period. When we travel to a different time zone, this pattern gets disrupted. During the first few days at a new destination, we may find ourselves awake in the middle of the night or falling asleep in the afternoon. Fortunately, there are things we can do to make the adjustment period more comfortable.

The process begins before leaving home. First, reserve a flight that arrives at your destination in the early evening. As soon as you board the plane, change your watch setting to reflect the time at your destination. This will help you adjust psychologically. Then, when you arrive, stay up until at least 10:00 local time. Avoid caffeine, large meals, and heavy exercise close to bedtime as these things can keep you awake no matter how tired you may be.

Finally, spend as much time as possible in the fresh air and sunshine. Exposure to the sunlight will help your biological clock adjust to the new time zone. Conversely, staying indoors will aggravate the effects of jet lag.

161. What is this article mostly about?

(A) How to stay healthy while traveling
(B) How to adjust to a new time zone
(C) How to fly more comfortably
(D) How to plan a business trip

162. What is recommended?

(A) Get up before 10:00
(B) Avoid eating until 10:00
(C) Go to bed at 10:00 or later
(D) Arrive at your destination by 10:00

163. According to the article, what will help you sleep better?

(A) Going outside
(B) Avoiding the sun
(C) Getting enough exercise
(D) Adjusting your mealtimes

ROGERS, MILTON, & COLE, PC
17 Willow Avenue
Moltonsburgh

May 10, 20—

To Whom It May Concern:

This is a letter regarding Ms. Amelia Spark, a former employee at Rogers, Milton, & Cole, PC. Ms. Spark began with our company as an intern soon after she graduated from university. At the end of her internship, we hired her on as a full-time legal assistant. –[1]– At the same time, she continued to take classes at the university, I understand with the goal of eventually going for an advanced degree. –[2]–

As well as being reliable and hardworking, we could always count on Ms. Sparks to be pleasant and helpful to everyone in the office. –[3]– These characteristics were especially helpful in Ms. Spark's dealings with clients. In fact, clients often specifically asked to work with her. –[4]–

We were sorry to lose Ms. Spark when she left us last month, but wish her much success with her decision to move to New York and in all her future professional endeavors. We know she will be a great asset to any firm she works with. Please don't hesitate to contact me if you require any further information.

Sincerely,

Stephen Cole

Stephen Cole

164. What will Ms. Spark use this letter for?

(A) To hire someone
(B) To get a new a job
(C) To get new clients
(D) To apply to university

165. What profession does Ms. Spark work in?

(A) Law
(B) Education
(C) Accounting
(D) Business

166. Why did Ms. Spark leave her job?

(A) She was fired.
(B) She became ill.
(C) She moved to a new city.
(D) She returned to school.

167. In which of the following positions marked [1], [2], [3], and [4] does the following sentence best belong?

"She worked diligently at that job, proving herself always eager to learn and willing to put in whatever time and effort a project required."

(A) [1]
(B) [2]
(C) [3]
(D) [4]

Questions 168–171 are based on the following article.

The Rockville Development Group (RDG) announced today a proposal for a mixed-use complex on the outskirts of Bingchester, close to Highway 10. The proposed complex includes 1,000 square meters of office space, 50,000 square meters of retail space, a parking garage, and several hectares of outdoor parking.

The announcement got a mixed reception. Bingchester City Council members hailed it as a boost to the local economy. "It will bring jobs. People will come here to spend money. What could be better?" proclaimed Council Member Miriam Hodges. But local business owners had a different opinion. "Its location can only hurt our businesses," said Bill Smithers, president of the Bingchester Business Owner's Association. "Look at the distance from the downtown shopping district. People driving down Highway 10 may stop at the mall, but they won't then drive the extra mile to spend money at our local shops." Environmental groups also expressed opposition to the proposal. "In addition to destroying acres of valuable agricultural land, water run-off from the pavement will dirty our local streams and rivers and damage natural habitats."

A spokesperson for RDG dismissed the opposition, saying, "This development has been five years in the planning. We have received all the necessary permits and are closely following government regulations. When it is completed, this project will be one of Bingchester's greatest assets. We expect to break ground before the end of the year." Construction will take close to two years to complete.

168. What is this article mostly about?

(A) Local business regulations
(B) The grand opening of a mall
(C) A plan to build stores and offices
(D) The revival of a downtown shopping district

169. What is a complaint about the project?

(A) It is too big.
(B) It harms farm land.
(C) It is too close to downtown.
(D) It will create parking problems.

170. Who is Miriam Hodges?

(A) A politician
(B) A shopper
(C) A builder
(D) A retailer

171. When will work on the project begin?

(A) By December 31
(B) Next January
(C) In two years
(D) In five years

GREG SAMSA	2:15
This is Greg in marketing. We're having a training workshop for new hires next Wednesday, and I'd like to reserve Conference Room 3. I checked the schedule online, and it's free all morning.	
BLANCA WHITE	2:20
I'm sorry. That room has been reserved for a client meeting. I'm a bit behind on updating the schedule and haven't put it up yet.	
GREG SAMSA	2:23
I don't know what to do. Room 3 is the only room big enough.	
BLANCA WHITE	2:25
How about Room 2? I believe it's available Wednesday morning.	
GREG SAMSA	2:27
The lighting in there is terrible. I can never see what I'm writing.	
BLANCA WHITE	2:29
Yes, we're going to fix that soon.	
BLANCA WHITE	2:30
How many people are you expecting?	
GREG SAMSA	2:33
At least 20.	
BLANCA WHITE	2:35
Then you could use Room 4. I'm sure you could fit 20 people in there comfortably.	
GREG SAMSA	2:39
Perhaps. But it's an all morning session, so we'll also need some room for serving refreshments during the break.	
BLANCA WHITE	2:43
The hall in that part of the building is fairly wide. I could have someone set up the refreshments just outside the door and that would leave you more space inside the room.	
GREG SAMSA	2:45
Do you think that will work?	
BLANCA WHITE	2:48
I'm sure it will. Why don't I meet you up there in 5 minutes, and I can show you where we will put the tables and how we can arrange everything.	
GREG SAMSA	2:50
Great. Thanks.	

PRACTICE TEST 5

172. What does Mr. Samsa need the room for?

    (A) A luncheon

    (B) A training session

    (C) Meeting with a client

    (D) Job applicant interviews

173. At 2:20, what does Ms. White mean when she writes, "I haven't put it up yet"?

    (A) She has not yet prepared the room for the meeting.

    (B) She has not yet determined which rooms are free.

    (C) She has not yet created the schedule for the week.

    (D) She has not yet posted the Room 3 reservation.

174. What is the problem with Room 2?

    (A) It has been reserved by someone else.

    (B) It is being repaired.

    (C) It is very small.

    (D) It is too dark.

175. What will Ms. White do next?

    (A) Get some tables.

    (B) Update the schedule.

    (C) Meet Mr. Samsa by Room 4.

    (D) Set up the refreshments.

Questions 176–180 refer to the following e-mail and survey.

To: Elizabeth Simons
From: Rosemount Hotel
Subject: Guest Satisfaction Survey

Dear Ms. Simons,

Thank you for choosing the Rosemount Hotel during your recent visit to Springfield.

Please visit the Internet link below. It will take you to our Guest Satisfaction Survey. We appreciate the time you take to fill out this survey as it enables us to provide you with the best possible experience at the Rosemount. Please follow this link to take the survey. We are sorry but we are unable to respond directly to feedback as the survey is conducted by a third party.

We hope your stay at the Rosemount was pleasant, and that we will see you here again soon. For billing or future stay assistance, please contact the following:
Billing inquiries—Mr. Perez: rperez@rosemounthotel.com
Future stay inquiries—Ms. Lee: klee@rosemounthotel.com

If you wish to opt out of future e-mails from the Rosemount Hotel, please follow this link to be removed from our list.

Again, thank you.

Harold Custer for the Rosemount Hotel

Rosemount Hotel
Guest Satisfaction Survey

Please rate the hotel staff:

	Excellent	Good	Fair	Poor
Professional attitude	✗			
Professional appearance	✗			
Knowledge of local area		✗		
Speed of check in process			✗	

Please rate your room:

	Excellent	Good	Fair	Poor
Cleanliness	✗			
Comfort of bed	✗			
Lighting	✗			
Internet connection	✗			

Please rate the fitness center:*

	Excellent	Good	Fair	Poor
Cleanliness				
Selection of equipment				
Condition of equipment				

If you experienced any problems during your stay, please explain:

I had to wait several minutes before someone was available to check me in. Then, the clerk had problems with the credit card machine. One other thing, I tried to use the fitness center, but by the time I got there (10:00 P.M.), it was closed.

Comments:

I thoroughly enjoyed my stay at the Rosemount. I was here this time for a client meeting but hope to return soon with my family for some sightseeing.

Your name: Elizabeth Simons

Date of stay: April 10–11

*Please leave this section blank if you did not visit our fitness center.

176. What is the purpose of the e-mail?

   (A) To ask for feedback
   (B) To explain a bill
   (C) To advertise the hotel
   (D) To confirm a reservation

177. Why should someone contact Ms. Lee?

   (A) To ask about a bill
   (B) To submit a survey
   (C) To make a hotel reservation
   (D) To be removed from the e-mail list

178. What problem did Ms. Simons have with the hotel?

   (A) The room cost
   (B) The comfort of the bed
   (C) The cleanliness of the room
   (D) The registration process

179. Why didn't Ms. Simons use the fitness center?

   (A) It was closed.
   (B) It wasn't clean.
   (C) She never exercises.
   (D) The equipment was in poor condition.

180. What was the purpose of Ms. Simons' trip to Springfield?

   (A) A family visit
   (B) A business meeting
   (C) A sightseeing tour
   (D) A conference

Questions 181–185 refer to the following schedule and e-mail.

```
┌─────────────────────────────────────────────────────────────┐
│                                                             │
│                          BOA                                │
│                 TENTH ANNUAL CONFERENCE                      │
│                    HALISTON HOTEL                           │
│                                                             │
│                       SCHEDULE                              │
│                                                             │
│   8:30–9:45          CONTINENTAL BREAKFAST (MAIN LOBBY)      │
│                                                             │
│   10:00 – 12:00      WORKSHOP SESSION 1                      │
│                      A: FINANCING YOUR BUSINESS (GARDEN ROOM)│
│                      B: MARKETING IN THE DIGITAL AGE (ROOM 3)│
│                                                             │
│   12:15–1:15         LUNCH (DINING ROOM)                     │
│                                                             │
│   1:30–3:30          WORKSHOP SESSION 2                      │
│                      C: SMALL BUSINESS HIRING PRACTICES (ROOM 2)│
│                      D: TRAINING YOUR PERSONNEL (MEZZANINE)  │
│                                                             │
│   4:00–5:00          SOCIAL HOUR (MAIN LOBBY)                │
│                                                             │
└─────────────────────────────────────────────────────────────┘
```

To: Bob Schumacher
From: Anne Kemp
Date: November 10
Subject: BOA Conference

Hi Bob,

I am attaching the conference schedule as you requested. I am really looking forward to it, especially since this is the first year I will be attending without being a presenter. Without that pressure, I will really have a chance to enjoy everything the conference has to offer.

I hope we can get together sometime during the day. I'd like to take the opportunity to discuss with you a loan I hope to get for expanding my business. I would really appreciate your advice on this matter as you have so much experience in this area and with the particular lender I hope to work with. Also I know you are active in the local Finance Educators Association and could perhaps point me to further resources. I plan to attend workshops A and C. I don't know whether you will be at either one of those, but we should make another time to get together to really have a chance to talk. I have a meeting with a colleague at noon, so I won't be at the conference lunch, but what about the social hour? Let's plan to look for each other there.

Anne

181. Who is this conference for?

    (A) Marketing specialists
    (B) Business owners
    (C) Personnel managers
    (D) Money lenders

182. Why did Ms. Kemp write the e-mail to Mr. Schumacher?

    (A) To invite him to go to the conference
    (B) To tell him about a workshop she will present
    (C) To make plans to meet with him
    (D) To suggest which workshops he should attend

183. Where will Ms. Kemp be at 1:30?

    (A) Main lobby
    (B) Dining room
    (C) Room 2
    (D) Mezzanine

184. In the e-mail, the word *active* in paragraph 2, line 4, is closest in meaning to

    (A) busy
    (B) ready
    (C) energetic
    (D) involved

185. What does Ms. Kemp want to discuss with Mr. Schumacher?

    (A) Borrowing money
    (B) Presenting a workshop
    (C) Organizing the conference
    (D) Arranging a social hour

Questions 186–190 refer to the following schedule, newspaper announcement, and e-mail.

Torryton 150th Annual National Day Celebration
Schedule of Events
Saturday

CRAFTS FAIR
Time: All Day   **Location: Torryton Park, Oak Walk**
Enjoy the shade of our city's famous old oak trees as you shop for hand-made items by local, national, and international crafters.

HISTORY EXHIBITS
Time: 10 AM–7 PM   **Location: History Museum**
Bring the whole family to see special National Day exhibits, inside the newly renovated History Museum. Special activities for the little ones include craft making and a film.

INTERNATIONAL FOOD FESTIVAL
Time: Noon–8 PM   **Location: Main and Maple Sts.**
Sample delights from all around the world as you stroll along the sidewalks of Main and Maple Streets.

SOCCER GAME
Time: 6 PM   **Location: Torryton High School Soccer Field**
Watch local teams compete for the coveted National Day Trophy.

CONCERT
Time: 8:30 PM   **Location: Torryton Park, East Field**
Relax under the stars while listening to music from local bands.

ANNOUNCEMENT
National Day Celebration
Due to the predicted bad weather, the City Council has announced several changes to this weekend's National Day celebration. All outdoor activities have been canceled, with the exception of the evening concert. This has been moved to the Torryton Theater. Like all the weekend's events, there is no charge for the concert. However, due to limited seating, tickets must be obtained ahead of time. Contact the City Arts Council to reserve your tickets. All indoor activities will proceed as scheduled.

To:	patr@ztown.com
From:	timrogers@river.com
Date:	June 11
Subject:	Torryton trip

Hi Pat,

Thanks for recommending the Torryton National Day celebration. I had a great time despite the weather. I guess you heard about that storm. Anyhow, there were still lots of celebration events going on. I was really sorry to miss the food festival, but maybe I can catch it next year. I saw the history exhibits early in the day, then I was lucky enough to get a ticket to the concert. It was fantastic. I'll give you a full account when I see you next week.

Tim

186. What is NOT true about the celebration?

   (A) It takes place once a year.
   (B) It includes a sports event.
   (C) It costs money to attend.
   (D) It is an old tradition.

187. Which activity is especially for children?

   (A) A movie
   (B) A crafts sale
   (C) An international meal
   (D) A walk on Main Street

188. Why didn't Tim go to the food festival?

   (A) It was canceled.
   (B) He wasn't hungry.
   (C) He didn't feel well.
   (D) It was too early in the day.

189. Where was Tim in the evening?

   (A) At the park
   (B) At the theater
   (C) At the museum
   (D) At the soccer game

190. In the e-mail, the word *account* in line 5 is closest in meaning to

   (A) bill
   (B) money
   (C) description
   (D) reason

Come to the new
Beeline Bistro
Use these coupons to take advantage of special offers when you visit us this month.

Beeline Bistro
***** *2 for 1 Special* *****
Choose any 2 entrees from our dinner menu for the price of one.

Offer expires March 31
One coupon per customer

Beeline Bistro
***** *Free Dessert* *****
Enjoy one free dessert with any lunch entree

Offer expires March 31
One coupon per customer

Beeline Bistro
*** *Sandwich Special* ***
Choose selected sandwiches from our lunch menu for just $6.99 each.

Offer expires March 31
One coupon per customer

Beeline Bistro
***** *Appetizer Tray* *****
Get 25% off our Appetizer Tray when you come in for dinner before 6:00 P.M.

Offer expires March 31
One coupon per customer

Beeline Bistro
113 Riverside Avenue
Serving 3 meals a day, seven days a week

Beeline Bistro

My husband and I tried out the new Beeline Bistro last week, and it did not disappoint! What a great dinner. It's still pricy, but we used a coupon and that made a big difference. They offer the same great selection as always. We skipped the appetizers and went straight to the entrees, and of course, couldn't pass up the great desserts. If you enjoy the old Beeline as much as we do, you're sure to like the Riverside version, too.

Penny Barlow

RIVERSIDE
Revival of a Neighborhood

The new restaurant and shopping district in the Riverside section of town is booming. Specialty clothing, book, and gift stores have popped up around the neighborhood. At the same time, numerous new eating places have appeared, and some old favorites have opened new locations there as well. The latter include the ever-popular Beeline Bistro. This is a wise move on the part of Beeline's owners, as the contemporary menu will surely appeal to the youthful residents of the neighborhood. The newcomer Café Cookie Cutter, just next door, is already *the* place to go for home-baked pastries.

In general, the concentration of restaurants in the area is a draw for other businesses as well, and on weekend evenings the streets are alive with shoppers, sightseers, and, most of all, people with money to spend. All in all, Riverside businesses are taking off.

191. What is suggested about the Beeline Bistro restaurant?

    (A) It is a new business.
    (B) It will be remodeled.
    (C) It has changed the menu.
    (D) It has opened a new branch.

192. Which coupon did Ms. Barlow use?

    (A) Free dessert
    (B) Appetizer tray
    (C) 2 for 1 special
    (D) Sandwich special

193. What criticism does Ms. Barlow have of the Beeline Bistro?

    (A) It is expensive.
    (B) It is too busy.
    (C) The menu is short.
    (D) The appetizers aren't good.

194. In the article, the word *concentration* in paragraph 2, line 1, is closest in meaning to

    (A) thinking
    (B) attention
    (C) crowding
    (D) shrinkage

195. What is suggested about Riverside businesses?

    (A) They are prosperous.
    (B) They are in a bad location.
    (C) They need more publicity.
    (D) They appeal only to young people.

AIRPORT TRANSPORTATION
All transportation services leave from the front of the East Terminal.

	Schedule	Destinations	Cost
City Bus #46	Every hour	Downtown, Parkview, Business District	$3.50
Train Station Shuttle	Every 30 min.	Central Train Station	$5.00
Hotel Shuttles	Varies	Neighborhood hotels	None
Taxi	Varies	Any	Varies

To:	m.reed@company.com
From:	s.chang@company.com
Date:	Friday, September 15
Subject:	travel

Melinda,

Thanks for doing such a great job organizing my trip. Everything has gone smoothly so far except for one little glitch at the airport. I was all set to take the downtown bus, as you suggested, because it stops right across the street from the hotel, but unfortunately it didn't work out because of the mess at the terminal, what with all the work going on, and then, of course, Friday is such a heavy travel day. I ended up having to pay for a taxi, which cost a good deal more, and I doubt whether it saved me any time. The traffic around here is horrendous. At any rate, I'm settled into the hotel now and getting ready for tomorrow's meetings. I'll let you know how everything goes.

Sam

NOTICE to Airport Users

The following changes to airport transportation have been put in place due to renovations and repairs being carried out at the East Terminal:

o All shuttle and taxi services now leave from the front of the West Terminal.

o Service from City Bus #46 is temporarily suspended. Those desiring to connect with other City Bus lines can take a shuttle or taxi to Central Train Station, which is serviced by buses #32, #57, and #75.

Please direct any questions or concerns to the Airport Office of Public Relations.

This notice is in effect from August 30 to October 15.

---

196. Which type of transportation is free to use?

(A) City Bus
(B) Train Station Shuttle
(C) Hotel Shuttles
(D) Taxi

197. Why didn't Sam take the bus?

(A) It doesn't go to his destination.
(B) It isn't in operation right now.
(C) It takes too long.
(D) It costs too much.

198. What does Sam suggest about the airport?

(A) It is crowded on Fridays.
(B) It is not cleaned regularly.
(C) It is far from downtown.
(D) It is close to his hotel.

199. What is happening at the airport from August to October?

(A) Construction of a new terminal
(B) Changes in shuttle schedules
(C) Reorganization of bus routes
(D) Remodeling of a building

200. In the notice, the word *direct* in line 10 is closest in meaning to

(A) advise
(B) manage
(C) express
(D) instruct

STOP

This is the end of the test. If you finish before time is called, you may go back to Parts 5, 6, and 7 and check your work.

ANSWER KEY
Practice Test 5

LISTENING COMPREHENSION

Part 1: Photographs

1. **A**	3. **C**	5. **B**
2. **D**	4. **A**	6. **C**

Part 2: Question-Response

7. **B**	14. **C**	21. **C**	28. **A**
8. **B**	15. **A**	22. **A**	29. **B**
9. **C**	16. **B**	23. **B**	30. **C**
10. **A**	17. **C**	24. **C**	31. **B**
11. **A**	18. **A**	25. **C**	
12. **C**	19. **C**	26. **A**	
13. **B**	20. **B**	27. **B**	

Part 3: Conversations

32. **C**	42. **B**	52. **D**	62. **A**
33. **D**	43. **D**	53. **C**	63. **C**
34. **A**	44. **C**	54. **A**	64. **D**
35. **C**	45. **D**	55. **D**	65. **B**
36. **B**	46. **A**	56. **A**	66. **B**
37. **C**	47. **C**	57. **B**	67. **D**
38. **A**	48. **B**	58. **A**	68. **B**
39. **B**	49. **C**	59. **B**	69. **A**
40. **D**	50. **B**	60. **C**	70. **C**
41. **B**	51. **A**	61. **A**	

Part 4: Talks

71. **A**	79. **C**	87. **C**	95. **B**
72. **D**	80. **A**	88. **C**	96. **C**
73. **C**	81. **D**	89. **D**	97. **A**
74. **B**	82. **B**	90. **C**	98. **D**
75. **D**	83. **B**	91. **A**	99. **A**
76. **A**	84. **A**	92. **D**	100. **B**
77. **B**	85. **C**	93. **C**	
78. **C**	86. **A**	94. **A**	

ANSWER KEY
Practice Test 5

READING

Part 5: Incomplete Sentences

101. **B**	109. **A**	117. **D**	125. **D**
102. **B**	110. **C**	118. **A**	126. **B**
103. **A**	111. **D**	119. **C**	127. **C**
104. **C**	112. **C**	120. **B**	128. **D**
105. **D**	113. **B**	121. **B**	129. **A**
106. **C**	114. **A**	122. **A**	130. **A**
107. **A**	115. **B**	123. **C**	
108. **B**	116. **C**	124. **C**	

Part 6: Text Completion

131. **C**	135. **D**	139. **C**	143. **B**
132. **B**	136. **B**	140. **B**	144. **C**
133. **A**	137. **A**	141. **A**	145. **B**
134. **C**	138. **C**	142. **D**	146. **D**

Part 7: Reading Comprehension

147. **B**	161. **B**	175. **C**	189. **B**
148. **D**	162. **C**	176. **A**	190. **C**
149. **B**	163. **A**	177. **C**	191. **D**
150. **D**	164. **B**	178. **D**	192. **C**
151. **C**	165. **A**	179. **A**	193. **A**
152. **A**	166. **C**	180. **B**	194. **C**
153. **D**	167. **A**	181. **B**	195. **A**
154. **B**	168. **C**	182. **C**	196. **C**
155. **C**	169. **B**	183. **C**	197. **B**
156. **C**	170. **A**	184. **D**	198. **A**
157. **D**	171. **A**	185. **A**	199. **D**
158. **A**	172. **B**	186. **C**	200. **C**
159. **D**	173. **D**	187. **A**	
160. **B**	174. **D**	188. **A**	

TEST SCORE CONVERSION TABLE

Count your correct responses. Match the number of correct responses with the corresponding score from the Test Score Conversion Table (below). Add the two scores together. This is your Total Estimated Test Score. As you practice taking the TOEIC practice tests, your scores should improve. Keep track of your Total Estimated Test Scores.

# Correct	Listening Score	Reading Score	# Correct	Listening Score	Reading Score	# Correct	Listening Score	Reading Score	# Correct	Listening Score	Reading Score
0	5	5	26	110	65	51	255	220	76	410	370
1	5	5	27	115	70	52	260	225	77	420	380
2	5	5	28	120	80	53	270	230	78	425	385
3	5	5	29	125	85	54	275	235	79	430	390
4	5	5	30	130	90	55	280	240	80	440	395
5	5	5	31	135	95	56	290	250	81	445	400
6	5	5	32	140	100	57	295	255	82	450	405
7	10	5	33	145	110	58	300	260	83	460	410
8	15	5	34	150	115	59	310	265	84	465	415
9	20	5	35	160	120	60	315	270	85	470	420
10	25	5	36	165	125	61	320	280	86	475	425
11	30	5	37	170	130	62	325	285	87	480	430
12	35	5	38	175	140	63	330	290	88	485	435
13	40	5	39	180	145	64	340	300	89	490	445
14	45	5	40	185	150	65	345	305	90	495	450
15	50	5	41	190	160	66	350	310	91	495	455
16	55	10	42	195	165	67	360	320	92	495	465
17	60	15	43	200	170	68	365	325	93	495	470
18	65	20	44	210	175	69	370	330	94	495	480
19	70	25	45	215	180	70	380	335	95	495	485
20	75	30	46	220	190	71	385	340	96	495	490
21	80	35	47	230	195	72	390	350	97	495	495
22	85	40	48	240	200	73	395	355	98	495	495
23	90	45	49	245	210	74	400	360	99	495	495
24	95	50	50	250	215	75	405	365	100	495	495
25	100	60									

Number of Correct Listening Responses ——————— = Listening Score ———————

Number of Correct Reading Responses ——————— = Reading Score ———————

Total Estimated Test Score ———————

ANSWER EXPLANATIONS

Listening Comprehension

PART 1: PHOTOGRAPHS

1. **(A)** A woman is looking at her wristwatch. Choices (B) and (D) correctly identify the bus in the background, but the woman is not watching it or riding on it. Choice (C) correctly identifies the tree in the background, but the woman is not planting it.

2. **(D)** The photo shows empty tables and chairs in front of some houses. Choice (A) is incorrect because the doors are closed. Choice (B) correctly identifies the benches, but there are no people on them. Choice (C) is incorrect because there is nothing on the tables.

3. **(C)** A man is standing in a grocery store aisle reading the label on a jar. Choice (A) correctly identifies the jar, but not the man's activity. Choice (B) relates *grocery store* and *food*. Choice (D) correctly identifies the shelves, but not the man's activity.

4. **(A)** A train stands in a station. Choice (B) is incorrect because there are no passengers in the photo. Choice (C) is incorrect because the platform is empty of people. Choice (D) confuses similar-sounding words *train* and *rain*.

5. **(B)** This statement correctly describes the woman. Choice (A) is incorrect because the man is not wearing a tie. Choice (C) is incorrect because the shelves are filled with books. Choice (D) confuses the *coffee cup* with a *coffee pot*.

6. **(C)** A chef stands in a kitchen. Choice (A) confuses similar-sounding words *kitchen* and *chicken*. Choice (B) correctly identifies the vegetables, but not their location. Choice (D) correctly identifies the plates, but not their location.

PART 2: QUESTION-RESPONSE

7. **(B)** This answers the question *Which*. Choice (A) repeats the verb *live*. Choice (C) confuses similar-sounding words *which* and *wish*.

8. **(B)** This answers the *yes–no* question with additional information about the time of the appointment. Choice (A) confuses similar-sounding words *appointment* and *disappointing*. Choice (C) relates the words *appointment* and *calendar*.

9. **(C)** *Susan* answers the question *Who*. Choice (A) repeats the name *Mr. Jenkins*. Choice (B) repeats the word *phone*.

10. **(A)** *Two months ago* answers the question *When*. Choice (B) confuses homonyms *here* and *hear*. Choice (C) repeats the word *here*.

11. **(A)** This answers the *yes-no* question about attending the conference. Choice (B) uses the related word *conferring*. Choice (C) confuses the meaning of the word *last* and repeats the word *month*.

12. **(C)** This is an appropriate response to the offer of a cup of coffee. Choice (A) confuses homonyms *wait* and *weight*. Choice (B) confuses similar-sounding words *coffee* and *coughing*.

13. **(B)** This is an appropriate response to the request to carry a box. Choice (A) would answer a *yes–no* question that is not a request. Choice (C) repeats the word *box*.

14. **(C)** This answers the *yes–no* question about the visitors' arrival. Choice (A) uses the related word *visit*. Choice (B) would answer a question about the arrival of something, but not of people.

15. **(A)** This answers the question about a preference. Choice (B) confuses similar-sounding words *train* and *rain*. Choice (C) confuses the meaning of the word *train*.

16. **(B)** This answers the *How long* question about time. Choice (A) relates *meeting* and *agenda*. Choice (C) would answer a *How long* question about size.

17. **(C)** The word *belongs* is the clue that this is the correct answer to the *Whose* question about possession. Choice (A) confuses similar-sounding words *closet* and *closest*. Choice (B) uses a plural pronoun, *they*, for the singular word *coat*.

18. **(A)** This answers the *Why* question with a logical reason. Choice (B) relates *bus* and *fares*. Choice (C) repeats the word *work*.

19. **(C)** This is a logical response to the invitation to play tennis. Choice (A) relates the words *tennis* and *racket*. Choice (B) confuses similar-sounding words *tennis* and *ten of us*.

20. **(B)** This answers the question *What*. Choices (A) and (C) confuse *weekend* with similar-sounding words *weakened* and *week*.

21. **(C)** This is a logical response to the comment about the short cord. Choice (A) repeats the word *cord*. Choice (B) confuses similar-sounding words *cord* and *bored*.

22. **(A)** This answers the *yes–no* question about possession of a car. Choice (B) would answer a *Which* question. Choice (C) would answer a *Where* question.

23. **(B)** *Noon* answers the *When* question. Choice (C) would answer a *Where* question. Choice (A) relates *arrive* and *time*, but it does not answer the question.

24. **(C)** The speaker responds to the comment about enjoying the play by agreeing. Choice (A) confuses the meaning of the word *play*. Choice (B) repeats the word *play*, but it does not answer the question.

25. **(C)** *Behind my desk* answers the *Where* question. Choice (A) would answer a *What* question. Choice (B) uses *left*, related to *leave*. *Where can I leave my bags?*

26. **(A)** This answers the *yes–no* question about John's presence at the party. Choice (B) is future tense, but the question is about the past. Choice (C) is not an answer to a *yes–no* question.

27. **(B)** *Fifteen* answers the *How many* question. Choice (A) repeats the word *many*. Choice (C) confuses similar-sounding words *fit* and *sit*.

28. **(A)** This answers the negative *yes–no* question about an office key. Choice (B) relates *key* and *lock*. Choice (C) confuses the meaning of *key*.

29 **(B)** This answers the *What* question. Choice (A) confuses similar-sounding words *talking* and *walking*. Choice (C) repeats the word *talking*.

30. **(C)** This answers the *Which* question. Choice (A) repeats the word *office*. Choice (B) would answer a *yes–no* question.

31. **(B)** This is a logical response to the suggestion to take a walk. Choice (A) repeats the word *take*. Choice (C) confuses similar-sounding words *take* and *make*.

PART 3: CONVERSATIONS

32. **(C)** The man says he is calling to ask how to get to the office from the subway. Choice (A) is incorrect because the man already has an appointment. Choice (B) is what the woman asks about. Choice (D) repeats the name *Mr. Wilson*.

33. **(D)** *Nothing easier* means that there is nothing easier than finding Mr. Wilson's office. Choices (A), (B), and (C) do not correctly explain the meaning of this expression.

34. **(A)** According to the woman's directions, the man will see the office building after taking a left onto Main Street. Choices (B) and (C) are other places mentioned in the directions. Choice (D) is incorrect because the man has to walk to another street after leaving the subway station.

35. **(C)** The man and woman both mention a room, and the woman quotes a price per night, so they are talking about a hotel room. Choices (A), (B), and (D) are things one might pay a deposit for, but they are not paid for per night.

36. **(B)** The man says, *That's more than I expected to pay*, and asks for something that costs less. Choices (A), (C), and (D) are all mentioned, but the man doesn't express any problems about them.

37. **(C)** The woman advises the man to *put a deposit down now*. Choice (A) repeats the word *later*. Choice (B) repeats the word *date*. Choice (D) is plausible but not mentioned.

38. **(A)** The man states that he will be on vacation. Choice (B) repeats the word *meeting*. Choice (C) is not mentioned. Choice (D) confuses similar-sounding words *reports* and *sports*.

39. **(B)** The man states that he bought a train ticket. Choice (A) confuses similar-sounding words *train* and *plane* and is confused with

the woman's mention of *flying*. Choice (C) confuses similar-sounding words *far* and *car*. Choice (D) is not mentioned.

40. **(D)** The woman says, *It'll take you forever to get there* and *I wouldn't have the patience*, which imply that she thinks the train is slow. Choices (A) and (B) are what the man says train travel is not. Choice (C) is related to the idea of slowness, but it is not mentioned.

41. **(B)** The woman mentions that the man is going to a party. Choice (A) confuses similar-sounding words *thinner* and *dinner*. Choice (C) relates *suit* with *meeting*. Choice (D) relates *suit* with *office*.

42. **(B)** The woman says, *You should wear a lighter color*. Choice (A) uses related words *cleaner's/clean*. Choice (C) repeats the word *fit*. Choice (D) confuses similar-sounding words *fit* and *rip*.

43. **(D)** The man says, *I think I'll change my tie*. Choice (A) is what the man has already done. Choice (B) repeats the word *opinion*. Choice (C) is what the woman wants the man to do, but he doesn't agree.

44. **(C)** The woman is playing golf with some friends and invites the man to join them. Choice (A) confuses similar-sounding words *work* and *walk*. Choice (B) confuses the meaning of the word *play*. Choice (D) repeats the word *lunch*.

45. **(D)** The woman says that the golf game is on Saturday morning. Choices (A) and (B) are confused with the similar-sounding word *fun*. Choice (C) is confused with the similar-sounding word *two*.

46. **(A)** The woman will call her friends tonight and tell them to meet at two instead of seven. Choice (B) is incorrect because she will call her friends, not visit them. Choice (C) is not mentioned. Choice (D) repeats the word *call* and confuses the meaning of the word c*lub*— the man mentions his golf clubs.

47. **(C)** The man asks the woman to *help me get this report done*. Choice (A) is related to the discussion about which bus the woman will take. Choice (B) is incorrect because it is the assistant who will make copies. Choice (D)

confuses similar-sounding words *report* and *record*.

48. **(B)** The man says that the office is *short staffed*, that is, there aren't enough employees. Choice (A) relates *copies* and *photocopier*, but there is no need to replace it. Choice (C) repeats the word *late*, which refers to the discussion of when the woman will leave, not when she arrives. Choice (D) is related to the discussion of the bus schedule.

49. **(C)** The woman says that she can *make the last bus leaving from Winwood Street*. Choice (A) is when the second-to-last bus leaves. Choice (B) is a time when a bus arrives in Berksville and is also the time that the woman will probably leave the office. Choice (D) is when the last bus arrives at its destination.

50. **(B)** The first man says, *We need to get together to work on the presentation*, and then the speakers discuss a day and time to do this. Choice (A) is incorrect because the speakers quickly agree on a place; it is the time that they discuss. Choice (C) repeats the word *appointment*, which is what prevents the woman from agreeing to the first suggested time. Choice (D) is related to the mention of different times and days, but it is not the topic of discussion.

51. **(A)** In this context, *That's no good* means *I can't do that*, and it is the woman's response to the first suggested meeting time. Choices (B), (C), and (D) don't fit the meaning of this expression in the context.

52. **(D)** One man says, *We really have to get going on this*, meaning *We have to start working on this very soon*. The other agrees, mentioning the due date: *Monday's coming up soon*. Choices (A), (B), and (C) are not mentioned.

53. **(C)** The woman says, *I'd like to get some business cards . . . .* Choice (A) confuses similar-sounding words *card* and *car*. Choice (B) relates *address* (which the woman wants to include on her cards) and *mail*. Choice (D) relates *Tuesday* (which is when the woman wants the cards to be ready) and *appointment*.

54. **(A)** The woman wants to order 250 cards, and the man says she will save money by ordering 500. Choice (B) refers to the description of the logo the woman wants on her card. Choice (C) repeats the word *Tuesday*. Choice (D) is related to the woman's *consulting* business.

55. **(D)** The woman asks the man to phone her when the cards are ready for pick up. Choice (A) repeats the word *address*. Choice (B) repeats *pick up*. Choice (C) relates *address* and *delivery*.

56. **(A)** The man is applying for a loan, so she is a bank officer. Choice (B) relates *house* and *real estate*. Choice (C) repeats the word *financial*. Choice (D) is who the man is.

57. **(B)** The man is interested in *taking out a loan*, that is, borrowing money. Choice (A) repeats the word *house*. Choice (C) is incorrect because the man already has a business; he wants to expand it. Choice (D) repeats the word *credit*.

58. **(A)** The man says, *That's a lot of paper. Do I really need to complete all those pages?* Choice (B) relates *risk* and *risky*. The man says he is a good risk, that is, he will surely repay the loan. Choice (C) repeats the word *information*. Choice (D) relates *account* and *accountant*.

59. **(B)** The man describes the parking policy as the one where employees *have to pay to park in the lot*. Choice (A) is not mentioned. Choice (C) is incorrect because employees lose assigned spaces as part of the policy. Choice (D) is contradicted by the correct answer.

60. **(C)** The women agree that people need to be encouraged to use public transportation instead of driving because the streets are too crowded with traffic. Choice (A) repeats the phrase *public transportation*, but no mention is made of whether or not it is quicker. Choice (B) repeats the word *crowded*. Choice (D) is related to the discussion of parking and driving, but it is not mentioned.

61. **(A)** If a plan doesn't *go over*, it means it won't be liked or accepted. Choices (B), (C), and (D) don't fit the meaning of the expression in this context.

62. **(A)** The speakers are discussing plans for a luncheon for a visitor from Tokyo. Choice (B) repeats the word *Tokyo*. Choice (C) is confused with *conference room*, the location of the luncheon. Choice (D) confuses similar-sounding words *seating* and *meeting*.

63. **(C)** The woman refers to next week's luncheon for Ms. Yamamoto. Choice (A) confuses similar-sounding words *soon* and *noon*. Choice (B) confuses similar-sounding words *door* and *four*. Choice (D) is not mentioned.

64. **(D)** The speakers agree that Ms. Yamamoto should sit near the door. Choices (A), (B), and (C) are not near the door.

65. **(B)** The woman asks the man to shampoo the carpets, wash the walls, and polish the furniture, that is, to clean the office. Choice (A) repeats the word *furniture*. Choice (C) repeats the word *walls*. Choice (D) repeats the word *carpet*.

66. **(B)** The man says, *We can have it all done by tomorrow afternoon at 5*. Choice (A) repeats the word *afternoon*. Choice (C) is when the woman has a meeting with a client. Choice (D) is not mentioned.

67. **(D)** The woman is going to write a check for the deposit. Choice (A) confuses the meaning of the word *check*. Choice (B) repeats the word *work*. Choice (C) repeats the word *client*.

68. **(B)** The woman asks the man about his *house hunting*, so he is looking for a house to live in. Choices (A) and (D) are related to the mention of an *office*. Choice (C) confuses the meaning of the word *suit*.

69. **(A)** When the woman suggests going to the café, the man says he would prefer *some place quieter* and the woman agrees, saying, *It's not really suited for talking*. Choice (B) is incorrect because the man says the café *is not expensive*. Choice (C) is incorrect because the woman says, *The food there's not bad*. Choice (D) is not mentioned.

70. **(C)** The man says, *So why don't you come to my office around noon tomorrow . . . .* Choice (A) confuses similar-sounding words *talk* and *walk*. Choice (B) repeats the words *house* and *going*. Choice (D) is incorrect because the

man suggests chatting in his office, not on the phone.

PART 4: TALKS

71. **(A)** The guest will speak about climbing in the Andes. Choices (B) and (C) are mentioned as things she does, but they are not the topic of the talk. Choice (D) is not mentioned.

72. **(D)** The speaker says the program will last *about an hour and a half total*. Choice (A) is the length of the film that will be shown. Choice (B) sounds similar to *15 minutes*. Choice (C) sounds similar to the correct answer.

73. **(C)** The speaker says that *coffee, tea, and snacks will be available in the lobby*. Choice (A) is confused with the words *book signing*. Choice (B) is confused with the mention of the guest's interest in photography. Choice (D) confuses the meaning of the word *sign*.

74. **(B)** The speaker apologizes for the delay that was caused by *maintenance work on the engine*. Choice (A) is related to the word *emergency*. Choices (C) and (D) are mentioned, but they are not the cause of the delay.

75. **(D)** The speaker says, *Please approach Gate 9 and line up single file*. Choice (A) is not possible, as the speaker says, *there is no seating in the boarding area*. Choices (B) and (C) are mentioned, but they are not what passengers are being asked to do.

76. **(A)** The speaker asks passengers to *check any large suitcases at the luggage counter before boarding*. Choices (B), (C), and (D) are all mentioned, but not as places to leave luggage.

77. **(B)** The speaker says, . . . *you need to be aware of a few minor adjustments to the schedule*, and that is mostly what she talks about. Choice (A) is confused with the mention of registering for one of the workshops. Choice (C) repeats the word *workshop*, but none are described, just named. Choice (D) is incorrect because lunch is over.

78. **(C)** The speaker says about that workshop, *anyone interested in attending it should visit*

the registration desk now. Choice (A) is where the social hour will take place. Choice (B) repeats the word *schedule*. Choice (D) is incorrect because the workshop has been moved to Room D.

79. **(C)** *I wouldn't miss that* can be a way of recommending something, meaning that it is too good to miss. The speaker is recommending that listeners go to the social hour. Choices (A), (B), and (D) don't fit the context.

80. **(A)** The speaker is speaking to tourists on a bus explaining all the places the bus will take them to. Choice (B) is not mentioned. Choices (C) and (D) are places they will visit.

81. **(D)** The speaker says, . . . *please take your seats now*. Choice (A) repeats the word *questions*. Choice (B) fits the context, but it is not mentioned. Choice (C) repeats the word *talk*.

82. **(B)** The speakers says that at noon *we are scheduled for lunch at the Blue Moon Restaurant*. Choice (A) will happen after the noontime lunch. Choice (C) is the entire context. Choice (D) is what the speaker is doing now.

83. **(B)** The speaker mentions *financial assistance, loans*, and *the money you need to start or grow your business*. Choice (A) is confused with the mention of workshops, Choice (C) repeats the word *employment*. Choice (D) is related to the topic, but it is not what is being advertised.

84. **(A)** The name of the loan program is *Small Business Assistance Program*, and the speaker also says, *We believe in supporting local businesses*. Choices (B), (C), and (D) repeat words mentioned in the talk.

85. **(C)** The speaker says, *Find out more about what we have to offer by attending one of our monthly workshops*. Choices (A), (B), and (D) are all plausible but not mentioned.

86. **(A)** The speaker begins by saying, *Let's go over the plans*, and the rest of the talk is about tasks that need to be done and who will do them. Choices (B) and (C) are incorrect because from the context, we can assume they have already happened. Choice (D) uses

the word *awards*, but there is no discussion about who will receive them.

87. **(C)** The speaker says that she *won't arrive until the ceremony begins*, which, according to the schedule, is 8:30. Choices (A), (B), and (D) are other times on the schedule.

88. **(C)** After describing the tasks to be done, the speaker ends by saying, *Who would like to do what?* Choice (A) repeats the word *hotel*, but calling the hotel is not mentioned. Choice (B) repeats the word *guests*, but sending them invitations is not mentioned. Choice (D) is mentioned as one of the tasks, but it is not what will be done next.

89. **(D)** *Things are looking up* means that things are improving. The speaker goes on to describe clearing skies and warmer temperatures, which are improvements in the weather. Choice (A) uses another meaning of *look up—research*. Choices (B) and (C) associate *higher* and *sky* with *up*.

90. **(C)** The speaker mentions *rising temperatures*. Choice (A) is the weather on Saturday. Choice (B) is the weather on Sunday. Choice (D) is the opposite of what the speaker says will happen—cloudy skies will clear up.

91. **(A)** The speaker says, . . . *bring along that umbrella if you venture out on Saturday as occasional showers are expected.* Choice (B) is confused with the colder temperatures on Sunday. Choice (C) repeats the words *enjoy* and *out*. Choice (D) confuses similar-sounding words *showers* and *flowers*.

92. **(D)** The speaker says that Joe Roberts is an accountant. Choice (A) is related to the mention of a *financial statement*. Choice (B) is related to the topic of appointments. Choice (C) is who the speaker is.

93. **(C)** The speaker says that Joe Roberts would like to meet with the listener and suggests a day and time. Choices (A) and (B) are plausible, but they are not the correct answer. Choice (D) cannot be correct because no previous appointment is mentioned.

94. **(A)** The speaker wants to know when the listener can meet with Mr. Roberts and leaves a phone number. Choice (B) is what Mr. Roberts

wants to do at the appointment. Choice (C) repeats the word *office*. Choice (D) has already been done.

95. **(B)** The found item is a jacket, that is, a piece of clothing. Choice (A) confuses similar-sounding words *jacket* and *package*. Choice (C) repeats the word *ticket*. Choice (D) repeats the word *blue*.

96. **(C)** The speaker says that the item was found in *the Track 10 waiting area*. Choice (A) repeats the word *track*. Choice (B) confuses similar-sounding words *floor* and *door*. Choice (D) is incorrect because we can assume the waiting area is inside, not outside, the station.

97. **(A)** The speaker says that the station manager's office is *across from the ticket counter*. Choices (B), (C), and (D) don't fit this description.

98. **(D)** There is a sale in the *produce section*, so it is a grocery store. Choice (A) associates *fruit* with *farm*. Choice (B) associates *bank* with *savings*. Choice (C) confuses similar-sounding words *closing* and *clothing*.

99. **(A)** The sale is for today only. Choices (B) and (D) confuse *today* with similar-sounding words *two days* and *Tuesday*. Choice (C) repeats the word *week*.

100. **(B)** The speaker says to *come back next week* for the weekly sale. Choice (A) confuses the usage of the word *check*. Choice (C) confuses the usage of the word *change*. Choice (D) confuses the usage of *check out*.

Reading

PART 5: INCOMPLETE SENTENCES

101. **(B)** This is a present tense verb that agrees with the subject *Registration*. Choices (A) and (D) do not agree with the subject. Choice (C) is a gerund or present participle and cannot act as a main verb.

102. **(B)** *Resign* means *leave a job*. Choices (A), (C), and (D) have meanings that don't fit the context.

103. **(A)** *If* introduces a condition. Choice (B) introduces a result. Choice (C) shows sequence in time, or introduces the result

of a condition. Choice (D) introduces a contradiction.

104. **(C)** To *renew* a contract means to *continue* or *extend* it. Choices (A), (B), and (D) have meanings that don't fit the context.

105. **(D)** The subject, *agreement*, receives the action rather than performs it, so a passive verb is required. Choices (A), (B), and (C) are all active verbs.

106. **(C)** *Another* in this sentence is a pronoun that refers to *another printer.* Either a noun or a pronoun is needed here as an object of the verb *buy*, and Choices (A) and (B) are not pronouns. Choice (D) is sometimes used as a pronoun, but it does not make sense in this context.

107. **(A)** *Because of* introduces a cause. Choice (B) introduces an alternative. Choice (C) introduces a contradiction and cannot be used with *of*. Choice (D) introduces a cause, but it cannot be used with *of*.

108. **(B)** *Gather* means *collect*, and can be used, as it is here, as an intransitive verb (a verb with no object). Choices (A) and (C) are transitive verbs—they need objects. Choice (D) doesn't fit the context.

109. **(A)** This is a base form verb following the modal *should*. Choices (B), (C), and (D) are not base form verbs.

110. **(C)** *From* is a preposition indicating the place where something starts, in this case, *the answer* from *the client*. Choices (A), (B), and (D) don't fit the context.

111. **(D)** *Investment* is a noun referring to money paid into something with the hope of future profit. Choice (A) is a verb. Choice (B) is a noun, but it refers to a person. Choice (C) is a noun, but it has a completely different meaning that does not fit the context.

112. **(C)** *Motivate* means to make someone want to do something. Choices (A), (B), and (D) don't fit the context.

113. **(B)** The verb *result* is followed by the preposition *in*. Choices (A), (C), and (D) can't follow *result*.

114. **(A)** *Largely* means *mostly*. Choices (B), (C), and (D) don't fit the context.

115. **(B)** *Likely* is an adjective meaning *probable*. Choice (A), when used as an adjective, means *similar*. Choice (C) means *nice* or *easily liked*. Choice (D) is a verb.

116. **(C)** *Before* is followed by a gerund. Choices (A), (B), and (D) are not gerunds.

117. **(D)** This is a noun used in this sentence as the object of the verb *requires*. Choice (A) is a verb. Choice (B) is a gerund. Choice (C) is an adjective.

118. **(A)** *Slight* means *very small*. Choices (B), (C), and (D) do not fit the context.

119. **(C)** *Although* introduces a contradiction. Choices (A) and (B) introduce a cause. Choice (D) introduces a result.

120. **(B)** *Showed up* means *appeared*. Choices (A), (C), and (D) do not fit the context.

121. **(B)** *Economize* is a verb, in this sentence, an infinitive verb following the main verb *need*. Choices (A), (C), and (D) are all nouns.

122. **(A)** *Who* is a subject relative pronoun with the antecedent *person*. Choice (B) is an object relative pronoun. Choice (C) is possessive. Choice (D), when used as a relative pronoun, refers to a thing, not a person.

123. **(C)** *Notify* means *inform*. Choices (A), (B), and (D) have meanings that don't fit the context.

124. **(C)** This singular verb agrees with the singular subject *Everybody*. Choices (A), (B), and (D) all need plural subjects.

125. **(D)** This is an adjective modifying the noun *offer*. Choice (A) is a verb. Choices (B) and (C) are nouns.

126. **(B)** This is the correct form for the verb in the *if* clause of a past tense unreal conditional sentence. Choice (A) is simple past tense. Choice (C) is a present tense conditional main clause form. Choice (D) is a past unreal conditional, but the form for the main clause verb.

127. **(C)** *Except* means *but* or *excluding*. Choices (A), (B), and (D) do not fit the context.

128. **(D)** *Faster than* is a comparative form. Choice (A) is not comparative. Choice (B) omits *than*. Choice (C) is superlative.

129. **(A)** *Her* is an object pronoun (follows the verb). Choice (B) is a subject pronoun. Choice (C) is a possessive pronoun. Choice (D) is a reflexive pronoun.

130. **(A)** This is a base form verb following the modal *could*. Choice (B) is an adjective. Choice (C) is an adverb. Choice (D) is a noun.

PART 6: TEXT COMPLETION

131. **(C)** This is a reflexive pronoun used to place emphasis on its antecedent (*list*). Choice (A) is a possessive pronoun or adjective. Choice (B) is a contraction of *it is*. Choice (D) is two separate words, not a correct reflexive pronoun form.

132. **(B)** The verb *need* is followed by an infinitive verb. Choice (A) is base form. Choice (C) is a gerund. Choice (D) is a future verb.

133. **(A)** The preceding sentence expresses a need to make registration easier, and this sentence explains one way that might be done. Choices (B), (C), and (D) are related to the topic of subscribing to an e-mail list, but they don't fit the passage in this place.

134. **(C)** *The* is a definite article referring to something that has been defined (the reader knows that the name and address fields referred to are the ones on the registration form). Choices (A) and (B) are indefinite articles and are used with singular nouns only. Choice (D) is used with singular nouns only.

135. **(D)** *Our* in this case refers to people who work for the moving company, including the writer of the notice. Choices (A), (B), and (C) would refer to groups or individuals that do not include either the writer or the readers of this notice.

136. **(B)** This is a logical reason for the suggestion to push rather than lift furniture. Choices (A), (C), and (D) do not fit the context.

137. **(A)** This is an adjective modifying the noun *base*. Choice (B) is an adverb. Choice (C) is a verb. Choice (D) is a noun.

138. **(C)** *Whichever* implies a choice among two or more things, in this case, among different options. Choice (A) refers to the manner of doing something. Choice (B) refers to time. Choice (D) refers to people.

139. **(C)** A job *application* refers to the process of seeking a job by submitting information. Choices (A), (B), and (D) have meanings related to the idea of asking for something, but they are not correctly used in this context.

140. **(B)** This is an adjective modifying the noun *positions*. Choices (A) and (D) are verbs. Choice (C) is a noun.

141. **(A)** *However* introduces a contrast and is similar in meaning and use to *but*—there are no job positions, but they will keep the applicant's information. Choices (B), (C) and (D) have uses that don't fit the context.

142. **(D)** After stating that there are currently no positions available, the applicant is invited to re-apply at a later date. Choice (A) is illogical—there is no reason to make an appointment since there are no current job openings. Choice (B) contradicts what was stated earlier in the letter. Choice (C) is irrelevant because the application has already been made.

143. **(B)** *Absence* refers to the state of being away from a place—the writer will be away from the office next week. Choices (A), (C), and (D) have meanings that don't fit the context.

144. **(C)** The adjective *available* is followed by an infinitive verb. Choice (A) is a future verb. Choice (B) is a modal + verb. Choice (D) is base form.

145. **(B)** *Get back* means return. The other choices have meanings that don't fit the context.

146. **(D)** The writer of the e-mail mentions that people might want to meet with her, so it is logical to follow that with the mention of availability for appointments. Choices (A), (B), and (C) are related to other things mentioned in the e-mail, but they don't fit the passage in this place.

PART 7: READING COMPREHENSION

147. **(B)** The ad is for a computer training course at a college. Choices (A) and (C) are confused with the headline for job seekers. Choice (D) is confused with the correct answer, but the

ad is clearly about a school, not a programming business.

148. **(D)** The ad states that the course is open to high school graduates. Choice (A) is confused with the location of the course—at City College. Choice (B) is the content of the course. Choice (C) is exactly what the ad says is not required.

149. **(B)** After mentioning her meeting in the café, she writes, "I'm still here." Choices (A) and (C) are other places she was earlier. Choice (D) is where Mr. Noda is.

150. **(D)** Mr. Noda is at the Sales Seminar, and Ms. Spurr means that she will meet him there and sit next to him. Choices (A), (B), and (C) do not fit the context.

151. **(C)** The coupon is good for a *purchase of $100 or more*. Choice (A) is incorrect because the coupon mentions *select*, or designated, products. Choices (B) and (D) are incorrect because other types of products are mentioned.

152. **(A)** The coupon expires on April 30. Choice (B) and (C) are confused with the provided contact information. Choice (D) is confused with the size of the discount.

153. **(D)** This is the name listed under *Bill to*. Choice (A) is the person who will receive the order. Choice (B) is the customer service representative. Choice (C) is the place the order will be sent to.

154. **(B)** This is the fee for *expedited*, or rushed, shipping. Choices (A), (C), and (D) are all plausible but not correct.

155. **(C)** The application form mentions a move-in date, rent, and lease, so it is an application for an apartment. Choices (A), (B), and (D) repeat words from details on the form but are not the correct answer.

156. **(C)** The form shows that the applicant owes $800 for the first month's rent. Choice (A) is the application fee. Choice (B) is the security deposit. Choice (D) is the total of all the fees.

157. **(D)** The form states that all apartments will be *re-carpeted prior to move in*. Choices (A) and (B) are things that can be requested.

Choice (C) is confused with the provided contact information.

158. **(A)** The phrase, *It's not just for skiing anymore*, suggests that most people know the place as a ski resort, and that the resort is now introducing new types of activities. Choice (B) is incorrect because it is a ski resort, so it must be open in the winter, as well. Choice (C) is incorrect because the quality of the accommodations is not mentioned. Choice (D) is incorrect because a price comparison with other resorts is not mentioned.

159. **(D)** This activity is not mentioned at all. Choice (A) refers to the mention of the *restaurant* and *chefs*. Choice (B) refers to the mention of *mountain biking*. Choice (C) refers to the mention of *swimming, sailing, and fishing*.

160. **(B)** The information states, *Reservations must be made 30 days in advance of your visit*. Choice (A) refers to the minimum stay length. Choice (C) refers to the months when the special rates are available. Choice (D) is contradicted by the correct answer.

161. **(B)** The article talks about how to adjust sleeping patterns to a new time zone. Choice (A) refers to the mention of meals, exercise, and caffeine, but they are mentioned here specifically in terms of managing sleep, not health in general. Choice (C) refers to the mention of jet lag and plane travel. Choice (D) refers to the context of business travel, but planning the trip is only mentioned in terms of managing sleep patterns.

162. **(C)** The article recommends to *stay up until at least 10:00*. Choices (A), (B), and (D) all mention *10:00*, but they are not what is recommended.

163. **(A)** The article says to spend time *in the fresh air and sunshine*. Choice (B) is the opposite of what is recommended. Choice (C) is confused with the mention of avoiding exercise close to bedtime. Choice (D) is confused with the mention of avoiding large meals close to bedtime.

164. **(B)** This is a letter of reference, so it will be used to get a new job. Choice (A) is what the

recipient of the letter will use it for. Choices (C) and (D) repeat words used elsewhere in the letter.

165. **(A)** Ms. Spark was hired as a *legal assistant*, so her profession is law. Choice (B) is related the mention of *university*. Choices (C) and (D) are not mentioned.

166. **(C)** The last paragraph mentions Ms. Spark's *decision to move to New York*. Choices (A) and (B) are plausible reasons, but they are not mentioned. Choice (D) is incorrect because Ms. Spark continued at her job while taking classes.

167. **(A)** The phrase, *that job*, refers back to the position of *legal assistant* mentioned in the previous sentence. Choices (B), (C), and (D) are not logical locations for this sentence.

168. **(C)** It is about *a proposal for a mixed-use complex* that will include both *office* and *retail* space. Choice (A) is related to the topic, but it is not the correct answer. Choice (B) relates *retail space* and *mall*, but there is no grand opening as nothing has been built yet. Choice (D) is related to the mention of *downtown* and *local shops.*

169. **(B)** Environmental groups oppose the project because it will destroy *acres of valuable agricultural land*. Choice (A) is related to the mention of the size of the project, but no one complained about it. Choice (C) is the opposite of the business owners' complaint—they think it is too far away to attract business to their shops. Choice (D) is related to the mention of parking, but no problems with it are mentioned.

170. **(A)** Ms. Hodges is a City Council member and, therefore, a politician. Choices (B) and (D) are related to the mention of retail space. Choice (C) refers to the Rockville Development Group.

171. **(A)** The RDG spokesperson says that they will *break ground*, that is, begin construction, *before the end of the year*, that is, by December 31. Choice (B) is the beginning of next year. Choice (C) is related to the amount of time it will take to complete the project.

Choice (D) is related to the amount of time it took to plan the project.

172. **(B)** Mr. Samsa asks to reserve a room for a training workshop for new hires. Choice (A) is confused with the mention for refreshments. Choice (C) is what someone else has reserved the room for. Choice (D) confuses *job applicants* with *new hires.*

173. **(D)** Mr. Samsa was not aware that Room 3 had already been reserved because Ms. White had not yet posted that information on the online schedule. Choices (A), (B), and (C) do not fit the context.

174. **(D)** Mr. Samsa writes about Room 2, *The lighting in there is terrible. I can never see what I'm writing*. Choice (A) is incorrect because Ms. White suggests that Mr. Samsa reserve it for himself. Choice (B) is what Ms. White says will happen in the future. Choice (C) is related to the fact that Mr. Samsa is concerned about getting a large enough room, but the size of Room 2 is not mentioned.

175. **(C)** Ms. White offers to meet Mr. Samsa in 5 minutes to show him how the refreshment tables for Room 4 can be arranged. Choices (A), (B), and (D) are all things Ms. White will probably do at some point, but she does not mention doing them right away.

176. **(A)** The e-mail asks the hotel guest to complete a *Guest Satisfaction Survey*. Choices (B), (C), and (D) are related to the hotel business, but they are not the purpose of the e-mail.

177. **(C)** The e-mail says to contact Ms. Lee for *future stay inquiries*, that is, to make plans to stay at the hotel. Choice (A) requires contacting Mr. Perez. Choices (B) and (D) are done by clicking on a link.

178. **(D)** In the survey, Ms. Simmons describes problems with *check in*, that is, registration. Choice (A) is not mentioned. Choices (B) and (C) are things she rated as excellent.

179. **(A)** Ms. Simmons says of the fitness center *by the time I got there (10:00 P.M.) it was closed*. Choices (B) and (D) are things she didn't rate because she didn't use the center. Choice (C) is incorrect because she wanted to use the center.

180. **(B)** Ms. Simons states the purpose of her trip as a *client meeting*. Choices (A) and (C) are things she plans for the future. Choice (D) is not mentioned.

181. **(B)** The topics of the workshop sessions relate to different aspects of running a business. Choices (A), (C), and (D) each refer to specific workshop topics, but not to the overall theme of the conference.

182. **(C)** At the beginning of paragraph 2 of the e-mail, Ms. Kemp writes, *I hope we can get together sometime during the day*, and making arrangements to do that is the main topic of the rest of her message. Choice (A) is incorrect because Mr. Schumacher already has plans to go to the conference. Choice (B) is incorrect because she states that she won't be a presenter. Choice (D) is incorrect because Ms. Kemp mentions which workshops she will attend, but she makes no suggestions for Mr. Schumacher.

183. **(C)** Ms. Kemp writes that she will attend Workshop C, which takes place at 1:30 in Room 2. Choices (A), (B), and (D) are locations of other events.

184. **(D)** Because of Mr. Schumacher's involvement in the local Finance Educators Association, Ms. Kemp thinks he might know of useful resources for her in her search for a loan. Choices (A), (B), and (C) are other meanings of *active* that don't fit the context.

185. **(A)** Ms. Kemp wants to discuss a loan. Choices (B), (C), and (D) all repeat words from the e-mail, but they are not the correct answer.

186. **(C)** The announcement states, *Like all the weekend's events, there is no charge for the concert*, meaning none of the events cost money. Choice (A) is a true statement because the schedule describes the celebration as *annual*. Choice (B) is a true statement because one of the events on the schedule is a soccer game. Choice (D) is a true statement because this is the 150th celebration.

187. **(A)** On the schedule, under History Exhibits, the schedule mentions a *film* (movie) for *the little ones* (children). Choices (B), (C), and (D)

are all activities that are not mentioned as being specifically for children.

188. **(A)** Tim wanted to attend this event but, according to the announcement, most outdoor events were canceled due to weather, and on the schedule we can see that the food festival was an outdoor event. Choices (B), (C), and (D) are all plausible, but they are incorrect reasons.

189. **(B)** Tim attended the concert, which took place in the evening and was moved from its outdoor location to the theater. Choice (A) is where the concert was originally scheduled to take place. Choice (C) is where Tim was *early in the day*. Choice (D) is incorrect because everything that would take place outdoors was canceled.

190. **(C)** Tim means he will give Pat a complete description of the celebration when they meet. Choices (A), (B), and (D) are other meanings of *account*, but they don't fit the context.

191. **(D)** It is referred to as *new* in the review, but the article makes it clear that this is a new location for an old business, not a new business entirely, so Choice (A) is incorrect. Choice (B) is not mentioned. Choice (C) is incorrect because the reviewer mentions *the same great selection*, that is, *the same great menu*.

192. **(C)** She used it for dinner, which eliminates Choices (A) and (D), good for lunch only, and she says they didn't have appetizers, which eliminates Choice (B).

193. **(A)** She says the restaurant is *pricy*. Choice (B) is not mentioned. Choice (C) is incorrect because she describes the menu (selection) as *great*. Choice (D) is incorrect—she didn't have the appetizers, but she does not mention a reason or say anything more about them.

194. **(C)** The article is about the many new restaurants in the area, so from the context we know that the idea here is *crowding*. Choices (A), (B), and (D) are other uses of the word *concentration*, but they don't fit the context.

195. **(A)** The article says that businesses are *booming* and *taking off*, that is, fast becoming

successful. Choices (B) and (C) are incorrect because the article suggests the opposite. Choice (D) is confused with the mention of the appeal of the menu to young people.

196. **(C)** The cost of the Hotel Shuttles is listed as *none*. Choices (A), (B), and (D) all have a cost.

197. **(B)** According to the notice, bus service to the airport is *temporarily suspended* because of work on renovations. Sam also says that he didn't take the bus because of the *mess at the terminal*, referring, in part, to the disruption caused by the renovation work. Choices (A), (C), and (D) are all plausible, but they are incorrect answers.

198. **(A)** Sam mentions that *Friday is such a heavy travel day*, implying that there were a lot of travelers at the airport. Choice (B) confuses the meaning of the word *mess* in this context. Choices (C) and (D) are not mentioned.

199. **(D)** The notice mentions *renovations and repairs being carried out at the East Terminal*. Choice (A) is confused with the correct answer, but it is an already-existing building that is being worked on, not a new one being built. Choice (B) is confused with the change in the location of the shuttles, but no schedule changes are mentioned. Choice (C) is confused with the mention of different bus routes, but no reorganization of them is mentioned.

200. **(C)** The idea is that people can *express*, or *talk about*, their questions and concerns with the PR Office. Choices (A), (B), and (D) are other uses of the word *direct*, but they don't fit the context.

ANSWER SHEET
Practice Test 6

LISTENING COMPREHENSION

Part 1: Photographs

1. Ⓐ Ⓑ Ⓒ Ⓓ
2. Ⓐ Ⓑ Ⓒ Ⓓ
3. Ⓐ Ⓑ Ⓒ Ⓓ
4. Ⓐ Ⓑ Ⓒ Ⓓ
5. Ⓐ Ⓑ Ⓒ Ⓓ
6. Ⓐ Ⓑ Ⓒ Ⓓ

Part 2: Question-Response

7. Ⓐ Ⓑ Ⓒ
8. Ⓐ Ⓑ Ⓒ
9. Ⓐ Ⓑ Ⓒ
10. Ⓐ Ⓑ Ⓒ
11. Ⓐ Ⓑ Ⓒ
12. Ⓐ Ⓑ Ⓒ
13. Ⓐ Ⓑ Ⓒ
14. Ⓐ Ⓑ Ⓒ
15. Ⓐ Ⓑ Ⓒ
16. Ⓐ Ⓑ Ⓒ
17. Ⓐ Ⓑ Ⓒ
18. Ⓐ Ⓑ Ⓒ
19. Ⓐ Ⓑ Ⓒ
20. Ⓐ Ⓑ Ⓒ
21. Ⓐ Ⓑ Ⓒ
22. Ⓐ Ⓑ Ⓒ
23. Ⓐ Ⓑ Ⓒ
24. Ⓐ Ⓑ Ⓒ
25. Ⓐ Ⓑ Ⓒ
26. Ⓐ Ⓑ Ⓒ
27. Ⓐ Ⓑ Ⓒ
28. Ⓐ Ⓑ Ⓒ
29. Ⓐ Ⓑ Ⓒ
30. Ⓐ Ⓑ Ⓒ
31. Ⓐ Ⓑ Ⓒ

Part 3: Conversations

32. Ⓐ Ⓑ Ⓒ Ⓓ
33. Ⓐ Ⓑ Ⓒ Ⓓ
34. Ⓐ Ⓑ Ⓒ Ⓓ
35. Ⓐ Ⓑ Ⓒ Ⓓ
36. Ⓐ Ⓑ Ⓒ Ⓓ
37. Ⓐ Ⓑ Ⓒ Ⓓ
38. Ⓐ Ⓑ Ⓒ Ⓓ
39. Ⓐ Ⓑ Ⓒ Ⓓ
40. Ⓐ Ⓑ Ⓒ Ⓓ
41. Ⓐ Ⓑ Ⓒ Ⓓ
42. Ⓐ Ⓑ Ⓒ Ⓓ
43. Ⓐ Ⓑ Ⓒ Ⓓ
44. Ⓐ Ⓑ Ⓒ Ⓓ
45. Ⓐ Ⓑ Ⓒ Ⓓ
46. Ⓐ Ⓑ Ⓒ Ⓓ
47. Ⓐ Ⓑ Ⓒ Ⓓ
48. Ⓐ Ⓑ Ⓒ Ⓓ
49. Ⓐ Ⓑ Ⓒ Ⓓ
50. Ⓐ Ⓑ Ⓒ Ⓓ
51. Ⓐ Ⓑ Ⓒ Ⓓ
52. Ⓐ Ⓑ Ⓒ Ⓓ
53. Ⓐ Ⓑ Ⓒ Ⓓ
54. Ⓐ Ⓑ Ⓒ Ⓓ
55. Ⓐ Ⓑ Ⓒ Ⓓ
56. Ⓐ Ⓑ Ⓒ Ⓓ
57. Ⓐ Ⓑ Ⓒ Ⓓ
58. Ⓐ Ⓑ Ⓒ Ⓓ
59. Ⓐ Ⓑ Ⓒ Ⓓ
60. Ⓐ Ⓑ Ⓒ Ⓓ
61. Ⓐ Ⓑ Ⓒ Ⓓ
62. Ⓐ Ⓑ Ⓒ Ⓓ
63. Ⓐ Ⓑ Ⓒ Ⓓ
64. Ⓐ Ⓑ Ⓒ Ⓓ
65. Ⓐ Ⓑ Ⓒ Ⓓ
66. Ⓐ Ⓑ Ⓒ Ⓓ
67. Ⓐ Ⓑ Ⓒ Ⓓ
68. Ⓐ Ⓑ Ⓒ Ⓓ
69. Ⓐ Ⓑ Ⓒ Ⓓ
70. Ⓐ Ⓑ Ⓒ Ⓓ

Part 4: Talks

71. Ⓐ Ⓑ Ⓒ Ⓓ
72. Ⓐ Ⓑ Ⓒ Ⓓ
73. Ⓐ Ⓑ Ⓒ Ⓓ
74. Ⓐ Ⓑ Ⓒ Ⓓ
75. Ⓐ Ⓑ Ⓒ Ⓓ
76. Ⓐ Ⓑ Ⓒ Ⓓ
77. Ⓐ Ⓑ Ⓒ Ⓓ
78. Ⓐ Ⓑ Ⓒ Ⓓ
79. Ⓐ Ⓑ Ⓒ Ⓓ
80. Ⓐ Ⓑ Ⓒ Ⓓ
81. Ⓐ Ⓑ Ⓒ Ⓓ
82. Ⓐ Ⓑ Ⓒ Ⓓ
83. Ⓐ Ⓑ Ⓒ Ⓓ
84. Ⓐ Ⓑ Ⓒ Ⓓ
85. Ⓐ Ⓑ Ⓒ Ⓓ
86. Ⓐ Ⓑ Ⓒ Ⓓ
87. Ⓐ Ⓑ Ⓒ Ⓓ
88. Ⓐ Ⓑ Ⓒ Ⓓ
89. Ⓐ Ⓑ Ⓒ Ⓓ
90. Ⓐ Ⓑ Ⓒ Ⓓ
91. Ⓐ Ⓑ Ⓒ Ⓓ
92. Ⓐ Ⓑ Ⓒ Ⓓ
93. Ⓐ Ⓑ Ⓒ Ⓓ
94. Ⓐ Ⓑ Ⓒ Ⓓ
95. Ⓐ Ⓑ Ⓒ Ⓓ
96. Ⓐ Ⓑ Ⓒ Ⓓ
97. Ⓐ Ⓑ Ⓒ Ⓓ
98. Ⓐ Ⓑ Ⓒ Ⓓ
99. Ⓐ Ⓑ Ⓒ Ⓓ
100. Ⓐ Ⓑ Ⓒ Ⓓ

ANSWER SHEET
Practice Test 6

READING

Part 5: Incomplete Sentences

101. Ⓐ Ⓑ Ⓒ Ⓓ
102. Ⓐ Ⓑ Ⓒ Ⓓ
103. Ⓐ Ⓑ Ⓒ Ⓓ
104. Ⓐ Ⓑ Ⓒ Ⓓ
105. Ⓐ Ⓑ Ⓒ Ⓓ
106. Ⓐ Ⓑ Ⓒ Ⓓ
107. Ⓐ Ⓑ Ⓒ Ⓓ
108. Ⓐ Ⓑ Ⓒ Ⓓ

109. Ⓐ Ⓑ Ⓒ Ⓓ
110. Ⓐ Ⓑ Ⓒ Ⓓ
111. Ⓐ Ⓑ Ⓒ Ⓓ
112. Ⓐ Ⓑ Ⓒ Ⓓ
113. Ⓐ Ⓑ Ⓒ Ⓓ
114. Ⓐ Ⓑ Ⓒ Ⓓ
115. Ⓐ Ⓑ Ⓒ Ⓓ
116. Ⓐ Ⓑ Ⓒ Ⓓ

117. Ⓐ Ⓑ Ⓒ Ⓓ
118. Ⓐ Ⓑ Ⓒ Ⓓ
119. Ⓐ Ⓑ Ⓒ Ⓓ
120. Ⓐ Ⓑ Ⓒ Ⓓ
121. Ⓐ Ⓑ Ⓒ Ⓓ
122. Ⓐ Ⓑ Ⓒ Ⓓ
123. Ⓐ Ⓑ Ⓒ Ⓓ
124. Ⓐ Ⓑ Ⓒ Ⓓ

125. Ⓐ Ⓑ Ⓒ Ⓓ
126. Ⓐ Ⓑ Ⓒ Ⓓ
127. Ⓐ Ⓑ Ⓒ Ⓓ
128. Ⓐ Ⓑ Ⓒ Ⓓ
129. Ⓐ Ⓑ Ⓒ Ⓓ
130. Ⓐ Ⓑ Ⓒ Ⓓ

Part 6: Text Completion

131. Ⓐ Ⓑ Ⓒ Ⓓ
132. Ⓐ Ⓑ Ⓒ Ⓓ
133. Ⓐ Ⓑ Ⓒ Ⓓ
134. Ⓐ Ⓑ Ⓒ Ⓓ

135. Ⓐ Ⓑ Ⓒ Ⓓ
136. Ⓐ Ⓑ Ⓒ Ⓓ
137. Ⓐ Ⓑ Ⓒ Ⓓ
138. Ⓐ Ⓑ Ⓒ Ⓓ

139. Ⓐ Ⓑ Ⓒ Ⓓ
140. Ⓐ Ⓑ Ⓒ Ⓓ
141. Ⓐ Ⓑ Ⓒ Ⓓ
142. Ⓐ Ⓑ Ⓒ Ⓓ

143. Ⓐ Ⓑ Ⓒ Ⓓ
144. Ⓐ Ⓑ Ⓒ Ⓓ
145. Ⓐ Ⓑ Ⓒ Ⓓ
146. Ⓐ Ⓑ Ⓒ Ⓓ

Part 7: Reading Comprehension

147. Ⓐ Ⓑ Ⓒ Ⓓ
148. Ⓐ Ⓑ Ⓒ Ⓓ
149. Ⓐ Ⓑ Ⓒ Ⓓ
150. Ⓐ Ⓑ Ⓒ Ⓓ
151. Ⓐ Ⓑ Ⓒ Ⓓ
152. Ⓐ Ⓑ Ⓒ Ⓓ
153. Ⓐ Ⓑ Ⓒ Ⓓ
154. Ⓐ Ⓑ Ⓒ Ⓓ
155. Ⓐ Ⓑ Ⓒ Ⓓ
156. Ⓐ Ⓑ Ⓒ Ⓓ
157. Ⓐ Ⓑ Ⓒ Ⓓ
158. Ⓐ Ⓑ Ⓒ Ⓓ
159. Ⓐ Ⓑ Ⓒ Ⓓ
160. Ⓐ Ⓑ Ⓒ Ⓓ

161. Ⓐ Ⓑ Ⓒ Ⓓ
162. Ⓐ Ⓑ Ⓒ Ⓓ
163. Ⓐ Ⓑ Ⓒ Ⓓ
164. Ⓐ Ⓑ Ⓒ Ⓓ
165. Ⓐ Ⓑ Ⓒ Ⓓ
166. Ⓐ Ⓑ Ⓒ Ⓓ
167. Ⓐ Ⓑ Ⓒ Ⓓ
168. Ⓐ Ⓑ Ⓒ Ⓓ
169. Ⓐ Ⓑ Ⓒ Ⓓ
170. Ⓐ Ⓑ Ⓒ Ⓓ
171. Ⓐ Ⓑ Ⓒ Ⓓ
172. Ⓐ Ⓑ Ⓒ Ⓓ
173. Ⓐ Ⓑ Ⓒ Ⓓ
174. Ⓐ Ⓑ Ⓒ Ⓓ

175. Ⓐ Ⓑ Ⓒ Ⓓ
176. Ⓐ Ⓑ Ⓒ Ⓓ
177. Ⓐ Ⓑ Ⓒ Ⓓ
178. Ⓐ Ⓑ Ⓒ Ⓓ
179. Ⓐ Ⓑ Ⓒ Ⓓ
180. Ⓐ Ⓑ Ⓒ Ⓓ
181. Ⓐ Ⓑ Ⓒ Ⓓ
182. Ⓐ Ⓑ Ⓒ Ⓓ
183. Ⓐ Ⓑ Ⓒ Ⓓ
184. Ⓐ Ⓑ Ⓒ Ⓓ
185. Ⓐ Ⓑ Ⓒ Ⓓ
186. Ⓐ Ⓑ Ⓒ Ⓓ
187. Ⓐ Ⓑ Ⓒ Ⓓ
188. Ⓐ Ⓑ Ⓒ Ⓓ

189. Ⓐ Ⓑ Ⓒ Ⓓ
190. Ⓐ Ⓑ Ⓒ Ⓓ
191. Ⓐ Ⓑ Ⓒ Ⓓ
192. Ⓐ Ⓑ Ⓒ Ⓓ
193. Ⓐ Ⓑ Ⓒ Ⓓ
194. Ⓐ Ⓑ Ⓒ Ⓓ
195. Ⓐ Ⓑ Ⓒ Ⓓ
196. Ⓐ Ⓑ Ⓒ Ⓓ
197. Ⓐ Ⓑ Ⓒ Ⓓ
198. Ⓐ Ⓑ Ⓒ Ⓓ
199. Ⓐ Ⓑ Ⓒ Ⓓ
200. Ⓐ Ⓑ Ⓒ Ⓓ

Practice Test 6

LISTENING COMPREHENSION

In this section of the test, you will have the chance to show how well you understand spoken English. There are four parts to this section, with special directions for each part. You will have approximately 45 minutes to complete the Listening Comprehension sections.

Part 1: Photographs

Track 55

Directions: You will see a photograph. You will hear four statements about the photograph. Choose the statement that most closely matches the photograph, and fill in the corresponding oval on your answer sheet.

1.

3.

4.

5.

6.

Part 2: Question-Response

Track
56

Directions: You will hear a question and three possible responses. Choose the response that most closely answers the question, and fill in the corresponding oval on your answer sheet.

7. Mark your answer on your answer sheet.

8. Mark your answer on your answer sheet.

9. Mark your answer on your answer sheet.

10. Mark your answer on your answer sheet.

11. Mark your answer on your answer sheet.

12. Mark your answer on your answer sheet.

13. Mark your answer on your answer sheet.

14. Mark your answer on your answer sheet.

15. Mark your answer on your answer sheet.

16. Mark your answer on your answer sheet.

17. Mark your answer on your answer sheet.

18. Mark your answer on your answer sheet.

19. Mark your answer on your answer sheet.

20. Mark your answer on your answer sheet.

21. Mark your answer on your answer sheet.

22. Mark your answer on your answer sheet.

23. Mark your answer on your answer sheet.

24. Mark your answer on your answer sheet.

25. Mark your answer on your answer sheet.

26. Mark your answer on your answer sheet.

27. Mark your answer on your answer sheet.

28. Mark your answer on your answer sheet.

29. Mark your answer on your answer sheet.

30. Mark your answer on your answer sheet.

31. Mark your answer on your answer sheet.

Part 3: Conversations

Track 57

Directions: You will hear a conversation between two or more people. You will see three questions on each conversation and four possible answers. Choose the best answer to each question, and fill in the corresponding oval on your answer sheet.

32. What does the woman ask the man to do?

   (A) Give her a ride to work
   (B) Lift something heavy
   (C) Take her shopping
   (D) Fix her car

33. Why does the man want to be at the office early?

   (A) To repair some office equipment
   (B) To get ready for a client meeting
   (C) To wrap some presents
   (D) To finish a report

34. What does the woman suggest doing?

   (A) Leaving later
   (B) Calling a client
   (C) Stopping at the library
   (D) Asking someone for help

35. What are the speakers discussing?

   (A) Getting the office cleaned
   (B) Renting an apartment
   (C) Buying furniture
   (D) Going out to eat

36. What problem do they have?

   (A) They lost the contact information.
   (B) They think the price is too high.
   (C) They can't find anyone to hire.
   (D) They don't like the schedule.

37. What does the man suggest they do?

   (A) Leave earlier
   (B) Offer to pay less
   (C) Meet somewhere else
   (D) Buy new furniture

38. Why is the woman talking to the man?

   (A) To invite him somewhere
   (B) To make a suggestion
   (C) To discuss a problem
   (D) To ask for advice

39. What is the man doing?

   (A) Watching sports
   (B) Writing a report
   (C) Cleaning his desk
   (D) Making a phone call

40. What does the man ask the woman to do?

   (A) Give him directions to the restaurant
   (B) Come back to talk with him later
   (C) Help him with his work
   (D) Wait for him at 7:00

41. What is the man renting?

   (A) Some furniture
   (B) An apartment
   (C) A heater
   (D) A car

42. What does the woman suggest the man do?

   (A) Request something larger
   (B) Look at other options
   (C) Rent for more time
   (D) Reread the agreement

43. What will the man do next?

   (A) Fill the tank
   (B) Sign a document
   (C) Go away for the weekend
   (D) Go to another rental agency

PRACTICE TEST 6

44. Why did the man make the call?

(A) To report a problem
(B) To make a complaint
(C) To order a product
(D) To ask for information

45. What costs $20?

(A) Standard shipping
(B) Express shipping
(C) Special packaging
(D) Guaranteed delivery

46. What does the man mean when he says, "That's it"?

(A) He's decided which products to buy.
(B) His questions have been answered
(C) He's chosen his shipping method.
(D) His order is completed.

47. What best describes this conversation?

(A) An introduction
(B) A staff meeting
(C) An interview
(D) A sales pitch

48. What does the man like most about his job?

(A) The pay
(B) The events
(C) The benefits
(D) The schedule

49. What will probably happen next?

(A) The man will answer the woman's last question.
(B) The woman will speak with Mrs. Patterson.
(C) The man will leave for the weekend.
(D) The woman will go home.

50. What is likely the purpose of the man's trip?

(A) To meet a client
(B) To take a vacation
(C) To take photographs
(D) To attend a conference

51. What do the women imply about the hotel?

(A) It is in a bad location.
(B) It is uncomfortable.
(C) It is too expensive.
(D) It is very noisy.

52. What will the man do next?

(A) Research other hotels
(B) Reserve a room
(C) Cancel his trip
(D) Take a nap

53. What kind of work are they hiring contractors for?

(A) Construction
(B) Decorating
(C) Transportation
(D) Editing

54. What will happen at the meeting tomorrow?

(A) They will write a quote for the project.
(B) They will meet the contractor.
(C) They will talk about the schedule.
(D) They will review the submitted quotes.

55. What was the problem with the last contractor?

(A) He didn't finish the work.
(B) He left the job site a mess.
(C) He was located too far away.
(D) He tore up the contract.

56. Where does this conversation take place?

  (A) Clothing store
  (B) Restaurant
  (C) Paint store
  (D) Bank

57. Why is the man there?

  (A) To apply for a job
  (B) To return an item
  (C) To order something
  (D) To make a complaint

58. Why does the man say, "The selection certainly could be better"?

  (A) He wants more time to make his choice.
  (B) He doesn't like the offered choices.
  (C) He hasn't ever seen better choices.
  (D) He needs help making his choice.

59. What are the speakers discussing?

  (A) A play
  (B) A concert
  (C) A business trip
  (D) A boxing match

60. What is the woman's problem?

  (A) She has to go out of town.
  (B) She doesn't like her seat.
  (C) She is busy tomorrow.
  (D) She can't get tickets.

61. What does the second man offer to do?

  (A) Plan a trip
  (B) Call his cousin
  (C) Buy some tickets
  (D) Go to the box office

Building Directory

1st floor:	Woolman & Fox, PC
2nd floor:	Gilchrist, Inc.
3rd floor:	Zenith Enterprises
4th floor:	HCR Company

62. Look at the graphic. What floor will the woman go to?

  (A) First floor
  (B) Second Floor
  (C) Third Floor
  (D) Fourth Floor

63. Why is she going there?

  (A) To start a new job
  (B) For a job interview
  (C) To look at an apartment
  (D) For a doctor's appointment

64. What does the man imply about his relationship with Mr. Gill?

  (A) He works near Mr. Gill.
  (B) He is a client of Mr. Gill's.
  (C) He has never met Mr. Gill.
  (D) He wants to work for Mr. Gill.

65. What will the woman drink?

  (A) Lemonade
  (B) Coffee
  (C) Water
  (D) Tea

66. Why doesn't she want pie?

  (A) She isn't hungry.
  (B) The pie is too hot.
  (C) She doesn't like pie.
  (D) She hasn't had lunch yet.

67. What will the man do?

(A) Have some pie
(B) Bake some buns
(C) Buy some bacon
(D) Make some toast

Florence Café

Lunch Specials

1. Tuna fish salad plate $13
2. Mixed vegetable salad $12
3. Baked fish with rice $16
4. Sautéed vegetables with rice $15

68. Why has there been a delay?

(A) The chef arrived late.
(B) There aren't enough servers.
(C) The restaurant is very crowded.
(D) There are some new staff working.

69. What does the woman imply about the restaurant?

(A) It has a good reputation.
(B) It is not well known.
(C) It is not very popular.
(D) It always has slow service.

70. Look at the graphic. What will the woman eat?

(A) Tuna fish salad
(B) Vegetable salad
(C) Baked fish
(D) Sautéed vegetables

Part 4: Talks

Track
58

Directions: You will hear a talk given by a single speaker. You will see three questions on each talk, each with four possible answers. Choose the best answer to each question, and fill in the corresponding oval on your answer sheet.

71. What is the purpose of this message?

(A) To explain rules
(B) To solve a problem
(C) To describe a schedule
(D) To introduce a special offer

72. What happens once a year?

(A) The park stays open late.
(B) There is a movie night.
(C) A discount is offered.
(D) A concert is performed.

73. Who can the listener talk to by pressing one?

(A) A musician
(B) An operator
(C) A sales agent
(D) A park manager

___

74. What is the topic of the workshop?

(A) Budgets
(B) Computers
(C) Investments
(D) Software

75. What does the speaker give each participant?

(A) A schedule
(B) A laptop
(C) A snack
(D) A chair

76. How many breaks will there be?

(A) 1
(B) 2
(C) 3
(D) 4

77. Where is this talk happening?

(A) On a plane
(B) On a boat
(C) At a hotel
(D) On a bus

78. What is the problem?

(A) Storage compartments are full.
(B) There are not enough seats.
(C) There is bad weather.
(D) Bags have been lost.

79. What has been delayed?

(A) Serving drinks
(B) The arrival time
(C) Showing a movie
(D) The departure time

___

80. What problem does the speaker have with the product?

(A) It doesn't have a cover.
(B) The fan doesn't blow.
(C) She can't turn it on.
(D) It doesn't heat.

81. When did the speaker buy the product?

(A) This morning
(B) Two days ago
(C) Last Tuesday
(D) Nine days ago

82. What does the speaker ask the listener to do?

(A) Replace the product
(B) Provide a refund
(C) Return the call
(D) Send a manual

83. What is the focus of the tour?

(A) Architecture
(B) Gardens
(C) History
(D) Parks

84. How will the group travel?

(A) Bus
(B) Van
(C) Foot
(D) Bike

85. What will the group do first?

(A) Have lunch
(B) Look at a map
(C) Visit City Hall
(D) Buy their tickets

86. Where would this product be used?

(A) In an office
(B) At a restaurant
(C) On an airplane
(D) In a private home

87. How many cups of coffee does the product make?

(A) 20
(B) 24
(C) 28
(D) 29

88. What are listeners asked to do?

(A) Place an order
(B) Try other products
(C) Ask for a free sample
(D) Look for information

89. What event is the speaker reporting?

(A) Approval of bridge plans
(B) Completion of a bridge
(C) Repainting of an old bridge
(D) Repair work on all city bridges

90. What are people waiting to do?

(A) Photograph the bridge
(B) Talk with the reporter
(C) Cross the bridge
(D) See the mayor

91. What does the speaker mean when she says, "It's hard to believe, but final costs came in well under budget"?

(A) She doesn't understand the budget.
(B) She's surprised the project cost so little.
(C) She thinks incorrect numbers have been given.
(D) She isn't certain what the total cost of the project is.

92. What is the book about?

(A) History
(B) Cooking
(C) Travel
(D) Memoir

93. What does the speaker mean when he says, "He jumped at the chance"?

(A) Roger decided not to take a risk.
(B) Roger immediately accepted a job offer.
(C) Roger was surprised to hear about the job.
(D) Roger looked for other work opportunities.

94. What will Roger do tomorrow?

(A) Cook a meal
(B) Eat at a restaurant
(C) Read from his book
(D) Travel to the Caribbean

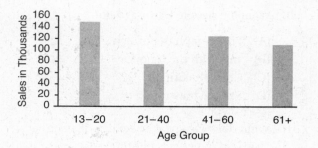

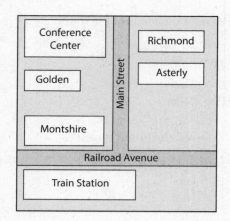

95. What type of product does this company sell?

    (A) Shoes
    (B) Clothes
    (C) Sports equipment
    (D) Construction materials

96. Look at the graphic. Which age group does the speaker want to focus on?

    (A) 13–20
    (B) 21–40
    (C) 41–60
    (D) 61+

97. What will the listeners do next?

    (A) Read a sales report
    (B) Work in groups
    (C) Have a discussion
    (D) Look at another slide

98. Who is Marc, most likely?

    (A) A ticket agent
    (B) A hotel manager
    (C) The speaker's boss
    (D) The speaker's assistant

99. Why does the speaker want to change her travel plans?

    (A) To go to a seminar
    (B) To add more meetings
    (C) To stay at a better hotel
    (D) To use a different form of transportation

100. Look at the graphic. Which hotel will the speaker prefer?

    (A) Richmond
    (B) Golden
    (C) Asterly
    (D) Montshire

This is the end of the Listening Comprehension portion of the test. Turn to Part 5 in your test book.

READING COMPREHENSION

In this section of the test, you will have the chance to show how well you understand written English. There are three parts to this section, with special directions for each part.

**YOU WILL HAVE ONE HOUR AND FIFTEEN MINUTES
TO COMPLETE PARTS 5, 6, AND 7 OF THE TEST.**

Part 5: Incomplete Sentences

> **Directions:** You will see a sentence with a missing word. Four possible answers follow the sentence. Choose the best answer to the question, and fill in the corresponding oval on your answer sheet.

101. Earn a good salary while building _____ job skills when you enroll in the City Tech carpentry program.

 (A) value
 (B) valued
 (C) valuably
 (D) valuable

102. The Whip cargo van can haul _____ to 5,350 pounds and comes with a rear back-up camera and security alarm.

 (A) over
 (B) up
 (C) before
 (D) in

103. The course is _____ for working professionals, so the class meets two evenings a week.

 (A) barely
 (B) rapidly
 (C) primarily
 (D) slightly

104. Greg Trist opens his art studio to the public on the first Monday of the month, which coincides _____ the city's monthly Art Walk event.

 (A) between
 (B) by
 (C) through
 (D) with

105. The executive team decided to use the pink and orange color _____ for the new laundry detergent logo.

 (A) appearance
 (B) photo
 (C) scheme
 (D) line

106. I strongly recommend _____ a contract with LL Logistics to handle our domestic deliveries.

 (A) sign
 (B) signed
 (C) signing
 (D) will sign

107. The landscaper said he _____ the hedges around the office when he comes next week.

 (A) trims
 (B) will trim
 (C) has trimmed
 (D) has been trimming

108. If you can wait a few minutes, Ms. Sato will attend _____ your problem as soon as she is free.

 (A) to
 (B) for
 (C) beside
 (D) in

109. Zasels' weekly coupon is good for 40% off items storewide _____ custom framing, furniture, and electronics.

(A) exempt
(B) having
(C) without
(D) except

110. Visitors to the factory must leave their personal _____ at the security desk and put on a protective coat and a pair of goggles.

(A) belongings
(B) costumes
(C) experiences
(D) appearances

111. While he is a team player and always on time, Daniel doesn't have the skills to do _____ job.

(A) he
(B) him
(C) his
(D) her

112. By signing this form, you _____ KM Recovery Group to act as your agent.

(A) authorizing
(B) authorization
(C) authority
(D) authorize

113. Full-time employees _____ attend the RSTLC annual conference at their department's expense with approval from their supervisor.

(A) be
(B) don't
(C) can
(D) won't

114. Unfortunately, the kitchen needs _____ repairs that have to be made by a trained plumber.

(A) marginal
(B) extensive
(C) minimal
(D) common

115. _____ budget reductions, the company will not be filling the currently available Marketing Supervisor position.

(A) Due to
(B) However
(C) Because
(D) In that

116. The remote control _____ programmed to work with the television in the lobby but not the break room.

(A) has
(B) be
(C) been
(D) is

117. The person _____ signature appears on the document is the one ultimately responsible for the deal.

(A) who
(B) who's
(C) whose
(D) whom

118. _____ until the last minute to turn in work is definitely not encouraged in this department.

(A) Wait
(B) Waiting
(C) To wait
(D) Wait for

119. You can sign up for the online training at your convenience _____ attend the next week's onsite training session in person.

(A) or
(B) so
(C) if
(D) as

120. The budget report had to be rewritten because some of the figures it contained were _____.

(A) acceptable
(B) inaccurate
(C) comprehensive
(D) calculating

121. The company has plans to _____ several neighboring properties, which will be used for expanding the manufacturing plant.

(A) inquire
(B) require
(C) expire
(D) acquire

122. _____ the client accepts the plan, the team has one month to complete the final design.

(A) Before
(B) After
(C) While
(D) Then

123. The best way to _____ approval from your supervisor is to consistently complete your projects on time.

(A) earn
(B) collect
(C) grant
(D) incur

124. When the renovations _____ complete, we will have a much more attractive and spacious office.

(A) are
(B) is
(C) be
(D) will be

125. The production team can _____ the photos if the client thinks they are too large.

(A) size
(B) resize
(C) sizeable
(D) sizing

126. _____ the shipment went out later than promised, the client decided to make another order.

(A) Because
(B) Therefore
(C) Despite
(D) Although

127. The prices quoted on the website _____ materials as well as labor, but not shipping and handling costs.

(A) include
(B) including
(C) inclusive
(D) inclusively

128. The Human Resources Department requires all applicants to provide references from their _____ employers.

(A) before
(B) advanced
(C) previous
(D) precede

129. You can choose to receive your paycheck by mail or opt for direct deposit into your back account _____.

(A) either
(B) instead
(C) alternative
(D) in addition

130. Last quarter's sales would have been better if the company _____ more in advertising.

(A) had invested
(B) has invested
(C) has been investing
(D) would have invested

Part 6: Text Completion

> **Directions:** You will see four passages, each with four blanks. Each blank has four answer choices. For each blank, choose the word, phrase, or sentence that best completes the passage.

Questions 131–134 refer to the following letter.

Dear Business Owner,

We are writing to let you ____ about our new company, Executive Dining,
          131

which provides catering services to local businesses. We cater everything from

elegant banquets to informal refreshments for meetings and workshops. We

have a variety of menus from which you can choose, and we can also tailor our

offerings to meet ____ specific needs. We do everything from set up to
         132

serving to clean up, and we can provide table settings, decorations, and chairs and

tables as needed. As the company's ____ , we have a combined 25 years of
         133

experience in food service and are both graduates of the National Culinary School.

____ .
134

Sincerely,

Elaine Mayfield and Georgina Simms

131. (A) know
    (B) knows
    (C) to know
    (D) will know

132. (A) its
    (B) our
    (C) your
    (D) their

133. (A) auditors
    (B) backers
    (C) clients
    (D) founders

134. (A) We believe you will enjoy the meal we have planned for you
    (B) We hope you will contact us to discuss your catering needs
    (C) We have put your next company banquet on our schedule
    (D) We look forward to meeting you at the end of the week

Questions 135–138 refer to the following notice.

NOTICE TO RIDERS OF RED LINE BUSES

_____. Therefore, Red Line service will be temporarily suspended at the Main
135
Street stop as of June 1. Passengers can use the Oakland Avenue or River Street

stops _____. Please check the City Transport Services (CTS) website for schedule
136
information for those stops. We apologize for any inconvenience this situation may

cause. It is part of the mayor's initiative to _____ bus service for all users. Please
137
_____ the CTS Public Relations office with any questions or comments.
138

---

135. (A) Buses are undergoing routine maintenance
　　 (B) Bus fares are scheduled to go up next month
　　 (C) The number of buses serving this line will increase
　　 (D) Renovations on selected bus shelters will begin soon

136. (A) also
　　 (B) despite
　　 (C) instead
　　 (D) nevertheless

137. (A) approve
　　 (B) improve
　　 (C) disprove
　　 (D) reprove

138. (A) contact
　　 (B) to contact
　　 (C) can contact
　　 (D) you will contact

Questions 139–142 refer to the following memo.

To: All Employees
From: Arthur Ivers
Date: February 10
Re: Annual Leave Policy

We have revised the company's annual leave policy.

_____.
139

• Leave requests must _____ a minimum of one month in advance.
                        140

• To request time off, please complete Form 54 and make one copy for your supervisor and _____ for the HR office.
                        141

• You may take no more than two weeks of leave at a time. If special circumstances require that you take more, please discuss it with your supervisor.

I will be happy to answer any questions you may have _____ the policy revisions.
                                                      142

Please stop by my office any time.

139. (A) Revisions need approval from the HR office
     (B) Please follow the guidelines in the handbook
     (C) Annual leave can be taken at any time of year
     (D) Here is the policy as it looks with the changes

140. (A) submit
     (B) to submit
     (C) be submitted
     (D) be submitting

141. (A) another
     (B) that one
     (C) some
     (D) this

142. (A) pertaining
     (B) regarding
     (C) concerns
     (D) relative

Hotel Comar

April 3

Dear Mr. Warren,

We have received your letter describing your stay at the Hotel Comar last week. _____.
143

We pride ourselves _____ our excellent customer service and strive
144
to make all our guests feel welcome and comfortable. Unfortunately, we did not meet this goal during your _____ stay. It was an unusually
145
busy time for us as we were hosting two conferences, and it was also the height of the tourist season. However, that is not an excuse for neglecting the comfort of all our guests.

We hope you will consider _____ to the Hotel Comar the next time
146
you are in town. We offer a prime location, fully-equipped gym, and a five-star restaurant. I am enclosing a coupon for twenty percent off the cost of your next stay with us.

Sincerely,

Amalia Knight
Manager

143. (A) Thank you for choosing to stay at the Comar during your visit to this city
(B) We were very sorry to hear that you had such an unpleasant experience
(C) We regret that we have no rooms available at that time
(D) Our hotel is known as one of the finest in the city

144. (A) on
(B) in
(C) of
(D) due

145. (A) upcoming
(B) final
(C) lately
(D) recent

146. (A) return
(B) returns
(C) returning
(D) to return

Part 7: Reading Comprehension

Directions: You will see single and multiple reading passages followed by several questions. Each question has four answer choices. Choose the best answer to the question, and fill in the corresponding oval on your answer sheet.

Questions 147–148 refer to the following webpage.

---

www.foodshopping.com

File   Edit   View   Favorites   Tools   Help

You are almost finished. Please review your order and then click **Confirm** to pay and get your groceries on their way. Your order will be on your doorstep before noon today.

Include any special requests or comments in the notes section below. We look forward to shopping for you.

ITEM	AMOUNT	PRICE
Bananas	1 pound	$0.99
Orange Soda (Store Brand)	6-pack	$3.99
Folder's Brand Milk Chocolate	1 bar	$2.15
Tomatoes	1 pound	$3.45
Walnuts, whole	1 pound	$8.50
	SUBTOTAL	$19.08
	SERVICE CHARGE	$8.00
	TAXES	$0.00
	TOTAL	$27.08

NOTES:

Please choose yellow bananas that are ready for eating.

Confirm

---

147. When will the order be delivered?

(A) This morning
(B) This afternoon
(C) Tomorrow morning
(D) Tomorrow afternoon

148. What does the customer request?

(A) Cold soda
(B) Yellow tomatoes
(C) Ripe bananas
(D) Chopped walnuts

Questions 149–150 refer to the following text message chain.

MILLIE WILSON Did you see the e-mail from the warehouse?	8:45
PAUL STONE No. Is there a problem with the shipment?	8:46
MILLIE WILSON It's not going out till tomorrow.	8:47
PAUL STONE No good. Peterson is not going to like this.	8:49
MILLIE WILSON Who?	8:51
PAUL STONE The client. The one who paid an extra thousand dollars for overnight delivery.	8:52
MILLIE WILSON He did? I had no idea. Let me make a few phone calls and see if I can get them to speed things up.	8:54

149. At 8:47, what does Ms. Wilson mean when she writes, "It's not going out till tomorrow"?

(A) The warehouse is closed today.
(B) The shipment will be delayed.
(C) She will wait to e-mail the client.
(D) The client has not yet made an order.

150. What does Millie offer to do?

(A) Call up the client
(B) Make the delivery herself
(C) Get the order sent earlier
(D) Return the thousand dollars

Questions 151–152 refer to the following expense report.

	Asterix, Inc. Expense Authorization				
	Employee: Roland Webb Purpose: Wilmont office training seminar				
Category	Date	Description	Notes	Amount
Airfare	Sept. 16, Sept. 21	Round trip, business class.	Seminar originally planned for week of Sept. 9. Amount includes $200 change fee.	$885
Hotel	Sept. 16–Sept. 20	$110/night x 5, at Atrium Hotel, Wilmont		$550
Car Rental	Sept. 16–Sept. 21	Zippo Rental Agency		$275

151. What fee is included in the cost of the airfare?

(A) Special meal
(B) Extra baggage
(C) First class upgrade
(D) Rescheduling charge

152. How many nights did the employee stay at the hotel?

(A) 1
(B) 5
(C) 6
(D) 10

Questions 153–154 refer to the following employment ad.

Part-time office assistant needed for small accounting firm. Will be trained in all aspects of the job including computer data entry, file management, and appointment scheduling. Must have pleasant manner and ability to provide excellent customer service. Must be proficient with word processing functions and able to learn software programs used in the office. Apply in person to Estelle Fox, 110 Grayson Avenue, Suite 10. No phone calls.

153. What is a requirement of the job?

(A) Proficiency in data entry
(B) Ability to program computers
(C) Knowledge of word processing
(D) Experience with appointment scheduling

154. How can someone apply for the job?

(A) Visit the office
(B) Send an e-mail
(C) Mail a résumé
(D) Call Ms. Fox

Questions 155–157 refer to the following article.

Richard Wenger, director of the Metropolitan Area Public Transportation System (MPTA), has announced that as of February 1 conductors on the MPTA's commuter rail lines will start accepting e-tickets on passengers' smartphones. Passengers can go to the MPTA website to purchase single-ride and round-trip tickets as well as weekly and annual passes, which are then sent by e-mail to the purchaser. Train conductors can scan the ticket or pass directly from the passenger's smartphones. Passengers can also choose to print their tickets, and the conductor will scan the printed copy. As an incentive to start using the new system, e-ticket purchasers will receive a 15 percent discount on all tickets and passes purchased during the month of February. Traditional paper tickets are still available for sale at ticket machines in most commuter rail stations. However, these tickets are being phased out and will no longer be available as of January 1st of next year. Mr. Wenger commented that surveys of commuter rail riders showed overwhelming enthusiasm for the new system.

155. What is this passage mostly about?

(A) A special discount
(B) A passenger survey
(C) A new kind of train ticket
(D) An increase in train fares

156. How are traditional tickets sold?

(A) On the web
(B) By machine
(C) From conductors
(D) At the MPTA office

157. The phrase *phased out* in line 21 is closest in meaning to

(A) displayed
(B) discovered
(C) distributed
(D) discontinued

Professional Certification

The Southeastern Interior Design Association's professional certification program offers three levels of certification for professional interior designers. The program is open to anyone who has been a member in good standing for at least one year. The Southeastern Interior Design Association's professional certificates are recognized by most interior design businesses and training programs in the country.

Certificates are awarded upon successful completion of a test. To take the test for any one level of certification except Level One, you must have passed the previous level test. While no coursework is required, we do offer classes and reading materials to help you prepare for the test.

Currently, certification tests are administered every six months at the association's headquarters in Savannah. A web-based test will be available by the end of next year. For information on certification levels, test preparation classes, or test registration, please request an information packet from our office: *info@sidassn.org*. Don't forget to include your member number in your message.

---

158. What is required to take a test?

    (A) Membership in the association
    (B) Completion of certain classes
    (C) Experience in interior design
    (D) Graduation from a training program

159. How often are the tests given?

    (A) Six times a month
    (B) Six times a year
    (C) Once a year
    (D) Twice a year

160. What should someone do who wants to take the test?

    (A) Enroll in a class
    (B) E-mail the office
    (C) Visit the website
    (D) Speak with an advisor

Questions 161–163 refer to the following flier.

Lightning Car Rentals

NEW: Damage Fee Waiver offer

Your standard rental agreement includes comprehensive insurance. However, if your rented vehicle is involved in an incident during your rental period, you could be responsible for a $500 damage fee that is not covered by insurance.

Renters who are aged 21 or over and haven't been involved in an accident in the past 12 months have the option to purchase a Damage Fee Waiver. These waivers are not a substitute for insurance coverage; they offer extra peace of mind against unexpected costs. The waiver must be added to the rental agreement at the time of signing.

Two Damage Fee Waivers are available.
• Half Waiver: For $10 per day of rental period, reduce your damage fee to $250
• Full Waiver: For $15 per day of rental period, reduce your damage fee to $0

Ask your rental agent to add this waiver to your rental agreement now.

---

161. Who can get a waiver?

(A) Any agency customer
(B) Drivers who pass a road test
(C) Customers who rent for a week
(D) People with a safe driving record

162. What is the waiver for?

(A) To extend coverage to 12 months
(B) To remove the age requirement
(C) To reduce or eliminate a charge
(D) To replace regular insurance

163. When should a waiver be purchased?

(A) When signing the rental agreement
(B) When making a reservation
(C) When reporting an accident
(D) When insurance is purchased

Questions 164–167 refer to the following online chat discussion.

Mija Kim [1:15]
How are the plans for Friday coming along? I haven't had an update in a while.

Jairo Perez [1:15]
I heard back from the caterers just this morning. They can accommodate my menu modifications, no problem.

Alba Jones [1:16]
At no extra charge?

Jairo Perez [1:17]
No extra charge.

Mija Kim [1:18]
That's excellent news. What about the room set up? Has anyone talked with Maintenance about that?

Alba Jones [1:20]
I did. They'll have tables and chairs for 50 all ready and arranged by 11:30, so the caterers can get in and set their stuff up. They said they want to be in there an hour ahead of time.

Mija Kim [1:21]
Fantastic! I got some more RSVPs last night. I think I've heard from just about everybody now.

Jairo Perez [1:21]
And almost everyone is coming, right?

Mija Kim [1:23]
It looks that way. So, with the caterers and the room arrangements all set, I guess that's it. We're good to go.

---

164. What is being planned?

(A) A workshop
(B) A staff meeting
(C) A demonstration
(D) A luncheon

165. What did Jairo change?

(A) The menu
(B) The schedule
(C) The number of guests
(D) The room arrangement

166. What did Mija receive last night?

(A) A guest list
(B) Invitation responses
(C) Room arrangement plans
(D) A message from the caterers

167. At 1:23, what does Mija mean when she writes, "We're good to go"?

(A) The guests are happy to be invited.
(B) It's time to set up the room.
(C) Everything is ready.
(D) She has to leave.

The question is all too common. You're new to the job market, having just finished your education. There's a lot of competition out there. How can you prepare for job interviews in a way that will help you stand out from the crowd? –[1]–

"It all boils down to one thing," says Evelyn Pritchard, former hiring manager at XQ, Inc. and now president of her own employment consulting firm, Pritchard, LLC. "Professionalism. That's the key. You've got to dress, talk, act like a professional." This may seem obvious, Pritchard explains, but many young people have a hard time grasping this concept. She offers the following advice for those setting out for their first job interviews. –[2]–

Appearance comes first. –[3]– You should dress like a professional. This means business suits for men and business suits or skirt and blouse combinations for women. Keep in mind that you don't want the color of your clothes to shout. Black, charcoal gray, or deep blue are best for job interviews.

–[4]– When you enter the room, introduce yourself with a firm handshake. Look your interviewer in the eye as you speak. Answer questions with confidence. Most important of all, keep your cell phone turned off.

168. Who would be most interested in this article?

(A) Hiring managers
(B) Employment agencies
(C) Mid-level professionals
(D) Recent college graduates

169. What does Ms. Pritchard mean in paragraph 2, line 1, when she is quoted as saying, "It all boils down to one thing"?

(A) It is important to stand out from the crowd.
(B) Her advice can be summarized in one word.
(C) People must work hard to look professional.
(D) Interviews are a key part of the hiring process.

170. What is suggested about clothes worn for job interviews?

(A) The colors should be dark.
(B) The suits should be clean.
(C) The skirts should be long.
(D) The clothes should be new.

171. In which of the positions marked [1], [2], [3], and [4] does the following sentence best belong?

"Acting like a professional is as important as looking like one."

(A) [1]
(B) [2]
(C) [3]
(D) [4]

Questions 172–175 refer to the following letter.

August 22

Stephanie Jackson
PO Box 110
Marston, NH

Dear Ms. Jackson,

I heard you speak last week when you were a guest on our local radio show, Green Energy Talk. I was very impressed with the depth of your knowledge about solar energy. I know a little bit about this subject myself. I belong to a small local organization called Sun Power that has the goal of bringing more solar power to our community. I have some familiarity with the different types of solar panels and have installed some on the roof of my house. They provide my family with most of our domestic hot water needs throughout the year.

As you are well aware, replacing fossil fuels with alternative forms of energy is crucial to our future, and I believe we need to spread the word and get more people on board with this. To that end, we are having an alternative energy fair in our community toward the end of next month. We would be very grateful if you would consider being one of our speakers. We wouldn't be able to pay you, but you would have the chance to sell your books there. If you plan to attend, I will need to hear back from you before the end of two weeks so that I can put you on the schedule. Thank you for considering my request, and I hope to see you in September.

Sincerely,

Fred Marquez

Fred Marquez

172. Why did Mr. Marquez write the letter to Ms. Jackson?

(A) To tell her about his organization
(B) To sell her some solar panels
(C) To invite her to an event
(D) To ask her for a job

173. What is indicated about Mr. Marquez?

(A) He is the president of the Sun Power organization.
(B) He wants to get people interested in his cause.
(C) He makes a living installing solar panels.
(D) He is an expert on solar energy.

174. What is suggested about Ms. Jackson?

(A) She has written some books.
(B) She is a friend of Mr. Marquez.
(C) She hosts a radio show.
(D) She travels frequently.

175. When does Mr. Marquez need to have Ms. Jackson's reply?

(A) In one week
(B) In two weeks
(C) Before September
(D) Before next month

Questions 176–180 refer to the following webpage and e-mail.

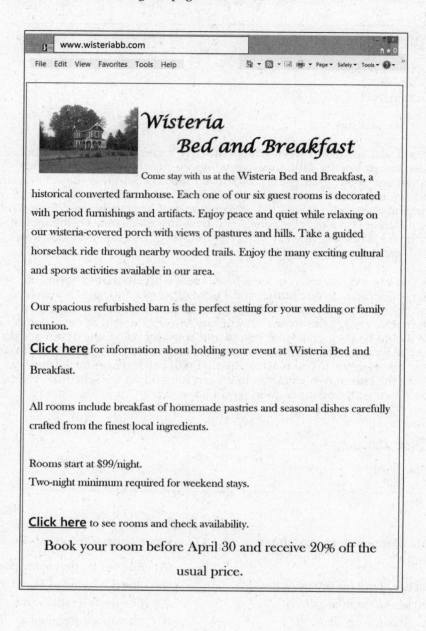

From: lsimmonsherbs@simmons.com
To: info@wisteriabb.com
Subject: introducing myself
Date: April 1

Hi,

I just saw your bed and breakfast website. It looks lovely. I noticed that you include local ingredients in your breakfast dishes. I am a local grower of herbs and flowers. I sell my products at local farmer's markets and also have a number of regular customers among the area's hotels and restaurants.

I would be happy to provide your business with fresh herbs and flowers on either a regular or as-needed basis. I can supply fresh herbs for your breakfasts and floral decorations for weddings that you host. In addition, you may want to consider providing your guests with fragrant herbal bouquets in their rooms.

I can come by your place any time next week to talk it over. In the meantime, I am attaching a list of herbs and flowers I have available, by season. Prices vary but are always competitive.

I look forward to hearing from you.

Lucinda Simmons

176. What is suggested about the Wisteria?

(A) It is a large hotel.
(B) It is in a rural setting.
(C) It has a flower garden.
(D) It has a modern design.

177. What can guests do at the Wisteria?

(A) Buy crafts
(B) Have lunch
(C) Host a party
(D) Work in the barn

178. How can a guest get a discount?

(A) Hold an event in the barn
(B) Stay at the Wisteria in April
(C) Stay for two weekend nights
(D) Make a reservation before April 30

179. Why did Ms. Simmons write the e-mail?

(A) To offer products for sale
(B) To make a room reservation
(C) To ask about buying the business
(D) To find out about holding an event

180. What kind of business does Ms. Simmons have?

(A) Farm
(B) Hotel
(C) Restaurant
(D) Event planning

From: drosen@mycompany.com
To: customerservice@marvelclean.com
Subject: cleaning
Date: December 15

Dear Marvel Cleaning Service,

I am interested in finding out about your cleaning services. I am currently located at the Octagon Towers, but plan to be leaving next month. According to the terms of the lease here, tenants must leave everything in good condition or be charged a penalty by the landlord. So, I need a service to come in and clean up after I have left, and a colleague at work suggested I contact you. I am contacting several services at this time, so that I can compare costs. Could you let me know how much you would charge to clean my place? Would you need to visit it first, or can you tell me the price based on size? It is an efficiency apartment, so it consists of just one large room.

Thank you.

David Rosen

Marvel Cleaning Service

"Big or small, we clean it all."

Leave the housekeeping to us. Whether you live in a palatial mansion or an efficiency apartment, we will make your home sparkle and shine.

Up to 3 rooms	....	$75
4–5 rooms	....	$125
6–7 rooms	....	$175
8 rooms	....	$200
over 8 rooms	....	Contact us

If your space is larger than 8 rooms, a customer service representative will discuss your needs with you and provide you with an estimate. We guarantee that our prices are always competitive. Call us when you need us, or arrange for regular weekly or monthly service.

Book your cleaning today.
customerservice@marvelclean.com
303-555-1212

181. Why does Mr. Rosen need to have his apartment cleaned?

(A) He is looking for a tenant.
(B) He is expecting visitors.
(C) He is moving away.
(D) He is hosting a party.

182. How did Mr. Rosen hear about Marvel?

(A) A co-worker recommended it.
(B) He found it on the Internet.
(C) His landlord suggested it.
(D) He saw the flier.

183. How much will it cost to clean Mr. Rosen's apartment?

(A) $75
(B) $125
(C) $175
(D) $200

184. What is suggested about Marvel Cleaning Service?

(A) It charges more than other cleaners.
(B) It cleans residences only.
(C) It doesn't serve one-time customers.
(D) It rarely cleans spaces larger than 8 rooms.

185. In the flier, the word *estimate* in paragraph 2, line 3, is closest in meaning to

(A) guess
(B) value
(C) analysis
(D) approximation

Questions 186–190 refer to the following webpage, e-mail, and review.

www.lannons.com

File   Edit   View   Favorites   Tools   Help

LANNON'S OFFICE SUPPLY

E-Z Folding Table

✳Special Promotions✳

Need extra work space? Holding a large meeting or luncheon? Desk too small? The E-Z Folding Table expands your space in just seconds. It quickly unfolds to accommodate up to 8 people. When you no longer need it, it folds back up to a compact size that fits easily in most closets. Black table top with chrome legs.

Buy now and save!

Small (seats 4)	$65
Medium (seats 6)	$85
Large (seats 8)	$110
Set of 3 (1 of each size)	$230

(Prices good though March 30.)

First-time customer? Use coupon code **Z54** at checkout for a 15% discount.

Click here to calculate shipping costs.

Free shipping on all orders of $100 or more.

From: noreply@lannon.com
To: miker@trex.com
Subject: your order

The following item(s) shipped today.

Item	Quantity	Price
E-Z Folding Table	1	$110.00
Tax		$6.50
Shipping		$0
Total		$116.50

Tracking no. 1205039299919111
You can track your order at *www.lannons.com/tracking*

★ ★ ★ ★ ★

By Mike Rivera on June 14, 2016

I received my Lannon's E-Z Folding Table last week. Everything was great until I went to put it away. It unfolds easily and is very sturdy and also attractive, but when I first folded it up to put away, I realized the clips were missing. These are needed because without them the table doesn't stay folded and you can't store it. I originally gave this product 3 stars because of this. However, I contacted customer service and they sent me the clips right away. The customer service person was very polite, and now that I have the clips, the table perfectly suits my needs. We use it in our office for our weekly staff meetings and everybody says it is very comfortable and convenient to use. Highly recommended.

186. What is suggested about the folding table?

(A) It is currently on sale.
(B) It is available only in March.
(C) It comes in a variety of colors.
(D) It is the website's most popular item.

187. Which table did Mr. Rivera order?

(A) Small
(B) Medium
(C) Large
(D) Set of 3

188. Why didn't Mr. Rivera pay shipping costs?

(A) He had a coupon for free shipping.
(B) His order cost more than $100.
(C) The company never charges for shipping.
(D) He forgot to include this on his order form.

189. Why did Mr. Rivera order the table?

(A) For client consultations
(B) For extra desk space
(C) For guests at a lunch
(D) For use at meetings

190. Why did Mr. Rivera change his original product rating?

(A) His use of the product changed.
(B) His co-workers liked the product.
(C) The company corrected a mistake.
(D) He listened to other reviewers' opinions.

Stoneybrook Dinner Theater

presents

Romeo and Juliet
by William Shakespeare

June 12, 13, 14, 19, 20, and 21

Enjoy a three-course meal followed by our own specially choreographed version of Shakespeare's classic tale.

Reserve your place now! Visit us online at *www.stoneybrookdt.com* or call us at 493-555-2121.

	Show only	Dinner and Show
per person	$50	$80
per couple	$90	$135

Dinner begins at 6:30, show begins at 8:00.

Three-course meal includes:

- Choice of soup or salad
- Entrée—beef, chicken, or vegetarian
- Dessert

From: estherwilson@acme.com
To: bobcharles@workplace.com
Subject: dinner theater
Date: June 12

Bob,

Are you interested in seeing Romeo and Juliet? My sister gave me some tickets that she can't use. They're for that Stoneybrook Dinner Theater place, so we'd have dinner first and then see the play. I've heard the food there is only mediocre, but the play got fantastic reviews.

The tickets are for June 21st. I won't be able to leave the office that day until a little after 6:00, and I really don't want to be late for the dinner, so I think the best plan would be for me to take a cab and meet you there. I hope you can come. I know it will be fun.

Esther

From: bobcharles@workplace.com

To: estherwilson@acme.com

Subject: re: dinner theater

Date: June 12

Hi Esther,

Yes, I would love to join you at the dinner theater. It sounds like a lot of fun, and it will be my first time seeing this particular play. I'll have my car with me, so I'll plan to pick you up. Then you won't have to worry about a cab. It only takes 15 minutes to get to the dinner theater from your office, so I think we'll make it just in time.

I know what you mean about the food. I've actually eaten there before. I suppose we could just skip the dinner and see the show only, but you already have the tickets, so we might as well enjoy it as much as we can. And I am really looking forward to seeing the play.

See you June 21st.

Bob

---

191. What is suggested about the meal at the dinner theater?

  (A) It is served after the show.
  (B) It includes dishes without meat.
  (C) It can be bought apart from show tickets.
  (D) It is highly-rated by restaurant reviewers.

192. How much did Esther pay for the dinner theater tickets?

  (A) $0
  (B) $80
  (C) $90
  (D) $135

193. How will Esther probably get to the dinner theater?

  (A) She will drive.
  (B) She will take a cab.
  (C) She will ride the bus.
  (D) She will get a ride with Bob.

194. What is suggested about Bob?

  (A) He doesn't like to see plays.
  (B) He has never seen *Romeo and Juliet*.
  (C) He thinks the play won't be very good.
  (D) He has not been to the dinner theater before.

195. In the second e-mail, the word *skip* in paragraph 2, line 2, is closest in meaning to

  (A) consume
  (B) improve
  (C) omit
  (D) jump

Questions 196–200 refer to the following itinerary, flier, and e-mail.

HR Manufacturers
Itinerary for: Siri Hakim
Wiltshire/Montague trip
April 10–April 15

Sunday, April 10	lv. 2:30 P.M. Breezeways Flight 23 arr Wiltshire 8:30 P.M. Rivera Hotel, Wiltshire
Monday, April 11	10 A.M. – 5 P.M. Meetings with Product Development Team
Tuesday, April 12	8:00 A.M. Train to Montague, tour of HR Manufacturers Plant Hotel Pine, Montague
Wednesday, April 13	9:15 A.M. Train to Wiltshire 2:00 P.M. Meeting with Marketing Department Riviera Hotel, Wiltshire
Thursday, April 14	8:00 A.M. Breakfast meeting with John Andrews 10:00 A.M. Tour of Wiltshire. 1:30 P.M. Presentation to Wiltshire staff
Friday, April 15	lv. 9:45 A.M. Breezeways Flight 567

Don't miss the 3rd annual Wiltshire

Business Expo!

Exhibits by businesses from all over the region
✔ See new products and innovations
✔ Find out about current best business practices

Workshops by renowned business experts

✔ Learn from some of the country's most respected business professionals.

(See other side for a list of workshop topics and a complete schedule.)

Bring your résumé!

✔ Recruiters from major companies will be available to meet with job seekers and discuss employment opportunities.

Wiltshire Conference Center
April 15–17

196. When will Ms. Hakim visit a factory?

(A) April 10
(B) April 11
(C) April 12
(D) April 13

197. What can people do at the business expo?

(A) Buy products
(B) Interview for jobs
(C) Learn to write résumés
(D) Find out about business loans

198. In the flier, the word *renowned* in line 6 is closest in meaning to

(A) trained
(B) famous
(C) experienced
(D) knowledgeable

199. What change does Ms. Hakim want to make to her itinerary?

(A) Add a day to her trip
(B) Move to a different hotel
(C) Have another staff meeting
(D) Stay in Wiltshire for the weekend

200. What is suggested about Ms. Hakim?

(A) She has never been to the Wiltshire office.
(B) She takes frequent business trips.
(C) She is looking for people to hire.
(D) She used to work in Wiltshire.

STOP

This is the end of the test. If you finish before time is called, you may go back to Parts 5, 6, and 7 and check your work.

LISTENING COMPREHENSION

Part 1: Photographs

1. **C**		3. **D**		5. **B**	
2. **A**		4. **A**		6. **D**	

Part 2: Question-Response

7. **B**	14. **B**	21. **B**	28. **C**
8. **A**	15. **A**	22. **A**	29. **B**
9. **C**	16. **C**	23. **C**	30. **A**
10. **A**	17. **C**	24. **C**	31. **A**
11. **C**	18. **B**	25. **B**	
12. **A**	19. **A**	26. **A**	
13. **B**	20. **B**	27. **A**	

Part 3: Conversations

32. **A**	42. **C**	52. **A**	62. **C**
33. **B**	43. **B**	53. **A**	63. **B**
34. **A**	44. **D**	54. **D**	64. **A**
35. **A**	45. **B**	55. **C**	65. **D**
36. **D**	46. **B**	56. **D**	66. **A**
37. **C**	47. **C**	57. **C**	67. **A**
38. **A**	48. **D**	58. **B**	68. **B**
39. **B**	49. **B**	59. **A**	69. **A**
40. **C**	50. **D**	60. **D**	70. **B**
41. **D**	51. **B**	61. **B**	

Part 4: Talks

71. **D**	79. **A**	87. **B**	95. **A**
72. **A**	80. **D**	88. **D**	96. **B**
73. **C**	81. **B**	89. **B**	97. **C**
74. **C**	82. **C**	90. **C**	98. **D**
75. **A**	83. **A**	91. **B**	99. **A**
76. **B**	84. **C**	92. **B**	100. **D**
77. **A**	85. **B**	93. **B**	
78. **C**	86. **A**	94. **C**	

ANSWER KEY
Practice Test 6

READING

Part 5: Incomplete Sentences

101. **D**	109. **D**	117. **C**	125. **B**
102. **B**	110. **A**	118. **B**	126. **D**
103. **C**	111. **C**	119. **A**	127. **A**
104. **D**	112. **D**	120. **B**	128. **C**
105. **C**	113. **C**	121. **D**	129. **B**
106. **C**	114. **B**	122. **B**	130. **A**
107. **B**	115. **A**	123. **A**	
108. **A**	116. **D**	124. **A**	

Part 6: Text Completion

131. **A**	135. **D**	139. **D**	143. **B**
132. **C**	136. **C**	140. **C**	144. **A**
133. **D**	137. **B**	141. **A**	145. **D**
134. **B**	138. **A**	142. **B**	146. **C**

Part 7: Reading Comprehension

147. **A**	161. **D**	175. **B**	189. **D**
148. **C**	162. **C**	176. **B**	190. **C**
149. **B**	163. **A**	177. **C**	191. **B**
150. **C**	164. **D**	178. **D**	192. **A**
151. **D**	165. **A**	179. **A**	193. **D**
152. **B**	166. **B**	180. **A**	194. **B**
153. **C**	167. **C**	181. **C**	195. **C**
154. **A**	168. **D**	182. **A**	196. **C**
155. **C**	169. **B**	183. **A**	197. **B**
156. **B**	170. **A**	184. **B**	198. **B**
157. **D**	171. **D**	185. **D**	199. **A**
158. **A**	172. **C**	186. **A**	200. **A**
159. **D**	173. **B**	187. **C**	
160. **B**	174. **A**	188. **B**	

TEST SCORE CONVERSION TABLE

Count your correct responses. Match the number of correct responses with the corresponding score from the Test Score Conversion Table (below). Add the two scores together. This is your Total Estimated Test Score. As you practice taking the TOEIC practice tests, your scores should improve. Keep track of your Total Estimated Test Scores.

# Correct	Listening Score	Reading Score	# Correct	Listening Score	Reading Score	# Correct	Listening Score	Reading Score	# Correct	Listening Score	Reading Score
0	5	5	26	110	65	51	255	220	76	410	370
1	5	5	27	115	70	52	260	225	77	420	380
2	5	5	28	120	80	53	270	230	78	425	385
3	5	5	29	125	85	54	275	235	79	430	390
4	5	5	30	130	90	55	280	240	80	440	395
5	5	5	31	135	95	56	290	250	81	445	400
6	5	5	32	140	100	57	295	255	82	450	405
7	10	5	33	145	110	58	300	260	83	460	410
8	15	5	34	150	115	59	310	265	84	465	415
9	20	5	35	160	120	60	315	270	85	470	420
10	25	5	36	165	125	61	320	280	86	475	425
11	30	5	37	170	130	62	325	285	87	480	430
12	35	5	38	175	140	63	330	290	88	485	435
13	40	5	39	180	145	64	340	300	89	490	445
14	45	5	40	185	150	65	345	305	90	495	450
15	50	5	41	190	160	66	350	310	91	495	455
16	55	10	42	195	165	67	360	320	92	495	465
17	60	15	43	200	170	68	365	325	93	495	470
18	65	20	44	210	175	69	370	330	94	495	480
19	70	25	45	215	180	70	380	335	95	495	485
20	75	30	46	220	190	71	385	340	96	495	490
21	80	35	47	230	195	72	390	350	97	495	495
22	85	40	48	240	200	73	395	355	98	495	495
23	90	45	49	245	210	74	400	360	99	495	495
24	95	50	50	250	215	75	405	365	100	495	495
25	100	60									

Number of Correct Listening Responses _____ = Listening Score _____

Number of Correct Reading Responses _____ = Reading Score _____

Total Estimated Test Score _____

ANSWER EXPLANATIONS

Listening Comprehension

PART 1: PHOTOGRAPHS

1. **(C)** A woman is standing at a podium speaking into a microphone. Choice (A) confuses similar-sounding words *microphone* and *cell phone*. Choice (B) correctly identifies the action of standing, but there is no store in the picture. Choice (D) refers to the woman's hands, which are visible, but she is not shaking hands with anyone.

2. **(A)** A man in a business suit is looking at a computer and writing notes with a pen. Choice (B) correctly identifies the glass of water on the table, but there is no waiter. Choice (C) correctly identifies the computer, but there is no salesman and the scene doesn't appear to be in a store. Choice (D) is incorrect because the man is reading from a computer, not a book.

3. **(D)** The photo shows teacups, a teapot, and a vase of flowers on a tray. Choices (A), (B), and (C) correctly identify objects in the photo, but not their locations.

4. **(A)** The photo shows a man and a woman looking at items in a store; the types of items make it appear to be a hardware store. Choice (B) refers to the rake the man is holding, but he is not raking anything. Choice (C) refers to the store location, but it incorrectly identifies the woman's action. Choice (D) correctly identifies the broom, but no one is sweeping.

5. **(B)** Two men are crossing the street. Choice (A) refers to the coffee cup in one man's hand, but no one is ordering coffee. Choice (C) confuses *suitcase* with the *briefcase* in one man's hand. Choice (D) associates traffic with the street scene, but there are no policemen in the photo.

6. **(D)** A freight train is seen in a country setting. Choice (A) refers to the water seen in the photo, but it is not a city scene. Choice (B) associates *train* and *conductor*. Choice (C) associates *train* and *railroad*.

PART 2: QUESTION-RESPONSE

7. **(B)** This answers the *yes-no* question about Sam's arrival. Choice (A) confuses similar-sounding words *yet* and *set*. Choice (C) repeats the name *Sam*.

8. **(A)** *A shop right across the street* answers the *Where* question. Choice (B) associates *coffee* and *cup*. Choice (C) would be a response to an offer of a cup of coffee.

9. **(C)** This is an appropriate response to a request for help. Choice (A) confuses the meaning of the word *show* in this context. Choice (B) confuses related words *printer* and *print*.

10. **(A)** This answers the *Why* question with a plausible reason. Choice (B) associates *lunch* and *sandwich*. Choice (C) repeats the word *desk*.

11. **(C)** *Fifteen* answers the *How many* question. Choice (A) confuses similar-sounding words *dinner* and *winner*. Choice (B) would answer a *When* question.

12. **(A)** This is an appropriate response to the remark about the lamp not working. Choice (B) would answer a *Why* question. Choice (C) confuses similar-sounding words *lamp* and *damp*.

13. **(B)** *Half an hour ago* answers the *When* question. Choice (A) relates *meeting* and *agenda*. Choice (C) repeats the word *start*.

14. **(B)** This is an appropriate response to the *yes–no* question about living in the neighborhood. Choice (A) repeats the word *neighborhood*. Choice (C) confuses similar-sounding words *neighborhood* and *good*.

15. **(A)** This is an appropriate response to the question about weekend plans. Choice (B) confuses similar-sounding words *plans* and *plants*. Choice (C) repeats the word *weekend*.

16. **(C)** *Fifteen minutes* answers the *How much time* question. Choice (A) confuses the meaning of the word *left* in this context. Choice (B) confuses similar-sounding words *much time* and *lunchtime*.

17. **(C)** This answers the indirect *Why* question with a plausible reason. Choices (A) and (B) repeat the word *open*.

18. **(B)** This is an appropriate response to the offer of help. Choice (A) associates *phone* and *message*. Choice (C) confuses similar-sounding words *phone* and *fun*.

19. **(A)** This is a logical response to the comment about the museum's opening time. Choice (B) uses a number, but it is not in the context of time. Choice (C) uses related word *opener*.

20. **(B)** *The leather one* answers the *Which* question. Choice (A) would answer a *Who* question. Choice (C) uses relate words *decided* and *decision*.

21. **(B)** *A biography* answers the question about reading. Choice (A) would answer a question about *eating*, not *reading*. Choice (C) confuses similar-sounding words *read* and *need*.

22. **(A)** This answers the *Where* question. Choice (B) would answer a *When* question. Choice (C) repeats the word *credit*.

23. **(C)** This answers the *yes–no* question. Choices (A) and (B) would answer a *When* question.

24. **(C)** This answers the *yes–no* question. Choice (A) confuses similar-sounding words *class* and *glass*. Choice (B) uses the word *sign* with a different meaning.

25. **(B)** This answers the *How much* question about cost. Choice (A) associates *air conditioner* and *degrees*. Choice (C) would answer a *How many* question.

26. **(A)** This answers the question *When will you be leaving*. Choice (B) would answer a *Why* question. Choice (C) would answer *When is your appointment*.

27. **(A)** This answers the *yes–no* question. Choice (B) uses the word *watch* with a different meaning. Choice (C) would be a response to *Thank you*.

28. **(C)** *Henry* responds to the comment about something *someone* did. Choice (A) associates *lights* with *turn on*. Choice (B) associates *lights* with *electrician*.

29. **(B)** The *Clinton project* answers the *What* question. Choice (A) would answer a *Where* question. Choice (C) associates *talking* with *sound*.

30. **(A)** The comment *You look nervous* is answered with a reason. Choice (B) uses the word *look* with a different meaning. Choice (C) confuses similar-sounding words *nervous* and *service*.

31. **(A)** This is a logical response to the *yes–no* question about a phone number. Choice (B) repeats the word *phone*. Choice (C) associates *number* and *five*.

PART 3: CONVERSATIONS

32. **(A)** The woman asks for a *lift*, meaning a *ride*, and the man talks about getting to the office, so the ride is to work. Choice (B) confuses the meaning of the word *lift*. Choice (C) confuses the meaning of the word *shop* (her car is in the shop, that is, at the mechanic's). Choice (D) is related to the fact that her car is in the shop, but it is not what she asks the man to do.

33. **(B)** The man says he has to give a presentation to a client and needs time to prepare. Choice (A) confuses similar-sounding words *prepare* and *repair*. Choice (C) confuses similar-sounding words *presentation* and *present*. Choice (D) repeats the word *finish*.

34. **(A)** The man wants to leave at 7:00, and the woman says, *Why don't you pick me up at 8:00*. Choice (B) repeats the word *client*. Choice (C) repeats the word *library*, the place where they will meet. Choice (D) repeats the word *help*—the woman offers to help the man, but she doesn't suggest asking someone else to do so.

35. **(A)** The woman says that she contacted the cleaning company, and later she mentions the good job they do on the floors, windows, and furniture. Choice (B) is associated with the mention of *floors*, *windows*, and *furniture*. Choice (C) repeats the word *furniture*. Choice (D) is associated with the mention of a *restaurant*.

36. **(D)** The man wants the office cleaned before his client meeting, but the cleaners can't come until Monday, which is after the meeting. Choice (A) is incorrect because

the woman says she contacted the cleaning company. Choice (B) is incorrect because they say the price is reasonable. Choice (C) is incorrect because they are hiring the cleaning company.

37. **(C)** The man says, *Why don't we plan to meet the clients at a restaurant instead of here?* Choice (A) repeats the word *earlier*. Choice (B) associates *pay* with *price*. Choice (D) repeats the word *furniture*

38. **(A)** The woman is going to a restaurant with a group of friends and asks the man to go with them. Choices (B), (C), and (D) are all plausible reasons, but they are not the correct answer.

39. **(B)** The man says, *I still have this report to finish.* Choice (A) confuses similar-sounding words *report* and *sports*. Choice (C) repeats the word *desk*. Choice (D) confuses similar-sounding words *all* and *call*.

40. **(C)** The man asks the woman to *work on the last part of it with me*, *it* meaning *report*, so he can finish on time to go to the restaurant. Choice (A) repeats the word *restaurant*. Choice (B) is not mentioned. Choice (D) repeats the time they will go to the restaurant.

41. **(D)** The woman mentions a *vehicle*, and the man mentions *GPS* and a *tank of gas*, so they are talking about a car. Choice (A) is related to the mention of *seats*. Choice (B) is incorrect because it is not something that someone can *bring back*. Choice (C) is related to the mention of *heated seats*.

42. **(C)** The woman says, *. . . you can keep it over the weekend, if you want it for a little longer.* Choice (A) is related to the man's request for a large vehicle. Choice (B) is plausible but not mentioned. Choice (D) repeats the word *agreement*.

43. **(B)** The woman has shown the man a rental agreement, and the man requests a pen. Choice (A) is what he will do when he returns the car. Choice (C) repeats the word *weekend*. Choice (D) is related to the topic but not mentioned.

44. **(D)** The man called to ask about shipping options. Choices (A), (B), and (C) are all plausible reasons, but they are not the correct answer.

45. **(B)** The woman says, *there is a $20 surcharge for express shipping*. Choice (A) costs $10. Choice (C) is not mentioned. Choice (D) is part of standard shipping.

46. **(B)** The woman asks, *Is there anything else*, meaning *Is there anything else you want to know*, and the man replies, *That's it*, meaning there is nothing else. Choices (A), (C), and (D) are plausible in the context, but they are not the correct answer.

47. **(C)** The woman asks about work and benefits and says, *If I'm hired . . . .* Choices (A), (B), and (D) are all plausible, but they are not the correct answer.

48. **(D)** The man says, *. . . the hours are great.* Choices (A), (B), and (C) are all things someone might like about a job, but they are not the correct answer.

49. **(B)** The woman asks a question about benefits and the man says he will take her to see Mrs. Patterson, who can answer that question. Choice (A) is incorrect because the man says that Mrs. Patterson is the one who can answer the question. Choice (C) repeats the word *weekend*, related to the mention of the work schedule. Choice (D) is contradicted by the correct answer.

50. **(D)** The man mentions that the hotel where he plans to stay is next to the conference center. Choices (A) and (B) are plausible, but they are incorrect answers. Choice (C) is confused with the photos the man says he saw on the hotel website.

51. **(B)** One woman says she couldn't sleep and then mentions the beds. The other woman agrees about the beds and adds that the rooms are small. All this adds up to an uncomfortable hotel. Choice (A) is incorrect because all the speakers agree that the price is *reasonable*, that is, *fair*. Choice (C) is incorrect because they say the hotel is *well located*. Choice (D) is a plausible reason for not sleeping, but it is not mentioned.

52. **(A)** The man says, *I'll look into some other possibilities*, meaning he'll research other

possible places to stay. Choice (B) is contradicted by the correct answer. Choice (C) is plausible in the context, but it is not mentioned. Choice (D) relates *sleep* and *nap*.

53. **(A)** The speakers are talking about a *renovation* project, and the contractor's trucks are mentioned. Choice (B) is related to renovation. Choice (C) is related to the mention of trucks. Choice (D) is something contractors might be hired for.

54. **(D)** The woman says, *Three contractors have submitted quotes, and the team is meeting tomorrow to review them.* Choice (A) repeats the word *quotes.* Choice (B) repeats the word *contractor.* Choice (C) repeats the word *schedule.*

55. **(C)** The man says, *we need a contractor that's based within 30 miles of the job site,* and the woman says that the last contractor *complained about the distance.* Choices (A), (B), and (D) are plausible in the context, but they are not the correct answer.

56. **(D)** The man is ordering checks at a place where he has an account, so he is at a bank. Choices (A) and (C) are associated with the mention of *colors and styles.* Choice (B) is associated with *order* and *check* (with a different meaning—at a restaurant *check* means *bill*).

57. **(C)** The man is ordering checks—he says he wants more checks and the woman shows him styles and colors he can order and says the order will arrive in two weeks. Choices (A), (B), and (D) are plausible, but they are not the correct answer.

58. **(B)** *Selection* refers to the variety of choices; when the man says it *could be better,* he means it is not good enough. Choices (A), (C), and (D) don't fit the context or the meaning of the phrase.

59. **(A)** They are talking about a show at a theater that has great acting and for which you need tickets, so it is a play. Choice (B) is an event that could take place at a theater and requires tickets. Choices (C) and (D) are things that require tickets.

60. **(D)** The woman called the box office and found out the show was sold out, that is, all the tickets had been sold. Choice (A) is what one of the man's cousins is doing. Choice (B) repeats the word *seat.* Choice (C) repeats the word *tomorrow*—the day that the cousin is going out of town.

61. **(B)** The man offers to call his cousin to find out if the cousin will give his tickets to the woman. Choice (A) repeats the word *trip,* but there is no mention of planning. Choice (C) is incorrect because he only offers to find out if the tickets are available, he does not offer to pay for them. Choice (D) repeats the words *box office*—where the woman called to try to buy tickets.

62. **(C)** The woman is going to see Mr. Gill at Zenith Enterprises, which is on the 3rd floor. Choices (A), (B), and (D) are the locations of other offices.

63. **(B)** The woman says she hopes to work with Mr. Gill and is going to see him for a job interview. Choice (A) is related to the discussion of work. Choice (C) confuses similar-sounding words *appointment* and *apartment.* Choice (D) repeats the word *appointment.*

64. **(A)** The man says that Mr. Gill's office is on the way to his own office and also that he hasn't seen the woman there before, both of which imply he works near Mr. Gill. Choices (B), (C), and (D) are contradicted by the correct answer.

65. **(D)** The woman says she prefers hot tea. Choice (A) associates *lemonade* with *lemon.* Choice (B) is what the woman says she doesn't want. Choice (C) is what the man will use to make tea.

66. **(A)** The woman says she had a big lunch and can't eat any more. Choice (B) repeats the word *hot.* Choice (C) is not mentioned. Choice (D) repeats the word *lunch.*

67. **(A)** The man says he'll have a piece of pie. Choice (B) repeats the word *bake* and confuses *buns* with the similar-sounding word *one.* Choice (C) confuses *bacon* with the similar-sounding word *baked.* Choice (D) repeats the word *toast.*

68. **(B)** The man says, *We're a bit understaffed today*, meaning there aren't enough staff members at work. Since the speakers are in a restaurant, that means there aren't enough servers. Choice (A) repeats the word *chef*. Choice (C) is plausible but not mentioned. Choice (D) uses the related word *staff*.

69. **(A)** The woman says, *Everybody knows the food here is worth waiting for*, meaning most people have a good opinion of the restaurant. Choice (B) is not mentioned. Choice (C) repeats the word *popular*. Choice (D) is related to the fact that there was a delay.

70. **(B)** The woman says, *I'll try the number 2*. Choices (A) and (C) include fish, which the woman says she doesn't like. Choice (D) includes vegetables, which the woman says she wants, but it isn't what she ordered.

PART 4: TALKS

71. **(D)** The message offers a discount on annual passes and explains the benefits of having a pass. Choices (A) and (B) are plausible but not mentioned. Choice (C) is associated with the description of the different activities that take place at the park.

72. **(A)** The speaker mentions the annual Evening Extravaganza, when the park stays open until midnight. Choices (B) and (D) refer to activities that are mentioned, but there is no mention of how often they take place. Choice (C) is the topic of the message, but there is no mention of how often a discount is offered.

73. **(C)** The listener can *talk to a representative about purchasing annual passes*, that is, a person who will sell them something. Choice (A) is associated with the mention of concerts. Choice (B) is associated with the context of talking on the phone. Choice (D) is associated with the topic of a park.

74. **(C)** The workshop will cover *stocks and bonds*, how to *help your money grow*, and *places you can put your money*. Choice (A) associates *money* and *budgets*. Choice (B) associates *laptops* and *computers*. Choice (D) repeats the word *software*.

75. **(A)** The speaker mentions *the schedule I'm passing out*. Choice (B) is what the participants were asked to bring. Choice (C) is what the participants might have later during the break. Choice (D) associates *seat* and *chair*.

76. **(B)** The speaker says, *We'll take one break after the first hour and then another at around eleven*. Choice (A) is confused with *one break*. Choices (C) and (D) are not mentioned.

77. **(A)** The speaker is talking to passengers, mentions a storm, and then says, *We cannot fly over or around it*. If they are flying, they must be on a plane. Choice (B) has passengers and a captain, but it does not fly. Choice (C) is associated with the mention of bags. Choice (D) has passengers, but it does not fly.

78. **(C)** The problem is a storm. Choice (A) repeats the phrase *storage compartments*. Choice (B) repeats the word *seats*. Choice (D) repeats the word *bags*.

79. **(A)** The speaker says, *beverage service will be suspended until further notice*. Choices (B), (C), and (D) are plausible in the context of plane travel, but they are not mentioned.

80. **(D)** The product is a heater, and the speaker says, *I haven't been able to get it to heat again*. Choice (A) is confused with the mention of the manual cover. Choice (B) is incorrect because the woman says that the fan blows. Choice (C) is incorrect because the woman says she can turn it on, and when she does, the fan blows.

81. **(B)** The speaker says, *I've had the heater for two days*. Choice (A) repeats the word *morning*. Choice (C) sounds similar to the correct answer. Choice (D) confuses similar-sounding words *fine* and *nine*.

82. **(C)** The speaker asks the listener to *phone me* to let her know if there is a way to fix the heater. Choice (A) is plausible in the context, but it is not mentioned. Choice (B) is what the speaker says she doesn't want. Choice (D) is incorrect because she already has a manual.

83. **(A)** The speaker mentions visiting buildings and looking at building styles. Choices (B) and (D) are things they will see, but they are not the focus of the tour. Choice (C) is related

to the *historic district*, the part of the city they are touring, but it is not the focus.

84. **(C)** The speaker mentions that they will *stroll* and *walk*. Choices (A), (B), and (D) are all plausible in the context, but they are not the correct answer.

85. **(B)** The speaker says she will show the group a map; this will happen before they set off on the tour. Choice (A) is the last thing they will do. Choice (C) is the first stop on the tour; they will do this after looking at the map. Choice (D) has already been done because the speaker says she has everyone's tickets.

86. **(A)** The speaker mentions using this product in a *break room* and with *colleagues*, so it is being marketed to office workers. Choices (B), (C), and (D) are all places where coffee-makers are used, but they are not the correct answer.

87. **(B)** The speaker says that the product *can make 24 cups at a time.* Choice (A) sounds similar to the correct answer. Choice (C) is confused with how long the coffee stays warm (*8 hours*). Choice (D) confuses similar-sounding words *time* and *nine*.

88. **(D)** The speaker tells listeners to visit the company's website *to find out about this and other fine Stenson's products*, that is, to look for more information. Choices (A) and (C) are other things a customer might do on a website. Choice (B) repeats the word *products*.

89. **(B)** The speaker is talking about an *opening ceremony* for a new bridge. Choice (A) is confused with the mention that the plans met with approval from city residents. Choices (C) and (D) are plausible in the context, but they are not mentioned.

90. **(C)** The speaker says, . . . *there is a long line of drivers waiting to be among the first to go across the new bridge.* Choices (A) and (B) are plausible but not mentioned. Choice (D) repeats the word *mayor*.

91. **(B)** *It's hard to believe* is a phrase used to express surprise at an occurrence, and Choices (A), (C), and (D) do not correctly interpret the meaning of this phrase.

92. **(B)** The word *cuisine* is included in the title. Roger has a career as a chef, and the book contains recipes. Choices (A) and (C) are mentioned. Choice (D) is plausible in the context.

93. **(B)** To *jump at a chance* means to *take advantage of a good opportunity*; Roger was offered a job as a chef, and he accepted it. Choices (A), (C), and (D) do not fit the meaning of the phrase or the context.

94. **(C)** The speaker says that Roger will be at a restaurant where he will *share excerpts from his book.* Choices (A) and (B) are associated with the place where Roger will be. Choice (D) is what Roger has done in the past.

95. **(A)** The speaker mentions *footwear*, which refers to shoes in general, and *sandals*, *slippers*, and *running shoes*, which are types of shoes. Choice (B) is associated with *footwear*. Choice (C) is associated with *running shoes*. Choice (D) is confused with *brick-and-mortar store*, which actually refers to a physical store as opposed to an online store.

96. **(B)** The speaker is concerned about the group with the *noticeably lower sales.* Choices (A), (C), and (D) all had higher sales, and there were no large differences among them.

97. **(C)** The speaker says, *I'd like to take a few minutes to talk over any ideas you might have.* Choice (A) relates *reported* and *report*. Choice (B) repeats the word *groups*. Choice (D) repeats the word *slide*.

98. **(D)** Marc is arranging the details of the speaker's trip, so he is her assistant. Choices (A) and (B) are incorrect because Marc is responsible for arranging more than just train tickets or hotels; he is responsible for both those things as well as meeting schedules. Choice (C) is related to the context, but it is unlikely that a boss would arrange trip details.

99. **(A)** The speaker wants to add time to her trip in order to attend Professor Obard's seminar. Choice (B) repeats the word *meetings*, but adding more is not mentioned. Choice (C) repeats the word *hotel*, but getting a better one is not mentioned. Choice (D) repeats the word *transportation*.

100. **(D)** The speaker says she wants a hotel that is as close to the train station as possible, and the Montshire is the closest. Choices (A), (B), and (C) don't fit this description.

Reading

PART 5: INCOMPLETE SENTENCES

101. **(D)** *Valuable* is an adjective describing the noun *skills*. Choice (A) is a verb or a noun. Choice (B) is a past tense or past participle verb. Choice (C) is an adverb.

102. **(B)** *Up to* means *as much as*. Choices (A), (C), and (D) have no meaning in this context.

103. **(C)** *Primarily* means *mainly*. Choices (A), (B), and (D) have meanings that don't fit the context.

104. **(D)** The verb *coincide* is followed by the preposition *with*. Choices (A), (B), and (C) are prepositions that don't normally follow *coincide*.

105. **(C)** *Color scheme* refers to a combination or arrangement of colors. Choices (A), (B) and (D) don't fit the context.

106. **(C)** The main verb *recommend* is followed by a gerund. Choice (A) is present tense or base form. Choice (B) is past tense. Choice (D) is future tense.

107. **(B)** The time expression *next week* indicates that a future verb is required here. Choice (A) is present tense. Choice (C) is present perfect tense. Choice (D) is present perfect continuous tense.

108. **(A)** The verb *attend* is followed by the preposition *to*. Choices (B), (C), and (D) are prepositions that don't normally follow *attend*.

109. **(D)** *Except* is a preposition meaning *not including*. Choices (A) and (B) are not prepositions. Choice (C) does not fit the context.

110. **(A)** *Belongings* means *possessions*. People are not allowed to take their possessions into the factory with them. Choices (B), (C), and (D) have meanings that don't fit the context.

111. **(C)** *His* is a possessive adjective, in this case, meaning *Daniel's* and modifying the noun *job*. Choice (A) is a subject pronoun. Choice (B) is an object pronoun. Choice (D) refers to a woman.

112. **(D)** A verb is needed here to act as the main verb of the clause. Choice (A) is a gerund or present participle. Choices (B) and (C) are nouns.

113. **(C)** *Can* is a modal, in this case, preceding the base form verb *attend* and meaning *are allowed to*. Choice (A) is grammatically incorrect. Choices (B) and (D) don't make sense in this sentence.

114. **(B)** *Extensive*, in this case, means *a lot of*. Choices (A), (C), and (D) have meanings that don't fit the context.

115. **(A)** *Due to* introduces a cause. Choices (B) and (C) need to introduce a clause, not a phrase. Choice (D) introduces a contradiction.

116. **(D)** This is a passive verb made up of the present tense form of the verb *be* and the past participle of the main verb. Choice (A) is not a form of the verb *be*. Choices (B) and (C) are forms of the verb *be* but don't have any verb tense.

117. **(C)** This is a possessive relative pronoun. The meaning is *the person's signature*. Choices (A) and (D) can be used as relative pronouns, but they are not possessive. Choice (B) is a contraction for *who is*.

118. **(B)** This is a gerund in the position of subject of the sentence. Choices (A) and (D) are base form or present tense. Choice (C) is an infinitive verb.

119. **(A)** *Or* introduces a choice. Choice (B) introduces a result. Choice (C) introduces a condition. Choice (D) introduces a cause or a comparison.

120. **(B)** *Inaccurate* means *not correct*, so *inaccurate figures* would be a reason for rewriting a budget report. Choices (A), (C), and (D) have meanings that don't fit the context.

121. **(D)** *Acquire* means *get* or *obtain*. Choices (A), (B), and (C) have meanings that don't fit the context.

122. **(B)** *After* introduces a time clause that describes the action that happened first, in

this case, first the client accepts the plan, then the team has one month to complete the design. Choices (A) and (D) would introduce the action that happens second. Choice (C) introduces an action that happens at the same time as another action.

123. **(A)** To *earn* approval means *to get approval* as a result of your actions. Choices (B), (C), and (D) have meanings that don't fit the context.

124. **(A)** This is a future time clause, so a present tense verb is needed. Choice (B) is present tense, but it doesn't agree with the plural subject, *renovations*. Choice (C) is base form. Choice (D) is future tense.

125. **(B)** *Resize* is a verb following the modal *can*. Choice (A) is a noun. Choice (C) is an adjective. Choice (D) is a noun or a gerund.

126. **(D)** *Although* introduces a dependent clause that describes a contradiction. Choice (A) introduces a cause. Choice (B) introduces a result. Choice (C) is a preposition and is not used to introduce a clause.

127. **(A)** *Include* is the main verb of the sentence. Choice (B) is a gerund or present participle. Choice (C) is an adjective. Choice (D) is an adverb.

128. **(C)** *Previous* is an adjective describing something from before, in this case, the noun *employers*. Choice (A) is a preposition, not an adjective. Choice (B) refers to something that is forward or ahead. Choice (D) is a verb, not an adjective.

129. **(B)** *Instead* is an adverb meaning *as a substitute*. Choice (A) would be correctly used in the clause that precedes *or*. Choice (C) is not an adverb. Choice (D) has the wrong meaning.

130. **(A)** The past perfect form of the verb is used for an unreal past conditional. Choice (B) is present perfect tense. Choice (C) is present perfect continuous tense. Choice (D) is the correct form for the main clause, not the *if* clause.

PART 6: TEXT COMPLETION

131. **(A)** A verb following *let* is in the base form. Choice (B) is present tense. Choice (C) is an infinitive. Choice (D) is a future verb.

132. **(C)** This possessive adjective modifies the noun *needs*, referring to the needs of the person addressed in the letter, so the second person form is required. Choices (A) and (D) are third person forms. Choice (B) is a first person form.

133. **(D)** The company founders are the people who started the company; they are the people writing the letter to introduce their new business. Choices (A), (B), and (C) have meanings that don't fit the context.

134. **(B)** This is a logical way to end a letter that introduces a new business. Choices (A), (C), and (D) all imply that there already has been contact between the writers and the recipient of the letter, and that is illogical since it is a letter of introduction.

135. **(D)** This is a logical reason for temporarily suspending service at a bus stop. Choices (A), (B), and (C) are about buses, but they don't fit the context.

136. **(C)** *Instead* means *in place of*. Passengers can use these stops in place of the Main Street stop. Choices (A), (B), and (D) have meanings that don't fit the context.

137. **(B)** *Improve* means *make better*. Renovating bus shelters is one way of making bus service better. Choices (A), (C), and (D) have meanings that don't fit the context.

138. **(A)** This is an imperative verb suggesting something that readers can do. Choice (B) is an infinitive verb. Choice (C) would require mention of a subject. Choice (D) is a command and would not be used on a notice of this sort.

139. **(D)** This sentence introduces the bulleted list that follows. Choices (A), (B), and (C) are related to the topic of company policy, but they do not fit the context.

140. **(C)** A passive verb is required here because the subject, *requests*, is not active. The requests don't submit themselves. Choices (A), (B), and (D) are reactive verb forms.

141. **(A)** In this sentence, *another* is a pronoun for *another copy.* The meaning *is one copy for your supervisor and one copy for the HR office.* Choices (B) and (D) don't make sense in this context. Choice (C) is incorrect because *some* refers to a plural noun, but a singular word is needed here.

142. **(B)** *Regarding* in this context means *about.* Choices (A), (C), and (D) have similar meanings, but they require the use of prepositions or adverbs. Choices (A) and (B) are followed by *to.* Choice (C) is preceded by *as.*

143. **(B)** The purpose of the letter is to apologize for a guest's bad experience, and this sentence introduces that idea. Choices (A), (C), and (D) are related to the topic of a hotel, but they do not fit the context.

144. **(A)** *On* is the correct preposition to use with the expression *to pride oneself on.* Choices (B), (C), and (D) cannot be used in this context.

145. **(D)** *Recent* refers to something that happened just a short while ago, and the first sentence of the letter tells us that this guest's stay happened *last week.* Choice (A) describes something that will happen in the near future. Choice (B) means *last.* Choice (C) is an adverb, so it cannot be used to describe a noun.

146. **(C)** The verb *consider* is followed by a gerund. Choice (A) is present tense or base form. Choice (B) is present tense. Choice (D) is an infinitive verb.

PART 7: READING COMPREHENSION

147. **(A)** The order will be delivered *before noon today,* that is, this morning. Choices (B), (C), and (D) don't fit this description.

148. **(C)** In the notes section, the customer asks for *yellow bananas that are ready for eating,* that is, ripe bananas. Choice (A) is incorrect because the customer didn't specify a temperature for the soda. Choice (B) repeats the word *yellow,* but it was not used in relation to tomatoes. Choice (D) is incorrect because the customer specified *whole walnuts.*

149. **(B)** This is Ms. Wilson's reply to Mr. Stone's question asking whether there is a problem with the shipment. Choices (A), (C), and (D) do not fit the context.

150. **(C)** Millie writes that she will try to *get them to speed things up,* that is, to get the shipment sent sooner. Choice (A) refers to the phone calls Millie will make, but they are to the warehouse, not the client. Choice (B) is not mentioned. Choice (D) refers to the payment made by the client for overnight delivery, but there is no mention of returning it.

151. **(D)** According to the notes column, the change fee is because the date of the trip was rescheduled from September 9 to September 16. Choices (A), (B), and (C) are all plausible reasons for an extra fee, but they are not the correct answer.

152. **(B)** The description of the hotel charge is *$110/night × 5,* which means the $110 nightly fee was charged five times. Choices (A), (C), and (D) are not mentioned.

153. **(C)** The ad states, *Must be proficient with word processing functions.* Choices (A) and (D) are what the assistant will be trained to do. Choice (B) repeats the words *program* and *computers,* but programming computers is not mentioned.

154. **(A)** The ad states, *Apply in person,* and then gives the address of the office. Choices (B) and (C) are not mentioned. Choice (D) is incorrect because the ad specifically states *no phone calls.*

155. **(C)** The article is about e-tickets on commuter trains. Choices (A) and (B) are mentioned, but they are not the main topic. Choice (D) is not mentioned.

156. **(B)** The article states that traditional tickets are for sale by machine. Choice (A) is how to buy e-tickets. Choice (C) is mentioned but not as a way to buy tickets. Choice (D) is not mentioned.

157. **(D)** *Phased out* means *discontinued.* Traditional tickets will be discontinued soon because e-tickets are being used. Choices (A), (B), and (C) have meanings that don't fit the context.

158. **(A)** The passage states, *The program is open to anyone who has been a member in good standing for at least one year.* Choice (B) is mentioned as an option, not a requirement. Choice (C) is plausible in the context, but it is not mentioned. Choice (D) repeats the phrase *training program*, which is mentioned as something that recognizes the certificates.

159. **(D)** The tests are given *every six months,* that is, twice a year. Choices (A) and (B) repeat *six.* Choice (C) is an incorrect interpretation of *every six months.*

160. **(B)** An e-mail address is provided for requesting information about test registration. Choice (A) is mentioned as an option for preparing for the test. Choices (C) and (D) are plausible in the context, but they are not mentioned.

161. **(D)** The requirements for purchasing a waiver are to be over 21 and to not have *been involved in an accident in the past 12 months.* Choice (A) is contradicted by the correct answer. Choices (B) and (C) are plausible in the context, but they are not mentioned.

162. **(C)** A waiver can reduce the damage fee from $500 to $250 or to $0. Choice (A) repeats the phrase *12 months.* Choice (B) refers to the age requirement for purchasing a waiver. Choice (D) contradicts the information in the passage: *These waivers are not a substitute for insurance coverage.*

163. **(A)** According to the passage, *The waiver must be added to the rental agreement at the time of signing.* Choices (B), (C), and (D) are related to the topic, but they are not the correct answer.

164. **(D)** *Caterers, menu, tables,* and *chairs* all indicate that food will be served, and this is the only choice that is a food event. Choices (A), (B), and (C) are events that colleagues might plan together, but they are not the correct answer.

165. **(A)** Jairo mentions *my menu modifications.* Choices (B), (C), and (D) are all mentioned, but they are not things Jairo changed.

166. **(B)** Mija writes that she got *RSVPs,* that is, responses to invitations, and she and Jairo go on to discuss the people that are coming, that is, the people who have been invited. Choice (A) is related but not mentioned. Choice (C) is discussed, but it is not what Mija received. Choice (D) is what Jairo got this morning.

167. **(C)** The expression, *We're good to go,* means *We're ready to get started,* and Mija mentions the things that have been all arranged—the caterers and the room. Choices (A), (B), and (D) don't fit the meaning of the phrase or the context.

168. **(D)** The article is directed at people who are *new to the job market* and have *just finished your education,* and who are described as *young people.* Choices (A) and (B) are incorrect because the article is for people who are seeking jobs, not people who are involved with hiring. Choice (C) is incorrect because the article is not for experienced people.

169. **(B)** The expression, *It all boils down to . . .* means *It can be summarized as . . . ,* and the word that summarizes Ms. Pritchard's advice— *professionalism*—soon follows. Choices (A), (C), and (D) don't fit the meaning of the expression or the paragraph.

170. **(A)** The article states, *Keep in mind that you don't want the color of your clothes to shout. Black, charcoal gray, or deep blue are best for job interviews,* which suggests dark colors. Choices (B), (C), and (D) are plausible in the context, but they are not mentioned.

171. **(D)** This sentence introduces the topic of the paragraph—how to act like a professional. Choices (A), (B), and (C) are not the right context for this sentence.

172. **(C)** He wrote the letter to ask her to speak at an alternative energy affair, that is, to invite her to an event. Choice (A) is mentioned, but it is not the main topic of the letter. Choice (B) is incorrect because there is no mention of his selling anything. Choice (D) is a plausible reason to write a letter, but it is not mentioned.

173. **(B)** Mr. Marquez writes about alternative energy: *I believe we need to spread the word and get more people on board with this,* that is, he wants to inform people and persuade them to his point of view. Choice (A) refers to

the organization Mr. Marquez belongs to, but there is no mention of whether or not he is president of it. Choice (C) is incorrect because the implication is that he has done this for his own family only. Choice (D) describes Ms. Jackson; Mr. Marquez has some knowledge but probably not an expert level.

174. **(A)** Mr. Marquez tells Ms. Jackson that she can sell her books at the fair, which implies that she has written some. Choice (B) is incorrect because it is implied that Mr. Marquez has never met her, or only heard her speak on the radio. Choice (C) is incorrect because she was a guest, not the host. Choice (D) is plausible, but there is nothing that implies this.

175. **(B)** Mr. Marquez writes, *I will need to hear back from you before the end of two weeks.* Choice (A) is not mentioned. Choices (C) and (D) are incorrect because the letter is dated August 22, so September will begin sooner than two weeks.

176. **(B)** The Wisteria is in a converted farmhouse with views of pastures and hills and nearby horseback trails through the woods, so it is in a rural setting. Choice (A) is incorrect because there are only six guest rooms. Choice (C) is plausible but not mentioned. Choice (D) is incorrect because it is in an historical farmhouse.

177. **(C)** Guests can rent the barn for a wedding or family reunion. Choice (A) confuses the use of the word *craft*. Choice (B) is incorrect because only breakfast is mentioned. Choice (D) repeats the word *barn*, but it is only mentioned in the text as a place for parties, not as a working barn.

178. **(D)** The information on the webpage states, *Book your room before April 30 and receive 20% off,* that is, make a reservation before April 30 to get a discount. Choice (A) is mentioned, but not in connection with a discount. Choice (B) is confused with when the reservation must be made. Choice (C) is mentioned, but it is not in connection with a discount.

179. **(A)** Ms. Simmons writes, *I would be happy to provide your business with fresh herbs and flowers.* Choices (B) and (D) would be reasons

to contact the Wisteria, but they are not the purpose of the e-mail. Choice (C) repeats the word *business*.

180. **(A)** Ms. Simmons is a grower of herbs and flowers, that is, a farmer. Choices (B) and (C) are mentioned as the types of customers Ms. Simmons deals with. Choice (D) is related to the mention on the webpage of holding events in the barn.

181. **(C)** Mr. Rosen writes that he is *leaving next month* and must leave his apartment in good condition to avoid a penalty. Choice (A) repeats the word *tenants*. Choice (B) confuses the word *visitors* with Mr. Rosen's asking whether someone from the service needs to *visit* his apartment. Choice (D) is a plausible reason, but it is not the correct answer.

182. **(A)** Mr. Rosen writes, *a colleague at work suggested I contact you.* Choice (B) is plausible, but it is not the correct answer. Choice (C) repeats the word *landlord*. Choice (D) is incorrect because Mr. Rosen asks for information (prices) that is on the flier, so it is unlikely that he has seen it.

183. **(A)** Mr. Rosen states that his apartment has just one room, and this is the price quoted on the flier for an apartment of 1–3 rooms. Choices (B), (C), and (D) are the costs to clean larger apartments.

184. **(B)** The flier mentions *mansion, apartment,* and *home,* which all refer to residences, and no other type of place is mentioned. Choice (A) is incorrect because the flier describes the prices as *competitive,* meaning they are similar to those of it competitors. Choice (C) is incorrect because the flier states, *Call us when you need us, or arrange for regular weekly or monthly service,* implying that customers are invited to hire the service for either one-time or regular service. Choice (D) is incorrect because there is information on pricing for larger spaces with no indication that this is rare.

185. **(D)** This refers to a price estimate, or an approximate price. Choices (A), (B), and (C) don't fit the context.

186. **(A)** It is on the website's *special promotions* page, and the listed prices are described as *good through March 30*, so they will change after that date. Choice (B) is incorrect because it is the current prices, not the product itself, that are available only through March. Choice (C) is incorrect because only one color combination—black with chrome—is mentioned. Choice (D) is not mentioned.

187. **(C)** According to the e-mail, Mr. Rivera is paying $110 for his table, and this is the price listed on the webpage for the large table. Choices (A), (B), and (D) have other prices, according to the webpage.

188. **(B)** The webpage states, *Free shipping on all orders of $100 or more*, and Mr. Rivera is paying $110 for his table. Choice (A) is confused with the discount coupon mentioned on the webpage. Choice (C) is incorrect because the webpage has a link for calculating shipping costs. Choice (D) is contradicted by the correct answer.

189. **(D)** In his review, Mr. Rivera mentions using the table for weekly staff meetings. Choice (A) is not mentioned. Choices (B) and (C) are uses suggested on the webpage.

190. **(C)** Mr. Rivera explains that a part (the clips) was missing and says that he originally gave a 3-star rating because of this, but then the company sent him some clips, and now he is happy with the product. Choices (A) and (D) are plausible, but they are not mentioned. Choice (B) is mentioned in the review, but it is not as a reason for changing the rating.

191. **(B)** The menu description includes the word *vegetarian* as one of the entrees. Choice (A) is incorrect because the flier states the dinner will be *followed* by the show. Choice (C) is incorrect—there are prices listed for *show only* but none for dinner only. Choice (D) is incorrect as Esther writes that the food is *mediocre*, and Bob agrees with her.

192. **(A)** Esther did not pay anything for the tickets; her sister gave them to her. Choices (B), (C), and (D) are prices listed in the flier.

193. **(D)** In his e-mail, Bob offers to pick up Esther with his car. Choice (A) is incorrect because it is Bob, not Esther, who will drive. Choice (B) is what Esther suggests. Choice (C) is not mentioned.

194. **(B)** Bob writes, *it will be my first time seeing this particular play*. Choices (A) and (C) are incorrect because Bob writes that he is *looking forward to seeing the play*. Choice (D) is incorrect because Bob writes, *I've actually eaten there before*, referring to the dinner theater.

195. **(C)** Bob means that they could *omit* the dinner, that is, not eat it because it is not likely to be good. Choices (A), (B), and (D) don't fit the context.

196. **(C)** According to the itinerary, Ms. Hakim will take a *tour of HR Manufacturers Plant* on April 12. Choices (A), (B), and (D) are other dates on the itinerary when she has other activities scheduled.

197. **(B)** The information on the flier states, *Recruiters from major companies will be available to meet with job seekers to discuss employment opportunities*. Choice (A) refers to the products that will be exhibited, but there is no mention of sales. Choice (C) repeats the word *résumé*, which is suggested that people bring with them. Choice (D) is not mentioned.

198. **(B)** *Renowned* means *famous*. Choices (A), (C), and (D) are not the correct meaning for this word.

199. **(A)** Ms. Hakim wants to change her return day from Friday to Saturday, so she can attend the business expo. Choices (B), (C), and (D) are plausible in the context, but they are not the correct answer.

200. **(A)** Ms. Hakim writes, *I'm really looking forward to finally having the chance to meet the Wiltshire team*, which implies that she has not been to the Wiltshire office before. Choice (B) is related to the topic of the e-mail, but it is not mentioned. Choice (C) is something she might do at the business expo, but she doesn't mention it. Choice (D) is contradicted by the correct answer.

AUDIO TRACK LIST

Track 1   Introduction

Listening Comprehension
Part 1: Photographs
Track 2   Skill 1—Assumptions
Track 3   Skill 2—People
Track 4   Skill 3—Things
Track 5   Skill 4—Actions
Track 6   Skill 5—General Locations
Track 7   Skill 6—Specific Locations

Part 2: Question-Response
Track 8   Skill 1—Similar Sounds
Track 9   Skill 2—Related Words
Track 10   Skill 3—Homonyms
Track 11   Skill 4—Same Sound/Same
                 Spelling but Different Meaning
Track 12   Skill 5—Suggestions
Track 13   Skill 6—Offers
Track 14   Skill 7—Requests

Part 3: Conversations
Track 15   Skill 1—Questions About People
Track 16   Skill 2—Questions About Occupations
Track 17   Skill 3—Questions About Place
Track 18   Skill 4—Questions About Time
Track 19   Skill 5—Questions About Activities
Track 20   Skill 6—Questions About Opinions
Track 21   Skill 7—Graphic
Track 22   Skill 8—Meaning in Context

Part 4: Talks
Track 23   Skill 1—Questions About Events
                 and Facts
Track 24   Skill 2—Questions About Reasons
Track 25   Skill 3—Questions About Numbers
Track 26   Skill 4—Questions About Main Topics
Track 27   Skill 5—Paraphrases
Track 28   Skill 6—Graphic
Track 29   Skill 7—Implied Meaning
Track 30   Skill 8—Multiple Accents

Mini-Test for Listening Comprehension
Track 31   Part 1—Photographs
Track 32   Part 2—Question-Response
Track 33   Part 3—Conversations
Track 34   Part 4—Talks

Practice Test 1
Track 35   Part 1—Photographs
Track 36   Part 2—Question-Response
Track 37   Part 3—Conversations
Track 38   Part 4—Talks

Practice Test 2
Track 39   Part 1—Photographs
Track 40   Part 2—Question-Response
Track 41   Part 3—Conversations
Track 42   Part 4—Talks

Practice Test 3
Track 43   Part 1—Photographs
Track 44   Part 2—Question-Response
Track 45   Part 3—Conversations
Track 46   Part 4—Talks

Practice Test 4
Track 47   Part 1—Photographs
Track 48   Part 2—Question-Response
Track 49   Part 3—Conversations
Track 50   Part 4—Talks

Practice Test 5
Track 51   Part 1—Photographs
Track 52   Part 2—Question-Response
Track 53   Part 3—Conversations
Track 54   Part 4—Talks

Practice Test 6
Track 55   Part 1—Photographs
Track 56   Part 2—Question-Response
Track 57   Part 3—Conversations
Track 58   Part 4—Talks